Also by Hedrick Smith

The New Russians
The Power Game: How Washington Works
The Russians

Rethinking America

HEDRICK SMITH

Rethinking America

1384461

Random House   New York

C l
oo- 3/738690

Library of Congress Cataloging-in-Publication Data
Smith, Hedrick.
    Rethinking America/Hedrick Smith.
      p.   cm.
    Includes bibliographical references and index.
      ISBN 0-679-43551-4
      1. Benchmarking (Management)—United States.   2. Technological innovations—Economic aspects—United States.   3. United States—Economic conditions—1981–   4. United States—Economic policy—1981–1993.   5. United States—Economic policy—1993–
6. Competition, International.   I. Title.
HD62.15.S62   1995
338.973—dc20   94-46664

Manufactured in the United States of America on acid-free paper
24689753
First Edition

To Jason Fuller
and the next generation of America's mid-kids
whose quality education is vital to America's future

Acknowledgments

Any book is a collaborative enterprise—certainly a book such as this one, which highlights collaboration as a major theme. I alone am responsible for its conclusions, but this book has benefited greatly from the cooperation, assistance, wisdom, and generosity of many people—my editor, academic mentors, journalistic colleagues, researchers, and news sources and people who opened their lives, schools, and businesses to me.

Several people deserve special acknowledgment for the very special contributions they have made to my work, and they have my most sincere gratitude:

Susan Zox, my wife, fellow traveler and reporter, first reader, first editor, and first believer in the value and validity of the concept underlying this book;

Kate Medina, my editor at Random House, whose commitment to this book was vital and whose intelligent, tough-minded editing sharpened the book's focus, forced me to clarify my thinking, and created a stronger interplay of problems and solutions;

John Paul MacDuffie of the University of Pennsylvania's Wharton School of Business and Howard Rosen, Executive Director of the Competitiveness Policy Council, whose thoughtful comments on the book's manuscript and on my PBS documentary series *Challenge to America* were immensely valuable on many occasions;

The two people who worked most closely with me, directing the research for this book through many long hours of hard work and devotion:

Anne Lawrence, whose thoughtful and well-organized management of the early phases of research was crucial to the book's conceptual formulation; and

Steve Johnson, who poured heart and soul into the pursuit of facts and facets of research too numerous to mention, and whose painstaking and diligent direction of the final phase of research was vital to bringing this book to completion;

Three scholars and experts who were especially generous with their help and their time:

Tom Rohlen of Stanford University, who shared his immense knowledge of Japan, its people, and their educational system;

Richard Smyser, writer, scholar, and longtime diplomat, who was my excellent tutor on Germany and its economy;

Anne Heald, who opened the way to my understanding of Germany's dual-education system and of the efforts of U.S. educators, businesspeople, and policymakers to bring the benefits of that approach to American teenagers; and

Finally, Janina Roncevic, my executive assistant, who not only can find any misplaced document or address but manages my relations to the world with invaluable equanimity and infectious good cheer.

I owe special thanks to four institutions and their leaders, whose support for this project was essential: Johns Hopkins University's School of Advanced International Studies and its Foreign Policy Institute, which has provided me with a congenial academic home and intellectual support under the leadership of Deans George Packard and Paul Wolfowitz; and the three foundations that funded the research and the extensive travel necessary for this book and for researching the PBS series *Challenge to America:* the Corporation for Public Broadcasting and its program directors, Don Marbury and Josh Darsa; the Tamaki Foundation of Seattle and its president, Meriko Tamaki Wong; and the German Marshall Fund of the United States, its former president, Frank Loy, and its program officer, Marianne Lais Ginsburg.

My colleagues in the production of the *Challenge to America* documentary series were kind to share so much of their reporting and thinking with me: Melinda Crane-Engel, the field producer in Germany, and Miho Kometani, the field producer in Japan; and the producers of the four programs—Gene Marner, Kathleen McCleery, Steve York, and the series executive producer, Phil Burton. I am most grateful to them all for their contributions to my learning and for my pleasure and satisfaction in producing that series together with them.

In Japan, I want to acknowledge the special assistance and hospitality of Karel van Wolferen, a Dutch correspondent and author whose comments and whose fine book on Japan educated me; of Yoshihisa Hayashi, the documentary producer from NHK and Walk Co., Ltd., whose support and interest opened many doors and helped me understand the Japanese; of Glenn and Sakie Fukushima, whose American and Japanese backgrounds and whose academic expertise and business experience provided countless insights; and of Marie Anchordoguy of the University of Washington and Leslie Helm of the *Los Angeles Times,* another couple whose rare combination of scholarship, reporting, and personal experience provided rich insights. Valuable help on Japan's business culture came from Michael Gerlach of the University of California at Berkeley; Clyde Prestowitz, Jr., president of the Economic Strategy Institute; and Kozo Yamamura of the University of Washington. Merry White of Boston University kindly shared her expertise on Japanese preschool and elementary education.

In Germany, I want to acknowledge the special assistance of Hans Decker, former vice chairman of Siemens in America; Fritz Pleitgen, chief of radio service at WDR, Cologne Radio and Television; and Tom Kielinger, chief editor of *Rheinischer Merkur;* as well as the help of Henning Wegener and Gisela Libal of the German Federal Press and Information Service, and of Agnes Gerlach of Inter Nationes, in arranging many contacts in Germany. For assistance and introductions, I would like to thank Jerry Livingston, former executive director of the American Institute for Contemporary German Studies; Gottfried Haas, press counselor of the German embassy; and Wolfgang Pordzig, director of the Konrad Adenauer Foundation in Washington.

In the United States, I benefited from the experience and understanding of the American corporate system of several scholars and practitioners. Michael Porter, Jay Lorsch, Alfred Chandler, Jr., Bruce Scott, and David Yoffie, all of the Harvard Business School, were most generous with their assistance, as were David Kearns, former CEO of Xerox; Edson Spencer, former CEO of Honeywell; Ray Marshall, former secretary of labor, who is now at the University of Texas; and Jeff Faux, director of the Economic Policy Institute in Washington, and his colleagues. Special help in the field of science and technology was rendered me by Frank Press, former president of the National Academy of Sciences; Charles Ferguson, author, technologist, and computer industry specialist; and Daniel F. Burton, Jr., president of the Council on Competitiveness, and his colleague, Erich Bloch. In the field of public education and policy, those who were particularly helpful were Gordon Ambach, president of the Association of Chief State School Officers; Ernest Boyer, president of the Carnegie Foundation for the Advancement of Teaching; and Tom Kean, former governor of New Jersey and now president of Drew University.

Jeffrey Garten, investment banker, author, and more recently under secretary of commerce, was a lively and provocative source of historical and contemporary comparisons of the German, Japanese, and American economic systems, as was Ira Wolf, formerly with the State Department and with Motorola in Japan.

As research associates, several people made significant contributions to the research memos that brought together the concepts and case studies that became the foundation for the *Challenge to America* documentary series and for this book. For that, I want to thank especially David Adelman, David Earling, Deborah Foster, Alan Hodges, Kevin King, and Monique Meier. For research and translation work done during the television production, I am grateful to John Greco, the research director, and to the staff of Belinda Lee, Susan Gray, Matthew Murphy, David Palmer, Aaron Stopak, and Ilja Teuchter. In the final phases of the book, I benefited from the research assistance of Stefan Sagner, Alison Watkins, and several interns—Brett Bell, Sue Driscoll, Megan Masson, Harriet Miskell, and Bageshree Vaze—and I express my appreciation to them all.

For some especially timely editorial advice and creative suggestions, I am most grateful to Jon Karp of Random House. My gratitude goes as well to Renana Meyers, for the many things she has done to steer this manuscript through Random House, and my copy editor, Lynn Anderson, whose careful, thoughtful editing saved me from many missteps.

Throughout this endeavor, the support and counsel of my literary agents, Julian Bach and Trish Lande, and of my friend Barry Frank of the International Management Group have been indispensable and much appreciated.

Hedrick Smith
Chevy Chase, Maryland
February 22, 1995

Contents

Introduction: Rethinking America   xvii

Part One: America Challenged
Mired in the Mind-Set of Success

1. New Mind-Set/Old Mind-Set—Challengers Versus Champions: 6
   Sharp Versus RCA—How Singles Beat Home Runs

2. The New Global Game—People, Quality, Flexibility, Trust: 34
   What GM and Mercedes Had to Learn from Toyota

3. The Success Reflex: 72
   IBM—Seeing Change as a Threat, Not as an Opportunity

Part Two: Education
Rethinking Schools for the New Global Game

4. School—Where the Race Begins: 100
   Teamwork or Tracking—Which Works Best?

5. High School—The Neglected Majority: 126
   Whose Mid-Kids Are on Track for the Global Economy?

6. Harlem—Teaching Habits of Mind: 152
   It's Not "Academic," It's "Real Life"

7. Wisconsin—Business and Schools as Partners: 173
   Youth Apprenticeships—A New Deal for the Neglected Majority

Part Three: Business
Matching Mind-Sets with the Competition

8. People: 196
   Protecting and Developing Human Capital

9. Partnership: 216
   The Turnaround at Ford—"We-We" Instead of "Us Versus Them"

10. Power Sharing: 234
    Owners, Managers, and Workers—"Sitting in One Boat"

11. Stakeholders Versus Shareholders: 262
    Gaining the Long-Term Edge in the Boardroom

12. The Network: 293
    Mitsubishi's Mutual Protection Society—The Corporate Clan

13. Counterattack: 317
    Motorola—No Market Sanctuary for the Japanese

Part Four: Public/Private
Government and Business as Collaborators

14. Europe's Grand Coalition: 350
    Boeing and the Challenge from Airbus

15. America's Industrial Partnership: 377
    Sematech—Reagan's Radical Rescue Plan

Conclusion

16. The Unfinished Agenda: 405
   High Performance and the Perpetual Revolution

   Bibliography   421

   Notes   427

   Index   451

Introduction: Rethinking America

The way we see the problem is *the problem.*[1]
—STEPHEN R. COVEY, *THE 7 HABITS OF HIGHLY EFFECTIVE PEOPLE*

Global competition is not just product versus product, company versus company, or trading bloc versus trading bloc. It is mindset versus mindset.[2]
—GARY HAMEL AND C. K. PRAHALAD, *HARVARD BUSINESS REVIEW*

There is nothing more difficult to carry out nor more doubtful of success nor more dangerous to handle than to initiate a new order of things.[3]
—NICCOLÒ MACHIAVELLI, *THE PRINCE*

This book is about the need for Americans to develop new ways of thinking—about ourselves as a people; about how we educate our children and run our businesses; and about how we can work together more effectively, to make America work better for more Americans.

We live in a world of explosive technological change and of intense global competition. In this restless new world, what is needed above all is a new mind-set—if America is going to sustain a high standard of living into the twenty-first century and to prevail as a global economic power in the long run. And, in fact, a new mind-set *is* being developed by the American Innovators whose firsthand stories I recount in this book.

Take Ford Motor Company. When Don Petersen became president of Ford in 1980, he was appalled. This company, once the pioneer of modern mass production, was in dire economic peril. It was losing customers and money at such a disastrous rate that Petersen was afraid it could not survive.

Ford's leadership decided that drastic measures had to be taken.

And so, like other embattled American companies in the 1980s and '90s, Ford slashed its production, shut down plants, and fired tens of thousands of workers.

But then Petersen and his colleagues discovered that these emergency measures were not enough to save Ford.

"It was the first time in my life when I could not see a solution," Petersen admitted. "On any other job I had taken, I had a pretty good idea of how to solve things after a month or so. This time, I had no idea—even after several months. We didn't have a solution to our basic problem."[4]

Only when Petersen and his top-level colleagues at Ford had exhausted all the traditional business fixes did they finally realize that what was wrong with Ford was Ford: What had worked for so long simply did not work anymore. They realized that what was needed was a deeper, more systemic change—a *rethinking* of Ford's entire way of doing business, inside and out.

In order to survive, let alone compete in the new global game, Ford Motor Company had to go through a cultural revolution from the ground up—and from the top down, starting with management's frame of mind.

A completely different way of thinking was necessary if Ford was going to win back its place in the new, dramatically more competitive global environment—an environment in which the rules of the economic game had shifted, without Ford's being aware of it.

And so Ford transformed itself from within. It adopted a whole new concept of how to do business. It rethought its old philosophy of management. It let go of old concepts about power, hierarchy, responsibility. It created new relationships among its people. It committed itself to a strategy of proactive participation, constant learning, and perpetual change.

This bedrock, fundamental change in thinking is what began Ford's turnaround in the early 1980s, a decade ahead of Chrysler and General Motors. At Chrysler, as at Ford, only when the *thinking* changed did Chrysler's fortunes begin to change. Later, that same process of rethinking also began at General Motors, though the transformation of GM has a long way to go; in fact, it is far from over even at Ford and Chrysler.

Yet Ford's turnaround represents the kind of deep process of systemic change that is needed throughout America—a revolution that reaches far beyond the world of commerce into many walks of American life—and especially in the way children are educated and the way young people are prepared for the new world of work; in how different parts of American society must learn to work together; in how America sees itself and in how Americans go about building a more promising, more reliable future in a world where America is no longer the uncontested champion.

The American Innovators—in schools, at work, in government, and in communities around the country—have understood that what is needed in America is a rethinking of old purposes, patterns, and priorities, and they have been moving ahead and, as a result, making America work better.

Many other Americans are still stuck in old-think, in trying out half measures and old fixes, as Ford did at first, and so they have been struggling or falling behind. But traditional fixes of the old system, as Ford found out, are not enough. New technologies and global competition challenge America at the very heart of its culture—its educational system, its industry, its economic system—from the top of American society to the bottom.

Over the past decade or more, the new game of global competition has shaken up the world's old economic order, just as the end of the Cold War has altered the old diplomatic order and left America unable to impose its political will on a disorderly world. In the 1980s and early 1990s, the new economic game challenged America's economic supremacy and ravaged its industries from the heartland to Silicon Valley.

Now, in the mid-1990s, America has made an economic comeback, but critical difficulties persist and more change is needed. As America readjusts, millions of Americans are being left behind. Millions more are uneasy about the future. Rivals in Japan, east Asia, and Germany have been going through their own difficult readjustments in the past two or three years, and they are now gathering strength to compete with new force in the years ahead.

What is more, the painful 1980s have left an imprint that has soured the mood of America even during recovery. Americans mistrust short-term gains because they understand that the short term is forever changing. In economics as well as in education, it is the long term that counts.

History and a Failure in Thinking

When people get into trouble, they often do what Don Petersen did at Ford: They look first at symptoms rather than at causes—at actions or inaction, rather than at a failure of thought.

When the new global economic challenge first hit America, the early reflex of many Americans was to check their performance: Were they *doing things right*? That is, were they operating as efficiently as they could? What could they do differently?

But the more important question was: Were they *doing the right things*? That is, did their vision, their concepts, and their strategy fit the present global reality? Or was there a failure in thinking?

History teaches us that countries crumble and whole civilizations collapse when their core ideas fail or become obsolete. That is one of the prime lessons of the collapse of the Soviet system after seventy years. Its ideology was so out of touch with reality, so unable to motivate a nation, that by the mid-1980s some Kremlin leaders launched what became a new Russian revolution. In the post–Cold War era, American and Western diplomacy has floundered, most strikingly in Bosnia, not for lack of military strength but for lack of a core idea that fits and responds to the new global reality: The old anti-Communist doctrine of NATO no longer provides a guiding, unifying purpose for collective security. America and the world suffer from a conceptual vacuum.

That malady of mistaken or outdated thinking afflicts American businesses and schools, too. Their problems and dilemmas shed light on the problems and dilemmas of the wider society in which they exist, and successful new strategies in business and education point the way to winning solutions for society as a whole.

Peter Drucker, a business strategist from Claremont Graduate School in California, makes the trenchant observation that major companies in America and worldwide have gotten into serious trouble in the 1980s and '90s because their *"theory* of the business"—the assumptions and rationale on which the business was built—"no longer fit reality."[5]

What is instructive is that America's most farsighted innovators have been wise enough to see that they face not only new competitors, but a new kind of economic competition—and that only a fundamental change in thinking, not piecemeal changes in behavior, can meet this new and continuing challenge.

In commerce, for example, the American Innovators realized several years ago that there had been a seismic shift in the way the global economy works. They saw that the old rules of business no longer applied and that the old levers of economic advantage had been powerfully altered by the new economic game—and that has wider consequences for society as a whole.

Size and scale, advantages long enjoyed by America, are now often liabilities, less desirable in the new competitive arena than flexibility and agility. Low cost has given way to quality as the premier touchstone of performance. Developing technology, while important, does not work without also developing the full potential of people who can apply the new technology. Virtuoso individuals and commanding CEOs cannot operate effectively without teamwork and production networks. Collaboration has become the name of the new game.

In almost every case, hardware is less important than human software. Machines and money can be moved anywhere in the world, and since they are universally available, they are less decisive for a country in the long run than the way its people learn, organize themselves, and become motivated for high performance.

Fortunately, there are positive lessons for the rest of us, and for America's future, in the experience of the American Innovators, whose reforms offer paradigms for American society as a whole.

Their experiences illustrate that rethinking America demands first of all looking closely at our old thinking—at specific companies and educators who did *not* see the new game coming and also at the mindsets that crippled them and may now be crippling other Americans.

Over the long run, for example, labor unions cannot protect their members' jobs by clinging to outmoded job classifications and refusing to share responsibility for corporate survival; nor can management sustain dynamic growth, as Ford's management tried to do, by decreeing mass layoffs and protecting its own power without ensuring long-term employment security and active engagement for its workforce. Similarly, teachers cannot achieve world-class performance by invoking the inviolate catechism of old methods, by resisting new partnerships with parents and business, or by ignoring the need for a new relevance in education to the world beyond the classroom; nor can parents and industry hope for the best results by leaving education to the professionals without becoming far more deeply engaged in the process and focusing more resources on learning. Finally, America cannot thrive as a democratic society as long as it is riven by divisions of income, skill, race, and place, which are raised to raw wounds by uncivil public discourse, nor until it has created a more democratic system of education.

The experience of the American Innovators shows the power of inclusion. It demonstrates the dynamic renaissance generated by sharing power and by tapping the minds of ordinary workers and students, who have long been treated as unimportant cogs in America's industrial machine. Companies such as Motorola, Republic Engineered Steel, Corning Industries, Southwest Airlines, and Levi Strauss have found that success springs from engaging the energy and imagination of their average employees.

In a larger context, then, rethinking America entails the recognition that people at all levels of society are the nation's most valuable asset and that the path to renewal for America lies in the engagement of as many people as possible in the common endeavor.

In industry, a daring minority has found certain keys to a winning strategy: that trust is their most powerful motivator, that people rise to the level of the responsibility they are given, and that learning is the engine of continuous growth. Similarly, daring educators have found that establishing trust, setting high expectations for all students, and providing every single student with close personal mentoring can stimulate high performance among troubled inner-city youth and can even conquer violence in schools. In the American heartland, businesses and high schools have demonstrated that the apathy of "the forgotten majority" of average, non-college-bound students can be overcome by giving them an education that is relevant to the economy of tomorrow and by inviting them to learn in the adult world.

Time and again, the American Innovators have found that in the new competitive environment the old adversarial game does not work as well as collaboration—a sense of shared interest, common responsibility, and mutual respect—though it has often taken an enormous effort to break the old stereotypes and reach across the barriers of mistrust. Their lessons about trust, engagement, and partnerships have wider importance for American society, which is so often preoccupied by searing divisions rather than focused on its common interests, its common ground.

The lesson from the Innovators for rethinking America, then, is the need to forge integrated strategies—to make connections between elements of American society that have been at arm's length or at odds in the past.

In the new economic competition, the pieces need to be fitted together more purposefully—management and labor, business and education, government and industry. For the new global game tests much more than the competitive level of American business and technology. It challenges not only America's commercial resilience but the capacity of disparate forces to work together. It tests not only the brilliance of America's Nobel Prize–winning scientists but also the ability of America's public high schools to deliver a world-class education to the vast majority of average American teenagers, who are the foundation of America's economic future. It puts on trial our values and priorities as a people. And it tests the capacity of our leaders and our economic and political systems to lift our sights from parochial short-term interests to enlightened long-term interests.

In both education and industry, the American Innovators have shown us the way. Their stories, case by case, show how more Americans—children, young people, workers, CEOs—can develop innovative ways of thinking, of learning, and of working together for a brighter future.

Benchmarking America—The Perplexing Questions

It was America's mounting economic troubles that prompted me, in 1990, to begin thinking about writing this book.

Like many Americans, I was troubled by the sight of America's industrial giants stumbling and by the disappearance of more than 2 million good jobs in a little more than a decade[6]—many of them shifted abroad by big American companies looking for cheaper foreign labor.

In the 1980s, so much of American industry had lost its competitive edge and so many American consumers had become dependent on foreign imports that the nation's total trade deficit in that decade ballooned to $1 trillion.[7] America became a debtor nation; by 1990, it was $650 billion in the red to foreign creditors.[8]

In an earlier book, *The Power Game: How Washington Works,* I focused on the competitive arena of politics—how America's government works and why it did not work better. That book combined an overview of how the elements of Washington's power system fit together with the personal stories of individual players from Ronald

Reagan to new-breed politicians such as Newt Gingrich and Dick Gephardt.

Now my focus has shifted to the America beyond the Washington Beltway, to what is happening out there in America, in our schools and businesses, that has been causing us to falter in another competitive arena—the marketplace. I wanted to find out how America's culture of commerce is working and why it isn't working better.

Here, too, the personal stories of people—from the boardroom to the classroom to the factory floor and the research lab—were important to me, the stories of both ordinary people and corporate CEOs in America, and in Japan and Germany as well. I wanted to find out why America had lost so much ground in the 1980s, economically as well as educationally; and I wanted to know who in America—or anywhere else in the world—was doing it better.

Many questions perplexed me:

•If, as we thought, the business world is driven by technology, how could General Motors invest $77 billion in new technology and still lose ground to a much less automated company, such as Toyota? What explains that seeming anomaly?

•How could an American electronics giant such as RCA simply disappear? Why had it failed to develop its own great inventions, while Sharp, an unknown midsized Japanese company, became a global leader by developing one of RCA's inventions?

•By contrast, how could Motorola first be driven out of consumer electronics by Japanese rivals and then turn around and become a winner, doing $1 billion a year worth of business *in Japan*?

I wondered what differences in mind-set had made Motorola a winner while GM and RCA had become losers in the new global economic game. How had the CEOs of these companies been thinking?

•Are there important differences in the ways that other societies operate? How could the Europeans, for example, start an aircraft consortium from scratch and overtake every American company in the field except Boeing? And how can Boeing hold the European competition at bay over the long run?

•What would cause Ronald Reagan, an ardent apostle of free enterprise, to set up a partnership between the federal government and private industry in the field of computer chips? And could that partnership fairly claim a role in America's comeback?

In the field of education, I wanted to see how children in other countries are being educated to prepare them for global competition and what America can learn from its rivals about helping young people make the often difficult transition from high school into the world of work. There, too, many questions nagged at me:

• At the primary level, does tracking by ability groups make sense? If so, and if America does more tracking in the early grades than countries in Asia, then why do comparative tests in math show that the highest-scoring U.S. schools fall below the lowest-scoring schools in Japan, China, and Taiwan—*by fifth grade?*[9]

• If so many average American high school graduates are having a tough time finding good jobs, how do Japanese high schools manage to place their students in jobs *before* graduation?

• Why is there such a big earnings gap between college-educated Americans and the non-college-bound, while the German system gives high school graduates an educational base that guarantees the vast majority good jobs and helps many others rise to become middle managers and top corporate executives?

• If American public schools are as hopeless as some critics suggest, how can an inner-city high school in Harlem graduate 90 percent of its students, year after year, and send 90 percent of its inner-city graduates to college—a record to be envied in more affluent suburban districts? And how can this school's formula for success be applied all around America?

For more than three years, I pursued the answers to these and other questions, traveling and reporting across America and in two other economic superpowers, Germany and Japan. I followed the trail of America's most hardheaded and open-minded corporate leaders and educators. Like them, I went abroad to "benchmark" America, as they like to say—to compare America's performance with that of its main rivals. Like these CEOs and American educators, I studied the practices and attitudes of our competitors, not as models to be copied, but as a lens for reexamining America's strengths and shortcomings, for rethinking America with a fresh perspective.

Talk of Change: People Usually Mean "Somebody Else Changing"

The changes undertaken in recent years by America's most agile and innovative companies have helped power America's economic recovery in the mid-1990s. They and others have become models, inspiring imitation abroad as well as at home.

But changing the way people think and behave does not come easily. Take a simple thing such as dieting: Millions of people try to diet every year; time after time they fail—because losing weight permanently means changing ingrained habits. Multiply that problem for the individual to the scale of a large organization—whether a business or a school system—and the challenge of change is enormous. As Machiavelli observed four centuries ago, "There is nothing more difficult to carry out nor more doubtful of success nor more dangerous to handle than to initiate a new order of things."[10]

Americans love to talk about change. We embrace the newest fads and fashions, the latest news, the freshest innovations—whatever's "hip" or "in" at the moment. Change is America's credo. We are a young nation that has thrived for two hundred years on tilting at the old order and on proclaiming that we are at the new frontier. In taste as well as in ideology, we want to be modern, up to date, leading edge.

Yet as David Kearns, the former CEO of Xerox, observed wryly: "Everyone likes to talk about change, but they're really talking about *someone else* changing. Change is onerous. . . . And often, therefore, big institutions don't make the changes until it's too late. One of the mistakes that I made at Xerox was doing too little, too late—several times in a row."

In fact, Kearns asserted, it usually takes a crisis to shake people out of their old ways. "Without outside pressure, such as the competitive pressure from the Northern Europeans or the east Asians," Kearns asserted, "you don't make those changes because they're too difficult."[11]

Jiro Aiko, a managing director of SONY, commenting in 1991 about America's complacency, declared with shocking bluntness: "What America needs is an *economic* Pearl Harbor!"[12] In short, unless the threat is overwhelming and unless it impinges directly on our vital interests, we Americans can be slow to react. And for many Americans, the global economic challenge crept up too gradually to set off alarms.

Still, here and there, private "Pearl Harbors" did galvanize people such as Don Petersen at Ford, David Kearns at Xerox, and Jack Murphy at Dresser Industries. In his shirtsleeves one warm September afternoon in his Dallas office, Murphy, the soft-spoken CEO of Dresser, recalled his own Pearl Harbor—the shock that woke him up to the deep-seated problems within Dresser. He had flown to Tokyo mainly as a precaution, to benchmark Dresser's performance against Japanese industry. Knowing that Dresser was the world's biggest producer of heavy oil-drilling equipment, Murphy was feeling confident about his company.

"We had no direct competitors in Japan. I figured we were the best in the world at manufacturing," Murphy told me. Suddenly his voice dropped: "Then I saw the Japanese—and I realized we had a long way to go." When Murphy landed back in Dallas, his colleague, Dresser President William Bradford, found Murphy "white faced—scared to death."[13] And Murphy went to work like a religious convert—he set about to rethink, transform, and rejuvenate Dresser Industries.

Sometimes the wake-up call comes from a totally unexpected quarter. For Procter & Gamble, it happened when P&G decided to market Pampers, its disposable diapers, in Japan. The company expected to impress Japanese consumers with American ingenuity and corporate prowess. Instead, confessed CEO E. L. Artzt, the Japanese housewife gave the American company a lesson in quality.

The typical Japanese mother is an extraordinarily demanding consumer because, according to Artzt, she has grown up in a business climate "where virtually every company manufactures products to a standard of zero defects, and she had come to expect that level of quality in every product."[14] And Pampers did not make the grade.

To meet the perfectionist standards of the Japanese housewife, Procter & Gamble had to reengineer its Pampers over and over again. Step by step, P&G made its Pampers lighter, more portable, more leakproof. Listening to Richard Laube, P&G's Pampers manager for Japan, you would think that P&G had created a new high-tech space suit for astronauts. "To survive in Japan," said Laube, "Pampers had to upgrade its product no less than four times in thirty-six months. This Pamper is now three times thinner than the original model. It's shaped for better fit, has a waist shield and leg gathers to stop leaks."[15]

Procter & Gamble eventually got it right, and its sales in Japan grew nicely. The improved Pampers were also marketed in the United States, so American consumers benefited from the perfectionism of their Japanese counterparts. From that experience, Procter & Gamble gained a new sense of the meaning of quality and, as Ed Artzt commented later, a new appreciation of Japan as "perhaps the toughest, most competitive, fastest-moving consumer market in the world." As Artzt observed, "One of the reasons the Japanese products are so successful in the U.S. and Europe is that Japanese companies sharpen their teeth—competing furiously against one another—in their own home market."[16]

When the global challenge first hit Americans with full force, however, the reflex of many corporate leaders was not to rethink their ways or their products but to deny that they had serious problems. Resistance to change was widespread, even among America's best and brightest. People blamed cheap Asian labor, foreign exchange rates, the lack of investment capital in America, the federal deficit. They blamed everything but themselves as the sources of the problem, and not until that finger pointing gave way to self-examination did their fortunes begin to change.

The Danger of Declaring Premature Victory

Now, even though America has bounced back in the 1990s, there is a danger in declaring premature victory and using America's recovery, while Japan and Germany have been in recession, as a reason to stand pat.

In 1993, for the first time since 1985, America was ranked by the World Economic Forum in Switzerland as the world's most competitive economy. Even so, the Forum warned of future U.S. decline unless America makes progress in such vital areas as education and worker training.[17]

After several years of humbling setbacks, the temptation to declare victory is strong. The triumphant cry "We've won. We're number one!" echoed in corporate America and the business press throughout 1994, with the implication that America was over the hump—that fundamental changes were no longer needed and there was really not much that America could learn from foreign competitors.

Yet while the picture has improved for America, trade figures offer little consolation for the long term. *Fortune* can trumpet that, in 1993, Chrysler made more profits than all of the Japanese carmakers put together—but Japanese producers still managed to win more than 23 percent of the American car and light truck market in 1994, while the

American Big Three were selling to less than 1 percent of the Japanese car market.[18]

Nor have the chronic economic migraines of the 1980s been cured. In 1993, the Japanese exported $28 billion worth of autos and auto parts to America, while American auto and auto parts exports to Japan were $26 billion less, or $1.8 billion. In 1994, U.S. automotive exports increased slightly (to $2.7 billion), but auto imports from Japan rose even more sharply (to $31.4 billion), so the automotive trade deficit widened to nearly $29 billion.[19]

In computers, chips, and telecommunications, the pattern was similar. In those arenas, Japanese exports to America in 1993 were $31.9 billion and American exports to Japan were only one sixth that level ($5.2 billion)—partly because the Japanese market is not truly open to imports.[20] By 1994, the picture in those sectors had improved somewhat, but the trade gap was still running $20 billion against the United States ($27.4 billion in Japanese imports versus $7.7 billion in U.S. exports to Japan).[21]

And there were other disturbing omens—the value of the dollar dropped to 100 yen, American middle-class living standards stagnated, corporate layoffs continued. More broadly, while America's overall economic growth in 1993–94 outshone Japan and Germany, what counts most is long-term performance. From 1979 to 1992, America's economic growth per capita averaged 1.1 percent a year, compared with 1.8 percent for Germany and 3.2 percent for Japan.[22] The gap was narrowed by America's comeback in 1993 and 1994, but, to recover from the past fifteen years, America had a lot of ground to make up.

Moreover, America's rivals have not been idle. Just as America made painful adjustments during its 1990–92 recession, Japan and Germany have lately been doing the same. As they have done throughout the postwar period, both countries were learning from America. They have engaged in their own restructuring, modifying their economic systems at the margins yet maintaining the most essential and distinctive elements: lifetime employment in Japan; power sharing and youth apprenticeship training in Germany. By 1994, the German and Japanese economies were turning up again, and economists were projecting new competitive tests ahead for America, especially from Japan and east Asia.

Finally, and most importantly, the process of change is steady, never ending. It stops for no one. That means that the process of renewal in both thought and action must be constant in order to ensure survival and success, as I believe the stories in this book demonstrate.

There is no such thing as the perfect plan, the final plateau. Improvement must be continuous; the revolution is perpetual.

The temptation to interpret America's economic recovery as proof that American industry has conquered the global challenge would misread the basic lesson of the American Innovators—namely, that the challenge to America—its businesses, its educational system, its culture of commerce—is permanent and unceasing and that a basic rethinking of America is essential if we are to attain a higher quality of life for ourselves and our children in the twenty-first century.

PART ONE

America Challenged

Mired in the Mind-Set of Success

Almost any opinion poll in the 1990s reveals a deep-seated anxiety among people about America's economic future.

No matter how much we are told that the economy is growing or how many new jobs are created, Americans feel they are on shaky ground. They worry about the future—both their own and their children's.

One symptom was the news in late 1994 that charitable giving in America had declined despite three years of American economic growth. When pollsters asked people why they were giving less at a time when the American economy was strong, more people said they were worried about not having enough money to take care of themselves in the future than had been worried a few years earlier, when America was in fact experiencing a recession. Nearly three people in four did not trust in their own economic future.[1]

One reason for this anxiety, of course, is the painful jolt America experienced in the 1980s: the competitive decline of one American industry after another. That experience left a deep uneasiness in people. The lives of millions of Americans were thrown into economic upheaval, and that experience left a special angst because the economic trauma had been so unexpected; it was so at odds with the gossamer optimism of the decade.

For perhaps the most prevalent popular image of the 1980s in the minds of many Americans was that of America Standing Tall Again, an image personified by the jaunty figure of a smiling, triumphant President—Ronald Reagan.

In the 1980s, America passed beyond the self-doubt of the Vietnam era and the political shame of Watergate. It was the decade in which America won the Cold War and became the world's only remaining superpower. Ideologically, America saw its beliefs and its way of life vindicated. Economically, too, America was growing. The 1980s was a decade in which the American economy generated several million new jobs, engaging more women in the workforce than the nation had ever known.

In retrospect, however, we can see that there was a hollowness at the core of America's resurgence. For the 1980s were, in fact, a time when seismic shifts were challenging America's dominance.

Nations in east Asia and Europe were growing faster economically than America was; they were overtaking America. Washington's politicians might claim an economic boom, but the hard fact was that America's economic growth was feeble by comparison with that of its rivals, the second lowest of nine leading economies—a per capita growth rate of 1.5 percent a year compared to 2.3 percent on average for Japan, Germany, France, Britain, Italy, Scandinavia, and Canada.[2] In terms of rising productivity—the engine of economic growth and a high standard of living—the 1970s and the 1980s were America's two worst decades in the twentieth century.[3]

At the commanding heights of the American economy, important pillars of the nation's industrial might were collapsing. American industry no longer had the United States as a captive market: American consumers had discovered that other nations made better products than American industry did, and they defected to Japanese-, German-, and Korean-made cars, television sets, appliances, fax machines, and computers.

Wall Street awoke late to the weaknesses of America's greatest companies, but out in the heartland ordinary people felt the pain sooner. The mass layoffs began in 1980 and rolled on until the early 1990s—300,000 at General Motors, 150,000 at Ford, 180,000 at IBM, tens of thousands more in steel, textiles, and the high-tech industries of Silicon Valley. For many of those who still had jobs, the news was demoralizing. The take-home pay of average Americans was actually lower in 1989 (by 13 percent in real terms) than it had been at the time of Richard Nixon's first inauguration in 1969.[4] In fact, the 1980s was the first decade since the Great Depression during which large numbers of Americans saw their living standard seriously decline.[5] At the same time, people in other countries were gaining: In the 1980s, ordinary Germans and Japanese were earning more than their American peers were.[6]

In these trends were severe warnings that something was seriously amiss in the American system and that changes were overdue. In fact, these omens were heeded by a number of America's leading innovators, some of whom figure in this book and in America's recovery in the mid-1990s. But more typical was the fateful immobility and the blindness of such American giants as RCA, General Motors, and IBM. All three were victims of attitudes and habits embedded in the American culture of commerce and typified by the mind-set of success.

Because, paradoxically, America was handicapped by the very fact of its long economic success.

Success brings power, wealth, and authority. It also carries with it the seeds of a potentially perilous cast of mind: the notion that one is immune to failure, an attitude of superiority toward competitors, a tempting and self-destructive conviction of one's invincibility and infallibility. Successful people, institutions, and nations are tempted to coast on past performance.

Most people have to scramble to keep up with the times, but the successful often suffer from a special myopia, a difficulty in seeing the onset of a new order, the rise of a revolutionary new way of doing things, the coming of a new game that will shatter the world of the comfortable and the complacent.

By the 1980s, America was afflicted with the success syndrome. In earlier decades, the military humiliation of the Vietnam War and the diplomatic humiliation of the Iran hostage crisis had chastened America as a political power. But America had been so successful economically for so long that many Americans found it hard to comprehend that America had to rethink its entire way of doing business.

The first step in rethinking America today is to understand the failed strategies of yesterday. Before moving on to explore winning strategies that America's Innovators have developed for the 1990s, we need to understand what actually happened in the 1980s—where and why so many intelligent people went wrong, what habits and mind-sets were—and still are—embedded in America's way of thinking, educating, and doing business, and which caused some of America's flagship corporations to stumble so badly.

These three stories—of how RCA, General Motors, and IBM stumbled in the 1980s—can serve as cautionary tales, with vital lessons for the years ahead.

1

New Mind-Set/Old Mind-Set— Challengers Versus Champions

Sharp Versus RCA—How Singles Beat Home Runs

> *If you're always going after the home run, there's a high possibility of going bankrupt. So in business as in baseball, maybe you have to settle for a bunt or a single.*[1]
>
> —ATSUSHI ASADA, EXECUTIVE VICE PRESIDENT, SHARP INC.

What could be more American than the home run—the crack of the bat, the ball a blur, streaking over the fence by inches or soaring majestically out of the ballpark and emptying the bases.

A home run is instant drama; it brings the crowd to its feet. A solo performer can wipe out the opposition with one swift blow. In an instant, he can become a hero. Few moments in American sports have a more mythic aura than that delicious instant when Babe Ruth, the incomparable Sultan of Swat, pointed to the right-field stands, dispatched a home run to that very spot, then trotted jauntily around the bases, tipping his cap to his roaring fans. That Ruthian feat is a quintessentially American moment—the cockiness, the delivery, the adulation.

In America, the home-run hitter is king.

Not so in the cultures of America's rivals. It is one of the mind-set differences that set America apart from our greatest economic competitors in the new global game. The Germans and Japanese, for example, emphasize teamwork over individual heroics, a more gradual scoring over the long term rather than the quick, decisive hit. Americans have long had a culture of champions, accustomed to winning. Germans and Japanese have a culture of challengers, intent on gradually catching up to the champions.

Americans do not mind that home-run hitters strike out more often than steadier, more pedestrian batters. Fans forgive the strikeouts if they can get the home runs. Sluggers are the heroes, the legends of the sport. Babe Ruth was the first giant; and over the years, American fans have watched other players chase Ruth's record-setting feats— first Roger Maris topping Ruth's once-unreachable record of 60 homers in one season, then Hank Aaron piling up the astounding lifetime total of 714 home runs, to eclipse Ruth's mark but not his memory. Each season, the home-run race becomes a captivating saga of individual prowess.

The home-run hitter is a fitting symbol for America's celebrity-driven culture, which glorifies the solo performance. Hollywood, the TV networks, sports, and industry all live and die by the star system. For in America, not only the sports culture but the culture of commerce has a love affair with the home run.

In business, the home run is a stunning, breakthrough invention (the Polaroid camera, the Xerox photocopy machine, the transistor) that produces a sudden economic gold mine. American industry is in thrall to the home-run mind-set. It is forever banking on a technological thunderbolt—a commercial "home run"—to change the game in one fell swoop and give some American company an unbeatable competitive advantage.

The home-run mind-set reflects a culture dominated by a short-term mentality, impatient money, and an all-or-nothing frame of mind that is quick to quit if the return on investment is not fast and handsome.

In other countries, the game—both the game of baseball and the economic game—is played very differently.

The Japanese brand of baseball, for example, reflects a very different cultural mind-set. Japanese teams may import a few American sluggers to add spice to their game, but the essence of the Japanese game is not a single winning stroke but a mosaic. The Japanese variant of America's national pastime does not idolize the megastar. Japanese baseball is an elaborate dance of teamwork, not a celebration of individual heroic feats. Its trademark is putting the pieces together patiently.

In Japanese baseball, the sacrifice bunt, the infield single, the walk, the stolen base, the precise craft of the sacrifice squeeze play, and how these elements are combined are appreciated more than the home run. The Japanese savor the slow, steady accumulation of runs, incremental progress rather than a sudden big coup.

In keeping with Japanese culture, Japanese baseball does not glorify the innate ability of the born star. It values relentless practice and hard work—committed striving for perfection. Less glamorous than the American game, Japanese baseball rewards perseverance and tenacity.[2]

Similarly, in Japanese business, the mind-set is different from that of America's culture of commerce. The Japanese path to ultimate success is *kaizen,* the incremental accumulation of skill and know-how, continuous improvement.

The Japanese are not known for stunning inventions and breakthroughs of global dimensions, but they have prevailed time and again and have won grudging respect for their ability to polish, perfect, and magnificently mass-produce the discoveries of others.

With the mind-set of challengers, not champions, they have pursued progress step by step, reaching out constantly for what is new and adapting it swiftly to the marketplace. They never stop to rest on their laurels. They labor tirelessly, making progress in tiny increments. Whereas Americans can often seem fickle and too quick to give up if their commercial home run does not materialize rapidly, the Japanese have been endlessly patient, and they have turned that patience to great national advantage.

The Consequences of the Home-Run Mind-Set

The champion mind-set and the home-run mentality offer one vital explanation why America's seemingly invincible commercial dominance was so terribly shaken in the 1980s.

In one field after another, American scientists would come up with brilliant inventions, only to see the Japanese and others take over production and reap the commercial benefits. The economic cost to America was devastating in terms of jobs and profits. Many an American company and its top executives tried to rationalize after the fact, but those explanations rarely got to the heart of the problem. Some U.S. companies recovered, by shifting to new lines of business. But for others, such as RCA, the home-run mind-set led to a story with life-and-death consequences, as we will see. The RCA story is a parable with a resonance that echoes through American life.

Not only did RCA ultimately disappear as a corporation, gobbled up by other companies that kept its name to market their products, but also America lost an entire new industry—the flat-display-panel industry. This industry turned out to be of vital importance worldwide in the Information Age—vital to computers, to telecommunications, to aircraft, to medicine, to defense, to many high-tech industries. Not only RCA but other leading American corporations made attempts to get into this field at various points in the 1970s and '80s, but they failed to turn America's technological edge into industrial leadership.

By contrast, Sharp of Japan turned this same RCA technology into a stunning rise from an unknown, run-of-the-mill electronics firm in the 1970s to a global powerhouse in the 1990s.

The difference in the destinies of RCA and Sharp lies in the difference in the mind-sets of these two companies and the mind-sets of their countries.

RCA: The Culture of Creativity

May 1968 was a high point for RCA, an American giant synonymous with the best in modern electronics and television. For decades, RCA had been at the forefront of the world in communications technology. In that year, 1968, RCA was at its zenith, enjoying record business, when it summoned the world press to its corporate headquarters in Rockefeller Center in midtown Manhattan. The press conference was called to celebrate a new invention, yet another testimony to RCA's strength and its creativity.

At that news conference, on May 28, 1968, RCA unveiled what it thought would be a new technological home run for the company.

The hero of that press conference was George Heilmeier, an enthusiastic thirty-two-year-old electrical engineer, and the leader of an eight-man research team at RCA's famed David Sarnoff Laboratories in Princeton, New Jersey.

For decades, Sarnoff Labs had revolutionized the world of communications. David Sarnoff, the visionary leader of RCA from 1930 to 1969, considered the labs and their 1,200 researchers and technologists the jewel of his corporate crown, the fount of the creations that had made RCA so hugely successful. Sarnoff Labs was famous for its spirit of free inquiry. It was a place where imagination, innovation, and creativity were valued above everything else. Its inventions had changed the world of consumers and the world of science. The first postwar TV set had been made at Sarnoff Labs. Color television had been invented there. Sarnoff Labs was the site of such important scientific breakthroughs as the electron microscope, sophisticated metal oxide transistors, solid-state amplifiers for satellites, and other marvels of modern electronics.

For five years, George Heilmeier and his team of young, free-spirited researchers had been secretly developing the technology for yet another technological revolution. What Heilmeier unveiled at the May 1968 press conference was a stunning innovation that pointed the way toward David Sarnoff's dream—creating "television on the wall," a television screen so flat and compact that it could be hung on the wall, like a painting, or put on a small shelf, like a book. This new invention—a flat, electrified display panel—held out the promise of incredible savings, convenience, mobility, and compact size, all great improvements over the cumbersome, bulky cathode-ray tubes of traditional TV sets.

Here was a revolutionary invention with untold commercial potential. By 1994, the flat display panel fitted with electronic circuitry would drive a $4-billion-to-$5-billion-a-year industry that was projected to rise to fifteen to twenty billion dollars annually by the year 2000.[3]

Along the way, a broad range of products would develop from this revolutionary invention. By the early 1970s, milky white display panels based on Heilmeier's innovation would be on tens of millions of pocket calculators and digital watches. Other applications of the technology would quickly multiply—display panels on industrial gauges, hotel clocks, home appliances, automobile dashboards, stock market tickers, medical imaging systems, and aircraft cockpit control panels. Later there would be vast armies of lightweight screens that would make possible the millions of laptop and notebook computers that would sweep the world in the late 1980s and 1990s. Still later would come video screens for handheld portable TV sets and cameras and eventually much larger screens for high-definition television.

A vision of twenty-first-century Information Age inventions—TV on the wall, video telephones—this was what Heilmeier and George H. Brown, RCA's vice president for research and engineering, presented at RCA's 1968 press conference to some fifty reporters, photographers, and network camera crews.[4]

"We showed all of the prototypes that we had built," Heilmeier recalled, "the electronically controlled window, the calculator displays, the electronic clock display. We showed some static displays of TV pictures."

Liquid crystal, a mysterious milky substance produced in nature by the octopus and squid, was the key discovery at the heart of the new commercial bonanza. Liquid crystal had long been of interest to scientists because it flows like a liquid but is composed of tiny crystals that, like diamonds, reflect light. RCA's Sarnoff Labs had been trying to improve the quality of color TV when its researchers had discovered that if electrical charges were applied to liquid crystal in certain patterns, the crystal would operate as a kind of camera shutter. When the molecules of liquid crystal were lined up in parallel rows, the crystal allowed light to pass through, making a dark image. When the liquid crystal molecules were twisted horizontally by an electrical charge, the crystal blocked light and reflected it opaquely, making a light image.

Heilmeier's team had turned this phenomenon of light and chemistry into a visual display, which they called an LCD—a liquid crystal display. They sandwiched an extremely thin film of liquid crystal—one thousandth of an inch thick—between two panes of glass, one coated with a reflector and wired in vertical and horizontal rows. By applying different charges of electricity to these rows on the display panel, Heilmeier's team created checkerboard patterns of light and dark. Manipulating the squares of light and dark, they could make simple numbers, letters, and pictures. Their early displays were pretty crude, but, as the technology was developed and perfected, the images would become much more fluid and sophisticated.

Heilmeier's liquid crystal display was commercially exciting because it required very little space and very little electrical power, far less than a conventional TV tube. Operating it would require a miniaturized electrical system, a system of microelectronics. Once that was developed, images could be produced on a small, portable panel operating at low power and low cost. It would take years to achieve the complicated graphics and moving pictures required for a television screen; yet the basis had now been created. So there was intense interest in what Heilmeier unveiled.

"There was a virtual explosion of press coverage—I mean, explosion," Heilmeier recalled. "It was picked up all over the world. It was carried on the nightly news. I mean, suddenly this was celebrity time. The folks in New York said, 'Gee, when we announced color TV, we didn't get this kind of response.' We spent, I would say, the next four to six weeks doing almost nothing but talking with people from the media. What a great time! We were all young. We were walking on cloud nine."[5]

This was a moment to savor for George Heilmeier, who would be named America's Outstanding Young Electrical Engineer of 1968 by the fraternity of electrical engineers, and who would later be awarded the National Medal of Science. It was also an hour of triumph for American science and research. For here was yet another in a galaxy of brilliant American discoveries that affirmed America's technological preeminence throughout the world. Since the end of World War II, this kind of innovation had helped secure unchallenged leadership of the global economy for American industry. This new invention was also a consummate achievement for one of America's great research centers and for the driving genius of David Sarnoff, who was forever challenging and inspiring RCA's most talented minds to generate new marvels to dazzle and delight the world and keep America at the industrial forefront.

RCA and Quick "ROI"—Return on Investment

What happened to George Heilmeier's invention graphically illustrates why America lost a great deal of its technological leadership and commercial supremacy in key economic sectors in the 1970s and 1980s.

This episode is the story of a giant corporation's fall and of the high costs of the old mind-set, the home-run mentality. It is an episode that has parallels with other American high-tech creations—color television, the transistor, the VCR, instant photography, the laser printer. These American innovations, like the flat display panel, were commercialized by other nations at great cost to both U.S. corporations, which saw their profits plummet, and millions of American workers, who saw foreigners get the jobs that Americans would have had, and once did have. So the LCD story carries crucial lessons for the 1990s.

"The loss of this display technology reveals fundamental weaknesses of the U.S. high technology system," the magazine *Technology Review* asserted in 1991. Not only RCA, but other American companies tried and failed to develop and mass-market liquid crystal displays, but all lacked the vision, the patience, and the grit to stick with developing the technology. The Americans wanted an obvious home run and a quick payoff; otherwise, they quit the race.

"Neither large nor small firms were able to match a dazzling innovation with the manufacturing muscle needed for commercial production," *Technology Review* asserted. "As a result, a vital technology developed in the United States slipped away."[6]

Ironically, despite its history as an innovator, RCA had become prone in the early 1970s to letting its new inventions get away, if those inventions did not realize what the corporate world calls quick ROI—return on investment.

As Heilmeier tried to move the LCD into commercial development, he ran into a serious malady at RCA—the success syndrome. RCA had become a giant of electronics with revenues of roughly $3 billion. Its corporate arteries were clogged with the cholesterol of success—echelon upon echelon of corporate bureaucracy and a corporate mind-set that resisted change. Once daring and innovative, RCA's management had grown cautious and conservative. The top brass had their eye on profits, not technological leadership. They were coasting on success, stuck in comfortable grooves, wary of unpredictable ventures.

Vested interests fought for the status quo. Each of RCA's main divisions was out to protect its established lines of business—in defense electronics, communications technology, the NBC television and radio network, and consumer electronics, especially color television based on the cathode-ray tube. These divisions of RCA had the self-assured tunnel vision of established champions. Sitting on top, they saw little need for or virtue in developing new and unproven technologies.

And as at many an American corporation, success had left a leadership problem. RCA was suffering from a loss of vision at the top; David Sarnoff was in the sunset of his career, and, while he was still nominally chairman at seventy-seven, he was fading in energy and influence. The running of RCA had been turned over to his son, Robert Sarnoff.

Still, the vacuum at the top was more than a matter of single personalities. Most significant was a problem common to many American corporations—a gap in technical competence and understanding at the top of the business. RCA was not led by executives with scientific training and technical experience, people with a keen grasp of the technologies that would shape the marketplace of the future. "Bob Sarnoff was not a technologist—he felt uncomfortable with technology," Heilmeier told me.

David Sarnoff, though not trained in science, had developed a feel for technology and had come to understand it from four decades of experience. But Bob Sarnoff had brought in a new breed of corporate executive, quite unlike those of his father's generation. Above all, the new breed were managers—marketing men, financial experts, business school graduates—people whose first devotion was to managing corporate stability, not stirring the pot with innovations.

In a company built on change, the agents of change had become pariahs—and that was the supreme cost of the success mind-set.

In this new incarnation of RCA, the free-spirited inventors at Sarnoff Labs had become an isolated universe whose spawnings were not always welcomed in the executive suite, because exploiting new technology inevitably meant disrupting existing operations. RCA's new leadership had developed a corporate attitude of standing pat. As the 1970s unfolded, they gained a reputation for what *Fortune* magazine called "managerial flat-footedness and missed opportunities."[7]

The Champion Mind-Set and the High Cost of Impatience

Appearances at that Rockefeller Center press conference in 1968 were misleading. On the surface, RCA seemed to be proclaiming a new thrust of corporate innovation and a major new line of business. In reality, RCA's senior managers had not yet really embraced the new technology. Some had learned from experience that converting an innovation such as Heilmeier's liquid crystal display into David Sarnoff's "television on the wall" would require patient investment and years of development. There would have to be many steps and intermediate products along the way. It would take a long-term commitment and a long-term strategy to realize the full potential of the liquid crystal display and to reap its commercial dividends. But RCA's corporate culture in the early 1970s was no longer geared to patient development.

One hope for Heilmeier was engaging David Sarnoff personally. In his prime, Heilmeier believed, David Sarnoff would have pushed very hard to develop the liquid crystal display panels. According to Heilmeier, the early Sarnoff "would have said, 'I want that right away!' and heads would have rolled" if a commercial product were not developed to his satisfaction.[8] In the 1940s and 1950s, David Sarnoff had frequently visited the labs and personally talked with RCA's research teams. But by the late 1960s, David Sarnoff lived in the corporate stratosphere, sealed off from direct contact with researchers by what Heilmeier called "a no-pass filter" of headquarters staff.

The Rockefeller Center press conference gave Heilmeier a rare opportunity to speak to David Sarnoff, who asked immediately "about the potential of this new discovery to build his dream, a flat-panel TV." Heilmeier told Sarnoff the potential was there, but it would take years to develop. But Sarnoff did not seize the moment. "He was an old man, he was tired," Heilmeier said. "And so, the intellectual vim and vigor that he radiated in his earlier years was not there."[9]

Without David Sarnoff's visionary patronage, the liquid crystal display project caromed off one internal obstacle after another. It was a victim of corporate impatience, of the success mentality, and of tunnel vision within RCA. At a minimum, Heilmeier and his colleagues told me, the vested interests in RCA saw this new technology as a distraction; at worst, a disruption—or even a challenge. For if the LCD project were successful, it would eventually put out of business RCA's big cash cow—its production of cathode-ray tubes for television sets. Huge factories would have to be shut down or converted from an old manufacturing process to a new one. That was both expensive and threatening to the status quo; hence the resistance.

Conceivably, RCA's top leadership might have seized on the technology had it promised an instant home run or had there been pressure to keep up with competitors. But RCA's management had become risk averse. Under competitive pressures, they had tried producing mainframe computers and videodiscs, but both efforts had ended in financial disaster. Also, the economic recession of the late 1960s had wounded RCA. So RCA's new leaders favored stability over the risks inherent in David Sarnoff's restless quest for constant innovation, and they felt no competitive heat to move fast on LCDs.

It is a large leap to go from crafting a few hand-tooled prototypes during research in the lab, as Heilmeier's team had done, to designing and engineering products that can be mass-produced. Commercial development demanded significant time and money and many competent people. RCA had all the skills and technologies necessary to develop the LCD, but the company's leaders gave it no special push; they left the LCD project underfinanced. Heilmeier may have been too shy, too young, and too low down in the corporate hierarchy to demand sufficient resources. Within RCA, the competition for money was fierce; the financial squeeze hit the LCD as soon as it moved out of research into product development. Corporate jealousies and turf battles slowed its takeoff. Heilmeier's team were reduced to mere consultants; responsibility for developing commercial products fell primarily to an operating division, whose heart was not in the task.

"The liquid crystal display work was turned over to the semiconductor division for productization," Heilmeier recalled. "They were interested in manufacturing semiconductors. For them, the LCD was a distraction. It wasn't their baby. It was completely out of their field. So, to say the least, the LCD wasn't welcomed by the product division."

The semiconductor division acted as if it wanted to sabotage the project, according to Heilmeier and his team. Even though this division made microelectronic chips, it balked at producing the special chips needed for LCDs. It assigned a weak marketing manager to check out the market potential for using LCDs on industrial displays, watches, and calculators. When he came back reporting that "there's tens of millions of dollars of business out there for this stuff," division higher-ups told him to try to sell other RCA products, such as Numatrons. When customers still wanted to try LCDs, the division chiefs ordered them to fork up money for product development.

"I don't really think that RCA knew the potential of what we had," said Joe Friel, Heilmeier's senior technician.[10]

"RCA wasn't prepared for the success of liquid crystals," Heilmeier commented. "They were said to be 'too difficult to make.' Liquid crystals were viewed as a threat rather than an opportunity by the product divisions."[11]

Diversification: Taking Your Eye off the Ball

The final crippling flaw at RCA was that its corporate managers took their eye off the ball. They were caught up in the American corporate fad of the 1970s—diversification. With their focus on the cash box and the bottom line rather than on maintaining and improving RCA's core competency in high-tech electronics, Bob Sarnoff's management team branched out into totally unrelated businesses. They were in pursuit of short-term financial success rather than long-term technological leadership.

"Bob Sarnoff had a different vision for RCA than his father," Heilmeier remarked. "His father saw RCA as a high-tech giant, constantly innovating. Bob Sarnoff at that time wanted to build a more stable company, and he felt that diversification was the vision of the future for RCA. He bought Hertz Rent A Car and Coronet Carpets and Banquet Foods, companies that were really quite different than the base business of RCA."

In the long run, diversification proved shortsighted and counterproductive. With its executive energies and its investment funds diverted into other fields, RCA took a beating in its core business. While it was off investing in carpets and rental cars, RCA was losing ground to the Japanese in consumer electronics. By the early 1970s, its manufacturing capability was slipping. Its products were no longer top quality. It was no longer paying close enough attention to detail, no longer investing enough funds and talent in the lines of business that had made it great. What it did, it no longer did well enough to meet the new competitive pressures from abroad.

The effort to commercialize Heilmeier's LCD suffered, as did other RCA operations, from the company's drift off its main course. Eventually, with constant pushing from Heilmeier, the research division, the marketing manager, and some interested customers, RCA set up prototype production for sample wristwatches and calculators using LCDs. But this halfhearted effort had little impact. The quality of the products was not good enough. The scale of the enterprise was too small.

"RCA tried to get into the calculator business, and they tried to get into the watch business using liquid crystal displays, and they failed," Heilmeier told me. "The Japanese beat them—built a better product at lower cost. And so there was no business momentum here at RCA to keep the torch alive."[12]

"RCA blew it—they tried to manufacture the display, and they failed miserably," was the blunter assessment of Larry Tannas, who headed a rival liquid crystal development project at North American Rockwell that also lost out to the Japanese. "They sold samples of LCDs, but they couldn't manufacture them in quantity. They just blew it."

Without a quick marketing success, RCA's top brass lost interest in developing liquid crystal displays. George Heilmeier, seeing no future at RCA for the innovation he had fathered, quit the company in frustration. He became a White House fellow and then moved to the Pentagon's research agency.

In 1973, just five years after the Rockefeller Center press conference trumpeting the LCD discovery, RCA bailed out of LCDs entirely. It sold its watch prototypes to Timex and its LCD patents to the Japanese. Its impatient managers, not having invested enough in resources or their own time to make LCDs a success, totally surrendered to others what would become a multi-billion-dollar market.

The maladies that crippled the LCD project epitomized a wider corporate pathology at RCA that contributed to the company's long, slow decline and its ultimate disappearance as a corporation.

Sharp: The Underdog Mentality

An entirely different dynamic was at work at Sharp, then a modest-sized manufacturer of radio and television sets and other consumer goods in Osaka, Japan's second largest city. The corporate culture at Sharp, and across Japan generally, was a stunning contrast to the corporate culture at RCA—and the differences were crucial to the destinies of both RCA and Sharp.

Sharp was focused on immediate applications of the new technology, even if they represented only modest progress, and was less demanding of big financial returns in the short run than RCA was. Sharp was driven by an underdog mentality. Its leadership was heavily steeped in engineering and therefore quick to grasp the potential of new technologies. Moreover, Sharp was given to patience and persistence, in the style of Japanese baseball, not to the uncertain lure of a technological home run.

Ironically, Sharp's reaction to the RCA press conference in 1968 was the opposite of RCA's own reaction: Sharp was galvanized into action. Sharp's scientists and executives recognized the great potential of LCD technology; developing it became central to Sharp's dramatic rise as a global powerhouse in high-tech electronics.

The way the word traveled to Sharp was fascinating in itself. One of the follow-up television broadcasts on RCA's invention was done by NHK, Japanese Public Broadcasting. In a special report on RCA in 1969, NHK spoke in awe of RCA's achievements, reporting that RCA had once "poured fifty billion yen (then $140 million) a year into the development of color television alone." For NHK's cameras, Heilmeier demonstrated to a Japanese reporter the prototype clock and other displays and he explained his work. The significance was not lost on NHK. "This research is expected to have various applications in the future," its commentator observed. "Making the flat-panel television with the liquid crystal would be quite an achievement. Thus, Japanese manufacturers are paying close attention to this."[13]

No one paid closer attention than Sharp. Traveling in Japan in 1993, I came across a Japanese scientist named Tomio Wada who had seen the NHK broadcast. At that time, Wada had been a thirty-two-year-old section chief at the central research laboratories of Hayakawa Electric Company, which later changed its name to Sharp. Wada told me about his reaction to Heilmeier's findings.

"I was quite excited because I saw something very new," Wada recalled. "I immediately knew this new kind of display would be used into the next generation."

Wada alerted his superiors. "We began to discuss the merit of using the LCD," he said. Sharp was impressed with the low power consumption of Heilmeier's innovation, the lack of glare on the display, and the thinness of the glass panel. They saw an immediate use for the LCD. "If we were to adapt this to the electronic calculator, we were sure that we could make the calculator smaller," Wada said. "So we had great interest in this new display."[14]

One vital difference between Sharp and RCA was that Wada could quickly get to the company's top executives, and they immediately understood the implications of what he told them.

Sharp's leadership, dating back to its founder, Tokuji Hayakawa, an engineer who had invented the Eversharp pencil, had a solid grounding in technology. Sharp's top executives were mostly engineers, as is typical in most Japanese manufacturing corporations. So the top brass closely followed leading-edge technologies. Also, in contrast to RCA's steep corporate pyramid, with its many layers of bureaucracy, Sharp's setup—again in Japanese style—had few layers from top to bottom and good horizontal communications among its divisions. Sharp fostered close contact among top executives, line managers, and senior researchers, a tradition that continues today despite Sharp's enormous growth.

In the late 1960s and early 1970s, Sharp was driven by the underdog's hunger to break into the big time and by a willingness to gamble on new technology to make its mark. It was dwarfed not only by such American giants as RCA, General Electric, and Westinghouse but by the major electronics firms in Japan—Matsushita, Toshiba, Hitachi, and NEC (Nippon Electric Corporation). It was looking for its own niche, and it was ready to stake its resources and its corporate destiny on creating a new product.

Although Sharp's leaders understood David Sarnoff's dream of a flat-panel television screen, Tokuji Hayakawa, the founder and president, and Tadashi Sasaki, vice president for technology, did not demand an instant home run. Hayakawa and Sasaki were looking for a competitive edge on one product, a stepping-stone on which to build and then to pursue *kaizen*, patient, step-by-step, incremental improvements.[15]

Sharp had another advantage: It was not handicapped by success. What Sharp saw and exploited—which RCA failed to see and exploit—was the enormous potential of the calculator market. Before the pocket calculator, for decades business had to rely on clunky, hand-cranked office calculating machines that weighed twenty to thirty pounds. Suddenly, in the early 1970s, an explosion of technology opened the way for replacing this basic office machine—for those who had the vision and also the skill to integrate the necessary technologies for a mass consumer market. The first calculators were crude and inefficient; they ran on batteries, and the batteries were always running out. One common model exhausted six small batteries in three hours. Once the low-power LCD was perfected, the life of a calculator jumped to a hundred hours.

So for Sharp, Heilmeier's LCD offered a huge competitive advantage in Japan's "calculator wars." Sharp could gain a big edge if it could beat its competitors into the market with lighter, more efficient calculators based on liquid crystal displays (just as Seiko led the way with LCD digital watches). With the mind-set of the challenger, and of patient *kaizen* improvement, Sharp saw that a lightweight calculator not only would reap early profits but would give Sharp a springboard for developing other applications of the LCD. That approach enabled Sharp eventually to move into laptop computer screens and high-definition television in the 1990s. Unlike RCA, therefore, Sharp was willing to start that long process—to tackle the difficult work of marrying liquid crystal technology with the microelectronic circuitry necessary to operate LCDs.

In the 1970s, Sharp poured $200 million into early LCDs.[16] That was a huge investment for a company of Sharp's size—and far more than RCA put into creating LCD products. Eventually, Sharp executives told me, Sharp invested several billion dollars in developing LCD technology and building elaborate high-performance plants for manufacturing flat-panel displays.

The original investment was a big gamble, according to Atsushi Asada, who as a young engineer of thirty-seven was picked by Sharp to head its team for developing LCDs and who is now Sharp's executive vice president. Sharp was betting the company on LCDs. "Without success in this area, there was no tomorrow for our shop," Asada admitted. "We were very ambitious. We had a passion—we wanted Sharp to be one of the leading companies in the electronics industry. We looked into the future, and we thought investment in this area was important."[17]

Manufacturing: A High Art Given Low Status in the United States

In the American scheme of things, the glory typically goes to the inventors of the original breakthrough. The follow-up implementation—manufacturing—has been looked down upon as secondary, boring, pedestrian. By the 1970s, very few major American companies were led by people who had made their careers in manufacturing divisions. The route to the top was through finance or marketing.

In Japan, by contrast, skills in manufacturing have been highly regarded and finely honed, while Japanese science has taken a backseat to science in America and Europe. America had long counted on its scientific lead to maintain its industrial lead, but during the 1970s and 1980s the balance of competitive advantage shifted in favor of expertise in manufacturing. Inventions in electronics were tumbling over one another so rapidly that each technological advance gave only a temporary edge until it was matched by competitors or overtaken by the next advance. The process of "reverse engineering"—taking apart someone else's invention, analyzing how it is put together, and then copying that invention or improving on it—became a high art not only in Japan but in Korea, Taiwan, Hong Kong, and elsewhere. Very quickly, reverse engineering nullified the inventor's advantage, especially if (like RCA) the inventing company failed to commercialize its invention while it was still a secret.

So, despite America's continued dominance in science, the Japanese attention to the art and science of manufacturing eventually enabled the Japanese to dominate one market after another in the 1980s. They were able to piece together the elements of the technical mosaic before anyone else did, and this accumulation of expertise generated competitive advantage and eventually leadership in industry after industry.

In the case of the LCD, Sharp had started from far behind. RCA had a five-year lead in the laboratory plus all the necessary electronic technology in its operating divisions. Yet while RCA chose to diversify into carpets and rental cars, Sharp set about mastering the unglamorous work of making LCDs.

Sharp had only the skimpiest information about the workings of the LCD, from the NHK broadcast. So it sent Wada's superior, a man named Mito, to Sarnoff Labs with four other Japanese researchers, to talk to Heilmeier. RCA would not let the Japanese photograph anything, but Joe Friel, one of Heilmeier's team members, remembers that two Japanese scientists made meticulous drawings of every item in their labs, while three other Japanese researchers asked voluminous questions.

Should RCA have been more wary of the Japanese visit? I asked Friel.

"Yeah, well, we opened it to the public," Friel responded. "We had the press conference, so basically we were telling them."

"Were you surprised at how fast they developed it?"

"They moved very fast, yes," Friel replied.[18]

Tadashi Sasaki, Sharp's vice president for technology, tried to make a deal with RCA for joint development of LCDs. "I wanted to make a trade: We buy RCA's liquid crystal, and they should buy the design technology for manufacturing the electronic calculator from Sharp," Sasaki told me. "RCA refused to make the swap. They said they were going to invest heavily on their own development of crystal. But really they wound up selling their liquid crystal operation to Timex. They said we must pay for the patent royalty. We had to pay about $3 million."[19]

Still, Sharp needed sophisticated microelectronic circuitry for operating the Heilmeier flat display panel. It tracked down North American Rockwell, which was developing its own LCD for a calculator. In one of its Pentagon contracts, Rockwell had also developed just what Sharp needed, a fancy transistor known as a metal oxide semiconductor. Unaware how aggressively Sharp was moving on the LCD, Rockwell sold Sharp the semiconductor patent for $2 million.[20] Like RCA, Rockwell was after a quick cash return on its technology, without seriously worrying about the longer-run consequences of its action.

Sharp went into a crash twelve-month effort to produce a mass-market LCD calculator by April 1973. The schedule was extraordinarily tight for designing the calculator, melding the technologies, constructing a factory, training the workforce, and going into operation. But Sharp did it—and became the first in the world to go into mass production of LCD calculators.

Rockwell, which had counted on marketing calculators in America, was totally surprised by the speed of Sharp's operation.

"Back then, no one could have envisioned what happened," admitted Larry Tannas, who headed Rockwell's LCD development. "The attitude at Rockwell was 'We have our U.S. market. They have their Japanese market.' We were ahead on technology. But we needed money. We got the technological jump and sold it to the Japanese. The Japanese were fast to exploit this breakthrough. The Japanese invested and made the technology manufacturable. Sharp succeeded in the consumer design. It had more finesse on the manufacturing side. We at Rockwell failed. They just overwhelmed us. They beat us at the game—in our own market. So we got out of the business in 1975."[21]

The Culture of *Kaizen*—Continuous Improvement

When I visited Sharp's huge electronics complex at Tenri, an hour's drive from Osaka, in 1993, they showed me a dazzling variety of liquid crystal displays. From the primitive products of Heilmeier's lab, this powerful technology had evolved through several generations. The small, cigarette-sized panels of the 1970s-era calculators had grown to large seventeen-inch television screens. What had once been in black and white was now in color. What had once been still-life images on a screen had become the swift action of a hockey game. What had been crude static numerical displays were now exquisite, fluid pictures of moving fishes and birds with the lifelike quality and color of Audubon bird prints, perfect in every detail. From one continent to another, surgeons could watch one another on liquid crystal displays, doing intricate operations in real time. As developed by Sharp, LCDs had opened an entire universe of visual communication.

The LCD story was typical of a disturbing pattern that took root in the 1970s and '80s: American firms losing market share to the Japanese and surrendering their leading positions in consumer electronics.

Ampex gave up on its magnetic videotape recording technology; they sold it to SONY, which generated a mass market worth tens of billions of dollars. SONY was quick, too, to jump on transistor technology for making TV sets, while American firms, such as Zenith, clung too long to the old vacuum tubes and got left behind. In calculators, Sharp, Casio, and Toshiba, three Japanese firms, were gobbling up the world market, making huge profits, and using that money to improve their calculators—either enlarging the display panels or shrinking the size of calculators to the thinness of credit cards.

From calculators, Sharp went on to develop new products using LCDs. It created new markets, reaping profits at each stage and then vigorously reinvesting to generate yet more new products. Sharp's strategy was to go for modest successes, one at a time, rather than go for broke, RCA style.

"It is difficult to keep hitting home runs," commented Atsushi Asada, the young engineer who had headed Sharp's LCD project. "The home-run hitter is also the strikeout king. And so, if you're doing business and if you're always going after the home run, there's a high possibility of going bankrupt. So in business as in baseball, maybe you have to settle for a bunt or a single, and this way the business is more stable."[22]

Central to this characteristic piece of Japanese philosophy is *kaizen.* For example, Asada explained, "We had to make screens thinner and thinner, more and more complex. This was research by industrialization."[23]

A fascinating concept: Innovation emerged not only from inventing new technology but from constantly perfecting one's skill at making things. This required not home runs but teamwork, precision, and patience. The mastery of new and exceedingly complex technologies did not come with one magical breakthrough. It took time and extraordinary skill to graft each new improvement onto existing microelectronics and chemistry, and to do it all with excruciating precision.

Over the years, the quantum jumps in technology repeatedly came from America and Europe, but the Japanese were the first to learn how to capitalize on them. Among these jumps were (1) the "twisted nematic" liquid crystal—ten times more powerful than Heilmeier's original "dynamic scattered" display; (2) a whole new family of organic compounds for LCDs; and (3) a leap from "passive" to "active" matrix displays, first demonstrated in the mid-1970s at Westinghouse Electric by a Hungarian-born scientist named T. Peter Brody.[24] Brody's new method was the biggest technological breakthrough of all. It dramatically increased the visual sharpness of LCDs and made motion easier to display by embedding a huge integrated circuit of transistors in each pane of LCD glass, so that every single point could be flashed on and off to create changing pictures.

It took years and billions of dollars to perfect that intricate technology, and the American home-run mentality was not geared to that protracted process. At Westinghouse, Brody, like Heilmeier at RCA, bounced from one division to another, scraping funds together. Then, as Westinghouse lost its market in color television to the Japanese, it killed Brody's project in 1979. Brody raised some venture capital and set up his own company, Panelvision, but he never could get to the manufacturing stage.[25]

Brody's experience fit a pattern: While the Japanese were playing *kaizen,* the Americans were playing all-or-nothing. At least fifteen American corporations—not only Westinghouse, RCA, and Rockwell, but IBM, Raytheon, General Electric, Exxon, Texas Instruments, GTE, and Control Data—got into and then gave up on efforts to develop flat-panel displays. Several Silicon Valley start-ups also made temporary breakthroughs in the 1980s but lacked the capital to go into manufacturing. Big American companies were wary of bankrolling these operations.

"Not only did the little companies lack the necessary capital, but the big companies were scared off by Japanese willingness and ability to throw enormous capital at the problem, suffer losses, and stick with the technology through thick and thin," commented Clyde Prestowitz, an experienced Reagan administration trade negotiator and author of *Trading Places,* an authoritative book on the Japanese-American economic rivalry. Prestowitz quoted Tsuyoshi Kawanishi, executive vice president at Toshiba, another LCD producer, as asserting that Toshiba "was prepared to lose money for ten years to gain leadership in flat-panel-display technology. No U.S. company has that kind of staying power."[26]

It was true that the Japanese were armed in the 1980s with "patient capital"—investment money patient enough to pursue a technology through a couple of decades to the big payoff. "Patient capital" is also a fruit of the long-term "singles" mind-set of the Japanese people; they save five times more of their money than Americans do, and private Japanese savings provide huge reserves of capital for industry.

But what many Americans underestimated was the unbeatable advantage the Japanese were gaining by gradually building their manufacturing know-how. While Brody struggled at Westinghouse to learn how to make his "active matrix" LCDs, Sharp was light-years ahead of him—putting hundreds of thousands, even millions of transistors onto the glass panels of its LCDs. Even a few defective transistors rendered the entire screen worthless. So perfection was crucial in making LCDs, and perfection required an unrelenting focus on quality and precision that came naturally to Japanese culture. That concentrated and continuous effort over twenty-five years is what produced the dazzling images I saw at Sharp's display center in Tenri in 1993.

The heart of Sharp's strategy, Atsushi Asada told me with quiet pride, was step-by-step investment. "We started with the electronic calculator, and we saw that it was successful," Asada said. "Then we turned to the electronic notebook computer. We always checked carefully at each stage whether this investment was worthwhile. But in the end, it totaled a few billion dollars."

Kaizen paid off. The Japanese left the Americans in the dust in the liquid crystal display industry. By the early 1990s, a few small American companies were still making flat-panel displays for specialty users such as the Defense Department. In 1991, these U.S. companies accused the Japanese giants of "dumping" sophisticated "active matrix" display panels below cost on the U.S. market, and the U.S. International Trade Commission slapped on a 63 percent penalty tariff. But that did not help. IBM, Apple, and other U.S. computer companies had become so dependent on Japanese LCDs that they moved computer assembly plants abroad to avoid having to pay the tariff. So that tariff cost the United States even more jobs.[27]

In hopes of leapfrogging the Japanese, Motorola teamed up on a new technology with InFocus, a small firm, in 1993, but that effort later folded.[28] The Pentagon, increasingly concerned by its dependence on Japanese flat panels for military uses, gave subsidized contracts to other small companies. Finally, the Clinton administration decided to try to get back into the LCD game by doing what American industry had given up on—investing in large-scale manufacturing capability in the United States. In April 1994, the Defense Department announced a $1 billion–plus public and private partnership to build four major LCD factories.[29]

The message was unmistakable: Singles had triumphed over home runs.

By the mid-1990s, Sharp and eighteen other Japanese firms controlled 95 percent of the world market in flat-panel displays.[30] Sharp, once an underdog, had become king of the hill. It claimed more than

40 percent of the global LCD market—$1.5 billion worth of business a year. It dominated the high-end, high-quality, high-price part of the LCD market. All across the board, Sharp had become an economic powerhouse. With more than $13 billion in annual income and nearly 65,000 employees, it was bigger than RCA had been in its prime.[31]

While Sharp was climbing, RCA fell. Not only did its core business suffer, its diversification strategy boomeranged. By the early 1980s, RCA was spinning off its side ventures in a frantic effort to raise money to save the mother company, but it was too late. In 1986, RCA was gobbled up by rival General Electric and its consumer electronics division was sold off to Thomson S.A. of France. RCA had become a victim of its own myopia—stuck in an old mind-set, coasting on past success, too shortsighted and impatient to follow through on its own best inventions.

Sarnoff Labs: The Brain Drain

For America, the story did not end with RCA's demise. Not only was an invention lost, a laboratory was figuratively lost, too—the Sarnoff Labs became a symbol of the brain drain in research that still plagues America in the 1990s.

RCA's Sarnoff Labs was one of American industry's scientific treasures. It ranked with a handful of renowned industrial research centers—AT&T's Bell Laboratories in New Jersey; IBM's Thomas Watson Research Center in Yorktown, New York; General Electric's labs in Schenectady, New York; and Xerox Parc, the Palo Alto Research Center in California. In its heyday, Sarnoff Labs had a staff of 1,250, 40 percent with Ph.D.s.

Within two years of General Electric's takeover of RCA, the staff of Sarnoff Labs had been chopped to seven hundred; one third of its scientists had been let go.[32] Not long after that, Jack Welch, CEO of General Electric, gave away Sarnoff Labs to a California research and consulting firm, SRI International, with an interim subsidy of $250 million in research funding for five years.[33] But SRI lacked the money to run Sarnoff Labs, so Sarnoff scientists had to hustle funds to finance their own research projects. That dramatically altered the labs' operation. The long-term theoretical research that had produced the labs' great breakthroughs had relied on corporate support and insulation from the market. In its new guise, Sarnoff Labs had to adopt shorter time horizons and research that was more targeted at quick commercial payoffs.

Like the LCD story, the fate of Sarnoff Labs (now renamed David Sarnoff Research Center) was a paradigm for the cutbacks in American corporate research during the 1980s.

"It's happening all over, and it has already seriously diminished research all over the country," observed Richard Williams, a Sarnoff physicist whose theoretical work had made possible Heilmeier's LCDs.[34] Williams ticked off industrial labs that were being shut down or cut back at U.S. Steel, Exxon, Eastman Kodak, Du Pont, General Motors, General Electric. "It's been a continuing trend over the past five years at least. Right now we're seriously underinvesting in technology in this country." The long-term implications worried Williams. "Weakening the large institutions that have created the technology we're living on now is probably a recipe for stagnation," he said.

Elsewhere, I heard similar warnings from scientists about the dangers of the short-term mentality that was undermining America's long-term economic strength.

Arno Penzias, a Nobel laureate in physics and the top scientific executive at the celebrated Bell Laboratories in northern New Jersey, told me that since the breakup of AT&T, Bell Labs' research staff had been sharply cut. AT&T's management wanted corporate research to produce big hits in the marketplace, Penzias said, and it had no patience with failures.

"If you want an eighteen percent return on your money every year, you can't afford to wait ten years," Penzias explained. "When I came here thirty years ago, it was assumed that if we produced knowledge, people would come along later and find ways to use it. Now, a much larger percentage of my people are working with short-term horizons—one to two years. To get our money's worth, we have to have really big breakthroughs. It changes your way of operating. To justify big investments, you can't afford to fail. That breeds caution. It slows down bringing new products to market. The Japanese bring lots of products to market, kill off the failures, and keep going. They do things incrementally. They hit singles. We have to hit home runs."[35]

James E. Carnes, president of the David Sarnoff Research Center, warned in 1992: "The U.S. is facing an R and D crisis that threatens our standard of living. We will not see the full impact of this crisis for another five to fifteen years—and then it will be too late."[36]

This ominous warning marked the reversal of half a century of technological supremacy. Since World War II, America had used its leadership in science and technology to provide for national security and to ensure its commercial and industrial leadership in high-technology industries. America's unmatched research universities had been generating unprecedented success in science; the Pentagon had fostered leading-edge applications; and American corporate labs had been turning science fiction into reality. Yet, by the late 1980s and early 1990s, prestigious advisory panels to the Pentagon, the Department of Commerce, and other federal agencies were warning that America was consuming its "seed corn," losing its edge in some key technologies, and not plowing enough of its profits back into the long term.

The facts were disturbing. By the second half of the 1980s, American spending on nondefense research and development by the government, industry, universities, and private patrons, which had previously risen at a rate of 7.5 percent a year, had stopped rising, according to the National Science Board. In 1990, America's civilian research spending actually fell, at a time when the research spending of foreign competitors was rising. The downward trend "should give us real concern for the continued vitality of our research enterprise," warned Dr. James J. Duderstadt, National Science Board chairman and president of the University of Michigan.[37]

For the first time, Japan was challenging America's traditional role as the world leader in overall support of industrial research. In August 1992, a National Science Board panel asserted that, not counting defense research, Japan and Germany had through the late 1980s and early 1990s spent a larger share of their national income on civilian research and development than the United States had.[38] The Competitiveness Policy Council, appointed by President Bush and the congressional leadership in 1991, seconded that grim assessment. In early 1994, the National Science Foundation reported that overall, the United States was investing only 1.9 percent of its national product on civilian R&D compared to 3.0 percent in Japan and 2.7 percent in Germany.[39] In industry alone, the Japanese in 1991 had virtually pulled even with American industry in R&D spending, in an economy only 60 percent the size of America's.[40]

And in the related area of new investment in plant and equipment, the Competitiveness Policy Council asserted, Japanese industry had invested more in 1989, 1990, and 1991 than American industry had.[41]

The steady commitment of funds to research had a practical impact. American scientists have continued to dominate the Nobel Prize circle, and their work is more frequently cited in scientific papers than the work of any other country's scientists. But by the mid-1980s, Japanese industrial firms began to equal or surpass American firms in new patents. In head-to-head competition within business sectors, Hitachi overtook IBM; Fuji passed Eastman Kodak; Toyota, Honda, and Nissan pulled about even with General Motors, Ford, and Chrysler, excluding the aerospace patents of the American carmakers. "This shows that the Japanese drive is pretty deep," observed Daniel F. Burton, Jr., president of the Council on Competitiveness, a private American business group. "It's not just microwaves and toasters and VCR's. They're capable of mounting a challenge in the most sophisticated areas of technology."[42]

Japan in the Mid-1990s: Squeezing the Towel

With Japan in recession since 1992 and America enjoying economic recovery during 1993 and 1994, America has improved its position. American research spending has slowly resumed its climb, while such Japanese electronics giants as Hitachi, Fujitsu, and Nippon Electric have trimmed back their research budgets from 1991 peak levels, though very modestly.[43] To offset that trend, the Japanese government has increased its spending on science and technology. What is more, other Japanese firms have protected their R&D programs by cutting costs in other areas such as entertainment, overtime pay, and staff size.

SONY actually increased its development spending during the Japanese recession. "If we cut research and development, we are cutting our future," said Minoru Morio, Sony's executive deputy president. At Toyota, a managing director, Tokuta Inoue, said that to prevent R&D cutbacks, "We are squeezing water from the towel"—making cutbacks almost everywhere else.[44]

One towel that Japanese companies were not squeezing, however, was their new practice, begun in the late 1980s, of setting up state-of-the-art research laboratories in America.

Very near the shrunken Sarnoff Labs in Princeton, New Jersey, Nippon Electric Corporation (NEC) founded a new long-term basic research center and recruited scientists from Sarnoff Labs, Bell Labs, Exxon, and Xerox, among others. NEC was spending $30 million a year to hire 60 to 100 American Ph.D.s to think long term and to create new types of computers.[45] Other Japanese corporations set up labs near leading American universities: Mitsubishi, near MIT in Cambridge, Massachusetts; Canon, near Stanford University in Palo Alto, California; Matsushita, near San Francisco and the University of California at Berkeley; Hitachi, near the campus of the University of California at Irvine.[46] Japanese firms said this was their answer to the repeated American complaints that Japanese industry had for many years been profiting from U.S. research without contributing its proper share to the common pool of knowledge. Now they were reversing that trend.

This new Japanese effort has aroused some fears of a brain drain of top American scientists and thinkers away from U.S. universities and companies. By one account, Japanese firms were paying $250,000 and up for senior scientists and $70,000 for fresh Ph.D.s—in some cases 20 to 30 percent more than the salaries at comparable American companies.[47] Frank Press, former president of the National Academy of Sciences, told me of his concern that the new Japanese research strategy would make it hard for American universities to hold on to their most promising young scientists.

The Japanese offer more than money—they offer a philosophy of patience. Research scientists report that Japanese firms have been reviving the atmosphere and conditions that used to exist at American labs, where contemplation and long-term fundamental research were encouraged and supported. George Heilmeier, in competition with the Japanese, remarked that the Japanese philosophy and working conditions are extremely attractive for American scientists. Instead of a constant and uncertain battle to find money for research year by year, he noted, American scientists find Japanese firms offering the opportunity to pursue long-term research, free of the burden of raising their own research funds or having to produce quick results for the market.

In short, the Japanese firms with their *kaizen* philosophy were taking the long view, just as Sharp had done on the LCDs, confident that this research strategy would ultimately achieve success.

"Is It Management or Leadership?"

The trends were disturbing to George Heilmeier, who in 1991 had become CEO of Bellcore, the research and development consortium of the seven regional Baby Bell companies, after a career at the Pentagon and Texas Instruments. America's most serious problems, he said as we walked around his old haunts at Sarnoff Labs, are not problems of performance but problems of mind-set. In his view, too many American companies are still treating research and development as an expense instead of an investment.

"When you start looking at research and development as an expense, you tend to be very, very shortsighted in your outlook," Heilmeier asserted. "Any good manager minimizes expenses. That's part of the reason why we've had some difficulties in this country. I think the Japanese have had a solid appreciation for the role of research and development in building businesses and building companies. Japanese management has focused on R and D as an investment."

What troubled Heilmeier, who in his late fifties was still bubbling with boyish enthusiasm, was that American business has too few top executives who understand technology, especially the technology that will change their businesses in the future.

"There are some companies that have executives who *do* understand the technology: Roy Vagelos, Merck; Andy Grove, Intel; Bill Gates, Microsoft; Norm Augustine, Martin Marietta," Heilmeier observed. "They all have something in common—their businesses are very successful. You'd think people would begin to understand that. But the Harvard Business School tells you, by golly, if you get an MBA from Harvard Business School, you can manage anything. But this is more than management—it's leadership, and Harvard Business School doesn't teach you anything about leadership. Management is all about running an enterprise in a smooth manner. Leadership's all about change.

"Now, you might say, 'Well, what do we need in this country, management or leadership?' It's not either/or, you need both. Unfortunately, in this country we've tended to swing the pendulum too far to the management side. Where in Japan the pendulum has swung very heavily toward the leadership side. It's not uncommon for Japanese CEOs to come up through the technical line."[48]

Over the years, Heilmeier had traveled often to Japan, where he was awarded a citation for the discovery of the LCD technology. Heilmeier felt some remorse that the Japanese, and not the Americans, had developed his LCD, but he also felt that was better than having it ignored. Moreover, his contacts with Japanese corporate leadership had underscored some important differences with America.

"The higher you go in a corporation in America, the more distractions you must deal with—dealing with regulatory matters, dealing with the Congress, dealing with various special-interest groups," Heil-meier said. "A CEO in this country finds it very difficult to delegate that responsibility.

"In Japan, it's just the opposite. The higher you go in a corporation, the more time you have to do strategic thinking about the business. Their management teams stay together for very long periods of time, so they know each other very, very well. Consequently, the CEO feels that he can delegate things to his subordinates, things that in the U.S. we can't delegate.

"In Japan," Heilmeier concluded, "the role of a CEO is to spend time thinking about the future of the business."

The long-term *kaizen* view, not the short-term home-run mind-set.

2

The New Global Game—People, Quality, Flexibility, Trust
What GM and Mercedes Had to Learn from Toyota

> *It's a special mentality of quality. Our car has a philosophy in the tradition of Karl Benz and Gottlieb Daimler, who said one hundred years ago, "We will produce the best or nothing."[1]*
> —MATTHIAS KLEINERT, COMMUNICATIONS CHIEF, DAIMLER-BENZ, IN 1991

> *In this age of rapidly changing technology, the winners in the business world from now on will be those companies who are most aggressive, creative and successful in implementing advanced technological concepts.[2]*
> —ROGER SMITH, FORMER CEO OF GENERAL MOTORS, IN 1984

> *Teamwork is everything.[3]*
> —TAICHI OHNO, FORMER CHIEF ENGINEER, TOYOTA, IN 1978

The most far-reaching changes in the global world of work over the last fifty years have taken place in the auto industry.

Technological advances have come more rapidly in high-tech industries, but in human terms—in terms of the way large numbers of people work, in the way people think about work—the greatest revolution has come in autos. And it is still going on.

Most Americans have noticed the external symptoms of change— the turmoil of mass layoffs, plants closing, regions reeling in economic distress, governments battling over trade quotas and "voluntary restraints."

But of more fundamental importance to everyone who works, and to every parent, student, and teacher, is the metamorphosis that has gradually unfolded inside the global auto industry—first in Japan, then later in America and Europe. *Inside* automobile assembly plants is where there has been a revolution to achieve higher quality and where that quality revolution has caused the greatest transformations in the nature of work.

What has changed most fundamentally is the greater responsibility being given to workers to take charge of ensuring higher quality and to take a proactive role in organizing their own work—responsibilities that in the past management jealously kept for itself. Inevitably, with greater worker self-management, the relationships between managers and workers have changed, and ultimately so has the matter of who has power in modern industry and how that power is exercised, day in and day out.

The auto industry has been both a model and a catalyst for change in many other economic sectors. Phil Condit, president of Boeing, Jack Murphy, CEO of Dresser Industries, and top executives in other branches of industry told me they have taken important cues from what has been happening in the global auto industry. The auto industry has had this ripple effect because its internal transformation has been so wrenching and profound that what in 1980 was considered a modern way of making cars is now obsolete—a fact experts knew but most of the rest of us were ignorant of. What is more, that significant shift in the production system for cars has had powerful implications for all manufacturing businesses—for that matter, all service businesses. It also has implications for how young people should be educated and prepared for the economic world of today and tomorrow.

This process of dynamic change originated in the automobile industry and was set into motion by a clash of cultures—the commercial cultures of America, Germany, and Japan.

We typically speak of automaking as one industry, and yet it is a mistake to think of that industry, or any industry, as being the same the world over. Over time, the trend is toward convergence; peoples learn from one another. But the various branches of an industry, such as automobiles, have developed differently in different parts of the world; they have taken on very different characteristics that reflect their cultural roots, the attitudes and historical experiences of their home countries.

And so, in fact, there has been not one auto industry, not one system for producing cars, but three very distinctive systems of production—mass production in America, craft production in Germany, and flexible production in Japan.

These three systems collided, and from that collision have come the lessons that today propel the process of change, not only in autos but in the world of work in general.

The Mercedes Mind-Set: Quality at Any Cost

In Europe, the oldest auto-manufacturing region in the world, the car was born in the nineteenth century as a luxury item for the aristocracy. This small, elite clientele demanded high quality; for them driving was initially a hobby or a sport, not a utilitarian mode of transportation. European aristocrats wanted a car that could maneuver easily on narrow, winding roads—"a driving machine," the Germans called it. High performance was essential. Low cost was far less important. Aristocratic tastes and demands fostered a German automobile industry in which production was on a relatively small scale and the engineering and craftsmanship had to be superb—features that came to be the distinctive traits of the German automobile industry, of companies such as Porsche, BMW, and Mercedes-Benz.

People in Germany hold science and technology in awe; engineering has a special mystique. The Germans have an undisguised romance with precision instruments, high-speed trains, intricate machine tools, high-fidelity optics, fine printing presses, automated lasers, and meticulously crafted consumer goods, everything from luxury cars to electric shavers, espresso machines, and children's toys. "The most popular field of study among male German university students is *maschinenbau,* or mechanical engineering," writes Harvard business economist Michael Porter. "Prestige in science and technology in Germany dates back a century. The world's first graduate schools, and doctoral dissertations requiring original research, were German inventions." In a book comparing the competitive advantages of eight nations, Porter asserts that German industry has maintained its edge by "an unfailing commitment to preserve technical leadership."[4]

A passion for quality is also a national trait. Pride in workmanship is in the marrow of German bones. It has its roots in the guild system, which dates from the Middle Ages. For centuries, master craftsmen have jealously guarded the quality of German products, held new workers to demanding standards, and put them through long, exacting apprenticeships and journeyman training. Maintaining high standards is the heart of this system, and Germans take it very seriously. The *Meister,* or master craftsman, is the ultimate authority—a highly regarded figure in German society, whether his craft is manual or professional. German plant managers and CEOs talk of their *Meisters* with great respect. Wagner's opera *Die Meistersinger* celebrates the German tradition of painstakingly working up to mastery. The novice has to apply to join the craft group, then be guided by qualified superiors to develop skill and expertise. Only after satisfying the trainers is the acolyte granted the opportunity to demonstrate merit—in Wagner's opera, to become a master singer by delivering a "master song."[5] Germans put great stock in this demonstration of mastery as an assurance of quality. It is quality that counts most.

As consumers, Germans are very demanding. If Americans look first at price and convenience, the German touchstone is value—by which they mean quality and durability. When Germans buy cars, shavers, blenders, furniture, appliances—anything—they expect to own them for a decade or more. Germans are less moved than Americans are by marketing, advertising, price cutting. They assume that quality and durability will cost more, and generally they prefer paying more to bargain shopping. In German homes, when I asked people when they had bought their appliances, often it was so long ago that they could not remember the last time they had replaced an oven, a toaster, or any other electric appliance. Ilja Teutcher, a German graduate student at Georgetown University in Washington, told me that in his family, three generations—his grandfather, his father, and himself—had for several years shared the same Braun electric shaver. He had inherited it after his grandfather had died. Five years later, Ilja told me, "I still have it, and it's working fine—not a single mechanical problem, and I expect to have it another five years."[6]

Germany's independent consumer agency, the Stiftung Warentest, the Foundation for Product Testing, is far tougher than America's *Consumer Reports.* Its ratings illustrate how fussy Germans are. Items that Americans would call excellent often rate only a "good" in Germany. In the January and February 1994 issues of *Test,* the foundation's magazine, for example, not a single product merited the highest rating—"very good"—and this was in a dozen different consumer lines, including coffee machines, baby high chairs, VCRs, and bicycle locks. At least twenty-five items were rated "insufficient" or "very insufficient."[7] In Germany, a high quality rating has to be earned.

And so it is with cars. In the world of luxury cars, Mercedes-Benz embodies the German pursuit of excellence. "It's a special mentality of quality," asserts Matthias Kleinert, corporate chief of communications for Daimler-Benz. "Our car has a philosophy in the tradition of Karl Benz and Gottlieb Daimler, who said one hundred years ago, 'We will produce the best or nothing.' "[8]

Throughout its long history, Mercedes has pursued the strategy of not merely providing superior quality but setting the standards of good taste and status. Cost and price were no object. Mercedes became so successful in the global high-niche market that by the mid-1980s not only hundreds of thousands of Europeans but nearly one hundred thousand Americans a year were shelling out whatever it took to buy a Mercedes.

"We have been *forming markets* with first-class quality—our customers have accepted that," Helmut Werner, the photogenic chairman of the Mercedes managing board, assured me one wintry afternoon in Stuttgart. "People identified themselves with the product, the car. They tried to 'buy themselves up' into a higher model. Their egos were defined by ornaments like gold, diamonds, sterling silver—our car. Quality was priceless."[9]

The epitome of Mercedes's status chic was the superluxurious S-car launched by Mercedes in early 1991. At that time, senior executives at Mercedes and BMW exuded confidence about their ability to beat back the upstart Japanese, who were just beginning to push into the luxury-car industry. Unlike the Americans, the Germans asserted, they had built a solid base on unparalleled German engineering, the superiority of German design and technology, painstaking customer service that cemented lifelong loyalty (Mercedes even calls to congratulate its customers on birthdays, wedding anniversaries, the births of their children), and the quality of German craftsmanship. "With the S-car, we felt we were launching the best car in the world," Helmut Werner later said. "It was a car for the ego and the glory."

At its debut in 1991, the S-car epitomized the German love affair with complicated engineering, sophisticated design, precision instrumentation, and what Mercedes proudly, if immodestly, terms "the striving for perfect solutions." This sumptuous new road cruiser was a proud technical achievement for Mercedes. Its special features filled a twelve-page glossy brochure and made fascinating reading for auto aficionados.

The technical perfection of the S-car production line at the Mercedes plant in Sindelfingen matched the technical extravagance of the car itself. The "marriage" of the S-car body and wheel undercarriage was performed with stunning efficiency in a few seconds by an expensive array of robots. Another mesmerizing spectacle was the mechanical ballet performed by a single agile robot with an entire 210-pound dashboard panel, filled with instruments and stretching the width of the car. Like a male dancer, the robot gently lifted the cockpit like a horizontal ballerina, swung the dashboard up into the air, pointed it head down over the hood of an approaching S-car shell, and then fluidly inserted it through the open windshield—with only millimeters to spare. The robot then dropped the dashboard neatly into place, while two other robots fixed it to the auto body.

But the personification of the Mercedes craft system of production were the *Meister*s walking among the machinery, hands clasped behind their backs like the Duke of Windsor, coaching other workers, consulting, answering questions, ensuring that the production ran smoothly. They were ubiquitous in their full-length blue lab coats, looking more like professors than factory foremen. They were the ones responsible for seeing that quality was built into Mercedes cars.

At the "cockpit" assembly area, where workers were inserting instrumentation and wiring into dashboards, Horst Rebmann, a stout thirty-six-year veteran at Mercedes, whose cinnamon curls fringed a balding pate, was in charge.

When I asked Rebmann how one becomes a *Meister*, his first response was the German formula: Take the demanding training courses under the auspices of the chamber of industry and trade. Then, more candidly, he spoke from his German soul: "But you can't learn to become a master craftsman just from training. It has to come from your heart, something younger people often don't understand."

As for Mercedes's quality, Rebmann gave credit to the precision of the design and engineering, and then he emphasized: "What you see today on the streets and in the market depends on people. Ninety percent is due to workers. Design can be created, but quality depends on the worker."

For Rebmann, the secret of high performance is training. The worker, said Rebmann, "sees how the automobile is supposed to look, and that's how he's brought up to standard. I am responsible for the training, to see that the workers learn their task correctly. And our system works."[10]

One reason it worked was that Mercedes went over every car with a fine-toothed comb before it went out the door. At the end of the assembly line was a massive inspection and rework area, a symbol of Mercedes's commitment to quality. Walking through that section, I saw armies of inspectors scrutinizing finished cars while workers hand-polished the finish, checked bumpers, tested brakes, fly-specked every interior detail, every component under the hood. Teams of blue-coated *Meisters* and experienced assemblers reworked every slightest defect, no matter how long it took. This extra, second effort at quality ensured perfection, but it was costly.

Unquestionably, German automakers have long taught the world a great deal about how to achieve superior quality. Yet even at Mercedes, this paragon of German manufacturing, there were flaws in the German system: Both cars and plants were overengineered, and costs were sky high.

The exalted S-car epitomized these problems. It had taken at least ten long years to conceive, design, and develop that car, an eon in the swift-moving market of the 1990s. The development cost had been staggering for a niche-market car—at least $1.5 billion. And when the S-car was unveiled at the Frankfurt Auto Show in 1991, it was castigated by German environmentalists and some of the German press as the devil of "three twos"—it cost 200,000 deutsche marks (roughly $130,000), it weighed two tons, and it only got about twenty kilometers (or twelve miles) to the gallon. Even in the narrow, high-end luxury market, those handicaps were going to hurt Mercedes; not only was BMW gaining ground in Europe, but the Japanese soon would be.

Throughout the 1980s, while the American automobile industry was under assault, the German luxury-car makers had largely been spared head-to-head competition with the east Asians, mainly because the Japanese had started by making low-priced cars. But in the early 1990s, the Japanese were moving upscale, partly to make more money in America, where an informal import quota limited the number of cars they could sell. In 1991, the Germans were just beginning to feel competitive pressure. It seemed unlikely that Mercedes could carry on its expensive quest for quality without lowering costs and getting cars to market much faster. I would return later to see how Mercedes would respond.

The General Motors Mind-Set: Mass Marketing

In America, with its wide-open spaces, long roads, cheap gasoline, and democratic ideals, Henry Ford turned the "driving machine" of European aristocrats into a mode of transport for the burgeoning middle class. The American car was mass-produced for a low cost and bought by customers who, in comparison with European aristocrats, did not know much about technology and were not discriminating about quality. As time wore on, a comfortable ride became essential; the American auto of the 1950s was the family road cruiser, a living room on wheels. Never mind the oversized interiors or the waste of fuel. Unlike Europe, America had space and gasoline to burn.

Achieving the low cost necessary for a mass market led to production based on economies of scale. Costs were cut by volume production. Quality, variety, and quick reaction to the market were of secondary priority. Henry Ford reportedly quipped that people could have "any color Model T they want, so long as it's black." Both the product and the production process were standardized so that relatively unskilled or semiskilled workers could perform the endlessly repetitive tasks of putting the car together, weld by weld, piece by piece. Unlike the Germans, with their low-volume craft production, American auto companies favored very large production runs of the same model of car to realize economies of scale. In this scheme, size was a great advantage; big companies did best.

General Motors epitomized the American system. It became the world's largest corporation—a giant among giants. By the early 1980s, GM's global empire reached into thirty-nine countries, with 950,000 employees and a gross income topping $80 billion. In 1980, as Chrysler and Ford were jolted by Japanese imports, GM felt impregnable—a citadel with such vast resources that it could overwhelm any challenger. In the American auto market, General Motors was Gulliver. Single-handedly, it nearly matched an entire world of Lilliputian competitors, accounting in 1978 for close to 48 percent of all passenger-car sales in the United States.[11]

General Motors had applied Henry Ford's philosophy to the hilt, and for decades it set a standard that the world tried to match. It won competitive advantage through sheer mass. Year after year, it piled up huge profits and gained a commanding grip on the popular-car market through enormous volumes of production, with cosmetic changes in trim and exterior design to differentiate models that were essentially the same under the skin. Its trademark was gigantic centralized production facilities. Its stamping plants churned out hundreds of thousands of fenders, doors, and body parts of all kinds and shipped them to assembly plants all over the country. GM was the most integrated of all car companies, American or foreign, producing 70 percent of its own parts, claiming to be saving and pocketing the profits that outside suppliers would have made. Its assembly plants often built just one car model—250,000 copies a year. Its organizational divisions spanned several makes of cars. Its designers used the same platform—the same wheelbase and undercarriage design—for Buicks, Oldsmobiles, Chevrolets, Pontiacs. Even when standardization produced look-alike boredom, GM stuck to the dogma of mass production.

The one disturbing omen, as Roger Smith took over as chairman and chief executive officer of General Motors on January 1, 1981, was that in 1980 GM had suffered its first financial loss in sixty years (a loss of $760 million), largely because of Japanese incursions into the U.S. car market. Roger Smith proclaimed his intention to meet this challenge with new thinking at GM.

At first blush, this seemed unlikely. In his thirty-one-year rise through GM's finance division, Smith had been a classic organization man, a company loyalist who did not rock the boat, though in his final years as understudy to outgoing GM Chairman Thomas Murphy, he had gained a reputation for strategic planning.

Very soon, the business press was lionizing CEO Roger Smith as a daring corporate reformer who was shaking up GM's old ways by reorganizing America's largest corporation. In March 1984, *Fortune* magazine headlined a profile "GM's Unlikely Revolutionist." It quoted Maryann Keller, an auto analyst on Wall Street and later the author of two well-respected books on the automobile industry, who declared: "GM is a whole new company now. Smith is standing history on its head."[12] *The New York Times Magazine,* in several articles about creative thinkers in America, singled out Roger Smith in April 1985 as "The Innovator." It described his efforts to inject new daring and new thinking into GM, proclaiming that Roger Smith had "directly challenged the corporate culture, the entrenched way of life of the monolith called General Motors. He is presiding over a top-to-bottom internal reorganization."[13]

In fact, the shake-up was less than it appeared to be, as we shall see. The real hallmark of Roger Smith's master plan for General Motors was technology. He embarked on the most ambitious and expensive investment program of any single industrial corporation in history. In a system devoted to Thinking Big, Roger Smith was Thinking Bigger. If RCA had missed the boat by ignoring its own new technology, Roger Smith was out to buy the best technology in the world, computerizing and robotizing all of General Motors in an attempt to drive down production costs and match lower-priced Japanese imports. With GM's massive financial reserves, he was determined to "leapfrog the competition," as he loved to say, and beat them into the twenty-first century.

"In this age of rapidly changing technology, the winners in the business world from now on will be those companies who are most aggressive, creative and successful in implementing advanced technological concepts," Smith confidently proclaimed at a GM management seminar in 1984.[14] He was such an exuberant apostle of technology that he chirped with boyish wonder about its potential for overcoming all obstacles, all opposition.

"I know this is going to sound crazy to you, but do you know what really impresses me? I saw a robot pick up an egg!" he gushed to Cary Reich, writing for *The New York Times Magazine.* "You show me a robot that can pick up an egg and I'll show you. . . . Well, it's fabulous! Picking up an egg! You know, most robots go squish, like that"—his hands squished an imaginary egg, yoke dripped down his sleeve— "That's what most robots do. . . . Those old robots we used to have— you know, the ones that looked like a duck drinking water—we don't even call those robots any more. We call 'em *junk!* Today, that robot's got to know whether that thing coming down the assembly line is a coupe or a sedan or a station wagon, and weld accordingly. That's what we call a robot now."[15]

So Roger Smith gambled on automation, robotics, computers, what he exulted in calling "the factory of the future." He spent $2.5 billion to buy H. Ross Perot's Electronic Data Systems to computerize GM's management, and he boasted that the new Saturn division would have a completely "paperless plant." He acquired Hughes Aircraft for $5 billion, counting on its large-scale integrated systems and engineering know-how to transform GM's manufacturing operations. He went into partnership with Fanuc, a Japanese robotics firm, so GM could make its own robots. He saw himself creating a high-tech corporation, what he proudly called "a different kind of automobile company."

Under Roger Smith's leadership, General Motors spent the staggering sum of $77 billion in new plants and equipment.[16] Year after year, at an unrelenting pace, even as GM was shutting old plants, Roger Smith was building new ones coast to coast, at a cost of $1 billion or more apiece. He was completely rebuilding old plants from top to bottom, equipping them with the latest computerized automation and armies of robots. Even in the mid-1980s, when some financial writers began to question this strategy, Smith plunged onward, investing $8 billion to $9 billion a year.

"We were driving the leading edge and sometimes when you do that, you go over the edge," Roger Smith later acknowledged in hindsight. "We made our mistakes. We went too far on some automation and not far enough on other automation."[17]

Roger Smith's high-stakes gamble on technology was a quintessential American response to the challenge of the new global game. It epitomized American faith in the marvels of science to solve the most difficult problems. It fit the pattern of America's long economic hegemony after World War II, using technological innovations to keep ahead of the world. It was not a break with GM's past, but rather an acceleration of old trends and of GM's basic strategy—economies of scale.

Central to Roger Smith's technology strategy was the goal of reducing GM's dependence on human labor. His overall target was to cut costs and to improve quality by reducing waste and inefficiency. Before "downsizing" became the American corporate fashion, his master plan envisaged thousands of robots replacing hundreds of thousands of assembly-line workers. Cutting the GM labor workforce, Smith later asserted, was not his sole objective, "but certainly that was one of the objectives—one of the prime objectives—and I think it was very successful."[18]

As an iron-fisted finance man, Roger Smith cut the company's workforce by 200,000 and slashed $3 billion from the corporate budget during his first two years as chairman.[19] Railing periodically against the United Auto Workers Union, Smith called on GM's workers to help fight foreign competition by giving back concessions to the company in pay and benefits. During GM's negotiations for a new contract with the UAW in 1982, Smith used the threat of automation as a club. "Every time the cost of wages goes up a dollar," he thundered, "a thousand more robots begin to look economical." Then right after the UAW signed a contract giving up $2.5 billion in wages and benefits, GM disclosed an expanded bonus program for its 6,000 managers.[20]

"Roger's a pretty cynical guy—he had a very low estimate of human nature," said Elmer Johnson, a former GM executive vice president who had once been groomed by Smith as his successor. "If you really have a very low estimate of the quality of your workforce, then you've got to depend even more on technology."

According to Johnson, Roger Smith did not trust organized labor, and he took a tough, shrewd line with the union. Johnson recalled that "Roger said to me in '87, 'You know, in '84 I pulled quite a good trick. I was able to sell them [labor] on a profit-sharing plan on a totally different formula from ours for the executives. Ours paid off handsomely, but the union never got a penny. Now what you've got to do, Elmer, is come up with another little trick.' "[21]

Smith took issue with Johnson's account. "That's a conversation that never took place," he insisted. "You don't go in and do a trick. You die from tricking the union. You just can't do that."[22]

Nonetheless, Johnson was correct that under the profit-sharing agreement approved by Roger Smith in 1984, GM's rank-and-file workers did not receive profit-sharing bonuses, even though GM was showing record profits and GM managers were receiving large profit-sharing bonuses.[23] In 1987, with Ford leading the Big Three automakers' labor negotiations and with Elmer Johnson supervising GM's bargaining team, a revised profit-sharing plan was approved. After that, GM's hourly workers did begin getting profit-sharing bonuses.[24]

Moreover, after his retirement as CEO, Roger Smith acknowledged that bitter labor-management conflicts had often crippled GM. "There's no question about that—there was a confrontational atmosphere," Smith conceded. "I think it was embedded not only on the union side, but on the management side."[25]

GM's Grand Flaw: Discounting People—Workers and Customers

Unfortunately for General Motors, Roger Smith's blind faith in technology proved to be a disaster.

By 1986, some people inside GM as well as some on the outside saw that GM's massive investments were not paying off. There were signs that even Roger Smith suspected that something was deeply wrong but did not know how to correct it. Despite his grand strategy, GM was far less efficient and productive than Ford or Chrysler, let alone its Japanese competitors.

An MIT study on the global auto industry found in 1986, for example, that a typical GM plant, one in Framingham, Massachusetts, took more than forty hours to assemble a car, compared to just eighteen hours at a Toyota plant.[26] Each GM car was costing more to produce than its competitors' were—24 percent more than Ford, 34 percent more than Chrysler—and Toyota and Honda were undercutting all three.[27] GM required a longer lead time than its competitors to design and bring out new models. What's more, GM was hobbled by defects and mass callbacks of its cars. Millions of once-loyal customers were walking away. In the American market, where the loss of even 1 percentage point of market share is worrisome, GM's market share plummeted from nearly 48 percent in 1978 to 36 percent in 1990. A year later, GM suffered a whopping financial loss of $7 billion in its North American operations.

What had gone wrong?

One thing was that Roger Smith's corporate "reforms" were largely ineffective reshuffling. For all the talk about his being the corporate "revolutionist," Roger Smith never shook GM's huge bureaucracy or its risk-averse top brass out of their complacency, their overconfidence. His corporate reorganization in 1984 had failed to break up GM's rigid hierarchies or break down the internal compartmentalization that made GM unresponsive to a fast-changing market. His few genuine innovations—a joint venture with Toyota Motors in California and the experimental labor-management power sharing at the new Saturn plant in Tennessee—had been kept apart from the main GM structure. Roger Smith had never brought their lessons into the company's mainstream.

Authentic change requires fresh air and freewheeling candor, but Roger Smith's top-down command style inhibited open debate. His imperial manner discouraged risk taking; it kept GM stiff and immobile. His commandments from on high stifled an entrepreneurial spirit and suppressed unpleasant truths. The cardinal rule under Roger Smith was: "Don't be a naysayer. The boss doesn't like bad news."[28] So deeply inbred was the habit of obedience during his tenure that one high executive blurted out: "At GM, the Chairman is God."[29]

An even more central problem than management style was leadership decisions—Roger Smith's technology strategy was a catastrophic mistake. It sounded good, but it was riddled with flaws.

Its first grand flaw was that it forgot the customer. GM had to predict the market long in advance, build its new plants, buy its robots, and stick to its plan, no matter what. But that plan was built on un-realistically rosy scenarios about the growth of the American car market, and it was insensitive to changing consumer demand. So General Motors was left with enormous overcapacity, and it was too muscle-bound to change.

The $77 billion was spent "very badly, without a plan," according to Thomas Wyman, a GM board member under Roger Smith and afterward. "Originally they thought in terms of fifty billion dollars, and they went over by twenty billion. But money was no object. The whole plan depended on our producing at ninety-five percent capacity to show a profit. But of course, you can't meet ninety-five percent all the time. Something like eighty percent—or less—is far more typical."[30]

The second grand flaw in Smith's technology strategy was that it was so antilabor that it ignored the vital role of workers to implement the strategy—to program, maintain, and work with the robots. "You cannot take technology and dump it on a current workforce—not educated, not trained to effectively use that technology on the plant floor—and expect it to work," asserted Harry Pearce, a high-level aide under Roger Smith and executive vice president of GM since 1992. As Pearce pointed out, robots require sophisticated maintenance and skilled workers to operate computer keyboards and the control apparatus, but GM had failed to provide its workers with adequate training.

A high-tech strategy "requires a significant effort before you ever put the technology in the plant, to attune and educate and prepare your workforce," Pearce asserted. "So that not only do they welcome it, but they understand it and they know how to use it and can apply it efficiently. Otherwise, you end up with a disenfranchised, disenchanted workforce, unable to use the technology. But you've spent the billions on the technology—so now your fixed costs go up, but your productivity doesn't. In fact, it may go down. It's the worst of all worlds."[31]

Most fundamentally, the premise on which Roger Smith's technology strategy was based—the belief that mass production is the world's most efficient manufacturing system—missed the revolutionary changes in manufacturing cars that had been pioneered by the Japanese in the 1970s. GM's top brass took the typical American view that Japanese carmakers had been able to break into the American market only by exporting small, fuel-efficient cars produced with low-cost labor during the oil crisis of the mid-1970s. Initially that had been true, but what GM failed to see was that the old GM system, once the best in the world, had been improved upon by the Japanese. By the late 1980s, Japanese labor costs had risen, virtually to a par with America's, but the Japanese share of the American market was still growing. The competitive advantage of the new Japanese system was its quality, its flexibility, its speed, its responsiveness to shifts in customer sentiment. Its strong suit was being small and agile, not large and lumbering.

"GM management was wrong," commented GM board member Tom Wyman. "All that investment turned out to reduce our flexibility and to prevent change."[32]

"Unfortunately, because we were so successful, we didn't see what was happening around us or elsewhere in the world," Harry Pearce admitted. "Because we were largely blinded by our own success, we continued to operate as we had thought we had learned to operate successfully—with a lot of plants, huge manufacturing capacity, very high volumes, vehicles that *we* would define as best suited for the customers—when, in fact, the industry was going down another path."[33]

In Pearce's view, one reason for the myopia of GM's top management was that it walled itself off from the world in the cloistered fourteenth floor of GM's headquarters, the Fisher Building in Detroit.

"Not only did we isolate ourselves from our workforce, salary and hourly, we isolated ourselves from our customers," said Pearce. "That isolation suggested to the world that we were a sort of an arrogant lot. But I'll tell you that arrogance is a real deficit when you're on the brink and you're staring down some of the toughest competition in the world."

And so, in the 1980s, for a solid decade, GM missed the lessons of the Japanese, and it wound up having to pay an enormous price in the 1990s, just to survive.

"We didn't see the Japanese preparing to do battle with us," Pearce admitted. "We didn't see them developing lean manufacturing techniques that ultimately were going to render us noncompetitive."

The Toyota Mind-Set: Flexible and Lean

In Japan, the car industry did not take off until after World War II, and then a dozen fierce competitors had to scramble for small niches in a tight market. Japanese roads were narrow and rutted; fuel had to be imported and was terribly expensive. Fuel economy was therefore critical, and Japanese cars had to be small and highly maneuverable. Like the Germans, Japanese consumers demanded high quality and long-term reliability, partly because they could ill afford to buy a new car every few years, partly because their culture values quality and precision.

In the early postwar years, Japanese carmakers found their consumers fickle, slow to develop brand loyalties. The car companies learned that small innovations could give them a market edge. So they constantly updated their models to cater to changing consumer tastes. Fast turnaround on design of new models was critical. A fast-changing market also dictated short, low-volume production runs; small runs required skilled and adaptable workers who were trained to do multiple tasks and to change equipment rapidly. In Japan, it did not make sense to stockpile great volumes of components for cars that might never be built or sold. Carmakers waited until the last minute to get supplies, and they waged an incessant war against waste, typical of a resource-poor nation where 125 million people are crammed into a space the size of Montana and where everyone learns to economize from an early age.

For sheer survival in their domestic market, Japanese auto companies had to master very different competitive virtues from those of Americans or Germans. Above all, they had to be fast, flexible, and economical.

Toyota is the high temple of this flexible Japanese system. The most progressive American executives and academic specialists on industry rate Toyota as probably the best manufacturing company in the world. By the 1980s, not only were Toyota's assembly plants the most efficient anywhere, according to an exhaustive MIT study of the auto industries of Europe, North America, and east Asia, but Toyota was the seedbed of a new kind of production system and of ideas that were revolutionizing the thinking of the best companies in America and Europe.

Yet on my first visit to an assembly plant at Toyota City, about three hours south of Tokyo on the high-speed train, I was not immediately impressed. There was nothing physically imposing about it—no dazzling modern technology. In fact, the Takaoka plant, an early Toyota flagship, was far less modern than the Mercedes plant at Sindelfingen or the General Motors plant I had seen in Pontiac, Michigan. In early 1991, it had only just finished installing automation that had been standard for several years in American auto plants—lines of robots in the body-welding line and the paint shop. Its assembly lines were conspicuously *not* high tech, and the Japanese considered that a virtue.

In fact, Toyota's competitive edge—its speed, its efficiency, its quality, its flexibility—did not spring primarily from anything physical or mechanical. Toyota's advantage was conceptual: It put customers and workers ahead of management and technology, and it insisted on simplicity in the way every piece of work was conceived and organized. Far more than Mercedes, Toyota paid heed to productivity, to avoiding waste and unnecessary costs, yet with no less commitment to quality. In contrast to Roger Smith, Toyota's leaders saw people, not technology, as their primary asset. Quality and productivity, in Toyota's view, depended on giving ordinary workers more—not less—responsibility in the production process, in improving operations, and in solving problems in Toyota plants. What is more, Toyota had been disciplined by the rough-and-tumble Japanese market to be literally customer driven—and from that fundamental fact flowed many important consequences.

Toyota's guiding thinker, its legendary chief engineer, Taichi Ohno, had expressed this cardinal rule simply: "We are now unable to sell our products unless we think ourselves into the very hearts of our customers, each of whom has very different concepts and tastes."[34]

In short, contrary to Roger Smith and other American executives, who operated as if *they* could decide and mass-produce the kinds of cars consumers wanted, the Japanese put the emphasis on listening to consumers. According to auto industry experts, Japanese carmakers were more willing to change in response to market research than were Americans or Germans. For example, American carmakers resisted environmental standards for years, treating them as a governmental intrusion into their business, but the Japanese executives whom I met at Toyota and Honda saw public demand for environmentally improved cars as a new selling opportunity, a chance to add attractive new features. In the early 1990s, they talked eagerly about developing electrically powered cars and making car bodies recyclable. They embraced change.

The key to responsiveness is flexibility—and flexibility demanded that Toyota make every aspect of its operation lean and nimble. In an ever-changing global market, flexibility is more essential than the best robots or the most imposing luxury car. What flexibility meant in practice, I saw, was the kaleidoscopic variation of different model cars in a rainbow of sizes, colors, and configurations that came tumbling off the assembly lines at Toyota plants. It was a world apart from the standardized production of GM plants.

In one day, the two assembly lines at Toyota's Tsutsumi plant, for example, rolled out ninety-one different types of engines on thirty-eight different models of cars, according to Assistant Plant Manager Hiroshi Tomomatsu, and he rattled off the export Lexus, the wide-body Camry, the Windom, the domestic Lexus, the Corona, the narrow-body Camry, the Corona station wagon, two-door coupes, four-door sedans, right-hand drive, left-hand drive—more different "flavors" than in a Baskin-Robbins ice cream store. For that day's production, Tomomatsu told me, the orders had come in from customers on a computerized system in the previous two weeks. That's how close to the market Toyota was.

In that brief span of time, Toyota had had to order all the parts, get them delivered to the right place at literally the right second, and keep track of how they flowed to meet the haphazard sequence of car bodies coming down the assembly line. It was a masterpiece of flexible organization.

Supreme flexibility is the prize achievement of the Toyota Production System. On that base, Toyota built a commanding position in the Japanese market and moved into America and Europe. The benefits were obvious. As Tomomatsu explained, if the Camry wasn't selling so well one month, the Tsutsumi plant stepped up output of Coronas without having to cut back its overall production. That was a crucial advantage over the GM plants, which were dedicated to producing just one car.

Toyota took the opposite view of size from GM's. It saw size as a problem, not an asset. Like a weight watcher, it was constantly fighting its own size. In late 1990, as Toyota was pushing deeper into the American market, strengthening its dominance at home, and launching the Lexus against the European luxury cars, its sixty-five-year-old chairman, Shoichiro Toyoda, was restlessly reorganizing the company's management as if Toyota were a company in deep trouble. He was ripping out two layers of middle management, stripping a thousand executives of their staffs, and moving the people to new operations.

"We felt we suffered from large-corporation disease," Toyoda asserted, even though his company was a fraction of GM's size. "It had become extremely difficult for top executives to convey their feelings to our workers. So we embarked on a cure. We have a saying: 'A large man has difficulty exercising his wits fully.' "[35]

Another area where Toyota had gotten a "flexibility jump" on American and German carmakers was in its rapid design of new cars. In the late 1980s, Japanese carmakers were on average about 1½ years faster in car design—and therefore closer to changing customer tastes—than American manufacturers were, according to two major studies. One study found that Japanese carmakers typically took forty-three months to move a new car model from initial conception into the hands of consumers, compared to sixty-two months on average for American and European carmakers—and Toyota was the fastest of the Japanese.[36]

According to Toyota's design chief, Senior Managing Director Akihiro Wada, the key was "simultaneous engineering," that is, doing several elements of design and engineering at once, instead of doing them in a compartmentalized sequence—initial design; then styling; then engineering the car; then redesigning the assembly process and retooling; then drafting specifications for the car's components. Traditionally, American carmakers did these operations one by one; often one stage would confront a problem and simply throw it back to an earlier stage. With each element working separately, the process would bog down. The American approach took far longer than "simultaneous engineering" does. The Japanese brought all the elements of the process together in one team, forcing them to consider one another's problems. It was hard to get started, but once major decisions were made, the different elements of the team pulled together more readily. Meshing all those phases at once takes extraordinarily good teamwork and communications—both of which are strong assets at Toyota.

Since the mid-1980s, Ford, Chrysler, and to a lesser extent GM have learned from Toyota and Honda. Former Ford CEOs Donald Petersen and Harold "Red" Poling told me that Ford had significantly narrowed the time gap for designing new cars. But they conceded that in the early 1990s Toyota was still ahead, still faster than any rival.[37]

A Toyota Advantage: The Flexible Family Pyramid

Another critical factor in Toyota's flexibility is its unique supply system, its corporate family. In this aspect of the business, as in other aspects, Toyota took the opposite tack from General Motors, which produced 70 percent of all the components for its own cars. That was GM's way of keeping control. GM exercised centralized command over its supply system; it had set up massive, centralized stockpiles of parts for assembly plants all across the United States.

Toyota decentralized the process. It got outside suppliers to produce 70 percent of its components and avoided the waste and overhead of stockpiling parts. It kept very low inventories; parts were made in response to changes in market demand. That was efficient, but it was also risky. Without large buffer stocks of parts, its system was fragile and vulnerable. Timing was everything. In Toyota's slogan, everything had to arrive "Just in Time." If one single part did not make an on-time rendezvous with the correct car body coming down the assembly line, that stopped the flow of cars and derailed the whole production system.

Toyota had to count on its suppliers. It took superior organization and constant attention to keep everyone in its system operating "Just in Time." But Toyota discovered that this effort kept everyone on their toes and doing their best all the time. "Just in Time" was not only a challenge, it was also a motivator.

At Toyota plants, this tightly timed supply process is visible everywhere. At the Tsutsumi plant, for example, the engine area of the assembly line is located near an unloading dock, and every twenty minutes a flatbed truck arrives with two dozen engines from a nearby engine supplier. There is space for two truckloads of engines in the unloading dock, so supplies are usually twenty to thirty engines ahead of the assembly line. Each new truck arrives just in time for the empty truck to have pulled out. No wasted space; no wasted time.

The complex electronics and computerized systems for Toyota cars come from Nippondenso, which was the electrical division of Toyota Motor Company until it was spun off as a separate company. Now a $12-billion-a-year giant, Nippondenso makes high-tech fuel injectors, airbag sensors, electronic displays, computers for engine firing, and suspension systems, not only for Toyota but also for other carmakers. But Toyota is by far its largest customer. Every day, Nippondenso sends a thousand truckloads of components to Toyota assembly plants.[38]

Multiply that by hundreds of suppliers in the region, and the roads around Toyota City are clogged with trucks racing to meet Toyota's just-in-time deadlines.

In fact, everything in Toyota City, home to 325,000 people, literally revolves around Toyota. The Japanese call it a "castle city," with rings of supplier firms radiating outward from Toyota Motor Company headquarters across Toyota's home province, Aichi Prefecture. Flying over Toyota City in a helicopter, I saw this network pattern: assembly plants and supplier factories, sun glinting off their roofs, marching off from the center in all directions. The older, more important subcontractors were in nearby rings; the newer, smaller suppliers, farther out.

From the air, I was getting an introduction to the feudalistic structure of Japanese industry—the parent company at the hub and its suppliers, all members of an industrial family, or *keiretsu,* gathered around it. They are interdependent. Toyota has an ownership stake in its main suppliers, and they have an ownership stake in Toyota. As the parent company, Toyota guarantees them work and sometimes steps in to tell them how to run their businesses more efficiently. They give Toyota new ideas for improving its cars, and they bear the main burdens of meeting crash deadlines and retooling for new cars. The long, close ties of this corporate family network are central to Toyota's success. The corporate network is a looser, more nimble arrangement than the internal supply system at General Motors, which is inflexible and hard to manage centrally. But the Toyota system, with its informal links, is more reliable than the haphazard dealings of a totally free marketplace.

"Long-term relationships are more efficient. You don't need lawyers. You can get along with fewer CPAs to guard against cheating," observed Kozo Yamamura, a Japanese-born American professor at the University of Washington. "The parent company has bargaining power with the subsidiaries. On Friday, it can demand just-in-time delivery and get delivery on Monday. Toyota's productivity increases, so overseas sales increase, so subsidiary companies get more work and their workers' wages go up. Another great advantage: Inside the *keiretsu,* information flows more efficiently. You don't have to be so secretive or protective about proprietary information. It allows the companies to do more flexible long-term planning."[39]

From afar, we see Japan's giants—Toyota, Mitsubishi, Nippon

Steel, Hitachi, SONY. But Toyota's success, and indeed the overall economic success of Japan, depends on the entrepreneurial drive and flexibility of small and medium-sized feeder firms with fewer than three hundred employees, which constitute close to 99 percent of Japan's enterprises.[40] In his book *The Misunderstood Miracle,* economic writer David Friedman argues that Japan is much more small business–oriented than America, its manufacturing output and employment less concentrated in big firms than in America. Decentralized production, according to Friedman, has given the Japanese economy its competitive edge; it is the main reason why Japan has been able to gain rapidly on America since 1970.[41] The decentralized feeder system certainly gives Toyota flexibility—an enormous competitive advantage.

A Radical Idea: Trust on Toyota's Factory Floor

Inside Toyota factories, the most vivid symbol of decentralized power—and a key to Toyota's high quality—is the ability of any worker to stop the assembly line in an instant.

Running like a laundry line over the heads of the workers in every Toyota plant that I visited was a white or yellow cord. It was within easy reach. One jerk on that cord would trigger loud music and flashing alarm lights. Coworkers would come running to try to fix the problem, but if that took more than thirty or forty seconds, the line would stop dead. Line stoppages were fairly frequent. Most were very short because Toyota's work teams are skilled at troubleshooting. No one got upset. Everyone understood that line stoppages were essential to Toyota's quality control. To workers, the stop cord showed management's confidence in them. It was a symbol of trust on the plant floor.

This single facet of the Toyota Production System illustrates the profound differences in philosophy between Toyota and General Motors. In Roger Smith's GM, stopping the line was an almost absolute no-no, unless someone's life was in danger. Output was the overriding goal. Traditionally, American carmakers told assembly-line workers to push for maximum output and not to worry about problems. Then, at the end of the line, quality control inspectors would hunt for defects and send defective cars to "rework" departments. In a typical GM plant, "rework" was a sizable operation with space for 200, 300, or

400 cars, as much as half a day's output. (In comparison, Toyota's Takaoka plant has 40 rework spaces, less than 10 percent of a day's output.) In the GM plants that I saw, the rework areas had lots of shiny new cars with something wrong. Heavy "rework" drives up costs, a major reason American carmakers long regarded cost and quality as trade-offs. Going for low cost meant sacrificing quality, or vice versa, and typically cost was the priority.

The Japanese had a radically different slant. They were bears about keeping costs down, but they were also as obsessive about quality as the Germans. A striving for perfection is a Japanese national trait, from the discipline imposed on children trying to master the complex calligraphy of written Japanese, to the precision of tea ceremonies, to the trimming of bonsai plants, to the precise, formalistic wrapping of gifts, layer inside layer inside layer. "Perfectability is a goal, a dream, a target," Karel van Wolferen, a Dutch journalist who has lived in Japan for twenty-five years, told me. "There is a 'perfect way' to do everything. Japanese strive for that perfection."[42]

In the auto industry, Toyota achieved quality in a radically new way. Unlike GM, Toyota saw low cost and high quality not as trade-offs but as complementary goals. Ironically, that insight came from an American management expert, the late W. Edwards Deming, whose advice was heeded by the Japanese long before it became popular in America. Deming taught that it was cheaper in the long run to get things right the first time (high quality) rather than to fix them later with rework and recalls.[43] Heeding Deming, Toyota decided that it cost less to stop the line, interrupt production, and take time right away to catch defective parts or to spot a faulty assembly process and to trace a problem to its source and fix it, rather than to keep working and then have to fix hundreds or thousands of defects at the end of the line.

That led to the single most revolutionary innovation of the Toyota Production System—putting primary responsibility for quality on every single assembly-line worker. Toyota told each worker to inspect continuously for defects in every component that he or she touched. Rather than let a defect go forward, the workers should stop the assembly line. Never send a car to a customer that is less than 100 percent perfect, Toyota told them.

Others use that slogan, too; the knack is making it work in practice. Toyota came up with an ingenious wrinkle. It told line workers to think of their customers not as unknown buyers in a distant city or country but as the very next worker down the assembly line. In other words: Don't pass a defective car on to your buddy. It was a powerful idea.

"Stopping the line is symptomatic of a different attitude toward workers," observed John Paul MacDuffie, an auto industry specialist at the University of Pennsylvania's Wharton School of Business. "A Japanese colleague, Haruo Shamada, came up with the term 'fragile' to describe the Toyota Production System. You take out quality control inspectors and make workers do it, and you have much greater dependence on workers. That's a fragile system. It means you have to create a very strong relationship with the workers."[44]

Toyota's Worker-Friendly Strategies: "Bottom Up"

Motivation is high in Toyota factories. Nowhere else in the world have I seen workers actually trot from one task to another. But the work pace is grueling, and it takes its toll. Maintaining morale requires a constant effort at worker-friendly strategies. Mikio Kitano, long Toyota's managing director for production, admitted that in good times, Toyota's labor turnover is high, say 25 percent among younger workers, a costly problem for Toyota. Young Japanese nowadays shy away from what they call "the three K's"—work that is *kitsui* (difficult), *kitanai* (dirty), and *kihen* (dangerous).[45]

"You should see how fast these guys work—it's brutally hard work," said Chris Donnegan, a young American management trainee at Toyota who was required to put in a month in an assembly plant as part of Toyota's orientation for new managers. "It's tough. It's dirty. It's hot. It's dangerous. But the Japanese stick it out. They persevere. They value perseverance and a certain hardness of character. They see American impatience and complaining as selfish, as a weakness. They have a word—*gaman*—forbearance, persistence. It's a big deal in Japan. The Japanese say, 'Japan is a *gaman* culture.' "[46]

To maintain worker morale and build bonds with workers, Toyota's management uses technology to ease the strain of work. Generally, technology is introduced not with Roger Smith's goal of supplanting workers but rather to support workers. Mikio Kitano, as Toyota production chief, favored controlling the pace of automation. At one stage in the late 1980s, a previous production chief was impressed by American automation and followed the American model at a new plant in Tahara. But it had too many robot breakdowns interrupting production, so when Kitano took over, he cut back the "excessive automation" at Tahara and used far less automation at newer plants on Kyushu Island. "It's important to install machines in a gradual manner," Kitano emphasized. "The trick is to make the workers familiar with machines, not to make them feel threatened, but to make them feel part of the process of installing machines."[47]

Phil Condit, president of Boeing, holds up Toyota as a model for melding manual and automated processes and for its criteria for introducing automation. "In Japan, the first thing you automate is the dangerous work," Condit told me. "The second thing is the dirty work, and third is the heavy work. In each case, it's the human concern—worry about people—that brings the automation. The Japanese automate in order to save humans."[48]

Another worker-friendly strategy for which Toyota is world famous is designing cars for easy assembly. Toyota design engineers make a fetish of reducing an assembly unit from, say, 100 parts to 19 parts or of designing "snap-on" bumper parts to make the work easier. They are renowned for simplicity of design. Auto companies the world over buy and tear apart one another's cars to see how they are designed and made, in order to pick up trade secrets and to benchmark their own performance. In 1990, eight carmakers in Europe, Asia, and North America were polled by a team from MIT, and they rated Toyota number one in the world at designing cars for ease of manufacture. Next came Honda, Mazda, Fiat, and Nissan. Ford was sixth; GM and Chrysler were further down the list. Design for ease of manufacture, the MIT study commented, means an easier job for workers as well as cheaper, faster, and more defect-free production.[49]

But the heart of Toyota's worker-oriented production system is teamwork and worker participation. "Teamwork is everything," wrote Taichi Ohno, the organizing genius of the Toyota system.[50] Teamwork is the Toyota litany. Plant managers never refer to "workers" but always to "team members." Foremen and supervisors are "team leaders" and "group leaders." The atmosphere in a Toyota plant is very democratic; perks are almost nonexistent. Team members and team leaders work elbow to elbow, wear the same work jackets, eat together in the same cafeteria, and while away their evenings together at beer drinking, *karaoke* sing-along parties.

Teamwork flows naturally from the importance Japanese culture attaches to group loyalty and responsibility. Toyota has tapped into historical experience. The core building block of a Toyota assembly line is a five-member team (sometimes a bit larger), which is an echo of the rice-tax system of two hundred years ago. Under this system, Japanese authorities made groups of five families responsible for paying their rice taxes together; if anyone came up short, others in the group had to make up the shortfall.[51] In a Toyota plant, the factory team members, like the rice farmers, have collective responsibility for one small section of the assembly line. Team members do morning calisthenics together, take breaks together, and share the workload. They divide up the tasks and rotate jobs. They all develop multiple skills, rather than being highly specialized as American autoworkers are. As part of their collective responsibility, the factory teams regularly hold "quality circle" meetings near the assembly line. Everyone is asked to chip in ideas on how to make the work easier and better.

What is crucial to worker motivation at Toyota is the workers' sense that management listens to them, takes them seriously, values their skills and advice. "These workers have been empowered compared to American autoworkers," Chris Donnegan told me. "In American factories, the structure is very hierarchical. In the Japanese system, there's much more worker participation." Not only do workers stop the production line with the pull cord, but workers (not supervisors) order new supplies of parts when their stocks run low.

Most important, Toyota encourages its workers to invent ways to improve their jobs. Toyota factories are literally dotted with simple mechanical devices, little rigs and dollies loaded with parts, Rube Goldberg contraptions that have been suggested and often built by line workers. No detail of production is too small to be perfected. Workers have proposed substituting plastic grommets for certain screws on a car body because they were easier to insert; they have suggested screens to shield their eyes; they have gotten engineers to change the height of the assembly line; they have urged inserting trenches or small platforms to make some operations easier; they have designed simple gravity-feed shelves so that boxes of new parts slide toward them as they work at the assembly line.

The pride of workers at the Tsutsumi plant was a gliding work chair called *raku-raku,* a worker proposal. It swung from a highly flexible overhead support arm, like a chair on a ski lift. As the empty car body moved down the assembly line, without doors or seats, a worker floated into it on the *raku-raku* and glided around easily from one point to another within a car, inserting dashboard components and tightening other parts in place. Compared to the old method of the worker getting into the car, sitting down, and having to move himself around, using the *raku-raku* was much easier. Quality and efficiency went up, and the workers liked the job better.

The key for Toyota managers is what they call the "bottom-up approach" to running the company: Find and fix the problems at the bottom and let solutions percolate upward. Give the workers power and responsibility instead of giving them commands from the top down, General Motors style. "The real spirit of Toyota," the Tsutsumi operations manager, Kazuwaki Gotoh, asserted, "is that everything comes up from the bottom, from the team members."[52]

Even allowing for some exaggeration, the revolutionary concepts at the heart of the Toyota system—its flexibility and its empowerment of workers—have sent waves of change into the world of manufacturing in Europe and America.

Mercedes: Benchmarking and Learning from Toyota

By the spring of 1993, Mercedes was on the defensive. The Germans had discovered that they were no more impervious to the Japanese challenge than the Americans had been. Mercedes's leaders were talking a different game. The new Japanese luxury cars, especially the Lexus from Toyota, were eating into their once-comfortable hold on the luxury-car market, especially in the "neutral" market of America. The Germans were astonished that Toyota could generate such high-quality cars so quickly and sell them for $45,000–$50,000. And they understood they had to change.

"Lexus is quite a challenge, and what the Japanese are doing is very, very impressive," Helmut Werner, the chairman of Mercedes-Benz, admitted to me, a grimace tinging his photogenic smile. "Therefore, yes, we are very much under pressure as far as costs are concerned, as far as efficiency is concerned. The Japanese are doing a very, very good job, at least some of them, and we have to accept this new challenge and do better."[53]

Werner contended that some customers would stick with brand loyalty and the snob appeal of a Mercedes, but he admitted that others were deserting Mercedes. "In the good old days, we *made* markets," Werner conceded. "Today, we have to understand how we can make ourselves attractive. The customers became more individualistic, and all of a sudden we were in a competition."[54]

To compete, Werner was moving Mercedes into smaller cars, like the 190 series, the "Baby Benz" for yuppies. He was accelerating development of new models from ten years to eight (still double Toyota's cycle time). Dieter Zetsche, the young new development chief, said Mercedes's engineers were going to have to make their cars less intricate and easier to assemble. Bruno Sacco, Mercedes's top designer, was more blunt: Mercedes would have to give up some of its impractical infatuation with technology. The S-car, he insisted, had been overbuilt; the engineers had been showing off. "There are a huge number of things the driver doesn't even see or appreciate," Sacco groused. "We have to look at what the market wants and not just perpetuate our idiosyncrasy for its own sake."[55]

The Germans, famous for heavy corporate hierarchies, were cutting back. One layer of bureaucracy was being cut from the headquarters staff at Mercedes and its parent company, Daimler-Benz. The factory workforce was cut back—14,000 in 1993 and nearly that many again in 1994, small by comparison with General Motors and handled mainly through attrition, but unprecedented for Mercedes. Management persuaded IG Metall, the autoworkers' union, to accept reductions in pay and benefits to help Mercedes to be more competitive. In Japanese style, Mercedes decided to move factories to overseas markets: It announced plans to build a $300 million factory in Alabama, with 1,500 jobs, to produce four-wheel-drive sports utility vehicles.

In the Sindelfingen factory, hallowed practices were under fire. Mercedes was taking the Toyota doctrine to heart. The rework area at the end of the assembly line, once a proud symbol, had become an albatross. Dieter Zetsche saw it as a prime target for cost savings.

"That's a typical waste area," Zetsche declared, in an echo of Toyota. "If you do it right the first time, you can forget about all that. There's no car manufacturer in the world where the rework activity would be zero, but it has to be very close to zero."[56]

Quality testing would continue, but Mercedes was moving to reduce the need for rework by experimenting with Japanese-style work teams and giving more responsibility for quality to line workers. "We had very experienced and well-equipped workers," Zetsche said. "We just didn't use their talents as much as we could have. Today, we give the responsibility to the worker."

Mercedes was experimenting with its own improvement on the Toyota system. Instead of keeping the auto body constantly moving on an assembly line, Mercedes periodically diverted it to "stop stations," where it stood still for twenty-five to thirty-five minutes while a team of four or five workers inserted components under the hood, into the trunk, and inside the chassis. Instead of each worker doing single, repetitive tasks every sixty or ninety seconds on a moving line, these teams had much more time to do many more tasks and to manage themselves. They split up the work as they chose, going at their own pace so long as they met the overall deadline.

Jörg Schuster, a worker and team leader in his early thirties, was enthusiastic about the new system. "The advantage is that there are fewer mistakes through better cooperation among the people," he told me. "When you work in such a close-knit group, there's a good spirit of cooperation. So if one person is finished with his work, then he can help the next person. Some people work faster, others slower, but we usually have no problem finishing in time. It helps if you can switch tasks. Then it goes better. On an assembly line, it would be monotonous."[57]

By comparison with the Toyota workers, the Germans didn't look to me as though they were working terribly fast. Nonetheless, Zetsche reported that this experimental teaming had increased the speed of production by about 25 percent and reduced defects by 80 percent. The key, he said, was the heightened sense of involvement and personal responsibility among the workers.

Mercedes was also trying out a new style of leadership, an elected team "spokesman" or leader (highly qualified but not officially a *Meister*). Zetsche had just come from a meeting of senior executives where a team leader had given a sharp critique of past mistakes and told how he and his team had found ways both to increase quality and to reduce the crew size.

"It's refreshing, and it's impressive how much you can achieve by looking at things from the bottom up rather than planning from top down," Zetsche said with a certain wonder in his voice. "Bottom up— there is really a big change."

Some old-line *Meister*s, used to being bosses, were resisting this change; but Horst Rebmann, the *Meister* in the cockpit assembly area, was adapting. He had seen the results of the new system: defects going down, quality going up.

"The workers have changed in the last thirty years," he explained.

"Before, the workers wanted to be told what to do and how to do it. They didn't want to think on the job. Today, the workers have a greater sense of responsibility. They want to think for themselves and be responsible for what they produce. It's more difficult to supervise today's workers than it was twenty or thirty years ago—but it's also a lot better."[58]

So Mercedes-Benz, the bastion of German craft production, had been pushed off its pedestal. The old standards, the old goals, and the German attention to superior quality were still in place. But Mercedes had been forced to incorporate the lessons of Toyota's flexible production into the German craft method. It could no longer rest on its reputation.

"We have to be the best in every regard," said Zetsche, "not only deliver the best product but deliver it for the lowest possible price. For some time we didn't live in the real world, as far as competition goes. Things changed. Today, competition is everywhere."[59]

GM: A Fifty-Fifty Joint Venture with Toyota

Even at General Motors, Roger Smith suspected there might be something to learn from Toyota. Most GM executives were skeptical that the Japanese had actually developed something new; moreover, they doubted that a Japanese system could work with a unionized American labor force. But according to former GM Executive Vice President Elmer Johnson, Roger Smith "began to smell something fairly important" and he wanted to "embarrass General Motors into seeing what was different about this production system."[60]

In February 1994, Roger Smith launched an experiment—a fifty-fifty joint venture with Toyota in Fremont, California. Toyota's contribution was thirty to forty top managers and its worker-centered production system. GM's contribution was fifteen or twenty officials, as observer-helpers, and a plant that GM had shut down for good in 1982. Roger Smith had invested $150 million to make the Fremont plant a state-of-the-art facility—but to no avail. GM management said the workforce was impossible, and it had laid off all five thousand employees.

The Fremont plant epitomized GM's worst problems: Quality was terrible, productivity was low, wildcat strikes were frequent, drug and alcohol abuse were chronic, absenteeism was bad, often running as high as 20–25 percent. GM Fremont had taken an average of thirty-six hours to make one car, more than double what it took in Toyota City. One big reason: hostile labor-management relations.[61] "When GM ran this plant, it was nicknamed 'the battleship,'" said Bill Childs, who became vice president and general manager for human resources in the GM/Toyota joint venture. "The plant is low and gray, like a ship floating on the sea. But it was nicknamed 'the battleship' because of what went on *inside* the building."[62]

The idea behind the joint venture, formally called New United Motor Manufacturing Inc., or NUMMI for short, was for Toyota to test its methods in North America and for GM to study the Toyota Production System in action. The plant would produce Corollas for Toyota to sell in America and Chevy Novas (essentially the same car) for GM. In November 1985, three years after GM shut down the Fremont plant, the first work shift of NUMMI went into full production, and the second work shift in April 1986. Total output averaged 950 cars a day.

To GM's astonishment, productivity at NUMMI doubled, quality and morale jumped way up, drug and alcohol abuse and absenteeism all dramatically declined.[63] The MIT study of the global auto industry found that, by 1987, NUMMI was operating almost on a par with Toyota's best plants. It was producing cars in nineteen hours, half its former time. Defects were one third of the former level. Parts inventories were cut from two weeks' supply to two days' supply, a dramatic improvement though still not down to the Toyota standard of two hours' supply.

All this had been accomplished without great cost. Toyota had invested $150 million in a stamping plant that it wanted to have right next to the factory, so it would not have to depend on GM plants in the Midwest. Even more impressive, most of the old workforce had been rehired. More than 80 percent of NUMMI's three thousand rank-and-file workers came from the old GM Fremont plant, and more than half of the workforce was minority, mainly African American and Hispanic. The United Auto Workers union still represented the workers.

"Everything looks the same—but everything is different," observed James Womack, who headed the MIT study team.[64]

A Revolutionary Change in Labor-Management Relations

What had transformed the Fremont plant was a near-revolutionary change in labor-management relations, a shift from bitter suspicion and confrontation to trust.

Toyota had insisted that everything change—the policy on layoffs, strikes, absenteeism, workers' responsibility, and power. According to Kan Higashi, Toyota's first chief operating officer at NUMMI, the toughest problem was to change how people dealt with one another and how they thought about their work.

"My focus was human relationships," Higashi told me. "Our concept comes from the strong belief in mutual trust between labor and management. We recognize them as human beings, and they see us as partners. In the United States, young people are trained how to debate. On very small issues, you debate in detail. You Americans come from many different cultures. You start from mutual distrust of each other, and you have to find something in common. In Japan, our homogeneity means we don't have to discuss in detail, item by item."[65]

The very first step taken by Bill Childs, as NUMMI's senior personnel officer, was a shocker: He hired back the old union leaders.

"I had only one condition—I asked them, as individuals, if they would commit themselves to the principles of cooperation and trust and to make this thing work," Childs told me. "All but one agreed. The GM people went bonkers. I had to go back to Detroit and explain what I was doing and why. Even Toyota had problems. They knew what had gone on. I said we had to start out with trust. Eventually everyone agreed."

The former Fremont plant workers wanted their jobs back and were worried about not being rehired. Toyota made an early public commitment to take on at least half of the former workforce. "The first thing I told the union leaders, 'We're going to rehire as many as we can,'" Childs recalled. "We hired blacks. We hired Hispanics. Women. The first group, on average, was over fifty-five. We hired people who couldn't read or write. What we were after most was a commitment to make this thing work."[66]

For Toyota, the biggest early hurdle was the union rules. Higashi emphasized that the Toyota system would not work if the United Auto Workers continued to insist that workers be specialized by more than 150 different job classifications. Toyota wanted just two job categories—assemblers and technicians—so that it could develop its team concept and move workers from job to job. Toyota also demanded tough rules on absenteeism, with the right to fire workers who repeatedly shirked their jobs by playing hookey on Mondays and Fridays or taking free holidays. Finally, Toyota demanded a ban on wildcat strikes; in fact, it wanted no strikes at all.

The UAW rejected Toyota's demands. "I'll never forget the first day," Higashi recalled. "Victor Reuther was still alive. He was pounding the table, 'We'll never give up our right to strike!' The union people showed us the old GM agreement, the old rules. We said, 'Why don't you throw out the old rules? It won't work with the old rules.' It took us six months. Finally, they trusted us. They agreed. I respect the union guys very much. They bravely took a big risk. Those job classifications and the right to strike—that was their security, their protection. They had to give that up and trust us."[67]

In return, in an unusual labor agreement, Toyota made a rare promise—a promise that matched what it promised its Japanese workers—it guaranteed that it would not lock out and "not lay off employees" unless the long-term financial viability of the company was threatened.[68] In 1988, for example, when market demand for Chevy Novas fell and production was down by nearly 40 percent, NUMMI did not lay off any workers.[69] In return, the UAW pledged not "to engage in any strike, sympathy strike, work stoppage, picketing, boycott, sick-out, slow down" or other work interruptions.[70]

Toyota sought quickly to convey a new attitude and forge a new climate. It flew about 450 team leaders to Japan for three-week training sessions to see the Toyota system in action. At NUMMI, its managers made a show of equality with the workers—no coats or ties, no special parking places, no special dining halls. Most important, Kan Higashi told the American workers that it was up to them to produce top quality and to stop the production line if necessary. For quite a while, he said, the American workers did not dare to take the risk of pulling the overhead cord to stop the line. But in time suspicions eased and there were line stoppages.

"If you want to get the trust and respect of the workers, management must show it first," Higashi said. "We didn't want people to come to work on the surface only. We wanted their brains as well as their bodies. Total involvement is very important to all of us."

GM's Corporate Culture Resists Change

NUMMI was a success, in production terms and eventually commercially as well. Its quality and productivity shot up, and eventually its cars sold well with American buyers. NUMMI proved that the Toyota system could work well with an American workforce, and that inspired Roger Smith to attempt an even more daring experiment in labor-management power sharing at the Saturn plant in Tennessee, which we will explore later in the book.

But NUMMI had very little impact on the GM mainstream—its army of regular plants all over America. Hundreds of GM plant and divisional executives went to NUMMI for short visits. Typical was the reaction of three managers from GM's plant in Framingham, Massachusetts. One suggested that NUMMI was operating with secret repair areas and secret inventories because he hadn't seen enough to add up to a "real" plant. Another brushed it all off: "They build cars just like we do." A third bristled: "All that NUMMI talk is not welcome around here."[71]

The bulk of GM's North American Division insulated itself from the influence of the Toyota system. For one thing, few GM people spent enough time at NUMMI to become immersed in the Toyota system. Those who worked at NUMMI for a year or more were swamped by the old attitudes and the massive bureaucracy when they returned to regular GM jobs.

By 1987, GM's top brass had gained enough experience to know the main features of the Toyota Production System and, as former Executive Vice President Elmer Johnson put it, to understand "how radically more efficient it is than ours—not only just efficiency, but the effect on the quality of the product. But the knowledge didn't seem to make a difference. We didn't seem to have the ability to execute change."

Johnson blamed GM's resistance on a corporate culture of "arrogance and overconfidence" bred by forty years of assuming that GM's market dominance was immutable. He quoted senior GM executives coming back from NUMMI saying, "Hey, don't tell me to change things, I'm doing just fine."

Roger Smith, who put much of the blame on union resistance, commented that GM managers saw no reason to change while GM was making record profits and they were reaping big bonuses.[72]

But according to Johnson, the most important obstacle was Smith's own failure to take charge and to push the NUMMI lessons into GM's main operations. "The orders weren't coming from on high," said Johnson. "There wasn't the commitment from on top."

Instead, Roger Smith pressed ahead with more robots and automation into the late 1980s despite the dropoff in GM's share of the American market, the lessons from NUMMI, and the confidential analysis by GM's finance division that Ford Motor Company, which had learned more from Toyota and had changed more radically, was earning more than General Motors on much less volume. Roger Smith stalled, asking for more reports, and he blamed others, such as James McDonald, GM president and chief operating officer, for GM's failures, according to Johnson.

"I think Roger was totally confused, totally, from '86 forward, certainly '87," Johnson asserted. "I'd hear him turn to Jim McDonald and say, 'Something is terribly wrong with *your* reorganization. You know, I'm a finance guy and I'm chairman of the board, but you're in charge of manufacturing and it's a manufacturing problem.' I think by this time Roger had become completely imbued with his role as Mr. Washington, Mr. Wall Street, and Mr. Celebrity."[73]

Typical of Roger Smith's legacy, of his failure to apply the lessons from NUMMI more widely, was the GM plant in Fairfax, Kansas; Smith had lavished $1 billion to rebuild and modernize that plant. "It is a showplace of automation—it probably has two hundred fifty different robots," observed Jim Harbour, an auto industry analyst and consultant for GM. "Yet they could never sell enough volume to keep the plant loaded."

Lack of flexibility was one critical obstacle. The Fairfax plant, according to Harbour, was built with a capacity to make 240,000 cars a year, but in 1993 it was making only about 100,000 cars. The Fairfax plant produced only one brand—the Pontiac Grand Prix—which was not selling very well, and the plant lacked the flexibility to build comparable cars such as the Chevy Lumina or the Oldsmobile Cutlass Supreme.[74]

The Fairfax plant was also plagued by GM's poor performance on designing cars for easy assembly. On this score, the Pontiac Grand Prix built at Fairfax was far behind the cars rolling out of the nearby Ford plant at Claycomo, let alone the Japanese cars, according to Harbour. So the Fairfax plant in the mid-1990s was still suffering from Roger Smith's grand mistakes—from GM's blind reliance on automated mass production, from the poor designs of his favorite series of cars, the highly vaunted "GM-10" cars, and from the false assumption that GM could anticipate consumer demand years ahead.

Finally, on the central lesson from NUMMI—worker empowerment, there had been no more than a halfhearted attempt at Fairfax. Because GM had cut back from 5,000 workers at the old Fairfax plant to 3,650 at the new plant in 1987, to 2,250 in 1991, experienced autoworkers were fearful about job security and distrustful of management. Back in 1987, they had been enthused when the Fairfax managers had announced plans to apply lessons from NUMMI and to introduce Japanese-style work teams and flexible production techniques at the new plant. Many workers got a month of training in NUMMI concepts.

As time wore on, however, the plant management had drifted away from the NUMMI strategy, several workers said. Lean production and the just-in-time supply system had been undermined, according to Art Dobbins of the chassis shop, by the old GM practice of stacking up extra buffer supplies to ensure the production flow. The plant's robots broke down so much that Dick Lynch, another worker, said the body shop constantly worked overtime.[75] Terry Mitler spoke of the poor design of cars for assembly. Art Dobbins had a such a serious problem installing fifteen-pound brake boosters under the hood with his left hand that the task left him and some coworkers with carpel tunnel syndrome. Despite repeated complaints, the problem had not been fixed.[76]

But the workers' greatest disappointment was the Fairfax management's failure to carry out the Toyota-NUMMI concepts of teamwork and worker empowerment to improve quality. "You've got workers who want to do it better, but if you get slapped down and somebody says, 'We know about it, let it go through,' then you give up," Terry Mitler reported. "Lean production is a joke. The team concept isn't really working. The bottom line is production over quality. Don't stop the line except in extreme situations, like safety."[77]

"Some of management is still in the same old frame of mind —they don't listen," agreed Barbara Bell. "They let cars go through, even knowing something's wrong."[78]

"There's no trust," said Art Dobbins. "Everybody resorts to the point-the-finger-at-the-other-guy. It's the same old bull."

...

General Motors had to go to the brink—nearly 300,000 layoffs since the early 1980s and $17 billion in losses from 1990 to 1992—before its board installed a new leadership ready to embrace serious change.

The new leadership that took over in 1993 under President Jack Smith, a principal figure in setting up the GM/Toyota joint venture, saw the need to shake up GM's corporate culture—to open it up to new ideas, drawing on Toyota's example. Jack Smith, who had run GM's successful European operation, reversed a lot of things Roger Smith had done. He began by reducing layers of management, breaking up GM's top-heavy central staff, rigorously cutting supplier costs, and shucking off some of the extra capacity that Roger Smith had built. In 1994, riding a booming car market, GM showed solid profits for the first time in five years, but its market share was still shrinking and its North American division was still struggling.[79]

Even with many plants running at full capacity and with improved financial fortunes, GM was still behind Ford and Chrysler on the critical yardsticks of quality and productivity—and far behind Toyota: In 1993, Chevrolets and Pontiacs, which accounted for more than half of GM's sales, had twice as many defects as Toyota cars. Catching up to Toyota was at least three years off. And by Jack Smith's own estimate, it could take GM until the end of the decade to match Toyota on productivity.[80]

It was significant that Toyota had finally become the primary standard by which the new GM leadership was benchmarking its performance. The goal of Jack Smith's team was to match Toyota, largely by embracing and applying concepts of flexibility, simplicity of design, leaner management, and improved relations with labor. For example, GM's designs of new cars for the late 1990s were simplified, cycle times were shortened, and design operations were integrated.[81] Toyota's hallmark of flexibility became a GM byword. "We've got to have highly flexible manufacturing facilities," said Executive Vice President Harry Pearce. "We have to be able to build three, four different models and platforms in a single plant, because you can't predict with complete accuracy the marketplace two, three, four years down the road."[82]

Worker empowerment did not get the same firm endorsement from GM's new leadership, although Jack Smith set out to improve his personal relations with the United Auto Workers leadership. At long last, General Motors was absorbing some lessons from the new game pioneered by Toyota. Still, there was a question of whether GM could successfully transform itself or whether it would be held back by its old mind-set. Success, even temporary success, once again loomed as a potential obstacle.

"I constantly worry that we will slip back into the complacency that got us into trouble in the past," confessed Harry Pearce. "We work every day at disabusing people of the notion that we have this thing fixed."[83]

3

The Success Reflex

IBM—Seeing Change as a Threat, Not as an Opportunity

> *What happened to this company was not an act of God, some mysterious biblical plague sent down from on high. It's simple. People took our business away.*[1]
> —LOU GERSTNER, CEO, IBM

> *We were like a dinosaur: They'd whack us on the tail, and three weeks later we'd feel it in our brain. . . . Most of the industry figured they could . . . spot us a six-month head start with our own technology, and they'd still catch up to us in the marketplace.*[2]
> —BOB CORRIGAN, IBM PC DIVISION CHIEF, 1990–94

> *IBM's strength is technology. Technology is not enough, though. They have to totally change the way they're doing business.*[3]
> —GLENN HENRY, FORMER IBM FELLOW AND EXECUTIVE

In the spring of 1985, Glenn Henry and his wife, Peggy, flew from Austin, Texas, to San Diego for the big event—IBM's annual "technical recognition" event honoring its brightest technical stars. This was an invitation-only affair at which IBM tipped its hat to the geniuses who were keeping it at the technological frontier.

Each year, IBM would select a couple hundred of its top technical achievers, fly them and their spouses to a choice spot, put them up at a posh hotel, and treat them like royalty. Amid professional accolades, occasionally an IBMer would be handed a surprise check as a reward for some stunning breakthrough. Once before at a similar event,

Glenn Henry had opened an envelope to find a check for $50,000 made out to him personally, for his invention of a new line of business computers.

By the mid-1980s, Henry had compiled a dazzling record at IBM. He was an unusual combination—a mathematician and a thinker with a practical bent, a computer romantic with the pragmatic grit and the leadership skills of a production manager. In eighteen years at IBM, Glenn Henry had been not only the chief conceptualizer of three mid-size computers for small and medium-sized businesses (IBM's System 3, System 32, and System 38 computers), but he had also been the manager who had put them into production.

In 1985, as Glenn Henry flew to the recognition weekend in San Diego, he was leading yet another important project—the production of IBM's first "workstation" computer. This was a high-powered desktop computer for people who needed a compact but especially potent machine—quality graphics and blinding speed. It was driven by a streamlined new chip and operating system called RISC (Reduced Instruction Set Computing).[4]

The mid-1980s were still the heyday of IBM. Seventy percent of the world's large mainframe computers used by governments and the biggest global corporations were IBM made, as were nearly half of the personal computers. For IBM, 1984 had been a banner year,[5] and, as John Akers took over as IBM's new chairman and CEO, he reported to IBM's stockholders in early 1985 that "IBM's prospects have never been brighter than they are today."[6]

So the "technical recognition" weekend in the spring of 1985 was a three-day fiesta of success, full of easy relaxation, corporate camaraderie, and a sense of confidence about IBM's future momentum.

The grand finale of that weekend, as every year, was the naming of IBM Fellows, the highest honor the company could bestow. Fellows were IBM's Hall of Fame. To be named an IBM Fellow was to be assured a job and salary for life and the freedom to choose one's own work. Each year, IBM named only two or three new Fellows.

In 1985, Glenn Henry was chosen an IBM Fellow. Three years later, in the summer of 1988, Glenn Henry jolted IBM—he quit, and he went to work as technical director for IBM's then-barely-known rival, Dell Computer Corporation.

Glenn Henry's resignation reverberated throughout IBM. It was unheard of—an IBM Fellow leaving Big Blue! This never happened, except perhaps when a Fellow left to pursue pure scientific research at a university. But to leave for another computer company—that was a shock.

"My wife was in shock for a year or two," Henry confessed in mid-1993, when I found him in a small, unpretentious office at Dell Computer in Austin, Texas, his jaw fringed with a salt-and-pepper beard, his shirt collar open at the neck.

Glenn Henry's departure was symptomatic of a rockslide that was starting inside IBM.

Within three months of Henry's departure, the executive to whom Henry had submitted his resignation, Dennis Andrews, director of the IBM Development Laboratory at Boca Raton, also resigned; he went to work for Xerox. Some time before, Frank King, another of Glenn Henry's bosses, had quit to join the software company Lotus. In 1988, Andy Heller, the brilliant young technologist who had taken over leadership of IBM's workstation project from Henry in 1986—and another IBM Fellow—also left. So did other bright stars—Joel Birnbaum, director of research, left in 1980 for Hewlett-Packard; John Moussouris, a key researcher, moved out in 1984 and went on to co-found two hot new companies called MIPS and Microunity; Bob Evans, a vice president and mainframe division manager, left to set up his own business in Silicon Valley. And there were more.

IBM was bleeding internally. It was suffering a brain drain. Some of its best people were quitting in disillusionment over how IBM was being run. They were frustrated by rigidity at the top, by how slowly IBM made decisions, by IBM's refusal to change, by its stifling of new ideas from its most creative people.[7]

"IBM was a good company, treated me well," Henry told me. "IBM Fellow is really a good deal, so leaving IBM probably wasn't the smart business move. I didn't do it for career or business reasons. I did it because I love computers and I want to work on computers. I want to work in the heart of the industry. I want to work where things are really happening, and I just got so frustrated that I couldn't deal with the overhead, the bureaucracy, the slowness [at IBM]. And I said I've just got to go work where I can love my work day to day."[8]

What Glenn Henry found intolerable was seeing the established powers at IBM squeeze the life out of some of IBM's best inventions.

Henry's own effort to put out an IBM desktop workstation computer had been delayed eighteen precious months by management's on-again, off-again indecision—a delay that made the difference, Henry said, "between a runaway success and ho-hum." Long before

Henry's effort was geared up, IBM's top brass had sat—for fifteen years—on the central concept behind the workstation, the RISC chip technology. Back in 1968, an IBM researcher named John Cocke had dreamed up the idea that computers could work faster if the basic, highly complex set of computer instructions on its microprocessing chip could be reduced. Hence RISC—Reduced Instruction Set Computing. But Cocke lacked high-level support, and it took him a decade to develop a prototype. Even then, in the late 1970s, IBM's leaders had not seized on this revolutionary idea. In fact, they had dallied so long that by late 1986, Sun Microsystems developed its own RISC chip and brought out a better workstation than IBM's. It grabbed the market that IBM should have had—and that it is still scrambling to get back.

One of Glenn Henry's breakthrough inventions ran into a similar stone wall. As an IBM Fellow, he set out in 1986 to create something entirely new—a "multimedia" PC, a combination of personal computer and TV set. A multimedia PC would not only do traditional computer functions, it would also be able to record and reproduce sound and high-definition graphics and pictures.

In the mid-1990s, multimedia PCs have become the market rage, and Glenn Henry was years ahead of the market. He and his team of thirty coworkers developed the prototype of a "multimedia" PC in 1987. Henry took that prototype to New York to show to CEO John Akers, the man who had personally anointed Henry as an IBM Fellow, and to other top IBM executives.

"This is the way of the future," Henry told them. "I want to try to get funding and make a product."

"And they said 'No,' " he recalled.

Henry was astonished. Here was a visionary product, but IBM's leaders lacked the vision to exploit it.

The same kind of high-level resistance blocked his next project, another attempt at a breakthrough that would open up new markets for IBM.

Henry gave up on IBM, and his departure underscored IBM's most grievous malady. Glenn Henry was a change agent within IBM, and, while IBM's corporate hierarchy recognized his technical genius, it rejected the very process of change that Glenn Henry stood for. In his eyes, IBM was deserting its grand tradition of innovation and creativity. It feared change—seeing change as a threat to IBM's established business rather than as an opportunity to do something new.

"If it can happen to IBM, it can happen to anybody," Glenn Henry asserted. "You have to change your business. . . . IBM's strength is technology. Technology's not enough, though. They have to totally change the way they're doing business."[9]

The Mystique of Leadership

IBM is a metaphor for America. Its long-unchallenged supremacy, its sudden steep decline, its partial recovery, and its improved but still-embattled future—all these mirror the experience of much of America over the past decade.

For half a century, IBM seemed invincible. No company better symbolized American high-tech supremacy. It was the most successful high-tech company in the world, always setting the global pace. IBM solved problems for governments and industries that were beyond the reach of any of its competitors. IBM utterly dominated information technology. In IBM's labs were invented many of the breakthroughs in computer technology, such as the memory chip, the RISC high-speed microprocessor, and a slew of computer models.

At its peak, IBM had more than 400,000 employees and annually spent up to $6 billion on research and development. It funded the greatest collection of talent in the computer industry—an industry on which all others have come to depend. Nobel Prize winners walked its halls and worked in its labs. Its two legendary leaders, Tom Watson, Sr., and Tom Watson, Jr., fostered a spirit of independent inquiry, high ethics, and hard work. And they nurtured the open clash of ideas, even to the point of tolerating shouting debates at management meetings.

Until the mid-1980s, IBM was the commanding leviathan of the computer world. It was riding on the mystique of leadership as well as on the reality of leadership. As Charles Ferguson and Charles Morris wrote in their book *Computer Wars,* IBM "was not just the flagship of American high technology, but almost the entire navy."[10] Only twenty years ago, IBM's computer sales were larger than *the combined sales of all other computer companies in the world.*

Like America, IBM became the world standard, the target of every competitor. In the 1970s, the Japanese government organized Japan's entire computer industry to try to catch up to IBM.[11] "Beat IBM!" was the exhortation chanted by engineers and computer programmers at Fujitsu and Hitachi as they slaved into the wee hours.[12] So aggressive were Fujitsu and Hitachi that in the early 1980s, they got caught trying to steal IBM's trade secrets in computer architecture and software. Together, they had to pay IBM more than $1 billion in compensation.[13]

From World War II until the mid-1980s, IBM embodied America's competitive advantage. Its humbling fall therefore came as a great shock to unsuspecting Americans. IBM's greatness multiplied the significance of its failure for the country.

Americans might discount the auto industry's troubles as symptomatic of Detroit's parochial ineptitude or as evidence of the personal blind spots of an individual CEO, such as Roger Smith at GM. The skidding fortunes of IBM, however, suggested that America's problems in the early 1990s were much more serious than the pathology of one old smokestack industry.

Once the symbol of America's high-tech supremacy, IBM suddenly stood for America's high-tech vulnerability. Policymakers in the Pentagon and in Congress worried about America's growing dependence on foreign suppliers for critical technologies.

Once the secure safe haven of the best and the brightest, IBM became a geyser of white-collar unemployment. After decades of robust expansion, it had to shut down plants and shuck off 190,000 employees. As IBM let go experienced managers, engineers, and Ph.D.s by the tens of thousands, it sent the unmistakable message that no one was immune from the shock waves of the new global challenge. This competition could not only savage blue-collar America, it could wreak havoc in gentrified white-collar suburbia as well.

Just to keep up with once-lesser rivals, IBM was suddenly scrambling for partnerships and alliances, in order to catch up on technologies that it had let pass by. Although IBM remained the world's largest computer company, its power was sorely diminished. Andy Grove, CEO of Intel, the leading chipmaker, observed shrewdly that "The most important measure of competitiveness is the direction of market share, up or down."[14] IBM's global market share fell from 38 percent in 1983 to 23 percent in 1990—a worse tumble than General Motors took in the 1980s—and its downward slide continued for another couple of years.[15]

In April 1991, CEO John Akers issued a belated wake-up call to IBM's legions. "The fact that we're losing market share makes me goddamn mad!" Akers thundered to a management seminar. He put out the word that if IBM's sales representatives lost a single customer, their jobs were at risk. "I'm sick and tired of visiting plants to hear nothing but great things about quality and cycle time—and then to visit customers who tell me of problems," Akers declared. "The tension level is not high enough in the business. Everyone is too damn comfortable at a time when the business is in crisis."[16]

Akers himself had been too complacent to grasp the depth of IBM's problems until it was almost too late. And so, reeling from $13 billion in operating losses in 1992 and 1993 and with IBM's stock plummeting, IBM's board ousted CEO John Akers and President Jack Kuehler. In desperation it turned to an outsider—Lou Gerstner, then chairman of RJR Nabisco—to rescue the sinking company.

How had this paragon of American supremacy fallen so badly?

Revolution from Below: The Attacker's Advantage

The textbook explanation at IBM was that Big Blue had been humbled by a technological "revolution from below."

The foundation of IBM's dominance had been the huge $10 million to $20 million mainframe computers that it leased and later sold to major corporations. These were computers massive enough to occupy entire floors of block-size office buildings. They were capable of handling nationwide reservations for American Airlines, automating the banking operations of Chase Manhattan, routing all the telephone calls for an entire region, or enabling Boeing to design aircraft.

Every few years, IBM would come out with a new family of mainframes—the "360 series," the "370 series," the "390 series." In between, IBM made itself indispensable to corporate clients with a stream of other improvements. Like a family doctor, IBM's approach was to invite its customers to tell IBM their problems and then to let IBM devise the cure, that is, to design their entire information systems. For IBM, this was a cozy and lucrative setup. It put IBM in control, and it kept big revenues rolling in steadily.

Suddenly, within one short decade, from 1980 to 1990, IBM lost control of the computer market. Its world was shaken to the core by the mushrooming power of small personal computers.

The computing power fused into the tiny thumbnail-size microprocessor chips that drive personal computers (PCs) and desktop workstations took several miraculous, quantum leaps in the 1980s. Within a few short years, the best of the workstation computers, no bigger than a PC, became 50 or 100 times faster than the massive mainframes of yesteryear.[17]

"The technology is changing at a ferocious pace," James McGroddy, IBM's vice president for research, told me. "In 1981, a microprocessor could handle a hundred thousand instructions per second; today, a hundred *million* instructions per second. It's a thousand times faster. As capabilities expand, people dream up new uses that were never imagined before. With PCs, people are not just replacing their accountants and their secretaries. They are restructuring their businesses, inventing entire new businesses based on information technology. Wal-Mart has made an entire industry out of inventory control. Frito Lay uses computer systems to tell exactly how much inventory of its products is in each supermarket. But even that does not satisfy them. Frito Lay wants to know exactly where each store is displaying its chips. So now they want a computer with a visual capability, so they can look at the shelves—not just count the boxes."[18]

Along with the technological sunburst came an equally powerful explosion in the marketplace.

McGroddy spoke with a touch of nostalgia about the 1970s, when IBM had only half a dozen competitors—Digital Equipment, Burroughs, Control Data, NEC (Nippon Electric Corporation), Fujitsu, and Hitachi. Building mainframe computers was so expensive and complicated that only a few big companies could afford to get into the game.

"We had half a dozen or a dozen competitors, and we were at war with them," McGroddy recalled. "We won that war—but in the meantime, we have fifty thousand or a hundred thousand new competitors."

IBM's old game had been blown wide open. During the 1980s IBM's clones—its technological twins—were swarming all over the globe. Basic computer technology had become universally available. Any little company could purchase the microprocessor—the "engine" of a PC—from Intel in Silicon Valley; it could buy memory chips from Japan and other components almost anywhere. Microsoft sold the basic operating software. So it took only a few dozen people to go into business assembling PCs. Like rabbits, the competition multiplied. Desktop computers poured by the millions out of Hong Kong, Taiwan, South Korea, Japan, Singapore, Germany, France, England, and scores of American companies such as Apple, Compaq, Dell, Packard Bell, and others.

IBM fell vulnerable to "the attacker's advantage," as Jim McGroddy put it. He meant that the new companies were continually coming up with new products to fill the gaps in today's technology. They were driving the process of change by moving into new market territory—what McGroddy called "the white space, the empty space."

"Most established companies don't pick at their own white space," McGroddy admitted. "They have the markets all assigned to one division or another. People have their own territory, their own mission. They have to produce and sell to established markets. So the reaction of the system [inside IBM] is to resist new inventions."

The reactions at IBM described by McGroddy were very revealing: "The first is 'What you're showing me is very small and uncertain. It's too risky—how do I know it will pay off?' The second reaction is 'I'm busy as hell, don't bother me. I can make a lot more money with incremental improvements in the products I'm already selling than with some newfangled thing.' And the third reaction is 'Hey, if that new thing succeeds, it will threaten my base and cut my own business out from under me.' "[19]

The fundamental problem at IBM, according to McGroddy, was that IBM did not realize that it had to cannibalize its own business, that its new divisions and its old new computers had to go head to head against its own established computer products and their divisions. In short, IBM needed to tolerate, and even encourage, internal competition—and without that internal ferment, IBM was doomed to decline.

"We didn't understand that *we* had to go into that unoccupied territory ourselves," McGroddy admitted. "Only in the late eighties did we come to understand that we had to put *our own* production out of business with new technology, or else *someone else* would do it to us."

The Mainframe Mentality

McGroddy's explanation made IBM's fall sound mechanistic, impersonal, inevitable. But in fact, the causes were human, highly personal, and avoidable.

IBM was not toppled by a "revolution from below" but by the die-hard resistance of the palace guard. IBM's wounds were self-inflicted.

IBM had a choice: Either embrace change, make internal adjustments, and ride with the new technology or keep the old game plan, let others take the lead, and suffer the consequences. Under CEOs John Opel and John Akers in the 1980s, IBM chose to stick with its old ways in a new game.

IBMers had their own name for the problem. They called it "the mainframe mentality." By this, they meant not only the rigid attachment of IBM's top executives and main divisions to a corporate strategy based on making and marketing large mainframe computers—"Big Iron," in industry lingo. Even more fundamentally, they meant the hidebound, self-centered effort of IBM leaders to try to control the growth of rival technologies—*within IBM itself*—despite the obvious fact that the computer world had burst beyond the capacity of anyone to control.

IBM suffered from the success reflex—a corporate reflex to protect the status quo. It remained stuck in the past, committed to the old formula that in the computer world, what is big matters because it has always produced success and paid handsome profits for IBM; and that what is small doesn't matter and has to be stopped from disrupting the comfortable world that IBM has created.

Most of IBM's leadership was so steeped in the mainframe culture that they could not envision a different future. Corporate IBM had become so accustomed to living off the enormous profits generated by its controlled, periodic upgrading of mainframe computers to captive corporate clients, who provided two thirds of IBM's vast revenues, that IBM's leadership resisted anything that would threaten this lucrative scheme. As Peter Drucker, the business strategist, put it, IBM's corporate hierarchy could not see that IBM's concept of its business had become obsolete.[20]

One reason for IBM's corporate myopia was that its senior management came to be dominated in the 1980s by people who did not understand computer technology well. Many came from backgrounds in marketing and business management, or from twenty years of selling mainframe computers, which were the only computer systems they knew.

Their limited technical understanding held IBM back, and it drove IBM geniuses such as Glenn Henry out the door. "Near the end, my manager in New York—I don't think had ever used a PC," Henry told me. "He certainly wasn't PC literate. But that was the person who was making the decisions about the PC business!"[21]

So instead of riding the tide of technological change, instead of taking the lead in innovation, IBM tried to fight the tide and slow the revolution.

"That's a change, because previously IBM had embraced change very aggressively and had been the leader in transformations in the industry," commented Charles Ferguson, a former IBM technologist and an expert on the computer industry.

It was true. In the 1950s and 1960s, IBM had reorganized and remade itself several times as each new technology appeared. Typically, IBM was among the first to introduce innovations in order to improve its competitive position. However, by the time the small-computer revolution came along, Ferguson asserted, "IBM as a company had changed, and its culture had changed, into one that wanted to protect an entrenched establishment rather than lead the industry in technical change."[22]

What's more, insiders told me, the sense of competitive urgency that had once driven IBM, as well as its tradition of honest and open debate, had been corrupted in the 1980s by corporate politics and turf wars. Seasoned executives were often motivated more by vested interests in their own products, divisions, and careers than by a long-term vision of IBM's technical leadership.

"They placed the advancement of their careers and their power inside IBM ahead of the interests of the company," said Ferguson, "and as a result they didn't admit mistakes, didn't make decisions that would have reduced their power, didn't permit competing points of view to be heard."[23]

Mice in the Elephants' Straw: The Mismatch of PCs and Mainframes

The irony of IBM's inflexibility in the late 1980s is that during its early development of personal computers, IBM had tried to change. It had proven—temporarily—that a big company does not have to be muscle-bound.

For that brief spell, IBM was quick and responsive to the market. Then, however, IBM reverted to mainframe myopia and smothered its own success.

In personal computers, Big Blue began behind the curve. The PC pioneers in the 1970s were upstart companies such as Apple, Tandy, and Atari. In the bowels of the IBM labs, some young computer "jocks" were building their own PC prototypes, but most senior IBM executives were uninterested. They patronizingly dismissed all this as "low-end computing." One vital exception was Frank Cary, IBM's CEO in 1980, who saw the potential of the home computer market. On his way to the top, Cary had tilted with IBM's mainframe apparatchiks just enough to introduce midsize computers, the family of computers on which Glenn Henry had worked.

In August 1980, Cary decided to make a run at desktop computers. He took extraordinary precautions. Cary understood the penchant within IBM for strangling its own infant technologies in the cradle. So Cary provided this effort with unprecedented protection—he made it a separate operation entirely outside the regular IBM structure.

Cary set a tough deadline: Within one year, he wanted IBM to match the Apple II home computer. To achieve that, he granted the project's leaders extraordinary independence. He liberated them from control by IBM's top-heavy bureaucracy. He exempted them from IBM's centralized quality control, from the standard requirement to buy all components from within IBM, and from the oppressive power and labyrinthine regulations of IBM's Standard Products Authority, which normally had to approve and monitor all new computer development.[24] These were some of the bureaucracies that later suffocated Glenn Henry.

The PC group were a happy band of self-styled renegades and mavericks. Located in Boca Raton, Florida, they enjoyed the informality of jeans, tennis shoes, and open-necked shirts, in defiance of the IBM dress code—dark suits and white dress shirts. They called themselves "the wild ducks," and their team leader was Don Estridge, an executive known for a freewheeling entrepreneurial style, pep rallies, big bonuses, and recruiting young computer jocks from lost lagoons in IBM's research centers.

To jump-start IBM's project, Estridge bought a basic PC microprocessor chip made by Intel and operating software from Microsoft, which then consisted of only a handful of people led by Bill Gates. In neither case did IBM buy the system outright; the ownership stayed with Intel and Microsoft, unwittingly leaving IBM dependent on these two suppliers. Like many American firms that were buying parts from Taiwan, Japan, Korea, or southeast Asia, IBM saw components as secondary; it mistakenly thought the crucial element was its know-how in putting the parts together.

What the Boca Raton "wild ducks" achieved was nothing short of phenomenal. They not only produced IBM's first PC by August 1981, but three years later, in 1984, IBM had the largest share of the PC market (41%) and a $4 billion business with ten thousand employees.[25] The PC business quickly exceeded Frank Cary's wildest dreams. In ten years, IBM sold 17 million PCs, and its rivals sold 83 million clones.[26]

What is shocking is that IBM then turned good fortune to bad. In 1984, John Opel, IBM's new CEO, decided to bring the renegade PC division back under central control, inside the regular IBM structure. Opel took away the freedom and flexibility that had generated success. To head the new operation, Opel chose Bill Lowe, an experienced mainframe executive and a classic corporation man, whom the "wild ducks" nicknamed "Mr. Flannel."

In typical mainframe style, Lowe and his aides tried to achieve IBM's control over the entire PC industry by seeking to impose IBM's technical specifications on any company that made a personal computer that was "IBM compatible"—or similar to IBM's. But the other firms refused, and IBM was too dependent on Intel's microprocessors and Microsoft's software to be able to dictate discipline to the market. So competition was a free-for-all, and IBM had to compete on equal terms with everyone else. Control had slipped through IBM's fingers.

Undercut by low-cost PC companies buying cheaper components abroad, IBM counted on its reputation for quality to maintain customer loyalty, but it made a disastrous mistake. Its mainframe-minded leaders failed to see that in the PC market, others, not IBM, were setting the pace, and they failed to keep up with that pace—because they were trying to protect IBM's own bigger computers.

In 1986, IBM forfeited technical leadership in the PC world to Compaq—a mistake that gave Compaq a break that is still hurting IBM in the mid-1990s. Intel was upgrading its "286" microprocessor to a faster, more powerful "386." When IBM's PC division wanted to buy the new "386," IBM's midsize computer division objected. They feared that a faster PC using a "386" chip would threaten IBM's midsize computer business. So IBM's top management vetoed IBM's use of Intel's faster "386" chip. Compaq and other PC makers, however, seized on the Intel "386" and leapt ahead of IBM. Now behind on both quality and price, IBM saw its share of the PC market fall precipitously.[27]

"There's no nice way to describe what IBM did to its personal computer business," Charles Ferguson declared. "A number of IBM executives, very senior executives, through a combination of arrogance and technical ignorance and inattention, made a series of inexcusably disastrous mistakes that resulted in IBM's share of the personal computer market going from fifty percent to less than ten percent in a decade."[28]

The heart of the problem was that inside IBM, two cultures were at war—the culture of the mainframe and the culture of the personal computer.

These two worlds are poles apart. They do not mesh. IBM's development of each new line of mainframes is methodical; major new developments come every four or five years. The deals are big deals, corporation to corporation. It is a predictable world; IBM, the producer, had always run it that way. "Your customers are corporate information specialists—they like stability and continuity," explained Bob Corrigan, who became head of IBM's PC division in 1990. "Big companies were investing zillions of dollars in those big computers. They want to be sure that what worked before will still work and they won't have to do too much retraining. Change is slow, and there's a long payback for the initial investment."[29]

The PC world is the opposite—disorderly and totally unpredictable. The rate of change is pell-mell, and the impetus comes not from producers, such as IBM, but from the rampant, ever-changing appetites of mass consumers. In the mid-1980s, like General Motors in autos, IBM was suddenly confronted with a market where speed, variety, and responsiveness were much more valuable than size and a leadership mystique.

"The PC world is completely different," said Corrigan, shrugging, palms up, as if to say, How had IBM's top brass failed to see this? "It didn't fit in with that traditional IBM system. When it was folded back inside the traditional IBM structure, it got smothered. It got lost in the huge business of producing and marketing those mainframes. So it lost touch with the market in every element—in responsiveness, in manufacturing, in development, in marketing."

Human talent was not the issue, according to Bob Corrigan, but it was absurd to expect the same design engineers to put together small PCs and massive mainframes, or the same sales representatives to market both personal and corporate computers. The PC operation suffered from the effort to marry those two disparate worlds.

Worse, the mainframe mind-set requires endless approvals before any new move can be made. As Corrigan took over the PC division, he said, "They told me that before you could launch a new model PC, you had to do a customer requirements survey. They handed me a 'Market Requirements Package.' It was in *eight looseleaf binders,* telling you every detail you had to study before you could even start selling something new. You had to go up the corporate ladder to get approval to do anything out of the ordinary."

By this point, Corrigan was grinning, lampooning IBM's legendary slow-footedness.

"People made an entire industry out of underpricing us—they would undercut us one day, and it would take us six weeks to decide to match them," he whined. "We were like a dinosaur: They'd whack us on the tail, and three weeks later we'd feel it in our brain. Most of the industry figured they could beat us by six months. We could invent something and license it to others. They could spot us a six-month head start with our own technology, and they'd still catch up to us in the marketplace. We didn't understand: Speed is the key in the PC market today."

While Bob Corrigan saw IBM's problems as massive incompetence, Jim McGroddy, the research division chief, saw animosity at work. Like Charles Ferguson and Glenn Henry, McGroddy believed the PC operation had been deliberately crippled by the mainframe palace guard. It was utter folly, he thought, to have stripped the PC division of its independence and brought it back inside IBM's main structure.

"Suppose you want to raise mice," McGroddy said with an Irish twinkle in his eyes. "Now you might conclude that, you know, what a mouse needs is a place that's nice and warm and cozy and whatnot. So you put these mice in the elephant's cage. And they find a nest in the straw that the elephant has there. What happens when the elephant finds the mice? He's probably going to step on them. The elephant doesn't want mice in its cage."[30]

Trying to Buy an IBM Laptop in a Hurry

My own personal encounter with IBM's flat-footed, elephantine ways came toward the end of 1992. I needed a laptop computer for my work in Germany and Japan and for traveling around America, and I had heard great things about IBM's new ThinkPad 700. It had a gorgeous flat-panel screen made by Toshiba and a red TrackPoint ball built into the keyboard. The color version was pricey—about $4,000—and all I needed was a word processor, so I preferred a black-and-white version, priced at about $2,600.

IBM had been running big newspaper ads, touting the ThinkPad 700 as the leading-edge laptop for people on the go: small, light, with a big memory, fast computing power, and a built-in fax. It got rave reviews from PC magazines. Just what I needed. But simply getting to see this IBM laptop in Washington, D.C., proved to be an ordeal to match a trip to Siberia.

Janina Roncevic, my executive assistant, and I began calling computer stores in Washington, only to discover that no one had a Think-Pad 700 in stock. The best-known computer stores in the shopping malls were not carrying *any* IBM PCs; IBM's retail network did not yet include them. Its only retail outlets at that point were Sears, Roebuck and Staples, a big office-supply supermarket. Staples, however, got only IBM's low-budget laptop. That version did not have the features I needed, and it was take-it-or-leave-it. I could buy it and then try to negotiate upgrades with IBM by long distance. So much for IBM's market flexibility.

Locating a real live ThinkPad 700 became a detective chase. We went outside Washington to Gaithersburg, Annapolis, Baltimore. I was ready to drive thirty or forty miles to see one. No store anticipated less than a month's delay in receiving the ThinkPad 700.

We tried the IBM dealer listings in the yellow pages. From their answering machines I discovered that IBM dealers operated strictly nine to five on weekdays; no evenings or weekend hours to accommodate working people. Evidently they weren't feeling too much market pressure. Besides, several dealers told me, they didn't sell to individual customers, only to businesses. I said I had a business, and then the truth came out: They, too, had no ThinkPad 700s for sale.

Finally, after scores of phone calls, Janina tracked down a Computerland business outlet in Rockville, Maryland, which was sharing one lone demonstration ThinkPad 700 with three other dealers. They were handing it around from one potential commercial customer to another for a few hours at a time. Computerland's turn was due in a couple of days, so they would let me see the demo—briefly. The salesman, Kurt Engelman, cautioned Janina that Computerland already had a thousand back orders and no prospect of an early shipment. Still, it was a worth a look. It was now early January 1993; I needed a laptop right away.

When I arrived, Kurt Engelman pulled out his ThinkPad 700 from behind a counter, like a secret cache of gold.

"I got some good news for you," he said. "We received a shipment of about four hundred last night in our warehouse out in California, which was sort of a surprise to me because I came in today expecting to see zero."

"Let me take a look," I said eagerly, playing the keyboard and testing the TrackPoint ball. It had a color screen with sharp, clear resolution. Great quality and a built-in fax modem. I asked about a black and white.

No black-and-white ThinkPads until March, Engelman said, and there was already a backlog of three thousand orders.

I asked him several questions about the quality of the display on the black-and-white version. He looked around vainly for fact sheets or pictures.

He shrugged. "I've never seen a black-and-white screen. This is the only demo unit I have from IBM."

My frustration burst out. "I've been around to a whole bunch of other computer stores," I said. "I can find a Compaq. I can find a Toshiba. I can find a Texas Instruments. They're on the shelves. You can try them out, put your hands on them, see if you like the keyboard, the display. Here I am, an individual customer, and IBM has told me they're really trying for my business. They've got these darn 700s advertised in the newspapers—"

"I agree, I agree," Engelman sympathized. "I feel the frustration, too—only from a sales perspective. Because I have customers that want to buy it. And it's like, 'Yeah, I would like to sell it to you, but I don't have it. Can you wait?' They're like, 'No, I can't wait.' And they start looking at other machines."[31]

That was my situation. I liked the IBM technology, but I couldn't wait until March. So I settled for another brand, at a better price.

Perhaps, I thought, the big picture might be different.

I went to the big semiannual Consumer Electronics Show in Las Vegas, where manufacturers showcase their best new offerings to retailers from all over the world. Amid IBM's dramatic displays of ThinkPads, voice-activated computers of the future, uncanny new cellular phones, and other technical wizardry, I met Anthony Santelli, a vice president of IBM's new PC company, and I told him my predicament.

"I hate to tell you," I said, "I'm buying a rival product because I've got to have one now. There have got to be a lot of people like me. What does IBM do for us?"

"We are right now putting a full-court press on building as many of these machines as we can—that's what IBM is doing," Santelli told me. "It's a blowout product."

Santelli is a born salesman, dapper, with flashing eyes, a white mustache, a liquid tongue, and expressive body language. I asked Santelli what was IBM's big problem.

"The thing that's evil in the IBM corporation—and we're going to eliminate—is the bureaucratic claw," Santelli replied, and his right hand popped up, fingers curled into an eagle's claw.

"Anytime a basic pricing decision had to be made," he said, "we'd have to go through meetings upon meetings upon meetings, to have people who were only superficially involved with the product and the market, but had a position of power. I don't know where it came from, some mythical power, but they had to vote. If you didn't get their vote, you couldn't move."

"So the market moved, and IBM didn't go with it?" I asked.

"The market moved. We studied it. We looked at it. And basically, we missed the market," Santelli moaned. "When we introduced a new product, a major question was not 'How are you against your competition?' but 'What do you do to our product line?' Again, the bureaucratic claw: Thou shalt not cannibalize the main line."

"You mean, don't hurt your own business," I said.

"Don't hurt our own business. Don't eat your babies."

Santelli insisted that IBM was changing; the PC company was going to go for new technology, even if that ate into IBM's old lines of business.[32]

Someone pulled Santelli away, so I went to find some retailers who were moving among the IBM, Apple, Compaq, and Toshiba display areas. Gregory E. Kinnear, who had a computer store in Denver, told me that from his viewpoint IBM was still too slow. He admired IBM's technology, such as the ThinkPad 700, and said that IBM's pricing had gotten better. But IBM was still not agile enough.

"The problem is, the market's not a stationary target, it's a moving target," Kinnear said. "As soon as they hit a price point, everybody else reacts. And you've got to react quick, or else you're still overpriced."

"Do others move faster?" I inquired.

"Absolutely, yeah. Compaq in their whole new revamp has moved much faster," was Kinnear's judgment. "In my store, Compaq has outsold IBM ten to one."[33]

Kinnear was in his thirties; perhaps he favored up-and-coming companies more than establishment IBM. So I looked around for an older retailer.

Samuel Semel, who had run a computer store in Elmira, New York, for many years, had been watching IBM's struggle, and he echoed Kinnear's judgment that IBM's PC operation was still hobbled by IBM's old ways.

"They brought the same people—the inertia, the typical IBM person, the dark-suit, white-shirt type of person," said Semel. "They are still very, very slow to react."

Semel was irked that IBM was segmenting the market rigidly and dictating to him which computers he should be selling—which lines were for home use and which were for the small-business market. Semel wanted to make those decisions himself, and he found IBM still too inflexible.

When I mentioned Santelli's claim that IBM had gotten rid of the bureaucratic claw, Semel snorted skeptically. "They've gotten rid of a lot of very, very good people. And the people that are on top, making these decisions, have no idea what the marketplace is like."[34]

The Battle to Change IBM's Corporate Culture

By the early 1990s, IBM was nearing the brink. From 1986 to 1993, CEO John Akers had to write off $28 billion in losses, as well as in pay for drastic personnel cuts and reorganization. In the PC market, IBM's sales were plummeting so badly by mid-1992 that IBM's $11 billion PC operation "would have gone right out of business" without a radical reorganization, according to Bob Corrigan.[35]

IBM faced two challenges: first, halting its steep decline just to survive; second, transforming its corporate culture.

John Akers, in his waning months as CEO, made desperate efforts to inject flexibility into IBM by decentralizing power. Akers's scheme was to break up the battleship of IBM into a "swift-moving fleet of destroyers"—a federation of thirteen independent companies, linked together under one corporate umbrella. But in January 1993, before he could carry out that plan, Akers was ousted by the IBM board of directors. He did manage, however, to break off IBM's PC division as a separate company to give it back the independence that had once enabled the "wild ducks" to achieve great results.

Changing the IBM mind-set—above all, instilling a readiness to change and a sense of collaboration—was Bob Corrigan's main task as head of the new PC company.

Corrigan, a thirty-year IBM veteran, knew IBM's problems. And so his first priority was not operational efficiency or new products but human relations—breaking down walls, healing rivalries within IBM, getting everyone to work together as a team. "When things get in trouble, people build fences—'not my fault, not my fault,' " Corrigan mimicked them. "My job was to put it back together as one whole. The hardest part is bringing the people back together."[36]

Corrigan's second catechism was speed—both moving swiftly to keep pace with changing technology and being responsive to consumer demands. "You've got to be quick," Corrigan said. To drive home his point, Corrigan put out the word: Let anyone undercut an IBM price and he wanted IBM responding *the very next day*—"not three weeks later, not two weeks later, the next day."

One test came quickly. On October 20, 1992, the day before Corrigan's PC company was going to announce its first new models, Compaq stole the march by lowering its PC prices. "So we had to change our price that very day—you should have seen it," Corrigan said. "We already had our ads prepared to go into the papers the next morning to announce our new computer. It took us about an hour to decide what to do on the price." IBM matched the Compaq prices. "At four that afternoon, our guys were calling around to the newspapers to change the prices in the ads."

Corrigan's injection of speed and teamwork rescued IBM's PC business from bankruptcy and produced a turnaround. In 1993, IBM's PC and laptop sales jumped 45 percent to nearly 4.5 million units, or 10 percent of the market. Very narrowly, IBM was the market leader,[37] but its lead in the PC market was short lived. In 1994, Compaq surged well ahead, and IBM fell to fourth place, behind Apple and a relative newcomer, Packard Bell.[38]

Solving IBM's problems has proven difficult. Not only have its costs remained high, but it has had trouble reading and responding to the market. Both problems are legacies of IBM's heavy-footed inflexibility. Even after two years of supposed reforms, the PC company in 1994 was still running short of ThinkPad laptops and producing too many of another model, the ValuePoint. Under top-level pressure, Bob Corrigan resigned, from IBM's embattled PC business.[39]

Moreover, even in the mid-1990s, IBM's mainframers are still in a time warp, fighting a rearguard battle. The Enterprise Division, which makes and markets mainframe computers, has been scrambling to protect its ties with its old corporate clients, the information officers of major corporations. It has been trying to slow the trend toward workstations, PCs, and the new alternative of massively parallel computing, in which armies of smaller computers strung together can work problems faster than big mainframe computers can. Worldwide, mainframe sales dropped from $30 billion in 1990 to $21 billion in 1993 (less than the $35 billion world market in small computers). IBM's market share in mainframes fell, too, as did its prices; to prevent total collapse, IBM has been feverishly trying to adapt its big computers for use as "servers" to networks of smaller computers.[40]

"As fast as we think we're going, it's not fast enough," Nick Donofrio, the new head of IBM's mainframe division, admitted to me in December 1993.[41] *The Economist* mockingly compared IBM's mainframe fixation to Custer's last stand.

But the fundamental fight at IBM has not been about PCs or mainframe computers per se; it has been over IBM's entrenched corporate culture, its insular, self-centered, slow-to-change mind-set.

Changing that IBM culture has become the primary target of Lou Gerstner, who took over as IBM's chairman and CEO in April 1993. The fifty-one-year-old Gerstner came to IBM from RJR Nabisco, where he had been CEO. Gerstner had no high-tech background; he did, however, have a reputation as an extremely effective, hard-driving manager.

At IBM, Gerstner won early press headlines by going after cost reductions, dramatically declaring that IBM would cut $7 billion by 1996. He kept reducing IBM's staff—trimming 35,000 employees on top of the 155,000 already cut by John Akers.

Gerstner is action oriented. He emphasizes performance over vision. When pestered by financial analysts to spell out his long-term strategy, Gerstner snapped back: "Strategy is execution!"[42] He did reorganize IBM's sales operation and the top management team, though most of his top deputies were holdovers. He brought in a few of his own people—in finance and in personnel—and, to market small computers, he replaced Bob Corrigan with his own longtime protégé, G. Richard Thoman from RJR Nabisco.

But Gerstner has been less of a radical than John Akers had become in his final year. He has rejected Akers's idea of splitting up IBM into separate operations, and he mocks the notion that size is IBM's problem.[43] "There is a misconception that small is always more beautiful than big," Gerstner told one interviewer.[44] On the contrary, Gerstner sees IBM's leviathan size as a source of strength, a vehicle for offering large corporate customers a full plate of computers and services.

The people at IBM, and their attitudes, are what Gerstner wants to change most. He has seen an urgent need to alter IBM's insular mindset, the IBM habit of deciding internally what the market needs instead of first listening to customers. He has chided IBM's managers to "squeeze the arrogance out" of their approach. At one session with managers, Gerstner declared bluntly: "We have been too preoccupied with *our own* view of the world."[45] Like an itinerant preacher carrying the new gospel to one IBM facility after another, Gerstner thundered to one gathering: "What happened to this company was not an act of God, some mysterious biblical plague sent down from on high. It's simple. People took our business away."[46]

To shake IBM out of its lethargy, Gerstner has appealed for "china breakers"—for innovators and mavericks, for the very kinds of people that IBM has lost, such as Glenn Henry. Urgency is Gerstner's message, his fuse for exploding IBM's old habits of mind.

Collaboration is another element of Gerstner's catechism. Mindful of the fratricide in IBM's past, he has set out to stanch IBM's villainous infighting. He prods divisions to work together and has decreed that for the sake of unity and efficiency, all IBM divisions, from the smallest to the largest computers, will use the same family of software and PowerPC (RISC) computer chips. In his first major management memo, Gerstner emphasized teamwork and collaboration.[47]

Whether Lou Gerstner has been bold enough in assaulting the IBM culture remains to be seen. His decision to keep IBM's old unified structure risks perpetuating the centralized system in which IBM's old guard can, as before, squelch innovations percolating up from below. His emphasis on collaboration is a potential invitation to endless coordination and delays, rather than market-driven swiftness. His requirement that all IBM computers use the same software and micro-processors could end up reviving IBM's stultifying conformism.

"I see a lot of the same old IBM," Glenn Henry remarked in mid-1994, after talking with old friends still at IBM. "Those divisions are supposed to be pulling together, but they're pulling in different directions. No one can do anything without the okay of the others."[48]

Another skeptic, Charles Ferguson, gives Gerstner credit for avoiding disaster by managing IBM's personnel, finances, and organizational structure much better than his predecessors did. "Without that, we could possibly have been looking at the largest bankruptcy in U.S. corporate history," Ferguson observed.

Nonetheless, Gerstner has left intact much of IBM's old strategy, including its fateful reliance on mainframe computers. Ferguson and others warn that if IBM continues on this path, it cannot recapture its former technical leadership; instead, it risks slow decline at some point in the future.[49]

Whether Lou Gerstner has succeeded in his modest push for a cultural revolution at IBM is also problematic. One IBM survey of 1,200 of its senior managers found that in spite of Gerstner's exhortations, 40 percent had not accepted "the need for change." In April 1994, a year after his takeover, Gerstner admitted to IBM shareholders: "When it comes to a results-oriented corporate culture, we're not there yet—not by a long shot."[50]

Gerstner has clearly shaken things up, in part by injecting uncertainty about long-term job security at IBM, once a hallowed tradition. Nonetheless, IBM remains resistant to change. And Gerstner chafes at the degree of resistance: "Everything takes too long. We have people here fighting decisions that were made three years ago."[51]

Gerstner's comments underscore the wider object lessons of the IBM story. Even the best of companies can get trapped by the inertia and the myopia of their own success. If they do not boldly introduce the innovations that render their past successes obsolete, competitors will—and that will hurt them more.

The ingrained mind-set that resists change causes self-inflicted wounds, and those are the most crippling wounds of all, because they are the hardest to cure.

The bottom line: Change is irresistible; run with it.

Part Two

Education

Rethinking Schools for the New Global Game

Winning in today's competitive world requires not only a new mind-set but a new kind of person.

In the old-fashioned, mass-produced assembly line pioneered by Henry Ford, the ordinary worker did a monotonous, unthinking robot job. He was seen as an extension of a machine. The worker attached the same widget, gunned the same welds, did the same bit of riveting hundreds of times a day, thousands of times a week. "Just follow orders and let us do the thinking" was the message from managers and engineers. For a job requiring modest skills, a general and not very demanding education was adequate. Employers did not worry greatly about school performance or even what courses a worker had taken in school. Finishing school was a mark of reliability, and employers hired high school graduates without much reference to their academic record.

In today's global economy, the strategy of mass production in industry has been overtaken by the flexible system pioneered by Toyota, a system that is geared to speed, responsiveness, and high quality. In one sector after another, technology has exploded. The modern corporation needs workers who know calculus and statistical process control, who can talk with talking robots, and who can program complex computer-run equipment. These qualifications are needed not only in manufacturing but in service industries and in virtually any business, large or small.

Work today is not just doing; it is, more than ever, thinking.

Today's corporation needs thinking, flexible, proactive workers. It wants creative problem solvers, workers smart and skilled enough to move with new technologies and with the ever-changing competitive environment. It needs workers accustomed to collaborating with co-workers, to participating in quality circles, to dealing with people high and low. Communication skills and people skills have become parts of the necessary repertoire of the modern worker.

Preparing young people for the modern work world imposes new demands on education. It requires rethinking old courses, old curriculums, old standards. What once worked well enough no longer fits today's reality. To be effective in the new competitive world, education needs to inculcate the habits of mind and the patterns of teamwork that have become the sources of competitive advantage. More than ever before, education needs to be relevant to the world outside the classroom, the world beyond graduation.

Rethinking education requires opening new connections between schools and business. In the past, Americans have tended to compartmentalize their lives and their problems: business in one compartment; education in a second compartment; science and technology in a third. We have treated the various arenas of American life as separate pieces, but now we need to fit the pieces together more consciously, as our foreign rivals do. And in the new global game, no connection is more basic and more vital than the partnership between business and education.

It is especially important to ensure a high-quality education for average students—the students who will be the backbone of our future workforce.

As a nation, America has been slow to adopt a national strategy to meet this new educational challenge. By contrast, America's most potent global competitors are pursuing well-integrated strategies to educate, train, and channel average youngsters from high school into the mainstream of their economies. In Japan and South Korea, a very high percentage of high school students are pushed through rigorous academic programs to provide a well-educated young workforce for industry. The German partnership of business and education provides modern, world-class schooling and training that is relevant to today's economy for the great majority of their young people. All three countries are investing purposefully in the rising generation in order to compete against the rest of the world from the high end—high skills, high quality, and a high standard of living.

In America, the new competitive game has spurred the beginnings of important educational reform. American educators and business leaders have gone abroad to study other countries and to benchmark America's educational performance against foreign rivals; and we will do the same in Chapters 4 and 5, in which American elementary and high school systems are benchmarked against schools in Germany and Japan.

The American Innovators in education, whether inspired by foreign examples or by original ideas, are creating new schools and new approaches from the ground up. In one case, a famous American educational reformer, Deborah Meier, has reached out to inner-city students in Harlem, students who were dropping out in great numbers. Meier's school has lifted these students to new levels of achievement. In another case, Wisconsin has taken a lesson from the German apprenticeship system and by doing so has opened up effective new pathways into the modern work world for average American high school students.

The challenge for America is to turn models like these, and others, into a broader movement of reform that will meet the educational needs of the new competitive game.

4

School—Where the Race Begins
Teamwork or Tracking—Which Works Best?

> *Since we study in groups, I want to cultivate their sense of cooperation.*[1]
> —SACHIKO IKEDA, JAPANESE TEACHER

> *I would like for each child to feel important . . . for each child to become independent.*[2]
> —CELESTE MOORE, AMERICAN TEACHER

> *We have to learn how to cope within a group. We don't live alone in the world. The world is heavily populated, and here is a small group that has to learn to live together.*[3]
> —ILSE LINDENBERGER, GERMAN TEACHER

A country's performance in the global game does not begin with its corporations. Rather, it begins in the mind-sets of its people—how people are taught to think, to deal with one another, to work together.

In other words, the race begins in school.

The first clues to what makes a nation tick—its distinct core values—can be seen in how children are educated. A society transmits its bedrock values through the upbringing of its young people.

Many people think of elementary school as primarily engaged in teaching basic skills—reading, writing, and arithmetic. But school is also the first institution outside the home that molds a child's behavior and social habits. The school is a mirror of society: It reflects the culture of the nation, and it imprints that same cultural archetype and mind-set on each new generation.

The patterns formed in elementary school, coupled with the way children are socialized in their families, deeply influence the way most people behave during their adult lives. Early school experiences shape people's outlook, their expectations of themselves as individuals and in relation to others, their codes of conduct. Not only do those early experiences have an enduring impact on individuals, they also set patterns of group interaction that affect the way people perform throughout business and industry.

Early socialization—different in each country—helps define and explain the particular strengths and weaknesses of the economic systems in America, Japan, and Germany.

Japan: *Wa*—Moving Along Together

Perhaps nowhere in the world do elementary schools set out more purposefully to draw young children into a web of mutual social relationships and to inculcate a spirit of cooperation and participation than in Japan.

In a Japanese elementary school, as in Japanese industry, teamwork and quality are emphasized. The Japanese teach their children to function as members of a group; this is true both in the family and in school. From an early age, Japanese children are taught the importance of relationships, interdependence, mutual obligations, and mutual responsibility. The group is the basic building block of society. The individual develops by participating in the group and cooperating with others; a child wins recognition through the success of his or her group, not for an outstanding solo performance.

In adult life, a high premium is attached to *wa,* or harmony. Open confrontation is frowned upon; all viewpoints are heard, and resolving differences is a primary social goal. As a homogeneous people, the Japanese do not have to cope with the wide ethnic differences that often divide other peoples. So highly prized is consensus among the Japanese that leadership is perceived not as the imposition of a strong individual will but as the art of inducing a group to reach consensus. The sage leader is a sheepdog shepherding a flock, not a lion growling commands.

The teacher in a Japanese elementary school operates from a similar frame of mind. He or she guides, like a coach; he or she does not deliver truth from on high. Knowledge emerges rather than being dispensed. Elementary education in Japan is not a mountain of material to be memorized; it is a voyage of curiosity and discovery.

The Japanese inculcate high standards and a striving for perfection by getting children to labor at mastering the details. Their view is that excellence results from hard work, not from natural ability or social background: Anyone who tries hard enough can achieve. As a consequence, Japanese elementary schools have an egalitarian spirit—high expectations for every child. Gifted children are not singled out for special opportunities, and slower learners are not consigned to a watered-down education. The children move along together. At school—as later, in a factory—everyone is a member of the team.

Judo Teaching: Using Student Energy

Certainly no individual school can represent an entire nation. Yet in my benchmarking of America, Germany, and Japan, I sought with the help of experts to find similar, average public schools in three industrial regions—in Toyota City, Japan; outside Kansas City, Missouri; and in Sindelfingen, Germany, outside Stuttgart—and I visited their second-grade classes.

At the Nomi elementary school in Toyota City, the face of Japan that I encountered surprised me. It did not fit cultural stereotypes.

Like many Westerners, I had heard that widely cited Japanese aphorism "The nail that sticks up higher than the rest gets pounded down." In short, don't stick out as an individual, restrain yourself. I had seen newspaper stories about the peer pressure among Japanese teenagers—the literal shunning of nonconformists—becoming so intense that it sometimes turned cruel and even violent. And so, at Nomi School, I expected to find stern regimentation: children in uniforms studying like robots, doing rote learning under relentless pressure to achieve, with strict schoolmarms imposing discipline.

Instead, in second-grade classes at Nomi School, I found a baffling lack of stress on academic achievement. Great freedom was given to the children, who were full of bubbly vitality. Teachers did not dominate the classroom; rather, they often stood aside, letting students lead the class with gentle coaching. In general, much more emphasis was put on encouraging student participation and stimulating their delight in the process of learning than on their getting the right answers.

"It's not a teacher-centered environment, not one in which authority is in some way irritating to the students," observed my companion, Tom Rohlen, a sociologist from Stanford University, who is a widely respected authority on Japanese society and on comparing educational systems.

"The teacher steps slightly aside, like in judo, where you use the energy of your opponent," Rohlen went on. "Well, the teachers here are using the energy and interests of the students, and they're letting things happen."[4]

At Nomi School—and Rohlen said this was typical of Japanese elementary schools—there was an atmosphere not of repressive orthodoxy, but of permissive freedom. The teachers encouraged spontaneity.

The result was a school charged with student energy. During recess and even during class activities, the seven- and eight-year-old second-graders were bursting with life—chatting with one another, moving freely about the classroom, comparing papers, making faces, clowning, prancing, and occasionally even screaming and falling on the floor.

Rarely did second-grade teacher Sachiko Ikeda stop the commotion in her class. Occasionally, she would introduce interludes of order and quiet, usually by asking the class leaders of the day—chores rotated so that everyone had a turn—to have the students sit quietly or to line up for another class. She introduced order in short spurts. Normally, however, Ikeda-sensei—*sensei* being the term of respect for a teacher in Japan and Ikeda-sensei being what everyone called her—tolerated a commotion that far exceeded what I saw in an American second-grade class outside Kansas City, Missouri.

"The Japanese view childhood as a time in which it's natural to be full of energy, [a time] to be completely open to curiosity," Rohlen explained. "To get the students just to be quiet artificially is to preclude some of that curiosity. So the teacher's idea is that a healthy class is one full of kids talking, raising their hands."

Ikeda-sensei's goal was to keep all the students engaged and interested in learning, so she allowed them a lot of leeway.

In a class on similes, Ikeda-sensei asked for examples from nature or the immediate surroundings, and when someone's pencil case hit the floor with a loud clatter, one bright-eyed boy, Kazuki Nakayama, quickly coined a mischievous simile: "Yuta dropped his pencil case. It sounded like lightning."

"Lightning? What's that?" one little girl asked.

"You mean thunder, not lightning," blurted out a boy next to Kazuki.

Ikeda-sensei kept quiet, letting the students debate for a few minutes. She was encouraging her eight-year-olds to make their own exploration, rather than instructing them quickly on the right answer. Engagement and participation were her primary objectives.

One technique often used by Japanese teachers is to have the class set a problem for themselves, then break up into small groups to work out answers; the groups report their solutions to the class. Japanese teachers are interested in getting many different answers, not just one right answer. This approach can take much longer than many an American teacher will allow, Rohlen explained, because the Japanese teachers invite answers that may be incorrect, in order to stimulate dialogue among the students. Then the children go back into their groups and discuss the various choices, gradually working their way to the right answer or to the possibility that there are several good answers.

"It's not the teacher modeling a correct answer so much as a teacher modeling a process of discovery," Rohlen pointed out. "It's not a victory of the smart over the less smart."

What is more, small-group work in class is also practice for problem solving in later life, similar to a Toyota work team dealing with factory problems in its quality circle. At Toyota, there is no textbook answer, only some methods that work better than others, and the best method emerges from group discussion. That is exactly how group learning works in class.

Mistakes, too, are an inevitable element of the work world. Mistakes have to surface and be addressed by the quality circle without placing blame, in order to improve the production process. Any worker's suggestion for improvement, no matter how outlandish, must be encouraged as part of the winnowing process toward the best solution.

Japanese second-grade teachers follow the same approach. Making mistakes is treated as normal, without any stigma. This is a marked contrast, educational experts note, to the normal practice in American schools, where mistakes are often targets of pointed criticism from teachers or, conversely, are buried or overlooked for fear of damaging a child's self-esteem or marking him a permanent failure.[5] At Nomi School, mistakes were frequent and not a worry; I never saw children chided for an incorrect answer. Quite the contrary: Teachers invited children to speak up, to try, even if their guesses were mistaken.

The Japanese view is that mistakes are opportunities to discover ways to a better answer and a method of drawing students into the process of learning.[6]

By Not Stressing Achievement, the Japanese Achieve More

In the early grades at Nomi School, the educational strategy is to make school enjoyable and comfortable, not demanding and forbidding. The primary objective is socialization—helping children adjust to the world of learning and the needs of social interaction. American schools work on socializing students in kindergarten and first grade, but the Japanese give that process emphasis up to the fourth grade.

The teachers at Nomi School take the view that students will ultimately perform best if they first find school inviting, if they are induced to participate in many activities, if they are led gradually into self-discipline and the proper way of doing things rather than being pushed into worrying about grades and performance. From first grade forward, all children are assigned tasks in leading little classroom routines—singing the morning song, picking academic games for the class, discussing a lesson or a problem, lining up for the next class, thanking one another at the end of the day. Year by year, they are drawn into good classroom behavior and concentration on their studies.

One school administrator told me that inculcating good social habits in the early years reduced juvenile delinquency in Japanese high schools and junior high schools and made learning more effective in the teenage years. Other educators said that by teaching the children to regulate their own behavior, the Japanese could have larger classes—on average, thirty-four students per class in Japan versus twenty-four in American primary schools—and that in the upper grades teachers spent less time on discipline, more on teaching.[7]

Nomi School does not believe in tracking children in the early grades. It makes no effort to group students by ability or even to push the fast students ahead rapidly.

In the school's computer lab, for example, Ikeda-sensei divided her thirty-one second-graders into two groups because there were not enough computers for everyone. First, the boys did arithmetic problems on the computers and the girls did written work in groups of twos and threes.

Kazuki Nakayama, the bright boy who had offered the simile about lightning, was the first to finish the programmed exercises on the computer. Kazuki impatiently called for new problems, but Ikeda-sensei had him redo the original ones. She gave her attention to students who were having trouble. When it came time for the girls to use the computers, Ikeda-sensei had Kazuki Nakayama do written exercises with two boys who had been having trouble; she told Kazuki to help them. That was typical; she and other teachers deliberately mixed children of differing abilities in their learning groups.

"In terms of what they can achieve or what they have done," Ikeda-sensei explained, "I want to keep the gap between them small."

Ikeda-sensei, an experienced teacher in her forties, was following the Japanese public school formula: moving students along together, according to a national curriculum and standards set by the Ministry of Education in Tokyo.

But more fundamentally, she was focused on goals she considered more important than academic attainment.

When I asked Ikeda-sensei what her principal aim was, she replied: "Teaching the children to be able to listen to others and teaching them to be considerate toward others. They're still quite self-centered, so I'd like to turn them into children who are capable of thinking about their friends. Since we study in groups, I want to cultivate their sense of cooperation."[8]

Here was a fundamental difference from the American approach. "This school or any Japanese elementary school in the early years," Tom Rohlen observed, "tries to socialize students to the entire environment and process of learning, much more than worrying about the exact content of some kind of academic learning."

This was a powerful idea, and it had a surprising academic payoff. Paradoxically, the Japanese were *backing into* achievement, rather than pursuing that goal directly. Although it might seem counterintuitive to Westerners, Japanese elementary schools were actually achieving more in math and sciences than American schools were, by *not* stressing achievement and grades.

The evidence lies in international tests such as those conducted over several years in Japan, America, China, and Taiwan by two well-known educational specialists, Harold W. Stevenson of the University of Michigan and James W. Stigler of UCLA. In their book *The Learn-*

ing Gap, Stevenson and Stigler reported that Japanese first- and fifth-graders easily outperformed their American peers in mathematical skills. After running tests in several schools in each of several cities— Minneapolis, Chicago, Beijing, Taipei, Taiwan, and Sendai, Japan, Stevenson and Stigler found "consistent and sobering indications of inferior performance by American children. . . . The *highest*-scoring American school falls below the *lowest*-scoring Asian school. . . . The inferiority of American children compared to Japanese children obviously begins early and grows worse as they pass through elementary school." When Stevenson and Stigler looked at the top 100 fifth-grade student scores among the four countries, 88 were from Japan.[9]

So the Japanese are doing better by concentrating on getting virtually every child engaged in learning and working hard. They get outstanding results by playing down individual performance and by maintaining high expectations for all. They do it by judo teaching—tapping the natural enthusiasm of the children—and by having teachers place their emphasis on encouraging effort and stimulating participation.[10]

Educating the Whole Person

Nomi School attaches top priority in the first four grades to what they call "educating the whole person," and the teachers use every conceivable opportunity to do so both in and out of class. They are more concerned, for example, about getting children to work in harmony and to take responsibility for cleaning up the school and serving one another lunch than they are about high marks in mathematics or Japanese grammar.

My first vivid impression of Nomi School, for example, was of the shoe racks. Japanese children take off their shoes as they enter the school, just as they do at home; they pad around school in slippers. Their shoes are stored by the doorways in large wooden racks of cubbyholes, as at an American bowling alley. At each doorway of the Nomi School, there are honeycombs of shoeboxes, stacked row upon row, five feet high and probably twenty feet long—several hundred cubbyholes in all, each filled with a pair of clean white tennis shoes (a few pairs were blue). Not a single stray pair of shoes littered the floor. Each pair was carefully lined up, the heels placed even with the outer edge of its box. A model of neatness and order.

The school principal, Gien Miwa, saw the proper care of shoes as a small lesson in self-discipline that the children would carry into the classroom and then into life in general. "In this way," he said, "they learn to treat things with respect."[11]

In educating the whole person, Japanese educators are relentlessly purposeful. Seeing school as a microcosm of society, they are forever dreaming up ways to teach habits that will be useful in later life—none more important than the habit of teamwork.

Every classroom at Nomi School has a wall chart that lists all the children as members of groups, or *hans;* there are six to ten *hans* per class. Chores are assigned to each *han*—providing the class leaders for the day, handing out notebooks, watering plants, and so on. Some teachers also use the *hans* as small learning groups. Whether in chores or academic learning, the emphasis is on teamwork. The *han* operates as a unit; its members earn recognition for achievement not as individuals but as a group. And the practice of cooperative work in the *hans* at Nomi School is training for collaborative work teams at any Japanese enterprise and any career, white collar as well as blue collar.

Nomi School leaves no opportunity for such social learning untouched. Even lunch has the conscious educational goal of having children take responsibility for themselves and show mutual support for one another.

At Nomi School, and all across Japan, lunch is served in the classroom—by the children. Each day a different *han* serves lunch to the whole class. The children don oversized white chef's coats and cook's berets and go off to the school kitchen for tureens of food, paper plates, and other paraphernalia. In the classroom, they dole out bowls of rice, curry sauce, fried fish, and cartons of juice, as classical violin music plays over the school's loudspeakers.

At lunch, too, I noticed that Ikeda-sensei stayed in the background, keeping an eye out for trouble but letting the children manage the entire affair. For all their antic energy, they were very considerate of one another. The entire class waited at their desks without touching their food until every last child was served. Only then did the class leaders fold their hands, prayer style, and lead the class in giving thanks, *Ittadakimas,* and the children begin to eat.

The end of the school day, at 3 P.M., brought another display of collective student responsibility. In Ikeda-sensei's second grade, the children pushed their desks to the back of the room, got out brooms, dustpans, and cloths, and began to clean up their classroom. That was going on all over the school. Everywhere, children were down on their hands and knees, brushing out corners, banging blackboard erasers out the windows, dusting and mopping—even in the lavatories.

Out in the corridor, where more teams were busily at work, I remarked to the principal about the beautifully polished floors. "Yes." Principal Miwa nodded. "One of the important elements of education is cleaning. Cleaning cultivates a beautiful and gentle spirit."[12]

It also creates a sense of solidarity and sacrifice, as well as a powerful attachment to the school, a feeling of ownership among the students. As Japanese parents say, serving meals and cleaning up makes school like home to the children.

The daily student cleanup, done all over the country, is also an important expression of Japanese values and priorities. Education money does not go to pay for custodians. It also rarely goes to pay for brand-new buildings, fancy equipment, or modern gyms. Nomi School was clean, sturdy, and brightly decorated with flowers and displays. But it was several decades old and pretty spartan; it had no frills. It also had no central heating, as I learned during a winter visit. Each classroom had its own kerosene stove, but the hallways were frigid. I could see my breath condense in the cold January air.

Nomi School is typical of the physical plants at other Japanese schools—buildings are pretty plain despite the fact that Japan spends a larger portion of its education budget on elementary schools than the United States does (America spends a larger proportion of national funds on higher education). Most of Japan's education money goes for teachers' salaries. "The school year is longer, and teachers are expected to work through the summer," Tom Rohlen explained. "These things lead to a very different allocation of resources—one that says teachers and teaching are more important. You don't find beautiful buildings or great facilities anywhere in Japan. But you find that the status of teachers has always been high. The word *sensei* is a sign of respect, of being paid well, and of having the trust of parents."[13]

The Home-School Connection: "Education Mom"

The final pillar of Japanese elementary schools is the close connection between home and school, the partnership between parents and teachers that experts have found to be absolutely crucial to high performance anywhere in the world.

Typically, Japanese parents take a deeper interest in their children's education than Americans do.[14] The secret of success for Japanese schools, many Japanese brag, is *kyoiku mama,* "Education Mom." At all levels of society, Japanese mothers esteem education and make sure their children attend school regularly. At Nomi School, typically fewer than 5 children out of 540 are absent on any given day—fewer than 1 percent, far below the American average of 6 or 7 percent. Having everyone in school regularly makes it easier to keep students on a rough educational par.

Communications between home and school in Japan are very close. At Nomi School, monthly parent-teacher meetings get almost 100 percent attendance, far above the skimpy turnout at the Missouri second grade I saw. Japanese mothers generally work less than American women and occasionally attend their children's classes. But the most regular contact—daily—is through a "communications notebook," in which parents and teachers write a steady stream of notes. This notebook is a common practice in Japan; almost every child has one. Ikeda-sensei showed me several in which short messages had gone back and forth—about homework, about behavior, about a child's mood or health, about happenings in the family that could affect the child. Both teacher and "Education Mom" sign off on each other's notes to close the circle of communication.

At Kazuki Nakayama's home, his mother oversees homework. Mrs. Nakayama gets home late—after 6 P.M.—because she is a teacher. Still, she said, "I make him do his homework in front of me, with his sister at the big desk in the living room and me between them."[15] Typical of the Japanese, Kazuki's parents have copies of his school textbooks and workbooks at home. Even in second grade, homework is a regular affair, even if for only a half hour, to inculcate the habit. Often homework requires parental involvement, for example, when the assignment includes reading aloud. Either father or mother has to sign the notebook saying that Kazuki has done the assignment.

Because Kazuki's parents were high achievers, both teachers and yuppies in their early thirties, there was a question in my mind as to whether they supported the school's egalitarian emphasis and its lack of tracking, even for bright children such as their own son.

Studies were important for Kazuki, Mr. Nakayama said, "but even more important is to have him develop a sociable nature. I would like them to nurture a spirit of mutual help so that, for example, a quick child helps a slower child or a coordinated child helps a less coordinated child, or this boy or girl who can run fast can help the slower runner. Group activities will tell them all how to help each other."[16]

That was the heart of the Japanese approach: More than test scores or good grades, these parents wanted their son's school to inculcate the cooperative, social attitudes and values that would make him a good member of Japanese society.

American Individualism: Miss Moore's Stars

Half a world away from Nomi School, in the suburbs outside Kansas City, Missouri, Linden West Elementary School in north Kansas City applies a very different educational philosophy.

Linden West preaches and practices American individualism in class; teamwork is largely left to sports or occasional projects. More conscious emphasis is placed on academics in early grades than at Nomi School. The strength at Linden West, as at most American schools, is in what it offers its best students—teacher attention, special programs, and ability tracking. It is up to the individual to take advantage of the opportunities. The connection between home and school at Linden West is generally weaker than in Japan, a pattern that studies show is typical of America.[17]

In some ways, Linden West is very much like Nomi School. In six grades, it has 500 children—about the same number as Nomi. Both are neighborhood schools. In Toyota City, Kazuki Nakayama and his friends walk to school; in north Kansas City, most kids ride the bus or are dropped off by their parents, both of whom generally work. Linden West is a bit above average for Missouri on statewide tests, similar to Nomi School's ranking in Toyota City. Located in the suburbs outside Kansas City, Linden West serves a mixed blue- and white-collar area of single-family homes. North Kansas City is ethnically almost as homogeneous as Japan—only 8 percent minority population.

Linden West is a much more modern and better-equipped facility than Nomi School; a new addition opened in 1990. The school is a handsome, spacious one-story brick building with a large new cafeteria, windowed classrooms, and airy corridors. The atmosphere is bright and inviting. For a typical class, the principal sent me to Miss Moore's second grade. Celeste Moore is a quintessential American primary school teacher—pleasant, energetic, outgoing, motherly, plump, a gray-haired veteran of twenty-five years of teaching, all at Linden West. She received her master's degree in education from the University of Missouri at Columbia.

Miss Moore follows the American educational model: Develop the individual. Her classroom celebrates the individualism that is bedrock America. Outside her classroom door is a display of "Miss Moore's Stars," with each child's name on an individual star. Inside, the classroom walls are decorated with charts showing individual achievement and responsibility. One wall chart has the names of all her students, showing their height and measuring their physical growth in recent months. Such a chart would never appear in a Japanese classroom because teachers there emphasize common characteristics, not differences that might embarrass some students.

Again in American fashion, Miss Moore has a "Helper's Chart" with tasks such as cleaning the chalkboard, emptying the wastebaskets, running messages and errands, and taking attendance, all assigned to individual students, not groups. By the windows is another chart showing every student's outside reading progress, with stars by each student's name for each book read at home or during recess or lunchtime. Some students, I saw, had fifteen or twenty stars; some had none. For a certain quota, students got a voucher for a free pizza at Pizza Hut.

"It gives them a little reward, and some children need to be pushed to read," Miss Moore observed.

I asked Miss Moore her main goal in teaching eight-year-olds.

"I would like for each child to feel important," she replied. "I would like for each child to become independent so they don't have to have the adult around to teach them and tell them what to think all the time. I want them to learn how to think, how to reason for themselves . . . and I want that they don't get discouraged by failure, that they keep going, that they keep learning, keep working at things. I want them to feel good about themselves, to become independent little people and yet learn how to cooperate with someone else."

Here was the educational philosophy of the land of opportunity— where the door to success is open to all, the teacher provides the means, and it is up to the child to be able and self-reliant enough to capitalize on the opportunity.

The bottom line for primary education, Miss Moore asserted, is "self-fulfillment, self-actualization."

Almost as an afterthought, Miss Moore added, "I also want them to learn something. If I'm teaching them a lesson, I want them to know something about that when I'm done."[18]

Correct Answers and Tracking by Ability Group

Like many American teachers, Miss Moore not only wants results, she wants correct answers, and she gives warm recognition to the students who produce them. The largest display in her classroom is a huge cat, a larger-than-life cutout with a smile to match, wearing a large sign reading "Purr-Fect." Pinned to the cat are spelling papers without a single error. Elsewhere in the classroom, other model papers are on display. "Correct" or "excellent" are words that constantly punctuate Miss Moore's dialogue with her class.

In a grammar exercise, for example, she had her students read un-punctuated sentences from the blackboard and then insert the proper punctuation. Among the first to recite was Raymond Utter—RL to his family and friends—one of Miss Moore's brightest children. Like Kazuki Nakayama, RL is a winning eight-year-old with big brown eyes and a shy tilt to his head when he smiles. He is attentive in class and nicely self-confident.

> RL, reading from the blackboard: "dad said i am flying to new york."
> Miss Moore: "Correct. I need a correction. Can you give me one?"
> RL: "The first 'D' on Dad needs to be capitalized."
> Miss Moore: "Correct. Why?"
> RL: "Because it's the beginning of a sentence."
> Miss Moore: "Correct. Very good. Jessica . . ."

After grammar, Miss Moore moved on briskly to arithmetic. She gathered her twenty-one students on the floor around her for an exercise in "calendar math"—a drill in math problems based on the day's date. It was March 3, and therefore, Miss Moore told the children, "We're going to be counting by . . ."

> Children: "Threes!"
> Miss Moore: "Threes, very good."

She called for examples of addition or subtraction that resulted in an answer of three. It was a waltz for the brighter students. One girl came up with the equation "52 times 2 equals 104 minus 101."

Miss Moore: "Equals three. Very good, Elizabeth."

After the better students rattled off eight or nine examples, the weaker students wanted their turn, and they slowly chanted their response.

Several voices: "One plus one plus one equals three."
Miss Moore: "Good . . . excellent. Boys and girls, you did a beautiful job."

During the drill, Miss Moore wrote each correct answer on the board, except the last one; beside each correct answer, she put the name of the individual student who had given that answer. Positive reinforcement.

For close to two hours, Miss Moore led her students through reading, writing, and arithmetic without a break or a recess. That was a marked contrast to the Japanese system of alternating periods of concentration with periods of letting off steam, and the attention of some of Miss Moore's students flagged.

Another contrast with Ikeda-sensei at Nomi School: Miss Moore was always at the center, always in command. She invited students to raise their hands and offer comments, but she did not stand aside to let the children lead the class or engage in an extended discussion on their own. She dispensed knowledge in exercises; she tested her students with oral multiple-choice questions. In fact, most of her exercises lent themselves to answers that were clearly correct or incorrect, rather than to some slower, more participatory process of discovery.

Miss Moore treated mistakes differently from her Japanese counterpart. She did not pause to use incorrect answers as opportunities for exploration. When slower students fumbled her questions, she was careful not to shame them, but she did not tarry to draw them out further or coach them into comparing various answers, as Ikeda-sensei had done. Miss Moore whisked along, looking for students who were on the mark.

Her class worked as one unit or else on individual assignments; she did not organize them into small learning groups or teams for academic games. When I asked about that approach, Miss Moore said that she used groups on occasion, but generally that was too time consuming and too much extra work for her.

However, there were special classes, she said, to accommodate the "wide range of natural abilities" among her students as well as ability groups. One child went one day a week to a program for gifted children; another, to a learning disability class; seven or eight, to remedial reading. In second-grade math, Linden West had four ability groups—fast, higher-average, average, and lower-average. RL Utter, the bright young grammar student, went across the hall to Mrs. Amy Streeter's room to join the "higher-average" math group, which was studying geometric shapes. According to Mrs. Streeter, a younger teacher, Linden West used ability groups because students "perform better when they are with people that go about the same pace and the same speed."[19]

In tracking second-graders, Linden West is typical of American public schools, which track earlier and more extensively than do other advanced nations, according to comparative studies.[20] At the high school level, Germans put teenagers into very different educational tracks, and the Japanese rank their high schools in academic order; but both countries frown on tracking in elementary school, especially as early as the second grade. They object that early tracking typecasts children into winners and losers and hurts the motivation and performance of students in slower groups.

Miss Moore herself had qualms about tracking. "In third grade, which I used to teach, our philosophy was that the smarter children could pull the lower ones along and that the lower ones were exposed to more," she said. "The second-grade teachers said, No, the lower one is not learning it. So this group of teachers sold the principal on ability groups."

One bottom line, certainly, was whether all the students, regardless of group, had to meet state or local achievement standards.

"In a way yes and yet in a way no," Miss Moore told me carefully. "In other words, a child can leave second grade and they still can't read sometimes, and yet we pass them on. At this elementary level, the parent has the final say about retention. It's not where the district says if they can't reach a certain level, or they can't add or they can't subtract, that they cannot go on. We can present this to the parents, and if the parent says 'No,' the child still moves on."

As testing by Stevenson and Stigler showed, the American approach was not paying off broadly. Compared to their peers in Japan, China, and Taiwan, "the American children's deficiencies in mathematics were pervasive" in the elementary years, the two scholars found. "The Asian students' superiority was not restricted to a narrow range of well-rehearsed, automatic computational skills, but was manifest across all tasks."[21]

Echoing those findings, specialists such as Tom Rohlen contend that one critical advantage for Japanese students is the length of the school year and the school week: Japanese schools put in 240 days per year compared to 180 days for American schools and 38 hours per week in Japan compared to 25 hours in America.[22] Another advantage cited by experts are the common curriculums and national standards that ensure that all Japanese schools toe the same line. A third point is the importance of maintaining high expectations for all students, rather than using ability groups, which may help the elite minority but undermine the motivation of average students.

Finally, the comparative study of America, China, and Japan underscored the crucial importance of two intangibles—making school a welcome place and not one where bored students hanker to escape; and how deeply parents get involved in their children's education.[23]

America at Home and at School: No Time for PTA

RL Utter's parents share the American dream of college for their son. RL's dad, Ray Utter, has been an autoworker for close to twenty years at the General Motors plant in Fairfax, Kansas, where global competition has sometimes forced him into temporary layoffs. Like many Americans, Ray Utter worried that the next generation, RL's generation, would not live as well as his own. He wanted RL to be well enough educated to "get him a real good job where he doesn't have to worry from paycheck to paycheck about making ends meet."[24]

Ray Utter thought Linden West was doing a good job, but his wife, Christie, who works at Ragan's Floral Shop, did not think that Linden West was doing enough with computers, which she saw as the wave of the future. "They really need more computers," she said. "That's probably where a lot of our schools are lagging behind."[25]

In fact, RL had a computer at home, and he was a master at Nintendo games, but at school he had no computer class. Some American schools, from inner-city Washington, D.C., to Seattle, Washington, are starting to use computers in the early grades, but computers are far from universal. At Linden West Elementary School, one lone computer sat in a corner of Miss Moore's classroom, but I never saw anyone use it—a contrast to the daily computer class for second-graders at Nomi School. The priorities were different: Nomi School had a far less fancy building than Linden West, but it did have a computer lab.

Homework was another area where Linden West was not keeping pace. Kazuki Nakayama got some homework every night; RL Utter normally had homework one night a week. That was typical: American elementary schools give less homework than the foreign schools investigated in *The Learning Gap* study.

One big problem, Miss Moore said, is parental priorities. She found it a chore to schedule homework so as not to interfere with all the after-school activities American parents set up for their children, which is far less of a problem in Japan or Germany.

"These children are involved in other activities—they go to skating, they go to baseball, they do different activities," Miss Moore explained. "And so we try to arrange homework where it's not too inconvenient and it doesn't take too long."

RL was conscientious. He liked doing math homework, usually without prompting, though his mother kept an eye out to make sure that it got done.

But contact between home and school was a sometime thing, especially by comparison with Japanese practice. Miss Moore held an annual conference with each set of parents, and the Parent-Teacher Association had monthly meetings. But participation was skimpy. "Last month I didn't have any parents from my class," Miss Moore reported.

Evidently the Utters were fairly typical. They went to the annual parent-teacher conference, but when I inquired how often they attended PTA, Christie Utter gave an embarrassed laugh. "Well, not very often," she said. "We don't normally make it, because we're not real together."

"PTAs are usually on Wednesday nights, and we bowl on Wednesday nights," Ray Utter added. "And I haven't been quite ready to give up my bowling to go to that."

To bridge the gap, Miss Moore once tried writing weekly letters to parents and found that it worked well. "But it's also very time consuming on my part," she said, "and so after a couple of years I kind of phased it out."

In sum, the vital link between home and school was weaker at Linden West than it was in comparable situations in Japan or Germany. Some families, of course, know how to step in and encourage their children, but many others do not. The American approach leaves that up to the individual. The American system lacks the simple, regular, socially accepted mechanism of the Japanese "communications notebook" for easily drawing all families into giving children the support they need to do their best performance in school.

"Melting-Pot" Germany: An Approach More like Japan's Than America's

Largely because of America's European heritage, Americans usually expect German elementary education to be similar to ours, or at least more like ours than the Japanese. But in fact, the opposite is true: The approach in Germany is more like Japan's than it is like America's. The reasons for this similarity lie in Germany's economic culture, which, like Japan's, puts a premium on cooperation and harmony, and in Germany's need to incorporate an influx of millions of foreign workers and new refugees from eastern Europe into German society.

Like the Japanese, German educators devote great attention in the early years to socializing their students. In terms of the development of the individual and the group, Germany stands between America and Japan. Nonetheless, in their classroom methods, German teachers are considerably more group oriented than Miss Moore at Linden West. Unlike the Americans but like the Japanese, the Germans decry tracking by ability in early grades; they mix fast and slow students in study groups. They believe in moving students along together at the same level, applying centrally set standards to all.

There are other similarities between Germany and Japan. The Germans have a longer school year than Americans (230 days compared to 180), and they are more demanding than Americans about expecting more homework at early ages. But, like Ikeda-sensei at Nomi School, German teachers work at making the early school years engaging, frequently varying the pace between concentrated study and allowing children to let off steam. Finally, in Germany as in Japan, teachers have a higher social status than they do in America, and the connections between school and home are close.

At first glance, however, the similarities with America catch the eye. Goldberg Elementary School in Sindelfingen, an industrial suburb of Stuttgart, looks like an architectural cousin of Linden West—a modern, flat-roofed, single-story brick building with spacious modern hallways that are decorated with student artwork. The children arrive in corduroys, jeans, and psychedelic-colored jackets that emulate those of the American heartland.

In ethnic terms, students in Germany today are almost as diverse as urban melting-pot America. In and around big cities such as Munich, Hamburg, Frankfurt, Berlin, or Stuttgart, as much as 25 percent of the population is ethnic foreigners, either workers invited in by West German industry since the early 1960s or refugees who have fled the bloodshed and turmoil in central Europe in the past five years. Today, Germany's 80 million inhabitants include about 6.5 million *Ausländer,* or foreigners, as most Germans call them. German elementary schools have become a mirror image of central Europe and the eastern Mediterranean region—Poles, Turks, Croats, Serbs, Greeks, Italians, Lebanese, Romanians, and Bosnians in class along with native Germans.

At Goldberg Elementary School, the names that Frau Ilse Lindenberger, the teacher, calls out in her second-grade class—Sirhan, Sebastian, Klaus, Claudia, and Nabri—reflect a multicultural reality that she must manage. Her challenge may compare with that of teachers in American inner-city schools, but her approach more closely parallels that of the Japanese. She begins each day with the students in a circle, singing a morning song of greeting in four languages—German, English, Italian, and Turkish. That "unity circle" is necessary, Frau Lindenberger told me, to bring children of radically disparate backgrounds together psychologically.

"Let's form our morning circle," Frau Lindenberger instructs the children. "Let's all think about what each of us has to contribute to make this day successful."

The children recite together: "I will do unto others what I would have them do unto me." Then, after wishing one another a good day in song, the twenty-four children share their personal feelings and hopes for the day, one by one, around the circle.

"At first, we have to collect ourselves and calm down, so that we can learn," Frau Lindenberger explained, in an echo of Ikeda-sensei at Nomi School. "I start off the morning with a song that involves movement. Their bodies need to move so that their heads can work again."[26]

A veteran of two decades of teaching, Frau Lindenberger sees her class as a microcosm of German society and the world; among her students, she seeks to inculcate habits of inclusion and harmony, of restraint on unbridled individualism. She often spends more time on teaching values and behavior than on teaching skills and subjects. In her view, the values of community and collaboration are social imperatives that must be taught in school, a need underscored by periodic German eruptions of violence against foreign immigrants.

She has posted "class rules" on a cabinet. They stress tolerance, respect, and mutual help—but say not a word about academics or individual achievement:

1. We are polite to each other.
2. When someone is speaking, we listen to him.
3. We don't trip one another.
4. We don't argue and fight.
5. We help one another.
6. We respect each other.
7. We don't call each other names.

The students had composed these rules, she said, as the minimum for getting along peacefully. "Sometimes it doesn't work—we have many disagreements," Frau Lindenberg admitted. "Sometimes we decide to add another rule."

The high priority this German teacher attaches to socializing her students reflects not only the tensions in her classroom but Germany's geographical place at the center of Europe. Unlike America, which is bordered by oceans and just two land neighbors, Germany has borders with nine countries.

"Where would we be if every person were selfish?" Frau Lindenberger asked. "We don't live alone in the world. The world is heavily populated, and here is a small group that has to learn to live together."

Germany's Grade-Free Learning Space

Like most schools in America, German elementary schools are oriented toward achievement, but they pursue it in ways that parallel the Japanese. Teachers must keep pace with a centrally set curriculum. Yet fifteen years ago, German primary schools abolished academic marks for first- and second-graders, to give those children what Frau Lindenberger calls "a grade-free learning space."

Having no marks frees the teacher from the need to classify her students by ability, and it enables Frau Lindenberger to work at keeping all of her students on as equal a level as possible, in spite of the social discrepancies among them. Some of the poorest immigrant children, who not only look and dress differently from German children, are living in terrible conditions—eight people sharing two rooms, three families sharing one bathroom.

"When I explain to the German children how difficult it is for their non-German-speaking peers," Frau Lindenberger said, "then they are prepared to help integrate their classmates. But this is daily work."

Her typically German approach to this problem is to arrange her class to work in small groups. Like Ikeda-sensei, she pairs fast and slow students, a bright German child with a Turkish, Romanian, Croat, or Serbian child who is struggling to speak German. The seating arrangement is crucial: Her students sit not at individual desks but clustered at worktables in groups of four or five. She encourages students to work together on arithmetic problems, on writing assignments, on class chores.

During a spelling and writing lesson, for example, Frau Lindenberger lectures on some intricacies of German syntax, and she calls on her best students, such as Claudia Schuster, to provide model answers. Then she has the students in their table groups write short essays. As at Nomi School, students are put in charge of grading each other's papers. Claudia Schuster, the bright girl, is paired with a Turkish boy. "Trade with him," Frau Lindenberger tells Claudia, "and then talk about the work with each other."

"It's important to help the others," Claudia told me later, beaming with pride at her responsibility. "Sometimes I see mistakes, and then I tell them where the mistakes are. I feel like I'm a teacher."[27]

Not only does this partnering parallel the Japanese approach, but so does the German method of alternating the classroom rhythm between hard work and relaxation. German teachers set their pace to the attention span of the children. Instead of one morning recess, typical in America, there are three or four recesses in Germany. Not only do German teachers break up the academic routine with songs and classroom games, they frequently shift between running the class, as Miss Moore does in the American school, and letting the students take the lead while they take a backseat, as Ikeda-sensei does in Japan.

The German theory is similar to the Japanese: Less can be more. Making school more lively and more fun achieves better academic results. Nothing spurs interest and student effort more than team competition among tables.

At a school in nearby Bürbligen, for example, I watched another second grade exploding in excitement over a team competition in multiplication. The teacher, Frau Scholz, had arranged the game so that each team's results depended not on its brightest student, but on all of its team members getting the right answers and moving around the room in four jumps, like American baseball players. That interdependence gave the bright students powerful incentive to drill the slower students in their multiplication tables before the game.

"It's not so important who is the best student," insisted Frau Scholz. "Teamwork is very important."[28]

Home and School: Coraising Children

German schools thrive as well on another partnership—parent-teacher cooperation and close communications, similar to those in Toyota City. "I can't educate a child without the help of the parents," Frau Lindenberger insisted.

She pursues an active stream of contacts with her students' parents—in addition to two major parent-teacher evenings each year. With so many foreign students, whose families are unfamiliar with German ways, Frau Lindenberger is often on the phone to parents in the evenings or dropping in on them for spontaneous visits. For more regular contact, she said, "we have a communications book" in which parents and teacher can share problems and insights.

Homework is another source of daily contact between home and school. At the home of Claudia Schuster, the bright girl who enjoyed "teaching" her classmates, it is her father, Jörg Schuster, a team leader at the Mercedes-Benz factory in Sindelfingen, who monitors Claudia's homework. In Germany, school lasts only a half day in the early years; like most German parents, the Schusters expect Claudia to do her homework right after lunch—*before* play and certainly before television. To emphasize their own priority on study, the Schusters have done what many German parents do (but which is not so common now in America)—they have provided Claudia with her own desk. Since Jörg Schuster's wife works as a beautician, he has arranged his work shift at Mercedes so that he can be home by early afternoon to go over Claudia's homework with her.

Although his daughter is one of the brightest in the class, Schuster endorses the absence of ability-group tracking at school. He likes the idea of Claudia's being asked to help slower students and has no prob-

lem with the foreign children getting extra help from Frau Lindenberger. "If the bilingual [foreign] children aren't doing as well and the
teacher looks after them, Claudia won't be neglected," Schuster asserted. "Claudia is learning a lot."

Moreover, Schuster is strongly in favor of recent trends in favor of
having children work more in groups rather than individually. In
Schuster's eyes, this is the wave of the future; it fits the new team methods in the work world.

"Group work in companies is becoming more and more common,"
Schuster observed. "There's probably no job that doesn't involve
some kind of group work. So when they learn early in school how to
conduct themselves in a group, it will be to their advantage later on in
their working lives."[29]

In a way that is fairly typical among Germans, Schuster speaks with
great respect of Frau Lindenberger as a teacher, his comments reflect-
ing not only his confidence in her personally but the generally high
esteem in which teachers are held in Germany. As in Japan, public
school teachers in Germany have considerable social authority. Many
German parents accept teachers instructing their children in social
values, in ways that mirror the Japanese system but that would trouble
some American parents.

Frau Lindenberger, for example, was gravely concerned about what
she saw as the pernicious influence on her students of violent programs on television. She had her students critique various programs,
draw pictures of the dismembered bodies and bloody murders they
had watched, tell one another how TV shows had scared them. Sitting
with her in a circle, they confessed and discussed their TV viewing
habits and then devised a set of TV-watching rules: "Too much TV is
harmful. One show per day is enough. I only watch thirty to forty-five
minutes of TV a day. I like days without TV. Playing is better than
watching TV."

Jörg Schuster and other German parents with whom I talked did
not object to such efforts by teachers to deal with values and behavior
outside of school. Like the Japanese, Germans are more inclined than
Americans to accept the authority of the teacher as well as the idea
that schools should teach values as well as skills and knowledge.

Perhaps this is because, as Jörg Schuster put it, he thinks of his
daughter's upbringing and education as a collaborative enterprise of
the parents and the school. "The most important task of the school is

to help raise the child along with the parents," he said. "That is, to coraise the child, to prepare the child for future employment. The school and the parents raise the children—together."[30]

At the elementary school level, as these stories indicate, Germany and Japan have been more purposeful than America in inculcating the values, the habits of teamwork and cooperation, and the mind-set of high expectations for all that lay a foundation for most of their children to move easily toward the world of work and business. Not only do international tests show that in terms of basic academic skills, Japanese and German students have outperformed American students, but the educational commitment in those societies has generally been stronger than in America, if measured in such terms as a longer school year, more daily homework, or more parental involvement.

What is more, the educational mind-set in Germany and Japan has been more inclusive—both in the classroom and in the community. Schools have forged strong links with parents, and, as we shall see, in high school they broaden those links to include business. The Germans and Japanese are not without their problems. But in terms of the new competitive game, both countries have set out not only to provide strong academic skills to the large majority of their children but also to make the relationships and work patterns used in elementary education relevant to the changing needs of society and the economy.

The American system invests its future primarily in the genius, creativity, and skill of the individual, and that has paid large dividends. Both the strength and the weakness of the American system are that it relies so heavily on the initiative and responsibility of individuals to get the most out of their schooling. Tracking students by ability in the early years works extremely well for the brightest and most affluent, who can afford the special track of private schooling. The children in the top brackets get pushed to the hilt and pointed toward the world's best universities. But along the way, many more average kids get a message from tracking that they're not meant for school or that they do not have the right "natural abilities" to go far. So they stop trying.

Not only may that disheartening and sometimes personally defeating process ultimately deprive many children of a true opportunity to do their best, it carries a steep price for society. For the average students in any society form the core of that country's workforce. If large numbers of average students move through elementary school and ultimately into high school less motivated and less well prepared than their peers in Japan and Germany, the burden on America's high schools will be too heavy. And ultimately, this educational shortfall will deny America one of the primary sources of strength in the new competitive game—a workforce with a world-class education geared to a rapidly changing global economy.

5

High School—The Neglected Majority
Whose Mid-Kids Are on Track for the Global Economy?

> *If they're not on the college-bound track, they're on the never-never track. . . . They cannot present themselves to employers and say: "I have the skills and aptitudes that are necessary in order to be a competitor in a global economy." They don't leave high school with a certificate that has any currency.*[1]
>
> —BERT GROVER, FORMER WISCONSIN SCHOOL SUPERINTENDENT

> *The German secret weapon is the education of the high school graduate who doesn't go on to university. . . . After you get through a German apprenticeship training program, you're simply the best-educated person in the world at your level.*[2]
>
> —LESTER THUROW, MIT ECONOMIST

> *The future now belongs to societies that organize themselves for learning. . . . Our most formidable competitors know this.*[3]
>
> —RAY MARSHALL AND MARC TUCKER, *THINKING FOR A LIVING*

For the average young people at American high schools, the educational system is stuck in the past, in a time warp.

Back in 1980, the American educational system fit the needs of the then-modern economy. But today, that system is as outmoded for many students, and as behind the competitive curve in education, as the mass-production system at General Motors has been behind the curve in making automobiles.

The two went hand in hand—GM's production system and the old-fashioned "general education" program of most U.S. high schools.

They were products of the same mind-set. GM mass-produced cars; it wanted workers who took orders and did assembly-line jobs by rote. American high schools mass-produced semiskilled human labor. Both did well enough—until their world changed.

Today, the old American educational model no longer fits the new competitive game. Old-style "general education" does not deliver enough thinking employees for tomorrow's economy. There is a serious mismatch between what the educational system tries to produce and what the job world needs, and the heart of the problem is a mind-set that ignores realities.

The curriculum and the educational priorities at most American high schools are geared to the college-bound; the dream of college sets the main agenda for American high school education. Yet economists assert that 70 percent of the jobs in the American economy do not require a four-year college degree, and educators report that 70 to 75 percent of American teenagers will not actually finish four years of college. Despite these numbers, the non-college-bound student—the average American high school student—is low priority in most American high schools.[4]

"The neglected majority." This is the term that Bert Grover, Wisconsin's state school superintendent for twelve years, gave to average American high school kids.

By "the neglected majority," Grover does not mean the dropouts or the troubled youngsters of the inner cities, or the better students, who are headed for America's university system, the best in the world. America leads the world at both the top and the bottom of the educational ladder—graduate schools and dropouts.

What worries Bert Grover and a growing body of experts is the great American middle. The young people in the middle, America's mid-kids, will be the backbone of our future workforce. They will provide the human resources for every business from high-tech electronics to manufacturing to banking to a multitude of service industries. Or else they will be a drag on the economy, doomed to lower living standards because they are no more qualified—or even less qualified—for modern business and industry than mid-kids in Malaysia or Mexico.[5]

What Bert Grover says is echoed by educators, state governors, and the heads of major corporations: Preparing mid-kids for high performance in the new work world is the key to whether America's standard of living will rise in the twenty-first century or continue to stagnate for the majority.

To see how well America is doing for its mid-kids in comparison to its global rivals, I visited three high schools in America, Germany, and Japan—and I focused on three average eighteen-year-olds at Blue Springs High outside Kansas City, Missouri; Yutakano High in Toyota City; and the Career School and the Mercedes Apprenticeship Center in Sindelfingen, Germany.

America: "Programmatic Anarchy" for the Average Teenager

Jason Fuller is a typical mid-kid from the heart of America: clean cut and crew cut, he likes all the things American teenagers are supposed to like—girls, cars, fast food, parties, and cash in his wallet. When I met Jason Fuller during the spring of 1993, he was in the final term of his senior year at Blue Springs High School in a suburb of Kansas City, Missouri. Jason has a soft-spoken, mid-South drawl, but he was husky enough to play tackle on the football team and to throw discus in track. He was friendly and talkative and seemed capable, but school bored him.

Rich Shatswell, Jason's stepfather since he was two years old, had long worked as an assembler at the General Motors plant in Fairfax, Kansas; his mother, Rosa, was an audit manager for Texaco. The family lived in a nice two-story home in a new housing development, and they kept the lawn neatly manicured.

In 1980, when Kansas City was a thriving factory town, high school seniors such as Jason Fuller could follow their fathers into factory jobs at the GM plants in Fairfax or in Leeds, Missouri, at the Ford plant at Claycomo, or at Armco or Allis Chalmers. Those jobs were their ticket to a good middle-class life. The standard high school course, "general ed," qualified them; any specific skills could be learned on the job.

Global competition changed all that. The GM plant at Leeds, Armco, and Allis Chalmers have all shut down; GM Fairfax has cut back from two shifts to one; other big plants and even most smaller companies want only people with special qualifications. Seniors such as Jason Fuller can no longer move right from high school into well-paying jobs, and many of them don't know how to cope.

Blue Springs High School, one of America's best, was rated triple A by the state of Missouri and cited by *The Wall Street Journal* in 1992 as one of the twenty top public high schools in America.[6] In 1992, its football team won the state championship, its band went to the Rose Bowl, and its choir sang at Carnegie Hall over Thanksgiving. Roughly 60 percent of Blue Springs' graduates went to four-year colleges and another 10 percent–plus to two-year community colleges.[7] That is above the national average: Only about half of America's eighteen-year-olds start college and half of those don't finish four years.

Yet Blue Springs High lacked an effective program for average non-college-bound students. It had bits and pieces, but, like America generally, Blue Springs had no integrated strategy for teenagers such as Jason Fuller.

In his senior year, Jason was taking four classes: a study hall, a tech course in electricity, a reading lab, and a class in marketing—the centerpiece of his program. The big attraction of the marketing class was that it enabled Jason and his classmates to get out of school at 11:11 A.M. to work at what were close to full-time jobs. In short, Blue Springs High left Jason with a watered-down hodgepodge of courses and no purposeful path into the future.

According to many American educators, Jason Fuller's predicament, with minor variations, is typical of hundreds of thousands of American high school students. "When it came to dealing with the needs of the non-college-bound—the neglected majority," declared former Wisconsin state school superintendent Bert Grover, "we had institutional and programmatic anarchy."[8]

One major reason is that the American way is to leave it to the individual student, supported by his family, to find a path into life. And yet, without giving young people clear guidance and providing an organized structure, the adult world is often just abdicating its guiding role in education to the uncertain whims of teenagers.

Jason Fuller's guidance counselor, Joellen Lightle, who had responsibility for half of the 650-member senior class, remembered that at the start of the senior year, Jason had been eager, as he put it, to "get out of high school and get on with my life." To Jason, she said, "That didn't mean more education. That meant a job, a real job."[9]

Boredom with seemingly irrelevant courses was one big impetus. Breaking away was another. But hidden beneath those symptoms, Mrs. Lightle suggested, was a deep fear about suddenly facing adult life and a feeling of inadequacy about making the big choices. "There's almost a panic to get a job and become independent," she said. "They want very much to feel that they're in control."

What Jason had really needed most was strong school support, direction, firm requirements, and an integrated, purposeful course structure. Blue Springs High provided that to students who were on its college prep track, but it was not geared to provide that same structure to the non-college-bound students. For them, it had a menu of electives.

One option was "Vo-Tech": three hours a day at a regional Vocational Technical Center, which offered courses in thirteen different crafts (auto mechanics, business computing, drafting, electronics, health care, and so on). But an older friend of Jason's had tried Vo-Tech, and it had not helped him get a good job; Mrs. Lightle did not recommend Vo-Tech on the ground that the center's equipment was badly out of date because industry was changing so rapidly.[10] The center's director, Walter Kennon, shared that worry.[11] Bill Oakes, an auto mechanics instructor, suggested another problem—a communication gulf between the guidance counselors and Vo-Tech. Oakes reported that the only time guidance counselors ever came to the Vo-Tech Center was to get their cars fixed cheaply by the students. "I've yet to see a guidance counselor come into my shop," Oakes bristled, "so how do they know what we have?"[12]

Jason found greater appeal in marketing class, which gave him a chance to make some money after school to keep his beat-up old 1970 Chevrolet Monte Carlo in gas and insurance. Like 700 other students at Blue Springs High (out of 2,000), Jason was driving his car to school every day. To support the car, Jason had been working for nearly two years after school, flipping hamburgers and waiting on customers at the Sonic Drive-in, and marketing class enabled him to keep that job.

It was the classic American teenage ritual: Get a car and become an adult. The problem was, Jason wasn't driving that car, the car was driving him. It was a distraction. While the car was literally taking him to school every day, it was actually taking him away from education. Jason was putting in thirty to thirty-five hours a week at the drive-in—much longer hours than he was putting in at school. The car and the job had diverted Jason from the real business of his high school years.

Jason represents a nationwide phenomenon. Two thirds of American high school sophomores, juniors, and seniors take jobs during the school year; seniors work the most—an average of twenty hours or more per week, according to Professor Laurence Steinberg of Temple University.[13] Steinberg and other scholars warn that while a modest amount of work may foster maturity and motivation, there is a serious danger when the job load gets too heavy. Ten hours is the break point;

less than ten hours of work, and grades typically rise, Steinberg's studies show; more than ten hours, and schoolwork and grades suffer; at twenty hours or more, the falloff is dramatic.[14]

Jason Fuller was far above the danger point, but no one at Blue Springs High stopped him or warned him off. In fact, marketing class made it easy for him to arrange those long hours.

Steinberg contends that excessive after-school work is a big reason why American high school students compare poorly against other countries on international tests. "Everybody worries why Japanese and German and Swedish students are doing better than we are," Steinberg says. "One reason is, they're not spending their afternoons wrapping tacos."[15]

For Jason Fuller, the Pieces Don't Fit Together

The test of Blue Springs High's approach was whether the marketing class and Jason Fuller's after-school job fit together as parts of a coordinated program that was helping Jason build long-term skills and develop a career path. This approach is taken at the high school level in several European countries, and very effectively in Germany, as we shall see. An effective work-study program requires a close working relationship between the school and the employer, to ensure that the academic program and the on-the-job training dovetail. Experts say that there also need to be firm performance standards for both the work-site training and the classroom work. At Blue Springs High, the connections were loose and standards were lax.

The central figure of the work-study program was Jerry Keister, the marketing teacher, a veteran of twenty years' experience in the classroom. Keister was supposed to be teaching the students about the world they were all eager to join as young adults—the world of work. Yet, from what I saw, his course stirred little interest. One morning, as Keister described how to extract tax information from a pay stub, three of the twenty-seven students were reading newspaper want ads, one was balancing his checkbook, a couple were dozing, and no more than eight or nine were bothering to take notes. Tests were mostly multiple choice, announced a week in advance, and Keister gave the class a day off beforehand so that students could bone up. The answers to essay questions were only about a paragraph long, he said.

The co-op jobs that Keister approved for his students, and in some cases helped them obtain, were limited in career potential. They were mostly low-skilled, entry-level jobs in restaurants, drive-ins, and retail shops. The tie-in between these jobs and his marketing course was tenuous; in Jason Fuller's case, there was no effort to coordinate his work with his electricity course. In fact, Keister told me that he accepted almost any job students could find. Jason said that there was little connection or discussion between Keister and his managers at the Sonic Drive-in, and he thought that was typical.

Even continuity of work did not seem to matter. Jason got into an argument with an assistant manager at the Sonic Drive-in; he quit and took a job filing and clerking for his aunt, who ran a tax counseling service from her home. Jason needed the new job to qualify for his midday release from school; Keister gave his permission.

In spite of Jason's job jumping, Keister asserted that Jason was laying the basis for a career after graduation.

"In what career?" I asked.

"Well, right now, we talked about the police." Keister replied. "He's interested in law enforcement."

Not having heard that before, I blurted out my skepticism: "He's been doing short-order cooking. He's now working for a tax accountant. How does that build a police career?"

"I get back to the basic skills," Keister replied. "We have so many students here that you can't have thirty-five different programs for every student. But, you know, you've got to learn how to work first of all. He knows he has to go to work on time, he knows he has to work so many hours, he knows he has to be loyal to that employer. And when he becomes a police officer, hopefully he'll say, 'Well, I remember that from class.' "[16]

Mrs. Lightle, the guidance counselor, was dubious about the career value of entry-level fast-food jobs for seniors. Instead of giving students serious training, she said, the businesses were using them to meet immediate needs. At best, she said, Jason Fuller and other Blue Springs seniors were getting some "job awareness," but no skills training.[17]

As Jason Fuller neared graduation, he himself suddenly had qualms about having dabbled aimlessly at minimum-wage jobs. I asked him whether anyone—Keister, Mrs. Lightle, or other teachers—had tried to help him develop a career or skills that would be useful after graduation.

"No, nobody really pushed me towards one," Jason answered. "It was pretty much my decision of what I wanted to do."

"And how do you feel about the decisions you made?" I asked.

"I feel like maybe somebody should have pushed me a little bit harder," he said. "Maybe I should've had somebody with a little bit more authority, such as my mom or dad or guidance counselor or teacher, help me out."[18]

Feeling at a dead end, Jason had gone to see an Army recruiter, hoping the Army would pick a career for him. His idea was to join the Army Reserves, but the reserves would give him only a few weeks on active duty after boot camp for job training—hardly enough to develop career skills. In the end Jason decided to join the Marines, and he landed in the infantry, much to his parents' dismay.

I went to see Ted Lewman, the principal, a good-looking man in his forties who is articulate about the importance of high standards, a good work ethic, and instilling the proper values. He was understandably proud of Blue Springs' twenty-eight honor students with straight-A, 4.0 grade point averages. Lewman had less to say about the school's programs for non-college-bound seniors, and I asked him specifically whether he felt the combination of marketing class and working after school at a drive-in constituted a well-organized program for students such as Jason Fuller.

"Well, I wouldn't think that the high school's responsible for the fact that he's a short-order cook," Lewman replied.

"Do you think that kid is going to compete with a Japanese and a German eighteen-year-old?" I asked.

Lewman flushed. After a pause he said ruefully, "That may be the toughest question you've asked. Because the school then becomes totally responsible for providing all the opportunities and the skills necessary for a young person to be competitive in the world market, and I'm not sure we're equipped for that to happen."[19]

In terms of the new competitive game, that response not only casts tens of thousands of Jason Fullers adrift, unprepared for the world beyond high school, but leaves them at a disadvantage to their peers in other countries. Jason Fuller was the victim of an old educational mind-set.

The fault lies not with Blue Springs High alone or with one misguided program. It lies with a general failure of American society and its educational institutions to develop programs and commit adequate resources to prepare American mid-kids for world-class jobs in a new competitive era. That failure deeply troubles such educators as Wisconsin's Bert Grover.

"If they're not on the college-bound track, they're on the never-never track," Grover declared passionately. "They're in an educational wasteland. They cannot present themselves to employers and say: 'I have the skills and aptitudes that are necessary in order to be a competitor in a global economy.' They don't leave high school with a certificate that has any currency."[20]

Germany: "Dual Education"—The Smooth Transition from School to Work

The Germans take a radically different approach to preparing their average teenagers for the global economy. They see each young person's skills as a social asset to be developed for the common good, as well as for individual fulfillment. In the German view, each teenager's growth is too important to society to be left just to the individual. The Germans believe the passage from school to work—one of life's most difficult transitions—has social ramifications; society, therefore, has a stake in seeing that this transition goes smoothly.

In Germany, many groups have come together to devise a workable national strategy. Whereas Americans compartmentalize the process—schools prepare students, businesses hire and train workers, and everyone trusts the market to sort things out—by contrast, the Germans have forged a system of partnerships and connections to ensure that both the individual's needs and the needs of business and industry are met. German schools, families, businesses, trade associations, chambers of commerce, labor unions, state governments, and the federal government all get into the act—all sharing the German conviction that it is essential to invest in people.

For centuries, one hallmark of the German economic system has been the apprenticeship tradition. It dates back to the medieval guilds and the practice of master craftsmen, or *Meister,* taking on young apprentices and fashioning them into qualified journeymen. Because the Germans put great stock in achieving high standards of craftsmanship, they set high qualifications for their workforce.

Alan Watson, a British author, observed in his book *The Germans* that "the very idea of entering a job untrained or employing somebody not specifically prepared for the work . . . is so alien in Germany" that everyone sees the necessity of a well-organized, well-run training and educational system for German youths.[21]

The sheer sweep and scale of the German program are impressive. Some 500,000 companies, professions, and public employers work closely with the public education system to operate a system of "dual education"—a combination of classroom courses and on-the-job apprenticeships in 400 different vocations. These range from modern electronics to journalism, from baking and bricklaying to marketing and office management, from hairdressing and health care to insurance and law.[22] Nearly two thirds of all Germans between the ages of sixteen and nineteen—or 750,000 a year—enter apprenticeship programs after tenth grade.[23] Typically, apprenticeships last three years; afterward, many apprentice graduates decide to go on to technical colleges or institutes for engineering degrees or advanced technical training. Apprenticeships are so highly regarded that even university-bound Germans often spend a couple of years in an apprenticeship program, to gain skills, self-confidence, and maturity. Many German firms now prefer up-and-coming managers to have both kinds of education—in an apprenticeship program and at a university.

What is striking about the German mind-set is its realism about the life prospects for youth. Germany, America, and Japan each winds up with roughly the same proportion of its young people graduating from college or university—around 30 percent. What distinguishes the Germans is their recognition in advance that most teenagers will *not* finish university. As a result, they take steps to provide good training and education for these young people, rather than letting them drift after an aimless high school education or after dropping out of college.

Instead, at age sixteen, all German high school students are given a tough set of exams, and two thirds are then channeled into the dual-education system of training for crafts, industry, and professions. That system, while not without its problems in matching every youngster to a desired career and to the changing needs of industry, has helped Germany avoid America's "neglected majority" of mid-kids. It has provided German teenagers with solid job skills and clear pathways into the mainstream economy and has historically given West Germany the lowest youth unemployment rate in Europe.[24]

The core of the German dual-education system is the heavy engagement of business and its close partnership with education. In the 1990s, West Germany's industries and crafts have been spending roughly $15 billion a year on apprenticeship training, and the program has been extended into the eastern states.[25] America, with nearly four times West Germany's population, would have to spend $60 billion a year to match the German effort.

The depth of German industry's engagement in this enterprise flows from Germany's high-performance strategy. One key to Germany's strong long-term export performance is its class of skilled workers; many German plant managers say that well-trained workers can do many things that Americans turn over to engineers. High wages and a high standard of living are taken as a given in Germany, even with the wage reductions of the past two recession years. To pay such high wages, German CEOs build their ability to compete globally on high quality—and that quality rides on a high-performance workforce and a superior educational and training system.

Training youth is accepted as a price of doing business in Germany, even in hard times, such as the past two years. As a practical matter, German businesses are required by their chambers of commerce and trade associations to provide training, or to pay the costs instead.[26] Most of German industry jealously watches over the dual-education system: Industry develops training courses, sets standards, does most of the training, runs the examinations, and certifies that apprentices meet Germany's tough quality standards.

Apprenticeship training, which takes place in many tiny shops and stores, is often big business. Siemens, the electronics giant, has a $15 million, six-story industrial building for training 600 apprentices in machining and electronics—from freshmen apprentices in dark blue coveralls laboring at industrial workbenches to senior class apprentices using state-of-the-art computer-programmed machine tools.[27] Near Stuttgart, Mercedes has two even more spacious and modern apprenticeship centers to train 4,000 apprentices.

To German companies, sound apprenticeship training is not only necessary for recruiting top-quality workers but a social responsibility, as I heard from Hartmut Welzel, former personnel chief at Ford Motor Company in Cologne. And it is smart marketing. German consumers regard good training as an indicator of high-quality products, Welzel told me. They will trust in a company's products only if the company has a reputation as a good trainer.[28]

In short, guaranteeing high-quality training to German youth has been woven into the fabric of German economic life.

For Roland Wacker, the Pieces Fit Together

Roland Wacker, a German eighteen-year-old, was in many ways a dead ringer for Jason Fuller, except that he was thinner and his hair was swept up into a high wave. Like Jason, Roland had been bored with schoolwork, he had no interest in college, and he was itching to get his hands on something practical. Like Jason's stepfather, Roland's father had worked in an auto factory and was now working for a parts supplier for Mercedes; his mother worked, too. The Wacker family lived in a modest two-story brick German row house in a blue-collar suburb of Stuttgart. Also like Jason, Roland had wheels; he proudly drove me in his little green 1979 Volkswagen Polo to the neighborhood café and bar where he met his friends.

But the parallels to Jason Fuller end there. Roland Wacker was on track to a mainstream job; he was in a high-quality apprenticeship program that paid him 900 marks, or $600, a month, during his training. Roland's academic program was demanding, and it dovetailed with the high-tech job training he was getting at Mercedes-Benz as an apprentice. The apprenticeship had actually stimulated him to work harder and take more interest in academics than he had when he was in school full time—because he had finally grasped how theoretical work improved his ability to learn his job.[29] For Roland, the pieces fit together.

At the Mercedes technical training center in Sindelfingen, Roland was taking an apprenticeship in industrial electronics. The training course was a fast track into a high-tech adult job. The Mercedes training center was absolutely up to date on technology, in stark contrast to the Vo-Tech Center near Blue Springs High.

Mercedes and its instructors were sparing no cost or effort to maximize what they were teaching Roland and his generation of apprentices. One afternoon, for example, Roland and two other senior-year apprentices were given a test by the *Meister,* the master craftsman who was their instructor: Find and fix the error the instructor had programmed into the electronic circuitry of the $1 million robot they had been using. The problem was like the real repair problems they ran into on the days when they were assigned to work in the Mercedes plant. To Americans, spending so much money on equipment to train high school–age apprentices might seem foolish; to the Mercedes instructor, it was only good sense. "We're training tomorrow's workers," he said.

A simple idea, and it testified to the high priority Mercedes placed on state-of-the-art training for its apprentices. They were not second-class citizens who were given worn-out equipment; they were important to Mercedes' future, to Germany's future.

The same purposefulness drove Roland's academic courses. Like all German apprentices, Roland divided his time between job training at Mercedes and classes at an academic center, called a *Berufsschule*—in his case, 3½ days a week in training, 1½ days in class. Unlike Jason Fuller, Roland was not getting watered-down academics. His physics course in electricity was a quantum leap above Jason's tech course in electricity. An instructor, Reinhold Wendel, commented that it was an old-fashioned idea that industrial work is mainly manual labor, because in the new economy technology plays a greater role. "These apprentices have to learn more theory because they're doing less with their hands," Wendel said. "But they're comfortable with that—they like it."

The Mercedes program was light-years ahead of the old American "general ed" course. Ironically, there was more "mind training" in this industrial program than in the classrooms of many full-time American academic high school programs.

"We teach them how to set goals," Wendel said. "That includes how to work in a team, how to get along with others. Second, we teach them certain methodological approaches to learning so that *they learn how to learn* about new subjects. We make sure that they don't simply become skilled workers who have to be told how to do everything. We want a worker who thinks on the job and has suggestions on how to improve things."[30]

The German program also had a heavy dose of pure academics—calculus, German language, economics, and a social studies course that gave Roland Wacker not only grounding in the German political system but a detailed discussion of the German tax system and how it finances the social security net. Somehow, the Germans were cramming a five-course load into a part-time classroom education, and Roland Wacker was taking it seriously, especially the final exams that loomed at the end of his apprenticeship.

"In technology, circuitry, in mathematics, economics, German, and social studies—the tests are pretty hard because it's a total of three and a half years of learning," Roland said. "You're tested on what you've learned during the whole apprenticeship program."[31]

Still, I wondered, was Roland Wacker, or any German youngster, ready at sixteen to pick a career path for life?

His parents described how at fourteen and fifteen, Roland and his classmates had begun talking with their families and teachers about careers. They had been taken by their schools to the career information and counseling centers that exist in every town and city. The one in nearby Stuttgart was a huge building, a fund of information—books, videos, pamphlets, and rotating job fairs and demonstrations. Young people were told how to get proper training, where to find jobs, what each job was like. They were stimulated to think about the possibilities and then helped to make a choice. Various trades offered try-out internships and job shadowing—or watching adult workers do their jobs. Roland tried an internship in sales, but he didn't like it—not enough action. Then he gravitated toward industrial electronics. His mother had seen the clues all along: the strobe light system and electrical gadgetry he had made as a boy; the computer and stereo system he had hooked up in his bedroom.

Roland's father, an apprentice in auto mechanics in his own youth, backed Roland's choice. He had pushed all three of his sons into apprenticeships. "It's definitely an advantage," he said, "a requirement for the future."[32]

Roland himself felt good about his choice. Instead of being bored in class, he was now stimulated as never before. "Back then I didn't do too much for school," he admitted. "But here, if you don't pay attention and get good grades, then you could get passed over and then you don't have a job. The pressure is there. . . . I do more for school now than I did before. The school and work complement each other. You need the knowledge you get from school in order to get ahead in the plant."[33]

Part of Roland's motivation in class was that he knew Mercedes would look over his whole transcript—academics as well as job training—before making a decision to hire him permanently after he finished his apprenticeship. This is an important feature of the German dual-education system—there is no job guarantee at the end, just as the company has no assurance that the apprentice will choose the company. Each has to impress the other during the apprenticeship. And the lack of a guarantee is a spur to do one's best.

One important question remained—did the Mercedes management

believe it was getting its money's worth from its investment in its apprentices?

Mercedes reckoned the full cost for each apprentice—his or her pay, training facilities, new equipment, teachers' salaries, everything—at about 100,000 deutsche marks (over $60,000). "If you accept that this is an investment into possibly a lifetime's work, then it's an excellent investment," asserted Helmut Werner, chairman of the Mercedes management board. "When they are through with that, you have a real first-class specialist."[34]

Hilmar Kopper: From Apprentice to Head of Deutsche Bank

The apprenticeship system in Germany permeates the economy—not just in blue-collar careers that Americans associate with vocational training but in such professional careers as banking, law, journalism, insurance, management. The formula is always the same—academic work integrated with practical on-the-job training; theory and practice together—dual education.

At a commercial vocational school, I met Nicole Rose, at eighteen finishing a banking apprenticeship and ambitious eventually to become a bank manager like her mother. Not only had Nicole taken courses in German and social studies as well as accounting, finance, economics, and banking, she had worked in the branch of a regional bank as a teller, doing computer work in the back office, and advising new customers. She had even been to Britain to learn about foreign banking.[35] The bank's chief training officer said that it was quite realistic for Nicole Rose, as an apprentice, to aspire to become a bank manager and to reach middle management—without a college education. Three of the bank's managing directors, he said, had risen from apprenticeships.[36]

In fact, I met quite a few German executives who had been apprentices; the highest ranking among them was Hilmar Kopper, the speaker or chairman of Deutsche Bank, one of the richest, most powerful banks in the world.

Kopper, who as a boy had made money on the black market after World War II selling scrap metal and used ammunition, had become an apprentice because his father could not afford to send Kopper to college. A family friend advised a banking apprenticeship on the grounds that knowing finance would always be useful. Kopper decided to give it a try, hoping later to make his way to university. But before that happened the bank offered him a job in New York, and his career at Deutsche Bank was under way.

Kopper had educated himself with reading and travel. At his home in the hilly suburbs outside Frankfurt, he had a personal collection of paintings and abstract sculpture by Scandinavian, Russian, and German artists.

I asked him whether, in the German system, having been just an apprentice without a university degree had been a handicap.

"Well, as a matter of fact, whenever I had time, I went to the university—for three years, I spent almost every evening there," he replied. "I never took an exam, but I think I've picked up quite a bit. . . . Still, I have no professional academic education."[37]

Kopper's career was testimony to the effectiveness of the German dual-education system and to the competitive advantage that Germans derive from their ability to fit the education and training of youth to the world beyond school.

"The German secret weapon is the education of the high school graduate who doesn't go on to university," asserts Lester Thurow, former dean of the Sloan School of Business Management at MIT. "At that level, after you get through a German apprenticeship training program, you're simply the best-educated person in the world at your level. They turn out an absolutely world-class worker, and it allows them to make very sophisticated products, use very sophisticated machine tools, and just operate technologies at levels that the rest of the world finds impossible to operate."[38]

Japan: "A Powerhouse of Education"

What characterizes the Japanese high school system is the intensity of the educational effort, the high demands set for all students—including those who are headed for the work world—and the unusual role of teachers in arranging job placements for their students.

Japan, like America, has nothing to compare with the German apprenticeship system at the high school level. In Japan as in America, companies prefer to do specific job training; high schools concentrate on completing a stiff core academic program. Since the early postwar period, the Japanese have had vocational high schools, but they are gradually being converted into regular high schools.

Like the Germans, however, the Japanese believe that putting young people onto a secure track into the mainstream economy is too important to society to be left to the individual. They have developed a strong support system for placing all high school students after graduation, including those not bound for college. In order to ensure a seamless transition from school to work, the Japanese system has forged closer ties between business and schools than exist in America. Recruiters from Japanese industry come right into the high schools during the last several months of the senior year, to get their pick of the graduating class for their blue-collar, clerical, or technical workforce. As a result, an extremely high percentage of non-college-bound Japanese high school seniors have lined up permanent jobs *before* they graduate.

The stakes at this stage of a Japanese teenager's life are extremely high. Japanese society is highly stratified, but it is also a meritocracy. Academic performance can lift a young person's fortunes or forever tarnish his or her destiny. How well a Japanese teenager does in high school sets the path for the rest of his or her life—whether that young person gets into university and how good a university, or what kind of company he or she will work for. One harsh reality of Japanese society is that not too many people get a real second chance if they do badly in high school. Most Japanese stick to their career paths—often with one employer for their entire lifetime—and therefore their initial point of entry into the adult world is crucial. It fixes their status and their standard of living.

Even getting into high school is serious business in Japan. High schools have their own entrance exams, and junior high school students compete citywide to get into the best high schools, public as well as private. In every city and province, high schools are academically ranked by the Ministry of Education, and the rankings are made public. The top schools attract the top students, offering them the best opportunities for getting into the top universities, which become pedigrees for the choice jobs in government, industry, and academic life; and so on down the line. Hence, all Japanese junior high school students slave to get as far up the ladder as they can. The competitive pressures are fierce. By junior high, even moderately affluent Japanese parents in Tokyo and other big cities send their children to *juku*s, or private cram schools, which hold evening and weekend classes, to prep for high school entrance exams. In big cities, half of the seventh-, eighth-, and ninth-graders take these cram courses, often at a cost of several thousand dollars a year.[39] In provincial centers, such as Toyota

City, *jukus* are far less prevalent and are attended by only about 10 percent of the students.[40]

Everywhere, the pressure is on to perform, even at an average school such as Yutakano High School, ranked fifth out of nine high schools in Toyota City. Like Blue Springs High School in America, Yutakano High takes great pride in getting more than half of its senior class of 460 into regional four-year universities. One quarter of the class went to two-year colleges, and more than a hundred students were headed for technical training courses or into the job market.[41] To motivate students, the teachers had stretched a large white banner from one end to the other of the corridor outside the senior classrooms; it bore the names of last year's graduating class and where each had gone to college or to work. The idea was to spur the current year's seniors to go all out.

High school in Japan is a far cry from elementary school. Gone are the freedom and the ebullient spontaneity of second-graders. The teenagers at Yutakano High show that same youthful energy as they chat and joke in the hallways or out on the baseball or soccer field, but, when the bell rings for class, they become subdued, focused, attentive.

"A powerhouse of education" is how Tom Rohlen described Japan's high schools. Rohlen, a Stanford University sociologist who for many years has benchmarked high schools in Japan and America, pointed out that *all* Japanese high school seniors are taking their second year of science, their sixth year of math, and their sixth year of literature since seventh grade. The math includes calculus, which is important in industry; almost every Japanese student takes calculus, compared to one third of the German students and only about 6 percent of American teenagers.[42] Because the Japanese school year is 240 days, compared to 180 days in America, Rohlen reckoned that Japanese teenagers finish high school with the equivalent of four more years of time in school than their American peers. Not surprisingly, their work is usually at the American college level.

"Whatever subject we're looking at, the amount that the students are doing here and the level they're going to reach is higher," Rohlen asserted. "It's almost not comparable. We're talking about kids in the middle of Japan getting a level of education that's maybe at the top five to ten percent of the American student population."[43]

Every high school in Japan has to meet the same rigorous standards, set by the Ministry of Education in Tokyo. So, even at

Yutakano, a week's spring vacation includes homework. One homeroom teacher, for example, urged students to plan their vacations "so that you can get your homework done easily. Finish early, and then think about the areas that you are not strong in."

The teachers at Yutakano High pack information into their students. One senior math class was deep into number sets and probability theory. In English, a woman teacher was drilling her students in grammar and punctuation and having them repeat passages of English conversation after her. In political economics, a tall, angular instructor was setting out the various forms of corporations and the provisions of "The Law Regarding the Prohibition of Monopolies and the Preservation of Fair Trade," writing furiously on the blackboard in impeccably formed Japanese *kanji,* or ideographs. The heavy emphasis on lecturing and note taking in Japanese high schools is patterned after the German and American universities of the nineteenth century, according to Tom Rohlen.

The Japanese also take the opposite view from Americans in their theory of personal development from childhood to maturity. Whereas Americans think that young children need to be taught self-discipline and teenagers should be given independence and autonomy as they approach adulthood, the Japanese in contrast believe in allowing freedom in the early years and then gradually reining children in, so that discipline is imposed in the high school years as adult responsibility looms on the horizon. "The funnel narrows and narrows," said Rohlen. "We give adolescents their freedom. In Japan, they say adulthood is serious business and now you're expected to really settle down, master an enormous amount of information, work hard."

A pragmatic economic mind-set is also at work. With methods that smack more of drill than of creative learning, Japanese high schools are training and hardening a work team for global competition.

"It seems very stifling to me," Rohlen commented. "It's far more information, by far, than American kids are used to having to field at this age. Whether they like it or not—and I would say that most [Japanese] students do not like this part of their life—they are being shaped as citizenry and as future workers in a way that makes them highly disciplined, well informed, and skilled in many of the kinds of things an economy can use."[44]

For Yasuteru Iyoda, the Teacher Makes the Pieces Mesh

At Yutakano High, Jason Fuller's counterpart was Yasuteru Iyoda, clean cut and crew cut, good looking, soft spoken, and rather serious. In his dark blue wool uniform, worn by Japanese high school students since the last century, Yasuteru looked like a Japanese naval cadet. His father, like Jason's stepfather, worked on the assembly line in the auto industry—for a supplier to Toyota. Like Jason, he was an average student. But there the parallels between the young American and the young Japanese ceased.

Even though Yasuteru Iyoda had no intention of attending a university, he had to take the full regular course load and the same exams as his college-bound classmates. No study halls, remedial reading, or watered-down tech courses for Yasuteru. He had to grind his way through courses on probability theory, Japanese corporate law, and the history of Chinese dynasties. Japanese companies, like universities, pay attention to academic results.

Employers in Japan are looking for dedicated hard workers, and they want new recruits who have shown they can learn. What is more, almost all companies require students to take the employers' own rigorous qualification tests, and Yasuteru Iyoda had to bone up for those. So he felt much more pressure than Jason Fuller did to get the most out of his senior year and to do his best academically.

Yasuteru Iyoda had neither the distraction of a car nor the competing demands of an after-school job. Like other students, he could take part in the wide variety of clubs, sports, and extracurricular activities that were popular with students at Yutakano High. But typically, students taper off their extracurricular activities in their senior year, in order to concentrate on studies—and that is what Yasuteru Iyoda did. Too much was riding on his senior-year academic performance for him to take time away from his studies to play on a sports team or be active in a club.

Yasuteru Iyoda's lack of a car typified the lifestyle of Japanese high school students. In fact, the most visible symbol at Yutakano High of the different lifestyles of American and Japanese teenagers was the ubiquitous presence of bicycles in Toyota City, of all places. Whereas the parking lot at Blue Springs High was jammed with seven hundred student cars, the area around Yutakano High was crammed with bike racks, and the bicycles were not fancy ten-speeds but basic utilitarian three-speeds showing plenty of wear.

"Japanese kids just don't have cars," Tom Rohlen remarked. "Their parents are expecting them to spend their high school years really studying hard."

What is more, that careful process of socialization in primary school, which is powerfully reinforced by the social order and conservativism of Japanese society, paid off. Japanese high school teachers spend very little time coping with disciplinary problems or worrying about dropouts. Yutakano's principal, Minoru Ogiso, said the dropout rate was only 1.1 percent in all of Aichi Prefecture, including Toyota City. He mentioned only two persistent discipline problems—smoking and motorcycles. Motorbikes and motorcycles were legal, but the school had barred them from its grounds.

"We've found out that when you get caught up in riding motorcycles and motorbikes, you lose any desire to study hard," Ogiso explained. "So we as educators have agreed with parents that we should prevent and correct this problem."[45]

The most striking feature at Yutakano High was that the teachers, instead of worrying about discipline, took on the task of ensuring that their students made a smooth transition from high school to the next stage of their lives, whether at a university, at a technical institute, or in a job. In the case of Yasuteru Iyoda and about fifty other students headed into the work world, responsibility for brokering the job hunt fell to Hiro Imai, a mild-mannered teacher of Japanese literature in his early forties. In Japan, as in America, Imai-sensei said, part of his job was preaching realism to Japanese parents who counted mistakenly on Yutakano High to get their children into some university. At first, he said, students felt the burden of their parents' expectations; but over time they would change their goals and decide to go after a job at some good company right out of high school.

Imai-sensei coached the students on their personal options and how the job market worked. In a career room, he displayed photos and personal letters from some of last year's seniors, reporting on how they liked their jobs. He urged the students to study company recruiting pamphlets. In one guidance session with eighteen students, he handed out a glossy brochure circulated by Toyota Tekko, a supplier firm in the Toyota family of companies. The brochure not only showed the company's vacation spa, gymnasium, and worker dormitories, it spelled out what the firm wanted in new workers.

"Please look," Imai-sensei instructed. "It says, 'We look for curiosity.' The brochure discusses the value of questioning. The company says they want their workers to stand up and question things."

Imai-sensei did not mince words about the recent hard times. Normally, with a nationwide labor shortage, Japanese companies aggressively hunt for new workers. By early 1993, in the midst of recession, Imai-sensei warned Yutakano's seniors that things would be tough; Nippondenso, the auto electronics giant, was cutting its new hires in half. "This recession will continue for one or two more years," Imai-sensei warned, "and what companies tighten up on most in order to survive is hiring."[46]

Later, he interviewed the students one by one. It was April, the start of the new school year in Japan, and student career plans were vague. Some girls talked of clerical jobs at big corporations. One boy wanted to go into banking. Like Jason Fuller, Yasuteru Iyoda thought he wanted to be a policeman. Imai-sensei checked with the students periodically, and he talked with their homeroom teachers about their interests. He did not want to put his credibility or the school's reputation on the line until he was sure that a student's intentions were firm. But once assured, he made contacts with the appropriate companies.

"I go to the personnel department directly to find out if there's a position open," Imai-sensei told me. "I'm the one who confirms this with the company."[47]

In Japan, with its tradition of slow consultation and consensus, such negotiations last several months. The companies want to follow the students' performance in school and to test them. Students may change their minds. Imai-sensei shepherds both sides. His strong suit is continuity: he nurtures long-term relationships with scores of companies, mostly in the region around Toyota City. He keeps track of the work records of previous Yutakano graduates at various companies and makes a point of mentioning their records to corporate recruiters as he pushes the career ambitions of the new seniors.

By July, the fourth month of the senior year, the academic pressures were intense and the tempo of the job hunt was picking up. Yasuteru Iyoda had changed his mind. He no longer wanted to be a policeman; he wanted to try for a job at the auto upholstery plant where his father worked. It was still not midyear, and the hallway outside Imai-sensei's career office became a waiting room for company recruiters. Imai-sensei, the literature teacher, was bargaining with industry: Give me more jobs for my students, and I'll send you my best prospects.

But jobs were tight. When the recruiter from Nippondenso said how few openings he had, Imai-sensei groaned. But the man from Sango, which makes mufflers and other components for Toyota, needed quite a few workers. Throughout the fall and into early 1994, Imai-sensei kept trying to match students to jobs. Students kept changing their minds, including Yasuteru Iyoda, who eventually decided to go for a job in the printing trade at a company called Kojima Press—and he got it. Like other students, Yasuteru felt an obligation to do well, not only for the honor of his family but for the school and next year's seniors.

"If graduates at some company work very hard and do really well there," he said, "then the company will think highly of the school and try to recruit more from the school. So for the sake of younger students, we must do our best."[48]

His point was telling. The school's track record was Imai-sensei's trump card in placing his seniors in good jobs. An implicit bargain was struck: The school pushed its students hard academically and prepared them well; employers took the school's guarantee; and the graduates protected the school's reputation.

A month before graduation in March 1994, Imai-sensei had met his goal. For the fifth year in a row, his batting average, as he put it, was "one hundred percent."[49] Even in recession times, he had lined up a job for every single student who wanted to go into the work world after graduation. That record was actually a bit better than that of the teachers who were coaching the university-bound students, some of whom had flunked the entrance exams and were planning to try again in a few months.

In Toyota City, some high schools did better and some did worse. But the performance at Yutakano High, an average high school, was no fluke. Nationwide, Tom Rohlen reported, the normal rate for placing high school graduates in universities, junior colleges, training programs, or jobs *prior to graduation* is 90 percent or better. A stunning benchmark for Americans.

The High Price of an Obsolete Mind-Set

By comparison with their peers in such countries as Germany and Japan, many average American young people have been held back not primarily by the poor performance of high schools but by an obsolete mind-set.

One of the harshest indictments of our system, as a system, came from a national bipartisan commission that included former labor secretaries from the Carter and Reagan administrations, corporate CEOs, and union leaders. The commission declared in 1990 that "America may have the worst school-to-work transition system of any advanced industrial country." Students not on the college track, it asserted, get "watered-down courses" and very little opportunity "for acquiring relevant, professional-level qualifications for occupations. The result is that typical high-school graduates mill about in the labor market, moving from one dead-end job to another until the age of 23 or 24. Then, with little more in the way of skills than they had at 18, they move into the regular labor market, no match for the highly trained German, Danish, Swedish or Swiss youth of 19."[50]

One root cause of the problem is that through the 1970s and '80s and even into the '90s, much of American industry treated average workers as a disposable resource, while America's global rivals saw training their workforce as an essential competitive advantage—a source of high quality and productivity. There are notable exceptions in American industry, and their number is growing. But, in comparison with other countries, most American businesses have not regularly made large investments in time and money in upgrading the skills of their frontline workers. According to one study, American employers in the 1980s spent about $30 billion a year on the education and training of their employees. Two thirds of that money was spent on college-educated employees, and 90 percent of the funds were spent by fewer than 1 percent of America's firms.[51] The classic American high-volume, low-cost, mass-production economy did not demand much from the mass of high school–educated workers. And the general education curriculums at many American high schools left large numbers of non-college-bound graduates without the skills needed to be competitive and world class in today's global economy.

The human price of that strategy has been high. Its consequences surfaced forcefully in the 1980s. When American businesses found that Koreans, Mexicans, Chinese, or Puerto Ricans could do semiskilled as well as low-skilled work just as well as American workers but for less money, American plants closed and hundreds of thousands of American jobs went abroad, and the Jason Fullers of America could not find good, steady work when they got out of high school. American families stayed afloat financially by having a second wage earner, usually the wife, join the workforce. While the American economy continued to grow in the 1980s, the living standard of the working middle class stagnated or went down.[52] And while the number of jobs in America has continued to rise into the mid-1990s, the quality and pay of the jobs of those with only a high school education have dropped.[53]

In short, the earnings gap has been growing between college-educated Americans, who generally have the skills to compete globally, and high school–educated Americans, most of whom do not. By focusing its resources on the college-bound, America's public school system has unintentionally become undemocratic, elitist. Among others, Thomas Kean, Republican governor of New Jersey from 1982 to 1990 and now president of Drew University, warns that this trend is creating a dangerous divide in America—the divide between the college-educated minority and the 70 to 75 percent who do not graduate from a four-year college.

"You follow them [the 70 percent] through, and their earnings haven't even kept pace with inflation, so they're losing—they're losing every day—and they see the vision of the new house and the new car disappear," Kean asserted. "You take the kids who go to college, they're all exceeding the rate of inflation. So you've got seventy percent of the kids going this way [his hand points down] and thirty percent going the other way [his hand points up], and you're not going to have that exist very long before this democracy is going to be in trouble. The seventy percent isn't going to allow the thirty percent to do that for very long."

As Kean and others see it, the disparity in earning power—and, behind it, in skills and the quality of education—is an issue threatening not only to America's capacity to compete economically but to the stability and cohesion of American democracy. "We cannot have unequal opportunity in this country," Kean has argued. "We have to go back to what Jefferson and Lincoln and everybody talked about—equal opportunity. And kids aren't getting it."[54]

Quite obviously, a keen sense of the perilous consequences that Kean cites and a growing awareness of foreign educational models for average high school students have spurred a new burst of educational reform in America in recent years. At the national level, both the Bush and Clinton administrations have promoted a campaign to raise America's national educational standards through the Goals 2000 legislation passed by Congress in 1994. At the state and local levels, there are scores if not hundreds of effective experiments at educational reform—important pioneering efforts, though still a tiny fraction of America's 110,000 schools in the nation's 15,000 school districts. So far, there is no national strategy being implemented.

One important theme among educational reformers has been to make American high school education more relevant to the world outside school. Some reformers have sought to reach out to minority students, who will be an important component of the American workforce in the year 2000 but who are currently dropping out of inner-city high schools at an alarming rate. Other reform efforts have focused on delivering modern job training and a classroom education to match, patterned after the German dual-education system. It is to these reform efforts that we now turn.

6

Harlem—Teaching Habits of Mind
It's Not "Academic," It's "Real Life"

We're trying not to make distinctions here between academics and real life. I'm trying to develop the same habits of mind here that I want the kids to bring to . . . everything they do in life. . . . Being educated is making connections, being conscious of society, of people's motivations. It is habits of mind which distinguish educated and civilized behavior from uneducated and uncivilized behavior.[1]

—DEBORAH MEIER, FOUNDER, CENTRAL PARK EAST SECONDARY SCHOOL

It's a community. I know the names of all the students in the school. Everyone in the school knows my name. . . . Students here sometimes complain that we're always in their face, and we are. We know them very, very well.[2]

—PAUL SCHWARZ, CODIRECTOR, CENTRAL PARK EAST

SECONDARY SCHOOL

The real problem in the nineties with education is replication. In the eighties, we didn't know really what to do. We knew the schools weren't good enough, and we weren't quite sure how to fix them. Now we have examples all over the country of people fixing them. And the question is whether or not we can replicate what's being done in the good schools.[3]

—THOMAS KEAN, FORMER GOVERNOR OF NEW JERSEY

The scene is East Harlem, Madison Avenue at 106th Street, a district of battered public housing, sidewalk graffiti, iron-grill fences, and storefront padlocks. This is a part of New York City where the toll of youth violence, gangs, arrests, teen pregnancies, and AIDS is an oppressive reality and where dropping out is as common as graduating.

In one public high school, Deb Meier, the school director, is talking quietly with two fourteen-year-old boys, one black, one white, asking them about a schoolhouse scrap—simple, factual, who-said-what and who-hit-whom questions.

Meier has become a celebrated educator since she founded Central Park East Secondary School in 1985 and made it a model of educational reform. She has helped redefine the three R's for American high school education: (1) Rethink the basic focus of education; (2) Raise the expectations for all students, even in Harlem; and (3) Restructure the school in terms of size, standards, and priorities. Central to her mind-set are ideas such as creating a community of close relationships among teachers, students, and families, and empowering teachers to run the school.

The results have been stunning—stunning for any school, and especially stunning for an inner-city school: The graduation rate at Central Park East is higher than 90 percent, and 90 percent of the graduates go on to four-year colleges, many in the Ivy League. Deb Meier's approach is catching lost youngsters and pulling them into mainstream America. Instead of a drag on the country, these teenagers are becoming assets to a modern economy.

I went to Central Park East Secondary School in mid-1993 to find out how Deb Meier and her faculty were achieving such success.

Deb Meier might be an academic icon, but she does not stand on ceremony. She is a hands-on teacher. In a loose blue denim blouse and skirt, she has the wind-tossed curly gray hair and folksy look of anyone's grandmother. But she is a wry, gritty New Yorker. Instead of complaining about how hard it is to teach inner-city kids, she takes pride in New York City as the "toughest and best" educational challenge in America.

I found Deb Meier talking quietly with the two boys who had been in a fight. The three of them, their heads in a close huddle, looked like coconspirators. Occasionally, when versions differed, Meier would ask for an explanation or would comment, "Can you imagine why he was upset when you called him 'Pussy'?" or "I think we'd better say 'allegedly' since you didn't see him do the hammerlock. You only heard about it." From time to time, she would enter some facts into a desktop computer. So it went, a quiet inquiry, probing, answering, compiling details. Her office, shared with two other staff members, was an open common room, but she ignored the commotion. For close to thirty minutes, she pursued her inquiry. Eventually, she made a computer printout, and she told the boys to check it carefully and to come back later.

Her dialogue had gone on so long that I had to ask why she had devoted so much time to a not-very-violent fight.

"Habits of mind," she replied.

I looked at her, puzzled.

"We're trying not to make distinctions here between academics and real life," Deb Meier went on. "I'm trying to develop the same habits of mind here that I want the kids to bring to everything we teach and to everything they do in life. So the way we deal with a fight is to get kids to sit down and write a report. And in this kind of situation, the questions I'm asking these two boys are the same questions we ask in History: What happened? Why? How did the war start? What are the consequences? Did the two sides understand each other? How could it have been averted? We critique their reports. We tell the kids, 'I can't read your handwriting.' 'Your spelling isn't correct.' Or 'You have to be clear—who is this "he" you mention?' Or 'What's your evidence?' 'I can't get what you're saying. You don't make your case well.' "

"So a school fight gets turned into a lesson in history and English?" I asked.

"They learn habits of mind—logic, perspective, making connections, being concrete, using evidence, building a case," Meier replied. "We have to demystify education, show kids that school is not separate from real life. When someone says, 'Oh, that's academic,' that means it's unimportant, it's irrelevant, it's only for getting from one grade to the next or getting a diploma, but it's not related to real life. We want our kids to make the connection between what they're learning in school and real life. This situation is very real to them, so we use it for teaching."

Her "habits of mind" are an echo of the thoughtful, proactive problem-solving mind-set that the most modern-minded corporations, from Toyota to Mercedes-Benz to Motorola and Ford, are seeking in their workers.

Most people think of schools as teaching subjects, Meier observed, and then they complain that schools don't graduate students who are ready to be good citizens, good workers, or even good family members.

"What these boys learn in this situation," she said, "is as important as civics. We want them to take responsibility. So we have to get them to tell us what happened—in a thoughtful way—and then examine how it happened. They have to see the connections between an insult and a fight, between a nation's bellicose talk and war. Being educated is making connections, being conscious of society, of people's motivations. It is habits of mind which distinguish educated and civilized behavior from uneducated and uncivilized behavior. We take that approach in everything we do in this school."[4]

This mind-set of using daily situations to teach habits of mind is a way of life at Central Park East. Other teachers swore by Meier's method of dealing with fights.

"It's a wonderful learning opportunity," said Paul Schwarz, codirector of Central Park East, with Meier. "It's one of the richest times to teach students. First of all, you have their attention—which is a big part of teaching."[5]

Students also mentioned the impact on them. Shadia Alvarez, a senior who had immigrated from the Dominican Republic nine years before and who had switched into Central Park East from another local school three years before, had expected to be punished for brawling with another girl, but instead, she said, "We had to write an essay about why we had a fight and how we could have prevented it and what the fighting really meant to us and if the reason we said we were fighting was really the reason. So, I mean, I wrote a four-page paper on why I had a fight and, I mean, after I read it, I felt like such an idiot."[6]

In fact, fighting is not much of a problem at Central Park East. Fights don't happen often, and, when they do, they are usually mild by Harlem's standards. The school does not permit weapons (possession of weapons leads to suspension). It has no metal detectors, and it does not frisk students. Its strong code of behavior condemns fighting, or even hitting back, unless your life is in danger. The school has an active conflict resolution center where students do the mediating.

Indeed, this school's hallways are conspicuously free of tension. Students say they consider it one place where they do not have to be constantly on guard. As they put it, Central Park East is their "safe haven" in Harlem.

A Powerful Community of Relationships

Achieving that peaceful environment is a remarkable achievement. A world of violence sits literally on the school's doorstep, and the students come directly into the school from that world. What creates the calm atmosphere, according to Deb Meier, is "the culture" of the school—the close bonds among the students and teachers, their mutual respect, their shared interests and goals, and, above all, the strong human relationships. The peaceableness of Central Park East, Meier asserted, "shows the power of a powerful community of relationships which people build around things that matter to them. That can have enormous impact."[7]

Central Park East operates from the premise that it is impossible to transform the process of teaching and learning and to raise the performance of its students without transforming the nature of human relationships in the school. Its faculty live by the insight that every student needs the nourishment of a close relationship with a caring adult, in order to be motivated to achieve and sometimes just to stay in school instead of dropping out.

In East Harlem, generating that motivation does not come easily. Students can enter Central Park East Secondary School—CPESS, as the kids call it, pronouncing the acronym "spess"—from anywhere in the city, as long as they have completed the previous grades successfully. Most come from the neighborhoods of East Harlem. Many are street kids; violence and confrontation have been their daily bread, and models of positive achievement have been rare in their lives. The student body is 40 percent black, 40 percent Latino, and 20 percent Asian American and white. CPESS runs from the seventh through twelfth grades. It is a public school with no special requirements for admission except two—prospective students and their parents must apply in writing and explain why they have chosen CPESS, and at least one parent must promise to work closely with the school. Every student for whom there is space is accepted.

Erran Matthews is representative. Erran was a tall, trim, highly personable, eighteen-year-old African American with jive and bounce. He was athletic, poised, and outgoing—a born leader with a wide, winning smile and a dark blue baseball cap that he wore everywhere. Yet, for all his innate talents, Erran had never used to care for book learning. He had grown up with an aunt, learning the arts of survival in a tough city. By his own account, Erran had been "a street kid," who, at his low point, 3½ years earlier, had been very violent and aimless and had never even thought about ultimately getting a job, let alone finishing high school.

"A lot of my friends back then are either in jail or dead," he told me. "I've been to one friend's funeral, you know, one I grew up with from first grade, and he died over an argument with some kid on a motorcycle. And when I heard he got shot up, it like hit me that Shawn was gone for good. I used to be crazier than Shawn. I would have been gone long ago. Only I said I wasn't 'going out' like that."[8]

The culture of Central Park East had touched Erran Matthews, broken through his old ways, drawn him in. Gradually, it had tapped his potential, given him purpose and direction. The heart of it, Erran said, was a sense of connection and close, meaningful relationships with people who cared about him. Central Park East had become Erran's family.

"I like the homey feeling that everybody knows each other, so I feel like they're my brothers and sisters," said this street-toughened young son of Harlem. "School—and *our school,* you know—is like two different things."

Other students echoed that strong sense of belonging and of bonding with the teachers and with fellow students.

"It's a small school, and that's a key," said Paul Schwarz. "It's a community. I know the names of all the students in the school. Everyone in the school knows my name. . . . Students here sometimes complain that we're always in their face, and we are. We know them very, very well."[9]

Schwarz, a former primary school teacher for twenty years, contended that the school's small size and close relationships are the most powerful antidote to youth violence—far more effective than guards or metal detectors. Schwarz blamed the level of serious violence in urban schools primarily on the impersonal anonymity at massive high schools, where teenagers feel lost and unknown.

CPESS works hard to ensure that every student has a network of relationships and to institutionalize individual, one-on-one mentoring. The core of that effort is its advisory system: Every teacher or staff member has ten to fifteen students as advisees. The advisory group, teacher and advisees, meet once a day for at least forty-five minutes in an old-fashioned homeroom situation. The talk at "advisories" often wanders far from academics. Students get into topics important to their lives—issues of homelessness, racism, and sexism in American society; violence in New York City; relationships at home with parents or brothers and sisters; homework and what time their parents insist they come in on weekends; their plans for after graduation.

"That advisory system means that each student is really rooted with an adult in a very positive, very important way," Paul Schwarz asserted. "I think that's the key to the lack of violence in this school."

The students' side of the story was told to me by Carlos Lavazzeri IV, a seventeen-year-old African-American junior who had come to Central Park East after a troubled tenth-grade year in a huge comprehensive high school, where he was constantly getting into street fights and periodic scrapes with the police.

Carlos wrote poetry and carried a book of his poems in a hip-pocket notebook, but no teacher at his old school had discovered his interest in writing. Nobody had even cared whether he was in class or played hookey, Carlos said, so he had spent a lot of time roaming the halls and the streets. "I mean, you got like five thousand students and nobody knows you." Carlos frowned. "So you try—they try to do what they can to be known, and that can cause fights and jealousy. Here, it's like you don't feel like you have to stand out, because the school makes you feel like you're an individual."[10]

Paul Schwarz, as Carlos's adviser, got to know Carlos well enough to uncover the secret of his poetry and to persuade Carlos to put some writing into shape to be published in *New Youth Connections,* a city youth newspaper.

Even with close personal mentoring, it was still not clear whether Carlos would make it to graduation. One teacher called him a young man with "a lot of raw talent, but a student on the edge." Carlos had slumps as well as bursts of creativity. Some bad habits lingered, such as playing hookey. But Central Park East jumped on that problem instantly. Once, Schwarz found out that Carlos was having stomach pains and got him to a hospital, where his trouble turned out to be appendicitis. At other times, Carlos was skipping school, and Schwarz intervened quickly to keep him from dropping out.

"People don't wake up one morning and say, 'I'm dropping out of school,'" Schwarz observed. "They get in the habit of not going to school, and it becomes easier and easier not to go to school. That's very hard to do here. Because if a student is absent for a day or two, we call home right away and talk to his parents and say, 'Is he sick? What's going on here?'"

At Central Park East, that task does not fall to an attendance clerk or a truant officer. It's done by the student's adviser, who usually has the student as an advisee for two or three years and gets to know both student and family quite well.

"I'm the expert on Carlos," Schwarz explained. "Every student in this school has an expert. That's my most important job, being the expert on Carlos and the other students I have in my advisory. I'm not his teacher, I'm his adviser. It's my responsibility to find out from his various teachers how he's doing in class. When his parents come to school and want to know about Carlos, I'm the one they come and talk to."

One student after another testified to the vital importance of that close mentor relationship. Erran Matthews said that three years earlier, when he had been in the depths, he had been rescued by the sports director, Mark Lutsky, and his adviser, Marian Mogolescu, a former humanities teacher. Shadia Alvarez told how her adviser, Shirley Hawkinson, a literature teacher, had pulled her back from the brink of dropping out of school.

"I have somebody who's there for me and somebody that I know cares about me just as much as I care about her," Shadia said. "If I have a problem, I know that I can stay with Shirley after class and just talk to her. She's also shed a lot of tears with me, so that's really nice."[11]

The school extends that sense of community and partnership to parents. It is helped by the parental promise, at the time of enrollment, to work with the faculty. The school claims 100 percent attendance at its regular parent-teacher conferences, remarkable for an inner-city school. Parents quickly become believers. Shadia's mother, Altagracia Faisal, remarked that being the mother of a teenager is not easy these days, so she welcomed the school's partnership. "I could call at any moment, I could show up any day of the week," she said, "and the teachers would stop what they are doing and see me and discuss any points."[12]

Central to the concept of community at Central Park East is mutual respect; and respect is a word that kept cropping up in conversations at CPESS. "We have a respectful relationship to each other, to the kids, and to their families," Deb Meier asserted.

Then, with a sudden, gritty passion, she protested the lack of respect at many New York public schools. "I think respect is an essential thing that is missing everywhere—schools in this city in which there isn't toilet paper in the bathrooms, or a mirror for people to look at, or towels to wash their hands, or doors in the boys' stalls," she declared. "Those are petty aspects, but they are very important statements of our disrespect for the young people who go to school. Often there is not a place for young people or for adults to engage in a conversation. That is a sign of disrespect. We don't treat schools as if they are essentially respectful relationships."[13] At Central Park East, she emphasized, "We work very, very hard in order that all the relationships in this school are respectful."

The Foundation: A World of Powerful, Interesting Adults

Teachers are the ultimate decision makers at Central Park East. That is how the school began in the mid-1980s, as one of a handful of schools set up by the New York City school system as experiments in alternative approaches to education. At Central Park East, the educational bureaucracy was set aside, and teachers were given great leeway and authority. Teachers were to set the school's curriculum, determine the graduation requirements and standards, decide how they would teach; and the teachers were accountable for the school's performance. Even today, the teachers at Central Park East continue vigorously to debate their goals and methods.

To Deb Meier, unleashing the power of teachers is the most vital element in rethinking and restructuring our approach to education. Without teachers feeling empowered, Meier said, Central Park East could not have generated the intellectual excitement that makes it the envy of other schools. In her view, the self-confidence of CPESS teachers was absolutely central not only to the creativity of their teaching but also to their influence with students. Teachers are poor role models for students, she said, if they are hampered, harassed, hemmed in by regulations, overburdened by paperwork, and overflowing with complaints about the school system. But they are strong role models, she asserted, if they are in charge of their work and show enthusiasm for it.

"What I think is important in this school is that the adults have created a world here that is first of all attractive to themselves, that's an interesting place, where they are powerful and interesting people," Meier observed. "And there's a possibility then for them to recruit kids, if you want, into the world of powerful and interesting adults, to make it seem feasible to kids that growing up might be a wonderful thing to do. You can't recruit kids to your club if you have made your club seem very unattractive. So, to start off with, this is a faculty that thinks they belong to an exciting profession."[14]

Teachers such as Shirley Hawkinson (literature), Marty Tuminaro (genetics), and Joe Walter (analytical geometry), all veterans of other schools, found Central Park East strikingly different. It was more liberating, they said, and hence more demanding—and more satisfying. They felt they had helped shape the school—the curriculum, their own courses, the overall goals, the standards for graduation. At times, they had prevailed over Deb Meier on key decisions. Their sense of ownership was strong.

Compared to other schools, Hawkinson asserted, teachers at CPESS have "more control and more power over what they're doing," and that enabled them to do the real work of educating. "In my previous schools, people were also interested in education," she said, "but it seems as if there were so many things operating against us, whether it was size, too many things to do, a structure that doesn't allow you to know your students very well."[15]

The size of the school was critical—a size driven by the need for immediacy and continuity of relationships, not only between teachers and students and their parents but among the teachers themselves. As they organized the school, the CPESS teachers insisted on being given time together. They felt that their interaction, their regular chance to debate and to work through what is good education and how to implement it, was critical to their success in class and the intellectual vitality of the school.

To Deb Meier, the best school size is driven by the need of the staff for the intimacy to hash out problems and to hone a unified message of learning for the students. Proper size also permits each teacher to teach no more than 40 students a week (instead of the usual 200), so teachers can really know their students individually and students can know their teachers personally.[16]

"You can't help people you don't respect, and you can't respect people you don't know," Meier insisted. "So the ideal school is three hundred kids. [CPESS has 450 in grades 7 to 12.] That's a size where the teachers can fit in one room around the table and talk to each other face to face. To send a powerful message to the kids, the staff has to be constantly in touch with each other, see each other's work, critique each other. The director can honestly know the staff. You can fail even in a small school, but not the way they fail in those big, big schools."[17]

By "school," Meier meant not a building but an educational unit. "A building is not a school, it's a building," she said. "A big building can house several schools."

In fact, at 106th and Madison Avenue, the building that used to be Jackie Robinson Junior High now contains three schools—a high school, a middle school, and an elementary school. Meier favored having all ages rubbing shoulders, to increase the sense of community. Teenagers behave better, she said, with small children around.

This logic seemed sound, but how can a big-city public high school afford small size, small classes for teachers, close mentoring relationships?

"We've made some hard choices," Paul Schwarz explained. "We've given up some things that I wish we didn't have to give up. We've given up a gym teacher. We've given up a music teacher. We don't have guidance counselors, we don't have deans, we don't have department chairs. We have taken virtually all our resources and used them to hire teachers, and we have more teachers than most other schools do."[18]

Slashing staff and school bureaucracy meant that teachers had to do everything. At Central Park East, they were generalists rather than specialists. They taught their specialties, but they often mixed disciplines by team teaching, *and* they had to act as mentors to their advisees, doing the college and career guidance work normally assigned to school counselors.

In terms of mind-set, teachers at Central Park East had to embrace change; they had to thrive on the stimulus of constantly creating new courses and new ways of reaching their students; and they had to be undaunted by teaching street kids from East Harlem. To Deb Meier, what they needed most was "lots of energy—not giving up easily."

"You have to have a very strong constitution for assuming that 'So it didn't work today, I'm going to try tomorrow,' " she said. "That frame of reference, that you don't expect easy answers and you get pleasure out of the difficult."[19]

Less Is More: Depth Instead of Breadth

The success of Central Park East rests largely on its willingness to break with orthodox American educational thinking. Its faculty does not believe in tracking. Like Japanese elementary school teachers, those at CPESS oppose dividing high school students into two groups—the naturally talented, who are headed for success, and the rest, who are written off as mediocre or less. Central Park East sets high expectations for all.

The school's approach is to emphasize depth over breadth, to train its students to master the critical habits of mind—examining evidence, making connections, developing perspective, imagining alternatives, seeing significance—rather than to make students memorize masses of material.

To those ends, Central Park East has broken out of what Deb Meier mocks as the "insane organization" of the standard curriculum—chopped up into forty-five-minute periods of separate subjects in which students are confronted with a parade of changing faces. "What business would operate that way—changing supervisors and coworkers every forty-five minutes?" Meier demanded.[20]

At Central Park East, the upper classes spend two hours in one class and do just two core academic classes per day. The point is to give more time for both academic training and hands-on experience in a few subjects, rather than a lot of seat time and "Carnegie credit units" in a menu of courses. In fact, Central Park East says, its students all wind up taking the rough equivalent of 3½ years of high school math and four years of English, plus science, history, the arts, and a language. But sometimes the material comes in a mix rather than as discrete subjects. Ninth- and tenth-grade classes, for example, engage in a semester-long exploration of the question "What is justice?" by reading books, watching movies, and comparing the American system with traditional Chinese systems of justice and the consensual system in West Africa. The justice course reaches across history, literature, social studies, and media.

"We have bought into the idea that less is more," Paul Schwarz explained. "We're not interested in covering a lot of material. We're not interested in a history course that says it's May, so we should be studying Truman now. We believe that if you study one thing in great depth and study it well, you'll be able to use your mind to study another similar situation. Therefore, we have not bought into the idea of studying all the biology facts that a traditional biology program would study. We take one particular issue in biology or history or social studies or literature and study it in great depth."

At CPESS, the object is to make students the activists—pushing their own learning curve, with teachers as catalysts and coaches but never lecturing to a room of students with heads down, scribbling notes. Joe Walter, a math teacher, asserted that from years of lecturing and writing examples on the blackboard for students to copy, he had discovered that "ten percent of them will probably be very attentive and very involved, and the other ninety percent will blank out."[21] At CPESS, Walter framed his math exercises to make students develop the material, make their own explorations. In one session, Erran Matthews, the street kid, was excited by a competition in which he and a partner were racing against five other pairs of students on an exercise that took twenty to thirty minutes to work through a complex set of real-life problems. In a literature class, Shirley Hawkinson touched off a lively debate by asking her students whether the way in which Shakespeare dealt with personal ethics and truth seeking in *King Lear* had relevance to life in Harlem. Semeika Smith, a senior, said she loved her science classes because the projects were related to the real world, such as studying infrared waves by analyzing microwave ovens.[22]

One of CPESS's trademark innovations is keeping education rooted in the real world: From eighth through tenth grades, all of its students must do two to three hours of community service once a week—reading to the blind, working in hospitals or day-care centers, serving in community environmental groups, counseling younger children at Boys' Harbor. In the last two years, every student must also do a work internship, roughly a semester long, at such job sites as a youth newspaper, the Shearson Lehman brokerage house, local businesses in Harlem, the New York City Council, or Mount Sinai Hospital. Both these requirements are intended to bring home to students the relevance of school to life, to give them practical outlets for learning, and to let them see that, in fact, people in the work world do use skills they learned in school.

For Graduation: Oral Exams and a Demonstration of Mastery

The boldest innovation at Central Park East was to do away with the standard written final exams as a requirement for graduation. The epitome of its reform philosophy was the alternative adopted by its faculty: Each student must demonstrate knowledge and mastery of different areas of study by presenting "portfolios" of work to a graduation committee and then defending his or her work before that committee.

At its founding, CPESS got a waiver from the normal graduation requirements from the New York City school system. To replace them, Deb Meier and her teachers turned to the work of Ted Sizer, a prominent educational reformer at Brown University, who has crafted an integrated approach to reforming education that is extensively employed at CPESS. Sizer argued that a high school diploma should be awarded based not on tests but "upon a successful final demonstration of mastery."[23] Sizer's argument was that not only are some students poor at test taking but even those who cram effectively for tests often quickly forget the material. It was Sizer who proposed instead that there be a demonstration, a performance, an exhibition of skill.

Central Park East translated Sizer's concept into the requirement that every student present fourteen in-depth portfolios and then appear before a graduation committee for oral exams on seven of these portfolios. Each student has a personal graduation committee composed of his or her adviser, one other teacher or CPESS staff member, a third adult of the student's choosing, and a younger student. The required portfolios cover such traditional subjects as math, science, literature, history, language, and the arts; they also cover less traditional areas, such as geography, media, autobiography, ethics and societal issues, physical challenge, practical skills, community service or internship, and life beyond graduation ("Why I need a diploma").

Shadia Alvarez, for example, wrote one project on her search for cultural identity after moving from the Dominican Republic to America. Carlos Lavazzeri was preparing a video about black-on-black crime.

As CPESS students start their junior year, they enter "the senior institute," and preparing portfolios becomes their healthy obsession. They are forced to develop self-reliance. They attend classes, but they also have a lot of independent study time. It's impossible for them to gather enough material for their portfolios without taking classes, yet even in class their primary objective is to develop the skills and the materials to build all fourteen portfolios. Typically, portfolios combine work done in class with work done independently. Simply submitting a class paper is rarely enough. It is up to each student, with the help of teachers and the coaching of an adviser, to organize and complete the fourteen portfolios. About three quarters achieve that in two years, about one quarter take three years (sometimes including a temporary dropout), and one student did it all in one year. But no matter how long it takes, *no one graduates* and gets a diploma without completing all fourteen portfolios.

"At other schools, you put in seat time, you have to take some tests, teachers will lower expectations, and it's possible for a student to graduate without being able to write or think very clearly," observed Marty Tuminaro, the genetics teacher. "Not so at this school—because we look at so many pieces of writing. I don't think a student can just slip on through."[24]

I watched Carlos Lavazzeri, the young poet, go through his first graduation committee. On his committee were Paul Schwarz; a math and science teacher named David Feldman; a tenth-grade student, Chyann Higgs; and his own father, whom Carlos had selected despite past tensions between them. They all sat around a small round table, but Carlos was obviously tense. For his first portfolio, he had submitted a thirteen-page autobiographical essay that was painfully candid, especially about his experiences at his last school—"the school from hell," he called it. Before the meeting, everyone on the committee had read his essay.

Carlos was asked the purpose of an autobiography. Self-discovery, he answered: "To get an idea of what helped make a person, like their childhood, their different experiences, what formed that person, what that person kind of did to motivate himself." Had he worked merely from memory? No, he said, he had taken a cue from the school's practice of making students write essays when they got into fights. "Like if something was bothering me or if I was hurt by something, I'd jot it down," he replied. "It was not like it goes away or it bothers me less—I just understand myself better when I read it back to myself." From those notes and from the recollections in his hip-pocket notebook, he had fashioned the essay.

Feldman, the math teacher, wanted to know if Carlos would now revise his essay. No, said Carlos, he would not change it because it rang true: "That's just how I felt, and I don't feel much different now than I did when I wrote it." Carlos's father probed him about the influence of religion, mentioned in an early passage about the boy's grandmother. He also wanted to know whether Carlos, who was now seeing some positive trends in his life, felt less negative about things in the past. Again, Carlos said the pain and the scars were real to him, but with the passage of time, he could see things more positively than he had been able to in the heat of the moment.[25]

The oral exam took about forty minutes, and then Carlos heard the committee's evaluations. Paul Schwarz called Carlos's autobiography "a strong piece of writing, and I was moved when I read it. It certainly met all of our expectations in terms of viewpoint, connections, evidence, voice, and conventions." Chyann Higgs, the student, echoed those comments. David Feldman told Carlos he should have "used more evidence" and stated more of a conclusion, but he admired Carlos's candor and his writing style, especially his flashes of humor and irony. Carlos's father, a teacher, had been surprised by the "very moving piece" his son had written. "It takes a lot of courage to reveal yourself like that to family or strangers," Carlos's father told him. "Your autobiography has touched me. I hope your writing gets a chance to touch people, because it will be a positive experience in a lot of people's lives. And I'm very proud of you."[26]

CPESS has only three grades for portfolios—satisfactory, unsatisfactory, and distinction. The graduation committee gave Carlos a "satisfactory-plus" (17 points out of 20) and told him that he could push it up to a "distinction" if he rewrote the essay in response to the critique. He also had to complete the portfolio requirement by submitting a personal résumé and a written family tree.

With the exam over, Paul Schwarz reached over and gave Carlos a friendly pat on the shoulder. Later, when I asked Carlos how he felt, he smiled shyly and looked at the floor. When he found his voice, he told me, "I feel like I've finished something. I feel like, you know, I can move on from here now. I feel a sense of completion."

Since passing such a committee fourteen times determines whether a student will graduate, critics inevitably question whether these committees are tough enough. So I asked Deb Meier for her response to those who say, "Look, your graduation committees, your portfolios, they're an interesting idea, but isn't that a way of lowering standards?"

"That's a critical question—what's it all for, and what happens afterwards?" she acknowledged. One way CPESS assesses itself is to invite outsiders—educators, businessmen, other teachers—to witness the process. But the main way is to follow the track record of CPESS graduates.

Of the first three graduating classes, she told me in 1993, "not only did ninety percent get into college but then ninety percent of those completed their first year and started their second year and are completing their second year of college. That is a phenomenal rate. That speaks to us that something happened that enabled them to handle an often less nurturing environment than this school, to know where to go for resources, for where to go for help, to have the stamina, the stick-to-itiveness, the grit, to survive and to succeed, which is far more important than any other quality that we can give them. It is that quality of character to handle that next stage."[27]

Among those I had met, Shadia Alvarez had been accepted at Syracuse and at Antioch College in Ohio and had picked Antioch. Carlos had another year of high school to go; by May 1994 he had completed several more portfolios before taking a semester off. He'd gotten married, had a job, and there was a child imminent, for whom he was taking responsibility. He was in regular contact with Paul Schwarz, vowing to finish high school and go to college.[28]

Erran Matthews, the street kid, had told me that in the old days he had never really thought about going to college. But as he approached graduation, he had a plan, a career, and a college all picked out.

"I'm heading to Cornell to be a doctor," he told me. "I want to be a doctor so I can start my children's center. But it is going to be called the Network, you know, where I network and get a lot of kids involved with different things that they have never been part of. I used to be like that. And I know how it feels to be by yourself and on the side, wanting to be involved. And I figure I never want that to happen to a kid while I'm around."[29]

Building on the Lessons of Central Park East

In less than a decade, Central Park East has established a remarkable record. With a profound shift in mind-set, a revolution in thinking and teaching methods, this school has demonstrated that public schools can work, even on the most difficult terrain. It has provided a success track into the mainstream for students—whether in East Harlem or in other inner cities—who are widely and inaccurately regarded by much of America as educationally beyond the pale.

The faculty at Central Park East has transformed what happens in the classroom and in students' performance, not only by making the curriculum, the graduation standards, and their approach to teaching more engaging and more relevant to life but also by building close connections between teacher and student, between school and home, between the school and the outside community. Central Park East cut frills, bureaucracy, and extracurriculars; it focused its resources on teaching. The teachers personalized the learning experience for *all* of their students by providing every single student with caring, one-on-one mentoring. Given the final responsibility for the results, the teachers at CPESS kindled an excitement among their students that stirred them to achieve at levels no one had expected.

Central Park East is such an effective model that the New York City school system is building on its example. In late 1993 and 1994, New York City opened eleven more schools in Manhattan, the Bronx, and Brooklyn, modeled on the philosophy and educational approach at Central Park East. Among them are the International High School, University Heights High School, Urban Academy, and Satellite Academies at Forsythe and Chambers. In addition, former CPESS teachers and codirectors have been picked to lead three other experimental schools in the city. Deb Meier has left Central Park East to help with the reorganization of several schools and to build the momentum of educational reform in New York City, even in the face of budget cutbacks forced by Mayor Rudolph W. Giuliani.

The Sizer Coalition of Essential Schools

More broadly, Central Park East is part of a growing nationwide movement for rethinking American education to make it more effective and more attuned to today's world.

Among the best known reform efforts is the Coalition of Essential Schools, led by Ted Sizer, former headmaster of Phillips Andover Academy and now a professor of education at Brown University. Developing the ideas of John Dewey, who preached decades ago that children learn best from experience, Sizer developed nine essential principles for revitalizing American schools.

Sizer emphasized the need (1) to focus on teaching students to use their minds, rather than on compiling credits; (2) to promote mastery of a few areas of knowledge, rather than offering exposure to a smattering of courses; (3) to set high expectations for all students; (4) to personalize learning; (5) to make the student the activist and the teacher the coach; (6) to build relationships of trust and decency; (7) to require exhibitions of mastery, rather than skill at test taking; (8) to encourage teachers to be generalists first, rather than specialists; and (9) to give teachers time for collective planning.[30]

All of the schools in Sizer's coalition must agree to these nine principles; they develop their own methods for implementing them, just as Central Park East did. From just a dozen schools in 1985, the Sizer coalition has blossomed to 178 schools across the nation by the fall of 1994—87 in cities, 67 in suburbs, 23 in rural areas.[31] Several hundred more have applied to join the movement.

The Comer Method

A parallel, and also successful, experiment that focuses on the parent-school connection as the primary agent for improving student performance is now operating nationwide, under the leadership of James P. Comer, a Yale University child psychiatrist who grew up in an inner-city black family.

Comer's thesis is that social development is vital to learning and that it is essential to overcome the social and psychological handicaps that alienate many poor inner-city children and hold back their academic achievement. His method is to overcome the barriers between home and school and to bring family and school into active partnership.

At two inner-city schools in New Haven, Connecticut, starting in 1968, Comer worked at getting parents engaged with the schools through various activities—a joint parent-teacher management committee for each school, the use of parents as part-time teacher helpers in class, and a multitude of joint family-school activities in neighborhoods where such events had rarely occurred. Even without academic reforms, Comer reported that discipline and attendance problems declined dramatically and achievement levels at the two schools shot up. Their students went from the bottom level in New Haven to near the top; they were well above national averages. Now the Comer method is being used in more than fifty schools in major cities across America.[32]

The New American Schools Development Corporation

A third major private reform effort, called the New American Schools Development Corporation, seeks entirely new, "break-the-mold" approaches to revolutionize public education in America. The effort, launched in 1992, was headed by David Kearns, former CEO of Xerox and Deputy Secretary of Education under President Bush. Support came from a coalition of American corporate leaders who were increasingly concerned that tinkering with the existing public school system would not achieve the quantum improvements they felt were essential.

The New American Schools Corporation invited reform ideas, received 686 proposals, and selected 9 "designs" for testing out in practice in 1993. The ideas vary widely, their only common features being a radical departure from existing school systems and an effort to make school relevant to life. One approach is built around experiential teaching and "educational expeditions," a variation on camping and boating expeditions run by Outward Bound in Colorado; another called Co-NECT seeks big jumps in learning levels by using computer networks, starting in kindergarten; a third turns schools into Community Learning Centers, operating year round, twenty-four hours a day, and mixing students of all ages.

To David Kearns, the challenge is not only to rethink American public education but to "scale up" the drive for educational reform so that by the year 2000, some 15 to 20 percent of America's public schools will be fundamentally restructured and operating in fresh, effective new ways.[33]

To speed the reform efforts, Walter Annenberg, the philanthropist who built a fortune in publishing, made a $500 million donation to educational reform in December 1993—$50 million to Ted Sizer's Coalition for Essential Schools, $50 million to the New American Schools Corporation, $50 million to New York City's expanding reform efforts, and more funds to James Comer's project and other reform efforts. Ted Sizer was put in charge of deciding how the remainder of Annenberg's funds would be allocated.[34]

The Goal of the 1990s: Replicating the Good Models

In short, after more than a decade of gloomy reports about the failings of American education, experiments in serious educational reform are gaining momentum. Not only the federal and state governments have become involved but business leaders as well. In 1994, Congress passed the Goals 2000 act, calling for the first time for national standards for American schools. But these standards were to be voluntary: It is up to states and communities to use those standards to gauge their own performance.

The two central questions that confront America in the mid-1990s on this issue are these: (1) Will most of America's 15,000 school districts learn from Deb Meier and other innovators and embark on serious reform, or will school boards, superintendents, and principals cling to the status quo? and (2) Will the reforms undertaken by schools be far reaching enough to have a significant impact on student performance?

The Education Commission of the States, a research organization partly supported by the states, reports that recent experience shows that a winning educational strategy requires fundamental restructuring of school curriculums, teaching methods, and goals. By contrast, the commission warns, shallow, "short-term, quick-fix approaches" can be counterproductive; piecemeal efforts can actually make things worse. But the commission found real and substantial payoffs from serious reforms: Where schools have undertaken careful, long-term "systemic restructuring," they have generated what the commission called "superior outcomes" in academic achievement.[35]

Nonetheless, resistance to serious reform remains strong at most American public schools, despite clear models of reform and despite a multitude of opinion polls expressing dissatisfaction with the existing educational system. Among America's 110,000 public schools, precious few have embraced systemic change. According to the Education Commission of the States, only 1 to 4 percent of America's schools have begun to undertake fundamental restructuring, and fewer than 1 percent have completed the process of change, which often takes five years or more. More than 95 percent of America's schools have stuck with the status quo.[36]

Resistance to change and uncertainty about how to change are the heart of America's problem in the 1990s, according to Tom Kean. "The real problem in the nineties with education is replication," asserts Kean. "In the eighties, we didn't know really what to do. We knew the schools weren't good enough, and we weren't quite sure how to fix them. Now we have examples all over the country of people fixing them. And the question is whether or not we can replicate what's being done in the good schools."[37]

7

Wisconsin—Business and Schools as Partners

Youth Apprenticeships—A New Deal for the Neglected Majority

If you want to meet the quality standards you need in international competition today, you've got to have trained people, very well trained. . . . We see the youth apprenticeship thing as a source of really sharp, young employees.[1]

—JOHN TORINUS, COMPANY CEO

We get what other kids our age aren't getting in high school. We get the knowledge, the experience that'll bring us to higher levels when we get out of high school. We'll have a good steady job and experience that no one else gets.[2]

—BRENDA RADOLL, HIGH SCHOOL APPRENTICE

We have nine career fields now for apprenticeships, and my dream is to have forty different kinds of apprenticeships in five years and six thousand to eight thousand young people in those programs.[3]

—BERT GROVER, FORMER WISCONSIN STATE SCHOOL SUPERINTENDENT

It is one thing to transform a school as Deb Meier did. It is another to try to transform a system. In America, sometimes it takes the bull energy of someone such as Bert Grover to begin to change the system.

In Wisconsin, people call Bert Grover "the buffalo." He is a big, strapping man with a barrel chest, a strong jaw, and a penetrating glint in his brown eyes. In normal conversation, Grover speaks quietly for a big man, but when he becomes passionate, the words come forth in great torrents. He has the zeal of a revivalist preacher.

As Wisconsin's elected state school superintendent from 1981 to 1993, Bert Grover set into motion a revolution in the state high school system. What others attempted piecemeal, Grover went after wholesale—youth apprenticeships, as a new way to prepare Wisconsin's average kids for the modern economy and to give industry the high caliber of people they needed.

In other states from Maine to Oklahoma to Oregon, reformers launched small-scale pilot programs of youth apprenticeships, styled after the German system; they focused on one industry or perhaps a handful. In Wisconsin, Bert Grover had a vision of sweeping, systemic change.

Grover got momentum built into the state's master plan, so that while the new approach started small, Wisconsin would eventually offer a menu of career pathways for average high school students, give them world-class training, and open up avenues to good jobs after graduation. Grover spent his last five years as superintendent pushing, prodding, cajoling the governor, state legislators, unions, teacher groups, state agencies, and business leaders into helping make that dream come true.

What drove Grover was the haunting image of a multitude of Jason Fullers—of average Wisconsin kids—being dumped into the work world after high school, lost and unprepared. That picture offended Grover's sense of fairness; he saw it as an enormous social waste.

"We hear constantly from the private sector that the non-college-bound graduates from our high schools have a diploma that isn't worth the paper it's written on," Grover asserted. "We've had this terrible floundering period for sixteen- to twenty-eight-year-olds, as they tried to find themselves in a Taco Bell, minimum-wage kind of economy. Some recovered and some didn't."

To sell his vision, Grover hammered at the mismatch between the loose and undemanding "general education" curriculum in traditional public high schools and the increasingly sophisticated needs of industry.

"Seventy-five percent of our children will not graduate from college, and they're going to be the workers of tomorrow," he asserted. "Eighty percent of the jobs will not require a baccalaureate degree. They will require a two-year associate degree, technical skills, a high level of competence in math and science and technology. All of those programs are available. It's just that our institutions didn't respond [to the changing economy], and they have left large segments of our children behind."[4]

For better performance, Grover advocated a new educational mind-set. Eventually other important people joined Grover's crusade and were better than he was at implementing his ideas. Tommy Thompson, the Republican governor, pushed the educational reform package through a Democratically controlled state legislature. Some business and community leaders, and even the statewide AFL-CIO, endorsed the project. But Grover took the lead in overcoming public inertia. In a country where college education is the universal ideal, Grover preached the need for greater realism, for accepting the fact that most young people would not finish college and that these average students had a right to an education that would prepare them well for a modern economy. It was time, he asserted, for rethinking old prejudices toward the non-college-bound, and for giving them new respect and new opportunities. What Wisconsin, and America, needed, Grover said, was "a whole new ethos" in order "to *democratize*" its schools.

The Needs of Business Stimulated Apprenticeships

Grover was inspired by Germany's dual-education system. After visiting Germany in 1988, he came away believing that the German system is more "democratic" than the American system, because it develops the potential of more young people and puts more young people on track toward a solid economic future. And he wanted people in Wisconsin to understand what Germans take for granted, namely, that modern education and training are the key: "If we can get a high-skilled, high-performance society, ultimately we raise the level and standard of living for all of our citizens."

Grover got a German-style dual-education program built into Wisconsin's blueprint for reforming its high schools. In the plan devised by various state task forces and passed by the legislature, Wisconsin's revised curriculum offers students three pathways: (1) "academic prep" for those headed to four-year colleges; (2) "tech prep"—a program of two years of high school linked to two years of junior college and organized according to broad career fields; and (3) two-year apprenticeships for high school juniors and seniors, tying together classroom education with work-site training and based on standards set by business as well as schools.

To those who protested that this was tracking, Grover replied: "We're tracking now. America has two tracks—the track to college and the track to nowhere."[5]

To those who pointed out that Wisconsin already had high school vocational courses, Grover contended that vocational training had "lost its authenticity," partly because of the social stigma attached to it but more importantly because vocational schools could not keep up with the latest technology and methods of business. As a result, said Grover, vocational students graduated "without marketable skills." Seventy percent of them, he said, are "never employed in anything remotely connected with their training."[6]

The antidote, in Grover's view, was to engage business and industry actively in education, so that business and education together would craft apprenticeship curriculums that were sound academically and also linked to the real world. This dual system would differ from normal vocational training because students would get extensive training at a real company, using today's technology and methods; because business would set performance standards and then certify the job proficiency of graduates; and because the schools would redesign their academic courses to tie classroom learning into the career skills that students were gaining on the job. The live connection with business and industry would be vital; it would stimulate teachers to rethink their courses and motivate students who were bored with school. As an added incentive, Grover got it established that student apprentices would be paid for hundreds of hours of job-site training.

Getting this program adopted took a fight. Many people in public and private institutions, even those who shared Grover's educational goals, resisted systemic change. For them, working with other institutions meant sharing power. Businesses would have to spend money, not only to pay apprentices but for the time of their experienced workers who would train the apprentices. Unions were worried about protecting their own apprenticeship programs. High schools balked at having to create new courses in "applied academics." Teachers felt awkward accepting ideas and pressures from industry. In some cases, high schools could not handle the new load and had to turn over teaching responsibilities to community technical colleges, and that generated institutional jealousies. Other frictions arose from the need for the Department of Education to share authority over an educational program with the Department of Industry, Labor and Human Relations. At every turn, the legislature debated and delayed.

Once, when a key piece of legislation hung in the balance in mid-1991, Grover blurted out, "I would roll a pea down the aisle of the state legislature with my nose—if I could get a majority vote on this thing."[7]

In the end, the demands of business finally broke the dam. In the early 1990s, Wisconsin's high-tech printing and graphic arts industry was in desperate need of more qualified workers and deeply unhappy with its new recruits from Wisconsin's high schools. In Milwaukee and the region to the north, the printing industry is an important employer. Some of Wisconsin's more progressive firms, mostly small and medium sized, were pushing into foreign markets, and they were using advanced technology. They were feeling the pressures of global competition, so they were willing to foot the bill of training high school students, as a long-term investment in upgrading their workforce. With the help of the printing industry's national trade association, several Wisconsin printers sat down with state educators to craft the first apprenticeship curriculum.

The program's beginnings, in the fall of 1992, were tiny—twenty-three apprentices at eight printing companies in two communities, West Bend and the Fox River Valley. But Grover's program finally had its first beachhead and a chance to prove itself.

Eric Baumann: "You Can't Compare It to School—You've Got to Be Mature"

For Eric Baumann, this new program was a godsend. It provided drive and purpose to his last two years in high school, and it opened a path into the work world.

Like Jason Fuller at Blue Springs High School and millions of other American teenagers, Eric was turned off by school. He was an average seventeen-year-old junior at Neenah High School near Appleton, about a hundred miles north of Milwaukee—certainly not flunking out, but drifting. Eric hated to read, didn't like math, and he was itching to work with his hands. He had no plans for after high school, except that, unlike his elder brother and sister, he knew that college was not for him.

So when Wisconsin announced its apprenticeship program in the printing trades in the summer of 1992, Eric Baumann signed up. His mother loved the idea. His dad was less enthusiastic.

"I feel all the areas of business should be participating in some type of apprenticeship program," said Mrs. Baumann, a lively, outgoing businesswoman who runs her own employment agency. "A lot of people I talk to are always concerned about their kids going on to college. But I see an awful lot coming into my employment service with a college degree who cannot find a job."[8]

Gary Baumann, Eric's father, was a bit hesitant because he was fearful that the new program would be "dumbed down" for the non-college-bound students. He himself had done a five-year metalworking apprenticeship after finishing high school in 1967. Now he had a good job as a pattern maker for the Neenah Foundry and a lovely suburban home outside Appleton. But as a high school student, he had felt the stigma of not being on a college track. He wanted to be sure that Eric's apprenticeship had a strong academic component.

"It is very important to us that Eric get a good education," Baumann told me. "And I've been worried that if the program isn't properly policed, you can end up with students washing windows and sweeping floors."[9] But Father, like Mother, went along with Eric's decision to become a printing apprentice.

Parental involvement was a hallmark of the Wisconsin program, from the initial decision of students to sign up to the parents' regular monthly meetings with instructors and administrators. Both Baumann parents became more deeply involved in Eric's education than ever before. They explained that their son was now involved professionally with adults in a business setting and they felt he required more parental supervision.

The academic side of Eric's apprenticeship turned out to be very productive, enough to satisfy his father. The apprenticeship was not an escape from academics; in fact, Eric had to buckle down seriously. Because Neenah High School could not revamp its curriculum fast enough, Eric and the other student apprentices went to Fox River Valley Technical for their courses in applied mathematics, chemistry for the printing trades, and computer graphics. They were in class two days a week and on the job three days.

Eric was surprised to find his attitude toward academics changing—he was even getting interested in his old nemesis, math. "I'm actually doing homework, now that I understand how it can be used in later life or on the job," Eric admitted. "I like this math better because it's more geared toward printing-type math. I have more motivation to do this kind of math than the math we did at school, because most of the stuff we did at school made absolutely no sense. But this stuff, working with fractions and decimals and percents, all these things that we use every day [in the plant]—it's very important."[10]

Eric's change of heart was typical of the other apprentices, according to Doug Paape, their graphic arts instructor. The key, said Paape, is giving these students a reason to learn by making their academic courses relevant to life outside school.[11]

Fox River Valley Technical College had also sought to keep its courses and its technology at the cutting edge. To match the operating level of local printing companies, the college had invested $30,000-plus in a new computer and sophisticated graphics software. Paape wanted to be sure that Eric and his classmates would be ready for today's jobs and for future growth. At Mid-America Printing Company, where Eric was working as an apprentice, one of his mentors, a computer graphics artist named Cindy Schey, commented that normal vocational programs and high school graphic arts classes were typically four years behind what industry was doing. But Eric's course was keeping up with the electronic revolution in graphic arts.[12]

Eric was the only apprentice at Mid-America Printing, where he was getting paid $4.50 an hour, enough to buy new stereo equipment and to save $200. Equally important for his motivation, he said, was being part of an adult business, rather than being stuck in class.

"You can't compare it to school," he said, laughing at the thought. "You're working with adults, and there's no screwing around. You've got to be mature about it. They're depending on you. I like physically getting in there, doing your job, and then having everybody look and say, you know, this is your product, you did a good job on it."[13]

His parents noticed changes in Eric—a maturing, a self-confidence, and slight changes in lifestyle. The hair, for example: In a year-old snapshot, Eric had been a freckle-faced sixteen-year-old with long hair streaming down his back to his waist.

Eric had thought he looked really good in long hair, but his mentors at Mid-America Printing told him that for safety reasons, he would have to tie it up in a ponytail. After a while, Eric said, he had decided that his long hair wasn't so important anymore, and so he had cut it off in favor of a high crew cut.

Even more dramatic was Eric's academic performance: His grades shot up. "Last semester I was on the honor roll," he said with a shy grin. Before the apprenticeship, he had never been on the honor roll; as he said, "Never even close to being on the honor roll."[14]

Although Gary Baumann still saw some teenage flippancy and immaturity in his son, Mrs. Baumann felt there had been a "one hundred percent change" in Eric. Most important, she said, "his self-esteem increased, and it got better and better as time went on. He was happier. He seemed very motivated. He had something of his own to talk about at the dinner table. Everything completely changed."

Near the end of his first year as an apprentice, Eric said he felt he had gained a leg up on his high school classmates. "I try to tell them that I'm getting all of this training and when I get out of school, I'm going to pretty much have a job," he said, "and these people haven't even started yet."

By the time his two years were finished, Eric Baumann graduated with better than a B average from Neenah High School. For a while he even toyed with going on to get a two-year college degree; three other West Bend apprentices did that, though the others went for permanent jobs right away. Mid-America Printing had a hiring freeze, but it kept Eric on as a temporary employee. Eric got impatient; he wanted a more settled job. Very quickly he found work at Printron, another printing firm nearby, bolstered in his job hunt by the self-confidence and the skills he had developed in his apprenticeship.[15]

John Torinus, Company CEO: $80,000 for Apprentices Pays Off

One of the business pioneers in Wisconsin's apprenticeship program was a tall, lanky, bespectacled CEO named John Torinus, owner of Serigraph Co., a midsized printing company.

Torinus was Bert Grover's most crucial ally in the state's business community. He was a prime mover in launching the apprenticeship program in Wisconsin, and especially in West Bend, about forty miles north of Milwaukee. As a firm believer in training at all levels, Torinus invested $80,000 in pay alone for his first crop of high school apprentices—and it paid off.

At Serigraph, Torinus had adopted an aggressive export strategy, and he saw the apprenticeship program as crucial to being globally competitive. He had bought the company in the mid-1980s and had moved it into foreign markets and into a high-tech, high-performance strategy. Torinus adopted Toyota-style work teams, expected his workers to master five or six jobs, and wanted his people to take responsibility for a product from beginning to end. And so he needed top-quality workers. Torinus was betting that the apprenticeship program was the best way to train them and to make a great leap forward in the quality and performance of his workforce. It was a long-term investment.

Moreover, Torinus was exploding with frustration over the recruits he had hired from regular high school courses. "We had illiterates— people who couldn't read blueprints, people who couldn't do simple decimals!" Torinus protested. "So we have an in-house school, which began as a remedial school to get people up to skill." But that was a drag on his company.

By 1992, Serigraph was doing roughly 30 percent of its business with foreign customers—in Singapore, in Brazil, in the border area of Mexico, and with Japanese companies operating in America. Among Torinus's hottest items were automobile dashboard and electrical equipment panels for Toyota and Nippondenso, a Japanese auto electronics firm. For McDonald's, Serigraph printed huge store signs in seventeen languages, from French to Chinese. At its four plants, Serigraph made everything from printed menus to instrument panels for almost every imaginable electrical appliance or piece of outdoor equipment. The printing was often very complex. One plastic panel for the interior of a GM car used twenty-one different colors and required special textures, hard coatings, and special adhesives.

"The quality pressures are almost excruciating," Torinus asserted. "To approach zero defects, for instance, we just have to have people who are sharp, all the way through our company—trained people, multiskilled people, people who can solve problems, people who can think for themselves, make decisions, fix things without any supervision—just do it."[16]

The clincher that sold Torinus on apprenticeships was a trip to Germany. As a member of the Governor's Commission on Youth, Torinus joined a delegation of Wisconsin business and political leaders who were looking at Germany's dual-education system. Torinus went to Germany a skeptic, puzzled over how the Germans could compete, with their six-week vacations, their thirty-seven-hour workweeks, their generous job benefits. He came back deeply impressed by the superb skills of German workers and the German commitment to training. He became convinced that Wisconsin—and America—needed to follow the German example.

In West Bend, Torinus became one of the architects of the dual-education system. He worked with West Bend High on the educational program, and he worked with the printing industry to craft a demanding set of requirements for the new apprentices—107 different job proficiencies to be mastered during their two-year program. At first, the high school teachers were uneasy about dealing with business, but eventually they designed new courses in "applied" academics—math, chemistry, and graphics for printing—to go along with the regular courses in literature, government, composition, and psychology. Another problem: The printing trades needed a waiver from Wisconsin's Child Labor Law to put student apprentices to work around their big printing presses.

Whatever the obstacles, Torinus helped overcome them, and when Wisconsin launched its dual-education program in the fall of 1992, Torinus signed up for more apprentices than any other employer in the state—a dozen in all, seven boys and five girls. One dropped out fairly soon, but the other eleven made it through the entire two-year program. In wages alone, each of these students cost Torinus $7,200 over two years (starting at a minimum wage of $4.25 an hour), not to mention the time of Torinus's trainers. The students were in the plant every day of the week; their day was split between mornings in school, middays onward in the plant, and back to school for extracurriculars in the late afternoon.

As an experimental program, this one had problems. One rough moment was when all eleven apprentices flunked a test in statistical process control given by Serigraph. Initially, the students, while disappointed, were inclined to pass off their failing grades as a bad test day. But for Serigraph, this was a litmus test of the seriousness of the program. Statistical process control was a core competency on which the company required solid performance. Rob Johnson, a quality engineer, did some remedial teaching, and all eleven apprentices passed the test on the second round. Then Johnson went to the high school to help ramp up the applied math course to meet industry's standards.

Torinus found that his firm spent more time teaching than he expected. "We're not getting a full $4.25 an hour's worth of value out of the students," he said. "But what I hope to get two years from now—three years from now if these young people go to technical college—is to hire these young people. They're going to be just superbly trained printers."

In fact, near the end of the first year, Torinus said, the program had "just exceeded my expectations." Some of his eleven apprentices were skilled enough on the multicolor printing presses to be taken on as backup print operators during summer vacation. "Incredible for seventeen-year-olds!" Torinus exclaimed.

The apprentices were buoyed by the responsibility they were being given in the plant, and they were stimulated by the new learning experiences. Brenda Radoll, who had been drawn to a printing apprenticeship by her interest in graphic arts and her general lack of interest in school, felt good about learning new math and graphic design skills on computers. Like Eric Baumann, she had gained a sense of self-confidence and a stronger motivation to learn; her grades, like his, had gone up. What had changed most, she told me, was her sense of direction and confidence about her future, a big contrast to her wobbly uncertainty beforehand. "I wasn't sure what I wanted and how I was going to get it," Brenda said. "And now I know exactly where I'm going."[17]

A year later, at the end of the two-year course, the results were impressive. All eleven apprentices at Serigraph had mastered every one of the 107 required proficiencies, and all got industry certificates along with their high school diplomas. Torinus hired nine of the eleven apprentices, including Brenda Radoll; the two others decided to go to junior college full time. Six of the apprentices hired by Serigraph started going to the local technical college part time, on the side.

In short, Torinus had begun to build up his new workforce, the students had landed good jobs, and most of them had gotten something they had not expected—new motivation to go on for more education.[18]

Torinus gave high marks all around, except for the one dropout and some initial resistance from teachers and a local union. But he had been surprised at how well the program had ended; overall, he said, the working partnership among students, parents, businesses, unions, and educators deserved an "A-plus." Only over time would he earn back his initial investment, but he was optimistic enough about that to take on more apprentices in each of the next two years.

"This has become apple pie and motherhood," Torinus chirped enthusiastically. "Everyone likes it—kids, parents, business, schools. Even the unions have come around."[19]

West Bend: Providing Good Options for *All* Young People

Word of the success of the programs in West Bend and Fox River Valley got out quickly, and that galvanized the growth momentum Bert Grover had hoped to achieve. In West Bend, not only did John Torinus take on more apprentices, but West Bend High School plunged into new career fields and expanded its partnerships with new employers.

"In West Bend it's caught on," Torinus said proudly.

In the second year, the fall of 1993, local banks and financial institutions took on nine apprentices, and more a year later. In the third year, the fall of 1994, another dozen apprentices got started in insurance and health industries—some at the local hospital and in medical clinics. That fall, West Bend had fifty apprentices in all and was making plans in 1995 to add two more career fields, auto technology and electronics, and modern machining and manufacturing.

"We're looking at an ag youth apprenticeship, we're looking at a small-business apprenticeship," Torinus added. "The idea is to make West Bend a town where all the young people have options, not just the college kids."[20]

Slow, steady development was what the program's architects had intended. They did not want a flash in the pan; they wanted to build a solid base for the future—both for business and for young people such as Eric Baumann and Brenda Radoll.

As John Torinus noted, the hardest, most time-consuming work was in launching a new field of apprenticeships; that took sustained effort, much more than for organizing traditional co-op or tech prep programs, because each new career field required forging new partnerships, integrating new groups of people. And that integration was essential to the program's success.

Each group of local employers, often joined by its national trade association, had to devise precise proficiency standards for the apprentices; then it had to work with high school teachers to hammer out brand-new course curriculums that both fit industry's needs and met academic requirements. Often, businesses had to give special preparation to their best workers to prepare them as mentors for the high school students. The high school decided that the system would work better if there were preparatory courses in the ninth and tenth grades, leading up to the apprenticeships. Career counseling and briefings for students and their parents had to be started in the seventh and eighth grades, to orient families to start thinking about these new pathways of education.

"It's not a rocket shot," Torinus commented. "It's slowly spreading."

Nonetheless, the sudden academic blossoming and maturing of the student apprentices and the quickening demand of local businesses for apprentices so impressed Mary Spacecki, the West Bend High School principal, that she and her faculty restructured the high school curriculum, based on occupational clusters. The school followed Bert Grover's formula—an academic prep pathway pointing toward four-year colleges; a tech prep pathway of two years of high school programs linked to a two-year technical college; and the apprenticeship pathway. West Bend High set up five apprenticeship pathways—one in industry, engineering, and technology; a second in health and human services; a third in arts and communications (printing); a fourth in business systems (finance and insurance); and a fifth in earth, ecology, and environment. It then eliminated the old general education track.

West Bend was a microcosm of the whole state. All across Wisconsin, the apprenticeship program caught on and picked up momentum. From twenty-two students in three medium-sized towns and seven businesses in 1992, it spread to urban centers like Milwaukee and Green Bay and throughout Wisconsin. By the fall of 1994, there were 450 apprentices from 85 high schools taking their dual education at school and at more than 200 businesses in nine different industries. The career fields included biotechnology, engineering technology, tourism/hospitality (hotels and motels), auto technology, and manufacturing, along with the other fields pioneered in West Bend. For the 1995–96 school year, further expansion is planned into electronics, agribusiness, and telecommunications.

Bert Grover's dream was happening. "We have nine career fields now for apprenticeships," he declared, "and my dream is to have forty different kinds of apprenticeships in five years and six thousand to eight thousand young people in those programs."[21]

The Innovators Versus the Status Quo

Not only in Wisconsin, but in states as diverse as Arkansas, Maine, Maryland, New York, Oklahoma, Oregon, and Pennsylvania, business-school partnerships are taking root and creating apprenticeship programs that are lifting average American high school students out of boredom and drift. In some cases, business groups and executives have taken the lead; in other cases, the spark of reform was fired by educators; in still others, by public officials.

In Tulsa, Oklahoma, for example, the crusading force for apprenticeships was the chamber of commerce. Industry had ebbed away from the Tulsa region so badly during the 1980s that the chamber's leadership was desperate to do something to save its local economy. Employers such as Tulsa's huge American Airlines repair facility, a large Rockwell International plant, Baker Oil Tools, Hilti International, T. D. Williams, and Webco were all complaining that local high school graduates did not fill their needs. The chamber sent delegations out to look at other educational systems, including Germany's apprenticeship programs. Impressed by the German model, the chamber put pressure on local businesses and educators to come up with a plan for Tulsa. The Tulsa formula is a four-year program: two years in high school, two years at Tulsa Tech (a junior college), and an on-the-job training component, all in four years. The price tag is steep—$50,000 per apprentice. In 1992, six companies put up the money. Some wanted to try one apprentice; others wanted several. That fall, Tulsa's first class of nineteen machine-tool apprentices got under way.[22]

In Boston, hospitals led the way. As one industry that did not nosedive during the 1990–92 recession, hospitals had the funds for new programs, and they were anxious about being able to find enough qualified new technicians to handle the growing health care burden. Educational requirements for health workers were spiraling because medical technology, computer software, and paperwork were becoming increasingly complex. That situation led in 1991 to the formation of Boston's Pro-Tech program, an alliance of seven hospitals with several high schools and an innovative group called Jobs for the Future, which has been a major force nationally in developing apprenticeships. The Boston program targeted inner-city minority students.[23] It was so immediately successful that by 1993, the hospitals had ninety-four health care apprentices, were looking for more, and the financial industry, Boston's largest employer, was clamoring for its own program. That program got under way in 1993, with seventy-five students.

Pennsylvania began with manufacturing apprenticeships and within three years had branched out into electronics, cellular manufacturing, equipment maintenance, and health care. By mid-1994, 350 students at sixteen different high schools were doing course work and taking job training at seventy-six different firms.[24] In Maine, Maryland, and upstate New York, apprenticeship programs were taking root in rural communities, too. In Oregon, driven by fears of long-term economic decline, the state legislature enacted a sweeping change in the state's school system in 1991 to orient part of its educational effort toward the work world.

In short, global competition and the aimless drift of many average young Americans have spurred a serious reform movement that embraces dual education—in school and on the job.

But whether this trend will be merely a passing fancy, a minuscule experiment affecting only a tiny fraction of the nation's high school students, or grow into a significant movement that will reshape the education and career opportunities of hundreds of thousands of young people is an open question.

The Clinton administration has thrown its support behind school-to-work programs, not only apprenticeships but other programs that tie work-site experience to education. As governor of Arkansas, Bill Clinton was a pioneer in launching apprenticeships at the state level. As President, he persuaded Congress in 1994 to pass a school-to-work transition bill authorizing a five-year, $300-million-a-year program to help underwrite model programs around the country in places such as Wisconsin and Boston.[25] Labor Secretary Robert Reich has relentlessly pressed the nation's economic, as well as social, need to provide more modern and sophisticated education and training—work and schooling combined—in the final two years of high school and two years of technical or community college, for masses of American young people. For America to compete in the twenty-first century, Reich asserts, this is the level of training most jobs will require; otherwise the living standards of America's middle class are doomed to stagnate.

So far, however, the message has not really sunk in with most people or even with most educators and business leaders. "If you look at us in terms of our future, we're still not doing a good enough job of educating all of our children—we're losing too many of them," President Clinton asserts.[26]

The administration itself, constrained by budget problems, has put up only a minuscule fraction of the necessary expenditure. West German business has been spending $15 billion a year on a nationwide apprenticeship program for a population roughly one fourth the size of America's. So to match the German effort, America would need to spend about $60 billion a year on apprenticeships. By government estimates, American business spends $30 billion a year on training employees and another $30 billion on remedial education for high school graduates who do not have basic work skills.[27] Some business leaders argue that it would be smarter to spend the money up front, during the high school years in apprenticeship programs, rather than do remedial education later. But most businessmen see education as the job of the schools.

Other resistance comes from unions fearful that high school apprentices will take their members' jobs and undercut their wage scales. Teachers resent the intrusion of outsiders into their classroom domain, forcing higher standards and new curriculums. Parents worry that their children will be tracked away from the dream of college. Many businesses shy away from going beyond charitable support of education to committing significant funds to apprenticeships. Conservatives and libertarians, ideologically opposed to government programs, deride public education in America as beyond redemption.

The biggest obstacle to change is the public mind-set, according to reform-minded public officials such as Tom Kean, the former Republican governor of New Jersey. "The American public doesn't really understand what's going on in schools," Kean told me. "They don't recognize it's *their* child who isn't getting the kind of education which would enable him or her to earn the kind of living that they deserve. I don't think we've yet really energized ourselves to understand that this is a national priority. This is really a crisis."[28]

Wisconsin's experience underscores the hard reality that opening up new pathways for average kids requires not only the synergy of an effective partnership of business and education but new attitudes of mind among parents and students as well as business, political, and educational leaders. Making American young people more globally competitive demands greater respect for the often untapped potential of the vast numbers of average kids who will not finish four years of college.

"This is a revolution in what we're asking of education," asserts Anne Heald, executive director of the University of Maryland's Center for Learning and Competitiveness. "It's not just that we're suddenly doing it so badly. It's that what we did in the past just isn't good enough. . . . The United States was actually an international innovator in creating universal education. The challenge now is to have universal *quality* education, not just for the top few but for *everybody.*"[29]

PART THREE

Business

Matching Mind-Sets with the
Competition

As our exploration of educational systems suggests, global competition is much more than a battle among multinational companies. Different economic systems are testing one another, and thus also testing the cultural patterns, values, and priorities of the nations in which they have taken root.

For Americans, the irony is that when we celebrated the triumph of the West over Soviet communism, we felt vindicated—not only because America had prevailed over the crumbling Soviet state but because America's economic system, capitalism, had won. Or so Americans thought.

Yet, as we have seen, America found itself in the waning years of the Cold War engaged in a fierce new global competition with its old allies, Germany and Japan. From that competition, Americans learned that there is not just one kind of capitalism but several. Each reflects the history, the values, and the commercial culture of that country. And each form of capitalism derives special advantages from the way it operates.

In their schools and in companies such as Toyota and Sharp, the Japanese have made flexibility, teamwork, and long-term thinking their hallmarks. The Germans have focused heavily on quality and technical leadership, with their traditions of fine engineering and craftsmanship at companies such as Mercedes-Benz and with their nationwide system of youth apprenticeship training.

Even more profound differences among the German, Japanese, and American economic systems lie beneath these signposts. The world's three most powerful capitalist nations differ greatly in their approach to people, to economic power, to the bedrock priorities of business, and to the importance of partnership and collaboration in society. And these differences affect performance—especially over the long run.

The defining core of American capitalism, of course, is individualism: Every man for himself, competing against all comers. America enshrines the entrepreneur, the daring tycoon, the all-powerful CEO, and the American genius of individual creativity. America has been shaped by a tradition of personal freedom and by the open frontier, which bred an easy confidence and the conviction that the welfare of society was served by the pursuit of individual gain.

The driving focus of America's laissez-faire economics is profits. America's governing commercial priority is the calculus of the bottom line: the best price, the lowest cost, the most lucrative deal. The market rules, deciding the fate of companies and of individuals. For an American CEO, the highest goal is return on investment to shareholders, although, in the 1990s, people noticed that when companies such as RCA, GM, and IBM focused too much on immediate financial results, both their shareholders and their employees got hurt in the long run.

In Japanese and German capitalism, a different mind-set is at work: Profit is not the only—or always the most important—criterion of success. Long-term growth and market share are often more important goals, and so the Germans and Japanese have tempered the free play of the market for the sake of social harmony and long-term national economic interests. Each country has fashioned a more cooperative form of capitalism than that which prevails in America. Collaboration, partnerships, and even power sharing are distinctive traits of the economic mind-set in Germany and Japan. And both countries consider these characteristics to be crucially important competitive advantages.

The Germans and Japanese, for example, attach great importance to the workforce as a national asset—the mainspring of growth. And so each country makes great efforts to train and retrain workers steadily in good times and to protect them in bad times. Both German and Japanese companies periodically compromise bottom-line profits for the sake of their employees and of stable labor-management relations.

A German or a Japanese CEO, moreover, must think differently from an American CEO. He must think not just about return to shareholders, he must balance the interests of various constituencies that have a long-term stake in the survival and growth of the corporation—employees, management, customers, suppliers, and local communities, as well as owners. In Germany, for example, top management must share power not only with a corporation's major owners but with its employees.

In rethinking their ways of operating, America's innovators have drawn lessons from foreign experience. Ford Motor Company, for example, has powered a turnaround with a new partnership between management and workers. Magma Copper and the Saturn division of General Motors have gone further than Ford, effectively using German-style power sharing and comanagement. Motorola has mounted America's most successful commercial penetration of Japan—and it has done so by honing techniques and strategies learned from the Japanese, in order to beat them in their home market.

In the realm of corporate governance, the revolts of boards of directors at General Motors and elsewhere have begun to check the power of the American Imperial CEO and to bring the wisdom of experienced outsiders to bear on corporate strategy. Their actions have spawned a movement to reform the powers and functioning of corporate boards in America. Growing employee ownership of large corporations has brought some increased employee representation in the boardroom. And respected American thinkers contend that American capitalism would perform much better in the long run were it to incorporate more of the collaborative mind-set of German and Japanese capitalism.

It is these differences in economic culture—and to the experiments of America's innovators—that we now explore.

8

People
Protecting and Developing Human Capital

Japan:
You must have the trust of the employees. This is our most important policy—to maintain the workforce and keep them happy. That's why we ensure them a job and pay. In the short run, this may not be profitable, but in the long run, this is profitable.[1]

—KOREMASA ANAMI, PERSONNEL DIRECTOR, NIPPON STEEL

Germany:
I am top manager, but I have special connection to the labor side—from my heart and from my function. I must think about the worker.... I know what a worker feels if he loses his job.[2]

—WOLFGANG WENZEL, PERSONNEL CHIEF, VSG STEEL COMPANY

America:
[T]he transition to a new career . . . [is] not a painless process. . . . I think more of the responsibility falls to the individual in America.[3]

—TOM USHER, PRESIDENT, U.S. STEEL

Change is disruptive and often cruel. In the harsh competitive environment of the 1990s, the pressure to adapt is unrelenting. Companies shrink; new companies emerge. People are forced out of aging industries and into a furious scramble to find places in newer, more dynamic industries—or else they are left to languish, unemployed or poorly employed, for months and years.

Not only are individuals' lives affected, but so is the whole economy. For how an economic system shifts people from the old order to the new order not only affects the people involved, it has an impact on a nation's standard of living and its competitive strength over the long term. If the transition is smooth, both the individual and the nation are strengthened. But when that transition fails, the lost jobs, the lost skills, the lost people are a high price to pay.

The capitalist economies of America, Germany, and Japan handle the transition from old to new quite differently. In America, the employee is quite literally the shock absorber. The individual, whether blue collar or middle management, bears the brunt of the painful readjustment. Not every society operates that way. In Japan, the company is the shock absorber; the company bears the burden, shields the worker from sudden unemployment, and works out the transition. And in Germany, society and the company share the burden of change.

Each of these three countries proceeds from a different mind-set, a different view of the employee. In the American system, the employee is disposable—a cog in the industrial machine to be discarded when management decrees and left to fend for himself in the marketplace. In Japan, the worker is treated as indispensable and is therefore protected, in the company's conviction that people are long-term assets whose full value will be realized when good times return. And in Germany, the philosophy is similar to Japan's, except that society helps foot the bill when readjustments are massive, as has been the case in recent years.

Japan: The Commitment Between Companies and Workers

The Japanese are known worldwide for their "lifetime employment" system—a system that guarantees jobs for life for permanent employees at Japan's major corporations, or about 40 percent of the nation's workforce.[4]

During the 1992–94 recession, Japanese companies came under enormous pressure to cut costs and abandon this system. In fact, they made modest changes, but overall they preserved the system essentially intact—both because of social pressures and because companies such as Toyota, Toshiba, and Nippon Steel considered it a long-term advantage to maintain their commitment to their employees. Lifetime employment was too beneficial and too integral to their way of operating to be abandoned.

As a people, the Japanese attach supreme importance to relationships, not only to the ties and obligations within the family but to bonding and loyalty in the work world, between a company and its employees.

On April 1 every year, at the start of what the Japanese regard as the new year in government, school, and business, a ritual ceremony of induction takes place in almost every large corporation in Japan. At this ceremony for all new employees—workers, engineers, secretaries, future executives—there is a formal, public exchange of vows. The employees make a pledge of perpetual loyalty to the company, and the company promises lifetime employment to its new employees. The sense of mutual obligation and commitment is powerful.

The Japanese call this ritual "the wedding ceremony," and it symbolizes the special nature of worker-employer relations in Japan.

As the Toyota Production System indicates, Japanese companies look to their workforce for competitive advantage. They believe in people more than in machines. Japanese companies invest heavily in their human capital—in regular retraining of employees and in protecting their jobs—and the companies reap the dividends of employee commitment, worker initiatives, and proactive participation. The mutual commitment has a payoff for both sides.

Major corporations offer a cocoon of paternalism to encourage workers to be dependent. Younger employees, whether management or frontline workers, are provided company dormitories and company cafeterias, which they use for many years. All employees travel to and from work on company allowances. And they enjoy myriad benefits, from sports facilities to vacation retreats to health insurance and life insurance. Even midcareer managers live in subsidized company housing or get low-interest company loans to buy their homes.

The process of personal bonding on the job is all-embracing. Many companies start the day with group exercises. Work teams take weekend trips together to cherry blossom festivals, historic monuments, or religious shrines. Getting together after work is another regular ritual, which often occurs several nights a week. People leave work together; to leave early, before everyone is finished, is frowned upon. Almost every supervisor, down to the team leader on the factory floor, gets a company entertainment allowance to take coworkers out after work for noodle soup, a plate of rice curry, a few beers, and sometimes an evening of *karaoke*—singing along with popular video recordings. Japanese bosses take an interest in their subordinates' private lives. Companies guide employees to suitable marriage mates, preferably within the corporate family.

In fact, the foundation of the employer-worker relationship in Japan is not a legalistic union contract or the financial bottom line; rather, it is a web of tightly woven relationships, feelings of closeness and trust, and, above all, mutual dependence, or what the Japanese call *amae*. It is similar, some say, to the feelings of dependence that a Japanese mother encourages in a child, as a means of control.[5]

To most Japanese, the company is more than an employer and a job. The company is a wellspring of personal identity. Working for an important Japanese company is a source of social status. Ask a Japanese about his work, and he will respond not by giving his employer's name but by invoking his team identity: "I am a Toyota man" or "I am a Mitsubishi man" or "I am a Nippon Steel man."

"The major principle of the Japanese corporation is what is called *employee sovereignty*—the company belongs to the employees, not to the shareholders," explains Eisuke Sakakibara, a senior official in the Ministry of Finance. "The level of participation in a Japanese corporation is much bigger than the level of participation of a typical employee in a U.S. company. . . . So you naturally become more loyal. You naturally think of the company's interests."[6]

Loyalty flows downward as well as upward. Employees, especially white-collar salarymen, sacrifice their private lives for their companies. They put in long overtime hours or pass up part of their vacation time, often without pay or receiving much less money than they deserve. And they expect the same loyalty in return. When times are tough, they count on the company not to lay anyone off. Reciprocity is the heart of the relationship.

Most major Japanese companies believe the lifetime employment system benefits them greatly. That practice took root during Japan's rapid economic expansion from the 1950s into the late 1970s. After World War II, Japanese companies faced chronic labor shortages. By promising lifetime employment, they were able to recruit and hold a good workforce. They retrained their workers constantly, to keep them abreast of the latest technology. Having made that investment, Japanese managers did not want to lose highly qualified workers to rivals. So, in bottom-line terms, it suited Japan's leading corporations to adopt a common code: lifetime employment within the corporate family.

Nippon Steel: The Company Benefits from Giving Job Security

The real test of any family comes when times are tough. The steel industries in Japan, Germany, and America, for example, have all hit hard times. All have been shaken by global overcapacity. New rivals have emerged (Korea, China, Nigeria) as the world demand for steel has been flattening.

Nippon Steel Corporation, the giant of Japanese steel companies, has felt the shrinkage: output and employment have fallen almost steadily from a peak in 1974, though in 1993 Nippon Steel was still number one in the world in output of crude steel—well over twice that of U.S. Steel.[7]

As it shrank, Nippon Steel went to great lengths to avoid outright layoffs and maintain its social compact of lifetime employment—even to the point of opening up satellite businesses as new "homes" for its employees.

Nippon Steel's philosophy is typical of Japanese management. It has operated from the premise that being globally competitive depends, above all, on stable labor-management relations, as Koremasa Anami, Nippon Steel's managing director for personnel, asserted. To get the most from its employees, Nippon Steel had to commit to their job security. "You must have the trust of the employees," said Anami. "This is our most important policy—to maintain the workforce and keep them happy. That's why we ensure them a job and pay. In the short run, this may not be profitable, but in the long run, this is profitable. With this kind of employment policy, we attract good people, and we train and retain them."[8]

According to Anami, Nippon Steel has benefited financially from harmonious relations with unions—it has avoided costly strikes and wildcat stoppages. Moreover, in bad times, the steel union has made concessions that helped the company make ends meet. Etsuya Washio, president of the Japanese Federation of Steelworkers' Unions, reported how in 1987 he had persuaded the union not only to forgo its normal annual demands for wage increases but to accept cuts in fringe benefits for workers' families, in profit sharing, and in the regular annual pay bonus. It was worth sacrificing to ensure the survival and recovery of Nippon Steel, Washio declared.[9]

The executives at Nippon Steel's Yawata Works, its oldest facility, located on Kyushu Island about seven hundred miles southwest of Tokyo, told me in detail about the payoff to the company from its commitment to job security for employees. Worker morale and efficiency were high, they said, and workers continuously helped management with quality improvements and efficiency measures. Every year Yawata Works saved about $80 million from the cumulative effect of efficiency measures suggested by employees, according to Deputy Superintendent Toshihiro Okuyama. The employees would never have made these suggestions without guaranteed job security, he said. Otherwise they would have feared that their cost-saving ideas would lose them their jobs.[10]

Moreover, he said, if the company wanted to maintain loyalty and high performance among younger workers, it had to treat older workers properly. As workers became too old to do heavy work or learn new technologies, Yawata Works eased them into lighter jobs, rather than suddenly dropping them. This gave younger workers confidence in their own futures, free from the nightmare of a sudden layoff.[11]

Yawata Works had been hard hit by the shrinkage in the Japanese steel industry. Its output in 1993 was just one half of its peak level in 1969, and its workforce had been cut back by 75 percent (9,800 employees, down from 44,000), yet Yawata Works had avoided firing anyone outright and had even hired some younger workers. Over thirty years, the main way of reducing the workforce had been normal attrition—about 20,000 people had reached retirement age or retired early, and another 5,700 had quit and gone back to the family farm. Some had had to quit because of injuries or disabilities, prodded into resigning by the company, but those numbers had been small, the company said.

Yawata Works had gone out of its way to protect the jobs of many more—10,000 had been transferred to other, more modern plants operated by Nippon Steel elsewhere in Japan; about 3,000 steelworkers had been retrained and shifted to jobs at Yawata Works as bus drivers, warehouse men, or mechanics and service workers, according to Nobuyuki Abe, Yawata's personnel manager.

But the most inventive way that Yawata Works had avoided layoffs, Abe said, was by starting up new subsidiaries and assigning lifetime employees to these new firms. It had, for example, spun off separate enterprises in engineering, chemicals, computer services, transportation, and warehousing, and had even opened a supermar-

ket. In May 1993, some 2,600 former Yawata managers, office employees, and frontline laborers were working at these ventures, just in
the local region—and Nippon Steel had this program going on nationwide. For all these people, remaining within the Nippon Steel family
was vital. The Nippon Steel connection was not only a matter of pride
and honor for them, it also meant that their wage levels were guaranteed at Nippon Steel levels, even if the satellite companies paid less to
other employees hired off the job market. For Yawata Works this was
a substantial commitment; it was spending about $70 million a year in
such wage subsidies and for worker retraining.[12]

One successful subsidiary was an amusement park called Space
World. Nippon Steel had built the public theme park near Yawata's
first steel mill. In fact, the rusting hulk of the original 1901 blast fur-
nace looms behind the park's modernistic, two-hundred-foot model of
the U.S. space shuttle *Discovery*. In the first two years after it opened
in April 1990, Space World attracted 3.6 million visitors.[13]

Among Space World's 350 employees, 150 had come from Yawata
Works. One was Masaru Hirayama, a trim, soft-spoken thirty-eight-
year-old who had worked for twenty years in steel casting and forging.
Hirayama had been sent for two weeks of training at Redstone Arse-
nal in Huntsville, Alabama, and had come home to be an instructor at
the theme park's "space camp," a large, modernistic training center
equipped with mock shuttle cabins, communications systems, moon
walks, and other simulators for astronaut training and space missions.
Every week, busloads of junior high school students rolled in, full of
excitement, for three-day courses; high school students got six days.
Space camp was a hit with them.

For Hirayama, who had become a junior manager, shifting to
Space World was a good career break. He had lost his steelworker's
hazard pay bonus, but, with overtime at Space World, he was about
even financially. And though he had always wanted to be a steelworker, Hirayama felt that Nippon Steel had kept faith with its promise of lifetime employment. In fact, he liked his new job with Space
World so much that he said if he were offered a chance to go back to
the steel plant, he would not take it.

"I think I have a better future here," Hirayama explained. "I think
Nippon Steel has treated its employees quite fairly, because we all
know that the demand for steel has been declining. Imports are developing from countries like Taiwan and Korea, and on top of that, we

have faced quite a drastic appreciation of the yen. So we know that Nippon Steel cannot rely on steel production alone for future expansion. So it's good that the company tries to give employees more opportunities by providing different jobs."[14]

In a Crunch, Employees Come Ahead of Stockholders

In January 1993, Japan felt the first shiver of fear that the lifetime employment system might unravel under the pressures of a steep recession. Pioneer Electronic Corporation ordered thirty-five middle managers in their fifties to resign and accept the company's early retirement bonus or else to face dismissal. Shock ran through the company. Pioneer's actions provoked popular indignation. The company's reputation was sullied and worker morale plummeted, according to the Japanese press. Several managers refused to resign, and the company backed down from its threat to fire them.[15]

Natsuomi Wakamura, a general manager at Nippon Steel, explained why. "This is a shame society," he said. "You do not act alone. You cannot escape family ties and obligations. You must always think about not bringing disgrace on your family." The company is a family, and in that family, parents (bosses), as well as children (workers), should not behave shamefully.[16]

Nonetheless, the lifetime employment system has been fraying at the edges, especially among white-collar workers and middle management, where there has been great inefficiency. There were some outright dismissals in the securities industry; with its boom-or-bust mentality, it operated by a different code from that of Japanese manufacturing firms. Those firings, along with the Pioneer episode, kindled open debate about the need for *risutora*—restructuring—by major corporations. With demand, profits, and productivity plunging, many Japanese businesses had to wrestle with the burden of excess white-collar staffs.

There was a lot of talk, but only modest action: Some companies lowered the normal retirement age from sixty to fifty-five; others offered generous terms of separation to employees—especially managers—over fifty; still others, such as Toshiba, stopped paying what had long been automatic annual pay increases for older employees who were unproductive.[17] Other firms resorted to *kata tataki,* "the tap on the shoulder." That is the practice of a boss prodding older, unpro-

ductive employees to retire early and, if they do not take the hint, stepping up the pressure by assigning them to "window seats"—desks off
by a window, without real duties.

The restructuring bug spread during 1993 and 1994. Companies
such as Nissan Motors, Japan Airlines, Nippon Telephone and Telegraph, and Toshiba announced they would each be shedding several
thousand employees. But the ethics of Japan's commercial culture
would allow only gradual change; the cutbacks would be phased in
over several years, so that, in fact, no outright layoffs were likely. All
the cuts could come from attrition and early retirement.[18]

From afar, this looked like the "downsizing" that swept through
corporate America in the early 1990s. But there was a crucial difference, illustrated by Nippon Steel's announcement in October 1993 of
plans for a three-year reduction of 7,000 employees. In the future, the
company said, it would hire more "temporary" employees in times of
expansion, people it could lay off during recessions. But Nippon Steel
President Takashi Imai stressed that no one would be fired and that all
"promises will be kept" to existing employees—even to the 7,000 people whose jobs were going to be eliminated. Those people would not
be fired, Imai asserted; they would be kept at guaranteed pay levels
and transferred to Nippon Steel's two hundred subsidiaries, which
were growing rapidly and which accounted for about one third of Nippon Steel's business.[19]

In fact, the bottom line was that Nippon Steel, with an annual loss
of 19 billion yen ($179 million) in 1993–94, preferred to cut its dividend
to shareholders in half, in order to avoid layoffs.[20]

Nor was it unusual for Japanese management to put employee interests ahead of the interests of shareholders. Japanese unemployment
reached 3 percent in July 1994, its highest level in seven years,[21] and
yet, by several estimates, Japanese companies were still carrying from
1 million to 3 million excess employees on their payrolls—testimony
to their continued commitment to lifetime employment in spite of
their financial losses.[22] In fact, a survey by the Japan Productivity Institute in 1993 found that nearly 90 percent of Japanese managers
planned to continue lifetime job security, with no more than minor
modifications.[23]

When American executives or economists extol the benefits of staff
cuts, the Japanese ask, "But how do you motivate the employees you
keep to do their best, if they see people all around them losing their
jobs?"[24]

Japanese managers have their eye on the longer term. They are worried that firing people will hurt morale and backfire against a company's efficiency. Another deterrent is management's fear that any company that jettisons lifetime employment will get a bad reputation and will then have trouble hiring good new employees once the economy recovers.

"Some industries in Japan, other than the steel industry, have laid off employees several times," observed Nobuyuki Abe, personnel manager at Yawata Works. "When they later tried to recruit new employees, no one wanted to work for them. If we once lay off our workers, then the company will get a bad reputation, and it will affect our recruiting effort negatively."[25]

Finally, Japanese managers are influenced by the core values of Japanese society, especially the commitment to long-term relationships. As Yoshihisa Hayashi, a documentary producer, put it, "If you fire somebody outright, you are not respected in Japan. Even tiny little companies try not to fire people. This comes from the idea of loyalty. Loyalty from employees should be answered by loyalty from employers—and loyalty is forever."[26]

The American Formula—Getting Lean and Mean at U.S. Steel

In America, U.S. Steel was hit by the same market crunch as Nippon Steel, and it adopted radically different tactics. In the managerial lingo of the 1990s, the company long known as Big Steel made itself lean and mean.

In volume, U.S. Steel surrendered its position as the world's biggest steel company to Nippon Steel. Rather than trimming output gradually and arranging a smooth transition to new businesses, U.S. Steel ruthlessly slashed its overcapacity and modernized a few selected plants, content to shrink its market share for the sake of profits.

In one decade, from 1983 to 1993, U.S. Steel cut its output from 31 million to 12 million tons a year. It shut down plant after plant, including the hot mills at the Fairless Works near Levittown, Pennsylvania, once a model of American production. Overall, U.S. Steel shrank its payroll from 90,000 to 18,000 employees.

With expensive new automation and a workforce cut to the bone, U.S. Steel made quantum leaps forward, according to President Tom Usher. In the mid-1990s, the company turns out a ton of steel in 3½ man-hours versus 11 man-hours a decade earlier. It is delivering a much higher quality product more efficiently than ever, using technology that matches the best in the world.

To make his point, Usher took me around the Edgar Thompson Works outside Pittsburgh, where U.S. Steel had invested $250 million in a new, automated continuous casting process that went into operation in 1992. With its computerized hot rolling mills, this plant is world standard, Usher said: "The product coming out of this plant is as good as any in Germany, any in Japan, any in Korea, any in the United States."[27]

Huge sections of the Edgar Thompson mill are operated by three or four workers in control rooms filled with closed-circuit TV monitors and computers. Workers are rarely visible on the shop floor. At one point, I asked Usher how many people worked around the clock in one shed which was as large as an urban railway station.

"On a typical crew like this, you'd probably see thirty workers," he replied.

"Instead of how many before?" I asked, meaning before automation.

"Several hundred," he said.

Usher volunteered that it was management failures that had gotten U.S. Steel into trouble. In the 1950s, he said, the top brass had not only misjudged the demand for steel, it had also missed the boat on new technology. While the Europeans and Japanese were installing "basic oxygen" technology, invented in Austria in 1952, American steel mills had stuck with the old "open-hearth" blast furnaces.

"It was only after twenty years of falling behind" that U.S. Steel woke up, Usher admitted. "If this had been recognized earlier, if they had moved quicker, the kind of transformation that took place in the eighties probably would have been done a lot easier and a lot less painfully."

In short, tens of thousands of workers had been laid off because management had bet on the wrong technology. I asked Usher whether U.S. Steel's managers had ever considered a Nippon Steel–style strategy of spinning off subsidiaries and assigning steelworkers to these new ventures, instead of laying off 72,000 people?

Usher's answer reflected the American mind-set. "I guess the concept of keeping them within the corporate family by attempting to spawn other business and so forth, I don't think we have," Usher said. "I don't think most American industries have taken that tack."

Management's priority was the return to shareholders and lifting U.S. Steel's stock price. And so, to cushion its shareholders against the cyclical ups and downs of the steel business, U.S. Steel spent $6 billion in 1982 to buy Marathon Oil, becoming USX in the process.

The United Steelworkers union protested that management should have put that $6 billion into modernizing more steel plants, instead of siphoning off its savings from the steel business to buy an oil company. Usher disagreed. It would have been smart to reinvest in steel, he said, only if steel could turn a profit. The huge Fairless Works near Levittown was an example. To modernize Fairless, Usher said, "you're looking at a bill that would probably run two billion dollars— an investment that no bank would look at and say it made any sense."

But did U.S. Steel's management feel a commitment to the tens of thousands of workers it had laid off?

"We certainly have an obligation to try and get those people on their feet—we don't just want to come in over the loudspeaker and announce, 'Have your desk clean and be out by noon,'" Usher replied. "I think [businesses] try to make the transition to a new career as painless as possible, but it's not a painless process. It's a difficult process. I think more of the responsibility falls to the individual in America."

An American Classic: Tim Reeves and "McJobs"

Tim Reeves was one of those individuals. He epitomizes the American middle class: clean cut, intelligent, a reliable worker, a family man. Yet just before Christmas 1992, when I met Tim Reeves, he was out of work. Along with a stream of other men, Reeves had come to Steelworkers Local 4889 in Fairless Hills, Pennsylvania, to pick up a free Christmas turkey and some canned goods for his family. He and the others were among 2,400 steelworkers laid off by U.S. Steel's Fairless Works in January 1991.

In nearly two years, Tim Reeves still hadn't found a job. His unemployment benefits had run out once already, and the extended unemployment pay voted by Congress in August 1992 would expire in six weeks. Tim was having trouble keeping food on the table and making his mortgage payments. Medical costs were a nightmare worry because he no longer had health insurance.

Like the Japanese steelworker Masaru Hirayama, Tim Reeves had gone into the steel mill right out of high school and had worked there nearly twenty years, eventually running an overhead crane. "In 1973, when I started there, it was, hey—this is the future," Reeves recalled. "But that's an eighteen-year-old thinking that, you know. Hey, the mill's going to be there forever, it's big, big business. . . . You start living the good life, and then all of a sudden, bang, you get hit with a layoff. It's devastating."[28]

At peak production, Fairless Works had 10,000 employees, but, starting in the mid-1970s, the layoffs came in waves.[29] By the 1990s, its grounds, massive enough to accommodate a dozen golf courses and equipped with its own railway, were a vast graveyard. The "hot mill," where steel is made, had gone dead. The only thing left operating was a cold-finishing plant with several hundred workers.

Of the 2,400 people laid off with Tim Reeves in early 1991, about one quarter had given up on finding a job and had taken retirement years ahead of time; another quarter had found some work, though usually at less than half their steel pay; and close to half were still out of work.[30] Social workers were helping these men and their families cope with their shattered lives—money problems, drinking, broken marriages, occasional violence, panic about the future, and the lost self-respect of middle-aged men who had always proudly supported their families and now suddenly felt like welfare cases.[31]

Some federal and state money was available for retraining workers, but, according to Joe Vandergrift, a former steelworker who had become a counselor at a center for displaced workers, there was not enough training money for all the laid-off workers. Worse, by the time additional funds were made available, many steelworkers could not afford to take retraining courses. Their unemployment benefits had run out, and they had to grab any temporary work that came along; that blocked them from serious retraining for a new trade, which could take several months and sometimes more than a year.[32]

Tim Reeves was among the lucky ones. Before Fairless Works was shut down, the company had sent him to Bucks County Community College for training in computer installation and repair. That had helped him get a government retraining grant—but not a job. Scouring the want ads in a typical Sunday paper in late 1992, Reeves would find only two or three job openings for a computer technician—and each time, there was a Catch-22.

"The worst two words I see in the want ads is 'Experience needed, two to three years,'" he protested. "That's the killer. I'll be thirty-eight next Saturday. Confidence is just about shot. Right now, I'm in separation from my wife after twenty years, and I'm sure that not having a job for two years has really played into it. . . . You're always looking for that light at the end of the tunnel. Right now, it's black."[33]

Eight months later, in July 1993, Tim Reeves's fortunes had improved. He had completed his junior college course, and he was fully qualified as a computer installer and technician. He still had found no work in that field, but he did have a job—doing clerical work on the night shift in the computer center at the community college where he had been studying. "Just to have a job again is wonderful," Reeves said with a smile.

The bad news was that he and his wife had divorced. To save money, Tim and his younger son had moved into the small home of Tim's elderly parents. On what Tim earned, he could not afford to pay for his own apartment and still cover his family obligations. Working the night shift meant missing his son's baseball games. But what really troubled Tim was his salary and the lack of future potential in his job.

"You always want to make the money that you made before," Reeves said. "I mean, the last three years I worked for U.S. Steel I made over $40,000 [a year]. Now I'm earning roughly a third of that. It's like starting over again. I'm not going to be able to go the rest of my life living at this salary. I'm never going to be able to afford to live in a home and have the things that I want. I've got to face the reality of the situation."[34]

Tim Reeves's story has become a modern American classic, not just for blue-collar workers but for middle managers, engineers, clerical workers, professionals with Ph.D.s, all hit by the "downsizing" strategy of American business.

The upturn in the economy in 1993 and 1994 rescued Tim and 6 million other Americans from the black hole of joblessness. In early 1994, Fairless Works hired back 150 to 200 workers, though no one knew whether these jobs would prove to be only temporary.[35] Across America, newspapers blossomed with stories about laid-off autoworkers, machinists, and construction workers who had finally landed jobs after long idleness. And the plot lines were remarkably similar: These people had signed on as cashiers or assistant managers at fast-food restaurants, sales clerks at discount stores, office workers in the service industry—for half their old pay or less. Among the 2,400 steelworkers laid off with Tim Reeves, retraining had not been much help—two thirds had not found work in their new fields. By 1994, only half had found full-time work. Fully one third were still out of work, and the rest were part-time workers. Among those who had jobs, the average pay was less than $17,000 a year, far below what it had been at U.S. Steel.[36]

"McJobs" was the put-down term used by these Americans to describe their new employment. Often it took two or three "McJobs" to equal the take-home pay from one old industrial job, and "McJobs" were legion. Temporary and part-time work reached record levels in 1994: More than one fifth of the nation's workforce—24.4 million Americans—had only part-time or temporary work.[37] Despite recovery, the number of manufacturing jobs fell by more than 8 percent from 1989 to 1994.[38]

Wal-Mart had become the nation's second largest employer after General Motors. Construction, mining, and manufacturing, where wages averaged from $530 to $630 a week, were shrinking, while service and retail businesses, where the pay averaged from $200 to $370 a week, were growing.[39] The Bureau of Labor Statistics reported in 1994 that, over the past decade, the average wage in America had fallen 5 percent, adjusted for inflation.[40]

This was the other side of the coin of record productivity that Tom Usher was reporting at U.S. Steel. In fact, in the last quarter of 1993, the U.S. Labor Department reported, the most impressive productivity gains—7.5 percent—came in heavy industry (automobiles, heavy machinery, durable goods, and steel); yet simultaneously the average hourly compensation of workers in those industries *fell* slightly.[41]

In short, stockholders were doing well, but workers were struggling—the opposite of the course taken in Japan.

Germany: The Company Must Have a "Social Plan" for Laid-Off Workers

With the huge burden of reuniting its eastern regions with the western part of the country, Germany was hit much harder by recession in 1992–94 than Japan was. As America recovered, Germany sank. At its worst, unemployment rose to nearly 9 percent in western Germany and nearly 18 percent in the east in early 1994, though by autumn those figures had fallen considerably, to 7.9 percent in the west and 13.8 percent in the east as the German economy recovered.[42] With its generous unemployment benefits, Germany was not only taking care of west German workers but pouring $100 billion a year into revitalizing the east.

In a shrinking industry like steel, what is distinctive about the German approach is how the burden of readjustment is shared. Any company that wants to cut back its workforce must come up with a *Sozialplan,* or social plan, to protect the workers' needs as the company downsizes. By law, the company has a responsibility to show how displaced workers will be cared for; it cannot simply fire people and walk away.

Because the shrinking of a major industry, such as steel, has such a wide social impact, restructuring is not solely management's affair. Many parties get involved—management, labor, regional chambers of commerce, and state and local governments. There must be agreement among management, unions, and state governments on the specific terms; they work together to ensure "social harmony."

In the 1990s, Germans are still haunted by the fear that explosive social conditions, brought on by mass unemployment, inflation, and recession, could trigger political extremism. They remember that Adolf Hitler rose to power in just such economic conditions, and so they are taking extreme precautions against letting that happen again.

The steel and coal industries are subject to special protections, partly because these industries have long been central to the German economy, partly because the links between German steel barons and the Nazis left Germans inclined to curb the power of steel-mill owners after the war. In 1951, Germany enacted laws that gave unions as well as owners and management a voice in how major companies operate, especially on issues such as workforce reductions.[43] The Germans temper the profit motive with a strong dose of "social responsibility" on the part of management—companies accept that both society and workers have a legitimate interest in how business operates.

By the mid-1990s, German steel companies were in such trouble that all sides recognized the need to retrench. Since the heydays of the 1950s and early 1960s, steelmakers such as Krupp, Thyssen, and Hoesch had already gone through several contractions. Still, German steel had too much capacity. With the highest-paid industrial workforce in the world,[44] German companies were being undercut by lower-cost competitors in Spain and eastern Europe as well as in Korea and China.

As the recession deepened in 1993, German steel company managers were pressing for workforce cutbacks. Tensions were rising. Steelworkers in the *Ruhrgebiet,* the industrial region stretching northward from Düsseldorf toward Holland and Hamburg, were marching in the streets to protect their jobs.

The state government of North Rhine–Westphalia, which governs the Ruhr area, feared the social repercussions of sudden, drastic cutbacks. And so it launched a major industrial reconstruction program —*Strukturpolitik*—to cushion the shock. The state government granted loans to new industries; it joined with businesses to set up technology transfer centers; it employed steelworkers to clean up old industrial sites; it prepared industrial parks to attract new industry; and it helped midwife the sale of dying coal and steel equipment factories to new environmental businesses, trying in every way to avoid shutdowns.

The steel companies also worked to ease the pain and disruption. In their "social plans," the companies joined with the state government and the steelworkers' union, IG Metall, to help steelworkers make a transition to new jobs and new specialities.

In early 1993, I saw this process at work at VSG Steel Company, a joint venture of three steel giants, Krupp, Thyssen, and Klöckner-Humboldt-Deutz. VSG was located in Hattingen, a Ruhr town where Thyssen had shut down a plant a few years earlier. Over fifteen years, VSG had trimmed about 60 percent of its workforce, either by attrition or by offering attractive "golden handshakes," as the Germans call their early retirement packages. As a result of these cutbacks, VSG Steel was already committed to spending DM 100 million (about $65 million) over the next five years, and the state would spend twice that amount.

By January 1993, VSG wanted to cut 550 of its 3,000 remaining workers. Wolfgang Wenzel, VSG Steel's personnel director, worked out retirement packages for about 300 workers, but he did not know what to do for 250 younger workers. For help, Wenzel took his problem to the personnel directors of the three parent steel companies, officials of IG Metall, the regional chamber of commerce, and the head of the state's employment agency.

"You can't just throw out people who have worked there for so many years," Wenzel asserted.[45]

Krupp, one of the parent firms, agreed to take a few workers on transfer. The state employment agency sought environmental cleanup jobs for a few others. But the main avenue for workers in their twenties, thirties, and forties was retraining in new career fields.

Germans approach the retraining of displaced workers with a different mind-set from that of Americans. Retraining in Germany is a collaborative effort, in which the old employer takes on a major responsibility. As part of its *Sozialplan,* VSG Steel had to set up a training center on its premises, buy all the necessary equipment, and arrange the courses. Displaced clerical workers were retrained in computers and software-related services, or in sales and marketing. Steelworkers got technical training in new fields—some, for example, as electricians and electronics specialists, two shortage trades in Germany.

Among that group was Uwe May, a thirty-six-year-old steelworker who had been with VSG for fifteen years. Like Tim Reeves, May was a crane operator. When VSG told him, in early 1993, that it no longer needed him, May said, "I felt trapped—I had never worked anywhere else, and so I felt I had no options." He leapt at the chance to take the two-year retraining course to become an electrician.[46]

Unlike the U.S. steelworkers at Fairless Works, May did not have to worry about making financial ends meet. The state and the company took care of him. During his two-year training program, VSG paid about half of May's salary, and the state paid the rest. IG Metall provided instructors and some funds for the course. VSG's big savings would come only in spring 1995, after the retrained workers had finished their course and moved off its payroll into new jobs.[47]

Uwe May had found the retraining difficult at first. "Imagine, for fifteen years nothing changes—and then, with the retraining, you realize you're still capable of learning," he said. "It's hard in the beginning, but once you're on the way, you get momentum." By mid-1994, other workers, who had taken shorter retraining courses, had gotten jobs; VSG, its situation improved, took some of them back. By November 1994, as May's course neared its conclusion, he felt he had gained both the skills and the flexibility he needed. "I'm sure I can find work," he said confidently. "It would be great to be part of something that's new, something that's just starting up, while I'm starting over again. We could grow up together."[48]

In this program, a typical German effort, all parties had come together to protect what Germans see as their most valuable competitive asset—their highly skilled workforce. In all, there are about a hundred such retraining centers in North Rhine–Westphalia, with the state government providing oversight as well as some funds to protect the displaced workers.

"Our money saves the companies money, but we don't do it for the sake of the companies, we do it for the people," explained Peter Harmel, an official in the state's economic development agency. "For us, the key is to keep the workers from becoming unemployed. They're harder to reemploy once they've been unemployed."[49]

In addition, the commitment of VSG Personnel Director Wenzel to ensure a future prospect for every single worker was in marked contrast to the attitudes of American management. "I don't want to say to people, 'I have no work, you must go,' " Wenzel declared, in his clipped, choppy English. "I am top manager, but I have special connection to the labor side—from my heart and from my function. I must think about the worker. I am responsible, and this responsibility does not come from the law alone. It comes from my heart and from my personal history. My father was a miner. And I know what a worker feels if he loses his job."[50]

I asked Wenzel which he put first—the profits of the company or the jobs of the workers?

"There must be an equal balance," Wenzel replied. It was his job to see that things were fair. "I must balance."

That's the German way.

As Steel Goes, So Goes the Nation

To a surprising degree, as steel goes, so goes much of the nation. The trends in the steel industry, while extreme, reflect wider economic patterns in Japan, Germany, and America. Caught in a sharp decline, the steel industries of the three countries have responded differently—and the differences reflect the contrasting values, priorities, and corporate ethics of each country.

In America, the market decides. Companies rise and fall, their fates riding solely on the bottom line. Management calls the shots to serve its own interests and those of shareholders. Millions of workers have found that they're expendable.

By contrast, in Germany and Japan, the market is not totally to be trusted. The power of management is limited—by custom in Japan, by law in Germany. For Nippon Steel or VSG, maximizing profits is not the only yardstick of success. The social ethic in both countries, plus strong unions in Germany, deters the kind of slash-and-burn cost cutting and downsizing that are common to American industry in good times as well as bad.

In Japan and Germany, shareholders have to accept lower returns in troubled times so that workers can be better protected, in order that all sides can benefit when the upturn in the economy comes. Those two societies and their corporate managers place a high value on social harmony, on long-term commitments, and on protecting people.

In competitive terms, German and Japanese corporations see job security as essential to job performance—to higher quality, productivity, and growth.

9

Partnership

The Turnaround at Ford—"We-We" Instead of "Us Versus Them"

Ford had a very top-down management system, with orders from on high, like an Army command system. We had to break that mentality.[1]

—DON PETERSEN, FORMER CEO, FORD MOTOR COMPANY

Years ago, we couldn't talk to our supervisors, let alone the plant manager. We were nobody, just guys throwing seats in cars. Now they listen to us. Now they correct the problems we tell them about.[2]

—BOB RUTOVIC, WORKER, FORD PLANT, SOUTH CHICAGO

I don't build the cars, the people here build the cars. I set the goals. I set the standards. But there's no one individual or no one culture—management or union—that builds this car. We build it together.[3]

—REG ANSON, MANAGER, FORD PLANT, SOUTH CHICAGO

When the tidal wave of Japanese competition hit Ford Motor Company in 1980, Ford's response was radically different from the reflex at General Motors—and in that difference lies the secret of Ford's much faster recovery.

Instead of betting on technology, Ford put its faith in people. Instead of distrusting its workforce, as Roger Smith did at GM, Ford's top executives gambled the fate of the company on putting new trust in its frontline workers.

Ford's top leadership concluded that the company's management echelons—not the workforce—was the main source of the company's problems and then set out to transform management's mind-set and culture.

Finally, Ford saw Toyota as a model to be learned from. Top people at Ford studied Toyota's flexible production system and then tried to apply its lessons at Ford. In fact, Ford's leadership turned to W. Edwards Deming, the American management guru who had coached the Japanese on the principles of good management and quality production, and Deming helped them launch a cultural revolution at Ford.

Red Ink: Catalyst for a New Managerial Mind-Set at Ford

What is most dramatic about Ford's turnaround is the sense of partnership generated between management and the rank-and-file workforce—the ways management found to tap the minds of workers for their suggestions for improving efficiency and quality and thus for putting Ford back onto a competitive path. But before Ford could energize its workforce, Ford's management first had to transform its own thinking.

Paradoxically, Ford was blessed by corporate poverty. It was strapped for cash. It could not afford the expensive decade-long technology drive decreed at General Motors by Roger Smith.

In the early 1980s, Ford's new leadership was in a state of shock at the deep inroads that had been made by Japanese carmakers. In two years, 1980 and 1981, Ford lost $2.5 billion. It was drowning in red ink, and its share of the American car market was skidding badly. Just to keep afloat, top management began throwing all excess baggage overboard. Production was cut back by 500,000 cars in one year; roughly 150,000 employees were laid off in 1980. In sheer panic, Ford battled to survive.

"When we first looked at the books, we couldn't believe how bad the situation was," recalled Don Petersen, who became president of Ford in 1980. "We weren't sure Ford could make it. The Japanese were delivering a better-quality car than we were—at a lower cost— and they could sustain that production at those lower costs for years."[4]

The loss of American consumer confidence in Ford cars was what most stunned Harold A. "Red" Poling, chief of Ford's North American Division. "The perception of the American public," said Poling, "was that we couldn't produce cars to match the Japanese quality—and unless we could change that perception, there was no future for any of us."[5]

The initial reflexes at Ford were to do anything to save money—cut production, close plants, slash the workforce. With American car buyers clamoring for fuel-efficient cars, Ford brought out the small, high-mileage Ford Escort. Then it gambled heavily on developing a new look, investing $3 billion in developing what years later became the successful Ford Taurus and Mercury Sable.

The first steps, however, were stopgap measures. Ford's leadership—Petersen, Poling, and Chairman Philip Caldwell—understood that. They understood that a more fundamental transformation was imperative. But they didn't know what to do.

As Don Petersen was casting about for new ideas and turning to outside consultants, a pivotal moment came when he saw a movie entitled *If the Japanese Can, Why Can't We?* That movie heavily quoted W. Edwards Deming, the management and quality expert.[6]

Up to that point, Deming had been a prophet without honor in his own country. He had been largely ignored by major American corporations even though he had found eager students abroad. His principles of management and quality production had instructed and inspired Japanese industry during its remarkable postwar buildup and its new challenge to American industry.[7]

At the core of Deming's management philosophy were a few simple principles: (1) Focus on long-term objectives, not on short-term profits; (2) Pursue quality as the primary objective, and let quality drive all other elements of corporate performance; (3) Get top and middle managers to surrender large portions of their power and push responsibility down to lower levels; (4) Make people the heart of the operation and tap the talents and energies of every single employee, especially frontline workers; (5) Create genuine collaboration and teamwork between management and labor.

Deming was eighty-one by the time Don Petersen invited him to help Ford in 1981. He had the solid, trustworthy, grandfatherly face of an old-fashioned doctor. But looks were deceiving. Deming could be stern and he took particular pleasure in lecturing CEOs, telling the top brass who had invited his diagnosis that they themselves were the heart of their company's problems.[8]

"We are in a new economic age, created by Japan," Deming liked to say. "Deadly diseases afflict the style of American management."[9]

At Ford, Deming took aim at the corporate mind-set. He prescribed a wholesale transformation of the mentality of Ford's management. He mocked those who blamed the company's problems on its workforce.

"Pleasant dreams," Deming wryly commented. "The workers are handicapped by the system, and the system belongs to management."

In Deming's bible, command-style management was a cardinal sin, and so was using fear as motivation—fear of job loss, fear of punishment, fear of a bad personal evaluation. "Drive out fear," advised Deming, "so that everyone may work effectively for the company."[10]

Initially, Deming's presentations did not go over well with many executives at Ford. Egos were bruised by his blunt, frontal attack on the corporate mentality. Some people had expected him to offer quick fixes, but his prescription would obviously take time to follow, and it would be hard to do.

Quite a few Ford executives brushed off Deming's advice, but Don Petersen took it to heart. "The most important thing I learned was to trust people, to believe in people, to use the human factor, especially the hourly worker," Petersen commented.

Petersen was rethinking the conventional wisdom of American management; with Deming's prodding, he was turning the managerial philosophy of mass production on its head. He was rejecting the dictum of Frederick Winslow Taylor, the time-and-motion management expert, whose theories and teachings had been dogma to American management for several decades. Taylorism is aimed at perfect efficiency; its premise is that there is a precise and perfect way for a worker to operate a machine. Taylorism seeks to eliminate every minute deviation from that perfect operation.

Petersen's views of Taylorism changed 180 degrees. In his words, he came to regard Taylor as "probably the most damaging person" for American corporate managers, because Taylor had preached a mechanistic mind-set—a mind-set that gave all power to management and production engineers and treated workers as mere extensions of machines.

"I came to see that the worker was often limited by the process [fixed by management] and could do nothing about it," Petersen said. "The process hemmed him in and forced him to do poor-quality work. Not only was the work bad, but it was demoralizing to the worker."[11]

"We had been treating our blue-collar workforce as a commodity," echoed Ernie Savoie, a Ford labor relations executive and later a vice president. The epitome of management's attitude was the jargon among managers and engineers about making a job "idiot proof" so that workers could not foul it up.[12]

With their new thinking, Petersen, Poling, and others at Ford took the opposite view—thinking workers were an asset and their input was needed; in fact, they were to be the primary movers in turning Ford around. "I came to see that the easiest people to motivate to perform better were the hourly [assembly-line] workers," Petersen told me. "They understood that their jobs were at stake. It was a matter of survival. And in the early eighties, they were full of frustration. They were angry that all the blame was being heaped on them for shoddy work and shoddy goods."[13]

Breaking Ford's Army Command Style: "Do It and Shut Up!"

The ingrained management style at Ford was not only the biggest obstacle to turning Ford around, it was also very hard to change. As Don Petersen observed, "Ford had a very top-down management system, with orders from on high, like an Army command system. We had to break that mentality." At the plant level, the authoritarian mode at Ford produced such bitterness and conflicts between labor and management that even today, the memory of those tensions is vivid among veteran line workers.

"Ten years ago, the supervisors did a lot of screaming," recalled Lucius Evans, a welder in Ford's South Chicago plant. "They were always hollering at the top of their lungs, instead of talking to us like we're human beings. We really had no input at all." Roland Dennis, another worker at South Chicago, bluntly recalled the old management style: "It was 'Do it and shut up!' "

With hindsight, some managers today admit their blind spots. "Many times we never explained what the outcome was supposed to be—we would simply say, 'Do the job!' " conceded Reg Anson, a Ford manager for more than twenty years.[14]

Don Petersen wanted a new kind of manager, one who would go down onto the shop floor, listen to the workers, get to know their problems, and enlist their help in boosting quality and productivity at Ford. Winning back the confidence of American consumers would require a quantum improvement in quality, "Red" Poling asserted, and that would require a virtual revolution in labor-management relations. In Poling's mind, Ford management had to get the employees "110 percent" behind the quality drive because "No one knows better what it takes to improve the quality than the people who are doing the job every day."[15] With experience in Ford's European operations, Poling had seen how a partnership between management and labor yielded higher performance.

And so a new, more cooperative partnership with organized labor became the foundation stone on which the Petersen-Poling team would build Ford's future.

As Ford's top operations executive, Poling began touring plant after plant, calling together the local factory managers and labor leaders at joint meetings and preaching the new gospel. Old-style Ford managers balked at sitting down with the labor leaders for a joint session with their boss; it had never been done that way before at Ford. But Poling insisted: These had to be joint sessions, in order to enlist everyone at Ford in a team effort to save the company.

Poling also ran into skepticism on the labor side. "At three of the plants that I visited," he recalled, "the union leaders said to me, 'Is this just another one of those blankety-blank programs, or are you really serious?' I said, 'Well, I can't tell you forever, but as long as I'm around, I'm serious.' And they said, 'We'll help you.' "[16]

It took several years to alter the ingrained habits and attitudes of management. For months on end, Ford ran retraining courses to force echelons of Ford managers to confront their old attitudes and to rethink their mind-set—to break down old barriers and to internalize a philosophy of teamwork and trust. There was a lot of resistance. Jealous of their power, managers fought against delegating their traditional authority and putting so much trust in ordinary workers. In the early months of this program, Petersen and Poling would be bombarded at the final session of each retraining course with angry questions from managers demanding what the top brass were doing to fix Ford's problems.

Discouraged at times, Petersen called California management expert Peter Drucker of Claremont Graduate School. "Am I on the wrong track?" Petersen asked.

Drucker urged Petersen to keep on. "If you get at least one third of the people with you, you'll make it," Drucker said.[17]

Gradually, the tone of those high-level training courses began to change. At the final session with Petersen and Poling, the division and plant executives stopped asking the top brass to fix their problems;

instead, they began to explain what reforms they intended to implement when they got back to their plants. Deming's message was getting through: Authority and responsibility were being pushed down from the top levels to plant managers; they saw that initiative had to come from below.

Powerful evidence began to accumulate that the corporate culture at Ford was being transformed, but change often came only *in extremis,* during an economic life-and-death crisis. In one case, Petersen recalled, Ford headquarters was ready to shut down an auto transmission plant in Sharonville, Ohio. The transmissions the plant was making were obsolete, and the plant itself was so inefficient that Ford could get better, cheaper transmissions built in Japan. Then something unprecedented happened: The people at the plant took the initiative of reorganizing the plant and reshaping their internal relations; they asked Ford's top management for an opportunity to compete against the Japanese.

"Management and labor as a team came to us, and they outbid the Japanese and won the contract for the new transmission," Petersen recalled. "It was the collective plant leadership, people getting together, who saved that plant."

Several years later, a similar scenario unfolded at a former tractor plant in Romeo, Michigan, where labor and management together devised a plan to convert the plant to producing engines needed for Ford's newest vehicles. Within a year, Ford management ranked the Romeo plant as producing the best Ford engines anywhere in the world.[18]

Even though Petersen became chairman and CEO of Ford in 1985, he played down his role in the reforms rippling through Ford's operating divisions. "I can't tell you about the most important changes at Ford, because they happened without me," he said. "I wasn't there."

For an American CEO, Petersen's modesty was uncharacteristic; but by Deming's standards, Petersen's arm's-length stance was the true measure of successful management. Bottom-up reforms had taken place at those Ford plants precisely because Petersen had applied Deming's principles of management. He had taken a backseat and empowered people at lower levels; in doing so, he had set a personal example of the new style of management that could be followed at each local Ford plant.

Survival at the South Chicago Plant: "When the Boat Sinks, We All Drown"

The Ford assembly plant in South Chicago was one of the most difficult places in the Ford network for carrying out the Deming revolution. In fact, as Ford cut back its operations nationwide, the South Chicago plant seemed a likely target for extinction.

The South Chicago plant, built in 1924, had once produced Model Ts for Henry Ford; by the late 1970s, it had become perilously inefficient. The plant took an average of thirty-four hours to build one car, nearly twice as long as it took at a Toyota assembly plant.[19] In 1979, the Ford Thunderbirds it made had so many defects that its employees were barraged with complaints by friends and neighbors who had bought the cars.[20] The workforce was heavily unionized, with a typical inner-city mix of minority and ethnic line workers. Labor-management relations were a cauldron of ill will.

Yet the sense of peril at the South Chicago plant galvanized its people to step back from the brink; it prompted labor and management to make compromises and reach for a partnership.

"I think we both realized over a period of time that we were in the same boat," asserted Arnold Banks, a veteran line worker who became president of United Auto Workers Local 551. "When the boat sinks, we all drown. We're all in the same boat. If this plant goes down for whatever reason, God forbid, then it affects everybody in here. And I think that everybody is aware of that. It's a survival thing."[21]

That survival instinct and the cultural revolution at Ford sparked a remarkable turnaround at the South Chicago plant.

In 1993, auto industry expert Jim Harbour rated Ford's South Chicago plant "a model of quality and efficiency"—one of the three top assembly plants in America operated by the Big Three U.S. automakers. Instead of producing 800 cars a day with nearly 3,800 workers, as it had in 1979, the South Chicago plant was turning out more than 1,200 cars a day with just 2,700 workers, usually on two ten-hour shifts. Instead of thirty-four worker-hours to produce a car, it took just eighteen hours—a pace nearly on a par with the Japanese. Quality, too, had dramatically improved. The number of defects per car was down by 80 percent.[22] And, as a billboard outside the plant proclaimed, the South Chicago plant makes the Ford Taurus, which in 1992 took over from the Honda Accord as the hottest-selling car in America.

Although Ford invested $178 million in the mid-1980s to reequip the South Chicago plant with 135 robots and other modern machinery, tooling up for the Taurus and the Mercury Sable, automation was *not* the reason for this plant's turnaround.[23] The South Chicago plant is hardly a showcase of technology; it is far behind most GM plants. In fact, the South Chicago plant reminded me of Toyota factories; it was an old building, and its assembly areas were sprinkled with the kind of simple, jerry-built contraptions that are a trademark of Toyota plants.

It was not technology, but people, who had produced South Chicago's success story.

The Language of Partnership: "We" Instead of "Them" and "Us"

One telltale sign of change at the South Chicago plant, and another echo of Toyota, was the language of partnership.

Many American CEOs have adopted the lingo of teamwork, quality circles, and worker participation. But often, nice words are not matched by reality on the plant floor. One acid test is to listen carefully to the pronouns workers and managers use when talking about each other. If ordinarily they talk in terms of "them and us" or "we and they," it is a signal that the two sides still feel far apart. But if the instinctive, natural lingo is an all-embracing and continuous "we," chances are that some important barriers have fallen and partnership is a reality.

Lucius Evans, a welder, underlined that change at the South Chicago plant. Under the old-guard management, "It was like 'You're there and we're here,' " Evans said, his hands flung wide apart. "But now it's like 'You're there and we're there also' [his hands close together]. All of us are in this together. So it's a big difference now."[24]

Arnie Banks, the union leader, said that over the years, the plant's managers had "learned to respect" the frontline workers. Other workers reported that managers were actually listening to rank-and-file employees and taking them seriously. Reg Anson, the plant manager, said simply, "I don't build the cars, the people here build the cars. I set the goals. I set the standards. But there's no one individual or no one culture—management or union—that builds this car. We build it together."[25]

The first step toward that sense of partnership began with "Red" Poling's visits to plants all over the country, to promote labor-management collaboration. A crucially important response came from the national leadership of the United Auto Workers union, which saw the danger of Ford's going under and moved to help the company. Doug Fraser, then UAW president, reached a contract agreement in 1982 with Ford Chairman Philip Caldwell that gave major financial concessions to Ford: It froze wages and benefits, delayed cost-of-living increases (critical to Ford's cash flow), and eliminated a dozen paid holidays over three years. The UAW also pledged there would be no local strikes.[26] The union reckoned that these concessions were worth more than $1 billion to Ford.

In return, the company agreed to new levels of labor participation in various programs, and management made a major new commitment to expand the retraining of workers to help keep them employable at Ford, a critical element of the new spirit of partnership.

Changing the Symbols of Power and Status

Removal of irritating symbols of power and status was often the most important indicator that new attitudes were taking root at Ford. At the South Chicago plant, for example, one of the most important steps was getting rid of the golf carts. The plant is huge—2.4 million square feet under one roof. It used to rankle ordinary workers that managers rode around the plant in golf carts, while workers had to walk the hard cement floors from one department to another. Rank-and-file employees resented the golf carts as symbols of management's attitude of superiority and the gulf between bosses and peons.

In the new era, the golf carts were thrown away as an anachronism, and, by the early 1990s, Plant Manager Reg Anson made a point of walking the plant floor every day. "I probably spend sixty percent of my day on the floor," Anson said. "I walk the plant to make a good example, to have an interface with as many people as I can. I try to make it quality time. It's something I enjoy."[27]

Anson makes himself approachable. From line workers to supervisors, people feel free to chase him down during his walking tours, to share a problem or to tell him some better way to run some facet of the plant. He is a familiar figure, loping along in his black zip-up windbreaker emblazoned with the insignias of both Ford and the UAW.

Anson's jacket, too, is an important symbol of the partnership effort at South Chicago. It is neither a management jacket nor a union jacket. "It's a plant jacket," Anson asserted. "It belongs to the plant. It's important that people know that the goals and objectives are common." The jacket, designed jointly by the management and the union in 1991 after the plant won the top Ford Q-1 Quality Award, is a popular symbol of pride and camaraderie. Workers and managers all over the plant wear that jacket.

To Arnie Banks, the union leader, the biggest symbolic change was "the stop button," which epitomized worker empowerment and the trust invested in workers by management. "The worker has the right to stop the line and do whatever she or he has to do to make the necessary changes," Banks asserted. To Banks, that was a concrete demonstration that Ford was practicing what it preached about worker participation. It was also confirmation that Ford was serious about putting quality ahead of output, since stopping the line meant sacrificing some output to achieve higher quality.

Banks was so proud of this innovation that he eagerly showed me how it worked. In some places, there was a cord to pull instead of a button to push; and so Banks found a cord, gave it a jerk, and the line of moving cars came to a dead stop. Banks, who is a few inches taller than my six-foot-two, beamed down at me, delighted by the power this system represents in the hands of an ordinary worker.[28]

For Reg Anson, this was an enormous change. Under the old Ford regime, the line stopped only if someone's life or limb was in danger or at the end of the shift. Giving workers power to stop the line for the sake of quality, Anson asserted, was a 180-degree turnaround by Ford's management.

Employee Involvement: A Religion at the South Chicago Plant

Ford, like Toyota, was making every single worker responsible for producing cars free of defects, instead of leaving that chore to the plant manager and the quality control inspectors. Reg Anson called that "driving back ownership" and responsibility for quality to the individual worker. Talking about that as a goal was one thing; it was another thing to motivate workers to want to produce high quality.

The first step was for managers to make quality their own top priority—and that was a revolution for Reg Anson. During twenty years at Ford, Anson had been taught Ford's gospel: Maximize output, turn out "a whole *lot of cars*, not a whole *lot of quality.*" And now, said

Anson, "it's kind of flip-flopped."[29] One way Anson underscored his new priority was by making a point of scanning cars carefully, checking for quality problems.

A second incentive for workers to take responsibility for high quality was pride. Ford had made the Taurus a quality car, so people at the South Chicago plant wanted to keep standards high. It was far nicer to hear the praise of your neighbors, Anson said, than to have them complain about the bad quality of Ford cars, as customers had once done.[30]

The most important motivation for rank-and-file workers, however, was for management to take them seriously, to encourage workers to state what was wrong and how to fix it, and to make them partners of management instead of treating them like mindless dummies.

Workers quickly noticed the change in management's approach. "Years ago, we couldn't talk to our supervisors, let alone the plant manager," said Bob Rutovic, a seventeen-year veteran at the plant. "We were nobody, just guys throwing seats in cars. Now they listen to us. Now they correct the problems we tell them about."

Rutovic, like other workers, talked about his new sense of involvement. Once, for example, he had gone to extreme lengths to combat a problem at the plant—the glass was falling out of the outside rearview mirrors. Driving home one afternoon on the superhighway, Rutovic noticed a Ford Taurus with the glass missing from its outside rearview mirror. "I flagged the guy down," Rutovic said. "He thought I was crazy."

At curbside, Rutovic asked the car owner for the details of how his mirror had broken. He took his report back to the plant, and that helped production engineers redesign the way in which the mirror was inserted and assembled. The fix worked, and Rutovic went back to the car owner's house and installed a new mirror, free of charge, to thank the owner for helping out the Ford plant by letting them study his car's problem.[31]

Rutovic's story illustrates the new mind-set among Ford workers. The more satisfied, the more challenged, the more engaged the workers were, the more creative all of them became. As Reg Anson put it, "I think we're tapping into the capability of the worker better than we ever did in the past"—tapping into the minds of workers, not just using their bodies.

With a program called EI—Employee Involvement—Ford institutionalized the process of getting its workers to rethink their own jobs and to analyze how the plant could be run better.

At the South Chicago plant, EI is a religion. Every day, between the day and night shifts, EI teams gather just off the line for a cooperative effort at devising ways to improve the plant's operations. Line workers, top management, maintenance crews, and supervisors all sit down together, some in their shirts and ties, some in jeans. Often the team leader is a frontline worker. In groups of ten or fifteen, people sit around picnic tables informally hashing over problems as small as why pin connectors in radio units are not making the right contacts, to the breakdown of line equipment, to a repetitive process that is causing worker fatigue or injury.

At the South Chicago plant, more than forty EI teams meet at least once a week to deal with specific customer complaints. In the electrical assembly area, for example, a team will go over customer problems with radios, audio systems, lights, headlamps, turn indicators—the small-parts problems that often require fixing under warranty, potentially a very costly bill for the company. Hence the need to fix the problem in the factory.

Employee Involvement teams do many things. They often send members to car dealerships to look at customer problems on the spot. They work with auto design engineers or with the production engineers in laying out the assembly line. And when management brings in competitive cars, such as the Toyota Camry or the new Chrysler cars, EI teams tear them down to take a close look at rival products. That stirs competitive juices and triggers creative thinking about how to improve Ford's cars.

Ford has learned that involving workers in EI teams works better than financial bonuses in motivating them to come up with new ideas. The EI system is far more effective than the old company "suggestion box," even though the suggestion system paid a bonus for good ideas and the EI system pays no bonus, according to Deborah Kent, a no-nonsense engineer who is assistant plant manager—Anson's number two. The only money involved is an hour of overtime pay that everyone earns for attending EI meetings.

Getting people involved is the key to getting ideas, Kent said. Moreover, Ford has empowered the EI teams to implement their ideas without getting top management's approval.

"We cannot have enough of these teams," Kent asserted. "We have reaped tremendous benefits from EI teams in our product quality as well as in our costs. We have thousands of suggestions that come out of these teams on a weekly basis."[32]

Worker-Inspired Widgets for Safety and Efficiency

The spirit of proactive worker initiative permeates the South Chicago plant. There are worker-inspired innovations everywhere.

One eye-catching Rube Goldberg contraption is an overhead device that helps roll seat covers over contoured foam car seats before they are installed in auto bodies. Traditionally that job had been done by hand, and the fit had to be so tight and smooth that workers suffered many hand and finger injuries in the process. Finally, some workers conjured up a fairly simple device that replaced human hands and that unrolls the seat cover onto the foam from the top of the seat to the bottom, like someone rolling on tight rubber gloves from the fingertips toward the palm.

That worker-inspired "widget," as Anson called it, had been a godsend. "In the past, we have had a very, very high incidence of medicals due to hand injuries," he said. "Since we got that widget, we have had hardly any medicals in the cushion department."

More than 150 such devices have been generated by workers and installed by the plant to improve safety and reduce stress.

No worker-inspired innovation stirs greater pride in the South Chicago plant than "the Chicago gun," so nicknamed as a spoof on Al Capone. It is a welding gun that looks like a 1930s gangland-style submachine gun. People in the plant came up with the "Chicago gun" because the original, very expensive welding guns on the robots, installed in the mid-1980s, kept breaking down or causing problems. Over the course of 2½ years, about sixty to seventy different line workers, toolmakers, electricians, and engineers combined forces to devise and build a new welding gun made of lightweight, durable ceramic. The gun went through five generations to be perfected.

The South Chicago plant has realized sizable production savings by installing about a hundred of the new "Chicago guns." They are a great improvement over the original guns—easier to operate, less prone to breakdown, and much cheaper to make and operate. The plant actually made a profit from its innovation by selling fifty to sixty of its "Chicago guns" to other Ford plants from Atlanta to Canada.[33]

The sense of participation in that project is keen—a vital factor in worker motivation. "A very important thread in all of this is owner-ship," Reg Anson commented. "If you can get ownership into a de-sign, ownership into a tool, ownership into anything you're using out in the plant, you're going to get more commitment to keep it running, more commitment to improve it, more people to help improve it, be-cause it belongs to this family, so to speak."

The Quid Pro Quo: Work Security

One fundamental element that made the new Ford partnership effec-tive was work security. A crucial question for the workers, of course, was whether their own improvements would work them out of a job. That is a common fear among employees all across the United States: Given management's fixation on cost cutting, blue-collar and white-collar employees want to know if they run the risk of eliminating some of their own jobs by suggesting ways to operate the plant or the office more efficiently. Without job security, as the managers at Nippon Steel pointed out, many workers are reluctant to participate actively in management's quality drives and employee involvement programs.

Understanding this natural fear and heeding Deming, Ford's man-agement has made major concessions and efforts to reassure its work-force. The company has refused to give absolute job guarantees, but after the mass dismissals of the early 1980s, Ford has gone to great lengths to avoid outright layoffs. It has periodically negotiated agree-ments with the UAW on fixed staffing levels at every plant, and it has accepted formulas that limit the pace of workforce reductions.

Most important, in recent years Ford has devoted large resources to massive retraining of workers, to open up new lines of work for em-ployees whose jobs are eliminated by efficiency measures. "Red" Pol-ing estimated the overall number of Ford workers retrained and upgraded in the tens of thousands. At South Chicago, Anson said, several hundred people had been retrained and moved into new jobs rather than being dismissed.

In fact, Arnie Banks, the local UAW president, emphasized that, since 1986, there had not been a single layoff at the South Chicago plant. For close to a decade, the only workforce reductions had come through normal attrition.

Ford had found many ways to use the assembly-line workers whose jobs were being squeezed out. Scores of line workers had been assigned by EI teams to go to dealerships to investigate customer complaints or to suppliers to work on quality problems with various auto components. Reg Anson had put some displaced line workers onto a full-time "ergonomics team," which was assigned responsibility for gathering ideas for reducing back strain, injuries, and other stress to workers. In its first few weeks, this team had come up with forty or fifty ideas that were being studied and implemented. Many other workers had been retrained as quality control specialists, gathering statistics on various elements of the production cycle. Others had gotten so good at their new jobs that they had become trainers for the plant's vastly expanded training program, financed in part by efficiency savings.

Heidi Tillotson, a fifteen-year South Chicago veteran, was typical. In the early 1990s, she had come off the line after her job was eliminated, but, like hundreds of others, she had not been laid off. "We recognized that Heidi had a skill we needed in the plant, and, being selfish, we used that skill," Reg Anson said. Ford had trained Heidi in statistics. What's more, she had gone to night school to get a college degree. She had written a paper on quality control about W. Edwards Deming.

The job shift had heightened Tillotson's motivation. She not only liked her new job but was reassured by the confidence that management had shown in her. She had become first a quality control specialist, then a trainer for other workers. She had also become a quality fanatic.

"I'm much more involved in the product" than ever before, she said with a laugh. "To the point that when I'm in a mall parking lot and I walk by a Taurus, I look at the fits. I drive my husband crazy! But I just feel more responsible for the car on the street."[34]

Anson's Formula: Trust, Respect, Good Human Relations

The partnership mind-set at Ford has yielded powerful dividends, both for the company and for thousands of its employees. It enabled Ford to rescue itself from the brink of extinction and to stage a dramatic comeback by the late 1980s, while General Motors continued to sink. For Heidi Tillotson and an army of retrained workers, management's new mentality and its commitment to worker participation have brought new life and hope to their careers.

Nonetheless, it would be wrong to imply that Ford has magically overcome all its major frictions and internal differences. Reg Anson, the South Chicago manager, and Arnie Banks, its union leader, typify the best of what Ford has achieved, as well as the limits on how far it has gone. They are an interesting couple: Anson, short, middle-aged, agile, and white; Banks, tall, lumbering, powerful, and black. In a friendly way, they acknowledge their differences. Banks makes no bones about his dissatisfaction with the soaring pay and stock options given high Ford executives, while the workers must make do with very modest pay increases and small payouts from their profit-sharing plan. Anson wants to introduce the Toyota team concept; Banks resists, fearing that eliminating the intricate labyrinth of job classifications throughout the plant would get rid of too many jobs too rapidly.

"I don't want it," Banks asserted. "I think today, without that change, we're one of the most productive plants in the world."[35]

So on that issue, Banks has an effective veto. But on other matters, Anson protects his managerial prerogatives. He consults with Banks but reserves the right of ultimate decision for himself. "I tell Arnold, 'I'll keep the keys to the plant, and you keep the keys to your union hall,' " Anson remarked.

Within those limits, their working relationship is cordial and collaborative—and that represents a big change in attitudes on both sides. "Ten years ago the process of negotiating was usually 'the management was evil' and 'the union was evil'—and 'If you jam me, I'm going to jam you,' " Banks observed. "The UAW and Ford Motor Company matured together over the last ten years. Labor and management, we've kind of come together. More hourly people are involved in some of the decision-making processes today than they ever were."

Anson keeps his door open to show Banks and his union committee "that I'm negotiable, that when I respond to them, their back won't be against the wall." Anson considered it crucial to the plant to preserve good relations and to keep the dialogue going.

"We don't always agree," Anson said. "We are family, and all families don't agree on everything, all right? But they learn to live with each other and somewhere they find common ground, and that's kind of how Arnold and I work. We don't yell, we talk. . . . Relations are the bottom line. You have to continually build relations, and you got to kind of bond it with trust."

This was Reg Anson's bottom-line formula for success. More than robots or big investments in modernization or brilliant engineering, the keys to the remarkable turnaround at the South Chicago plant have been trust, respect, and a sense of partnership.

10

Power Sharing

Owners, Managers, and Workers—"Sitting in One Boat"

All Germans have within their souls a bit of Hegel, the philosopher who believed in the reconciliation of opposites. Everything is a series of systems of cooperation, a series of networks, a series of reconciliations.[1]
—RICHARD SMYSER, SCHOLAR

Look at the number of strikes we had—almost none. . . . Look at the readiness [of workers] to really work and contribute, to learn. . . . All this, of course, was part of that method of consensus between workers' representatives and management—and it has contributed to the success of our company.[2]
—EDZARD REUTER, CEO, DAIMLER-BENZ

If you involve people in decisions that affect them, you get better decisions, and decisions that are implemented faster. And you get a successful enterprise.[3]
—SKIP LEFAUVE, PRESIDENT, SATURN CORPORATION

When Helmut Werner was proposed as the new chief executive of Germany's Mercedes-Benz in 1992, he had to pay a call on a veteran Mercedes worker named Karl Feuerstein. No decision on a new CEO could be made without Feuerstein.

Werner was the candidate of the top management of Mercedes' parent company, the giant German transportation firm Daimler-Benz. The main owners also favored Werner. For nearly six years, Werner had run Mercedes' trucking division, and he had won a reputation as a cost cutter and a resourceful global competitor.

But for the top job at Mercedes, the backing of top management and the owners was not enough. Werner also needed the approval of the workers, whose leader was Feuerstein. And Feuerstein's approval was not automatic. So, hat in hand, Werner drove the forty miles from Mercedes's headquarters in Stuttgart to the company's plant in Mannheim, where Feuerstein worked.

Feuerstein had been on the Mercedes payroll for thirty years, beginning on the assembly line at Mannheim. But years ago, he had been elected the full-time chief of the employee Works Council at Mannheim and later chief of the Works Council for all Mercedes factories. So now, Feuerstein was the top labor leader elected by the 230,000 employees of Mercedes-Benz, the highest representative at Mercedes of IG Metall, the German metalworkers' union. And he had an office right on the Mannheim factory premises—an office, a secretary, and everything else it took to run that office, all provided by Mercedes, as is typical in large German companies. That office is where Werner and Feuerstein met.

The two men are quite different. Werner is an elegant, silver-haired executive with a university degree in business economics, a taste for expensive suits and fine wines, and a lifestyle developed by years in the upper echelons of big German corporations. Feuerstein, a man in his fifties, cuts a Pickwickian figure—portly, balding, and bourgeois in a houndstooth tweed blazer and horn-rimmed glasses—and yet his office is decorated with a photograph of Karl Marx, sayings from *The Communist Manifesto,* and proletarian placards of historic May Day marches bearing slogans of labor solidarity: "Freedom, Equality, Brotherhood" and "Unity Makes Strength."

Feuerstein's power and authority derive not only from being the top labor leader at Mercedes but from the extraordinary leverage that position gives a worker like him in the power-sharing system at Mercedes—and at all major German corporations.

Under the German system, a company's employees are automatically entitled to half of the seats on the company's supervisory board. Karl Feuerstein was the leader of the worker delegation on the supervisory boards of both Mercedes and its parent firm, Daimler-Benz.

On the board, the ownership can technically outvote the labor representatives, but that is not the tradition at Daimler-Benz or Mercedes. The leadership has concluded that it is far wiser over the long run to achieve consensus on major decisions, so that labor, management, and owners can operate in tandem on matters of central importance. And what issue is more important than choosing a new chief executive?

In practice, Edzard Reuter, the CEO of Daimler-Benz, and Hilmar Kopper, its supervisory board chairman, never force through the choice of any top executive over the opposition of the employees. Every managing director, every top manager, has to get labor's approval. This approach involves risks. Twice during Reuter's tenure as CEO, his personal nominees for top management posts have been rejected by the worker representatives. "I personally was extremely unhappy about that," Reuter admitted, but he bowed to labor's will. Reuter felt it was essential to have senior managers who "will be accepted by [the workers], because the managing directors will have to work together with them for years and years."[4]

The selection procedure drives home to each new senior executive the importance of being able to get along with labor, much as the process of Senate confirmation drives home to American cabinet appointees the need to get along with Congress.

"You can be tough, but you must have a reputation of being fair, open, communicative—this is what the workers want," said Hilmar Kopper, the Daimler-Benz supervisory board chairman.

To Kopper, it was essential that worker representatives form their own firsthand impressions and not be forced to accept a candidate on management's say-so. "They should form their own view, what sort of person is that—professionally, personally, character, and so forth," Kopper said. "So they sit down and talk with them."[5]

And so, for these reasons, Helmut Werner needed to meet face to face with Feuerstein and then with all the employee representatives on the Mercedes board. In fact, the worker leaders demanded several meetings, and Werner consented.

"We mainly discussed how he planned to work with the labor representatives in the company," Feuerstein told me. "For you, in America, this might seem odd. But we feel that we should talk to candidates and ask them what their relationship to labor and to the works councils is, what they envision as good leadership for the company, how they intend to deal with problems between management and labor. It's an important process."[6]

By Feuerstein's account, the meetings were cordial but quite frank. Werner had joined Mercedes in 1987, coming from a high position in another company; the Mercedes labor leaders knew him as chief of the truck division, and his record made them uneasy. Werner's reputation as a cost cutter pleased the owners, but it had earned him a reputation among rank-and-file workers as "a hard-core rationalizer [cost cutter] without any human considerations," as Feuerstein put it.

Werner had been less inclined than other Mercedes executives to consult with the works councils on major matters affecting personnel. And so, with Germany heading into recession in 1992, Feuerstein and his labor colleagues feared that Werner would demand large layoffs— something Mercedes had never experienced in its seventy-year history. While the labor leaders accepted the need to cut costs and even to reduce staff, they wanted to see this done gradually with protection for the people involved. They wanted Werner's assurances that he would work with them.

According to Feuerstein, the talks with Werner were tough but very helpful. Werner, however, tried to play down the significance of these sessions. It was "not the time for deals" to be struck between a prospective CEO and the labor leaders, he insisted.[7] Nonetheless, he did make promises to do more in the future to consult the worker representatives on all important issues—and Feuerstein held Werner to those promises. In the end, Werner said enough to persuade Feuerstein and the others to give him a chance.

And so, with labor's assent, Helmut Werner was elected the chief executive of Mercedes, and he took over formally in May 1993.

Germany's "Economic Miracle": The Payoff of Power Sharing

Stunning as that episode is to many Americans, it is just one example of the extraordinary system of power sharing at the commanding heights of the German economy. Germans take for granted a system of consensus capitalism and power sharing that most Americans would find truly revolutionary.

On German corporate boards and in factory works councils, employee representatives have a voice in and a vote on every major issue of corporate strategy—diversification; mergers and acquisitions; whether to shut down plants or keep them open; whether to expand or to cut back the workforce; where and by how much; how large a dividend to pay to shareholders; and, in the case of Daimler-Benz, whether to build a new plant in Germany or Alabama.

This unique system of power sharing took root during Germany's remarkable recovery after World War II. There were precedents in the late nineteenth century in German laws promoting or requiring factory councils for workers. But it was the immediate postwar period that embedded the culture of power sharing in German laws and customs.[8]

The war left Germany devastated—a "frozen sea of shattered ruins," in one graphic account. Germany's great cities—Berlin, Cologne, Düsseldorf, Stuttgart, Hamburg, Munich—all had been pummeled into empty shells by the Allied air campaign against Hitler's Third Reich.[9]

"This country was totally destroyed—everything was destroyed," Edzard Reuter recalled. "So everybody, management and workers, labor, employees, had to begin from anew—*together*. And in the early postwar period, they quite well understood that this can be achieved only if one works together, and not if one fights each other."[10]

Lifting themselves from the rubble of war, Germans learned the absolute imperative of collaboration and cooperation—for the sake of national recovery. If they were to get back onto their feet, catch up with the victorious French, British, and Americans, and put Germany into the front ranks of the world, they could not afford the tensions, or the waste of energy and resources, caused by social conflict and division.

"You can't build up a destroyed country without a consensus between workers and management," said Karl Heinz Kaske, former CEO of Siemens, the electronics conglomerate. "It's not a consensus on details, it's a consensus on the basics. Of course, we negotiate, and we do so in a very tough way, [but] . . . in no sense do I view the union leaders as class opponents."[11]

After the war, Germans vividly remembered the high price of a divided society. The shattering of the Weimar Republic, Germany's earlier experiment in capitalism and democracy, had spawned the extremes of nazism and communism before World War II. In postwar Germany, no one wanted to risk reviving the class warfare that had opened the way for Hitler. Cooperation between labor and capital was preached by the towering conservative chancellor, Konrad Adenauer, and his Christian Democratic Union. German conservatives enacted laws that gave labor power on German corporate boards and mandated a system of cooperation—what analyst Richard Smyser has called "the reconciliation of opposites."[12]

And for Germany, corporate power sharing has paid off handsomely.

By the end of the 1980s, West Germans could point to a national output that was almost as great as that of Britain and France combined. In the 1990s, this system has helped make Germany the world's third largest industrial economy, after America and Japan.[13] For Germans, their astounding postwar recovery, "the economic miracle," was testimony to the validity of Adenauer's "social market capitalism"—tempering capitalism with the idea that workers and owners are not antagonists but must share power and responsibility.

Daimler-Benz: The CEO Does *Not* Sit on the Board

What makes Germany's consensus capitalism so distinctive is the diversity of the people and the forces the German system brings together.

The German way is epitomized by the makeup and operations of the supervisory board at Daimler-Benz. Every quarter, in one room, this board gathers the management of Germany's most powerful corporation; the leaders of the nation's strongest trade union; and the owners of the corporation, which include all three of Germany's largest banks as well as other major German industrial enterprises. As one German MP observed, the people around the octagonal table in the Daimler-Benz boardroom have as much power to influence the direction of their nation's economic policies as Tokyo's famous Ministry of Trade and Industry (MITI) does for Japan.[14] For decisions taken by the Daimler board often set the pattern for the rest of Germany.

No one pretends that the contending forces represented on that board do not have their differences and their conflicts, often lasting for months on end. But the hard fact of power sharing instills in them the mind-set of finding common ground and reconciliation, without sharp confrontations and public posturing.

The arithmetic of the Daimler-Benz supervisory board compels its members toward compromise. The board has twenty members: ten members from the owners' side and ten members representing the employees. The head of the owners' group, the board chairman, has a tie-breaking vote but has never used it.

The owners' group has long been led by Deutsche Bank, Germany's largest bank, which owns 28 percent of Daimler-Benz. The employee delegates represent white-collar as well as blue-collar workers, but in the main they are the leaders of the metalworkers' union, IG Metall. Seven come from within Daimler-Benz factories and its subsidiaries (led by Karl Feuerstein); three are top officials from the union's national headquarters.

The head table offers a symbolic snapshot of German power sharing: The board chairman is Hilmar Kopper, a tall, engaging, internationally known banker—the head of Deutsche Bank; the deputy chairman is Karl Feuerstein, the worker from Mannheim.

One big surprise: the chief executive of Daimler-Benz, Edzard Reuter, is *not* a member of the corporation's supervisory board. He has *no vote* in its deliberations. Instead, the chief executive of Daimler-Benz is the head of a lower board, the managing board of directors of Daimler-Benz, which runs the company day to day. At the supervisory board, Reuter has to report to his superiors—the owners and employees. He has to win *their* approval for management's strategies.

By law, every German company with more than 2,000 employees operates in a similar way. It is the German way.

"This is communism!" one American auto executive exclaimed to Eberhard von Kuenheim, former managing chairman of BMW.[15]

"Codetermination"—*Mitbestimmung*—is what the Germans call it. By American standards, it comes close to comanagement, though German executives insist they have their prerogatives. Especially at large firms, German power sharing extends far beyond the fifty-fifty split of power on the supervisory board. It operates at the factory level, too. There, a works council elected by the workers must be consulted by management on all the major matters of running the plant—work shifts, hiring, firing, layoffs, holidays, work conditions.

At the Mercedes factory in Sindelfingen, for example, the plant management, pushing Helmut Werner's drive to cut costs, wanted to wipe out 650 jobs in the upholstery shop. Management said that outside suppliers could provide the car seats, cushions, and other upholstery more cheaply. Erich Klemm, head of the plant's works council, demanded a chance to save the jobs, and the workers themselves, mostly women, proposed many little cost-saving measures—enough to meet the outside competition. So about 400 jobs were saved and 250 women were shifted to other work at Mercedes.[16]

In sum, Edzard Reuter explained, codetermination really amounts to "coordinating decisions in the factory, in the workshop, in the office—and this has continued in the whole of the postwar period, this basic feeling of commonly sitting in one boat."[17]

In fact, all three parties in the Daimler-Benz troika—owners, management, and workers—testify that codetermination has been good for their interests.

Too good for some, Edzard Reuter commented dryly as Germany's recession was deepening in 1993. Daimler's management, and German management generally, he said, had been lulled by Germany's prosperity in the 1980s and had been too generous to labor. By 1992, Reuter wanted to roll back some wage increases and worker benefits, to become more cost competitive. When he was in a hurry to cut costs, Reuter chafed at the time-consuming process of joint decision making. Still, in 1993 and 1994, worker representatives on Daimler's board, and on other boards, saw that their company was in trouble and made important concessions that saved billions of dollars for German corporations. So Reuter did get help from the system.

Over the long haul, he asserted, there is wisdom in a system of power sharing. Management had to learn to "include the understandable interests of labor in our decision-making," he said, and labor leaders had to think about "the strategic development of their company" and its financial good health. Reuter's bottom line: Codetermination has been a big plus for Daimler-Benz.

"Look at the number of strikes we had—almost none, or very few days of strikes," he said. "Look at the readiness [of workers] to really work and contribute, to learn. Look at the setting up of an educational system inside the company. All this, of course, was part of that method of consensus between workers' representatives and management—and it has contributed to the success of our company."

Endorsement also came from the other side—from Franz Steinkühler, the national president of IG Metall in the 1980s and early 1990s. With 3.2 million members, IG Metall is the strongest union in the entire industrialized world; in Germany, it has jurisdiction over several key industries—steel, autos, aircraft, machine tools. It is rich enough to afford a headquarters staff of more than 700, its own economists, and a mainframe computer; its senior officials sit on the supervisory boards of most of Germany's biggest corporations. Steinkühler was one of three national officers who were members of the Daimler-Benz supervisory board.

Power sharing affected Steinkühler's strategy as a labor leader. He did not often call his union out on strike, and when he did, the strikes were short—to make a point, not to cripple a company.

"A strong union needs to strike less to achieve its goals than a weak one," Steinkühler asserted.[18] He much preferred the leverage of inside bargaining with management.

Codetermination had not only won German workers the highest wages and benefits in the world, Steinkühler contended, but that same system made it possible during the 1993–94 recession to manage the difficult shrinkage of jobs and reduction of wages and benefits in steel, autos, and other industries—without social conflict. Codetermination provided a mechanism for heading off big troubles before they exploded.[19]

"Without codetermination, management and industry would make decisions on their own, with negative consequences," Steinkühler declared. "Then the unions would have to move in with their Red Cross first-aid kits after the train wreck. We don't want to run around with first-aid kits. We want to sit at the front of the locomotive, to help decide on the route taken and the speed chosen."[20]

In short, for labor, having an inside track within a corporation such as Daimler-Benz and taking part in the major decisions was far better than the typical labor union tactics of confrontation and a power struggle.

For the workers, the inside track had paid off; but for Franz Steinkühler, being an insider was ultimately his Waterloo. In May 1993, he was officially accused of making a profit on the stock market by trading on inside information on Daimler-Benz. In Germany, insider trading is not a crime, but it is taboo in business circles. Steinkühler denied the accusation, but he had to resign his union presidency.[21] His place on the Daimler board was taken by the deputy head of IG Metall, Walter Riester.

The Vital Chemistry That Makes Power Sharing Work

The success of Germany's consensus capitalism depends on not only the fact of power sharing but the mind-set of power sharing.

At Daimler-Benz, for example, the fifty-fifty split of board seats between owners and employees could easily deteriorate into a pattern of bloc voting and confrontations. But all sides are committed to preventing bloc voting, which would undermine the whole idea of power sharing, according to board chairman Hilmar Kopper, who represents Deutsche Bank's interests on the board. "You must break up bloc voting," Kopper insisted. "We are all forced to sit together and find solutions from the very start."[22]

In fact, German law gives Kopper, as board chairman, an extra vote to break ties. If the Daimler board splits 10–10 on an issue, the chairman can call for a second ballot, cast his double vote, and, as the Germans say, "pull the chain." But Kopper reported proudly, "I've sat on many boards, but I have never used my second vote."[23]

On occasion, Kopper had threatened to use his second vote—much as Franz Steinkühler had threatened strikes—and the threat, on either side, was sometimes enough to break a deadlock. But, as Kopper pointed out, "You can't threaten very often."

The danger in such a confrontational approach, he asserted, is that it can undermine the climate of trust nurtured at Daimler-Benz. To Kopper, as to many other German executives, synergy is preferable to muscle; and so Kopper works the arts of persuasion. Although he is an owner, he has cast himself as the middleman between management and labor—a practice typical of German board chairmen.

Kopper is a quintessential product of the German system. He grew up on a farm and never went to college; he finished high school, trained as a banking apprentice, and worked his way to the top. A strapping six-foot-two, Kopper has a friendly, direct manner. He is a leader in the collegial German style, oriented to mediating and bargaining rather than to giving commands, and to long-term, evolutionary changes. He is respectful of employees, fair minded, and unostentatious.

Kopper's relationship with Feuerstein, the labor leader, exemplifies the essential chemistry of codetermination, shared power between labor and owners.

For management, Kopper serves as the first litmus test for a new idea; if the executives can't sell *him,* they won't get anywhere with the board. If Kopper likes a management proposal, he will try to enlist Feuerstein. Sometimes, if Kopper is undecided, he will sound out Feuerstein before giving management his opinion. Over the years, Kopper observed, labor leaders such as Feuerstein come to know the business side so well that they think very much like managers. Kopper had come to put so much trust in Feuerstein's judgment that if Feuerstein dug in his heels on an issue, he could turn Kopper around.

"Someone like Herr Feuerstein identifies himself deeply with Daimler-Benz," Kopper said. "This is his life. He wouldn't say 'No' just for the fun of saying 'No' and being difficult. He wants to help the company. So you have to convince him that this is good for the company. He may still at the end say 'No.' But then maybe he has a very good reason, and then you'd better go home and think again yourself."[24]

One case came to Kopper's mind—an instance when the Daimler-Benz management wanted to shut down an office equipment plant and dismiss its 4,000 employees; this was a plant Daimler-Benz had absorbed when it bought the AEG corporation. Feuerstein had opposed the layoffs. For eighteen months, arguments dragged on. Daimler's management finally agreed to shift many of the employees to other Daimler-Benz plants, to finance an industrial park on the old plant site, and to provide loans for some employees to set up their own small businesses. Only then did Feuerstein agree to closing the office equipment plant.

Yet for all the past successes of German codetermination, the recession that took hold in Germany in 1993 posed serious new tests. In 1993, Daimler-Benz reported its worst performance since World War II—a $1 billion loss, partly as a result of $2 billion allocated to job reduction and retraining programs.[25] After nearly half a century of unbroken successes, Daimler-Benz for the first time had to confront the need for the kind of painful restructuring that had hit the German steel industry years earlier.

The agenda for the board meeting in April 1993, for example, was full of prickly issues. Mercedes had reduced its workforce by 14,700 workers in 1992, and Helmut Werner, the rising CEO, wanted to cut another 7,000 workers in 1993—a figure that would triple before the year was out. Then, despite the recession, Edzard Reuter wanted to spend $370 million to buy Fokker Aircraft, another in his string of acquisitions, although the payoff from the purchase would not come for several years. One complication for the worker board members was the press revelation that Daimler-Benz was even richer than previously known. It had tucked away DM 4 billion ($2.5 billion at then-current exchange rates) in hitherto undisclosed pension reserves—and yet Werner wanted to cut costs by reducing the workforce. Finally, management wanted board approval to build an auto assembly plant outside Germany—its first ever in the United States.

For Feuerstein and the worker representatives, it was a tough agenda. For months, these issues had been batted back and forth informally in Feuerstein's private talks with Board Chairman Kopper, Reuter, and others. It was in that informal give-and-take that consensus was usually forged and real decisions were taken; the board meeting was often a formality.

Feuerstein knew the game of power sharing well. He was very pragmatic. While he naturally took the side of the workers, he understood management's reasoning, and he was not contentious. Rather than forcing deadlocks, he sought trade-offs.

Feuerstein was realistic enough to see that recession was forcing manpower cutbacks all over Germany and that more workforce reductions at Mercedes were inevitable. Feuerstein's goal was to minimize the pain. For him, the disclosure of $2.5 billion in financial reserves was a windfall. Instead of paying a dividend from these funds, as some owners wanted, Feuerstein proposed leaving the money with the company and using part of it to finance generous bonuses to encourage older workers to take early retirement, making it unnecessary to fire anyone outright. Management and owners bought his approach.

Feuerstein had mixed feelings about Reuter's plans to spend $370 million to buy Fokker Aircraft. Amid talk of cutbacks at Mercedes, he disliked seeing Daimler pour still more money into the aircraft industry (he had balked at an earlier acquisition of Messerschmidt). But Feuerstein saw the business logic: Fokker produced planes that no other Daimler division made, and, most important, Feuerstein observed, Daimler-Benz had "about three thousand workers whose job it is to fill contracts from Fokker, and if our company doesn't buy Fokker and it folds, then those three thousand jobs could be gone." So he was in favor of that acquisition.

Management's proposal to build an auto-assembly plant in Alabama was more difficult. Edzard Reuter at Daimler and Helmut Werner at Mercedes argued that American autoworkers cost less than German workers. But management sugarcoated the pill by promising that the American plant would not compete with its German plants; the factory in Alabama would make only a new four-wheel-drive sports vehicle for the American market.

"That does bother us," Feuerstein admitted. "It does hurt. Because we naturally would rather have had it built here in Germany. They have explained their reasons, and we think that argument is not unreasonable."

Once again, Feuerstein had his eye on the long term. He knew that Mercedes was planning to go after a new segment of the European market with a new line of smaller cars—"city cars," they were being called. If Feuerstein went along with the American plant for a sports-utility vehicle, he wanted the new plant for "city cars" to be assembled in Germany, or at least most of their components to be German made.[26] While Feuerstein had no guarantees, he was building a strong case for a quid pro quo. In late 1994, the company decided to build the "city car" plant in France, with most components to be made in Germany. That was typical—power sharing meant give-and-take.

During the recession, that give-and-take continued. Daimler was able to get back into the black in 1994, helped by concessions from the metalworkers' union on a shorter workweek at reduced pay, as well as an agreement that increases in general pay levels would fall slightly behind the rate of inflation. Labor concessions in 1993 and 1994 were worth several hundred million dollars to Daimler-Benz.[27] Mercedes's management worked with labor to avoid outright layoffs, mostly through "golden handshake" retirement packages; although more than 30,000 jobs were cut back in 1992–94, only a few hundred were actual layoffs.

That pattern was repeated in steel, chemicals, and other key industries. At Volkswagen, labor's compromises rescued the company *and* jobs. In November 1993, IG Metall agreed to a four-day workweek with about a 10 percent reduction in pay; that saved the company up to $1 billion and protected 30,000 workers from being laid off.[28]

In short, codetermination helped cut companies' costs when the economy was contracting, just as it had helped boost workers' pay when the economy was expanding.

At Daimler-Benz, as elsewhere, the adjustments were far from easy, but the company's leaders—from Helmut Werner, the new chief executive, to Karl Feuerstein, the worker from Mannheim—adjusted to the harsh economic realities peaceably.

Once the economy improved and the big German companies were showing good profits again, IG Metall went on strike for a share of the gains. But the German power-sharing system had gotten both sides through a dark period. As board chairman Hilmar Kopper put it, "Despite all the difficulties, it all happens in a rather civilized manner."

The Old American Mind-Set—Confrontation

In America, history and culture have shaped a very different pattern of labor-management relations. In recent years, some American companies have been notable for developing cooperative relationships with unions and innovative power-sharing arrangements. But historically in America, the more prevalent climate has been one of labor-management confrontation.

In the half century from the 1880s to the 1930s, economic conflicts were often violent. Names such as Haymarket Square, Pullman, and Homestead ring with the echoes of industrial warfare in America. Even after unions became more accepted during the New Deal era and during the Great Depression, relations between the corporate giants and major industrial unions were still antagonistic and adversarial. One enduring pattern of America's culture of commerce has been the open, ongoing power struggle between Big Business and Big Labor.

With union membership sloping off from a peak of 20 million members in 1978 to 16.6 million in 1993, labor has been on the defensive.[29] During the Reagan presidency, political attitudes toward unions hardened. President Reagan broke a nationwide strike by air traffic controllers in 1981, and that example was followed by several sharp labor-management confrontations in the private sector—at Eastern Airlines, Greyhound, Caterpillar, Phelps Dodge, Ravenswood Aluminum, and Pittston Coal. All suffered financial losses, and Eastern paid the ultimate price: It went out of business.[30]

The belligerent trench warfare at Caterpillar, world-famous maker of huge excavating and earthmoving equipment, tractors, wheel loaders, graders, and paving machines, illustrates the contrast between the traditional mind-sets in German and American labor-management relations.

The conflict at Caterpillar has also marked a puzzling abandonment of a very successful effort at German-style collaboration on the factory floor. After suffering through eight costly strikes between 1958 and 1982, Caterpillar's management turned in the mid-1980s to a new policy of worker participation, which Caterpillar called the Employee Satisfaction Process. Two successive Caterpillar CEOs, Lee Morgan and George Schaefer, worked hard at establishing better relations with the United Auto Workers union, which represented nearly 30 percent of the company's employees. Frontline workers were given responsibility to reorganize the flow on assembly lines, purchase machinery, and work with supervisors to solve many problems. The plant at Aurora, Illinois, became a model of employee involvement. Morale soared.

"People really enjoyed coming to work," Al Weygand, bargaining agent for UAW Local 145, recalled. "You could actually sit down and have a cup of coffee [with supervisors]. They listened to you. They took your suggestions, and they got back to you."[31]

"For the first time, I felt when I went to work, I made some difference," said Richard Clausel, a UAW factory floor representative. "It gave me satisfaction thinking you were more than just a welder or machine operator."[32]

Efficiency and productivity shot up. Management calculated that employee suggestions generated $10 million in savings. The Aurora plant's example spread, and both quality and earnings rose companywide. Caterpillar launched a $2.5 billion program to modernize its plants. Output leapt from $7.3 billion in 1986 to $11.4 billion in 1990. Earnings rose handsomely in the late 1980s. Most important, Caterpillar withstood the challenge of its Japanese rival, Komatsu, Ltd., and remained number one in the world, exporting close to one third of its sales.

Caterpillar: "How Much Is It Worth to Run Your Own Company?"

In 1990, after Don Fites took over as Caterpillar CEO, the cooperative atmosphere of the previous five years decidedly cooled. Fites, a hardball manager determined to assert his leadership, was bent on making Caterpillar even more competitive—cutting costs, laying off employees, reorganizing the corporate structure, speeding the work process, stepping up the design of new products.

In 1993, Fites asserted proudly that twenty-one new products had been introduced at the Aurora plant and that, companywide, Caterpillar had cut inventories and reduced average manufacturing time for a complicated piece of heavy equipment from twenty-five days to nine days.[33] In thirty months, Fites had eliminated 4,000 managerial slots through attrition; that continued a long trend of workforce cutbacks, from 90,000 workers in 1978 to 50,000 in 1993.[34]

Fites's most celebrated trademark was his confrontation with the United Auto Workers. On the surface, the central issue was "pattern bargaining," the UAW's practice—similar to that of the German metalworkers' union—of including the same terms, the same pattern, in its contracts with all members of an industry group, such as the automakers (Ford, Chrysler, and General Motors) or the farm and heavy equipment makers (Caterpillar, Deere and Company, J. I. Case, and others). Fites wanted to break the pattern; he wanted better terms than Caterpillar's competitors were getting. In early 1991, nine months before Caterpillar's contract with the UAW expired, Fites began running full-page newspaper ads declaring that pattern bargaining was "a relic of the 1950s" that was handicapping Caterpillar in the global marketplace. "A pattern agreement for a company like ourselves that has a stated strategy that we're going to be globally competitive from a U.S. manufacturing base doesn't make any sense," Fites asserted.

In early 1991, Fites demanded eighty-nine concessions from the UAW membership on wages and benefits.[35] A year later, Fites had changed his terms to a level only marginally below those accepted by John Deere (wages at $21.00 per hour by 1997, full medical coverage, pension increases, and job security for all UAW employees, by name, for six years). But he still adamantly opposed pattern bargaining on principle.[36] Tensions had been so sharp that the union, to the regret of some members, was not prepared to accept the sweetened package.

This deadlock suggested that the real issue for both sides was power and control; pattern bargaining was just a symptom of a larger problem—the refusal to give and take.

Fites was out to assert his control and to check the increasing influence of the UAW within Caterpillar, whereas the union wanted to spread the practice of worker participation and power sharing to new areas. Fites objected; collaboration was not his priority.[37] He spurned the UAW's proposal for the kind of joint decision making Daimler-Benz practiced—decisions, for example, on which components for Caterpillar products would be made at Caterpillar plants and which components would be bought from outside suppliers. To the UAW, the sourcing of components was of major importance to labor as well as to management; having components made at Caterpillar helped to protect good jobs for Caterpillar's workers. To Fites, union involvement in decisions about where to make components was a power grab, an invasion of management's turf.

"You can't have a system whereby a union can say, 'No, you have to make that product—we have a right to make a sourcing decision here, or [to] veto your sourcing decision,' " Fites declared. No power sharing; management alone would decide. In Fites's words, the nub was this: "How much is it worth to run your own company?"[38]

The confrontation exploded into the open in the fall of 1991. As the old contract expired, the union struck a Caterpillar plant in Decatur, Illinois, on November 4, 1991; five days later, Caterpillar retaliated by locking employees out of other plants. Tensions quickly escalated. Lines hardened, and the power struggle grew ugly. Efforts at compromise failed.

On April 1, 1992, after Caterpillar's workers had been off the job for 165 days, Fites dropped his ultimate bomb—the threat to hire permanent replacement workers unless the 12,500 striking UAW members returned to work at once. The UAW agreed to return to work—without a new contract. Fites had won the power struggle, and he imposed his terms.

In March 1993, nearly a year after the strike had ended, I visited the Aurora, Illinois, plant. Production was under way, but tensions were smoldering. The old joint worker-management teams had been abolished. Here and there, workers wore black T-shirts showing two boxers fighting and the logo "Cat Vs. UAW." Others had caps with the slogan "No contract, No peace" or buttons showing Don Fites and George Bush (who had been defeated in the 1992 election) and the caption "One Down and One to Go." A few days earlier, the local press had reported that fifty union representatives had been fired for wearing the Bush-Fites button but then had been reinstated. Some union men, however, had been taken off good assembly-line jobs and been ordered to clean toilets.[39]

The union was taking a hard line, too. Al Weygand said that as a protest against Don Fites's terms, union members were "working to rule," that is, doing only the minimum required for their jobs but contributing nothing more—making no extra effort.

Listening to Don Fites and Al Weygand was to hear descriptions of two totally different worlds.

Weygand: "This plant, now, it's back in the scenario that used to be in the fifties. It's terrible. It's in total disarray. There's no trust. It's constantly a bitter battle."

Fites: "Heaven knows, we're ready to start negotiating tomorrow morning if they're interested, and we always have been. We'd prefer to have a contract, our employees would prefer to have a contract . . . but we're not going to do anything to jeopardize our global competitiveness."

Weygand: "We made 'em number one. They want to talk about being globally competitive. You got to have your workforce in a climate of doing things together. . . . How you get it leaner and meaner is through smarter management, not by attacking your workforce. That's not smart."

Fites: "Our relations with the Detroit UAW are probably at an all-time low. But I think the average employee out there is not nearly as unhappy as the international union is with us."

Weygand: "We're teaching the employees to work to rule. They're not doing anything more than exactly what that foreman says. They're checking their brain when they walk in the gate. The only thing Caterpillar has is their back."

Fites: "There's no work to rule going on in our plants. Otherwise, I couldn't stand here, look you in the eye, and say we have record quality and record productivity."

Weygand: "Their productivity has dropped drastically. They're having a bunch of problems in meeting orders and 'build' schedules."

Fites: "Actually, we're shipping way ahead of our shipping schedule in Aurora right now. . . . We had one month where we ran behind, and that's when we were trying to introduce several new models."

Weygand: "In 1991, Don Fites would walk through the shop and shake hands with everybody and have one-on-one conversations with them. That would not happen today—no way. They'd boo him—they literally would boo him. The last time Gerry Flaherty [a group president] and Glenn Barton [another group president] showed up at the Aurora facility, our employees chased them clear to the Aurora Airport and picketed the airport. They would do the same thing with Don Fites."

Don Fites denied any problem, saying that he "wouldn't have any concern" about his security in visiting the Aurora plant. The only problem, he said, was sometimes "these things get turned into media events."

Privately, others in Caterpillar's management cast doubt on Fites's bravado. I asked to do a television interview with him at the Aurora plant against a backdrop of earthmoving equipment, but a senior Caterpillar executive told me that would be impossible because of concerns about Fites's safety in that plant.[40] When we asked to interview workers at random, Caterpillar restricted us to interviewing two workers, handpicked by Caterpillar. As a condition of our filming in the plant and doing an interview with Fites elsewhere, Caterpillar insisted that the filming be kept absolutely secret in advance.

Despite the obvious frictions, CEO Don Fites contended that his get-tough tactics with the union had paid off handsomely for Caterpillar: The company was number one in the world, with record market share, quality, and productivity (Fites had made almost identical claims for Caterpillar in 1990—*before* his showdown with the union). In fact, Caterpillar did rebound to a prosperous year in 1993: $11.6 billion worth of business and a solid profit of $662 million. But this 1993 business volume was only a fraction more than Caterpillar's $11.4 billion volume in 1990 (less volume, if inflation was taken into account), and its 1993 profits roughly equaled the $622 million in losses that Caterpillar had suffered in 1991 and 1992.[41]

Nonetheless, for all Caterpillar's obvious strengths and efficiencies, a cloud of uncertainty hung over the company: The atmosphere of acrimony and economic guerrilla warfare persisted inside Caterpillar plants. There were nine wildcat strikes in the two years after the UAW went back on the job in April 1992. In 1994, the National Labor Relations Board issued ninety-two charges of unfair labor practices against Caterpillar, and on June 21, 1994, some 14,000 UAW members at eight Caterpillar plants in Illinois, Pennsylvania, and Colorado walked out on strike in protest against Caterpillar's labor practices. For months, the strike stretched on. As one news headline put it, "Labor Rift Promises Both Sides Bitter Harvest."[42]

Don Fites had his counterstrategy—drafting 6,000 of Caterpillar's office employees and managers to work in the plants, reinforced by job-hungry temporary workers. Over time, 4,000 of the UAW strikers returned to the job, so that by October 1994, Caterpillar management defiantly reported having produced 1,000 big machines since the strike began. In 1994, Caterpillar reported record sales of $14.3 billion and profits of $955 million.[43] Don Fites said Caterpillar could maintain its siege operations "as long as we need to." The UAW insisted it would hold out "one day longer than Caterpillar."[44] Finally, in January 1995, Caterpillar agreed with the UAW to work toward a resolution through a federal mediator.[45]

Whatever its short-term gains and losses, the perpetual power struggle between Caterpillar and the UAW seems a damaging pattern for the long term, compared to the German system of power sharing. Caterpillar may struggle on, even prevail on its own terrain, but trends under way elsewhere in America make clear that the mind-set of confrontation is a legacy of America's past, rather than a harbinger of its future.

A New American Mind-Set: Experiments in Power Sharing

America's corporate mind-set has recently been full of change. American innovators are transforming the power relationships between workers and management in many different ways.

Companies such as AT&T, Corning Glass, and Eaton Manufacturing, like Ford, have built new competitive strength on cooperative partnerships with their unions. But the quiet revolution in labor-management relations has been carried even further at places such as Magma Copper and Republic Engineered Steel. These companies have not only empowered their workers on the shop floor, as Ford did, they have drawn labor into sharing the power of running the business.

Like Ford, Magma Copper acted out of desperation. In the mid-1980s, it was heading for financial disaster. The bottom had fallen out of the world copper market, and labor-management relations were abysmal. The company gambled on power sharing to turn things around. It let high-performance work teams run their own operations, and productivity shot up elevenfold. The company gave workers training not only in basic reading and arithmetic skills but in problem solving and business management, and it drew them into joint decision-making at the divisional level. Cost savings were so great that, by 1993, the company paid workers an annual bonus that averaged $4,700 and invested $140 million in a new mine.[44] It set up a high-level steering committee, seven from labor and seven from management, to advise the CEO and to decide on all labor issues.

Magma Copper stopped short of full comanagement, but its version of power sharing generated a stunning corporate recovery. As CEO J. Burgess Winter put it, the company's "union-management alliance" was "a major competitive advantage."[45]

Saturn's Daring Innovation in Comanagement

By far the most radical departure in U.S. labor-management relations—and certainly the most widely heralded innovation in German-
style joint management—is Saturn, the company-within-a-company
set up by General Motors.

What distinguishes Saturn is power sharing between labor and
management at every level of the enterprise from the shop-floor work
unit to the Strategic Action Council, which runs the Saturn Corporation.

GM created Saturn as an experiment to compete head to head with
the Japanese small cars that were luring away millions of American
yuppie car buyers. Paradoxically, Roger Smith was Saturn's patron:
He invested $5 billion to build the Saturn plant, even though Saturn's
basic concept cut against the grain of his domineering management
style and his distrust of organized labor.

What triggered Saturn's creation was a GM management study in
1983. That study concluded that there was no way GM could build a
small car to compete with the Japanese on quality and price under the
restrictions of GM's existing labor contracts and GM's rigid management system. So GM told a group of ninety-nine GM managers and
UAW leaders to dream up something entirely new.

What emerged by 1985 was not just a new car but a radically new
form of company, a daring innovation in organizing and running a
midsize American corporation.

The new plan reflected the philosophy of teamwork, collaborative
leadership, and long-term partnership that Deming had developed
with the Japanese. Saturn, however, went much further than Toyota
had done. It embraced the joint decision making of Germany's system
of codetermination and deep worker participation in all aspects of the
corporation—from managing people and capital resources to setting
corporate strategy to deciding on car models, suppliers, and marketing approach.[46]

The principles crafted by the Group of 99, and approved in 1985 by
the Saturn Corporation and the United Auto Workers union, read
like a script written by Deming. Although he had no involvement, the
Group of 99 had been exposed to his thinking. To develop the Saturn
concept, they logged 2 million miles of travel while studying forty-nine
GM plants and sixty benchmark companies in other countries. At the

most successful companies, they found certain common guiding principles:

—"People were the company's most important asset"
—"Equality was practiced, not just preached"
—"Total trust was a must"
—"Everyone in the company had ownership of the company's failures and successes"
—"Quality was a top priority for maintaining customer satisfaction"
—"Union and management were partners who shared responsibility for ensuring the success of the enterprise"[47]

Saturn's credo, according to the company's president, Richard G. "Skip" LeFauve, was to create for its workforce "a sense of belonging in an environment of mutual trust, respect and dignity."

Saturn's goal was to meet not only customer needs, employee needs, and supplier and dealer needs, but also the needs of the environment and the local community. Every decision of Saturn, LeFauve asserted, would be consistent with Saturn's philosophy, and that philosophy would not be sacrificed to short-term market pressures. Significantly, Saturn's articles of faith omitted the traditional U.S. corporate priority on maximizing stockholder return.

The union leadership at Saturn agreed that labor had to act responsibly to promote the corporation's success—that Saturn had to meet competitive standards of quality, productivity, market share, and long-term profitability. But the UAW wanted these goals to be balanced off with the interests of workers in stable employment, high wages, good working conditions, and an effective voice in the enterprise. The union asserted that Saturn's unconventional partnership should be based on the premise that "long-term employment security cannot be negotiated independent of the economic performance of the firm, nor solely through collective bargaining *after* all strategic decisions have been made by management."[48]

In short, labor had to be in on the takeoffs of important decisions if it was going to suffer through the landings and accept the consequences—an echo of power sharing at Daimler-Benz.

Saturn was a team creation and has been a team effort. A strong partnership at the top, between LeFauve and Michael Bennett, president of UAW Local 1853, was essential. Together, LeFauve and Bennett have fashioned a unique system of labor-management relations. LeFauve, who as a young engineer had learned from an old foreman the importance of involving people, agreed to unprecedented union involvement in managing Saturn.[49] In response, Bennett's UAW agreed to give up seniority and the myriad job classifications that unions traditionally use to protect jobs and that severely restrict the flexibility of American corporations. LeFauve insisted that to make the partnership and consensus decision making work, "each party must put something at risk."[50] Bennett agreed to make 20 percent of the workers' pay dependent on meeting certain quality and productivity standards.

With GM's capital, Saturn built a brand-new plant in Spring Hill, Tennessee, took on 5,300 unionized GM workers laid off by GM plants and facilities in thirty-four different states, and targeted its start-up for 1990. Typical of GM's largesse under Roger Smith, Saturn got everything. It was a highly integrated operation; it made its own engines and transmissions, had its own foundry, and relied on very few common parts with other GM cars. Its domestic content was extremely high—98 percent from North America.

But people were the key. Recognizing that a new mind-set was crucial to Saturn's success, Mike Bennett, the UAW leader, persuaded the Saturn management to provide from 350 to 700 hours of retraining for all new workers. That training was both to inculcate in the workforce the new philosophy and work ethic at Saturn and to teach UAW members skills in problem solving, decision making, budgeting, business planning and scheduling, cost analysis, job design, accounting, ergonomics, and statistical methods—skills they would need to be effective partners with management.

When the new Saturn car finally appeared in July 1990, it was a smash hit with its target market. It was a smartly styled subcompact with a plastic body that offered high quality, reliability, and fuel efficiency at a modest price—$10,000 to $12,000. Those were precisely the characteristics that had caused millions of affluent, college-educated, under-forty American yuppies to desert U.S. carmakers and buy Japanese. By late 1994, Saturn had lured back 700,000 such buyers, half of whom said that without Saturn they would once again have bought foreign makes.[51] According to J. D. Power & Associates, the Saturn car quickly established one of the lowest defect rates among American-made cars. Its customer satisfaction was incredibly high, ranking behind only the Japanese luxury brands Lexus and Infiniti.[52]

But behind that early market success were internal struggles at virtually every step. Applying Saturn's idealistic principles was tough in practice. The standard top-down organizational chart was replaced by "decision rings" at all levels, and the "decision rings" operated by consensus. The basic building block was the fifteen-member work unit on the shop floor, which had the right to hire its own members and was responsible for its own efficiency and quality. Middle management was layered with 375 one-on-one partnerships—a manager and a worker comanager, jointly picked by the UAW and management; the two of them jointly made operational decisions. That was the plan developed by Saturn's architects.

Saturn's Growing Pains: Overcoming Old Mind-Sets

Theory is one thing; practice is another.

Most Saturn managers came from GM, and many had the old-fashioned GM mind-set. Only a few at the top had been in on Saturn's creation and were true believers.

So when the UAW pressed for full power sharing, the GM-style managers resented the intrusion. There were many clashes. In picking suppliers, the UAW wanted Saturn to develop long-term partnerships, Toyota style, with unionized GM suppliers; managers wanted freedom to get the best deal anywhere they could. The union coached its preferred suppliers to jack up quality and hold down price, and they got most, but not all, of the contracts. In selecting dealers, the union's demand for a voice met immediate resistance from Saturn's marketing managers, who subsequently relented when the union made a pledge to dealers to produce high-quality cars. A third major area of contention was whether to broaden Saturn's product line by adding a convertible or a station wagon first. Some marketing managers wanted the convertible; the union preferred the wagon because of anticipated production problems with the convertible. In the end, the wagon won out.[53]

In short, the Saturn method did not eliminate conflicts. In fact, it actually stimulated new conflicts because it was raising many new issues and involving many more people in decision making. Over time, however, issues were resolved, and people got used to a new process of debate before reaching decisions. Moreover, Saturn had the German advantage—an extensive apparatus for resolving conflicts.

LeFauve, the chief executive, remarked that while it often took longer at Saturn to make decisions with the union in the room with management, things moved more smoothly once decisions were made. "If you involve people in decisions that affect them," LeFauve told me, "you get better decisions and decisions that are implemented faster. And you get a successful enterprise."[54]

One case where Saturn's unique system speeded things up was air bags. Saturn cars had not originally been scheduled to get inflatable air bags until 1993, but air bags were a high priority for Saturn's well-educated young market segment. In 1991, Saturn's joint leadership told its engineers to come up with a plan to put air bags into the 1992 model. Freed from the ponderous GM bureaucracy, Saturn put together a small product development team, and it moved very fast: The air bags were in on the driver's side by March 1992.[55]

Saturn's worst time came in 1991, when its workers staged a temporary production slowdown while the UAW was negotiating a contract renewal. Workers wearing black armbands with the slogan "Stop Defects" accused management of sacrificing quality to GM's pressures for higher output. Saturn's management insisted that it was not abandoning quality as a goal but rather making a "transition from quality at any cost to quality at least cost." LeFauve, the president, concluded that the basic problem was a breakdown in communications between the engineering division, located in Troy, Michigan, and the worker comanagers. Through give-and-take, the issues were worked out and a new contract was signed—without a strike or even the formal presentation of union demands. But it had been a close call.

"If management had not held the union in high regard," LeFauve commented, "the partnership could have dissolved at that very dangerous point."[56]

The UAW leader, Mike Bennett, was constantly contending with foot draggers and dissenters among the workers. Some protested that Bennett was too cozy with management, too concerned about the company's success. One faction called for a return to traditional arm's-length relations with management. They wanted the worker comanagers elected by the union membership, like shop stewards in other GM plants, rather than being jointly picked by labor and management.[57] Bennett argued that this change would put personal popularity ahead of ability to handle the job, and it might undercut the whole power-sharing scheme. In a union referendum in January 1993, 71 percent sided with Bennett in favor of keeping the partnership contract.[58] When Mike Bennett ran for reelection in UAW Local 1853 in March 1993, he faced three rivals. One rival wanted to go back to the traditional ways of operating—for example, overtime pay instead of Saturn's salary and bonus plan based on Saturn's performance. The overtime plan would have cost Saturn $60 million and added $200 to the sticker price of each car. Bennett opposed that change, and he barely won reelection in a runoff, by 52 to 48 percent.[59]

As in any start-up company, Saturn needed time to turn a profit. The plant was built to produce 320,000 cars a year at full capacity, on three shifts. But in 1992, with only two shifts operating and its dealership network still being developed, Saturn made 200,000 cars and lost $700 million. Finally, with volume rising, Saturn began making a profit in May 1993, and it paid each worker a $1,000 bonus. In 1994, the plant had a record annual output of 281,000 cars. Both 1993 and 1994 were milestones—each was a profitable year.[60]

With its teamwork approach, Saturn had a way of turning embarrassments into advantages. In spite of its vaunted quality record, Saturn had to recall 380,000 cars in the fall of 1993 because faulty wiring near the alternator was causing sporadic engine fires.[61] With brilliant marketing, Saturn turned the normally gloomy task of a car recall into a celebration of its customer service, welcoming its buyers home with flags flying and elaborate courtesies.

Saturn's Predicament: Being GM's Stepchild

As Saturn has developed a new corporate culture and the mind-set of power sharing has taken root, it has had to contend with a basic problem—its dependence on General Motors. After his retirement from GM, Roger Smith said that he had hoped that Saturn's collaborative method would spread to other parts of General Motors and that the failure of GM to absorb more of Saturn's revolutionary approach had been "a heartbreak" to him.[62] In fact, the influence worked in the opposite direction. As GM's subsidiary, Saturn is ultimately governed by GM. Despite its own functioning system of comanagement, Saturn is linked to a larger corporate world that still operates in the old ways. Its power-sharing philosophy is regarded as a maverick idea by many at GM headquarters, even among GM's new leadership.

"If they didn't have Saturn already," said one industry analyst, "they wouldn't do it."[63]

For one thing, Saturn gets some components from GM plants, and it is occasionally afflicted by GM's problems elsewhere. For example, with its Japanese-style just-in-time delivery schedules, Saturn was forced to shut down temporarily in September 1992, when GM's metal-fabricating plant in Lordstown, Ohio, was struck by the UAW. Another problem is that GM keeps rotating middle managers in and out of Saturn; these managers require time to get into the Saturn way of doing things and then return fairly soon to the GM mainstream. That constant rotation undermines the incentive for them to make Saturn's mind-set their own. Yet another difficulty: Saturn's strategy and philosophy are geared to building a customer base for the long term, and pressures from GM headquarters for very-short-term profits cut against the grain. But the greatest problem is Saturn's need to expand, coupled with its dependence for investment capital on a GM top management whose priorities lie elsewhere.

For long-term growth and profitability, Saturn needs a minimum output of 500,000 cars a year, according to Donald W. Hudler, Saturn's vice president for sales, service, and marketing. And that requires opening a second plant. Initially, Saturn's management favored another new plant in Tennessee, while the local UAW leadership urged using a shut-down GM plant, to reemploy laid-off GM workers. The bottleneck was at GM headquarters. GM's new leadership team under CEO Jack Smith has been desperately looking for ways to cut costs and close plants until GM can get itself back on an even keel, and no one has been prepared to bankroll an expansion of Saturn.

Skip LeFauve, Saturn's president, makes the case that Saturn has shown it can win strong customer loyalty in America and that now Saturn is ready to go after foreign markets—even to take on Japanese carmakers on their home turf.[64] But GM's leadership hesitated. It put off a decision on a second Saturn plant, and in late 1994 it brought Saturn back into the GM mainstream, as part of a new small-car group. By having Saturn share more parts, technology, and engineering with other GM plants, GM management hoped to achieve economies of scale. The test will be whether Saturn's new power-sharing approach will galvanize other GM plants to higher performance or whether Saturn will lose its independence and see its success crippled, much as IBM's once successful personal computer division was smothered by being reintegrated into the IBM mainstream. One sign that GM's top brass wanted to protect Saturn was the appointment of Saturn President Skip LeFauve to head the new small-car unit.[65]

In four short years, Saturn and its groundbreaking experiment in power sharing have already made their mark on the American corporate landscape.

From a standing start, Saturn has established its niche in the American car market. It showed quickly that this new kind of American company could deliver top-quality cars to its target customers at attractive enough prices to win a sizable market share back from the Japanese. By inspiring strong consumer loyalty, Saturn made itself a permanent presence. As Skip LeFauve likes to say, "We're counting on being around for another hundred years."

Even more fundamental has been Saturn's success at establishing a model of corporate power sharing within a company where fractious labor-management relations, which often cost GM dearly, were the rule. Saturn had little experience in America's industrial history to draw upon. Saturn has demonstrated, nonetheless—as has Magma Copper—that the new mind-set of comanagement and power sharing can and does work in America.

11

Stakeholders Versus Shareholders
Gaining the Long-Term Edge in the Boardroom

Germany:

Shareholders in this country tend to allow companies to take this medium-term approach. They say, "It's fine. Do this. You don't have to maximize tomorrow. We would be very pleased if you optimize over the next four to five years."[1]

—HILMAR KOPPER, CHAIRMAN, DEUTSCHE BANK

America:

The U.S. system of allocating investment capital is threatening the long-term competitiveness of American firms and the long-term growth of the national economy. . . . American industry invests at a lower rate and on a shorter-term basis than German and Japanese industry in many areas.[2]

—MICHAEL PORTER, HARVARD BUSINESS SCHOOL

We've created capitalism without capitalists. We created this game where the only thing those people could do is "play Wall Street"—buy and sell, takeovers, leveraged buyouts. . . . They couldn't go into industries and plan long-run strategies.[3]

—LESTER THUROW, MIT ECONOMIST

In the 1990s, few issues of global competition have been more hotly debated than the relatively short-term focus of American industry, compared to rivals in Germany and Japan.

Evidence of trouble has abounded. One symptom of the problem was Sharp's patient development of computer display panels and emergence as a world power in electronics, while RCA looked for quicker profits in rental cars and frozen foods. Another symptom was Europe's painstaking twenty-year buildup of a new aircraft consortium, Airbus Industrie, which overtook all American rivals except Boeing in the civilian airliner industry.

Against this trend, there have always been exceptional American companies, such as Motorola, Hewlett-Packard, Cargill, Wal-Mart, and Boeing, that have forgone quarterly gains for the sake of longer-term strategies. But many more U.S. corporations have felt the pressure to show Wall Street quick financial results or else see their company's stock price suffer. Warnings have come from many quarters that this market-driven strategy is shortsighted—a long-term competitive disadvantage for America.

In recent years, one major study after another has reported that both Japan and Germany have been investing in non-defense-related industrial research and development at significantly higher rates than American corporations have.[4] Another alarming trend was that Japanese industry was investing more than American industry was in new plant and equipment as the 1990s began.[5] A blue-ribbon industry group, the Council on Competitiveness, brought out a massive report in 1992 that chided American industry for "missing the mark" in its approach to the long term.

American venture capitalists won high marks in this study for patient backing of high-risk start-ups. But the council's study, prepared by Harvard Business School, took established corporations to task for inadequate investments in precisely those areas most crucial to developing long-term competitive capabilities—research and development, human resource development and employee training, building close supplier relationships, and accepting start-up losses to gain beachheads in foreign markets.

Comparing the investment strategies of top American and top Japanese firms in nine key industrial sectors, the Harvard study found the Japanese leading in six pairups: Toyota over General Motors, Nippon Electric Corporation over IBM, Komatsu over Caterpillar, Nippon Steel over USX, Bridgestone over Goodyear, Kao over Procter & Gamble. American companies such as Kodak, Merck, and General Instruments narrowly led their Japanese peers in films, pharmaceuticals, and telecommunications equipment. But the overall pattern was unflattering to American business.

"Many American firms invest too little in those assets and capabilities most required for competitiveness," the blue-ribbon panel asserted, and American firms often "waste capital" on acquisitions and takeovers unrelated to their core business.[6]

What very few people did was to seek the roots of the problem in American industry or to match the American mind-set with the mind-set of rivals overseas.

American corporate leaders frequently blame the abysmally low level of savings in America, especially compared to that of Japan and Germany (Japan 14.8%, Germany 11.3%, U.S. 4.5%).[7] With considerable justification, they contend that the low American savings rate leaves American industry short of capital for long-term investment.

But comparison of American firms with the operation of firms such as Germany's Daimler-Benz or Japan's Mitsubishi Corporation reveals more fundamental causes for the short-term mentality in America and the longer-term mentality in Germany and Japan.

The deeper causes lie in the corporate cultures of the three countries: who owns the company; who sits on the board of directors; what stake they have—or do not have—in the enterprise; what influence do stock markets have on corporate objectives; and does the CEO have a free hand or is he subject to checks and balances by people with intimate knowledge and a stake in the company's long-term future—in short, what role and power do the major corporate stockholders exercise. All these are vital factors, and on every point the American system operates differently from the systems in Germany and Japan.

Germany: The Stakeholder Mind-Set at Daimler-Benz

During the oil crisis of the mid-1970s, the late shah of Iran tried to buy more than 25 percent of Germany's largest company, Daimler-Benz, from a German industrialist named Friedrich Karl Flick. The West German government became alarmed because, in late 1974, Kuwait had previously purchased a 14.9 percent stake in Daimler-Benz and Iran had bought 25 percent of another of Germany's foremost firms, the Krupp steel empire. If Kuwait and Iran together were to hold 40 percent of Daimler-Benz stock, they could dominate the company. It was the closest any major German corporation had come to a hostile takeover.

But Daimler-Benz had a guardian angel in Deutsche Bank, which was the largest owner of Daimler-Benz, with a 28 percent interest. The bank had gained its large stake in Daimler-Benz by making loans to the auto company, starting in 1924, and often taking equity in the company rather than calling in all its loans.

Now, in 1975, encouraged by Chancellor Helmut Schmidt, Deutsche Bank stepped in to protect Daimler-Benz and its own stake in the company.

The bank set up a special trust (Mercedes Automobil Holding) to buy nearly all of Flick's holdings—the 25 percent ownership that the shah of Iran had been after. Deutsche Bank said it was acting to "prevent the shares from going into foreign ownership . . . [and] to insure the corporate independence of Daimler-Benz."[8] This purchase gave Deutsche Bank a majority of Daimler's shares, and the Federal Cartel Office warned there would be an antimonopoly investigation if Deutsche Bank exercised its full voting power. The bank promised to resell part of its new bloc of shares within a year. But twenty years later, Deutsche Bank still has the shares and majority control, guaranteeing Daimler-Benz against any unfriendly takeover.[9]

That close interlocking relationship with its principal owner and stockholder has been extraordinarily valuable to Daimler-Benz over the decades—not only defensively but offensively as well.

As the major corporate owner, Deutsche Bank has operated as an active collaborator with Daimler-Benz in its long-term corporate strategies and so has the company's union, IG Metall. The bank has stuck with Daimler through ups and downs, intimately acquainted with the running of the company and throwing its influence and financial resources behind policies that made sense for the long term.

And for Daimler-Benz, having its main bank inside the corporate tent has been a great competitive advantage.

Hilmar Kopper, the chief executive of Deutsche Bank and simultaneously chairman of the supervisory board of Daimler-Benz, contends that the bank's long-term stake in the company has made for sounder strategies and policies at Daimler-Benz. "It enables them to do the right things, things that will be ultimately right, that is, in the medium term or long term, and not to follow short-lived strategies," Kopper asserted. "I think it provides for continuity. You do not zigzag through economic cycles, but you try to follow a rather straight line."

That patient, long-term vision is vintage German investment philosophy. German investors are not driven, as many Americans are, to go after a quick killing and then to cash in their profits. According to Kopper, "Shareholders in this country tend to allow companies to take this medium-term approach. They say, 'It's fine. Do this. You don't have to maximize tomorrow. We would be very pleased if you optimize over the next four to five years.' "[10]

Deutsche Bank has been instrumental, for example, in enabling Daimler CEO Edzard Reuter to carry out his strategy of diversification.

In the early 1980s, Reuter, who was then the corporation's top financial officer and planner, anticipated the pressures and limitations of the global automobile market. Both at that time and then as chief executive, starting in 1987, Reuter has engineered the transformation of Daimler-Benz from a luxury-car maker into a multifaceted conglomerate. He has pushed Daimler into buying up companies in aerospace, jet propulsion, high-speed rail systems. He has pressed the company into building on its own strengths to form subsidiaries in financial systems, insurance, and microelectronics.

This ambitious—and controversial—strategy of Reuter's required both great sums of capital and great amounts of patience, in order to give these investments sufficient time to pay off. To succeed, Reuter needed durable support, not only from Deutsche Bank but from the other members of the Daimler-Benz supervisory board, including its worker representatives.

The key to this long-term thinking at Daimler-Benz is the stakeholder mind-set on the corporate board.

Germans consider it vital to the effective operation of Daimler-Benz, or any similar corporation, that every member of the corporate supervisory board has a direct, personal stake in the survival and success of Daimler-Benz. That goes not only for owners but for the labor board members as well, most of whose jobs depend on the company's survival and success.

The major owners of Daimler-Benz are banks, financial institutions, other corporations, and wealthy families, all of whom maintain long-term connections to the company. Each of the board's twenty members has personal, in-depth experience in the company's affairs. None is an outside director with only a cursory knowledge. None has been put on the board as a friend or colleague of the CEO, as on many American corporate boards; in fact, the rules governing German corporate boards virtually rule out cronyism on the board.

Daimler's board members represent very different constituencies and very different perspectives. What they have in common is their stake in Daimler-Benz. None of the twenty members is a mere token shareholder; each one is an authentic *stakeholder* in Daimler-Benz.

The stakeholder mind-set on the board has several consequences. The first is an overriding concern with the company's long-term survival, growth, and preeminence. This moves German managers and boards to invest heavily in training their employees and in going after technical leadership. Quarterly performance is of far less consequence, except as an indicator of long-term prospects. Higher stock prices rank very low on the lists of German boards, CEOs, and managers, as they do in Japan (German and Japanese CEOs generally get no stock options), though surveys show that achieving higher stock prices is essentially the top priority for American CEOs (who get richly rewarded in stock options).[11]

Another consequence of the stakeholder mind-set in Germany is that the plans and strategies of the CEO are subject to rigorous examination by knowledgeable board members. People with their own money or jobs on the line scrutinize management performance and take a very close look at management's proposals. Well-informed and engaged board members ensure that decisions are well tested before the corporation gets committed.

This means, for example, that to carry out his long-term diversification at Daimler-Benz, CEO Edzard Reuter had to work the process of consensus making on the supervisory board like a German chancellor nursing a ruling political coalition. Reuter had to rally and hold together his key constituencies, capital and labor, to gain the time and patient capital that he needed.

Even so, Reuter insisted, one major competitive advantage of the stakeholder mind-set on Daimler's corporate board is the way this mind-set nurtures and sustains long-term strategies. Without the board's engagement, he told me, his diversification strategy could have crash-landed, as a result of inadequate or impatient financing by his banks or strikes by autoworkers angry at the diversion of resources into other sectors. Getting decisions from stakeholders with strong views and intimate knowledge of the company might take time, Reuter said, but once a decision is reached, they see the merit in staying on course.

The picture of a German corporation that Reuter painted was not of a hierarchical structure with an omnipotent CEO at the apex; rather, it is a network of cooperative relationships.

Leadership is collegial, more a matter of consensus building than of giving orders. Not only is compromise and negotiation built into the German system of power sharing by law, but German CEOs have grown comfortable with a collaborative style of leadership. American CEOs might be accustomed to making key decisions and getting rubber-stamp approval from passive boards, but German CEOs such as Edzard Reuter see merit in the techniques of inclusion.

"I would really not have ever dreamt of being arrogant enough to decide on a thing like that—the long-range strategy—without coming to a consensus with our owners and with our basic employees' representatives," Reuter insisted. "Because what I'm doing is not for just today or tomorrow. It's for the day after tomorrow, and maybe at that time I will not be there anymore myself. So how could I be so arrogant as to undertake that [strategy] on my own decision—and nothing else?"[12]

German Banks and the Web of Stakeholder Alliances

Large corporations in Germany are a web of stakeholder alliances, such as the one at Daimler-Benz, with the main German banks at the core of these interlocking networks.

German laws permit major banks to play a far more active and influential role in industry than banks in the United States. Over the past century—and the big ones have existed that long—German banks have accumulated great wealth, and they exercise great power. Alliances between big banks and big industry are so common that Germany's economic system has been called "alliance capitalism." One West German study in the mid-1980s concluded that banks, as holding companies, held the majority voting share in twenty-seven of the thirty-two largest industrial firms.[13]

Deutsche Bank is the archetypal German stakeholder. It was founded in Berlin in 1870, a year before Bismarck unified the modern German state, and ever since then the bank's fortunes have risen and fallen with those of Germany. Deutsche Bank financed the buildup of German industry in the nineteenth century and early twentieth century. After World War II, the Allies broke up Deutsche Bank into ten regional banks; but as West Germany rose from the ashes of war, so did Deutsche Bank, reuniting its fragments in 1957. Since then, the bank's surging growth has matched the miracle path of West Germany's economy, the bank's global assets rising to more than $200 billion by 1990.[14]

Deutsche Bank's stake in German industry is pervasive. It holds sizable stakes in nearly eighty German industrial and commercial companies—not only 28 percent of Daimler-Benz, but also 25 percent of Europe's largest department store chain (Karstadt) and 25 percent of Germany's largest construction company (Philipp Holzmann); 31 percent of a huge heavy engineering firm (Klöckner-Humboldt-Deutz); roughly 25 percent each of two large china and textile firms (Hutschenreuther and NINO); and 10 percent or more of other companies in oil and petroleum, insurance, tires, machinery, sugar, household appliances, concrete, and silk.[15]

The bank's vast holdings give it a powerful voice all across German industry. Deutsche Bank executives sit on some four hundred corporate boards.[16] Hilmar Kopper, its top executive, sits on eight boards (German law sets a limit of ten board memberships per person). And this is fairly typical, not only of Kopper's senior colleagues but of top executives at other major German banks.

As stakeholders, German banks provide major German firms with steady financial support, management advice, market information—and protection from hostile takeovers. Krupp, the Ruhr-based steel and engineering company, could not have modernized and restructured itself in the 1980s without steady backing from Deutsche Bank.[17] In 1985, Deutsche Bank arranged for a friendly takeover of the financially ailing electronics giant AEG by Daimler-Benz.[18] Continental Tire faced a takeover by the Italian firm Pirelli in the early 1990s, and Deutsche Bank saved the German firm.

Deutsche Bank epitomizes the German approach. Its hallmark is the enduring stakeholder connection, in bad times as well as in good times. "For us, banking with a corporation is not hit and run," asserts Hilmar Kopper, the Deutsche Bank chief. "It's not deal based. It's relationship based. We believe in relationship banking."

Even if Deutsche Bank occasionally gets hurt in the short run,[19] its eye is on the long term. That's the German way.

America: The Shareholder Mind-Set—Absentee Owners

America operates from a different mind-set—*the shareholder mind-set.*
Ownership in most publicly held American corporations is usually

fleeting, amorphous, and detached. It is scattered among millions of shareholders, a constantly churning mass, who buy and trade, driven primarily by short-run stock performance rather than by a company's long-term health and prospects.

As *The Economist* observed, American and British shareholders are like gamblers at the track "placing a bet on tomorrow's race."[20] If a stock looks like a winner, they may double their ante; if it looks like a loser, they cash in and drop out. Here today, gone tomorrow. On the American stock market, a "long-term" investment for tax purposes is for one year—and people want that reduced to six months; in Europe or Japan, one year is regarded as a short-term investment.

Unlike German stakeholders, most American shareholders do not think of themselves as owners. In fact, most individual shareholders now invest in mutual funds or in stock index funds; they are largely unaware of which companies they theoretically own. Even those who hold stock in individual companies care little about influencing the management behavior of those companies. In the main, their goal is to realize quick, high returns, and that shareholder mind-set puts pressure on management to focus on cost cutting and short-term payoffs. It does not encourage patient development of products, technology, markets, or the skills of the human workforce.

Over the past two decades, the individual investor has been largely eclipsed, except as a buyer of mutual funds. Nearly two thirds of the stock in America's large companies is held by institutional investors— pension funds, mutual funds, insurance companies, college and university endowments, and the like.[21] In theory, institutional investors with large funds to manage over the long term should be stable owners. But in the hothouse atmosphere of Wall Street, institutional money managers feel pressure to maximize the performance of their portfolios, quarter by quarter, even day by day, by jumping funds from one stock to another. Rapid turnover has become the name of the game for institutional investors. One study found that, on average, institutions investing in corporate equities in the mid-1980s were selling three of every four stocks in less than a year.[22] Another study found that American institutional investors trade ten times more frequently than similar investors in Japan.[23]

The American system, of course, has strengths. Having a multitude of shareholders spreads risks. Antitrust laws keep the market open for entrepreneurs and for new firms to challenge long-dominant companies. A wide-open capital market has provided funds to make America a creative hotbed of start-up firms and cutting-edge technologies. But as the studies of the Council on Competitiveness indicate, the pattern of floating, absentee ownership in America has serious drawbacks, when pitted against global rivals.

The most serious flaw is the disconnection between the mass of shareholders and the managers who run companies. Essentially, they communicate through the stock market instead of face to face, as on a German corporate board. And the volatility of stock shares and stock prices beams a powerful signal to American CEOs: Produce quickly, or face a decline in your company's stock.

"American owners—individual and institutional—have a very limited voice in corporate governance," observe business economists Jay W. Lorsch and Elizabeth A. MacIver. "They rarely hold sufficient shares in a company to gain a seat on the board, and the proxy voting process makes success unlikely in opposing incumbent management and directors. The best method to express dissatisfaction is for owners to sell their shares. This . . . pattern of investor behavior gives America's managers and directors a clear message about the goals of their owners: 'Improve earnings quarter by quarter and we will hold or increase our investment. If earnings decline, we will sell.' "[24]

The Go-Go Eighties Accentuate America's Short-Term Mind-Set

The market pressures on the American CEO to adopt a short-term, defensive mind-set were compounded by the takeover, merger, and buyout mania of the go-go eighties, and by the massive floating of junk bonds and corporate debt to finance the buyout binge.

In both Germany and Japan, the survival of the company—in the interests of owners, employees, clients, and home communities—is management's primary objective. Not so in America. Between 1977 and 1987—one short decade—157 of the 400 large companies listed in *Standard & Poor's* had simply disappeared—either shut down or bought out. The dollar value of mergers between 1985 and 1987 was more than $520 billion, ten times the level of the mid-1970s.[25] Again in 1994, corporate takeovers leapt to the level of $300 billion a year.[26]

In the 1980s, deal making became a driving obsession. Companies were bought, carved up, and sold off piece by piece by corporate raiders who had little knowledge of, or interest in, running these companies but who had found they could milk solid firms for handsome profits by selling off their assets, slowing down investment, and pocketing the cash flow. Some 480 companies and another 560 subsidiaries or divisions were devoured by private buyouts in the 1980s;[27] the volume of leveraged buyouts leapt from $3.1 billion in 1981 to $67.4 billion in 1988.[28]

Corporate raiders contend that the threat of takeovers imposes healthy discipline on management—to perform well or face being gobbled up by outsiders. But corporate executives protest that the takeover threat undermines sensible long-term strategic planning. That threat "breeds a climate of fear," asserted Philip R. O'Connell, former senior vice president of Champion International Corporation, forcing corporate leaders to focus unwisely "on short-term results and defense mechanisms that often place additional high burdens of long-term debt on their companies. [That] not only makes companies more vulnerable . . . but also undercuts product development, innovation and international competitiveness."[29]

It took massive borrowings to finance all that wheeling and dealing and to repay all the corporate debt. Much of the payback money came from cutting long-run investment in plant and equipment or in the research and development of technology for the future. So, as the crescendo of mergers and buyouts mounted in the late 1980s, American corporate investment for the long term leveled off and eventually declined. Many companies felt compelled in self-defense to divert funds from long-term R&D into buying back their own stock; this way, they could drive up the stock price and make their stock too expensive for hostile raiders to buy.

In a very real sense, the American eighties were a battle for control of the financial resources of American corporations. The binge of buyouts and mergers, as one business analyst remarked, put big money into the hands of "the manipulators, not the innovators"—the quick-buck artists over the long-haul investors.[30]

What came into sharp relief was the vacuum of authentic ownership in the American system.

The Rise of Managerial Capitalism—"Capitalism Without Capitalists"

American capitalism had once operated like capitalism in Europe and Japan, with wealthy families, banks, financiers, and other institutions playing a substantial and active ownership role in large firms. But over time the wealthy families and their heirs became less active, reaping their fortunes from the sidelines. And the financiers who had put together the big corporations were gradually eased out by corporate managers.

This trend was broadened in the 1930s, during Franklin Roosevelt's New Deal, when Congress passed the Glass-Steagall Act, which barred commercial banks from owning shares in ordinary corporations, and the Securities Exchange Law, which prevented all major financial institutions from sitting on corporate boards. In the 1930s, those laws had little impact, because institutional investors held only about 6 or 7 percent of the stock of publicly held corporations in America. Today, institutional investors own more than 60 percent of that stock, and they are still barred from sitting on corporate boards and taking an owner's role in overseeing management, as such institutions do in Germany and Japan.

"We've created capitalism without capitalists," asserts MIT economist Lester Thurow. "We created this game where the only thing those people could do is 'play Wall Street'—buy and sell, takeovers, leveraged buyouts, and all that kind of thing. They couldn't go into industries and plan long-run strategies, R and D strategies, [strategies for] how do we run the Japanese or the Germans out of this business. And what you end up with is an industrial system where there are no owners. . . . We've created capitalism with speculators, and capitalism with speculators doesn't work."[31]

Into the ownership vacuum stepped the professional managers, and America evolved into what business historian Alfred Chandler aptly termed "managerial capitalism."[32]

By 1950, according to Chandler, a new managerial class dominated most U.S. corporations, and few owners had any direct say in running enterprises. "Even the legal fiction of outside control was beginning to disappear," Chandler reported. In 1963, one study of America's 200 largest nonfinancial companies found that 169 were "management-controlled"; in only 31 did a family or group own more than 10 percent of the stock, and in only 5 did any owner have majority control.[33] By the late 1980s, ownership had dispersed even further. Only 8 of the nation's 50 largest companies had *any* ownership blocks greater than 10 percent; in none did any owner have majority control.[34]

Over time, the all-powerful CEO became the dominant force in American capitalism. By comparison with the intricate power sharing of Germany and the family-style networks of Japanese capitalism (which we will explore later), the American CEO has been king of the hill. Rarely does he have substantial owners looking over his shoulder, closely gauging his performance to protect their personal stakes in the company, as Edzard Reuter does on the supervisory board at Daimler-Benz.

The U.S. Corporate Board: Where Are the Stakeholders?

In theory, the boardroom is the nexus of power in the American corporation. The board of directors is supposed to act on behalf of the mass of absentee owners, the shareholders, to ensure the company's growth and to oversee management's performance. Like the supervisory board in Germany, the American corporate board is theoretically the final authority, not only a sounding board for the CEO but a check and balance on the CEO.

But, as Adam Smith pointed out two hundred years ago, this Anglo-American form of capitalist authority has an inherent flaw when the directors are not authentic stakeholders—when they lack a significant personal ownership stake.

"The directors . . . being the managers of other people's money," wrote Adam Smith, "it cannot be well expected that they should watch over it with the same anxious vigilance with which the partners in a private co-partnery frequently watch over their own. . . . Negligence and profusion, therefore, must always prevail, more or less, in the management of . . . such a company."[35]

The legendary Scottish economist had put his finger on what some critics consider a most grievous failing in American capitalism—the passivity of most corporate boards. They are often manipulated by an imperial CEO and rarely, if ever, called to serious account by stockholders. In the corporate board, *The Economist* observed, "the Anglo-American stock market has created a vacuum at the heart of capitalism."[36]

With the financial calamities at major corporations such as GM, IBM, Sears, Kodak, Westinghouse, and American Express in the early 1990s, a few U.S. corporate boards woke up belatedly and staged sensational shake-ups—typically long after the dire straits of their companies were common knowledge. But those boardroom revolts were the exceptions.

In the American boardroom, there is a long tradition of quietism and clubby camaraderie. Bad management decisions have rarely been seriously challenged until it was too late, and sometimes not even then. The CEO typically controls the board's agenda; he has the knowledge and the expertise, plus a high-powered staff to serve him and the time to study every issue in detail. By contrast, the board's part-time directors fly in for a quarterly or monthly meeting lasting one day. They are swamped with papers and presentations; rarely do they have time to discuss major proposals among themselves; and typically they are eager to get back to their own businesses on time. So power and procedure are tilted in favor of the CEO.

What is more, rocking the boat has been frowned upon in most corporate boards. William Woodside, chairman of Sky Chefs and retired CEO of Primerica, told *Fortune* magazine how he had been ostracized as a director at Nabisco Brands after blurting out his criticism of the company's candidate for a successor to Nabisco's president, Ross Johnson. "Nobody spoke to me at the next two board meetings," Woodside said. "It was a no-no. Socially, I'd pulled a tremendous gaffe."[37]

Many directors regard their function as advising the CEO, not challenging him. As one specialist wrote, most corporate directors regard their board appointment as "more of an accolade than an obligation" to play a vigorous role.[38] Graef Crystal, a longtime consultant on executive compensation to many corporate boards, described the typical American board as "a Potemkin village."

In the 1980s, Crystal observed, the CEO's proposals rarely met strong objections from board members. "Remember," said Crystal, "if you're on the board, you look to the end of the table and there is the boss, the chairman of the board. And if you've grown up being conscious of power relationships, you understand that this is the boss and you treat him deferentially."[39] An uppity board member, Crystal noted, risks being ousted by the CEO, cut off from the perks of the corporate jet, luxurious accommodations, and $30,000 a year or more in director's fees.

Here was a crucial point: Unlike in Germany, where the CEO does not have a seat on the supervisory board and the board chairman is a substantial outside owner, most American corporate CEOs also serve as chairman of the board. This makes an American CEO his own judge and jury. He can handpick board members. In practice, most boards are composed primarily of executives from inside the company, whose career paths depend on the boss, and of CEOs from other companies, who are often friends of the boss. According to one study, 69 percent of the outside directors on the boards of America's 1,000 largest companies are CEOs of other companies.[40] The rationale is that experience qualifies CEOs as directors. CEOs, however, are also part of the executive fraternity, unlikely to harass another CEO. Not only are CEO-directors often old friends and golfing buddies of the CEO-chairman, they often swap appointments to one another's boards. And, as directors, they observe the Golden Rule.

The absence of owner-stakeholders makes for passivity on corporate boards, observed MIT's Lester Thurow, a veteran of several boards. "These boards are very loathe to intervene," he said. "The board members may be very important citizens, but when you're put on a corporate board and you're not a big owner, how are you suddenly going to be aggressive? We don't have that day-to-day involvement of an owner-board of directors."[41]

The well-known corporate investor Carl Icahn agreed. Icahn recalled the 8 A.M. board meetings of a firm in Cleveland. "Literally half the board is dozing off. The other half is reading *The Wall Street Journal*," Icahn said. "And they put slides up a lot and nobody can understand the slides. . . . The chief executive officer at that time was a very intimidating sort of guy . . . and he was in control of the board. I mean, nobody could say anything. I was the only one who owned any stock, so I had an interest. I wanted to know what the hell was going on."[42]

How Well Do Stock Options Work in Generating High Performance?

The test issue on which American corporate boards first got caught napping—and the hottest button among shareholders in the early 1990s—was skyrocketing CEO pay packages.

Many large American corporations had been operating on the rationale that the way to get CEOs to think long term was to offer them rich stock options. The theory was that the CEO would ensure that the company performed well, since he would profit personally as the company's stock price rose. That sounded logical, but often it did not work out in practice.[43]

Graef Crystal, a longtime expert on executive pay who later joined the faculty at the University of California in Berkeley, asserts that most stock bonus schemes have a perverse effect—they encourage

CEOs to adopt policies that will have a positive short-term impact on stock prices, and thus benefit them personally, rather than to think long term for the sake of the company.[44]

For more than twenty years, Crystal worked inside corporate America, making $650,000 a year as a compensation consultant helping to put together golden bonus deals and stock options for CEOs. Crystal was a true believer that money could motivate CEOs to higher performance. That was what corporate CEOs wanted to hear, and Crystal made their case to their corporate boards. But while he was still on the inside, Crystal began to have doubts, and so he tried to persuade CEOs and corporate boards to be less lavish with stock options and pay packages. Inevitably Crystal's outspokenness cost him clients. He got fired.

After going on his own in 1988, Crystal admitted misgivings about having served as the minion of corporate CEOs. "I don't think I was ever for sale—at least not consciously for sale," Crystal told *The Washington Post*. "But I acted in the full realization that if I didn't please the client, I wouldn't have that client for long."[45]

When he started writing business columns questioning CEO pay levels and their rationale, Crystal found himself squeezed out of *Fortune* and *Financial World*. Later he told *The New York Times:* "I can't find a niche anywhere in any American magazine that has advertising in it. Because my enemies are going to be out there threatening to pull their advertising."[46]

So, armed with a database and inside knowledge of the pay systems of many of America's 500 major corporations, Crystal produced his own newsletter.

By this time, American CEOs were being paid the moon, mainly through enormous grants of stock options—and sometimes outright gifts of a couple of million shares of company stock. Before the mid-1980s, it was rare for a corporate CEO to be paid $5 million in one year. In 1991, the two highest paid were Robert Goizueta of Coca-Cola at $86 million and Leon Hirsch of U.S. Surgical at $118 million;[47] in 1992, the highest pay went to Thomas Frist, Jr., of Hospital Corporation of America at $127 million;[48] and in 1993, Michael Eisner, CEO of Walt Disney Co., set the all-time corporate record of $203 million. Nor were they alone. In 1993, for example, seventy-five top executives made more than $5 million—twenty-four of those made more than $10 million, eight topped $20 million.[49]

After studying the performance records of 370 major American firms over five years (1989–93), Graef Crystal could not find any rhyme or reason to the CEO pay levels of America's top twenty performing companies.

"I can get someone to run Wal-Mart for about a million dollars a year," he observed, "but it takes eighty million dollars to motivate the chairman of Coke and a huge amount of money [$203 million] to get Michael Eisner at Disney. It's just all over the map."[50]

There was "no correlation whatsoever" between CEO pay and company performance, Crystal insisted, no pattern connecting big pay with top performance or low pay with poor performance.

He did a special analysis of long-term stock options. In 1988, he said, the options granted to individual CEOs ran from almost nothing up to $200 million. Five years later, he said, "The answer is—there's no relationship" between the size of option grants and how well the companies did.[51]

There is commonsense logic to these findings, Crystal contended. He recalled a conversation from his former life as a corporate pay consultant, in which he asked an unnamed CEO whether this CEO would "work harder" for more money, and the boss barked back that he was already slaving tirelessly for the corporation. Then Crystal asked whether the CEO would "work smarter" for more money, and the boss replied that he was already doing his best. "Well, if you won't work harder for more money, if you won't work smarter for more money, and you're in your late fifties and your behavioral patterns are well ingrained," Crystal inquired, "then why do we assume that if we give you a two-million-share option that you will act differently than if we give you a one-million-share option or no option at all?"[52]

Crystal added that U.S. corporate boards have often undermined their own rationale of using stock options to promote long-term performance by making outright gifts of stock to executives, thereby guaranteeing their CEOs a huge profit regardless of company performance. Or else, he said, boards keep offering CEOs new options at lower prices if the company's stock price falls, so that, even after a bad performance, the CEO has a chance to make a killing, even if the company's stock price never gets back up to its previous level.

Other evidence supports Crystal's conclusions. For when American companies got into trouble in the early 1990s, bad performance did not slow the rising tide of CEO pay. In 1990, for example, *Fortune* magazine found that among companies that had a 20 percent drop in earnings that year, CEOs got pay increases averaging 7.6 percent;

among companies with a 30 percent decline in earnings, CEO pay went up 6.1 percent.[53] In 1991, Westinghouse Electric CEO Paul Lego got a 41 percent net increase in his pay and options while his company lost $1.1 billion;[54] Rand Araskog of ITT earned $11 million while his company's stock price skidded 20 percent; and Stephen Wolf of United Airlines netted $18 million while his company's corporate profits dropped 71 percent.[55]

Nor did the pay-for-performance theory stand up well in international comparisons. In the late 1980s and early 1990s, while Japanese companies were matching or beating American rivals, CEOs at large American companies were getting paid much more than their Japanese peers. In 1990, Crystal calculated that several hundred major U.S. companies paid their CEOs an average of $3.2 million, compared with $1.1 million in Britain, $800,000 in Germany, and $525,000 in Japan (though the Japanese chiefs got more corporate perks).[56] In Germany, the highest-paid CEO, Peter Tamm at the Axel Springer publishing empire, was making about $2.7 million, a far cry from the top American CEOs, who were pushing $100 million, according to *Forbes* magazine.[57] In Japan, poor performance brought lower pay: When the economy began nosing down in 1991 and profits dwindled, the heads of Hitachi, Fujitsu, Japan Airlines, and IBM Japan announced a 35 percent cut in their base pay.[58]

For the American economy, perhaps the most perverse effect of CEO stock options is that the formula for their personal financial success is not investment and growth; rather, it is often disinvestment and shrinking the corporation.

The stock market, for example, quite predictably shoots up the stock price of a company that announces cutbacks and layoffs, long before the actual results of "downsizing" are clear. The stock market's quick rise in response to "downsizing" becomes a powerful incentive for stock option–rich CEOs to engage in "corporate restructuring" that involves layoffs and cutbacks, even though follow-up surveys indicate that only about one third of the time does the company actually gain a competitive advantage from downsizing.[59]

"Rising pay packages for CEOs and worsening job security for many ordinary working people are often driven by the same phenomenon: the relentless pressure from financial markets to drive up stock prices," observes economist Margaret Blair of the Brookings Institution.[60]

This new dynamic stands on its head the classic pattern of corporate motivations and incentives that drove the American economy during its long postwar expansion. From 1950 to 1980, the American corporate gospel was growth. As American corporations, especially those in manufacturing, grew, they generated enough cash flow and earnings to pay handsome dividends to shareholders, to pay rising wages to workers, and to generate capital to finance further expansion. In those years, stock options were relatively modest. Growth was the primary yardstick of managerial success—and growth was the basis for yearly cash bonuses.[61] And that growth philosophy built long-term success—for the company and for the American economy.

But in the 1980s, things changed dramatically. In an effort to attract capital, many American companies switched their performance yardstick for CEOs from growth to the return delivered to shareholders; and massive stock options were the main motivating mechanism.[62]

So how well did American shareholders fare?

Morgan Stanley studied total return on investment in the decade from 1983 to 1993 in the stock markets of leading industrial countries. Germany, Japan, Hong Kong, and almost all of Europe outdid America. Out of thirteen countries, the shareholders of America came in last.[63]

Inside GM: How Roger Smith Finessed the Board

For America's corporate boards, CEO pay was only the tip of the iceberg. A far more serious problem was their failure in the 1980s to pay close attention to corporate strategies.

General Motors offers a prime case study. Roger Smith plunged GM into a $77 billion investment spree in new plants and automation, but instead of leapfrogging the Japanese, as Roger Smith had promised, GM fell on its face. By 1986, Roger Smith's misguided strategies were apparent inside the company as well as outside, according to Elmer Johnson, one of Smith's closest lieutenants.

Where was GM's board of directors? Why didn't they spot the problem and challenge Roger Smith's mistaken strategy?

"We weren't challenged adequately by our best outside directors—because we didn't provide adequate information so they would know where they ought to be challenging us," acknowledged Harry Pearce, deputy chief of GM's legal division under Roger Smith and now GM's executive vice president.

"The seventy billion dollars was spent very badly, without a plan—except that it must be healthy to do this sort of thing," asserted Thomas Wyman, a member of the GM board since 1985. "The board had nothing to do with this—that's the tragedy. The board never has anything to do with it. That's the tradition at GM and in most American corporations."[64]

Given the GM board's membership, that sounds incredible. The GM board had included some powerful and experienced people—John G. Smale, chairman and CEO of Procter & Gamble; Wyman, a former chairman and CEO of CBS and later chairman of the American arm of the Warburg investment bank; Dennis Weatherstone, chairman and CEO of J. P. Morgan; Edmund T. Pratt, Jr., chairman of Pfizer; J. Willard Marriott, chairman and CEO of Marriott Corp.; Charles T. Fisher III, chairman and president of NBD Bancorp; Marvin Goldberger, president of the California Institute of Technology; Anne L. Armstrong, former ambassador to Great Britain; the Reverend Leon Sullivan of Philadelphia; and, later, Ann McLaughlin, former secretary of labor; and Thomas E. Everhart, the new president of the California Institute of Technology.

Instead of drawing heavily on the advice of this board, GM management made poor use of the board's talents and expertise.

"We spent more of our time trying to manage the board, setting our agenda for the board, controlling the information flow to the board," admitted Harry Pearce. "That's not the way you get the best out of your outside directors. You get the best by putting your toughest problems on the table and inviting their comments and seeking their solutions. If you simply bring good news and explain the brilliance of your own strategies, you will never know when you're going down the wrong path."

Had the GM board been merely a rubber stamp? I asked Pearce.

"Too much," he conceded. "It was too rigid, too controlled. There was too little open debate, too few questions asked. The ambience within the room was such that questions were discouraged—not openly, but indirectly discouraged."

Had Roger Smith's style inhibited people?

"Well, Roger is a very strong personality," Pearce replied. "He's a take-charge sort of guy, and I don't know that he wanted an aggressive, open debate at the board level."[65]

Not only Roger Smith's hard edge but GM's might had daunted the outsiders, according to Elmer Johnson, once Roger Smith's executive vice president. "They were so awestruck by the size of General Motors that nothing in their companies prepared them for $10 billion a year going out for new investment," observed Johnson. "It took me four years before I felt that I had doped it all out."[66]

Each board meeting was carefully scripted. Roger Smith was the impresario. "All those presentations were previously screened by Roger," Johnson said, "and every presenter had to present the thing in writing, go over with Roger's finance people before they could go up there [to the board]. Then there was usually no time for questions, because we had to move on to the next thing."

GM's board had functioned for so long with the CEO making uni-lateral decisions and the board cheerleading that Smith found it easy to steamroll his directors. He had a core of support within the board from his full-time management team—at one point, seven inside man-agement directors versus fifteen outside directors.

"With twenty-two people round the board table, see how much *real* talk there is," commented Wyman, the outsider from CBS. "There would be a big exposition given the board and a big fat book, and the board would approve three hundred twenty million dollars for robot-ics investments at the Mansfield, Ohio, plant. And you know that three hundred twenty million in a GM boardroom is like your taking me to lunch for forty-two dollars. You could have five of these pro-posals come up at one session. There was no possibility of the board really understanding the proposal and debating it."

That is typical of corporate boards, Wyman said, and the term "board approval" is something of a misnomer. "It was technically re-quired that the board approve, so it was all done very meticulously," Wyman recalled. "Every proposal was passed with a board vote, and a record was made. So Roger Smith could go back to the minutes of those meetings and say, 'The board approved everything I did.'

"But when the VP for advanced engineering gets up and says, 'These are the machines, this is the technology, this is how it looks, this is what will put us ten years ahead of everybody,' it's hard to resist going along. There are a few questions, of course—at the board meet-ing, over lunch—but nothing serious. It's pretty formidable when you're dealing with an organization of that size and people of that ex-pertise and experience are giving you recommendations. The board felt, 'This is the responsible way to go. This is the courageous way to go. We are investing in our future.' There are clichés—'investing in our future'—while Ford and Chrysler are going 'on the cheap.' And in a few years we're going to reap the benefits of our wisdom in taking these hard steps now.' "[67]

As GM's problems became more apparent in the mid-1980s, dissenters surfaced, most notably H. Ross Perot, and they were eased out. As part of Roger Smith's automation and computerization strategy, GM had bought Perot's company, Electronic Data Systems, for $2.5 billion. Perot had been given a seat on the board and had repeatedly faulted Smith for mismanaging both companies by focusing too much on finance to the jeopardy of manufacturing. In 1986, Perot was paid $700 million for his GM stock and pushed off the GM board.[68] Executive Vice President Elmer Johnson also began questioning Smith, and Smith turned so chilly that Johnson quit GM in 1988.[69]

The grumbling among board members grew as GM moved toward Roger Smith's scheduled retirement in 1990. GM's North American operation was losing money. Roger Smith was no longer accepted as the oracle; at least eighteen months before his retirement, Wyman disclosed, the outside directors wanted him gone. Still, no move was made to oust him. The attitude on the GM board, according to Wyman, was "Look, you've got to live through this. It's pretty embarrassing, but we're going to have a real car man [Robert Stempel] in here in a year or two, and then we'll be okay."

Roger Smith even finessed the board on the choice of his successor. Robert Stempel was an insider, a management man, handpicked by Smith. The board simply went along.

"The selection of Stempel was automatic—as is traditional at GM and other companies," Wyman recalled ruefully. "These things evolve over three, four years. There are no surprises in a system like that. The board has nothing to do with it. No one objects, because it isn't good form. The table at Versailles is so big that nobody speaks up. So's the table at GM—and nobody speaks up there either."[70]

GM Board Revolt: "It's Embarrassing to Wake Up So Late"

It took a total disaster—an economic earthquake—to jolt GM's board members out of their inertia and into acting like stakeholders.

When Robert Stempel took over on August 1, 1990, the outside directors imagined a new dawn. Stempel had climbed the ranks of manufacturing, and the board pinned great hopes on him to get GM back to the practical work of making cars. Even Ross Perot chirped cheerily: "It's a terrific day for GM and a terrific day for the country!"[71]

But Stempel was too much of a company man, too steeped in the old GM mind-set, to make radical changes—and radical surgery was what the board's outsiders sensed was needed. Stempel asked the board to give him time, but the board was growing impatient with half measures. "Stempel was not all that different—Stempel was a supporter of Smith, he was a believer," Wyman recalled. "He had not learned any of the lessons. He just went along with the old strategy, and so did the board."

For a while—but revolt was percolating.

Sometime in 1991, the eleven outside directors led by Smale, the former CEO of Procter & Gamble, did total immersion to plumb GM's deepest problems. They met without the knowledge of the GM hierarchy. They sent faxes back and forth daily. They noticed that in Europe, Jack Smith, GM's vice chairman for international operations, had turned things around by cutting down the central staff, tightening supplier costs, quickly adding new models and dropping duds. Even though, in December 1991, Stempel announced plans to close twenty-one plants and lay off 74,000 employees by 1996, the restless directors were dissatisfied. They did not see him cutting back enough on GM's top-heavy management structure or shaking up the complacent corporate mind-set.[72]

Still the board hesitated.

What finally galvanized the directors into action was GM's $7 billion loss in 1991. "It took that seven-billion-dollar loss to really wake us up," Tom Wyman admitted. "What we did was pretty exciting, but it's also embarrassing to wake up so late."[73]

The GM board revolt came in two shots. In April 1992, the cabal of eleven outsiders forced the demotion of two key vice presidents; removed Stempel as chairman of the board's executive committee; installed Smale, the outside director, in his place; and made Jack Smith, the hero of GM's profitable European operations, president of GM and number two to Stempel. Six months later, at the end of October 1992, the outsiders completed their corporate coup. They made Stempel resign, named Jack Smith GM's CEO, and installed Smale, the leader of their revolt, as board chairman.

This sweeping shake-up was extraordinary. These were the first top-level executive demotions at GM since 1920. Stempel was made the sacrificial lamb, forced to take public blame for a decade of GM's mismanagement. But in fact, with Roger Smith still sitting on the board, the outside directors were really repudiating Roger Smith—his strategy, his mind-set, his handpicked team of successors, and, most important, the autocratic methods by which he had manipulated the board itself.

The irony was that these actions were taken not by hostile outsiders but by people whom Roger Smith had brought onto the board. Now, by naming their leader, John Smale, as board chairman, they were doing something unheard of at GM: They were deliberately limiting the power of the CEO, and they were asserting the board's independent power of oversight. It was a precedent-setting corporate coup.

"This is nothing short of a revolution and it is symbolic for all industry in this country," asserted Maryann Keller, author of two insightful books on the auto industry. "This should shake up every corporation where CEOs have been sleeping."[74]

In fact, by shattering the invincibility of the imperial CEO, the GM board revolt did trigger a chain reaction. Within a year or two, institutional investors and newly activist boards forced the departures of John Akers from IBM, Jim Robinson from American Express, Joseph Canio from Compaq Computer, Ken Olsen from Digital Equipment, Kay Whitmore from Eastman Kodak, Harvey Weinberg from Hartmax, James Ketelsen from Tenneco, and Paul Lego from Westinghouse, among others. At Sears, Roebuck, the board trimmed the power of CEO Edward Brennan. At Chrysler, it rebuffed Lee Iacocca's bid to stay on past normal retirement age.

Grassroots Reform: Shareholders Acting like Stakeholders

At the grassroots level, the GM revolt also spurred a new activism among shareholder groups and employee pension funds, which pressed many corporate boards to heed the long-term interests of stakeholders, rather than bow to the pressures of the corporate CEO.

None made a bigger splash in taking up the cause of corporate reform than CalPERS, the California state employees' pension fund, the largest in the nation with $80 billion in assets. CalPERS began to rethink its role as a corporate stakeholder. "In the eighties all of us were thinking of ourselves as investors, not owners," said Dale Hanson, CalPERS president from 1987 to 1994.[75] Hanson shifted CalPERS from being a mere manager of its members' money to being an engaged corporate owner. With its enormous stock holdings, CalPERS could not jump into and out of the market; it had to stick with companies over the long term. So CalPERS began to think about how to use its ownership stake to influence corporate behavior by developing ongoing relationships with management—what it called "relationship investing."

By law, CalPERS was barred from holding seats on corporate boards; and despite its size, it was still a small minority investor in corporations. With 4.3 million shares of General Motors stock, for example, CalPERS held only 1 percent of the total—far from enough to win a proxy fight but plenty to make its weight felt. In the ten to twenty firms in which CalPERS had a sizable stake, Dale Hanson and his staff set about jawboning management and pressing for corporate reforms—by mail, by phone, in face-to-face meetings, and by using the media to increase the pressure.

At Hercules, Polaroid, Salomon Brothers, Time Warner, and USAir, CalPERS put the heat on for appointment of more independent directors; at Control Data and the Ryder System, it demanded more open corporate communications with shareholders; at American Express, Dial, IBM, ITT, and eight other firms, it demanded changes in the executive pay system and truly independent compensation committees, to replace the friends of the boss. American Express CEO James Robinson quickly agreed. Rand Araskog at ITT bowed to an overhaul of his pay package. CEOs at Ford, IBM, and Avon took voluntary pay cuts in 1992 to head off the popular pressures.[76]

Shareholder public interest groups took up the campaign for corporate reform, as did employee pension funds from New York, Massachusetts, Wisconsin, and elsewhere. In 1992 and early 1993, CEO stock options became the target of angry protests. Shareholders showed up at corporate annual meetings, fuming over plummeting stock prices, demanding ceilings on CEO pay, and calling for the ouster of corporate boards for their oversight failures. Another shareholder tactic has been to use the courts to break up the cozy fraternity in the boardroom. In 1993, more than seven hundred lawsuits were filed against companies and directors on issues of corporate governance and accountability. The Investor Responsibility Research Center reported that more than half the companies in *Standard & Poor's* 500-stock index—companies such as Bethlehem Steel, Occidental Petroleum, Motorola, and Coca-Cola—were using directors whose firms provided them with professional services. Stockholder activists charged that this was a clear conflict of interest—that "affiliated directors" were too beholden to management to qualify as truly independent directors.[77]

Even the government, under the probusiness Bush administration, promoted corporate reform. For many years, the Securities and Exchange Commission had barred shareholders from petitioning corporate boards on the pay issue, asserting that this was a matter strictly for management. But the howls of outrage became so great that, in 1992, the SEC relented. That fall, the SEC issued new regulations dictating that corporate compensation committees be composed entirely of outside directors and requiring annual proxy statements to spell out more clearly the pay packages of top executives and to disclose "interlocking directorships"—cases in which CEOs were swapping seats on one another's boards and thus positioning themselves to raise one another's pay. The SEC also relaxed its earlier ban on communications among large shareholders, making it easier for pension funds and other owner groups to get together to put pressure on companies.

Congress took additional steps. In 1993, the Clinton administration pushed through a bill to deny corporate tax deductions for CEO pay above $1 million, but not before corporate lobbyists inserted an enormous loophole—the right of corporate boards to pay any amount whatsoever, tax free, so long as pay was linked to some performance standard, however low or vague. One favorite corporate tactic for beating the $1 million limit was to replace cash pay with "quickie options" that could be exercised within a year, thus defeating the whole purpose of long-term options. Other reform ideas, such as requiring corporate pay packages to be ratified by shareholders, never got off the ground.

In fact, as the economy picked up steam in 1993 and 1994, the protest over CEO pay cooled. In California, CalPERS faced political pressures. Corporate chiefs appealed to Republican Governor Pete Wilson to pack the CalPERS board in order to either oust or cool off its reformist president, Dale Hanson. While the legislature would not go along with expanding the CalPERS board, the mere effort had the intended effect, according to Graef Crystal, who was a consultant to CalPERS.[78] In late 1994, Hanson left CalPERS to take a private-sector job, saying that he no longer saw CEO pay as being a serious problem,[79] and his replacement, Jim Burton, has not been given to high-profile activism.[80]

Nonetheless, as the American economy rebounded from recession in the 1990s, CEO pay continued to rise handsomely. When the 1993 corporate pay packages were disclosed, there was a new record high. *Business Week*'s response was a headline: "Their Cup Runneth Over—Again."[81]

The new shareholder activism has led some, such as Harvard Professor John Pound, to suggest that the future American CEO "will look less like an emperor than like a Congressman," forced to balance constituencies.[82] Others saw shareholder activism as too much of a good thing. Robert Pozen of Fidelity Investments in Boston, a major mutual fund group, cast most institutional investors as "reluctant activists" who generally did not want to be drawn into a larger, more activist role in corporate life. Pozen spoke for many who preferred to remain mere shareholders—not stakeholders.[83]

Prescription: More Stakeholders on U.S. Corporate Boards

Within the corporate world, serious efforts have been afoot to institutionalize checks and balances on American corporate CEOs, in order to improve long-term corporate performance.

The General Motors board has expanded on its model. In March 1994, the GM board issued a corporate manifesto that engraved in stone basic changes to ensure the independence of corporate boards and to put limits on the unchecked power of the CEO. The GM board issued twenty-eight guidelines to make permanent the key elements of its 1992 boardroom revolution. The GM guidelines called for a company's outside directors, as a group, to select their own leader—if not the chairman of the board, then their own "lead director"—as a counterpoint to the CEO. Outside directors, the GM manifesto asserted, should meet several times a year, independently of management; should receive all proposals for board meetings in advance in writing, in order to have time to weigh and discuss them; should have "complete access" directly to all managers, without having to go through the CEO; should do a formal annual review of the CEO's performance; and should choose all new directors themselves—and not allow the CEO to pack the board with his own choices.[84]

Dale Hanson of CalPERS hailed this as a "Magna Carta" for American corporations. Other advocates of corporate reform, such as Jay Lorsch of Harvard Business School, saw the GM guidelines as a model for other corporate boards. "This legitimizes boards taking a tougher look at CEOs," Lorsch said. "We're already seeing some of these things happening."[85] GM's example was indeed energizing other boards. John Smale was getting private protests from his CEO friends, who strenuously objected to GM's call for boardroom independence and who resented the intrusion of their boards into what the CEOs regarded as their own prerogatives.

In other arenas, there have been calls for more basic reforms to engage stakeholders in governing U.S. corporations, in order to protect wider interests than are now being served and to encourage better long-term strategies.

At least twenty-five states have changed their laws on the accountability of corporate directors in recent years, permitting—and, in effect, prodding—corporate boards not just to think about their shareholders but also to take into account the interests of other constituencies. Among those who want a boardroom voice for their very real stake in companies are states, cities, and communities, which often grant tax breaks or raise substantial local bond issues to invest in local infrastructure in order to lure companies to their region, and which must contend with the painful impact of layoffs, shutdowns, and hostile takeovers.[86]

Other reformers have called into question the assumption that companies and their boards should be guided exclusively by the interests of shareholders, especially in terms of near-term stock prices.

The mass of fleeting, absentee shareholders has far less stake in an American corporation than do its workers, its managers, or its long-term customers and suppliers, asserts economist Margaret Blair of the Brookings Institution. The rapid turnover of shareholders, she argues, undermines the claim that the primary objective of management should be to raise stock prices for shareholders. Blair advocates a more general objective—"maximizing total wealth" for several constituencies: products for consumers, jobs for managers and workers, and profits for shareholders. Others would add markets for suppliers and economic stability for home communities. Membership on corporate boards should reflect these diverse interests, Blair contends, as well as accommodating such long-term institutional investors as pension funds.

"Boards must understand that they are the representatives of *all* the important stakeholders in the firm—all whose investments in physical or in human capital are at risk," Blair asserts.[87]

American corporations would improve their long-term investment performance by having their corporate boards include such constituencies as institutional investors, workers, customers, suppliers, and home communities, according to the study done for the business-led Council on Competitiveness by Harvard Business School. With these long-term stakeholders represented, the study contended, American corporate boards would be more like their German and Japanese counterparts, less prone to shortsighted, market-driven investment strategies and wiser in many respects, especially in their investment strategy for survival and long-term growth.[88]

The Harvard study proposed a package of reforms. At its core were proposals to alter the ownership structure and board membership of American corporations through changes in public policy. One recommendation is to revoke the New Deal–era legislation banning banks from owning corporate stock. Another step would be to lift the limits on the level of ownership permitted to pension funds and mutual funds. The study also recommends allowing institutional investors to hold seats on corporate boards, so that their knowledge and engagement can influence long-term corporate strategy.[89] In addition to putting these major owners onto corporate boards, the most radical proposal is to "encourage board representation by significant customers, suppliers, financial advisers, employees, and community representatives"—all the long-term stakeholders with interests in the company's success.[90]

Here was a call for fundamental changes in American corporate governance, well beyond the piecemeal changes generated by the corporate board revolts. And if such reforms were to be carried out, according to the Harvard–Council on Competitiveness study, there were good prospects of long-term gains for American corporations—a "more flexible, more responsive and even better informed" system than those of Japan and Germany.

One significant trend that is slowly pushing American corporations toward such reforms is the growth of employee ownership of companies. In recent years, as American companies have run into trouble, employees have stepped in to save their jobs by becoming significant part owners at such companies as United Airlines, Avis, Procter & Gamble, Chevron, Polaroid, Allied Signal, Paine-Webber, Knight-Ridder, TWA, Pittsburgh Plate Glass, and Northwest Airlines. Eleven million American workers own a stake in some 9,000 companies; at 250 major firms, employees own more than 20 percent of the company.[91] By the year 2000, experts predict, more than one fourth of the companies traded on America's major stock exchanges will be more than 15 percent owned by their own employees, and more than 25 percent will be owned by pension funds in general.[92]

So far, employee ownership is rarely reflected on corporate boards. But what lies ahead is new employee activism on this issue, as well as moves to amend labor laws that discourage employee participation in management.

Organized labor, taking a leaf from Germany, has periodically pushed for board representation. In 1980, Chrysler's management voluntarily took Doug Fraser, president of the UAW, onto its board for four years. In 1992, Lynn Williams, president of the United Steelworkers, made union representation on steel company boards a condition of a new contract.

Tom Usher, president of U.S. Steel, conceded that for too long U.S. Steel had made decisions affecting union members and their families and communities without hearing their views, and that the company needed "to do a much better job" of soliciting input from labor representatives. But Usher adamantly opposed putting worker representatives onto corporate boards, and he had the strong backing of Charles A. Corry, chairman of USX, the parent company of U.S. Steel.

"There still has to be somebody that makes the decisions, and that is the role of management," Usher asserted. "Comanagement—if you say that you have to have agreement on both sides—is not something that will work in the long term."[93]

Six months later, in February 1994, U.S. Steel changed its mind. Along with National Steel, Inland, Bethlehem, LTV, Acme, and Wheeling-Pittsburgh, U.S. Steel accepted a union representative on its board under its new contract with the United Steelworkers. Lynn Williams, the Steelworkers' president, had changed Usher's mind. "It was the last thing that was done," Williams said. "I told him there wouldn't be a new contract unless this was accepted."

Williams saw this as a crucial breakthrough. He believed that while the union nominee would obviously be outvoted on the board, his mere presence would change the dialogue in the boardroom. It would give the union advance notice of any major move planned by management and thus an opportunity to work things out, German style, before a confrontation, American style. Williams had made union representation on the board a *cause célèbre* because he—like John Smale—felt that a sharing of power or a limit on the power of a CEO had to be institutionalized; Williams felt that the company would be better served by having its major stakeholders heard in its board-room.[94]

Still, it is a serious question whether the GM board reform, the burst of shareholder activism, and proposals for bringing more stake-holders onto U.S. corporate boards foreshadow a thoughtful reshaping of American corporations or are mere flashes in the pan. Is all this just a temporary reaction to the failures of the 1980s and the 1991–92 recession, or do influential Americans see real benefit in modifying America's managerial capitalism by giving voice to more of the real stakeholders in American business?

Some reformers foresee the eclipse of the imperial CEO in America. I am skeptical. No less committed free-market capitalists than Adam Smith and Carl Icahn have warned that unless a corporate board in-cludes real long-term stakeholders (significant owners and employ-ees), outside directors have neither a powerful enough self-interest nor sufficient clout to check management and prevent the kind of slow, massive disaster that befell General Motors under Roger Smith.

12

The Network

Mitsubishi's Mutual Protection Society—The Corporate Clan

> *One of Japan's major contributions to modern industrial organization is the industrial group . . . known in Japanese as . . . keiretsu.*[1]
>
> —CHALMERS JOHNSON, SCHOLAR

> *There is no contract—no formal institution. A* keiretsu *is the mentality of mutual trust. . . . It's a sort of mutual insurance. It brings members of the* keiretsu *stability, efficiency, and less fuss in doing business.*[2]
>
> —NAOHIRO AMAYA, FORMER VICE MINISTER OF INDUSTRY AND TRADE

> *These groups operate as communities of shared interest, shared capital, and shared risk. . . . They can look at a problem and deal with it from A to Z, from manufacturing, sourcing, production, financing, to distribution, to after-sales. They can cut the whole network.*[3]
>
> —KENNETH COURTIS, BANK ECONOMIST AND HISTORIAN OF JAPAN

Television's cliché images of financial markets are fast-cut visuals of the frenetic, arm-waving human melee at some stock exchange. The Chicago Board of Trade or the New York Stock Exchange comes across as a wild rugby scrum—a swarming squall of humanity and a mind-rattling cacophony of voices. It is remarkable that, in that bedlam, thousands upon thousands of swift, intricate transactions can be consummated, many hinging on the mere fraction of a point and the volume running daily into trillions of dollars.

Compared to that global stereotype, the Tokyo Stock Exchange seems subdued. On a typical weekday morning, when I saw it, the nods and antic miming of the blue-jacketed floor traders were almost leisurely. Not a single voice was raised. As the tote board flashed a record of purchases and sales, the Japanese floor traders did not seem to have enough to do. Some were scanning the pit looking for business. In fact, what was striking was not how much was happening, but how little.

The slow-motion scene was all the more memorable because the Japanese economy was in recession and stock prices were going down. Major Japanese companies were reporting losses. Economic insecurity was a constant topic in the press. Yet there was no visible rush to unload shares. For even in a collapsing market, roughly 70 to 75 percent of the shares of big companies virtually never change hands. They are held permanently by what the Japanese call *antei kubunushi* ("stable shareholders").[4]

Stable Shareholders: "Keeping One Another Warm"

Why be a stable shareholder in a falling market? Why would anyone hang on to shares in companies that were losing money and foresaw more losses ahead?

The answer not only provides the secret to the stamina and vitality of Japan's most powerful companies, but it reveals a central strength of Japan's special form of capitalism—its network capitalism.

This system helps explain the resilience of the Japanese economy to external shocks and pressures, as well as the capacity of Japanese companies to sustain investments in long-term research and new plants during economic downturns. It explains why Japanese companies often come out so well in the global game of exports. And it also explains why newcomers—especially foreigners—have such difficulty getting a foothold in the Japanese market.

Japan's "stable shareholders" have a very different mind-set from Americans who buy stock. These Japanese shareholders are not profit-hungry investors chasing fat dividends, capital gains, or a spike in stock prices. Rather, they are members of a corporate fraternity—a network; they are usually business partners and associates of the companies in which they hold stock. The main investors in Japan are not individuals but banks, insurance companies, and other corporations.[5]

But unlike institutional investors in America, Japanese institutional investors do not buy stock for "ROI"—return on investment. What they are buying into is not investments but relationships—business ties that resemble the ties of a family. Their main objective as owners is not to make money but to cement and protect their network of important business relationships over the long run.

The ups and downs of the stock market do not shake Japanese companies out of their relationships, nor out of their shares. In fact, by sticking together through the worst downturns, Japanese companies demonstrate their family-style loyalty to one another.

The core of their mutual bonding is a pattern of reciprocal ownership within a network of companies known as a *keiretsu*. The *keiretsu* member companies do business with one another and hold one another's shares. Their mutual investments are not massive; rather, they are a web of small investments, each company taking 2 to 4 percent of the stock shares in each of about fifteen other companies within the *keiretsu* network. So the clan typically holds about 30 percent of a *keiretsu* member company's stock, though at the top of the biggest groups the clan owns even more—more than 50 percent.[6]

Through reciprocal shareholding, the main Japanese companies keep most of their shares *off* the market. That suits them. They are willing to forgo big stock gains in order to have the safety net of protection from their business partners. These Japanese companies rise and fall, rise and fall, and rise again together—always together. That way, no matter how bad things get, they never have to worry about hostile takeovers or going out of business. They all survive to play again another day.

The code of mutual ownership is so strong that even in the worst of times, no *keiretsu* company would dare sell another clan member's stock to an outsider for fear of being branded *murahachibu*—a corporate leper, ostracized and vulnerable to having its own shares dumped by angry *keiretsu* brothers.[7]

As the Japanese say, by holding one another's shares, Japanese businesses "keep one another warm."

Interlocking ownership has many advantages. In bad times, it spares management from straining to pay dividends; it lets companies use their resources to build for recovery—while they are weathering the storm.

"Their system is structured such that they can invest huge amounts of money for a long period of time to gain market share—they don't need a return on their investment in three months like American companies do," commented Marie Anchordoguy, a specialist on the Japanese economy at the University of Washington. "Americans, we hit a blip, we just stop investing, and then, when the market picks up, we start investing. . . . The Japanese invest all the way through the recession. They can only do that because they aren't tied to the stock market."[8]

In fact, in the depths of the 1992–94 recession, the pace of investment did slow somewhat in Japan, but not much—not nearly as much as American corporate investment had slowed during the earlier 1990–91 downturn in the United States.

Inside the Network: Mutual Trust, Mutual Protection

Understanding Japan's sources of competitive advantage means understanding the *keiretsu* system—its network mind-set and its way of life.

The relationships and patterns of behavior in the *keiretsu* are the embodiment of Japan's culture of commerce, so different from the commercial culture in the Anglo-Saxon West.

Within a *keiretsu,* the most important bonds are intangible. The cohesion of these corporate networks is based on a strong sense of moral obligation to others in the group and to the group as a whole. Cross-sharing of stock formalizes those obligations, but relationships are the key: They are long-lasting, mutual, and almost always personal, rather than formal and legal.

"There is no contract—no formal institution," explained Naohiro Amaya, an important former vice minister of industry and trade. "A *keiretsu* is the mentality of mutual trust. . . . It's a sort of mutual insurance. It brings members of the *keiretsu* stability, efficiency, and less fuss in doing business."[9]

The lifestyle and mind-set of the *keiretsu* reach beyond economics into daily life. There is a tribal loyalty within a *keiretsu,* a sense of belonging, and a team spirit that impels many Japanese people to buy their *keiretsu*'s make of car, use the *keiretsu*'s consumer goods, and drink the *keiretsu*'s brand of beer.

Let an American corporate raider such as T. Boone Pickens try to buy his way into Toyota's *keiretsu* of auto components companies and demand seats on the board of a Toyota *keiretsu* member company, and the whole Toyota clan joins ranks to block him and run him out of the company he bought into.

Paradoxically, however, *keiretsu* networks are looser and less monolithic than vertically integrated U.S. companies, which own their subsidiaries and exercise a centralized command. In a *keiretsu,* there is no central management, no holding company secretly manipulating the entire apparatus, no CEO ensuring unity of command and embodying the corporate persona.

In Japan's six main horizontal *keiretsu,* each of which has some big member company operating in every major sector of the economy, every company is legally independent. Relationships are more brother to brother than father to son. Group actions are decided not by some patriarch but Japanese style, through the informal process of consensus. That way the companies in a Japanese *keiretsu* avoid collisions. They move together in harmony—as communities of shared interests.

Keiretsu member companies draw strength from the complex interrelationships that knit the *keiretsu* together—interlocking ownership, overlapping boards of directors, exchange of executives, long-term buyer-supplier relationships, sacrifices made by stronger companies for weaker members in hard times, and the mounting of joint ventures in good times. To its members, the *keiretsu* offers support and linkages far more valuable than any one member could find in deals struck in a wide-open marketplace.

The internal ties of the *keiretsu* network are binding but not rigid; not restrictive but reinforcing. Mutual ownership, for example, entails a much closer relationship than mere voting of stock proxies once a year. It is the basis of mutual influence. Companies gain a long-term stake in one another's performance. Like family members, they are inextricably bound together; and like family members, the company presidents watch one another's performance very closely. Crossownership, therefore, puts strong peer pressure on management to perform well.

The *Keiretsu* Way: How Mazda Was Rescued by Its Network

Some Western free-market economists contend that the mutual obligations and internal ties within the *keiretsu* are inherently inefficient because they limit the free play of the market. But experts on Japan say the opposite.

Chalmers Johnson of the University of California at San Diego, a leading specialist on the Japanese economy, asserts that *keiretsu* are "one of Japan's major contributions to modern industrial organization."[10] Kozo Yamamura of the University of Washington explains that the Japanese network system, with its code of mutual trust and obligation, creates efficiencies that Americans often overlook.

"There are less transaction costs to enforce contracts," Yamamura observed. "You don't need lawyers. Using lawyers is a very expensive way of settling disputes, and the Japanese do not like it. You have fewer accountants to guard against cheating, and you don't have to be so suspicious or protective when you have some proprietary information. The system works through consensus."[11]

And by consensus, the network rescues members in trouble.

A case in point is the campaign mounted by the Sumitomo group, one of the six big horizontal *keiretsu* networks, to save Mazda Motors, its automobile sector company, in the early 1970s. Mazda was close to bankruptcy. It had run into trouble marketing cars with a pioneering rotary engine.

The Sumitomo *keiretsu* could not afford to see Mazda go under, so it mobilized support to keep Mazda afloat. Sumitomo banks put up loans and funds to carry Mazda through its roughest period. Other group companies took workers from Mazda to help it reduce its payroll. Throughout the *keiretsu* network, Sumitomo companies made sure to buy Mazda cars, trucks, and other products, and they sold components and supplies to Mazda on favorable terms. With *keiretsu* backing, Mazda recovered and then joined the battle in the American car market of the 1980s and '90s.[12]

Keiretsu can operate offensively, too, to move into new industries and to underwrite the heavy costs of building a globally competitive position. The muscle of the *keiretsu* system was demonstrated to the American microelectronics industry in Silicon Valley in the mid-1980s, during the global glut in computer memory chips.

A few years earlier, Japan's electronics giants—encouraged by the Japanese government—had set out to overtake the American superiority in computer chips, and suddenly the world was swamped with too many producers. American companies started dropping like flies in 1985 and 1986. Fairchild, Mostek, AMD, and National Semiconductor were driven out of business or bought up by other companies.

Intel and Motorola gave up on memory chips and focused on micro-processors. But the Japanese electronics firms, protected by the deep pockets of their *keiretsu* partners, not only survived but kept building for the future.

That comparison nettled Clyde Prestowitz, a former U.S. trade negotiator. From 1984 to 1986, Prestowitz noted, the U.S. semiconductor industry lost about $2 billion, roughly 30,000 people were laid off, research and development budgets were drastically slashed, and stocks plummeted. "But in Japan," he noted, "no companies went out of business. No one was laid off. Share prices in electronics companies went up. Overall production capacity was increased by 40 percent, and R and D spending went up."

Prestowitz asked Tsutomu Kawanishi, vice president of Toshiba's semiconductor operations, how Japanese semiconductor companies could endure losses of $4 billion between 1984 and 1986 and still justify more investments to their owners.

"We really don't have to make much of a justification," Kawanishi replied. "Our group thinks that semiconductors are fundamental. So we're going to lose money this year, but we are not going to leave the business. Our group considers the technology important. We watch our market share and the investments of our competitors—NEC, Fujitsu, Hitachi—and we keep pace with them."

Since the leadership of Toshiba's network had made a strategic decision that computer chips was a crucial sector, it threw the *keiretsu*'s resources behind Toshiba and rode out the hard times, in order to build long-term market advantage.

"No U.S. company has that kind of staying power," Prestowitz commented.[13]

Toshiba was the beneficiary of both of the two main kinds of *keiretsu* in Japan—vertical and horizontal.

The vertical *keiretsu* are mainly production networks that operate top to bottom in one industry, with the final production or assembly company at the apex of the pyramid, supported by a descending structure of thousands of suppliers: Toyota and Nissan in cars, for example, or Toshiba and Hitachi in electronics.

The horizontal *keiretsu,* such as the Sumitomo network that saved Mazda, spread across the entire span of the economy. These corporate networks embrace hundreds of member companies, but at the core each group has just one company working in each key sector—steel, automobiles, oil, electronics, computers, shipping, finance, insurance, cement, construction, beer, cameras, and so on. At its hub, each horizontal *keiretsu* has its financial arms—a "main bank" and an import-export trading company—which provide the financial bloodstream to nourish the entire organism.

When people speak of Japan, Inc., it is the six main horizontal *keiretsu* they usually have in mind—Mitsubishi, Mitsui, Sumitomo, Sanwa, Dai-Ichi Kangyo, and Fuji (or Fuyo). Toshiba is a member of the Mitsui network, and that is where it got its big financial support.

The six big *keiretsu* networks dominate the Japanese economy. They control 40 percent of Japan's total bank capital, and they handle two thirds of Japan's trade and commerce. They do two thirds of Japan's construction; they make 45 percent of the cars and heavy machinery; they handle 60 percent of the shipping and more than half of the steel production and real estate businesses, and they control about 40 percent of its electrical and chemical industries.[14]

The heart of these six big clans consists of just 188 companies—.01 percent of the 1.7 million firms in Japan. And yet these core companies and their corporate networks control close to 30 percent of Japan's total GNP, according to Kenneth Courtis, a Canadian-born economist with Deutsche Bank in Tokyo who is also a professor of Japanese history.

"So if the *keiretsu* get pulling in one direction," Courtis said, "they can pull pretty much the rest of the economy with them."[15]

Marunouchi: The Economic Heart of Japan

If one place in Tokyo represents the epicenter of Japan, Inc., it is Marunouchi, one of the most exclusive and expensive commercial districts in Japan—or anywhere in the world.

The Marunouchi district enjoys a prime location. It sits just at the edge of the Imperial Palace and Gardens, not far from the most important government ministries, and a quick walk from the Japanese parliament building, the Diet. Marunouchi is the crossroads of political and economic power in Japan, the Japanese equivalent of New York's Rockefeller Center, though its architecture is less imposing and decorative. Marunouchi's buildings are solid, utilitarian, and uniformly serious. So is the army of dark-suited commuters pouring out of the Marunouchi metro exits or the old gingerbread Tokyo Railroad Station nearby.

This choice piece of Tokyo real estate is home to the Mitsubishi *keiretsu,* one of the six big corporate networks.

Block after block, the commercial fortresses of the Mitsubishi clan stretch out before the eye—Mitsubishi Corporation, Mitsubishi Bank, Mitsubishi Heavy Industries, Mitsubishi Electric, Meiji Mutual Life Insurance, Mitsubishi Construction, Mitsubishi Estate Company, Mitsubishi Petrochemical, Tokyo Marine and Fire Insurance, Asahi Glass, Kirin Brewery, Nikon cameras, Mitsubishi Gas Chemical, Mitsubishi Plastics, and on and on. In fact, the Mitsubishi presence is so overwhelming that people simply call this area "Mitsubishi Village."

As David Sanger, former Tokyo correspondent of *The New York Times,* quipped to me, it was almost as if someone had decided to buy up Wall Street.

The story of that choice plot of land carries an important message to foreigners who are intent on pressing the Japanese to break up their close-knit *keiretsu* and to open up Japan to more foreign trade.

In 1890, the Mitsubishi *zaibatsu,* as the commercial empires of wealthy Japanese families were then known, acquired about eighty acres of wasteland on the then-outskirts of Tokyo for what was considered the exorbitant price of about $1 million. Now, by some estimates, the land is worth $80 to $100 billion.[16]

After World War II, Mitsubishi almost lost its grip on that precious land. The U.S. occupation forces were dissolving the prewar *zaibatsu,* which had played a central role in the buildup of Japanese economic and military power before World War II and the arming of the Japanese war machine. On American orders, the old Mitsubishi real estate corporation, the formal landowner, was split into three parts and, as Tsuneo Wakai, president of Mitsubishi Bank, recounted, "a green-mailer [financial blackmailer] bought up all the stock in one of the three companies." The Mitsubishi companies were alarmed to see their network landlord in trouble, and they rallied to buy back the real estate company and to bring ownership of the land back within the corporate family, where it has remained safely ever since.[17]

That little episode tells a great deal not only about the collaborative operations of modern *keiretsu* but also about how the Japanese as a people, when confronting hardship or external pressures to change, preserve the relationships and arrangements they find natural and advantageous.

That pattern of doggedly reviving elements of the old Mitsubishi *zaibatsu* in the new form of *keiretsu* was repeated many times. The

U.S. occupation command split up the various companies of the Mitsubishi *zaibatsu* into 139 separate entities. But with patience, purpose, and tenacity, these fragments of the old Mitsubishi clan patiently reknit their bonds and restored the old organism in the new, looser form of *keiretsu.* That process of rebuilding has gone on, stone by stone, into the mid-1990s. Like other *keiretsu,* the Mitsubishi clan has steadily consolidated its network to match rivals abroad.[18]

Because the new postwar networks had to abide by the letter of the antitrust laws that the American occupation authorities imposed on Japan, the new *keiretsu* were less monolithic and more flexible than the old *zaibatsu.* Ironically, that greater flexibility became a competitive advantage in the fast-changing global economy of the 1980s and '90s. And so, unwittingly, the American occupiers helped modern Japan become more competitive by their ineffective efforts to quash the old Japanese system.

"Rather than doing away with the controlled prewar and wartime industrial system, the occupation actually reinvigorated it," Karel van Wolferen, a Dutch journalist who has lived in Japan for the past twenty-five years, has written.[19]

That rebuilding process has made the Mitsubishi *keiretsu* a formidable force. In 1993, its twenty-nine core companies (not to mention the hundreds of other companies in its network) did more than $325 billion worth of business—more than the *combined* operations of General Motors, IBM, General Electric, Du Pont, and Boeing.[20]

Mitsubishi's "Old Boy" Network: Blocking a Hostile Takeover

In Marunouchi, you can catch a symbolic glimpse of the might of Mitsubishi just before noon on the second Friday of each month.

For at noon sharp, the clan elders—the presidents and chairmen of the twenty-nine core companies—arrive in their black chauffeur-driven cars to gather in the Mitsubishi Club, on the eleventh floor of the Mitsubishi Electric building, for the regular monthly luncheon of the *shacho-kai,* the President's Council. This is a ritual common to all the big *keiretsu.*

The titular head of the Mitsubishi family—formally the "coordinator" of what is colloquially known as *kinyo-kai,* "the Friday Club"— is sixty-five-year-old Minoru Makihara, the balding, bespectacled president of Mitsubishi Corporation, the global trading company and main overseas investment arm of the Mitsubishi network.

Although Makihara was born in Britain, educated in the United States at St. Paul's School in Concord, New Hampshire, and Harvard, and spent twenty-two years of his career in Seattle, London, and New York, he is very Japanese in his leadership style. He has the thoughtful, soft-spoken manner of a respected elder whose words carry great weight but who does not throw his weight around. True to Japanese preference, Makihara is tasteful, impeccable, and understated. "I am a very traditional person, fairly Japanese in my thinking," he told one interviewer. His Mitsubishi lineage is unimpeachable: His father was a Mitsubishi executive and his wife is the great-granddaughter of Yataro Iwasaki, the autocratic founder of the Mitsubishi empire in 1870.[21]

Moreover, while Makihara's foreign experience prompts him to urge modest changes and more openness in the Japanese economy, he is a strong advocate of the *keiretsu* system, asserting that it has served Japan very well, both at home and abroad.

Yet Makihara makes light of the Mitsubishi clan gathering on Fridays, eager to put to rest any suspicion that the monthly Friday Club luncheons are crafting a global master plan. The presidents and chairmen have only fifteen minutes to eat, and the fare is unpretentious. "My favorite," he said, "is curry rice"—white rice with a splash of curry sauce, a commoner's dish.

Often the main event is a guest speaker from the Bank of Japan, or perhaps a traveling former American official discussing world affairs or economic trends. The Mitsubishi VIPs also talk about pet charities; but they make no big business decisions because, according to Makihara, the Friday Club is not a policymaking body. Real business is done at the lower levels. By Makihara's account, the gathering is primarily for general talk, for socializing, and for renewing the brotherhood of "the old boys' club" in the *keiretsu.*[22]

Nonetheless, at times of crisis or on issues crucial to the Mitsubishi network, talk at the Friday Club can become serious. According to Dodwell's *Industrial Groupings in Japan,* the most authoritative encyclopedia of Japanese business, the agenda before the elders of the various big clans is often heavy. Typically, Dodwell's asserts, *keiretsu* leaders meet regularly not only to discuss the general economic situation, but "promising business, the state of R & D, maintenance of intra-group trademarks and company names and labor problems, as well as to make decisions on joint investment in new industries, on the allocation among members of political contributions, conducting of public relations activities for the entire group, rehabilitation of financially troubled group companies, key personnel appointments, etc."[23]

Makihara conceded that the most important business items at the Friday Club focus on collective efforts "to preserve the credibility and dependability of the Mitsubishi name" and jealously to guard the reputation of "the three diamonds," Mitsubishi's famous trademark, drawn from the crest of samurai warriors.[24]

Translation from Makihara's lieutenants: Friday Club members may discuss such delicate issues as helping some member company in trouble; avoiding questionable partners abroad; keeping members off one another's commercial turf; stopping interlopers from cashing in on Mitsubishi's good name; and preventing takeovers by outsiders.[25]

One classic case involved blocking an unfriendly foreign or outside takeover of Mitsubishi Oil.

For years, half of Mitsubishi Oil's stock had been owned by Getty Oil, which in 1984 was about to be bought out by Texaco. Getty had been a passive owner, but since Texaco showed every intention of selling off the Mitsubishi Oil shares to raise money, the Mistubishi clan was fearful that Getty's successor would not be so passive. Indeed, there were signs that the shares might fall to Kuwait Petroleum Company or to a domestic Mitsubishi rival, Nippon Oil Company. The Mitsubishi Friday Club swung into action. It blocked the move—by mobilizing the collective financial resources of the Mitsubishi group and negotiating a $335 million buyout from Texaco.[26]

With or without such dramatic action, the Friday Club is most important for its symbolism and for the sense of cohesion that it nurtures. Membership is a matter of high prestige. In a society where such totems have great value, the Friday Club delineates the elite of the *keiretsu*—and everywhere within the Mitsubishi empire, the "Friday Club companies" are always spoken of with special warmth and respect as blood brothers.

Simply because it takes place, and because of who its participants are, the monthly meeting of the Friday Club conveys to all—to Mitsubishi employees, to the larger business community in Japan, and to rivals abroad—the power and reach of the Mitsubishi clan's corporate network.

The *Keiretsu* Overseas: The Network Advantage

Whether competing at home or in the global game, Japanese companies gain important leverage from their network system.

Like the Germans, they gain strength from their ability to marshal capital collectively and from their insulation from the short-term pressures of the market.

From Minoru Makihara's perspective, these are two major advantages that a Japanese CEO derives from the corporate network and its system of stable stock ownership.

"This system allows us to think in terms of a long-term vision not affected by daily fluctuations in share prices," Makihara stated. "The knowledge that we have stable shareholders who are interested more in the long-term prospects of a corporation is extremely helpful in allowing us to plan."[27]

Time and again, the Mitsubishi *keiretsu* has marshaled "patient capital" for ventures with a long-term payoff. In 1985, for example, when the Japanese government deregulated the satellite broadcast market, the group rapidly raised $460 million to set up the Satellite Communications Corporation. It was a collective enterprise. The financing was put together by Mitsubishi Corporation and Mitsubishi Bank, and the management was organized by Mitsubishi Electric, the family firm with expertise in the field.[28]

And according to Mitsubishi literature, every single Friday Club company anted up capital for the new venture, including Nikon cameras and Kirin beer, which hardly have a natural business interest in satellite communications. But this is how the system works: The three main players kicked in the big capital, followed by two tiers of other family members, some companies each owning 5 percent of the stock in the satellite communications venture, others each owning just 0.5 percent. Whatever the share, the fact that everyone participated signaled both solidarity and the pressures of conformity, once the family elders had given the project the go-ahead.

Nor was participation a mere formality. After some failures, two communications satellites—Superbird A and B—were successfully launched in 1992, and, by early 1993, large white satellite dishes were sprouting on the rooftops in Marunouchi like so many white sky mushrooms. The Mitsubishi companies were beaming in-house broadcasts to their affiliates from one tip of Japan to the other. Minoru Makihara delivered a New Year's greeting message to Mitsubishi Corporation's 9,600 employees in Japan, and the company was putting out twice-a-day newscasts about the customers and ventures of the Mitsubishi network. At this stage, only about 20 percent of the satellite time had been sold to paying clients, but the Mitsubishi clan could afford to be patient for the commercial payoff, because they were sharing the risk. The system was working as it was supposed to.

That same network method works overseas. The Friday Club guided the Mitsubishi network into a major petrochemical venture in Saudi Arabia; the lead was taken by the core group, and most, though not all, of the other Friday Club members took part. Indeed, after the Iraqi invasion of Kuwait in August 1992, the hot topic at one Friday Club session was what to do about the collective financial exposure of group companies in Iraq and Saudi Arabia and whether to evacuate their people from Saudi Arabia. Another major venture that got a push at the Friday Club was the Mitsubishi Motors auto production and marketing operation in America, based on a joint venture with Chrysler.

The reach of the Mitsubishi empire is awesome. From Marunouchi, it stretches into 110 countries from Australia and China, to Saudi Arabia and Kuwait, all across central and western Europe, to the Americas, both North and South. The "Friday Club" companies have joint ventures all across the world—among them, joint operations with big American firms such as Westinghouse, Monsanto, Caterpillar, Chrysler, and Boeing.

To Minoru Makihara, the *keiretsu* approach offers Mitsubishi a built-in competitive advantage as the Mitsubishi corporate clan builds its network of global enterprises. In fact, corporate alliances—even with companies from other countries—are the cornerstone of Makihara's global strategy.

"On any major project, like in the CIS countries [the former Soviet Union] or in the Middle East, where country risks are ballooning, I think there have to be more and more strategic alliances," Makihara asserted, "between Japanese and U.S. companies, European companies, Asian companies, and so forth. Not just to hedge risks, but to pool the best expertise and knowledge of various issues, areas, subjects."[29]

Because of the way Japanese *keiretsu* networks are organized, they are well poised to exploit opportunities in the developing world, especially in the exploding economies of east Asia, according to Ken Courtis, a Deutsche Bank economist in Tokyo.

"These companies are able to work as systems," Courtis commented. "They can look at a problem and deal with it from A to Z, from manufacturing, sourcing, production, financing, to distribution, to aftersales. They can cut the whole network. They can move money around these *keiretsu* from one company to another. They can share risks across the *keiretsu*. They can move people around from one company to another. In fact, the best people are typically moved around from one company to another, so they get a feel for how the *keiretsu* operates. But at the same time, each of these companies operates in competition with other companies in the constellation—competition for capital, for the best people in the group. It's through the joint collaboration and competition that these companies are able to both maximize their return and minimize their risk."

The ability of the Mitsubishi family, and others like it, to provide a "full-service universe" for any market or product gives Japanese network capitalism a global competitive advantage. As Courtis put it, "The *keiretsu* could go to Vietnam and say, 'You're producing coffee, but this coffee is so bad that no one in the world can drink it. We will take that coffee. We will process it. We will upgrade it. We will market it, have it distributed. We will then put the funds in an escrow account. With those funds we will be able to buy you the machinery that you require and the know-how to upgrade your production. We'll install those for you.'

"They can turn the whole buckle, whereas our companies come in and say, 'We can sell you the machines, but we can't help you with the marketing.' Or a bank will come in and say, 'We can give you the financing, but you'll have to stitch the rest of it together.'

"That's why in this world of really integrated, global competition, these *keiretsu* are operating at such a tremendous advantage to our [Western] companies."[30]

The Mitsubishi *Keiretsu:* Transplanted into America

For Americans, the most stunning demonstration of the financial power of Mitsubishi—and one of the sharpest blows to the collective economic ego of Americans—was the Mitsubishi network's purchase in 1990 of a controlling share of Rockefeller Center, one of the quintessential symbols of American capitalism.

As things turned out, Mitsubishi may have overreached itself in that purchase and paid too much for that prestigious piece of property. By 1994, even wealthy Mitsubishi was having trouble meeting the mortgage payments.

Rockefeller Center, however, was merely the highest-profile symbol of the Mitsubishi presence in America. It also built up a far less visible, but more muscular, industrial empire in the United States. It fought off General Electric to buy Aristech Chemical Corporation of Pittsburgh for $877 million. It picked up the Verbatim subsidiary spun off by Eastman Kodak, launched a $150 million joint venture in Chicago for futures trading, and acquired a $400 million power plant in Virginia.

From sea to shining sea, the Mitsubishi *keiretsu* has developed an operating network worth more than $4 billion. It has a forklift plant in Texas, a cement factory in California, television-assembly plants in Georgia and the Rocky Mountains, a high-tech computer chip and semiconductor wafer complex in Durham, North Carolina, and a joint auto assembly plant with Chrysler in Bloomington, Illinois.[31]

In America, as in Japan, the Mitsubishi group companies operate in family fashion, providing one another with business, supplies, customers, money, and mutual support. Diamond-Star Motor Corporation, the joint venture with Chrysler, for example, gets components from twenty-five different Mitsubishi companies located in the United States and Canada. Its car air conditioners come from a plant in Rancho Dominguez, California, operated by Mitsubishi Heavy Industries; windows are made by Asahi Glass in Bellefontaine, Ohio; steel products come either from Mitsubishi International Company's operation in Joliet, Illinois, or Mitsubishi Steel in Milton, Ontario; starters and cruise controls are supplied by Mitsubishi Electric's plant in Cincinnati; engines and transmissions are delivered by Mitsubishi Motors in Japan.

Diamond-Star Motors does not rely exclusively on the *keiretsu* supply chain. In equipping the plant, it passed over robots from Mitsubishi Heavy Industries, and in assembling cars, it buys antennas, brakes, ball bearings, lighting and electrical equipment, seats, and other supplies from American firms. But much of the business stays in the family.

The buildup of Mitsubishi assets in the United States has been a well-oiled team effort that has often unfolded in careful phases. As the trading and overseas investment arm of the group, Mitsubishi Corporation, headed by Minoru Makihara, together with its American subsidiary, took the lead in making deals and organizing the finances. They put up the original funding, usually joined by Mitsubishi Bank and Mitsubishi Trust. But as the deals progressed, more and more members of the corporate family were drawn in as investors and partners. For example, five *keiretsu* members bought the California cement factory.

Buying Aristech Chemical Corporation was more delicately managed—possibly to avoid running afoul of U.S. antitrust law. The purchase was spearheaded by the same trio—Mitsubishi Corporation, Mitsubishi Bank, and Mitsubishi Trust; but four months after they made the purchase, a large portion was sold off to four family firms with businesses allied to Aristech Chemical—Mitsubishi Gas Chemical, Mitsubishi Kasei, Mitsubishi Petrochemical, and Mitsubishi Rayon. According to *Business Week,* Mitsubishi's American lawyers headed off a rival bid from GE Plastics by threatening to raise an antitrust case against General Electric on the ground that GE's acquisition would concentrate too much market share in basic chemicals in one company. But Mitsubishi Corporation had no such drawback because, in America, it is a trading company with no involvement in chemicals. Even after other Mitsubishi group companies got involved, no U.S. antitrust action was brought against Mitsubishi, because technically all of its companies are legally independent of one another.[32]

Other Japanese companies, such as Toyota and Honda, have established their feeder networks in the United States, prompting congressional demands for investigation into whether Japanese *keiretsu* operations in America violate U.S. antitrust laws. Jack Brooks of Texas, longtime chairman of the House Judiciary Committee, charged in 1990 that Japanese automakers, with their *keiretsu* cross-holdings and exclusive supply contracts, were "importing this anticompetitive system to the United States" and damaging the American auto parts industry.[33]

In April 1992, U.S. Attorney General William Barr announced the intention of the Bush administration to use American antitrust laws against foreign companies and cartels that were found blocking purchases from American companies through internal collusion. The Reagan administration had tried the antitrust strategy in the early 1980s, but it had yielded little and was abandoned in 1988 in favor of trying to negotiate changes in Japanese cartel practices.[34] The new threat of antitrust action in 1992 remained just that—a threat, underlining American frustration but yielding no significant results.

Construction *Dango*s Versus the U.S. Navy

The close—and closed—relationships in Japanese *keiretsu* have become a neuralgic point in trade disputes between the United States and Japan.

As the annual American trade deficit with Japan ballooned from $1.7 billion in 1975 to $60 billion in 1987 and to $65 billion in 1994,[35] one American president after another—Carter, Reagan, Bush, and Clinton—has demanded that successive Japanese governments take steps to open the Japanese market. Americans have charged unfair discrimination by the Japanese against all manner of imports from rice, cosmetics, automobiles, and aluminum baseball bats to cellular phones, sophisticated medical equipment, and supercomputers.

Over the past two decades, under outside pressure, the Japanese have gradually eased their official barriers—tariffs, foreign currency restrictions, and some bureaucratic regulations. Trying to correct the trade imbalance quickly, the Reagan administration in 1985 devalued the dollar from about 240 yen to about 160 yen, to make Japanese goods more expensive in the United States and American goods cheaper in Japan. But that did not cure the American trade deficit with Japan. In fact, after a temporary dip, the trade deficit rose again, and in 1993, with the exchange rate hovering just above 100 yen to the dollar, the trade deficit was back up to nearly $60 billion, despite new efficiencies and improvements at major American corporations.

Increasingly, Americans came to see that the problems lay not just in the weaknesses of various American industries, such as steel, textiles, automobiles, and consumer electronics, or in official Japanese government barriers, but in the obstacles built into the *keiretsu* networks. Not only Americans but west Europeans and other Asians complained that Japan's low level of manufactured imports pointed to structural barriers to trade. The heart of the difficulty was what Dutch author Karel van Wolferen aptly termed the "structural protectionism" of the Japanese network mind-set.[36] The Bush and Clinton administrations came to share that view.

"The major impediments to the Japanese market are rooted in the unique character of Japanese business organizations and their distinctive relationships with one another and with the Japanese government," wrote Laura D'Andrea Tyson just before her appointment as chairman of President Clinton's Council of Economic Advisers.[37]

American businesses made the case that the exclusive "old boy" networks of a third kind of *keiretsu,* the distribution *keiretsu,* made it impossible for American firms to get a foothold in Japan's retail market. They protested that the links within the vertical automobile supply *keiretsu* for Toyota and other Japanese carmakers were so binding that in 1990 American firms could land only about 1 percent of Japan's $120 billion auto parts market.[38] And finally, they argued that cartellike collusion and rigged bidding in the Japanese construction industry, among the horizontal *keiretsu,* was shutting out big American construction firms from a fair shot at contracts on huge Japanese public works projects, such as the new Kansai International Airport in Osaka, Japan's second largest city.[39]

The U.S. government got a firsthand taste of collusion in the construction industry when scores of Japanese companies formed a cartel to bid on $150 million worth of projects at a U.S. naval base outside Tokyo between 1984 and 1987. According to the Japanese Fair Trade Office and press reports, Japanese construction firms had developed a practice of parceling out market shares and portions of contracts. They would hold a *dango,* a secret meeting, at which Japanese contractors would decide among themselves which companies would make the low bids and land contracts on public works projects. By agreement, the other construction companies would make their bids higher than that of the predetermined winner. In the case of the American naval base, the *dango* was ironically nicknamed *Seiyukai,* which translates as "Friends of the Stars and Stripes." The U.S. Navy uncovered the *dango* operation and claimed that it had been the victim of $35 million in overcharges. Eventually, the United States collected $32.6 million in damages from ninety-nine Japanese firms, which reluctantly acknowledged their involvement in the *dango.*[40]

After that episode, Japanese officials promised more open bidding practices on public works projects, including the $8 billion airport construction at Osaka. But after the highly experienced team of Westinghouse and AEG, its German partner, lost out on a large "people mover" project to a relatively inexperienced Japanese bidding team representing two major *keiretsu,* foreigners again cried foul.[41] Bechtel was awarded a $2.5 million share of an airport design project in tandem with six Japanese firms. But the U.S. government accused the Japanese of discrimination, contending that the Bechtel contract was such an insignificant scrap of the $8 billion total project that it was a transparent sop to try to silence criticism rather than a real effort to reform the *dango* cartel.[42]

While Japanese ministries insisted that the *keiretsu* were not to blame for America's trade problems with Japan, Minoru Makihara of Mitsubishi Corporation acknowledged to me the difficulties foreigners face in doing business in Japan "because companies in Japan tend to establish long-term relationships." The problem, he said, is "not just confined to Mitsubishi group companies. Any Japanese company, or any individual for that matter, likes to establish relationships, extend those relationships, and build further relationships or business on such relationships. So it's a difficult market to break into, and I think Japan has to make it an easier market to break into."[43]

U.S. Supercomputers: *Keiretsu* Resistance

One field that the U.S. government made a *cause célèbre*—and in which it gained some headway—was supercomputers.

An American firm, Cray Research of Minnesota, had pioneered the field of ultra-high-speed computers in 1976, and by the early 1980s, it had established its global leadership, dominating both the American and European markets.

Cray symbolized American high-tech preeminence in a cutting-edge area. Its supercomputers were designed for highly complex calculations such as simulating atomic explosions, creating multidimensional weather maps, and testing airflow over cars or aircraft. Supercomputers are so fast that, in 1991, a supercomputer could do in one minute the same volume of calculations that would require ninety-six hours on a desktop computer. Supercomputers were big-budget items, costing $8.5 million apiece, and by the early 1990s, the global market for supercomputers was running at more than $1 billion.

Despite its world leadership, Cray was unable to break into the Japanese market for a decade. While Cray was held at bay, the Japanese Ministry of International Trade and Industry (MITI), which had sponsored Japan's development of other large computers and computer chips, pressed the main Japanese electronics firms—Nippon Electric Corporation (NEC), Hitachi, and Fujitsu—to develop supercomputers; MITI also provided $121 million to promote R&D.[44] The first Japanese supercomputers appeared in 1983, and they were the first to be sold on the Japanese market. Takehito Kato, a technical expert and Cray's marketing manager in Tokyo, was stunned because, even as a Japanese, he saw Cray's superiority. In part, he blamed Japanese snobbism toward American goods—"some kind of tendency of Japanese people to think Japanese technology is ahead of anyone else."[45] But American computer experts saw the hand of the Japanese government guiding the sales in order to bolster homegrown super-computers as a strategically important industry.

In 1985, Cray saw its first opportunity for a breakthrough in Japan. Automobile design engineers at Nissan Motors met with Kato and de-cided they wanted a Cray supercomputer, with its leading-edge soft-ware, to help them with structural design, with calculations on fuel economy, and ultimately with crash simulations. On tests of real prob-lems, as opposed to theoretical speeds, Nissan managers were satisfied that the Cray performed better than its Japanese competitors did. NEC, Hitachi, and Fujitsu had no software comparable to that used by the Cray supercomputers.[46]

Nonetheless, after months of internal debate, Nissan's top brass vetoed the purchase of a Cray supercomputer and ordered its engi-neers to buy from Nissan's *keiretsu* partner—Hitachi.

"Technical people in Nissan didn't want the Hitachi," said Marie Anchordoguy, a specialist on high-performance computers. "I mean, Hitachi's supercomputers are really the worst. No one buys Hitachi machines. So Nissan leaked it. They called Cray here [in Tokyo]. The engineers called the U.S. embassy here, and they said, 'We really want a Cray. Please help us.' "[47]

Armed with the Nissan leaks, the American embassy notified Washington, and the U.S. trade representative's office called foul. Washington put pressure on the Japanese government. The United States made the point that if Nissan and other Japanese carmakers wanted to keep selling more than 1.5 million cars a year in America, Japan had better open up its supercomputer market, especially in the auto industry.

Eventually, in 1986, the Japanese government told Nissan to buy the Cray supercomputer. With the ice broken, Nissan bought a second Cray and a third, and other Japanese carmakers followed suit. So gov-ernment pressure worked—partially.

As an outsider, Cray continued to have problems in Japan. It found some customers among automobile, chemical, and electronics compa-nies, but it was far from doing as well in Japan as it did elsewhere in the world.[48] Cray did best with independent companies. The *keiretsu* bonds were no longer impenetrable, but they were still a barrier.

Cray's biggest hurdle was the system of cozy relationships that *kei-*

retsu companies have with government agencies, institutes, and universities. Japanese universities, like commercial companies, have regular *keiretsu* ties, established by the Ministry of Education: Tokyo University with Hitachi, Kyoto University with Fujitsu, Osaka University with NEC, and so on, among the nine main national universities.[49] Japanese software writers and big computer makers feather one another's nests. In one celebrated case, scholars from Osaka University favored a Cray supercomputer, only to be ordered by their university and the Ministry of Education to stick to their traditional supplier, NEC.[50]

The *keiretsu* system posed another severe handicap to Cray—Japanese supercomputer makers offered 80 to 90 percent discounts to universities and government agencies, discounts that were underwritten by the *keiretsu* system. Cray could not match the Japanese electronics giants. Its only product was supercomputers; if sales fell, Cray's survival was at stake. NEC, Fujitsu, and Hitachi had a whole line of electronic products; their profits in other areas could cover their losses in supercomputers, plus they could tap the financial resources of their *keiretsu*. So, unlike Cray, they could afford to take losses on their supercomputers year after year.

In addition, the Japanese firms had an inside track—they were privy to advance information on which government institutions were getting funds to buy supercomputers and what their requirements were. Often, Cray's Japanese competitors had submitted bids to government agencies before Cray even knew of the selling opportunity. In 1987 and again in 1990, the U.S. government protested these practices. Official U.S. pressure helped Cray sell four supercomputers to government institutes—four out of thirty-eight sold, well below Cray's 20 percent of the private-sector market and a far cry from the 80 percent market share the company had in the rest of the world.[51]

Even getting that far takes government pressure to break the *keiretsu* stranglehold, commented economic specialist Marie Anchordoguy. "In fact," she said, "many Japanese people say, 'Pressure us. Pressure us. We need foreign pressure to make these changes.'"

But in the supercomputer case, Anchordoguy pointed out, "U.S. trade policy treated the symptoms of the problem and not the disease. The disease is the structural differences that enable Japanese firms to operate for ten, fifteen years, losing money. It's not an easy thing to deal with. But if you just put a little Band-Aid on these things, you're never going to get at the real problem."[52]

Trying to Attack the Structural Problem

Tired of Band-Aids, the Bush administration decided to target the "structural impediments" to trade that are built into the Japanese system.

In July 1989, President Bush and Trade Representative Carla Hills launched special negotiations to push for more vigorous enforcement of Japan's antitrust laws, more open procurement procedures, and administrative steps to break up the restrictive practices of Japanese network capitalism.

In April 1990, President Bush and then–Japanese Prime Minister Toshiki Kaifu signed an agreement in which Kaifu promised to relax the iron grip of the *keiretsu* networks on retail trade. Visiting Japan in early 1992, Bush celebrated the opening of two toy supermarkets by the American chain Toys "R" Us. But this was tokenism.

The Bush administration never achieved the fundamental changes it sought; the problem was passed on to the Clinton administration, which also ran into a brick wall.

Such longtime academic specialists on the Japanese economy as Chalmers Johnson warn that "It is totally futile for Americans to try and open up Japan." They emphasize that the political leaders with whom American presidents negotiate do not wield real power; that power is in the hands of a permanent bureaucracy that steadfastly resists changes that encroach upon *its* power to administer the Japanese economy. What Americans forget, Johnson says, is that "The Japanese prime minister appoints twenty people to the government; Clinton appoints four thousand," and the Japanese bureaucrats "are like the E-ring of the Pentagon"—dug in and determined to protect their bureaucratic turf.[53]

Indeed, after five years of off-and-on structural trade talks, the Clinton administration issued a trade report in April 1994 that echoed the familiar charges: Japan's *keiretsu* networks pose "special market access problems" because many Japanese companies remain "relatively closed to establishing new relationships with foreign companies." Moreover, the report stated, the Japanese government still maintains a "high degree of economic regulation that impedes the entry of foreign firms" into retail trade.[54]

In sum, things are pretty much still at square one.

As a result, three American administrations have acquiesced, in effect, to trying to join the Japanese system rather than to keep pressing for systemic change.

The U.S.-Japanese trade agreement most widely hailed by Americans as a success, the Semiconductor Agreement of 1986 negotiated under President Reagan, did not seek to reform the Japanese *keiretsu* networks. Rather, it went after a target share of the Japanese computer chip market for foreign firms. In that agreement, the Japanese government promised to help foreign computer chip companies achieve "their goal of a 20 percent market share" in Japan within five years. That meant roughly a doubling of foreign sales.[55] Hitting that target took a bit longer than planned, but the goal was reached in late 1992.[56]

Similarly, President Bush used his final summit meeting in Japan, in January 1992, to pursue a similar path for the American auto industry by seeking and obtaining Japan's promise to increase its purchase of automobile components from American firms from $9 billion to $19 billion by 1995.[57]

The Clinton administration carried on that approach, pushing for more access and numerical gains in telecommunications, medical equipment, cellular phones, supercomputers, and other fields.

All these moves, by three very different presidents, represent a Japanese-style quota approach, typical of the *keiretsu* system, not the American-style free-market philosophy.

The lesson is that the network mind-set at work in Japanese corporate families, and the competitive advantages that the Japanese see in network relationships, have so far proven more enduring than the competitive efforts of a host of American companies and the policies of several American presidents.

13

Counterattack

Motorola—No Market Sanctuary for the Japanese

> *One cannot allow one's competitor to have a sanctuary, be-*
> *cause—in military parlance—an enemy can go across the*
> *border, rest, load his pistol, and come down and do mis-*
> *chief. And you can't do enough harm [to him] if you don't*
> *pursue him back over his border.*[1]
>
> —BOB GALVIN, MOTOROLA CEO, 1959–87

> *If you're going to play in the major leagues, you'd better*
> *play with the best players in the world. In the electronics*
> *industry, many of the best players in the world are Japa-*
> *nese companies, and you had better be able to compete with*
> *them head to head in their home market.*[2]
>
> —GEORGE FISHER, MOTOROLA CEO, 1988–93

> *Most companies will not play hardball because they are*
> *afraid of being retaliated against without knowing it. Our*
> *view is that if we didn't play hardball, we'd be out of busi-*
> *ness. It was hardball that got us in here.*[3]
>
> —IRA WOLF, FORMER EXECUTIVE, NIPPON MOTOROLA, LTD.

Bob Galvin is a gentleman. He has a courteous, kindly manner, a friendly, open face, a trusting way with others. As a corporate leader, he is attentive to his people, respectful, and compassionate.

And yet Bob Galvin's gentle blue eyes and soft-spoken way can be misleading. They belie his grit and tenacity, his combative spirit. Unlike other high-profile American CEOs, who court media and public attention, Galvin is not given to explosive tirades or flamboyant posturing. His personal style is understated. Yet on three continents, I never encountered any more aggressive competitor than this quiet-mannered man who for nearly three decades ran Motorola as chairman and CEO.

When Bob Galvin talks about global economic competition—especially when he talks about the Japanese—he purposefully chooses the metaphors of warfare.

"One cannot allow one's competitor to have a sanctuary," he declared, "because—in military parlance—an enemy can go across the border, rest, load his pistol, and come down and do mischief. And you can't do enough harm [to him] if you don't pursue him back over his border."

It galled Bob Galvin that for so many years Motorola's Japanese competitors were able to enjoy what he called the "riskless scenario" of a protected home market where they could sell their goods at exorbitantly high prices, reap enormous profits, and pile up huge treasuries to finance their export drive into America. To break up that Japanese game, Galvin considered it imperative for Motorola to penetrate the Japanese market—not only to generate profits but to impose the discipline of competitive market prices on Motorola's Japanese rivals—and thus force them to operate on close margins at home.

"If the Japanese or any other competitor have a sanctuary in their home market, they will continue to build their strength there—if they wish to do mischief in one's native market here—and one is at a tremendous disadvantage," Galvin said. "That's an age-old principle. Very few businesspeople understand it. But we knew we couldn't let them stand alone in Japan without our having access in that marketplace as a significant competitor. So that principle drives our company and should drive every company."[4]

Motorola's Patient Campaign: Singles Instead of Home Runs

Galvin's counterattack strategy became a paramount priority at Motorola. Galvin and Motorola pursued it in unconventional ways that went against the grain of typical American corporate behavior in the 1980s. Galvin used Japanese strategies to battle the Japanese.

As one of the first American corporate leaders to take a personal interest in Japan and to anticipate the Japanese economic challenge to America, Galvin took the long view. He went for a steady stream of singles, instead of trying for a home run. Unlike the typical American corporate head, who focuses on early profits and quarterly results,

Galvin had Motorola concentrate on gaining market entry, establishing a beachhead in Japan, and going after market share rather than earnings. Galvin's instinct was to pursue a patient, persistent strategy in Japan. Motorola set up offices in Tokyo in 1962 but the company did no significant business in Japan until 1975. And not until 1979 did Motorola turn its first modest profit in Japan.

By the early 1980s, Motorola had escalated its trench warfare with the Japanese electronics industry, and Galvin, like a corporate Paul Revere, was running ads in business publications about "Meeting Japan's Challenge."

A decade later, in the early 1990s, Motorola's tenacity was paying off handsomely. In 1992, while the Big Three American automakers were complaining that the Japanese market was hopelessly closed to outsiders, Motorola was doing nearly $1 billion worth of business in Japan.[5]

The company's path to success is a virtual how-to handbook for other companies.

One of Bob Galvin's first precepts is renewal—a persistent, restless reinvention of Motorola's focus and objectives. He does not allow coasting on past success, the fatal flaw of the corporate leadership at RCA, IBM, and General Motors.

Central to renewal is Galvin's dedication to keeping alive the flow of fresh thinking by fostering a climate of bracing candor and contention at Motorola. He has encouraged fierce arguments over the company's policies and methods, and that process of rigorous debate has been a constant spur to cast off outdated habits of mind and to generate new ideas.

Rather than complain about the difficulties of breaking into the Japanese market, Bob Galvin used the demanding standards of the Japanese as a chinning bar for pushing Motorola to ever-higher performance.

In the late 1970s, he became one of the first American CEOs to preach the gospel of quality and to accept what was then the iconoclastic view that high quality went hand in hand with lower costs. An intellectual disciple of Deming, Galvin used the objective of quality to transform the entire company.

He was also one of the first corporate CEOs to look to unconventional alliances for success in the new global economic game. While many American CEOs scorned the U.S. government and held it at arm's length, Galvin and Motorola turned repeatedly to the government as an ally in their battle to penetrate Japan. At every stage of Motorola's counterattack, government pressures on Japan were essential to success.

Another hallmark of Motorola, one that was integral to Galvin's pursuit of quality, was a rare commitment to virtual life employment for Motorola's workforce. Like Ford and a few others, Motorola and Galvin believed their workforce was a priceless asset. Galvin went to unusual lengths to put that conviction into practice. While many American companies, convinced that they could not match low-wage Asian labor with American workers, were closing their American plants and shifting production overseas, Motorola refused to displace and lay off its American workforce. It built new leading-edge plants in the American heartland during the mid-1980s and used its ethnic American workforce to do battle with the Japanese. To make that strategy work, Motorola created perhaps the most extensive training program for any corporation its size.

On training, as on other matters, Motorola in the 1980s adopted the mind-set and methods of its Japanese rivals. And, believing that the best defense is a good offense, Galvin used those Japanese techniques to take the commercial offensive against the Japanese on their home ground.

Qualifying for Japan: Technical Perfection and Political Clout

Motorola's first big commercial battle with the Japanese came over pagers. That battle, beginning with the process of qualifying to do business in Japan, generated an internal revolution at Motorola that transformed the company.

But Motorola began its battle with the Japanese on the defensive.

Since the late 1920s, Motorola had built its business around consumer electronics, as a producer of car radios, home television sets, and other household appliances. When Japanese companies saturated the American market in consumer electronics in the 1960s, Motorola was forced to abandon that field. In 1974, Bob Galvin grudgingly approved the sale of Motorola's bleeding Quasar TV business to Matsushita of Japan.

By this time, Galvin realized that Motorola had to refocus its business. He had watched longtime American competitors like Philco and RCA disappear under the withering competitive assault because they were too rigid to change. "They didn't renew, they didn't think of putting themselves literally out of business [their old business]," Galvin asserted. "They all stayed doing what they were doing yesterday."

In Galvin's eyes, sticking with a once-successful but fading business is a fatal strategic mistake.

His father, Paul Galvin, the founder of Galvin Manufacturing, Inc., which later became Motorola, had drummed the idea of "renewal" into him. By that, Paul Galvin meant never being content merely to ride the success of an established line of business but, instead, periodically reaching for some new venture or invention in order to revitalize the company. So in the 1970s, Bob Galvin, a business visionary, set out to reinvent Motorola. He left consumer electronics and shifted the company into making computer chips and building on its core strengths in radio communications, in the new forms of pagers and cellular telephones.

As a pioneer in pagers in the late 1970s, Motorola rapidly established itself as the world market leader. Riding that early success, Bob Galvin decided to go after the Japanese market. He saw an opportunity in some large contracts being put out to bidders by Nippon Telegraph and Telephone (NTT), then a state monopoly and the only buyer of pagers in Japan. But Motorola collided with the whole closed system of Japan, Inc.—ingrained nationalism, technological protectionism, and the cozy business networks of Japanese *keiretsu.*

In 1980, NTT ruled the roost in Japanese communications. As a state monopoly, NTT was more powerful than AT&T had been in America before its breakup, and NTT was used to doling out shares of its equipment contracts to Japan's main electronics giants. It balked at having an American firm intruding on Japan's cartelized high-tech electronics industry and competing with NTT's traditional suppliers.[6] And so it rebuffed Motorola many times. Their meetings were so icy, Motorola executives reported, that the American company finally appealed to the U.S. government to help open up the closed Japanese game.

"We had to get Washington's help to fight our way into the competition," recalled George Fisher, who headed Motorola's effort to penetrate Japan and who would succeed Bob Galvin in 1988 as Motorola's CEO. Fisher enlisted Robert Strauss, President Carter's special trade representative, to apply pressure on the Japanese government to give Motorola a chance to bid on NTT's pager contracts.

Political muscle worked—but only to a point. Motorola got entrée to the bidding process, only to discover that it had to clear another hurdle. It needed to be formally qualified to do business in Japan, and the Japanese were skeptical that American products could meet NTT's demanding standards. "The Japanese didn't believe that we could meet their cost, reliability, and time schedule requirements," Fisher said. "Frankly, we weren't quite sure how we could do it either."[7]

The ordeal of getting technically qualified was like an icy swim in January—a shock to the system but stimulating.

The intensity of that effort energized Motorola; teams of Motorola engineers took the Japanese technical requirements as a personal challenge. "We had to spend hundreds of thousands of dollars to get our specs [technical specifications] translated into Japanese, and we had to have scads of meetings with the Japanese to satisfy them," said Jim Caile, a marketing vice president. "It took tenacity and patience, a *lot* of patience. Other U.S. companies throw up their hands at this stuff. They say it's too much to stomach. But we were determined to make it."[8]

Susumu Cho, a Japanese engineer who was working for Motorola and who is now executive vice president of Nippon Motorola, described Motorola's frenzied efforts to modify its pagers and raise their quality to meet NTT's standards. In the final four months before the September 1980 deadline, Cho and his fellow engineers were working seventeen hours a day, seven days a week; they took no holidays except July 4. Once a week, they pulled an all-nighter, working around the clock.

"That's the greatest degree of teamwork, cooperation, and camaraderie I had ever seen," Cho recalled. "Finally, we hand-carried the designs and a hundred and fifty pager samples to Tokyo and delivered them the day before they were due for testing."

Japanese inspectors immediately spotted flaws—scratches on the pager housings. The inspectors told Motorola to replace the housings on eight pagers. "Everything had to be perfect," Cho said.[9] Ultimately, Motorola made the grade. In November 1980, it earned a coveted seal of approval as a "recognized supplier" to NTT and then won a piece of NTT's contract for pagers.

Nippon Motorola, Galvin's Japanese subsidiary, undercut the prices of Japanese pagers, and within a few years Nippon Motorola built up its sales to capture about 30 percent of the Japanese pager market.

Up to that point, Japanese firms had been charging very high prices and pocketing a hefty profit. But as Motorola's market share grew, Japanese firms cut their prices in half to match Motorola's.

Then the Japanese retaliated against Motorola in the American market. "As soon as we made it in Japan, a couple of Japanese companies, NEC and Matsushita, came after our market—to teach us a lesson and to attack our base," George Fisher said. "They came in and cut costs fiercely."

By early 1982, Motorola was losing money on its American pager business.[10] It accused the Japanese of "dumping" their pagers way below cost—selling them for less than half the price they charged in Japan. Motorola filed an official trade complaint with the U.S. Commerce Department and Federal Trade Commission, and it won a ruling in 1983 that imposed a penalty tariff of 106 percent on Japanese pagers.[11] But that tariff did not deter the Japanese; they kept aggressively targeting Motorola's customers—and won some of them.

At first, Motorola's top brass assumed that its own pagers were superior to Japanese pagers and that price cutting was the only reason Japanese pagers were selling in America. Like the leadership at General Motors, Motorola's senior executives were as skeptical of the quality of Japanese products as the Japanese had been toward Motorola when Motorola had been trying to qualify its pagers for sale in Japan.

"In the late 1970s, we were in a denial stage," George Fisher admitted. "We were number one worldwide in market share, and that kind of success breeds arrogance. People stop listening to their customers and to their employees. We kept hearing how the Japanese were penetrating our market with very low costs and a good product. We denied it. We went through this period of denial for a couple of years—denying that they're as good as our customers were saying they were. Denying the fact that they could produce at lower cost than we could."[12]

The Spur of a "Healthy Spirit of Discontent"

Bob Galvin remembers when the alarm bell first rang for him. It happened at a meeting of senior Motorola executives in April 1979. The long session was just about to wrap up when Art Sundry, a division chief, bluntly spoke up. "Good meeting," he said, "but we're not on the right subject. Our quality stinks!"[13]

Bob Galvin, who prided himself on fostering what his father had called "a healthy spirit of discontent" within Motorola, welcomed Sundry's splash of cold water.

What made Sundry's comment so provocative was that Motorola was then selling to about 75 percent of the American market, and Sundry himself headed the company's most successful division. His jarring verdict was in keeping with Motorola's corporate code—a code of candor that gave the company its edge and drive.

Contentious debates are a hallmark among the armies of electrical engineers at Motorola and among a corporate leadership drawn mostly from technical backgrounds. People argue passionately about the pros and cons of any corporate issue, and those passionate debates are an essential ingredient of Motorola's corporate culture.

The bracing tension at Motorola initially unhinged George Fisher when he shifted to Motorola from AT&T's Bell Laboratories in the mid-1970s. "I was shocked at the level of internal discontent—discontent with what we're doing, self-criticism," Fisher admitted. "It didn't take too long before I realized it was a very healthy characteristic of the company, a real strength. Meetings were contentious—still are contentious—not particularly polite, not particularly orderly. But they did get a lot of differing views out on the table, somewhat in a raucous way."[14]

Bob Galvin, delighted by Art Sundry's blast against Motorola's "stinking" quality, seized the occasion to propel Motorola into vigorous self-examination. He launched the process of "reinventing" Motorola that ultimately produced a massive shift in the company's thinking—and a competitive payoff that continues today.

"We had to teach ourselves to be scared—in effect, face the gallows!" Galvin declared. "There was a growing threat of Japanese ascendancy in many marketplaces. So we actually took courses to show what the threat to America was. And that really began to stir our juices."[15]

Motorola also checked the quality of Japanese pagers, and, as George Fisher recalled, "That put us through hell! We tore apart the Japanese pagers and found out that they were very, very good. That woke us up to what trouble we were in. We won our dumping case against the Japanese, but despite that victory, their prices were still beating us. So we had to drop our prices to meet their competition. Then we had to figure out how to radically redesign our pagers so that we could make money at these lower costs—and still boost our quality."[16]

What was chilling to Motorola was that Japanese pagers were so durable and reliable: Motorola's pagers failed sooner and more often than the Japanese models. Worse, the Japanese were using the same parts and components that Motorola was, according to Richard Bretow, senior vice president and director of quality, "but they were building their product one thousand times more defect-free."[17]

The Japanese were "the best thing that happened to us," said another Motorola executive, Ed Bales, "because they threatened our survival."[18]

The New Paradigm: High Quality and Low Cost Go Hand in Hand

From painful comparisons and from trial and error came the most critical paradigm shift in Motorola's thinking over the past fifteen years—the refutation of the old business calculation that high quality spells high costs and the revolutionary discovery that striving for higher quality actually lowers costs. That shift in thinking turned Motorola upside down.

"We had to change the way we manufactured," Ed Bales said. "We would find defects and send them to be reworked. We did not want to waste those circuit boards. Big mistake. Every time they were reworked, we were increasing the chances of early failure for customers. We thought we were saving the company money by fixing defects. But actually, we were creating customer dissatisfaction."

Motorola learned the Deming lesson: Get the design and production of pagers, cellular phones, cars, or any other item right on the first try. It takes more time and probably costs more in the short run, but over time that approach reaps savings because it prevents defects and difficulties from multiplying by the thousands or millions during mass production.

Eventually Motorola concluded that it did not even make sense to fix defects that were spotted during production. It was better to throw out those items, Ed Bales explained, because it was precisely those items, once fixed and shipped to consumers, that most often broke down after they had been sold and that came back to haunt Motorola in the form of customer complaints and service repairs under

Motorola's warranties. Fixing a defect during production still meant Motorola was shipping a defective product. So Motorola tossed away all lemons, no matter how minor the flaw; that approach saved money in the long run.

"It just stands to reason," Bob Galvin said. "If you don't do things a second time, you don't have to repair, you don't have to correct, you don't have to take cognizance of the problem. Quality absolutely saves money. We embraced that starting in the early eighties."[19]

Achieving quality both to satisfy customers and to generate corporate savings became a crusade at Motorola, and Bob Galvin was its evangelist. He operated on the premise that if he wanted everyone in the company to pursue superlative quality, then, as CEO, he had to make superior quality his own uncompromising objective. At senior executive meetings, Galvin would dispense with the standard reviews of manufacturing, finance, human relations, and so on, and focus immediately on quality. On many occasions, Galvin's meetings never left that topic, because quality touched everything else. Galvin spoke of quality not so much as a managerial objective but, almost reverently, as "a philosophy, a way of thinking." He described quality as a "culture" that was the driving force for the entire company, driving everything—technology, investment, production, marketing, human relations, recruitment, every facet of Motorola's operations.

George Fisher described quality as "the single banner" under which Motorola transformed itself—"understanding that quality is broader than just how we make a product. Quality is in all the processes with which we run the company—how we treat our people, how we treat our customers, how we develop products."[20]

Six Sigma: A New Definition of Quality—Virtual Perfection

The pursuit of the Holy Grail of quality led Motorola step by step to a new perception of the meaning of quality.

Motorola executives thought they had been doing pretty well in the early 1980s by achieving a 99 percent defect-free rate, but, in retrospect, George Fisher almost mocked the notion that 99 percent had been good enough. By the time Motorola was putting several hundred thousand integrated circuits onto a single computer chip, Fisher pointed out, a 1 percent failure rate ran into thousands of bad transistors. The problem took a quantum jump by the early 1990s, when the number of transistors on a single chip had leapt into the millions. In the future, Fisher foresaw a single chip being implanted with 1 billion transistors, and, at that level, 99 percent perfect, he said, "leaves you with ten million bad transistors—and I don't think you want that device."

The restless quest for quality meant changing everything Motorola did. It meant redesigning many products, such as pagers, to have fewer parts. The more parts, the more human handling, the more processes that could fail, the more defects, the less reliability. Simpler design reduced all those potential failure points. The quality drive required radical improvements in production technology—more efficient machines for producing and assembling components. High-quality production also demanded a simpler, easier work flow in Motorola's plants to remove inefficiencies and hazards. As at Ford's South Chicago plant, achieving these improvements meant giving workers more responsibility for quality and inviting many more suggestions from workers. Every step, every tiny detail contributed something.

Almost inevitably, Motorola's quality crusade was forever accelerating. It kept setting new goals. Seen from the valley below, each one seemed like an impossible mountain, but, once scaled, the peak no longer looked so impressive. In fact, as a quality standard, the new level always seemed inadequate as soon as it was achieved, because the best American, Japanese, and European companies were chasing the same Holy Grail. With everyone's quality becoming ever higher, Motorola had to keep setting new, higher targets.

"We set out in 1981 to go after a tenfold improvement in quality," George Fisher recalled. "People thought that was unbelievable! Reach up tenfold in five years? Once we achieved it, we continued our benchmarking [of competitors] and looked around and saw that wasn't a fast enough rate of improvement."

In fact, Motorola achieved its tenfold improvement ahead of time and decided to go after another tenfold improvement in quality—a 100-fold improvement between 1981 and 1991. With momentum from the first phase, progress came faster in the second five years, so suddenly the goal was upped once again—to virtual perfection.

"We set our Six Sigma program in 1986–87, which was to virtually reach perfection—roughly three parts per million defect rate—in a five-year period," Fisher said. "Once again, people said, 'Oh my God! I have no idea how we're going to get there!' But guess what? A lot of our businesses got there. On the average, the company improved over a hundred and fifty times in that five-year period. We saved over two billion dollars in that period through reduced defects and [savings on] the cost of poor quality. Our people achieved things that we thought were impossible."[21]

Six Sigma has become an incantation at Motorola. In one day at Motorola, I heard Six Sigma invoked at least a hundred times. In mathematical terms, Six Sigma literally means only 3.4 deviations, or defects, for each 1 million tries, or 99.99966 percent perfect. It means McDonald's producing only three bad hamburgers per million, or your fax machine having only three paper jams or other failures per million pages, or only three runs per million pairs of panty hose.

To convey Six Sigma in layman's language, Motorola produced an advertisement showing golf pro Lee Trevino. "For me to hit that level of consistency," Trevino said, "I'd have to go thirty years without missing a single putt."[22]

Knife-Edge Decision: Start a New Plant in Malaysia or in Illinois?

One vital test for Motorola—during an episode that took the company's internal transformation still deeper—was whether an American workforce could match the perfection-minded Japanese, on both quality and cost.

The test came on a new field of battle with the Japanese—cellular phones. The question for Motorola was whether to shift production of cellular phones to Asia as a cost-cutting measure or try to compete against the Japanese with American workers.

Once again, Motorola had pioneered a new technology. It had created an entirely new commercial arena—cellular phones. In their basic technology, cellular phones are a Buck Rogers modernization of the old walkie-talkie radios that Motorola had produced for American GIs during World War II. In 1980, Bob Galvin saw these mobile phones as a potential $10-billion-a-year global business. Motorola produced a breakthrough invention, but its two-year jump on a world of competitors was ruined by eighteen months of delays in getting approval from the Federal Communications Commission to make and market cellular phones in the United States. By then, Japanese competitors were on Motorola's heels.

Japan's electronics giants had reacted immediately when Motorola test-marketed its cellular phone in Scandinavia in 1981. The Japanese are experts at reverse engineering—taking apart someone else's invention, analyzing how it is made, and producing a competitive version with very minor variations, as a way to avoid patent-infringement suits.

The Japanese moved so fast that when Motorola's first cellular phones went on sale in the United States in 1983, virtually every major Japanese electronics firm—Fujitsu, Hitachi, Kokusai, JRC, Matsushita, Mitsubishi, Oki, NEC, and Toshiba—was selling a rival cellular phone in the American market within a few months. By late 1984, the Japanese were slightly outselling Motorola; they had captured roughly 40 percent of the small but rapidly growing American market. Once again, Motorola accused the Japanese of price dumping—selling cellular phones for more than $2,000 in Japan but less than $1,000 in America.[23] Once again, the U.S. government ruled in Motorola's favor and imposed tariff penalties on the Japanese. And once again that ruling did not cure Motorola's problems.

By 1986, still under fierce assault by the Japanese, Motorola had to pare its costs drastically. "This was the moment of truth for cellular," said Susan Hooker, then working in the cellular phone division. "We were in deep trouble—the Japanese reliability was better, and their costs were lower. We were selling at a loss just to stay competitive. We were not able to manufacture this product in Illinois at a competitive price. There was a decision made to go offshore."[24]

For many American companies, meeting Japanese and other global competition in the 1980s meant moving plants offshore, mainly to east Asia, where labor costs were lower. Motorola Vice Chairman Bill Weisz and President John Mitchell were inclined to follow that trend. Motorola already had plants making semiconductor components in Malaysia. Weisz and Mitchell sent a team led by Dan Pryzbylski, then head of cellular manufacturing, to check out sites in east Asia for a new state-of-the-art cellular phone factory. Pryzbylski and his team came back recommending a site in Malaysia.[25]

That recommendation triggered a roaring battle within Motorola over where to put the new plant—in Malaysia or in Arlington, Illinois, a suburb northwest of Chicago. Wolf Pavlok, who was a member of the survey team and later became general manager of the cellular division, said the arguments were stormy. The majority of the survey team urged putting the cellular assembly plant overseas; they were impressed by the capabilities of the Malaysian workforce. With modest training, they said, Malaysians could do the job well—at 20 percent of the average pay of Motorola's American workers.

But a minority of the survey team, including Pavlok, took an unconventional view: "No, let's keep the jobs here, and let's be competitive." They argued that labor costs are only a small fraction (5 to 6 percent) of the total costs of high-tech devices such as cellular phones and that the wage differentials between Malaysia and America would be offset by U.S. tariffs imposed on cellular phones shipped from Malaysia into America. Support came from George Fisher and others, who asserted that technology was changing so rapidly and flexibility in production was so critical, it was smarter to build the new cellular factory near Motorola's engineering center outside Chicago, for easy back-and-forth between the designers and the manufacturing group.

"It was a hot debate—and a hot execution," Pavlok recalled. "I mean, it was a gamble. If we were to not execute and meet the challenge, we would not be here today."[26]

One other factor seemed to move Bob Galvin, and ultimately Weisz and Mitchell, too, in favor of building the new plant in Illinois. That was national and regional pride, a determination to prove that American workers could compete head to head with the Japanese. So finally, in 1986, Motorola picked a site at Arlington, Illinois, not far from Motorola headquarters at Schaumburg, for its new cellular plant and a major new design facility.

Back to School at Forty: New Skills and New Self-Respect

Motorola's leadership was in for a shock: Half of its regular assembly-line employees did not have the minimum skills required to work in the new cellular plant.

The company's response to that skills gap was critical to its future: It seized on the problem to lift the company to new heights.

If Motorola was going to meet the Japanese challenge, the new plant had to operate at peak efficiency. Plans were made for a high-performance workplace; the Arlington plant would embody everything Motorola had learned so far. It was not only slated for state-of-the-art robots and automation, but production engineers set up a new work flow based on workers' suggestions. Motorola had discovered that its plants were disorganized jumbles; they were not laid out efficiently. Engineers concluded that a straight assembly line, from one end of the factory to the other, was bad for communication among work teams. So the new Arlington plant would get U-shaped lines to keep workers in close visual and voice contact.

Moreover, the new cellular plant required the best rank-and-file workforce Motorola could muster. More than any previous Motorola operation, the new plant would rely on self-directed work teams and on line workers' taking responsibility for quality and process control. For maximum flexibility, Motorola also wanted the workers to be interchangeable—that is, to master multiple skills and multiple jobs, so that they could move easily from one part of the operation to another.[27]

The new plant needed about 3,000 workers. Motorola counted on recruiting them from its other plants in the suburbs northwest of Chicago. There was an avalanche of applications. Motorola's personnel office administered a battery of tests, and when senior executives checked the basic competency level of the applicants, they were stunned.

"We found that about fifty percent of the applicants either didn't have fifth-grade arithmetic skills or seventh-grade reading skills, which were the minimum levels we had established," George Fisher said.[28]

Motorola's workforce in the blue-collar suburbs northwest of Chicago was melting-pot America—eastern European, African American, Hispanic, French Canadian, Portuguese. Many of these workers, longtime employees of Motorola, were upset by the testing and by the bad results. Miriam Nielsen, a French immigrant who had put in fourteen years at Motorola, was one of thousands who failed the tests. The whole process baffled her. She was shocked and afraid.

"All of a sudden they wanted you to know how to read, how to speak, how to count, and we didn't know to what level until we took the test," Nielsen recalled. "We didn't know why we were doing that [test]. They were talking about new processes, and being able to compete world class, and so forth. I was worried about losing my job."[29]

Nielsen had joined Motorola in 1973 as a fresh immigrant, speaking broken English. She still speaks with a French accent but quite understandably. But in 1987, she had trouble reading and doing math. She was not alone.

Motorola had many workers who communicated with one another in Polish, Lithuanian, Spanish, or Portuguese, relying on a foreman or supervisor whenever English was needed. This would not work in the new plant, because the robots and other automatic devices were computer programmed to give voice messages in English when they had run out of components or to alert line workers to a malfunction. To manage robots and other automation in the new plant, workers had to be at home in basic English, and they needed basic math for various quality controls.[30]

Shocked by the low English and math skills of its workforce, Motorola's management launched a massive retraining effort for workers such as Miriam Nielsen. Local high school graduates offered no practical alternative—not only did they lack work experience and discipline, but only about 10 percent of them could pass Motorola's recruitment tests. So Motorola gave hundreds of employees a choice: If you want to work in the new factory, sign up for classes in English and math. Otherwise, stay where you are, but be aware that older plants will gradually be phased out or modernized.

The prospect of school frightened many middle-aged employees. "I was already in my mid-forties, and I was afraid I was going to be too old," Nielsen confessed. "Going to school and taking classes, I thought, 'At forty, oh my goodness, what am I going to do?' . . . We could take the class or refuse. Well, of course, I agreed to take the class. I wanted to try. I wanted to save my employment."

The experience proved to be reassuring. Motorola eased the difficulties by absorbing all the expense. Most employees were trained in classes, but some were too ashamed to show that they were functionally illiterate. Motorola provided them with personal tutors, sometimes retired Motorola employees; others were taught by their own children with computer software developed by Motorola for home learning. After six weeks, most employees took a second battery of tests, and the vast majority passed the basic competency levels needed to work at the new cellular phone plant.[31]

At the new plant, Miriam Nielsen and her coworkers found the work more stimulating and rewarding than at their old plants, and their bonds of loyalty to Motorola were strengthened, because the company had not used the tests as a pretext for getting rid of people.

"Motorola took care of us," said Miriam Nielsen. "I am very grateful to the company. Not only did they help me on my test, help me keep my job, but they helped me in my self-respect. I realized that taking classes was not so difficult. So I went out and I took classes on my own. I took typing classes. I felt wonderful. We all felt very grateful.

We felt that the company was not against us. It was trying to help us."[32]

"To Be Competitive, a Company Must Be Competitive One Person at a Time"

The crash training effort at the new cellular phone plant was a watershed for Motorola. It transformed the company.

Just as the painful discovery about the superior quality of Japanese pagers had provoked Motorola's quality crusade, the shock of discovering the low level of competence among its employees caused Motorola to undertake a massive training program. Motorola went far beyond what Ford had done—retraining displaced workers or upgrading the training of a certain group of workers for new job assignments, such as those at the cellular plant. It committed itself to continuous, regular—and universal—training throughout the company, from the lowest level of new recruits, custodians, or food service workers up to the very top, including the CEO.

"We came upon the fundamental principle that to be competitive, [a company] must be competitive one person at a time," Bob Galvin told me. "You must be as good [as] or better than the best counterpart of your class of job in the world."[33]

Galvin exempted no one, including himself. "Well, I knew there were Japanese executives who were smarter than I was, so I knew I needed a mentor," he said. "And so we needed a school to teach me and everyone else. We went into very elaborate education, so we could aspire to be as good as the best of anyone who had the similar job anywhere in the electronics industry."[34]

At its headquarters in Schaumburg, Illinois, the company set up Motorola University, which built up to a full-time staff of 230, plus 450 contract teachers. Motorola has miniuniversities at its facilities near Boston, Phoenix, Austin, Singapore, Yokohama, Edinburgh, and London. The curriculum is huge; the course descriptions fill many loose-leaf binders.

On a typical day, new workers are being taught about teamwork and problem solving; other workers are being trained in basic communications and computational skills; and a group of division managers and engineers is engaged in role-playing exercises designed to improve their management skills. One large room houses an entire tabletop assembly line, with several workstations—a robotic arm, visioning camera, computer station, quality checkpoint, and customizing area, all simulating the process of making pagers. This facility is used for many purposes: to show managers the results of their investment decisions on automation and what the capabilities and limitations of the equipment are; to give design engineers a look at problems in work flow or production engineering; to introduce new workers to the equipment and methods at Motorola.

The company estimates that an employee who stays with Motorola for forty years will work in ten different major areas during that career, and training is crucial for making all those career shifts. Many courses offer specific skills. Others introduce workers to new equipment and technologies, the result of Motorola's studies on how to overcome employee resistance to new technologies.

"A lot of technology is very slow to be implemented because people are afraid of it—afraid it's going to replace their jobs, just afraid of the complexity of it," explained Bill Wiggenhorn, Motorola's vice president in charge of training. "What we found was that you spend all that money on the technology, but unless you place it in the work environment in a way in which people understand what it's going to do and the implications, you're going to have a disaster."

As with quality, Bob Galvin was the leading zealot for training. When division managers balked, complaining that they could not afford either the cost of training or the loss of their employees during the training time, Galvin would tell them that, in reality, training cost them less than nothing. Galvin scoffed at the attitude of many companies that training is too costly, especially for frontline workers, except on matters of safety and health.

"We literally get back in terms of more effective work—in the quarter in which the training is presented—a value greater than the simple cost of that particular classroom," Galvin told me. "It just passes the commonsense test that if you teach people how to engage in a statistical quality control analysis, and they're on a problem-solving team, and it cost maybe fifty to a hundred dollars to put them through that course, within three months they will have probably caused a ten- or twenty-thousand-dollar savings as a result of their better thinking process. . . . In general, we believe the ratio of the gain we get from training versus cost is about thirty to one."[35]

And so Motorola provides every single one of its 107,000 employees at least one workweek in class per year—no small achievement for a $12 billion company. Its ultimate goal is to raise the required level gradually to one month of training per year for everyone. Overall, former Motorola CEO George Fisher estimated in mid-1993 that Motorola was investing $200 million a year in training—"and I say 'invest' and not 'spend,' " Fisher emphasized, because he saw training not as a cost to be avoided but as an investment in the company's growth.

"If you believe that your employees are a cherished asset and are with you for a long period of time—and we believe virtually in lifetime employment," Fisher said, "then you've got to admit that it's essential that we retrain, reeducate our people regularly through their careers."[36]

The Test: Head to Head with the Japanese in Their Home Market

With its quality drive and its training program in high gear, Motorola was ready for the big game—Bob Galvin's counterattack against the Japanese in the cellular phone market.

By the mid-1980s, Japanese electronics firms were pressing Motorola hard in the American cellular phone market. Galvin was eager to put Japanese manufacturers under pressure in their home market. Motorola already had a good foothold in the Japanese pager market, and it decided in the mid-1980s to go after the Japanese cellular phone market as well.

To George Fisher, then Galvin's number two, Japan was the supreme test of the excellence that Motorola had been striving to achieve. "If you're going to play in the major leagues, you'd better play with the best players in the world," Fisher declared. "In the electronics industry, many of the best players in the world are Japanese companies, and you had better be able to compete with them head to head in their home market."[37]

In many ways, the Japanese market is ideal for a company such as Motorola, with its small matchbox-sized pagers and cellular telephones that fit into a cupped palm. As Ira Wolf, a longtime Motorola executive in Tokyo, told me, the Japanese love *keisho tampaku*—small, thin, light, compact things.[38] They delight in the micro, the miniaturized, version of anything. They also take great pleasure in intricate packaging. They will wrap a birthday present in half a dozen layers of paper or tissue, each layer delicately folded into a perfect pattern, the perfection of the package as important as its contents. And they are gadget freaks, zany about the latest technological wizardry of any kind. Any new marketing wrinkle, however slight, will stir excitement in Japan.

Tokyo's Akihabara district is built on that fetish. It is perhaps the largest discount consumer market in the entire world—acre upon acre of multistoried emporia crammed to the ceilings with every conceivable electronic toy, convenience, or appliance and constantly swarming with throngs of Japanese bargain hunters.

The entire sprawling region of Akihabara is testimony to the Japanese hunger to test and possess the latest innovations of modern science and industry. It is here that companies such as SONY and Matsushita do their market research, not as American firms do, by conducting protracted market and opinion surveys before they launch a new product, but by bringing out a steady stream of new models and variations of Walkmen or miniature TVs or minicameras until they hit the most popular combination of features. That constant testing in the marketplace is one important way in which the Japanese get the jump on their competitors.

"If you can serve a Japanese customer, you can serve anyone," said Jim Caile, Motorola's vice president for cellular phone marketing. "They are very sophisticated and demanding customers. You know how service oriented they are. All you have to do is blink, and someone appears with a tissue to wipe your eye."[39]

Phase One: Reagan Pressure—Getting a Foot in the Door

Despite its world leadership in cellular technology, Motorola had to wage a ten-year diplomatic and commercial war to get the right to sell its cellular phones throughout Japan.

Although Motorola had proven its high technical competency with pagers and had gained a solid position in the Japanese pager market, it still ran into the closed club of the *keiretsu* networks and the tight ties between Japanese business and government. In fact, the grudging respect that Motorola had won from its Japanese rivals for the high quality of its pagers only made the Japanese all the more determined to block Motorola from establishing new beachheads in Japan.

Only by appealing to three successive American presidencies—the Reagan, Bush, and Clinton administrations—and by mobilizing their political muscle at critical junctures was Motorola able to carry out Bob Galvin's counterattack.

Motorola first saw a potential opening for its cellular phones when Prime Minister Yasuhiro Nakasone decided to copy the Reagan administration's policy of economic deregulation. With the breakup of AT&T in the United States as a model, Nakasone's government announced in 1985 that it would deregulate the Japanese telecommunications industry. It planned to privatize Motorola's onetime nemesis, the government communications monopoly, Nippon Telegraph and Telephone Corporation (NTT), and to invite competition in the Japanese communications market.

For Motorola, this promised a chance to compete. It had run into a stone wall in 1984, when it had first approached NTT and the Ministry of Posts and Telecommunications (MPT) to propose selling its cellular phones in Japan. Deregulation offered Motorola a way around NTT, a chance to find a different—and more willing—Japanese partner. The promise of deregulation spawned a couple of would-be Japanese competitors for NTT. Motorola allied itself with one of them, DDI, a new telephone company put together by SONY and Kyocera, a huge Japanese ceramics and electronics firm.[40]

But when DDI and Motorola tried to obtain a license from the MPT, they ran into the ultimate "old boys' club," the tight network of Tokyo government and business leaders that sets the rules for the Japanese market. Within Tokyo's corporate-government establishment, SONY had long been regarded as a maverick outsider, and Kyocera was a latecomer, a relatively new company based in Osaka, Japan's second city. Motorola's partners were not among the old-line, blue-blooded Japanese firms that form the inner circle in Tokyo. So NTT and the ministry threw up barriers to block Motorola and the SONY-Kyocera partnership (DDI). Motorola feared that it was being frozen out by the MPT, in order to blunt its technological advantage and to give Japanese companies a protected market and time to catch up to it.

The Reagan administration entered the fray, and there ensued a diplomatic battle royal between the governments in Washington and Tokyo. The harder the Americans pressed, the more the Japanese dug in their heels. Tokyo's business leaders claimed that their "baby" companies were no match for the "giant sumo wrestlers" from America,

IBM and AT&T. As the American trade deficit with Japan ballooned, the Senate voted 92–0 to demand that Japan open its market, raising the specter of congressional retaliation.

Ultimately, Motorola benefited from Washington's strident public pressure on Prime Minister Nakasone, who did not want his friendly ties with President Reagan torpedoed by a trade dispute. Motorola was also helped by a major rift within the Japanese government—the rivalry between two Japanese ministries, the Ministry of International Trade and Industry (MITI), which favored opening the market to avoid triggering protectionism in the U.S. Congress, and the Ministry of Posts and Telecommunications, which wanted to keep control of its bureaucratic turf.[41]

After more than a year of squabbling, Washington and Tokyo struck a compromise agreement that allowed Motorola to get its foot in the door—but there was a catch.

The MPT refused to let Motorola operate nationwide. It divided Japan into two territories. The most lucrative market was the Tokyo-Nagoya corridor, which holds about 60 percent of the country's population and which was allocated to NTT and another new company, Nippon Ido (organized by Toyota and Nissan). DDI, Motorola's Japanese partner, was allowed to compete against NTT in the secondary market—the rest of the country, much of it rural but including a major prize—Osaka, Japan's second city. In the Osaka region, DDI would set up a phone system, market Motorola's cellular phones, and buy from Motorola hundreds of millions of dollars of relay equipment, computers, and other ground gear for a cellular infrastructure.

In Osaka, unfortunately, there were more delays—some bureaucratic and some connected with the difficulties in installing the infrastructure for a new phone system. Japanese regulations also put a damper on Motorola's access to customers. The laws ban sales of mobile phones; they can only be leased. So Motorola was totally dependent on its distributor, DDI.

Even so, Motorola's phones made a hit in Osaka business circles; by 1991, Motorola claimed to have picked up 100,000 cellular subscribers, about half of the Osaka market. That was no small feat against NTT and its army of Japanese suppliers.[42]

Very soon, however, Motorola confronted new handicaps. The digital technology used by Motorola and DDI differed from the traditional analog technology used by NTT and the other company operating in the Tokyo region, Nippon Ido. So when Motorola's

Osaka customers traveled to Tokyo or Nagoya, their Motorola cellular phones did not work in that region. Technology was putting a crimp in Motorola's gains.

Once again, winning access to the Tokyo market became crucial.

Phase Two: Bush and Hardball—Prying Open the Tokyo Market

Unwittingly, Japanese authorities handed Motorola an opening to the Tokyo market. In midsummer 1988, Motorola found what it saw as evidence that the Japanese government was welshing on the 1986 trade agreement with Washington.

At that time, the Japanese government had barred Motorola and DDI from operating in the Tokyo-Nagoya corridor on the ground that there were only two available radio bands, which it had allocated to NTT and Nippon Ido. But in 1988, Motorola discovered that a third system had been surreptitiously allowed to operate in the Tokyo region—the radiophone system of a Tokyo taxi company. Motorola saw that as proof of sufficient radio-band capacity to accommodate DDI and Motorola in Tokyo.

Internally, Motorola was divided over what to do. Its Japanese executives opposed picking a new fight with the Japanese government. "Listen," they argued, "we're doing good business in Japan. We're making money. Let's not rock the boat."[43] They feared that a confrontation would jeopardize Motorola's lucrative phone business in Osaka and its pager business all over Japan.

To Bob Galvin and other senior American executives, however, the track record proved the value of being tough. "Most companies will not play hardball because they are afraid of being retaliated against without knowing it," said Ira Wolf, a senior Motorola executive in Tokyo at that time. "Our view is that if we didn't play hardball, we'd be out of business. It was hardball that got us in here."[44]

So Motorola took its case for access to Tokyo to the Japanese government, but its appeals and protests got nowhere.

Finally, in early 1989, Motorola decided to go public—on two tracks. It adopted a high-profile diplomatic strategy, and it stepped up the commercial pressure on its Japanese competitors. At a press conference in Washington in April 1989, Motorola made a splashy announcement unveiling a brand-new product, its Micro TAC cellular phone. At that time, the Micro TAC was a marvel of miniaturization, weighing only 10.7 ounces, far lighter than anything the Japanese had produced. Knowing that it was a couple of years ahead of its Japanese rivals, Motorola was counting on big press play to build consumer demand for its new phone—in Tokyo as well as in Osaka.

The second track of Motorola's strategy was an official complaint to the Bush administration accusing Tokyo of violating the 1986 trade agreement and arguing that Motorola and DDI should be awarded a radio band for their cellular phone service in Tokyo.

Once again, Motorola was going high profile, escalating its market problems into another diplomatic storm. Its case touched all the raw nerves of the 1984–86 battle over telecommunications. Special Trade Representative Carla Hills threatened retaliation against Japanese communications and electronics imports unless Motorola was given access to Tokyo. The issue became such a political hot potato that, in July 1989, Tokyo sent a top power broker, Ichiro Ozawa, then secretary-general of the ruling Liberal Democratic Party, to strike a deal with Hills. To prevent an escalating trade war, Ozawa promised Motorola access to the Tokyo market.

Hardball had paid off, or so it seemed.

But once again, there was a catch. Instead of granting the new Tokyo-area phone channel to Motorola's regular Japanese partner, DDI, the Ministry of Posts and Telecommunications ordered Nippon Ido to build the system for Motorola's cellular phones in the Tokyo region. The problem was that Nippon Ido used technology that was incompatible with Motorola's. Putting in a new Motorola-style digital system involved huge expense, and Nippon Ido was in no hurry to make those investments.

Also, Motorola was at a terrible marketing disadvantage to NTT and its allies. In May 1993, four years after the Tokyo market was supposedly opened to Motorola, I went looking for a cellular phone in Akihabara. Laox, one of the biggest, best-known electronics stores in Akihabara, had two displays with ten sample phones.

The most prominent display, at counter height, had four phones offered by NTT. Typical of the Japanese way of doling out shares of the market to all the big firms, these four phones were made by four different companies—Matsushita, Mitsubishi, NEC, and Nippon-denso—but all four phones carried the label of NTT, the phone company and distributor.

The second display was tucked down below the counter, at knee height, with six phones in an uninviting jumble. This batch bore the label of Nippon Ido in Japanese and Tokyophone in English. One of those was a Motorola phone, though Motorola's name was not on it.

I told the counter clerk that for my work in Japan I needed a mobile cellular phone, and he immediately recommended the NTT phones. They were "mover phones" with a roaming capability, he said, for operating all around the country.

According to the clerk, the other phones—the Tokyophones, including Motorola's model—worked only in "certain areas." Since this contradicted Motorola's assertion that its phone now worked nationwide, I asked the clerk to check further. He came back with instruction booklets and maps showing that the Tokyophones worked in part, but not all, of the Tokyo-Nagoya district; moreover, he said, they could not reach other parts of the country, such as Osaka.

Nippon Motorola officials had told me that their phones did require a simple attachment to make them compatible with the existing systems in Tokyo. I asked the clerk about that.

Ah, yes, an attachment, he said. Yes, it was possible to buy an attachment for the Tokyophone, and it would work in other areas of the country, too.

The clerk did not know immediately how much the attachment cost, but it turned out to be quite inexpensive—in fact, the Tokyophone plus the adapter was actually cheaper than the NTT phones. The Motorola phone was the cheapest of all.

Suddenly the clerk's mood changed. He told me helpfully that the Motorola phone was very popular with Japanese businessmen; they considered it very high in quality.

But how do your customers find out about the Motorola phone, I asked, since you did not recommend it or give me any information until I asked many questions.

Oh, he said, Japanese businessmen know before they come into the store which phone they want. They go right to the Motorola phone and order it.

What about other customers who do not know in advance, I asked. Do they ask questions and discover the Motorola phone?

Oh, no, he said. Japanese customers do not ask so many questions as you do. They buy the NTT phones that we recommend.

Phase Three: Clinton Threats—Overcoming the Japanese Stall

In short, Motorola faced many obstacles despite the official promises that the Tokyo market would be opened to it.

By mid-February 1994, nearly five years after the Japanese had promised Motorola a level playing field, Motorola had signed up only about 10,000 cellular subscribers in the Tokyo region—10,000 compared to nearly 1 million for NTT and its partners.[45] This ratio was way out of kilter with Motorola's experience in Osaka, where it had 49 percent of the market.

What made these results even more incongruous was Motorola's continuing technological leaps ahead of its Japanese rivals. In 1991, soon after Japanese companies had caught up with Motorola's Micro TAC, which weighed 10.7 ounces, Motorola came out with a far lighter version, Micro TAC Ultralite, which weighed only 7.7 ounces. In other world markets, the Micro TAC Ultralite was a hot item, but it was not moving well in Tokyo.

Once again, Motorola moved its marketing problems into the political arena. It turned to the Clinton administration for help, accusing Nippon Ido, its government-assigned partner in the Tokyo area, with foot-dragging. In five years, Motorola charged, Nippon Ido had built only half of the necessary telephone relay stations in the Tokyo-Nagoya area. So, in fact, Motorola's service was patchy and hence was not yet an attractive buy to Tokyo customers.

The Motorola bombshell burst amid another major trade donnybrook between Washington and Tokyo—this time over opening up Japanese markets in telecommunications, insurance, auto parts, and medical equipment. President Clinton's personal efforts to break the deadlock with Prime Minister Morihiro Hosakawa broke down in a dramatic failure on February 11, 1994. Four days later, the Clinton administration threatened to impose trade sanctions unless Japan lived up to its 1989 promise to allow Motorola to operate in the Tokyo market. A month later, an agreement was reached. Under orders from the Japanese Ministry of Posts and Telecommunications, Nippon Ido promised to step up construction of cellular telephone relay stations to make Motorola's cellular service available to 95 percent of the Tokyo-Nagoya corridor by the end of 1995.[46]

The lesson was clear: Motorola had gotten action both by achieving technological leadership and by getting political help from three successive American administrations. Neither tactic would have been sufficient without the other.

Targeting the Japanese market was crucial to Motorola's world leadership. Bob Galvin had used the counterattack strategy both to put pressure on Motorola's Japanese competitors and to drive Motorola to new heights of quality, innovation, and product leadership.

The Japanese challenge became not a cause for complaint or a retreat into protectionism but a catalyst for transforming Motorola into a high-performance company committed to the highest possible development of its workforce. Bob Galvin put his disciples into a frame of mind in which they were constantly drawing lessons from going head to head with the best in Japan.

The rules for success in Japan, according to Susumu Cho, executive vice president of Nippon Motorola, were a handbook for Motorola worldwide: "Attention to details. Make no excuses for problems or mistakes. We learned that Japanese customers had very low tolerance for failure to meet commitments."[47] While George Fisher was still CEO of Motorola, he, too, insisted that the Japanese market had taught the importance of fundamentals: "Is your quality as good as theirs (and they're the best)? Are your costs world class? Is your product what the customer really wants? And can you deliver that product on time?"

Then Fisher underlined a final lesson—that in Japan, simply being the best is often not enough. It takes collaboration between business and government to pry open the market opportunities.

"You have to use every tool in the book to make sure you get an opportunity to compete," Fisher asserted. "We did that in Japan. We didn't just use our technical abilities and our operational abilities. But we used our involvement with both the U.S. and the Japanese governments to make sure we got a fair chance to compete over there."[48]

Fisher differed with the view among many American business executives that the American government was their enemy.

"Quite the contrary," Fisher said emphatically. "I think that companies that don't recognize that the government has to be an ally are going to find it very, very difficult to compete effectively in the world's marketplaces where you're competing with governments *and* companies—countries such as France, Germany, Japan, where government and industry do work together."

"Today," Fisher went on, "you've got to look outside the borders of the U.S. and understand that it's going to take all the power we can put together in this country to compete effectively around the world. That means that government and industry have to work better together. It's absolutely essential."

PART FOUR

Public/Private

Government and Business
as Collaborators

In the new global game, one salient difference that sets the American mind-set apart from that of its two major rivals is the sharp line that Americans normally have drawn between the public and private sectors.

Both Germans and Japanese regard with astonishment the traditional stand-off between business and government in America. Each of these two countries is accustomed to merging public and private interests to a far greater degree than Americans could imagine doing. From experience, both know that government and business can join forces to serve the competitive interests of the entire nation.

In fact, during the past two decades, both Germany and Japan have mounted serious economic challenges to American domination in strategically important commercial arenas—Germany in commercial aircraft, Japan in computer chips. And they have done so by marshaling the combined forces of government and business. Neither country fully trusted market forces alone to ensure the nation's interest. Companies that were left to their own devices not only would despoil the environment but would sometimes refuse to invest in industries that were vital to the nation's long-run development. And so, even when it cost consumers more in the short run, the German and Japanese believed that the long-run well-being of the nation and its people was served by government entering into a partnership with business. Economics was to serve not merely private profit but also national economic power.

The modern industrial strategies of Germany and Japan have historic roots in the capitalistic system in each country. These strategies date back a full century to the industrial development of modern Germany under the conservative-minded Iron Chancellor, Count Otto von Bismarck, and to the rise of modern Japan under the Meiji Restoration. The Germans and Japanese, having industrialized later than Great Britain and America, were driven in the nineteenth century by the compulsion to catch up with the Anglo-Saxons, the world leaders. In both Germany and Japan, the catch-up strategy was for government to provide guidance and support to private industry, in order to focus and mobilize the nation's resources for long-term growth.[1]

This pattern was repeated once again after World War II—more powerfully and purposefully in Japan than in Germany. Nonetheless, it has seemed natural to both the Germans and Japanese that government should take the lead and point the way in important commercial sectors.

Americans, with their laissez-faire economics, have placed their faith in the invisible hand of the free market to ensure the most efficient and wisest development of the national economy. And America's belief in free-market economics staunchly opposes government intervention in industry.

America's practice, however, was less pure than its doctrine. During wartime, Americans have accepted government direction of industry to mobilize the nation; and during the long Cold War with the Soviet Union, even free-market conservatives allowed a large loophole in laissez-faire economics for the government to support defense industries. And since defense contractors such as Boeing, General Motors, and IBM also make commercial products, the subsidies and support that they have received from the Pentagon have helped these companies, and many others, develop and market new inventions and technologies to the civilian economy.

The ending of the Cold War, however, has made it harder to justify such governmental support for purely military purposes—just at a time when the commercial challenge to America from abroad has sharpened.

And so Americans have begun to rethink and readjust to the new game of global competition. Even a conservative president such as Ronald Reagan saw fit to launch a government-business partnership in the crucially important computer chip industry when it seemed about to collapse under competitive assault from Japan. More recently, the Clinton administration has modestly expanded Reagan's example of the public-private partnership called Sematech into other industries. Confronted by public-private partnerships abroad, some American executives at such leading companies as Boeing, Intel, Motorola, Eastman Kodak, General Motors, Ford, and Chrysler now advocate a government-business connection as a natural element of the new competitive game.

14

Europe's Grand Coalition
Boeing and the Challenge from Airbus

> *Over the past twenty-one years, the European governments have helped finance Airbus's development of a whole family of aircraft. Airbus has gotten twenty-six billion dollars in government subsidies. . . . That's an unfair advantage against a company like ours.*[1]
>
> —FRANK SHRONTZ, CEO, BOEING

> *Airbus would not have stood a chance against American producers without massive development, production and marketing support during its first 25 years.*[2]
>
> —LAURA TYSON, AMERICAN ECONOMIST

> *Boeing in the first twenty years of commercial aircraft also incurred huge losses. . . . In the United States, there was tremendously big indirect [government] funding. It's continuing . . . several billion dollars per year, which goes to the aeronautics industry . . . either through NASA or the Department of Defense or whatever.*[3]
>
> —JÜRGEN THOMAS, VICE PRESIDENT, DEUTSCHE AIRBUS

For Boeing, the painful moment of truth is easy to identify—Tuesday night, June 16, 1992, and the morning after.

Boeing, the world's number one manufacturer of civilian airliners, was in a head-to-head battle with Airbus Industrie, the European aircraft consortium, for a huge commercial airliner deal.

United Airlines needed new jetliners to replace its aging fleet of Boeing 727 trijets. Boeing and Airbus were each out to sell United 50 to 100 new planes, at $30 million to $40 million each.

This was the opportunity the Europeans had been striving for.

Governments and companies in Germany, France, Britain, and Spain had formed the Airbus partnership in 1970 in order to challenge America's dominance in an industry that Europe's leaders considered strategic—strategic in the economic as well as the military sense. It was an arm of national might, an embodiment of a nation's economic prowess and sophistication. Europe wanted an aircraft industry to prove it could play in the big leagues with America and Japan.

Going for the United contract was a crucial test for Airbus. It had already sold planes to Northwest, Eastern, and major foreign airlines around the world—but never to United.

On four previous occasions, Airbus had competed with Boeing over a big order from United, and each time Boeing had won. This time, Airbus was determined to prevail, and it had two powerful weapons—a technological edge and a financial advantage.

On June 16, 1992, Jean Pierson, chairman of Airbus Industrie, and Dean Thornton, then president of Boeing's Commercial Airplane Group, each flew to Chicago to meet separately with United Airlines Chairman Stephen M. Wolf.

Over dinner Tuesday evening, Pierson made an all-out pitch for Wolf to buy the most popular plane Airbus had ever built—the 150-seat, twin-engine Airbus A320.

Pierson, a hard-driving French executive, argued that the Airbus A320 was technically superior to the rival Boeing 737-400: The Airbus plane offered better fuel economy. It had 15 to 20 percent more range without refueling. It boasted more advanced electronic controls—a computerized flight deck and avionics so modern that it could be flown by a two-member crew instead of the usual crew of three, saving United big money on crew costs.

To make the deal financially irresistible, Pierson said that Airbus would provide United not only with tens of millions of dollars' worth of extras in parts inventories and training but also with the attractive option of "a walk-away lease"—United could lease the planes initially and decide later whether to buy them or to return them to Airbus and walk away from the deal.

The next morning over breakfast, Thornton made the pitch for Boeing. He reminded Wolf of the long ties between United and Boeing— for fourteen years, United had bought only Boeing planes. The Boeing 737-400, he said, was a new, updated version of an airliner with a proven record since the 1960s.

Buying the 737-400, Thornton argued, would give United the advantage of "commonality." That was Boeing shorthand meaning that United pilots and mechanics already knew how to fly and maintain the nearly five hundred Boeing airliners in the United fleet, and therefore it would take very little training for them to learn the wrinkles of the new 737s. Shifting to Airbus, Thornton noted, would require time and large training costs for United's air and ground crews to learn an entirely new flight system.

Thornton was even willing to stretch Boeing's financial terms. Normally Boeing opposed leasing; it preferred outright purchase. But, not to be outdone by Airbus, this time Boeing agreed to leasing, but for fewer planes than Airbus offered.[4]

The answer came quickly. Steve Wolf flew to France and made a $3 billion deal with Airbus. He ordered fifty Airbus A320s and took an option on fifty more.

Boeing was thunderstruck. "It was a big kick in the butt," admitted Larry Clarkson, Boeing's vice president for Planning and International Development.

"I have to admit that we were not sufficiently aggressive in the beginning. When we woke up to the fact that they [United] were seriously considering something else, we may have been a little late," Clarkson said. "I think that we evolved into a sense of false security. We thought we had a lifetime commitment, sort of, from Steve [Wolf]—and we found out differently."[5]

At first, Boeing executives blamed the United deal on sweet financing from Airbus. They were feeling heat from the bargain prices that Airbus was offering, in order to penetrate the American market. "Airbus has put some tremendous price pressure on us," Clarkson conceded.

Only grudgingly did Boeing's leadership admit a deeper problem— that Boeing was not competitive enough: It had lost the technological edge.

In the battle for United's order, Larry Clarkson conceded, Boeing had pitted a plane of the 1960s (the Boeing 737) against a plane of the 1980s (the Airbus A320). Phil Condit, Boeing's president, acknowledged that Airbus had forged ahead with its easier, more efficient fly-by-wire control systems and other technological advances.

Boeing had been stung. While it was still the global leader, it took heed from its defeat at United. Its top brass had watched Airbus start from scratch and overtake big, successful American aircraft manufacturers such as Lockheed and McDonnell Douglas. And they were no longer treating the Airbus threat nonchalantly.

"We are concerned," Larry Clarkson admitted. "We don't want to be the next IBM or General Motors."

America: The Stakes Are High, and the Deck Is Stacked

In their battle against Airbus, Boeing and other American aircraft manufacturers contended that the deck was stacked against them. They cast their battle as a competition between American private enterprise and an unholy alliance of governments and businesses in Europe.

In the early 1990s, Boeing Chairman Frank Shrontz blamed much of Boeing's woes on the unfair advantage Airbus Industrie had gained from subsidies from the governments of France, Germany, Britain, and Spain.

"Over the past twenty-one years, the European governments have helped finance Airbus's development of a whole family of aircraft," Shrontz asserted. "Airbus has gotten twenty-six billion dollars in government subsidies—that's the U.S. government's estimate."

Shrontz conceded that costs were not the only consideration for European governments in developing a world-class aircraft industry. "It's image, it's jobs, it's nationhood," Shrontz said. "But those subsidies amount to sixty percent of the development costs of a new plane—about eight million dollars for every plane Airbus has built. That's an unfair advantage against a company like ours, which has to finance the development of its own planes."[6]

In answer, the Europeans pointed out that America's civilian airliner industry had also gotten its start—and established its global leadership—with heavy governmental support. Boeing and other American planemakers had lived off government contracts after World War II, insisted Jürgen Thomas, vice president of Deutsche Airbus, the German partner of Airbus Industrie. "Boeing in the first twenty years of commercial aircraft also incurred huge losses, like Airbus," Thomas said. "In the United States, there was tremendously big indirect funding" from the U.S. government to the aircraft industry.

Even today, Thomas said, American companies are getting financial support for developing new aviation technologies. "If you look at the published reports, well, it's several billion"—and he emphasized the word billion—"several billion dollars per year, which goes to the aeronautics industry in the United States, either through NASA [the space agency] or the Department of Defense or whatever."[7]

Boeing's Larry Clarkson conceded that Boeing had benefited from military and space contracts, but he sought to treat that indirect aid as different from the direct subsidies given to Airbus. "Our issue," said Clarkson, "has always been with the direct subsidies, which, of course, we have never gotten."[8]

Thomas of Airbus replied that the government funds granted to Airbus were actually long-term loans, not subsidies, and those funds were "all repayable" since Airbus had to operate like any commercial firm.

Fundamentally, Thomas had history on his side. America's dominance in commercial jet aircraft had, in fact, been established after World War II with substantial financial support from the U.S. government. Coming out of the war, the Americans had had the lead in long-range aircraft. The German and French aircraft industries had been decimated by war, and the British had concentrated their wartime production on fighters and smaller planes, while America had produced large transport aircraft and bombers, such as Boeing's famous B-17 and B-29 bombers. After the war, defense contracts had kept Boeing afloat financially while its commercial airliner business lost money for two decades.

Government financing had paid for the development of the planes that provided a head start in civilian airliners for Boeing, Douglas, and Lockheed. Boeing's first big commercial passenger jet, the Boeing 707, had been a civilianized version of the U.S. Air Force KC-135 tanker, funded by the Pentagon. The Boeing 747 had drawn on engines and other technology developed for the C5A transport, another Pentagon project. Later, Boeing had adapted several government-financed technologies for its 757 and 767 jet airliners from the aborted supersonic transport (SST) project.[9]

So, as a financial backer and a catalyst for new technologies, the U.S. government had enabled Boeing and the American aircraft industry to achieve global leadership—and there were good reasons why.

The stakes in the aircraft race are high. Almost since the dawning of the air age, major countries have seen aircraft as a strategic industry, both for military purposes and for economic strength. The military advantages are obvious, but, more broadly, being a world leader in aircraft is a badge of manufacturing prowess and technological supremacy.

The aircraft industry not only provides premier high-wage jobs, it stimulates advanced industrial research and development in many fields. Modern aircraft represent the fusing of many technologies— leading-edge computers, state-of-the-art electronics, advanced materials, sophisticated jet engines. Feeder industries supply millions of components for a single airplane. In America, the supplier network reaches into almost every state of the union.

No other sector of manufacturing has projected American commercial and technical supremacy more than the aircraft industry. Certainly none has recently been more lucrative in world trade, and Boeing has been the star performer.

In a period of rising American trade deficits, no other company has contributed more to America's flow of manufactured exports than Boeing. During the 1980s, when the U.S. car industry was reeling and the computer chip industry was being savaged, Boeing maintained its regal domination in commercial aircraft. With nearly $30 billion in yearly sales, Boeing held roughly 60 percent of the world market. Boeing Chairman Frank Shrontz could boast that exports of jet airliners had amounted to $17 billion in 1990 and that Boeing alone had accounted for $13.5 billion.[10] That was a better export performance than any other single American firm in any sector of the U.S. economy.

The future stakes are also enormous. In 1992, Boeing officials estimated that 11,678 commercial jets would be sold by the year 2010— with a total price tag of about $857 billion.[11]

If American manufacturers capture 78 percent of the market (the American share in 1987),[12] that would be worth about $668 billion. But if Airbus keeps on gaining (and Boeing depends heavily on foreign subcontractors), the American share could drop to 55 percent, worth about $471 billion—a loss of nearly $200 billion.

The impact of such a loss on both jobs and America's trade balance is substantial. "Every time a $50 million airplane is sold by Airbus instead of Boeing," commented Ira Magaziner, a management specialist, "America loses about 3,500 high-paying jobs for one year . . . [and] a minimum of $30 million of net exports."[13]

Europe: Rising from Nowhere to Challenge the Champion

It was the American stranglehold on the global airliner market in the late 1960s that provoked the Europeans into what was an outlandishly bold and risky idea—a multinational partnership.

At that time, Boeing, McDonnell Douglas, and Lockheed were building more than 90 percent of the world's jetliners, and Europeans chafed at America's dominance. Europe's government-owned airlines (Air France, Lufthansa, BOAC) were alarmed by their dependence on America, just as Americans would become alarmed in the 1980s at America's dependence on Japan for civilian and defense electronics and computer chips.

No European aircraft company, however, could compete with the U.S. aircraft companies. So in 1970, to break the American monopoly, the Europeans created something new: a multinational *keiretsu*—Airbus Industrie. It was an alliance of France's Aérospatiale, British Aerospace, Spain's CSA, and Germany's Messerschmidt, with other companies added later.[14]

Since these companies were no match for the Americans, the Europeans put together a business-government partnership—the kind of public-sector–private-sector alliance that the Germans under Bismarck, and other Europeans, had used to build up their economic muscle and catch up to the leaders.

Industry provided market sensitivity and a capacity for innovation. Governments provided "patient capital" for long-term development, as did the Japanese *keiretsu*. Haunted by the American specter, the main nations of Europe swallowed their age-old rivalries and jealousies and pooled their resources.

For the Europeans, Airbus was much more than a commercial venture. It was the embodiment of European pride and prestige, of the Gaullist dream of rejuvenating the lost glory of Europe and projecting a united Europe as a global economic power. Earlier efforts with the French Caravelle airliner and the Anglo-French Concorde had failed to challenge American dominance of the aircraft industry. With Airbus, European politicians promised their peoples not only jobs but proof that Europe was a major player in the new global game, able to compete with the giants of America and Japan.

In fact, the most determined push for Airbus came not from industry but from politicians, such as the Bavarian conservative leader Franz Josef Strauss. Later, in the 1980s, Chancellor Helmut Kohl's government, working with Deutsche Bank, prodded Daimler-Benz into buying and revitalizing Messerschmidt and pulling together pieces of Germany's dormant aircraft industry under one roof—Deutsche Airbus.[15]

For two decades or more, it took the deep pockets of the European governments to keep Airbus alive. Governmental involvement was essential. The costs, risks, and scale of such an enterprise are staggering—as much as $2 billion to $5 billion and ten years' time to develop one new airliner. It can take another ten years and the sale of 600 planes to break even—to amortize all the costs of developing the plane, building new factories, and mounting the production runs.

"Airbus would not have stood a chance against American producers without massive development, production and marketing support during its first 25 years," wrote Laura Tyson in 1992, before becoming President Clinton's chief economic adviser. "It takes years of losses for a new firm to develop a family of aircraft and to produce them on a large enough scale. . . . [T]he upfront development costs and technological risks pose insurmountable barriers to the entry of new competitors through market means."[16]

The Keys at Airbus: "Patient Capital," Teamwork, and Innovation

In its infancy, Airbus suffered every imaginable growing pain. As the newcomer, Airbus had to wedge its way into the marketplace and build credibility. To achieve that, Airbus had to unify its cumbersome network of national companies; it had to produce a family of airliners; and it had to offer striking technological innovations.

Its first nightmare was integration—just integrating the design and manufacturing capabilities of several countries. The normal complexities of engineering planes were compounded by linguistic and cultural barriers.

The first Airbus plane, the Airbus 300B (a 250-seat, midrange jetliner) melded a rear fuselage from Germany's Messerschmidt, wings from Britain's Hawker-Siddeley, other wing segments from Holland's VFW Fokker, landing gear from France's Messier, door and tail sections from Spain's CSA. The final assembly was done by France's Aérospatiale in Toulouse.[17]

That plane was well designed and well built, but it was a commercial disaster.[18] Airbus had trouble landing customers. The government airlines Air France and Lufthansa loyally bought nine planes before the A300B's maiden flight in October 1972; then orders dribbled in, bit by bit. But purchases stopped dead in 1976, and Airbus went sixteen dark months without a single sale. Finally, in desperation, it leased four A300Bs to Eastern Airlines in 1977 for $1 apiece. A year later, Eastern bought the four planes; later, it took twenty-eight more. By the end of 1979, Airbus's total sales had reached 111 planes.[19]

Nearly a decade after its birth, Airbus was still far behind the Americans and still losing big money.

What is more, to be competitive, Airbus needed a full family of modern, wide-bodied aircraft to meet the various needs of commercial airlines. That meant going back repeatedly to its four government sponsors and asking for more billions—and patience to allow time for this strategy to work.

Slowly, the Airbus fleet grew. By 1987, Airbus had added three planes—the short-range A310 and the innovative A320 and A321, both good for U.S. coast-to-coast flights. Then, in the late 1980s, it made a big leap into much bigger transoceanic planes (the A330 and A340) that directly challenged the Americans. That gave it more offerings than American firms such as Lockheed and McDonnell Douglas had. Airbus matched Boeing at every market niche except for the 747 jumbo jet.

In its production operations, Airbus gradually achieved an unparalleled level of commercial teamwork among European peoples, better known historically for their hostility than for their harmony. Common computer systems and software eased problems of communication and made possible common engineering standards. At assembly centers such as the one in Hamburg, where the A321 airliner is put together, work units are multinational. British and Spanish teams work closely with the Germans to make sure that the wing and tail sections (built in Britain and Spain) fit properly with the body; French teams operate the equipment for final flight tests. Components are flown from one country to another in a fat, oddly shaped transport plane nicknamed "the Super Guppy," because it looks like a giant tank fish. It is capable of "swallowing" an entire aircraft fuselage lengthwise and then carrying it to another part of the Airbus network in another country.

But the special mark of Airbus has been the pioneering technology of its airliners. As the underdog, Airbus gambled on innovative technology as the way to break into the global market. Throughout the

1980s, Airbus offered one daring innovation after another, and that strategy made Airbus a serious contender to the American planemakers.

"We were the newcomer in the market, and the newcomer has to have an edge on everybody who is already there," explained Gustav Humbert, the Hamburg plant manager for Deutsche Airbus. "The newcomer can have an edge on economy, and he can have an edge on technology. We tried both—to say to airlines, 'Hey, your operating costs can be reduced.' "[20]

The first big Airbus innovation was to build wide-bodied jets powered by only two engines, instead of three or four. In the years after the OPEC oil embargo caused fuel prices to soar in Europe and North America, two-engine planes were a big hit with the airlines because they saved so much on fuel.

A second big innovation was to develop highly computerized aircraft control systems that revolutionized the array of dials, switches, gauges, and video screens that cram an aircraft flight panel. The new Airbus computerized system fed far more information to the pilot and copilot, and in a more digestible form, than the old system had. One payoff for the airlines was that the third man in the cockpit, the flight engineer, was no longer needed since computers monitored all the plane's operating systems. That, too, represented a saving for the airlines.

Airbus reduced the work of pilots by introducing electrical fly-by-wire systems, run through computers, in place of the old hydraulic systems. These digitized controls are so efficient, according to Gustav Humbert, that for a normal flight "you really don't need a pilot in the cockpit, because the instruments are working so well."

Each plane has backup systems in case the main system fails, but Humbert contended that the systems are so good that pilots are needed only to start the aircraft; after that, the autopilot can fly anywhere without the pilot. "You can even land with the autopilot," he said. "Airlines do this very often."

The payoff for Airbus's innovations took time, but when the payoff came, it came with a rush. The 1980s were a boom time for Airbus.

Initially, Americans disparaged Airbus's gains, asserting that Airbus had a captive market in Europe, especially with the government-owned airlines in France and Germany. American aircraft firms also accused European governments, notably the French, of putting political pressure on Third World governments to buy Airbus planes for their national airlines, using the enticement of landing rights in Europe in return for the purchase of Airbus planes.

But there was much more to the Airbus story than that. By the 1990s, Airbus had made itself a formidable force in the global aircraft market. It was reaping the harvest of its pioneering technology—especially with the A320, the plane that embodied the most innovations. Even before the A320 began flying in 1987, Airbus had 294 orders for the A320 plus 182 options to buy. Its first big breakthrough in the American market was a sale to Northwest Airlines in 1987 for more than a hundred aircraft (an order cut back in 1993 because Northwest was losing money).

In 1990, Airbus achieved a commercial breakthrough—its first profitable year since 1970—and American firms felt the direct impact of Airbus's success. McDonnell Douglas saw its share of new passenger jet orders worldwide fall from 22 percent in 1988 to 15 percent in 1990, and Boeing fell from 59 percent to 45 percent, while Airbus moved up from 15 percent to 34 percent of the new orders. Indeed, not counting the Boeing 747, because Airbus has no comparable model, Airbus actually got more orders in 1990 than Boeing did.[21]

With its full fleet of aircraft, Airbus had surpassed first Lockheed and then McDonnell Douglas to become the number two planemaker in the world. Airbus had achieved what once had been considered nearly unattainable: It had gone from ground zero in 1970 to more than 30 percent of the world market for new airliners. Overall, by the end of 1991, Airbus had sold 785 airliners, and another 990 Airbus planes—worth $68 billion—were on order.[22] Airbus was a powerhouse.

In a field where it had long been said there was room for only one or two companies to survive and profit over the long run, Airbus stood with Boeing in the survivors' circle.

And Airbus was pressing its challenge. Thirty percent of the world market was no longer enough, John Leahy, Airbus senior vice president, declared in mid-1994. "Our goal now is fifty percent," Leahy said. "There's no reason we can't do it."[23]

Boeing's Response: Create Your Own Alliance—with Japan

The momentum of Airbus galvanized Boeing. After losing that big sale to United Airlines in 1992, Boeing accelerated the internal changes it had begun in the late 1980s.

"If you stop, you're dead—because the other guy is going to catch you," Boeing President Phil Condit said in mid-1993.

"The U.S. automobile industry very clearly did not see that challenge fast enough," Condit observed. "They were watching each other, they weren't watching the world, and they let the Japanese get ahead of them. Today, you'd have to say that about IBM. It wasn't that there weren't smart people there. There are. But the challenge of changing—when you need to change—wasn't strong enough.[24]

"U.S. industry has the capability, the skill, the resources to be number one," Condit asserted, "but it doesn't fall in your lap."

Boeing took dramatic action.

First came a calculated gamble. To meet the challenge from Europe, Boeing reached across the Pacific to build up a production network with the Japanese. It drew several of the strongest members of the main Japanese *keiretsu* into producing larger and larger proportions of Boeing's newest airliners. Japanese firms took on production of about 20 percent of the airframe for Boeing's 777, a stunning new computer-designed airliner slated to come off the assembly line in mid-1995.

Gaining Japanese participation is one way Boeing can offset Airbus's government subsidies: By getting the Japanese to foot a sizable portion of nearly $5 billion in development costs of the 777, Boeing spreads its own financial risk.

What is more, Japanese participation helps Boeing sell planes in Japan—no small advantage when Boeing and Airbus are competing head to head worldwide. Although the two rivals scrap for every sale, each takes it for granted that Airbus has an edge in western Europe and Boeing has an edge in America. But Asia, which lacks major aircraft producers, is a neutral market, and it is also the world's fastest-growing market for commercial aircraft. In Asia, no country looms as large as Japan. Outside America, Japan is Boeing's best prospective market, likely to take $60 billion worth of new planes by the year 2010.[25]

"Having a [manufacturing] presence in Japan is clearly an important part of selling airplanes in Japan," Phil Condit asserted.

I asked Larry Clarkson if Boeing had an agreed quid pro quo with the Japanese—a guarantee that Boeing will get the lion's share of jetliner sales in Japan in return for granting Japanese industry a large share of Boeing's subcontractor business.

"I can't show you a piece of paper, but the facts speak for themselves," Clarkson replied. "Japanese industry is a partner on the 767 [airliner], and Boeing's largest foreign customer for the 767 is All Nippon Airways; Japan Air Lines is a significant customer. We are a partner with the Japanese on the 777, and both Japan Airlines and All Nippon were early launch customers."[26]

In the aircraft business, "launch customers" are the most important. They make it possible for a company to go ahead and build a new plane; their purchase orders guarantee a sizable chunk of business while the plane is still in the design and development stage. A launch customer is so critical to the birth of a new plane that there is a chicken-and-egg relationship: No one can say which came first, the plane or the launch customers, because without launch customers an aircraft manufacturer would have no plane. That is how closely the Japanese airlines were tied in to the creation of the 777.

Some American trade experts fear that Boeing is creating a Frankenstein, building up the Japanese aircraft industry as a future rival. Clyde Prestowitz, a former U.S. trade negotiator and specialist on Japan, says Boeing may be digging its own grave in the twenty-first century, by transferring its technological know-how to Japanese firms. The Japanese, Prestowitz asserts, have an "eat Boeing" strategy: gradually to accumulate knowledge and experience from each successive Boeing plane until they can make entire planes on their own.[27]

Some Boeing labor leaders share that fear. Tom Baker, who in 1992 was head of the Boeing local of the International Association of Machinists and Aerospace Workers, told me bluntly: "The Boeing Company is very foolish in offering the 777 technology to Japan. The aerospace industry is the only remaining industry where America is first."[28]

Japan: "Techno-Nationalism"

In Japan, as in Europe, the aircraft industry has long been nurtured by the government. The government-business partnership operated before and during World War II, and it is active today.

More explicitly than any other major country, Japan identifies national security with industrial power; it draws little distinction between military and civilian technology. This was true in the nineteenth century, during Japan's drive toward industrialization, and it has again been true in the past half century. In both periods, Japan feared

foreign domination. Driven by an acute sense of insecurity and vulnerability, Japan adopted a strategy of aggressive national economic development. "Techno-nationalism"—the ideology that national power
derives from technological and productive supremacy—is the term
given to Japan's strategy by Richard Samuels from MIT, an American
expert on Japan's aircraft industry.[29]

The aircraft industry is at the heart of Japanese "techno-nationalism." To Japanese economic strategists, the aerospace industry is crucial not only to supplying Japan's Self-Defense Forces with military
aircraft but also to Japan's rise as a global economic power. They see
that a sophisticated aviation industry offers technological spin-offs to
other sectors. The U.S. Occupation authorities shut down the Japanese aviation industry after World War II, but they allowed it to re-
vive during the Korean War. Since that time, Japanese leaders have
nursed the dream of restoring Japan to the place of world power in
aviation.

Among Japan's industrial policymakers, aerospace has ranked as
one of three key technologies for the twenty-first century. The Ministry of International Trade and Industry (MITI), which has master-
minded the postwar development of the Japanese steel, electronics,
microchip, and computer industries, has given aerospace high priority. Every ten years, MITI puts out a "vision" statement setting priorities for the decade ahead, and each decade, starting in 1970, MITI has
ranked aerospace at the top, along with information technology and
nuclear power.[30] By the early 1990s, MITI had poured as much government money into developing jet engines as into computer research.

In the postwar period, 80 percent of Japan's aircraft production has
been military. Japanese firms have built nineteen different American
military planes and helicopters, from the Korean War–era F86 fighter
plane to the modern F16 fighter-bomber, under licensing or coproduc-
tion agreements with the United States.

The most sensational—and controversial—Japanese venture has
been the FSX project (for Fighter Support/Experimental), launched
because MITI, Diet members, the Japanese defense establishment,
and heavy industry all wanted Japan to build its own modern jet
fighter, based on licensed American technology. Because the FSX
project created a furor in Washington, the Japanese backed off a go-it-
alone strategy. In 1987, they announced the codevelopment of a
"lightly modified" American aircraft by Mitsubishi Heavy Industries
and General Dynamics. But even that arrangement marked a signifi-

cant shift: For the first time, the Japanese were taking the lead and the Americans were the junior partners. Richard Samuels sees the FSX project establishing Japan as a "technological power of the first rank."[31]

In the global *commercial* aircraft market, Japan has yet to become a major player, though in recent years Japanese aircraft manufacturers have stepped up their work on civilian aircraft. Back in 1957, MITI launched and subsidized the building of the first all-Japanese airliner, the YS-11, by a consortium of Japanese companies. The YS-11 was a short-range, sixty-five-seat turbojet—technologically sound but poorly marketed. Its financial losses were heavy. Follow-up projects never got off the ground, and so MITI switched to a strategy of partnerships with foreign aircraft companies.[32] Hence the importance of Boeing's willingness to collaborate with the Japanese.[33]

At MITI's urging, Japanese companies went after, and won, contracts to provide components for the Boeing 737, 747, and 757 airliners, each time getting a slightly larger share. When Boeing built the 767, the Japanese share of production took a quantum jump—to 15 percent of that plane. Japanese companies became more than mere subcontractors; they gained a financial stake in the project, earning a fee on each aircraft sold. When Boeing began the 777 project, the Japanese aircraft companies asked to become full-fledged equity partners. Boeing refused. It kept the old arrangements, but it expanded its partnership with the Japanese, upping their share of production to 20 percent.[34]

The "Friendship Club": MITI Calls the Shots for "The Heavies"

Japan's government-business partnership in the aircraft industry operates similarly to that of Airbus Industrie, but its ties are closer. It capitalizes on the network mind-set of the *keiretsu* companies.

The main corporate players are known simply as "the Heavies"— Mitsubishi Heavy Industries, Kawasaki Heavy Industries, Fuji Heavy Industries, and Ishikawajima-Harima Heavy Industries. These huge industrial corporations make ships, generators, and other heavy equipment as well as planes. Each Heavy belongs to a different *keiretsu,* and so, in theory, they are supposed to compete. In practice, they more frequently collaborate. In aircraft, they operate as a cartel (nicknamed "the friendship club")—with MITI calling the shots. This pattern has been fostered by the government since the First Aircraft Industry Promotion Law of 1954.[35]

Over the years, MITI and the Japan Defense Agency have parceled out aircraft contracts to ensure that typically all the cartel members have gotten a share of a big contract. The prime contractor role has been shifted around, but each company has gotten a piece of the action. The general pattern has been for Mitsubishi Heavy to get 40 to 50 percent of the business, Kawasaki Heavy about 25 percent, and Fuji Heavy around 20 percent and for the rest to go to Ishikawajima-Harima Heavy or various small firms.[36]

To no one's surprise, this is roughly how the work shares got allocated for the Boeing 777. According to Japanese executives, the Heavies divvied up the work and then negotiated a deal with Boeing through the Japan Aircraft Development Corporation (a consortium of the Heavies overseen by MITI). As in Europe, government involvement was essential. In fact, a Mitsubishi executive reported that the Heavies would never have made the Boeing 777 deal without MITI's blessing and seed money. The ministry put up 20 percent of the Japanese development funds, which in total ran to several hundred million dollars.[37]

The main Japanese player is Mitsubishi Heavy Industries, which built 18,000 aircraft for the Japanese war effort and which is known for perhaps the most famous fighter of World War II, the Zero, a plane that won the respect of American pilots for its speed and maneuverability.

Today, Mitsubishi has regained its reputation for excellence in aircraft manufacturing. For the Boeing 777, Mitsubishi makes the aft-fuselage panels and all eight entry doors, which are complicated to design and fabricate. Boeing engineers are high on the quality of Mitsubishi workmanship. Outside of Nagoya, the plant in Komaki displays Mitsubishi's versatility. Scores of white-shirted Japanese engineers work on computer linkups to Boeing facilities in Seattle; automatic riveters piece together huge fuselage sections; and blue-uniformed Japanese machinists perform other tasks with meticulous care. Literally within a few feet of the Boeing area, another part of Mitsubishi's plant is devoted to making components for McDonnell Douglas planes. Nearby, Japanese fighter planes go through final assembly and inspection. The range and quality of Mitsubishi's work in that one plant is impressive.

With such capabilities, I heard, Japanese industry chafes privately at being relegated to being a mere "parts supplier" and itches to move out on its own. And so I asked Koichi Shiraishi, deputy manager of Mitsubishi Heavy's operations in Nagoya, whether Mitsubishi or the Heavies as a group would like to produce their own airliner. His intense brown eyes brightened.

"We are just talking about it, you know, about a smaller commercial airplane, maybe around a seventy- to ninety-seater," Shiraishi replied. "The market size in Japan is too small. [Foreign] competition is severe. So we have to study the business before we start this project. We need some support from the government. They have to make it a 'national project.' "[38] In short, no move without MITI's go-ahead.

In Tokyo, at MITI, officials said that the ministry was not yet ready to approve an independent Japanese airliner. They evidently recalled the storm in Washington over the FSX. For now, one senior official said, "More and more international joint ventures or partnerships make sense."[39] Indeed, the Heavies have been talking with Boeing about building an eighty-passenger jet.[40]

Simultaneously, the Japanese are honing their skills on another critical part of making aircraft: MITI has organized a consortium of the Heavies to work with Rolls-Royce, Pratt & Whitney, and other foreign firms to develop a hypersonic jet engine for the twenty-first century. So MITI is methodically promoting Japan's acquisition of the most critical technology and know-how for building civilian jetliners.

"As the Japanese get better and better, the world aircraft manufacturers depend on them more and more and they get a bigger share of the business," observed an economics specialist at the U.S. embassy in Tokyo. "It's probably only a matter of time before the Japanese know how to do the whole job themselves."[41]

At Boeing, senior executives defended the risks they are taking with the Japanese. According to Larry Clarkson, Boeing is trying to manage the risk by retaining control of the "core competencies," the most sensitive elements of aircraft manufacturing: the design, engineering, and production of wings; the cockpit avionics; and the process of "integration," the complex meshing of all the intricate elements of design and production.

Dean Thornton, longtime head of Boeing's commercial airplane group, argued that Boeing has had no choice: It had to link up with the Japanese Heavies as a preemptive move to keep the Japanese from going into joint ventures with Airbus or cash-starved McDonnell

Douglas. Both of those Boeing rivals had, in fact, approached the Japanese about collaboration.[42]

Nonetheless, Phil Condit admitted that Boeing had thought long and hard before drawing the Japanese Heavies so deeply into producing the Boeing 777.

"You don't go into any kind of a partnership with your eyes closed," Condit conceded. "There is always a risk that in fact you will be supporting the growth of a potential competitor. On the other hand, if you try to play all defense, you aren't going to win. You need good partners. You need to establish worldwide contacts . . . and it is better to keep moving forward to maintain your competitive position than it is to sort of hold on to everything and hope that nobody finds out what you do. Technology moves very readily. You can't hold it in a barrel. If you adopt a defensive strategy, other people find it out anyway."[43]

Boeing: Lessons from Japan—Zen and Teamwork

Condit had another reason—a more positive reason—for Boeing's links to Japanese industry: Boeing was not just teaching the Japanese Heavies its technological secrets; it was also learning important lessons from the Japanese, and it was applying those lessons to gain an edge over Airbus.

The prime example was the way that Boeing was building its new 777, a long-range, 375-seat airliner. Its size and capacity are just a market niche smaller than the giant 747's, yet the 777 will be a lot cheaper to operate.

What first caught the eye of aviation writers about the 777 was technology. Boeing was finally learning from the innovations of Airbus. The 777 has two engines instead of four; just two pilots in the cockpit; digitized fly-by-wire controls; more computers on the flight deck; and its own addition, flat-panel displays replacing the old TV-style monitors.

One eye-popping wrinkle was the radical way in which Boeing had designed the 777. It was quickly dubbed "the paperless airplane" because it was the first aircraft in history to be 100 percent digitally designed—and then preassembled, in 3-D, on computers. The design effort was massive. In Seattle's Puget Sound area, more than 2,200 individual computer workstations were linked to the largest mainframe computer installation in the world—eight IBM 3090-600J mainframe computers using three-dimensional interactive software developed by Dassault Aviation in France.

The three-dimensional computer simulations eliminated the need for the costly full-scale test mock-ups normally needed to check on whether the two million parts and components of a plane will fit together. Computers could check the fits better. A computer, working like a brain scanner, can peer deep into the interior of any section, such as a door, and make certain that no part blocks or rubs against any other. It is all done to a precision of several thousandths of an inch.

Yet Phil Condit, who had run the 777 program before becoming Boeing's president in August 1992, did not consider all this dazzling technology to be Boeing's greatest breakthrough on the 777. In fact, Condit tended to discount technology as the secret to competitive success.

Thoughtful and down to earth, Condit had made several intensive study trips to Japan in the 1980s. From the Japanese, he had learned Zen-style patience, the philosophy of gradual improvement, and the importance of people. In fact, Condit sounded like executives at Toyota and Sharp.

"The idea that you can win big by investing in higher technology, designing a fancier flight deck, is very tempting to our engineers," Condit observed. "We Americans tend to look for the home run, the big leap forward, the technological breakthrough that will put you clearly ahead. If I learned anything in Japan, it's that they have been willing to settle for little incremental gains that add up to more, over time, than a few great leaps forward."[44]

Another lesson that Condit had internalized was that high-tech solutions and complex processes are not always the best.

"One of the things we saw at Toyota was simplicity," he said. "You don't automate everything with high-tech robots. You simplify tasks, make it easier. It doesn't have to be an expensive laser-guided robot. It can be a simple thing that aids the guy doing the job to do it easily and correctly every time. Think through your processes, and then simplify them."[45]

The philosophy of gradual, cumulative improvements may have appealed to Condit because of the long life span of aircraft. Since a plane will be on the market for thirty years, he explained, it is far more important to get things right than to get into the market first with a new invention. Over the long run, enduring value will be more important than dazzling new features. Condit may have unconsciously been rationalizing. After all, for nearly a decade, Boeing had been behind Airbus on technology; it had waited to see whether Airbus innovations caught on or flopped. Once new Airbus technologies were proven and popular, Boeing had adopted them.

Condit's greatest lesson from the Japanese, however, did not concern technology at all. It concerned people.

Condit had become passionate about the overarching value of teamwork—among Boeing's employees, with its suppliers, with its customers. And he asserted that the teamwork mind-set is powering a new resurgence at Boeing.

"It's tempting to think of a company in terms of buildings and tools and products," said Condit, who was trained as a mechanical and aeronautical engineer. "In the end, a company is no more or no less than its people—the bright ideas they have, the way they work together."

As Condit was rethinking how Boeing had traditionally operated, he saw innumerable obstacles. "Companies tend to erect [internal] barriers," he remarked. "We pick languages that are different. Finance people talk a different language than structural engineers. Structural engineers talk a different language than control systems specialists. And that tends to isolate them."

The biggest single change in the way Boeing is building the 777, Condit asserted, has been "the emphasis on teaming."

"It is getting engineers, tooling people, factory people, finance people, marketing people, into design-build teams that work together and try to solve problems out ahead," he said. "Our old system tended to be very linear. Engineering designed it, handed it over to tooling. Tooling made tools, handed them to manufacturing. Manufacturing made parts, tried to put them together. . . . And so having manufacturing people, tooling people, and planners up in the design team meant that everything would fit together better."[46]

The Boeing Wrinkle: Have Your Customers Live in Your Factory

Condit's rethinking of the way Boeing works is an unmistakable echo of Toyota. Except that Boeing has added a revolutionary wrinkle—it has made customers part of the Boeing team. It brought the airlines directly into the 235 design-build teams that developed every major component of the 777.

Like many other American executives, Condit and Boeing Chairman Frank Shrontz talk constantly about being customer driven. In practice, they have carried this concept much further than others have. Condit calls it "listening aggressively." People correct him and say, "You must mean intently." And he replies, "No, aggressively—you've got to close your mouth and listen a lot of the time. It's that tremendous, aggressive focus on your customers and what their needs are."

In listening to customers about its 777 airliner, Boeing was making the best of its predicament. It was behind its rivals. In 1991, McDonnell Douglas had beaten it to market with the MD-11, an airliner for the market niche that Boeing intended for the 777. Airbus had targeted its A340 and A330 airliners to bracket that same market niche, and these planes were a year or two ahead of the Boeing 777. So, as Boeing began designing the 777, it could learn things by getting reactions to its rivals' planes from the airlines.

That was hardly a new approach—except that Boeing had the daring idea of bringing eight airlines right inside the Boeing family. These eight airlines—United, American, Delta, All Nippon Airways, British Airways, Japan Air Lines, Quantas, and Cathay Pacific—were made members of Boeing's design-build teams.

"I live here at Boeing," Gordon McKinzie, a United Airlines official, told me. "We're right inside the Boeing factory. We're in buildings we've never had access to in the past. We're up there with the real design engineers, and in the past we could not even get past the lobby. So now we have our Boeing badges and we get into the core design groups of these airplanes."

It was a radical change for McKinzie, a veteran of United's dealings with Boeing.

Previously, when United had ordered a new plane, it would go over the specifications with Boeing, make choices about which engine to use and what cabin configurations it wanted, and pick other options. Then it would make a down payment and periodic production payments, and it would wait five years while the plane was being built, hoping eventually to receive the plane it had ordered. Boeing was pretty good at customer service; nonetheless, there were always a few things that came out differently from what United had expected. If there were serious problems, they usually led to a nasty fight with Boeing. But all that happened too late to change anything important.

"We've always wondered why they reacted so violently to [our] changes, and now we know," McKinzie admitted, after having lived inside Boeing as it designed and built a new plane. "It's a very complex, very intensive process."

On the first day McKinzie had attended a design-build team with Boeing engineers, he had felt awkward. "It was like one of these 'Why am I here?' type things," he recalled. "The Boeing engineers had never seen a customer before—really, literally, they had never seen a customer. We felt uneasy. Somebody likened it to wandering into the ladies' locker room. I felt that way from time to time. I was getting a lot of stares about 'Why are *they* [customers] getting into our process?' And 'Why should we be sharing our secrets and frustrations?' "[47]

Phil Condit agreed that the Boeing people had been extremely defensive at first. For one thing, the airlines often disagreed with the initial ideas of Boeing designers. For another, they sometimes disagreed among themselves, even on big issues such as the plane's wingspan or how to fit the 777 into their different airport loading areas. Each airline, of course, had its own plan for dividing up the plane's interior between first class and economy and placing the galleys and the toilets. Boeing heard so many different plans that it built special flexibility into the interior design of the 777. Battling all that out, with customers in their midst, was awkward for Boeing's engineers.

"Designing an airplane's tough—it's hard work, it's complicated," Condit emphasized. "And nobody wants a customer wandering around, seeing you struggling with 'How am I going to solve this problem?' We'd like to have it all done and cleaned up before somebody comes in and looks."

Nonetheless, Boeing began to see payoffs after the first shock wore off. "Once you get over that hurdle, then the customer can tell you things that you never knew," Condit said. "They aren't great big breakthroughs. They're little things that, taken together, make a dramatically better product."[48]

How little—and yet how important to the airlines—was underscored by Gordon McKinzie. One perennial problem with Boeing planes to which Boeing engineers were oblivious, McKinzie said, was the size of the latches on the access panels used by mechanics to service airplanes. According to McKinzie, the latches are "about as big as your thumb, but when you're wearing heavy gloves in the winter in Chicago in a snowstorm, and you try to open those little doors with those little tiny latches, you've got to take your gloves off and freeze your fingers to open the latches. It seems like a simple thing, but Boeing never knew it."

He described problem after problem, some minor, some quite technical and complex. One problem revolved around how high the fuel tanks were off the ground. Even though the 777 is not as large as the 747, its engines are larger (because it has only two engines, versus four on the 747), so its wings are thirty-one inches higher off the ground. All of United Airlines' fueling trucks had been built to service the 747 or smaller planes, so the fueling tanks on the 777's wings would be out of reach.

"At United, we thought, unless we go and buy new fueling trucks all over our system—there's about twelve hundred trucks—or unless we have fuelers that are eight feet tall, there's no way we could reach that panel," McKinzie said. If the new 777s had been delivered that way, there would have been a major blowup between Boeing and United.

Inside the design-build teams, United and the other airlines asked Boeing's engineers to move the refueling panel closer to the ground. "And they said, 'That just can't happen. We've designed the wing, and it's done!' " McKinzie recalled. "But after putting a little bit of consensus airline heat on the problem, we got them to move the fuel panel down the wing towards the fuselage, and because the wing is tilted upward, that panel is now two feet closer to our stand. So now we can reach it. Don't need eight-foot mechanics, don't need new fueling trucks, and we're all set."

For Boeing, United was a particularly important customer. Not only had its CEO, Steve Wolf, chosen the Airbus A320 over the Boeing 737, but United was *the* prime launch customer for the 777. In October 1990, Wolf had placed the first order for thirty-four planes, with an option to buy thirty-four more. United's order had triggered Boeing's decision to move the 777 toward production. So keeping United happy on the 777 was critical, and Boeing was cementing that tie by including United's Gordon McKinzie, among others, in the design-build teams.

To underscore Condit's point about that kind of teamwork, Boeing christened its first 777 plane "Working Together."[49]

Beating Airbus on Its Home Ground

A crucial test for Boeing was whether drawing customers into the design-build teams would help in Europe against Airbus.

British Airways was a special target of Boeing. It is always under pressure to buy from Airbus Industrie because British Aerospace is one of the main partners in the Airbus consortium. But British Airways, which had become a private firm in the 1980s, has been freer than government-owned airlines such as Air France and Lufthansa to make its own choice. And so Boeing went head to head with its 777 against the Airbus A330 for a sale to British Airways.

Boeing invited British Airways to join the Boeing design-build teams, and that special involvement paid off: British Airways had an input on the 777 design, and in late 1991, it placed a $3.6 billion order to buy fifteen Boeing 777s and took an option on fifteen more.

Some of the reasons emerged in the spring of 1993, when Sir Robert Ayling, group managing director of British Airways, was given a demonstration of a full-sized cabin mock-up of the 777.

Because of the way the cabin was designed, with its floor at the widest part of the 777's body, the 777 cabin is wider than the cabins of the Airbus A330 and the McDonnell Douglas MD-11. Boeing's mock-up let airline buyers sit down and test the headroom and seat width of the three planes.

Sir Robert remarked on "the really good feeling of space" in the Boeing plane. "It's almost as though you're in the conventional interior of a house," he said. "Very striking."

After diplomatically pointing out that British Airways had other Airbus planes, Sir Robert Ayling said his airline had picked the Boeing plane "because for us, the economics of this aircraft were superior, and that was the telling factor."[50]

Even so, Phil Condit would not rest easy. Over twenty years, he had seen Airbus become a tough competitor, hard on Boeing's heels. Looking ahead twenty years, Condit expected no letup in the pressure from Airbus. "I expect they'll be right there—and we'll know they're there," he said.

Boeing: Public-Private Partnership Is Vital

Already, Boeing has learned many lessons from its competition with Airbus. One is the importance of partnership. Boeing has moved into closer collaboration with the Japanese, and Boeing executives predict more strategic alliances ahead because the cost of developing a new plane has become prohibitive for a single company. Boeing is drawing the Chinese into its production network and has signaled its readiness to talk to some Airbus partners about joint exploration of a super–jumbo jet.

After seeing the reliance of both Airbus and the Japanese Heavies on their governments to help defray the high costs and heavy risks of developing new planes, Boeing also wants the benefits of government-business collaboration in America.

The government's first job, Boeing CEO Frank Shrontz asserted, is to "assure a level playing field," so he was especially pleased in April 1992, when the Bush administration finally won the European Community's agreement to put a ceiling on direct governmental subsidies for new aircraft. The ceiling was set at 30 percent, about half of what Airbus had been getting. Shrontz also wanted American taxes modified to encourage investment and research.[51]

But the next generation of Boeing's leadership, Phil Condit and Larry Clarkson, is looking for more concrete help from the U.S. government. With the Cold War over and Defense Department budgets under pressure, they believe that winning in the new game requires that the government continue financing the development of basic new technologies. In the past, Boeing has received vital help from testing its airfoils and new designs in extraordinarily expensive wind tunnels provided both by NASA and by European governments, and from government-financed research in new technologies.

Condit sees clear roles for both parties in a public-sector–private-sector partnership, with industry developing and commercializing new technologies on a research foundation financed by government. "I think that [on] the fundamental technology developed," Condit said, "whether it is for high-speed commercial transport, or supersonic or advanced subsonics, more efficient airplanes, cleaner-burning engines—there is a clear role that government has in laying that foundation."

Clarkson suggested an even bigger step—rethinking the ground rules for commerce in America. In light of the big consortiums operating in Japan and Europe, he advocated reexamining and revising American antitrust laws, such as the Sherman Anti-Trust Act and the Clayton Anti-Trust Act.

Those laws "date from the end of the last century, when our only concern was trade and commerce inside the borders of the United States," Clarkson pointed out. "Today, take a company like Boeing, seventy-five percent of our sales are offshore, and yet our business laws in many ways hamper us. They put us at a disadvantage. It is time that we look at those laws and see how they ought to be revised to help us be more competitive."

Pristine laissez-faire economics, with a totally hands-off approach by government, is unrealistic, given how Japan and Europe operate, in Clarkson's view. "I think the United States government and industry should have a partnership," he said. "I think it is necessary if we are going to compete successfully in the next century. It is clear that our competitors and their governments have that kind of partnership. And if we are to compete on a level playing field, then we've got to do it, too."[52]

The Bush administration disliked this approach, but President Clinton picked up the partnership idea quickly. He moved the Defense Department's Advanced Research Projects Agency from working solely on military-oriented research to serving civilian industry as well; his first budgets included expanded funding for fundamental research to benefit commercial industries, including aviation.

Very quickly, too, President Clinton personally joined the global aircraft competition. He and other senior administration officials lobbied the government and royal family of Saudi Arabia to place a huge new order for airliners with Boeing instead of Airbus. And in February 1994, the White House heralded Saudi Arabia's decision to order $6 billion worth of planes from Boeing and McDonnell Douglas, shutting out Airbus.[53]

The American tactics in pursuing the Saudi deal signaled a shift in thinking. For that deal not only represented a commercial victory for the American planemakers, it signaled that the American government under President Clinton has turned activist—as ready to engage in global economic competition as the governments of Europe and

Japan are. Nor was the Clinton administration alone. It was following in the footsteps of the Reagan administration, which launched a government-business partnership to rescue the American computer chip industry. Even among political and economic conservatives, the new global game is changing the American mind-set.

15

America's Industrial Partnership
Sematech—Reagan's Radical Rescue Plan

> *Government policies have shaped the course of international competition in microelectronics virtually from the inception of the industry. . . . In none of the countries studied did a semiconductor industry come into being solely as a result of the "invisible hand" of the market.*[1]
>
> —THOMAS R. HOWELL ET AL., *CREATING ADVANTAGE*

> *Sematech managed to get U.S.-based competitors together in one place, so we could consider issues that were larger than any of us—technological road maps. . . . Sematech was a vital ingredient . . . in helping the U.S. semiconductor industry recover.*[2]
>
> —ANDY GROVE, CEO, INTEL

It was fear of catastrophe—a fear bred by the conspicuous success of the Japanese and the appalling collapse of American leadership in computer chips—that provoked America's most radical venture in industrial policy during the past three decades.

It was President Reagan who sanctioned this policy. Reagan thrust the U.S. government into a partnership with fourteen American high-tech companies to form a research and development consortium called Sematech, in the hope of rescuing the American computer chip industry.

The launching of Sematech, in December 1987, marked a remarkable shift in strategy for Ronald Reagan, an apostle of free-market economics who normally opposed an activist government and often mocked the bureaucratic ineptitude of what he called the "puzzle-palaces on the Potomac."

The fact that a conservative Republican such as Reagan would support Sematech—in an effort to steal back some of Japan's thunder—testified to the mood of desperation in Washington and Silicon Valley about the alarming trends in the semiconductor industry in the late 1980s. The Pentagon, the computer industry, and a host of other American industries that are dependent on computer chips were increasingly worried by America's sudden, growing dependence on Japan in this vital sector. Losing out in computer chips, moreover, was a grievous blow to America's commercial pride. Americans had discovered, indeed, had created, the world of computer chips in the 1960s, and in the mid-1970s, American firms had accounted for 70 percent of global sales in computer chips.

By 1987, however, America's computer chip industry was reeling. Its loss of dominance in the mid-1980s had been so extraordinarily swift that it had left both industry and government in a state of shock. In 1987, the American share of the worldwide market had fallen to just over 40 percent—and it was still skidding toward a low of 37 percent in 1988–89. By comparison, the Japanese share of the global computer chip market had nearly doubled in less than a decade—to 51 percent.[3]

"If you go back twenty years ago, there was such an arrogance in the American semiconductor industry that we believed we were unassailable, that no one could ever catch us," recalled Bill Spencer, a Xerox group vice president in the 1980s who later became the second president of Sematech. "By 1985, we had lost market leadership—something that nobody believed would ever happen. Well, then, everybody believed that the business was lost: It's just like color television. It's just like stereos or other things. The Japanese have taken this market over. It's gone. And so it was in that fit of depression that Sematech was formed."[4]

Borrowing a Strategy from Germany and Japan

With Motorola, the government had helped one company to penetrate the Japanese market. With Sematech, it was setting out to rescue an entire industry.

The Reagan administration was attempting to do what the Kennedy and Johnson administrations had considered doing—having the government intervene to promote a project in civilian industry, in their case the building of a supersonic transport. Jimmy Carter had also tried this approach, unsuccessfully, with the Synthetic Fuels Corporation—attempting to use government direction and support to galvanize the energy industry, an industry vital to the nation's economic health but suffering from global competition in the late 1970s.

In fact, the American computer chip industry had gotten its start under the wing of the government. In the 1960s, the Pentagon and the space agency, needing computers for ICBMs and Apollo spacecraft, had financed the critical research that had produced American breakthroughs on transistors, integrated circuitry, and computer chips. But that was long ago, and in the name of national security and for defense industries, even conservatives had been willing to make exceptions to the doctrine of laissez-faire economics.

A proactive government industrial policy in the civilian economy—on a consumer product such as computer chips—was, however, another matter.

In principle, industrial policy was anathema to the ideologists of "Reaganomics." By targeting the computer chip sector as a strategic industry that needed and deserved a shot in the arm from the government, Sematech cut against the grain of conservative antipathy to government interference with the natural workings of the marketplace—by what George Bush derisively rejected as the government's "picking winners and losers." Sematech embodied a blatant reversal of Reagan's declared determination to slash the size of the federal bureaucracy and reverse the legacy of governmental activism left by the New Deal.

Only a catastrophe, real or imminent, could have moved Ronald Reagan to become the patron of Sematech. The original push for Sematech, which had come from IBM and the computer chip industry, had won early backing from liberal Democrats in the Senate, but most congressional Republicans had initially been resistant. President Reagan was persuaded to back Sematech and sign the law creating Sematech by his old and trusted friend, Defense Secretary Caspar Weinberger, a former corporation attorney. Weinberger had been moved by the alarming assessments of his technical advisers about America's dangerous predicament in the critical field of microelectronics—computer chips and their allied technologies.

And so Sematech—an acronym for "semiconductor manufacturing technology"—would attempt something that Americans had come to accept in defense and space but that was unprecedented in the consumer sector of the civilian economy. It would combine the resources of the federal government with the talents and resources of the best and brightest in the American private sector. Every year, the government would put up $100 million, matched by $100 million from its private business partners, to conduct research on and development of new technologies that would help restore American leadership in the computer chip industry.

At its outset, the fourteen members of Sematech included four major computer companies—IBM, AT&T, Digital Equipment, and Hewlett-Packard; the five major American merchant chipmakers—Intel, Motorola, Texas Instruments, Advanced Micro Devices, and National Semiconductor; and other important companies such as Rockwell International, NCR Corporation, Harris Corporation, Micron Technology, and LSI Logic. These commercial firms, taken together, controlled 85 percent of American chipmaking capacity.

DARPA, the Pentagon's Defense Advanced Research Projects Agency, was the government partner in Sematech, the contributor of federal funds. But one crucial principle was that Sematech would be led and managed by private industry.

In the game of global competition, Sematech represented America's borrowing a leaf from the Germans and Japanese. It epitomized the kind of governmental activism with which German and Japanese capitalism had long been at home and the kind of government-business partnership which those two peoples regarded as essential to building national power. In fact, it was just such a Japanese strategy that had put the American computer chip industry into a hole.

For years, Japan's Ministry of International Trade and Industry (MITI) had assigned a top priority to Japan's becoming the world leader in computers and chips, and the Japanese government had used subsidies, incentives, protectionism, and government guidance to Japanese industry to achieve that end. In the early 1970s, MITI had orchestrated a highly calibrated offensive against IBM by a variety of Japanese firms.[5] Then, in 1975, MITI had summoned Japan's electronics giants and focused them on overtaking America's supremacy in computer chips, the most vital components of computers. The Japanese, argued Peter Drucker, the Claremont, California-based management expert, were pursuing a strategy of "adversarial trade" in which the aim is not just to win customers but to "gain market control by destroying the enemy . . . to drive the competitor out of the market altogether rather than to let it survive."[6]

The Semiconductor Industry Association described the battle in computer chips as not just a contest among different companies but a competition between America and Japan—"between *differing national economic systems.*" Individual firms might swim against the tide, the association commented, but "there is substantial evidence that Japan's rise and America's consequent relative decline in the 1980s was in large measure attributable to fundamental differences in the Japanese and American versions of capitalism . . . most importantly, in the relationship between government and industry."[7]

By the early 1980s, the government-directed Japanese assault had driven Japanese industry to a level equal to America in the technology of making memory chips. By the mid-1980s, the Japanese had forged ahead, leaving the American industry in disarray and collapse.

"We pioneered the field of semiconductor memory devices, and we were being decimated—killed—by the Japanese," recalled Andy Grove, CEO of Intel, the company that had invented the transistor and that had patented early computer chips.[8]

Computer Chips: "Upstream" to Almost Every Business

The real danger to America lay in the importance of computer chips— their ubiquitous applications. They had become vitally important not just for the computer industry but for practically every facet of the American economy.

A computer chip, tiny as a fingernail, is the key building block of the Information Age. It is as important to the new economic era as oil and steel were to the Industrial Age. The computer chip is the nucleus of modern microelectronics.

Computerized chips are in practically every device we touch. They are in state-of-the-art industrial equipment, robots, automated machinery; they are in microwave ovens, VCRs, washers, and dryers. In cars, they regulate temperature, fuel flow, engine timing, radios, clocks. In fact, the electronic circuitry and gadgetry in a car are now so extensive that they cost more than the steel for an auto body.

"If you control microelectronics and computers, you control the world." This blunt assessment came from Craig I. Fields, who ran DARPA during the Bush administration. "There's no industry that does not depend on information technology," Fields said. "If you are a banker, an automaker, if you're in food processing, construction, or making shoes, you need information technology. We've got to have the best information technology in the U.S. to survive."[9]

Experts such as Fields and Frank Press, president of the National Academy of Sciences from 1981 to 1993, worried not only that the Japanese were dominating the chip industry but that they were getting stronger "upstream."

In the argot of technology strategists, there is a stream, or "food chain," in any economy. At the end of the line, or "downstream," are the final users—banks, carmakers, food processors, ordinary consumers. Downstream is what we see in our daily lives; upstream is where the most critical battles take place. At the downstream end of the industrial "food chain," final users are dependent on the computers or computerized devices embedded in their equipment. In turn, computers are dependent on the next stage "upstream"—microprocessor chips that run computers and memory chips (known as DRAMS, pronounced *dee*-rams) that store information and software operating systems. Still further upstream, the companies that make computer chips are dependent on the semiconductor "tool" industry—the industry that makes the expensive high-precision equipment that produces computer chips.

By 1987, not only had America lost its dominance in making computer chips, it was in desperate decline "upstream," the semiconductor tool industry, as well. In 1979, nine of the ten largest semiconductor equipment suppliers in the world had been American; a decade later, Japanese firms were in four of the top five positions, and only four American firms were still in the top ten.[10] At Digital Equipment Corporation, for example, its former CEO, Ken Olsen, told me that, in 1980, 90 percent of the extraordinarily expensive high-tech equipment at the company's chip-fabricating plant in Hudson, Massachusetts, had been American made. But a decade later, only 30 percent was American made and nearly 70 percent was Japanese made. "We have to have the best," said Olsen, "and the Japanese provide us superlative quality."[11]

To Ken Olsen and other American executives, the implications of the Japanese dominance in the semiconductor tool industry were ominous. Digital Equipment, IBM, and other computer makers feared becoming perilously overdependent for their equipment on tool companies that were part of the same *keiretsu* networks to which the Japanese computer companies belonged. In a trade crisis, the Americans feared, the Japanese equipment companies would supply their *keiretsu* brothers but would turn off the "upstream" spigot and halt the flow of the newest Japanese technology to American companies. In fact, by the late 1980s, American companies did complain that they were getting slow delivery of leading-edge equipment and computer components from Japanese suppliers. One American company said that delays by its Japanese suppliers had cost it $1.4 billion in lost sales.[12]

The Americans were particularly alarmed that Japanese companies were steadily buying up the best small high-tech equipment makers in the United States. The squeeze of global competition was weakening these relatively small, independent American firms. They were often starved for cash and thus hard pressed for funds to finance their newest inventions. Financial weakness made them vulnerable to takeover by rich Japanese electronic giants, and that is just what happened. The takeover trend mounted to the point where in just three years, from 1987 to 1990, nearly forty leading U.S. semiconductor tool firms were bought out by the Japanese.[13]

The Gulf War: America's "Smart Bombs" Had Foreign "Brains"

Not only American industrial leaders but the Pentagon and U.S. intelligence agencies became alarmed at the trends in high-tech microelectronics. The Defense Science Board, a prestigious group of advisers to the secretary of defense, warned in 1988 that the U.S. military had become "dangerously dependent" on foreign supplies for critical technologies.[14]

Three years earlier, the Pentagon itself had issued the disturbing assessment that Japanese companies were leading in twelve of twenty-five critical aspects of the computer chip industry and American companies in only five (there was rough parity in the other eight). To avoid dependence on the Japanese, the National Security Agency, which has the job of electronic eavesdropping on other nations' most top secret messages, began an elaborate effort to build its own chip-fabricating plant. But the NSA could not avoid using Japanese suppliers for the equipment to put into its plant.[15] Another Pentagon report in 1987 disclosed that twenty-one of America's leading-edge weapons systems relied on computer chips from abroad and that seven types of crucial military components were available only in Japan.[16]

These problems came to a head during the Persian Gulf War in 1991. Americans watching the Pentagon's public relations videos showing American precision-guided missiles and "smart bombs" homing in on Iraqi targets were impressed by the dazzling display of what they assumed was American technology. Little did most people realize that the high-tech "brains" inside America's "top-gun" weapons often came from Japan, Thailand, France, Britain, or Germany. American industry *could not produce* this technology—not at the quality and speed needed for Operation Desert Storm.

In combat, therefore, American GIs and commanders were perilously dependent on other nations. Japan and Thailand were vital suppliers of chips for the computers that aimed and fired the guns of the Abrams tanks, the Air Force's Sparrow and Sidewinder missiles, and the Army's TOW antitank missiles and Maverick air-to-ground missiles. Among the other crucial pieces of foreign-made equipment were battery packs from France and Japan to power command and control computers; British radio gear and avionics; and French transistors to help beam signals among allied aircraft so they could identify friend from foe.

So crucial were these foreign parts and so low were American stockpiles during the Gulf War that on nearly thirty occasions the Bush administration turned frantically to foreign governments to get help in rushing components to the front.[17]

In the case of Japan, America's wartime dependency was a delicate issue, because many Japanese people saw parallels between the American air attacks around Baghdad and the American bombing of Japanese cities during World War II. In fact, Taizo Watanabe, the Japanese Foreign Ministry spokesman, disclosed that the Japanese government had run into difficulties in helping rush Japanese supplies to the American war effort because of "a strong abhorrence" among the Japanese people to exporting weapons. The government had responded by saying that Japanese electronic components could be for civilian as well as for military use and that Americans, not Japanese, were putting them into weapons systems. Even so, Watanabe said, the sale of Japanese parts for American weapons "meets some psychological resistance."[18] The implication was that in the future, America would not always be able to rely on Japanese support.

The precarious dependence of American forces on foreign technology, which surfaced during the Persian Gulf War, had been obvious to Pentagon insiders four or five years beforehand. Defense Secretary Weinberger, for example, was told that half of the computer chips for the fire-control radar in American F-16 fighters had come from

Japan—not just because the Japanese products were cheaper but because Pentagon procurement officers considered Japanese microelectronics superior to what American firms were producing.[19]

In early 1987, the Defense Science Board called America's eclipse in the computer chip industry an "unacceptable situation." The board urged the government to take steps to rescue the U.S. semiconductor industry; otherwise, warned its chairman, Norman Augustine, president of Martin Marietta, the American chip industry "will die in the not-too-distant future."[20]

That dire assessment persuaded first Secretary Weinberger and then President Reagan of the critical need for Sematech.

Sematech: Collaboration on "Precompetitive Technology"

The mere formation of Sematech required a radically new mind-set at some of America's leading high-tech corporations.

For not only were government and private industry pooling resources on a civilian project, but fiercely competitive rivals such as AT&T, IBM, Motorola, Intel, and Texas Instruments were agreeing to collaborate on research and development that was competitively important to each of them. In 1984, Congress had paved the way for an earlier consortium, and ultimately for Sematech, by passing the National Cooperative Research Act, amending U.S. antitrust laws to make it possible for American companies to join in collaborative research without risking federal prosecution.[21]

Even so, Sematech's start was rocky. Mistrust and wariness among traditional competitors plagued its early operations, despite the willingness of IBM and AT&T to contribute their leading technologies to Sematech.[22] Its first president, the legendary Bob Noyce, one of the inventors of the transistor, had trouble melding the different corporate cultures of Sematech members—the courtly manners of establishment IBM and AT&T; the brash informality of California upstarts such as LSI Logic and Advanced Micro Devices; the open, argumentative style of Intel and Motorola.

What's more, getting some of the companies to face up to their real problems was not easy. In the 1980s, the leading U.S. electronics firms blamed their difficulties mainly on lack of capital. The Japanese *keiretsu* networks, they pointed out, could spend American rivals into the ground.

But other American firms, especially Intel, Motorola, and IBM, knew better. Their assessment was that the American chip industry had lost its competitive edge. This was not just a matter of money but of quality, cost, efficiency, and the lack of cooperation between American chipmakers and their equipment suppliers. Reformers noted that the close links within the Japanese industry had been crucial to its success. The private market in America was not working the way it was supposed to, according to Bill Spencer, who took over in 1990 as Sematech's president after Bob Noyce died.

To launch its operations and to pull its members together, Sematech decided to build its own chip-fabricating plant. Early on, some people wanted Sematech to produce the world's most advanced chips; others, however, said that production was not Sematech's mandate—that it would put Sematech into competition with its members. And so, instead, Sematech focused on an even more critical goal—tackling the problems "upstream" by improving the high-tech equipment that would go into American chip fabs. Sematech's chip fab would serve as a test bed for new American technologies. It would function as a catalyst and goal setter for developing "precompetitive technologies" to improve the competitive capabilities of the entire U.S. chip industry. Sematech would use its funds, its plant, and its staff of experts to spur and support the development of the world's best chipmaking technology. In that way, Sematech would help rebuild the foundation of the U.S. chipmaking industry and help American chipmakers get back on top.

A Computer "Chip Fab": A World of Exquisite Precision

For Sematech, or any private company, building a chip-fabricating plant—"chip fab" in industry lingo—is an enormous and costly enterprise.

A chip fab is industry's highest striving to date to produce the perfect environment. Perfection, cleanliness, predictability are its inviolable laws. Nothing is left to chance. All possible impurities are extracted. Temperature, humidity, motion, and physical environment are rigorously controlled to within one degree of constancy.

Like a medieval castle with a treasure at its core, a chip fab is constructed with ring after ring of defenses to keep out alien elements and intruders. It has its moats, outer walls, middle walls, inner walls, passageways, gate locks, and, finally, its inner sanctums—the "clean rooms"—where its complex technology is honed to perfection.

In as many ways as the human brain can invent, the heart of a chip fab is sealed off from ordinary human existence so that it will remain uncontaminated by any foreign impurity as tiny as a nearly invisible piece of lint or as fine as a single human hair; uncontaminated by unfiltered breathing; untroubled by any motion, from the punishing power of tornadoes, hurricanes, and earthquakes to the subtle shakings of the fab's foundations caused by the underground rumble of passing traffic.

In Germany, Wolfgang Ganser, the director of a chip fab run by Siemens at Regensburg, took me through its outer works, which are typical of those of any modern chip fab. In a huge, high-ceilinged "attic," we climbed among miles of aluminum tubing nearly a foot in diameter. That tubing funneled purified cool air down through the ceiling into all the workrooms on the main fabrication floor. The falling curtains of cool air constantly washed away impurities in the work areas, and that cool air was recaptured, refiltered, repurified, and recycled—five hundred times per hour.[23]

The antiseptic universe of the chip fab is crammed with exotic and expensive high-tech "black boxes"—optical steppers, gas plasma etchers, ion implantation devices, scanning electron microscopes, and robots—performing feats of staggering technological precision. With computers, people monitor the intricate sequence of operations, but the most important tasks cannot be entrusted to human hands because mere mortals are not manually precise enough.

The pieces of equipment in a chip fab cost as much as $2 million to $4 million each, plus another $500,000 each to install, with all their piping, circuitry, and computer controls. Each chip fab needs more than two hundred pieces of this precious equipment. And so building a modern chip fab costs close to $1 billion.

The "Clean Room": Cleaner Than a Hospital Operating Room

Entering a computer chip fab is like stepping into a space-age world. It is a science fiction preview of the twenty-first century, an eerie and impersonal world, blindingly white, a world of near-perfect purity and silence.

The heart of a fab is the "clean room," or, actually, many clean rooms. At Sematech's headquarters in Austin, Texas, CEO Bill Spencer took me into this inner sanctum.

Since human beings are the greatest contaminators, extraordinary precautions must be taken to wash away people's impurities. En route to the "clean room," I had to brush off my shoes on several different welcome mats, walk across a "sticky floor" that pried off any remaining particles, and, finally, put ankle-high slippers over my shoes. I left behind my suit jacket and my reporter's notebook and pens, and in my shirtsleeves I took an air bath in a narrow passageway built like a cattle chute, while air jets in the walls pelted me at every level.

Finally, I began the laborious process of wriggling into a white bunny suit—first a hair net and skin-tight, surgical-style latex gloves; then coveralls from head to toe; then a set of boots to go over the shoe covers that I had put on previously; and, to cover my head, clear safety glasses, a hood, and a full face mask. Not a centimeter of my flesh was left exposed.

The final passage to the "clean room" was through a set of revolving doors, to ensure an air lock. Everything in the "clean room" had to be lint free, so the staff had special lint-free paper and a simple stylus for note taking.

The "clean room" was a bizarre world of strange creatures, all shrouded in bunny suits like walking mummies from another planet. The bunny suits were made of special Gore-Tex material, completely lint-free. Each uniform cost about $300, so that Sematech spent nearly $2 million just for fab uniforms.

Every single one of the 500 technicians and engineers who works in the "clean rooms" at Sematech, or at any chip fab, has to go through this elaborate suiting up daily. Not just once, but two or three times a day; to eat or to handle other necessities, people have to come out of the "clean rooms" because eating is far too contaminating to be allowed inside.

"Clean rooms" are classed on the basis of their purity—Class 100, Class 10, Class 1—the lower the number, the cleaner. To qualify as Class 1, a "clean room" has to have on average less than one particle of any kind in each cubic foot of pure air.

Sematech's "clean rooms" were Class 1—freer of impurities than a hospital operating room.

The Chip

The focus of this compulsive obsession with cleanliness is the computer chip.

To the naked eye, a chip looks as flat as a dime, but modern chips are in fact multistoried, microscopic honeycombs of transistors, layer upon layer. A 64-megabit memory chip (which can store 64 million bits of information) has 24 infinitesimally thin layers, each with hundreds of thousands of transistors etched into its highly polished silicon surface.

Etching the wafer and embedding microelectronic circuitry into each layer requires 20 to 25 extremely precise operations. So a 24-story chip must go through nearly 500 such operations. To complete that cycle takes seven weeks, working nonstop twenty-four hours a day.

The dimensions of the task and the speed with which chip fabs' technology is changing are staggering. Every three years, technology quadruples the number of transistors on each chip, producing a quantum leap in the power and capacity of chips. In 1971, a chip held 2,300 transistors; today's 16-megabit memory chips have 20 million transistors.

In concrete terms, the leaps in technology mean that, in 1985, a 1-megabit memory chip could hold about thirty pages of typed text. In the mid-1990s, the 16-megabit memory chip can hold five hundred pages of typed text. And by the year 2005, Bill Spencer predicts, a memory chip should be able to hold 4 billion bits of information—enough to record two full sets of the *Encyclopaedia Britannica*.[24]

The secret of the ever-exploding power and capacity of computer chips is the thinness of the microelectronic circuitry implanted on the chip surface.

To pack ever more transistors onto the layers of a chip, the circuitry must constantly be made finer and finer. It is already microscopically fine, far beyond the capacity of the human eye to discern. On a 16-megabit memory chip, for example, the circuitry is about 0.5 micron in width, or about 1/100th the thickness of an individual human hair. According to Spencer, Sematech's supplier companies have achieved 0.35 micron and are pushing to reach 0.10 micron, or about 1/500th of a human hair, in the next few years.

This precision must be achieved not once or several times but every time, to link up every transistor on every layer of every chip. Hence, the enormous precautions over cleanliness. The tiniest speck of dust will ruin a chip. Several specks could ruin a whole eight-inch silicon wafer containing 200 to 300 chips; and one large wafer is worth $50,000 or more.

The challenge to America by the late 1980s was that the Japanese, with their money, their perfection mind-set, their close ties between chipmakers and "upstream" equipment suppliers, and their culture of teamwork, had mastered the demanding task of producing the world's most advanced, most perfect memory chips.

Sematech's job was to help American industry recoup, in order once again to take on the Japanese head to head.

Step One: Saving the Last U.S. Firm from Foreign Takeover

Since the secret of magnifying the power of computer chips is the thinness of the lines of circuitry, the most critical technology in chipmaking is the ultraprecise equipment that imprints the line patterns on the chip's surface. That is done through optical lithography or photolithography. Because it is so central, lithography sets the pace for all advancement in chipmaking.

Photolithography works like an extraordinarily precise camera, with the chip as the negative. Chip wafers are coated with a chemical film, then exposed to light waves transmitted through a mask to form the desired pattern on the chip. Once the pattern is etched onto a wafer full of chips, the circuitry itself can be implanted.

The pattern for each chip is done separately. After doing one chip, the photolithography machine steps on to the spot for the next chip. It repeats that process more than two hundred times per wafer. From this stepping process, photolithography devices are known as "wafer steppers," or just "steppers."

Sematech's member companies recognized that it would be impossible to make the world's most advanced computer chips without the world's most advanced "steppers." But by the late 1980s, American capabilities in this vital technology were on the verge of being wiped out. And so Sematech put a very high priority on restoring America's competitive capabilities in photolithography "steppers."

"This is the heart of it—one third of the semiconductor equipment industry sales is lithographic equipment," asserted engineer Papken der Terossian, CEO of Silicon Valley Group, which makes lithography equipment. "Without being able to photograph the thin lines, all the processing that you do afterwards is useless. We're talking about the future of an eight-hundred-billion-dollar global electronics industry, in which America is losing its market share. We [America] are behind in this technology today. We have less than ten percent of the global market."[25]

In fact, the crisis in lithography was a major reason why Jack Kuehler, then IBM's executive vice president, had pushed so hard in the mid-1980s for the creation of Sematech. IBM was scared of becoming hostage to Japanese lithography equipment makers, which were members of the *keiretsu* networks of its fiercest rivals in the computer industry—NEC, Hitachi, Fujitsu, Mitsubishi, and Toshiba. By 1990, two Japanese firms—Nikon and Canon—had a near stranglehold on the photolithography business. Nikon had 65 percent of the world market; Canon had 25 percent.[26] In fact, Nikon's semiconductor business had become bigger than its camera business. Unless American industry could rebuild an independent, world-class capability in lithography, companies such as IBM, Intel, Motorola, and Texas Instruments would be vulnerable to being cut off by their Japanese suppliers.

America's back was against the wall. By 1989, only two small American firms—GCA and Perkin-Elmer—were still making photolithography equipment, and the Japanese were trying to buy Perkin-Elmer. Since World War II, Perkin-Elmer had been a world leader in precision optics; its components were used in the Hubble space telescope. Back in the 1970s, Perkin-Elmer had been the world leader in optical lithography, but by 1985, it had fallen technologically behind its Japanese competitors. Its lithography division was losing so much money that Perkin-Elmer was desperate to sell it off.

In its final, desperate effort to leapfrog the Japanese, Perkin-Elmer had spent about $100 million to invent an entirely new step-and-scan "stepper," called Micrascan; it did three chips at once, instead of one. This new technology promised to be both more productive and more accurate than anything that had gone before, and its potential had attracted Japanese attention.

Perkin-Elmer needed another $100 million to $200 million to develop and perfect the step-and-scan technology. IBM had been investing in Perkin-Elmer's research, but neither IBM nor any other American firm was ready to spend $200 million to fund the rest of the research or to buy Perkin-Elmer's photolithography division. In 1989, American firms were feeling strapped for investment funds. Moreover, they were reluctant to go head to head against the Japanese *kei-retsu,* both because the Japanese had built up such a lead in the chip industry and because the Americans dared not offend Nikon and Canon—and risk losing their Japanese suppliers.

Perkin-Elmer, feeling abandoned by American industry, turned to Japan for a buyer and found Nikon ready. As Horace G. McDonnell, Perkin-Elmer's CEO, put it: "We found ourselves in the position of having a technology for an industry that had moved to Japan." In November 1989, Nikon was on the verge of buying Perkin-Elmer's lithography division, when howls went up in Congress calling on the Bush administration to block the Japanese takeover.[27] In 1988, Congress had passed a law empowering the U.S. government to block any foreign takeover of an American company that might endanger national security. But President Bush and his commerce secretary, Robert Mosbacher, refused to use that power. As laissez-faire conservatives, they believed that the government had no business saving any company that could not compete on its own or that could not attract American investors.[28]

Sematech disagreed. In concert with IBM and others, it moved to keep the critical Perkin-Elmer technology in American hands. Nikon, a member of the Mitsubishi group, which had stirred up a furor in America by buying Rockefeller Center, backed off from buying Perkin-Elmer to avoid another public outcry. That enabled IBM to orchestrate the formation of an American consortium to buy out Perkin-Elmer's optical lithography division in early 1990. The lead was taken by Silicon Valley Group, a supplier of high-tech equipment for the chipmaking industry. IBM put up $3 million, Perkin-Elmer kept a temporary financial stake, and Silicon Valley Group eventually invested $43 million.

Equally important, Sematech and IBM ensured SVG's future. To fund continuing research on the breakthrough Micrascan "stepper," Sematech pledged $20 million for research and development, matched by $20 million from IBM and another $10 million from DARPA. In addition, IBM gave Silicon Valley Group a promise to buy $80 million worth of its "steppers" if the technology proved out well.[29]

Those research funds and the promised sales to IBM rescued the once-doomed American technology. And keeping Perkin-Elmer in American hands turned out to be critical. In 1993, GCA, the only other U.S. firm capable of producing lithography "steppers," shut down for good.

"It's *very* important technology," Sematech's Bill Spencer asserted. "Silicon Valley Group now is the only remaining U.S. supplier, and we feel it's important that they be successful."[30]

Step Two: Generating the Synergy Mind-Set and Retaking the Lead

Sematech's main contribution to the computer chip industry—and to Silicon Valley Group's successful development of new technology—was to generate a mind-set of collaboration.

Sematech stimulated progress by moving the computer chip industry from a mentality of dog-eat-dog wariness and arm's-length ignorance to a focus on common problems and cooperative solutions.

"Sematech managed to get U.S.-based competitors together in one place, so we could consider issues that were larger than any of us—technological road maps," asserted Andy Grove, CEO of Intel. "What direction are we heading [in] in photolithography collectively? What are the missing pieces? Can we fund research in those missing pieces to help all of us get better?"[31]

At Sematech's headquarters in Austin, Texas, senior executives, engineers, and scientists from its member firms defined the common needs for "precompetitive technology"—the future foundation of the U.S. semiconductor industry. Companies such as IBM, Intel, AT&T, and Motorola remained fierce competitors, but they derived a collective benefit from research projects done by Sematech with government laboratories at Sandia, New Mexico, and Oak Ridge, Tennessee, as well as from closer working relationships with equipment suppliers such as Silicon Valley Group.

"During war, Americans always cooperate, but in a peacetime we never cooperate," observed Papken der Terossian, CEO of Silicon Valley Group. "Sematech acted as a catalyst to bring the user and the manufacturer, like us, together—with their engineers and our engineers [working] for the common purpose of making the best tool [stepper] available. That simple catalyst and that simple change in culture has made this possible."[32]

Sematech carefully nurtured Silicon Valley Group's development of new, world-class photolithography steppers. Sematech engineers and technical experts, drawn from its member companies, worked with SVG to perfect the Micrascan technology. Sematech prodded SVG to develop a new, more advanced version—Micrascan II—for more advanced computer chips, the 64-megabit memory chips of the mid-1990s. And Sematech helped SVG measure its progress against world standards by testing the reliability of SVG's new step-and-scan stepper at the Sematech chip fab.

At Xerox, Sematech CEO Bill Spencer had learned the hard way that American high-tech equipment, no matter how impressive its technical capabilities, had a reputation for breaking down sooner than Japanese equipment did. Even American companies were gun shy of buying American-made equipment, especially new technology from a new supplier, such as SVG, that was competing against time-tested Japanese firms such as Nikon and Canon.

To break that pattern, Sematech—like Boeing's Phil Condit—examined how the Japanese operated and then adapted those lessons to America.

"We knew that their universities are not better than ours. We knew that the average intelligence of Japanese and Americans aren't that different. So what are they doing differently?" asked der Terossian, the Armenian-American engineer who runs Silicon Valley Group. "We found out that they are cooperating much more closely—the suppliers and users—and the government has helped them. They are providing a catalytic environment for industry to work together."[33]

In short, the Japanese were gaining a crucial competitive advantage because, within their *keiretsu* networks, high-tech equipment suppliers such as Nikon and Canon were getting early feedback on their new technology—*while it was being developed.* That early feedback enabled Japanese equipment makers to get a jump on American competitors.

Before Sematech's creation, American equipment suppliers and chip companies typically got together only when they were ready to buy and sell equipment, *after the equipment was already fully developed.* That was very late in the game—often too late for the suppliers to fix their expensive technology to satisfy big customers. The American equipment makers needed feedback much earlier.

Sematech arranged that vital process of early feedback, and that was one of its most crucial achievements. "We have teams of engineers from each of the member companies [chipmakers] using that equipment and finding out what's wrong with it, where it doesn't come up to standards set by competitors," Bill Spencer said, "and then making changes so that when that machine [Micrascan] does go into production, it will be as good as our [Japanese] competitors'."[34]

By mid-1993, after more than two years of work with Sematech,

SVG's Micrascan II technology had become what der Terossian called the world's "most advanced camera."

The joint Sematech-SVG effort had restored America's technological leadership in photolithography.

According to der Terossian, SVG's "stepper," Micrascan II, had achieved an ability to etch lines of 0.35-micron thinness, the level needed for the 64-megabit memory chips. But Bill Spencer wanted Sematech to check the reliability and durability of this new technology in extensive tests—*before* it was taken to the global market.

That careful approach paid off. By mid-1994, SVG's "steppers" were winning acceptance from very sophisticated customers. In all, more than forty Micrascan machines, each worth about $4 million, had been ordered—twenty by IBM; another fifteen in all by Intel, Motorola, Texas Instruments, and Advanced Micro Devices; a handful by Toshiba, Samsung, and Hyundai.[35]

But recovery had its price. From start to finish, development of the first two Micrascan "steppers" had cost American industry and the government roughly $300 million. But if SVG were, in fact, to succeed in becoming the market leader and to build momentum for the next stepper (0.25-micron lines for the expected 256-megabit memory chips of the late 1990s), it would be a crucial achievement for American industry.

"It's been expensive," conceded Sematech's Bill Spencer, "but if we wind up with all that technology coming out of the U.S., it would be quite a coup."[36]

Photolithography was becoming a showcase for Sematech's comeback strategy.

The Comeback of the American Chip Industry

By 1992, five years after Sematech was set up, the American chip industry was on the rebound. In terms of global market share, American chipmakers had pulled roughly even with the Japanese. And in 1993, the Americans moved slightly ahead of the Japanese and regained global leadership.

No one, including Bill Spencer, claimed that the American recovery was all, or mainly, the work of Sematech, though Spencer quipped humorously, "We did a rain dance—and by 1992, it rained pretty hard. So I think we should take some credit."[37]

Nonetheless, Spencer gave the major credit to American computer chip companies. Intel, for example, had made a stunning turnaround.

After teetering dangerously in the mid-1980s, Intel had made itself the world's premier chipmaker by the early 1990s—by rethinking its basic strategy. Intel abandoned to the Japanese the field it had pioneered—memory chips. It conceded Japanese superiority in moving steadily from one generation of memory chip to the next, with ever-expanding capacity.

Intel bet its future on making microprocessors—the chips that run personal computers by embodying their instructions. The design and architecture of microprocessors are more complex than those of memory chips. Developing microprocessors to match the ever-changing software for personal computers requires great agility. Intel's leaders, Gordon Moore and Andy Grove, saw that challenge as the toughest part—and also the most imaginative part—of the chip business. That was a competitive arena in which American ingenuity and creativity were an advantage against the Japanese. Intel's strategic gamble paid off handsomely. It has become the global market leader in microprocessors.

Politics and diplomacy also played a part in the recovery of the American chip industry. The Reagan administration put strong pressure on the Japanese government to open up its home market to U.S. chipmakers. In 1986, the Japanese government signed an agreement that set the target of raising the foreign share of computer chips sold in Japan from 8 percent to 20 percent by 1991. It actually took a year longer than that, but getting the Japanese to buy 20 percent of their computer chips from American suppliers in 1992 was vital to the American chip industry's recovery.

Another important contributor to that recovery was the continuing boom in personal computers in America. The rocketing expansion of the American PC market provided an ever-expanding outlet for American chipmakers.

Even so, people like Andy Grove of Intel, Bob Galvin of Motorola, and Jack Kuehler of IBM, as well as Sematech's longtime backers in Congress and elsewhere, give Sematech significant credit for reviving the ailing chip industry and restoring the "upstream" equipment industry to health in the 1990s.

"Sematech was a vital ingredient in our recovery—in helping the U.S. semiconductor industry recover some of the lost ground in terms of global market share," Grove asserted. "It did measurable good to the industry. . . . It was an industrial town hall where technologists from a dozen different companies would get together and work together on projects."[38]

In bottom-line terms, Grove and Galvin both felt their companies had gotten more than their money's worth from the $100 million or so that each company had put into Sematech. In 1993, both were pushing to continue Sematech for several more years.[39]

Even Sematech's outspoken foes, such as T. J. Rodgers, CEO of Cypress Semiconductor, acknowledge that it has generated positive results. "Sematech has done some good," Rodgers conceded. "But that's not the issue. The issue is: Is it worth a billion in taxpayer dollars? And the answer is no."

In fact, the taxpayers' investment in Sematech has actually been $780 million since 1988.[40]

Rodgers's objection was that Sematech and its government subsidy had offered "a free ride to the big companies." While Sematech's membership has been open to any American company in the field, Rodgers said that its dues structure was unfair to smaller companies such as his. (Under the Sematech formula, his company would have had to put up $2.5 million a year; had that amount been only $1 million, Rodgers said, he might have joined.)

Rodgers also criticized Sematech's original plan to make its technology breakthroughs available only to its paying members for one year, before offering those new technologies to other companies. And he praised Bill Spencer for changing that rule and making the technology immediately available to the entire U.S. chip industry.

But Rodgers's main opposition was to the government's playing any role in the civilian economy. "I have a religious opposition to the government giving money to my competitors," Rodgers declared. "World competition is like going into the Olympics, and there comes a time when you walk into the ring and you fight and that's it. And Uncle Sam can't lift the weights and he can't train you. Either you're ready and you can compete, or you're not ready and you lose. And the concept that the government can step in and make companies competitive is preposterous."[41]

Intel's Andy Grove, a fierce marketplace competitor, took issue with Rodgers. "These things are often turned into religious arguments, talking about free markets and all of that stuff," Grove observed. "Using air traffic as an analogy, airlines compete, but they need an airport. They don't build their own airports. They have to collaborate. They have to pay taxes. They have to pay fees to some municipality to put an airport in place so they can do their stuff. . . . The infrastructure of our industry—some foundation technologies whose development Sematech helped—is akin to the airport for us. Now, I don't hear anybody complain about the building of airports being anticompetitive. It fosters competition by permitting the airlines to do their work. That is how I view what Sematech has done."[42]

Bill Spencer and others at Sematech stress that Sematech has not been a typical government program or a "free ride" for industry, as T. J. Rodgers contended. Sematech's advocates point out that the private sector put up half the money for Sematech and watched over its operation to ensure against waste.

Moreover, people such as Bill Spencer, Andy Grove, and Bob Galvin argue that Sematech has not been a case, as President Bush put it, of the government's "picking winners and losers." Sematech's leadership and personnel all came from industry. Sematech's contributing member companies sat on its board, and they determined its strategy and its priorities. These arrangements ensured that Sematech was attuned to the marketplace and that it would operate for the benefit of the industry.

Nonetheless, government engagement and support are crucial to success, according to a global study done by the U.S. Semiconductor Industry Association, entitled *Creating Advantage.* The study found that the free market had never generated a computer chip industry anywhere in the world.

"In none of the countries studied did a semiconductor industry come into being solely as a result of the 'invisible hand' of the market," the association said. On the contrary, it asserted, at every crucial stage of the industry's development—(1) the American start of the industry, (2) the Japanese ascendancy, (3) the European effort, (4) the entry of Taiwan and Korea, and (5) the U.S. revival—government support had been essential. And where the government had played no role, as in the modern economies of Hong Kong, Canada, Australia, and New Zealand, no chip industry emerged.[43]

Nonetheless, once Sematech had achieved momentum for the long term, it favored phasing out government funding. Its 1995 government grant was reduced, and it proposed doing away with the entire subsidy in 1997. Sematech was making the point that government help had been crucial for a high-tech industry in crisis, but a permanent crutch was not needed.[44]

Sematech: A Model for Other Industries?

In the new global game, with other governments openly helping strategic industries, the Sematech experiment raises the question of whether the U.S. government should take a similar role in other critical economic sectors. Can the Sematech formula be transferred to other industries of strategic importance to the industrial food chain?

T. J. Rodgers's response is "definitely not." David Kearns, former CEO of Xerox, which considered joining Sematech and decided against it, says "maybe." Andy Grove asserts that high-tech innovation is inherently risky and requires a mind-set of experimentation, of accepting in advance that some experiments will succeed and others fail. Grove sees Sematech as a success that justifies more experimentation in public-private partnerships.

"You can't sit there and argue—Is industrial policy good, is industrial policy bad, in the abstract," Grove asserts. "Kind of like arguing how many angels can dance on a pin. You got to try things and then take a look at it empirically. . . . This worked, so let's do another one."

That attitude has been shared by the Clinton administration. Nor is it unprecedented in America for government to play an instrumental role in advancing certain critical industries.

As Boeing's experience demonstrates, the U.S. commercial aircraft industry was given an enormous boost in developing civilian airliners by the Pentagon's funding of long-range military aircraft after World War II. At times, the government has gotten rival aircraft developers to share their ideas and technology.

Earlier in American history, the U.S. Post Office gave wobbly new American airlines a boost by paying them for carrying air mail. In another sector, RCA—the Radio Corporation of America—got its start during World War I with support from the navy, which once owned 20 percent of RCA.[45] Republican presidents, as well as Democratic ones, have often fostered such support for industry, but they have usually linked it to military needs. That same vein of policymaking persists in the post–Cold War era, endorsed by political conservatives. As the Pentagon's weapons procurement is phased down, the Defense

Department has sought appropriations for defense-oriented industries, arguing the need for maintaining a "warm production base" in various industries—"a carrier-shipbuilding base," "a tank-industrial base," "a high-powered laser technology base," and even a "small-arms base."[46]

What is new in the 1990s is the modest but growing government support for and collaboration with civilian industries in order to make America more competitive in the new global game, with or without the rationale of defense needs.

Early in 1993, the Clinton administration took the important symbolic step of dropping the "D" from DARPA, the Defense Advanced Research Projects Agency, so that, as ARPA, it could handle civilian or "dual-use" (defense and civilian) research and development projects as well as purely military projects. Soon after, the president's new National Science and Technology Council proposed realigning the work of the seven hundred government laboratories run by the Departments of Energy and Defense, NASA, and other agencies, in order "to increase their contribution to commercial competitiveness," as a White House memo put it.

In the 1994 budget, the White House moved to cut the Pentagon back from 60 percent to 50 percent of the federal government's annual $73 billion research budget, using some of that reduction for fundamental research in pure science and some for applied research in civilian-oriented industries, including communications and computer technologies for the Information Superhighway.[47] Congress would not go that far right away, but by the 1996 budget the Clinton administration achieved that fifty-fifty split of R & D funding.[48] Strong endorsement for shifting the research emphasis toward the civilian economy came from the Competitiveness Policy Council, which represents business, labor, and the public.[49] Some critics mocked such a shift as a "technology pork barrel" and a "high-tech gravy train," but the U.S. Chamber of Commerce and the National Association of Manufacturers applauded the effort.[50]

One typical project was the decision of the Big Three automakers to pool their research efforts and to work with the Commerce Department to develop radically more fuel-efficient cars, at a potential cost of up to $500 million.[51] The Pentagon's reconstituted ARPA allocated another $68 million to promote research into electric cars and vehicles with hybrid power sources, for military and commercial uses.[52]

In a technically sensitive area, the Energy Department announced a

$52 million program to strengthen the nation's lead in supercomputing by using its two premier nuclear bomb-building laboratories at Los Alamos, New Mexico, and Livermore, California, to work with sixteen commercial firms to find ways to readapt software developed for the military to industrial uses in the civilian economy.[53]

By far the largest parallel to Sematech, however, was the Pentagon's decision in April 1994 to spend $580 million—to be matched by private industry—to put the United States back into competition in the making of flat-panel displays, the field that RCA, Rockwell, IBM, and many other American companies had abandoned to Sharp and other Japanese firms.

The Pentagon saw flat-panel displays as essential not only for portable computers but for a myriad of military uses—for example, in aircraft cockpits, fire-control displays in tanks, military command-and-control centers. Earlier, the Clinton administration had provided $100 million in funding for research in flat-panel technology; now, the Pentagon would help fund construction of four world-class production facilities. One rationale bore a striking resemblance to that for Sematech. The Pentagon said that Sharp, the world's dominant supplier of flat-panel displays, had stated that it would not supply technology or products directly to the U.S. military or supply U.S. defense contractors with customized display panels for military use.[54] As with Sematech, military need was cited to justify government subsidies to a leading-edge commercial industry.

Quite literally, the flat-panel project had brought events full circle from RCA's loss of that technology to Sharp.

Here was America reentering a competitive arena that its leading companies had abandoned. Here was America adopting the strategy of industrial targeting and government subsidies that it had decried for so many years when that strategy was used by the Japanese and Europeans to assault America's commercial hegemony.

Here was the implicit assertion that the market had not worked to serve the nation's interest and that government had to stimulate industry to undertake what was in industry's long-term interest but was too costly in the short run for industry to undertake without government help.

Here was yet another instance where the tidal changes in global competition had caused a fundamental rethinking and readjustment in America's traditional economic mind-set. Like other changes, the creeping industrial and technology policy begun by the Reagan administration and carried on by the Clinton administration came under fire from the new Republican-dominated Congress. Even where it survives, this policy is unlikely to be successful in every instance.

Yet, in the spirit of Intel's Andy Grove, America is experimenting with public-private partnerships, because both some business leaders and policymakers see that strategy as America's best chance for winning in the new global game.

Conclusion

16

The Unfinished Agenda
High Performance and the Perpetual Revolution

*You've got to reorganize the work for high performance,
decentralize the decisions, have a participative system. . . .
A high-performance organization is an efficient learning
system.[1]*

—RAY MARSHALL, FORMER SECRETARY OF LABOR

*To the degree that we can create a trusting environment,
people will respond. Trust is a tremendous motivator and a
great energizer.[2]*

—BOB GALVIN, FORMER CEO, MOTOROLA

*We used the total quality management process. Fortu-
nately, it worked and we were able to turn things around,
gain back market share, and compete effectively against
the best in the world.[3]*

—DAVID KEARNS, FORMER CEO, XEROX

By rethinking their old ways, America's Innovators have not only
powered an American resurgence in the 1990s, they have fashioned
the components of a high-performance strategy for America.

What is both interesting and instructive is that the changes which
the Innovators have been making mirror the wider changes in the
world at large. They complement a historic pattern.

For just as the American government has discovered in the post–
Cold War era that the United States cannot impose on other nations
the American notion of a world order, American business has learned
that it can no longer impose its hegemony on the global economy.

Similarly, within the innovative corporation, the towering individual—the imperial CEO—can no longer succeed by dominating the

company like Gulliver commanding an army of obedient Lilliputians. In today's economic game, a company must be a far more collaborative human enterprise.

In fact, the paradigm shift in the world at large is reflected in the common themes of the Innovators—their emphasis on people, teamwork, learning, long-term strategies, "patient capital," new partnerships, power sharing, and, ultimately, the joining of economic forces and institutions that have often clashed in America's past.

In short, the globalization of the economy and the explosion of technology have caused a centrifugal dispersal of power—outward from the old power centers.

Only those agile and supple enough to move with the new flows of competitive advantage can ride the tide. Others who have clung to the old order and the old hierarchies of power have been punished by tidal change.

The first step of America's Innovators was to reject the old status quo—and then to reframe their own mind-set. Armed with fresh thinking, the Innovators were then able to transform their organizations, whether schools or businesses, from the ground up.

Ford achieved a dramatic turnaround in the 1980s while General Motors careened into decline, because Ford's leadership grasped how thoroughly the nature of competition had been altered and because Ford was willing to make radical changes in its management philosophy. That same willingness to abandon the old formulas of success and to reach out to new opportunities enabled Motorola to thrive while IBM floundered. Rethinking saved Xerox, whereas RCA stood still—and perished. A new collaborative mind-set toward suppliers and customers enabled Boeing to withstand Airbus, while McDonnell Douglas and other American planemakers were overtaken.

In education, too, recognition of the need for fundamental change and a willingness to go against the grain inspired effective reform. Bert Grover in Wisconsin and Deb Meier in New York City saw that the American system was not delivering on its promise of universal education, and so they abandoned the conventional wisdom in education to create new schools and new programs that are relevant to preparing young Americans for tomorrow's global competition.

And today, despite America's recovery, the Innovators understand that their agenda remains unfinished—because, in the new global game, the only constant is change. The name of the new game is perpetual revolution.

The Daring Minority: Keys to High Performance

America's Innovators, who are still the daring minority, have been pursuing and implementing what has become known as "a high-performance strategy"—a strategy that not only puts their companies and schools at the leading edge but also delivers the American people a high standard of living.

America's choice is between that high-performance strategy—a strategy that requires high skills and delivers a high standard of living—or the alternative strategy that sets the target of low costs and low wages and gradually forces down the standard of living of average Americans to Third World levels, a strategy still pursued in many American companies.

As Ford Motor Company learned, achieving high performance requires a redefinition of work and of the relationships among people who work together. It means not only using the backs of workers but tapping their minds—and that entails giving more responsibility and autonomy to the ordinary worker and to the work team on the factory floor.

At its cellular phone factory, Motorola discovered that putting a company at the leading edge requires a melding of technology and human skills. Being that flexible requires a looser, less hierarchical, less command-driven system, one that invites innovation from everyone in an organization.

Since technology is ever changing, keeping pace means that human skills and human organization must be continuously upgraded. Success for Motorola, therefore, requires an ever-expanding commitment to education and learning for every employee.

This combination of rethinking the nature of work, decentralizing decisions, and setting up a participatory system, according to Ray Marshall, secretary of labor to President Carter, "is the only way that we're likely to be competitive on terms that maintain and improve our incomes."

The most important attribute of a high-performance workplace, in Marshall's eyes, is not a company's level of technology or its productivity, but whether it is what Marshall calls *"an efficient learning system."*

That point is worth underscoring. The climate for learning is essential to high performance, Marshall asserts, "because what technological progress really means is substituting ideas, skills, and knowledge for physical resources, and if you have an efficient learning system, you will be successful."[4]

If constant learning, constant technological change, and constant improvement are the engines of long-term success, as Marshall and many others contend, they demand that people work together in new ways—to exchange ideas, to develop new processes, to absorb new technology, to invent new products, and to achieve high performance. People at every level—from frontline workers to engineers to top management—are crucial to that endeavor. Ideas must flow from the bottom up as well as from the top down.

Maintaining an open flow of ideas is essential to high performance, and that open flow of ideas depends on an atmosphere of trust and security in which workers and managers alike can feel safe in sharing ideas that will generate innovations or greater productivity, even if that brings a change in their personal job assignments. People need to feel confident that collectively they will generate new work, so that greater efficiency in their old work does not lead to layoffs.

Trust, then, is the essential ingredient for high performance, according to Motorola's longtime CEO, Bob Galvin. "To the degree that we can create a trusting environment, people will respond," Galvin emphasized. "Trust is a tremendous motivator and a great energizer. If our people know that we believe in them, they will respond because they are trusted. That is a motivation factor that is almost unbeatable."[5]

American Innovators such as Bob Galvin at Motorola, Red Poling at Ford, and Skip LeFauve at Saturn—and others at companies such as Levi Strauss, Corning Glass, and Magma Copper—have understood the need for mutual trust between management and workers. They are part of a daring minority that has crossed a cultural divide. Many American businesses have not yet firmly embraced the conviction that trust, security, and a strong sense of partnership are essential in order to institutionalize the high-performance strategy.

The pervasive job insecurity in America today, and the traditional adversarial tensions in many American companies, are barriers to the trust needed for a high-performance workplace, according to Ray Marshall, now an economist at the University of Texas.

"An adversarial system is not a good learning system," asserts Marshall. "I'm not going to share any information with you if I think that I'm going to lose in the process. And if you're a manager and you believe that your power diminishes because you share information with me, then we're not going to learn much from each other. And therefore cooperation becomes terribly important to being an efficient learning system. . . . Most American workers believe that if they improve productivity, they lose their jobs. Well, that's not much of an incentive. And that's the reason job security becomes an important part of a high-performance system."

The late W. Edwards Deming, the American management guru, made a similar argument. "Drive out fear" among your employees, Deming admonished American CEOs, so that people will work effectively together in teams, rather than being driven by an every-man-for-himself mentality.[6]

The Downside of Downsizing

The current fashion of downsizing—deliberate, repeated layoffs—at some of America's most profitable corporations runs counter to the philosophy and strategy of the high-performance workplace set out by Deming, Marshall, and Galvin.

Experts differentiate the recent rash of corporate downsizing from earlier recession-inspired cutbacks and the massive restructuring of companies such as General Motors and IBM, which had to revamp after they had lost huge chunks of their market share.

The waves of layoffs since 1992 reflect a different approach—a long-term strategy of shrinking profit-making companies in good times. In fact, downsizing has become so pervasive that more than 85 percent of the *Fortune* 500 companies—profitable companies such as AT&T, BankAmerica, General Electric, Johnson & Johnson, NYNEX, Procter & Gamble, RJR Nabisco, Sears, and Xerox (after the retirement of David Kearns)—have lopped off sizable numbers of employees in the past five years; 100 percent say they plan more layoffs in the next five years.[7]

The downsizing strategy stands on its head the classic dictum of American industry voiced by Alfred P. Sloan, the former chairman of General Motors: "Growth is essential to the good health of an enterprise. Deliberately to stop growing is to suffocate."[8]

Today, the corporate dogma is "Smaller is better."

Layoffs win points for corporate CEOs with Wall Street and boost the value of executive stock options, although recent experience, company by company, shows that, in practice, cutting staff typically has fallen dramatically short of making the improvement in competitive performance that money managers expect.[9]

In corporate America today, downsizing is like dieting: Everyone is doing it, so people try it again and again, even though few achieve the desired results.[10] As one wag put it, the fixation with downsizing has become the new "corporate anorexia."[11]

Despite its popularity, downsizing in the late 1980s and early '90s has often failed to achieve its proponents' objectives, economists report, because typically slashing staff has not been "part of a thoughtful strategy to redesign the whole corporate structure and culture. Instead it's an almost panicked reaction to pressures and problems, administered with the sheeplike justification that everyone else is doing the same thing."[12]

In terms of achieving high performance in the long run, the problem with downsizing is that employees are treated as costs to be cut rather than as assets to be developed.

Layoffs undermine trust and the morale of employees who remain on the job; layoffs breed anxiety and a sense of betrayal. The sheer process of downsizing pulls decision-making power to the top of an organization, creates a hunkering-down, self-protective mood among employees, leaves managers averse to risk taking and less tolerant of failures, and increases internal infighting over shrinking resources, according to several studies. In such an atmosphere, teamwork becomes more difficult, and information—especially bad news—is not widely shared because of internal corporate fear and distrust.[13]

While these intangibles may not show up immediately on the bottom line, all of them hurt a company over the long run because they undermine the whole notion of employee empowerment and the crucial process of idea sharing that the American Innovators have found most effective. In fact, many companies that have engaged in layoffs have discovered that their productivity was worse off afterward, even though they continued more rounds of downsizing. "Sometimes companies did it three, four, and five times, but still didn't hit their expense-reduction targets," commented one specialist.[14]

Nor is this negative assessment simply the conclusion of academics and critics. The American Management Association, in a survey of 713 companies released in late 1994, reported that in the previous twelve months, nearly half of these companies had cut their staff an average of nearly 10 percent, but that "the goals of increased profits and greater productivity are unrealized for many firms." These were the conclusions of the companies themselves: "Productivity gains have been even more elusive. . . . The surest after-effect of downsizing is a negative impact on employee morale, which suffered in 86% of all firms reporting [personnel] cuts any time since January 1989."[15]

Another survey of more than five hundred corporations done by Wyatt and Company, a management consulting firm, found that while 60 percent of the companies reported that downsizing resulted in lower costs, only one third reported that it resulted in increased productivity or competitive advantage. More than half the companies wound up by replacing some of the dismissed workers. In an echo of both Bob Galvin and Ray Marshall, Wyatt and Company recommended a different strategy for U.S. corporations—engaging in an authentic process of *corporate renewal* to "foster an environment that is *conducive to learning*" and to motivating employees.[16]

It is telling, moreover, that innovative companies such as Ford and Motorola have gone to great lengths not to resort to layoffs for the past several years, in the conviction that the security of their workforce is essential to high performance. Rather than focusing on cost cutting, Ford and Motorola have sought to expand into new lines of business in order to absorb workers displaced by efficiency measures, rather than laying people off.

The bedrock strategy at Ford and Motorola, as well as at other companies such as Levi Strauss, Magma Copper, and Anheuser-Busch, has been to pursue competitive advantage by developing reciprocal loyalty between the company and its workers through job security and long-term investment in regular retraining. It is a strategy that has paid handsome rewards.

Finally, as a strategy of deliberate, long-term shrinking, downsizing has serious implications for the American economy.

It has already been painful to a wide swath of Americans, especially as American companies have expanded their production facilities abroad.[17] The combination of workforce cutbacks at home and expanded hiring abroad by American companies has contributed to the stagnant or declining living standards of much of the American middle class. It has pushed hundreds of thousands of well-paid blue-collar workers into lower-paying service jobs or part-time or temporary work. Nearly 20 percent of the Americans who lost their jobs from 1991 through 1994, for example, had not found work by November 1994, and nearly half of those who did find jobs were earning less than before.[18] The constant pressure of job cutbacks keeps wage levels down, so that the historic link between rising productivity and rising wages in American manufacturing has been broken. Productivity and profits have continued to climb over the past twenty years, but the take-home pay of the average worker has gone down in real terms.[19]

Some economists suggest, moreover, that the permanent strategy of layoffs, even in good times, may actually hurt the long-term growth of the U.S. economy. For that strategy accentuates the income gap between the executive class and the working class in America, and some studies indicate that the trickle-down economics of a two-tiered society, with large income inequalities, is not the best way to stimulate growth.

In what have been the most rapidly growing capitalist economies in the world, the "miracle economies" of Hong Kong, Singapore, South Korea, Taiwan, and—until its recent recession—Japan, the income levels of top corporate bosses have been much closer to the pay of ordinary workers than has CEO pay in America, and some economists see a connection between income equity and national economic growth.[20]

There is little question that the relatively modest income disparities in Japanese industry contribute to the strong sense of social solidarity among the Japanese people and to their willingness to accept belt tightening and extra devotion to the job in hard times for the sake of both company and country.

In America, it remains an open question how long rank-and-file workers who are falling behind economically will continue to tolerate growing disparities in earnings without social protest. The economic anxiety of Americans is a pervasive fact of life, widely reflected in opinion polls. *Time* magazine summarized the American mood in a headline: "We're #1 and It Hurts."[21] Labor Secretary Robert Reich talks about the new "anxious class" of Americans—"millions of Americans who no longer can count on having their jobs next year, or next month."

In the midterm elections of November 1994, public anger over economic insecurity exploded—at government and politicians, rather than at corporate America and its managers. Yet even some corporate leaders and business magazines have commented that the social compact between employer and employee has been stretched to the breaking point in America, and that the bonds holding American society together have been frayed by the economic tensions caused by downsizing.

The Dangers of Letting Overconfidence Stop the Process of Change

Resilience has always been an American strength. With its adaptability and ingenuity, corporate America has scrambled back from the dark days of the early 1990s. One proud emblem of its recovery was the judgment of the World Economic Forum in Switzerland that, in 1993, the United States had once again become the world's most competitive economy—after eight years of Japanese domination.[22]

But if resilience is an American strength, the 1980s showed that one American weakness is overconfidence. The danger in the 1990s is that corporate America will overinterpret its success and fail to push ahead with the unfinished agenda of reform.

America's recovery from the panicky years of the late 1980s was largely driven by the stark fear of competitive failure. Many a corporate CEO launched a cultural revolution in his company out of fear that the company would fail on his watch. As David Kearns of Xerox observed, it takes that outside competitive pressure to force people to make difficult changes. Today, with that acute sense of peril now eased, complacency has once again become a risk. The battle cry "We're Number One Again" becomes an excuse for saying the battle is over and America has all the answers.

In 1993 and 1994, for example, corporate interest in competing for the prestigious Malcolm Baldrige National Quality Award dropped off sharply. In the late 1980s and early 1990s, the Baldrige award became a spur and a symbol to leading American corporations to drive for higher quality. But enthusiasm for the quality movement has slackened during the U.S. recovery.[23]

In 1994, some American automotive factories, in their rush to cash in on good times with high output and high profits, were reverting to an old pattern—slacking off on quality and on long-term worker retraining.[24] General Motors, for one, boosted productivity by working factories at backbreaking overtime schedules—a tactic that has hurt quality in the past and that got GM into trouble with American car buyers in the 1980s.

In spite of Detroit's improvements, moreover, the American automobile industry still lags behind its Japanese rivals. In 1993, for example, the auto and auto parts industries accounted for close to $30 billion of America's trade deficit with Japan, and 1994 only worsened that trade gap. Ford's new CEO, Alexander J. Trotman, observed that, after slipping for a year or two, in 1994 the Japanese "have been coming back strongly. They're not going to change in the foreseeable future, except to get tougher and more efficient."[25]

The most savvy Americans understand that recovery has been generated not only by America's hard-won improvements but by the drop in the dollar's value from 130 yen to roughly 100 yen to the dollar between 1992 and 1994. Japanese industry, hit with a whopping 30 percent increase in the prices of its exports to the United States, has been hard pressed to maintain export levels; American industry has gained a major competitive advantage from more favorable currency exchange rates with Germany as well as Japan.

But history carries a warning: When the Japanese were hit with a similar dollar devaluation in 1985, it took them about two years to readjust; a similar two-year adjustment to the current dollar devaluation would end in late 1995. American industry could be hit hard, too, if the value of the dollar rises on the back of the American economic recovery.

No less a partisan of corporate America than Jack Welch, the CEO of General Electric, has raised the flag of caution. "If the Japanese are prepared to compete at 90 yen to the dollar, the U.S. must be prepared to compete at 130 yen to the dollar," Welch warned in October 1994. "Until we are, we delude ourselves if we think we are in control of our own fate."[26]

And despite the surge in America's industrial productivity in the 1990s, McKinsey & Company, the respected management consultant firm, reported that Japanese firms were leading American firms in 1993 in productivity in several sectors—automobiles, auto parts, metalworking, steel, and consumer electronics—while the Americans had an edge in computers, soaps and detergents, food, and beer.[27] Japan's Achilles' heel is in the groaning inefficiency of its domestic service sector.

Nonetheless, throughout their recession, the Japanese have kept building for the future. In 1993, for example, the Japanese savings rate was roughly 23 percent, compared to 3.1 percent in America—and those savings translated into an enormous capital for Japanese industry, according to Ken Courtis, an economist with Deutsche Bank in Tokyo. In fact, in the depths of its worst recession since World War II, Japan was virtually matching America dollar for dollar in capital spending—in 1993, about $720 billion, or roughly 18 percent of national output, went for new plants and equipment. By comparison, capital spending by American business, in the midst of the U.S. economic expansion, was only slightly greater—about $740 billion in 1993, or about 12 percent of the nation's gross output.[28]

In other words, the Japanese during a downturn were mounting a proportionately more ambitious building program than the Americans were during an upswing.

The Long Term and the Pattern of Partnerships

The crucial lesson in these investment figures, as well as in the winning strategies of the American Innovators, is that, for a high-performance strategy, the long term is where the focus needs to be. Short-term gains are perishable without the underpinning of the right kind of rethinking and reform for the long term. What looks good at the top of the business cycle can lose its luster at the bottom.

What is instructive is that as America's Innovators focused on the long term, they often broke new ground by turning to new arrangements of partnership, collaboration, and power sharing. The mind-set of cooperation ripples through each of the areas we have examined— educational reform, labor-management relations, corporate governance, industrial policy.

The pattern of new partnerships now dots the American economic landscape—in the joint ventures of business and education to develop high school apprenticeship programs; in the labor-management cooperation at companies such as Ford, Saturn, and Magma Copper; at the state level, in networking between small and medium-sized companies and universities, regional technical centers, and state agencies to promote exports, technology transfer, and new management methods.

Probably the most eye-catching partnership of recent years is Sematech—in large part because Ronald Reagan, an ebullient advocate of the free market, gave birth to this unusual peacetime collaboration of the federal government and the private sector, as well as to the equally radical working partnership among corporate rivals.

What makes Sematech a powerful precedent for the 1990s is that in order for Sematech to emerge, both public policy and private thinking had to change—and did. America's antitrust laws were relaxed to permit the cooperative research and development done by Sematech. Now, eight years later, some of America's most competitive multinational corporations have seen great enough benefits from this cooperative effort to keep financing Sematech's effort as government support is phased out.

In short, Sematech did something critical for this important American industry that the free market did not do: It committed the "patient capital" and an industry-managed strategy to promote the development of precompetitive technology that serves the whole computer chip industry over the long term.

In very different ways, Boeing has pursued another radical new form of networking by bringing airline customers inside the company to peer over the shoulders of Boeing engineers as they design new aircraft. Despite the early difficulties, this new approach—adapting the methods of Europe and Japan—has generated new ideas, new business, higher quality and productivity, and other dividends that were missing in the old arm's-length American approach.

What is more, Boeing, like Chrysler and some other American corporations, has moved into closer long-term relationships and guaranteed contracts with some of its own main suppliers, mimicking the Japanese *keiretsu* networks. Bringing in important Japanese subcontractors was a price Boeing paid for large aircraft orders from Japan Air Lines and All Nippon Airways. But even in America, Boeing has seen a competitive advantage in surrendering some of the absolute freedom of the marketplace and its traditional reliance on low-cost bidding in favor of steady partnerships with long-term subcontractors. That is a pattern that Chrysler and Saturn have both followed in the automobile industry and that IBM, Motorola, and Apple have been trying to develop in the computer industry.

Even bolder than Boeing's approach is the idea put forward in a study circulated by the Council on Competitiveness—namely, that American corporations would be better off forging long-term strategies by having a company's real stakeholders (its owners, its workers, its managers, its customers, its suppliers, and the home communities of its major plants) represented directly on corporate boards.

In a few instances, U.S. corporate boards have actually started to include labor members on their boards, either in response to labor-management negotiations (U.S. Steel and others) or when companies in trouble have been partly or wholly bought out by their employees (United Airlines).

Making it a more general practice to include important stakeholders on corporate boards would require changes in public policy—amending laws to allow banks, employee pension funds, and institutional investors to hold sizable shares of corporations, as well as to permit their representatives to sit on corporate boards and to act like owners, watching over the management of their investments.

This would mark a major change in America's business culture, a fundamental rethinking of the rules of ownership and governance in American corporations. Yet the study done by the Harvard Business School minces no words in asserting that this "stakeholder" form of corporate governance would bring important long-term advantages to American companies and to the U.S. economy as a whole by fostering a greater commitment to long-term research and development, long-term investment in training and upgrading the American workforce, and other long-term strategies.

"A reformed U.S. system would be more flexible, more responsive, and even better informed in allocating capital than those in Japan and Germany," the joint Harvard–Council on Competitiveness report asserts. "The gains will accrue not only to investors and to firms, but also to the rate of long-term productivity growth, competitiveness, and the prosperity of the U.S. economy."[29]

The Agenda in School-to-Work Education

Probably no social partnership holds more potential for both immediate and long-term impact on America's future—and none is more important for achieving a high-performance strategy—than the budding cooperation between schools and some businesses on educational reform, especially in the development of school-to-work programs for the vast numbers of high school students who are not college-bound.

Traditionally, American business has treated its involvement in schooling as a part-time charitable activity. But, as the work-study apprenticeships in Wisconsin, Pennsylvania, Maine, Oklahoma, and Massachusetts illustrate, some business leaders have understood that not charity but their own enlightened self-interest compels them to become more directly involved in improving public education to make it more relevant to the work world and to provide business with a modern, well-educated workforce.

Unfortunately, this is not the practice of the majority of enterprises in America. In the 1994 report of the Competitiveness Policy Council, a tripartite government-appointed group representing business, labor, and the public, James Renier, the former CEO of Honeywell, warned bluntly: "As a society, we are throwing away the future productive capacities of a growing portion of our people. . . . The competitive potential of the economy as a whole is diminished by our inability to tap the full potential of all members of our society."[30] Renier's comments apply not only to school dropouts but to high school graduates, who have been falling behind economically.

One major national survey, released in early 1995, found an alarming gulf between businesses and schools in America, in contrast to the close ties between those two sectors in Germany and Japan. The survey, done for the Education Department by the National Center on the Educational Quality of the Workforce at the University of Pennsylvania, reported that American employers and educators are generally moving along separate and different tracks. "What's really scary is that you have the education folks and the employment folks, the supply side and the demand side, and they don't understand each other's language," said one specialist on workforce education. "Employers have given up on the schools and by giving up, they've lost their ability to influence them."[31]

Despite reporting that at least 20 percent of their workers lack needed skills, many employers in the survey were skeptical of the ability of high schools to prepare students for the workplace and shied away from hiring graduates fresh out of school. They preferred instead to rely on "temporary" services and to wait to hire new workers in their mid-20s. Unlike German and Japanese employers, the survey found, American employers tended to disregard school grades and evaluations and to focus on attitude, behavior, and job experience. And despite the talk in American business about innovative work practices such as self-managed work teams, multiskilled workers, and job rotation, the survey found these new approaches were being used by far fewer businesses than expected. "If it indeed is true, as many argue, that the organization of the workplace and the quality of the workforce is going to be the central factor in keeping us competitive, there's not much evidence here that we're utilizing the best practices," observed Joan Wills of the Institute for Educational Leadership, a private, nonprofit research agency.[32] Especially with rising levels of technology and complexity in many jobs, the sharp cutbacks in youth job training and the educational Goals 2000 program voted by the Republican-led House of Representatives in early 1995 was shortsighted.

As we have seen, the job world is rapidly changing under the pressures of the new competitive game. The pursuit of a high-skills, high-wage, high-performance strategy has exposed a serious gap in America's traditional high school education for average students. College remains the universally proclaimed goal for American youth, yet labor experts point out that 70 percent of the jobs in America in the year 2000 will *not* require a four-year college degree.

For example, technical occupations, which already account for 20 million Americans and one of every four new jobs, are expected to grow more dramatically in the years ahead than most other kinds of work. Labor specialists project a rising demand for paralegals, radiology technicians, computer programmers, medical records technicians, drafters, engineering technicians, emergency medical technicians, science technicians—people whose skills and responsibilities blur the old lines between white-collar and blue-collar jobs.[33]

These are all fields that require a solid high school education and perhaps some junior college—generally a far better education than most high schools have been offering most of the average American teenagers who have gotten their diplomas in recent years. The problem of an educational shortfall is compounded by the fact that demographers expect that ten years from now there will be 3.9 million fewer workers between the ages of twenty-five and thirty-nine than there are today.[34] So demand will increase as supply is decreasing, and that will add to the pressures on high schools and junior colleges.

In his book *Reinventing Education,* IBM's CEO Lou Gerstner underscored the enormous handicaps to U.S. industry of the nation's educational shortfall. He cited a survey by the National Association of Manufacturers that found that "thirty percent of companies cannot reorganize work activities because employees can't learn new jobs and twenty-five percent can't upgrade their products because their employees can't learn the necessary skills." Poor schooling is such a competitive drag, Gerstner wrote, that corporate America must spend $30 billion a year on remedial education for its new workers and is losing $25 billion to $30 billion more each year because of low levels of worker literacy—a total of $60 billion annually.

Gerstner concluded: "We can't squander $60 billion and remain competitive."[35]

The challenge before American industry is whether it is prepared to rethink its role in education: Will it continue to spend or lose that $60 billion by waiting for the problem of inadequate schooling to land on its doorstep—in its factories and in its offices? Or will it do as German industry does—reach out to form a partnership with educators? For the sake of high performance, will American business both participate in—and invest something like $60 billion in—a massive effort to lift the quality of education for average American teenagers and open up pathways of success for this long "neglected majority" in scores if not hundreds of careers?

Such a collaboration in education would be a model of social partnership for many other arenas of American life.

This kind of partnership is no longer an untested idea. In the field of educational reform, as in labor-management relations, corporate power sharing, and the collaboration of the public and private sectors, America's Innovators have pioneered the way.

The question now is whether other Americans are ready to rethink old ways, to learn from the Innovators, and then to apply and adapt their lessons in order to move America to higher performance and a higher quality of life in the coming generation.

Bibliography

Aerospace Facts and Figures 1990–91 (Washington, D.C.: Aerospace Industries Association of America, Inc., 1991).

America's Choice: High Skills or Low Wages! Report of the Commission on the Skills of the American Workforce (Rochester, N.Y.: National Center on Education and the Economy, 1990).

Anchordoguy, Marie. *Computers Inc.: Japan's Challenge to IBM* (Cambridge, Mass.: Harvard University Press, 1989).

———. "Japanese Policies for the Supercomputer Industry." (Washington, D.C.: U.S. Government Printing Office, 1991).

Benedict, Ruth. *The Chrysanthemum and the Sword: Patterns of Japanese Culture* (Rutland, Vt.: Charles E. Tuttle Co., 1974).

Blair, Margaret M. "CEO Pay: Why Such a Contentious Issue?," *The Brookings Review,* Winter 1994, pp. 23–27.

———. *Ownership and Control: Rethinking Corporate Governance for the Twenty-first Century* (Washington, D.C.: The Brookings Institution, 1995).

Blasi, Joseph Raphael, and Douglas Lynn Krause. *The New Owners: The Mass Emergence of Employee Ownership in Public Companies and What It Means to American Business* (New York: HarperBusiness, 1992).

Bluestone, Barry, and Irving Bluestone. *Negotiating the Future: A Labor Perspective on American Business* (New York: Basic Books, 1992).

Bottoms, Gene, Alice Presson, and Mary Johnson. *Making High Schools Work* (Atlanta: Southern Regional Education Board, 1992).

A Brief History of Mitsubishi 1992 (company publication).

Brooks, Jack. "Possible Violations of U.S. Antitrust Laws by Foreign Corporations," testimony before the House Judiciary Subcommittee on Economic and Commercial Law, May 3, 1990 (Washington, D.C.: U.S. Government Printing Office, 1990).

Burstein, Daniel. *Yen! Japan's New Financial Empire and Its Threat to America* (New York: Fawcett Columbine, 1990).

Carnes, James A. "The Crisis in R&D," in *Sarnoff: Fifty Years of Vision,* special supplement (Princeton, N.J.: Sarnoff Laboratory, 1992).

Chandler, Alfred P. *The Visible Hand: The Managerial Revolution in American Business* (Cambridge, Mass.: The Belknap Press, 1977).

Chiappetta, Robert. "Restructuring Japanese Style," *Inside/Outside Japan,* February 1994, p. 3.

Choate, Pat. *Agents of Influence: How Japan Manipulates America's Political and Economic System* (New York: Touchstone, 1990).

Christopher, Robert C. *The Japanese Mind* (New York: Simon & Schuster, 1983).

Clark, Rodney. *The Japanese Company* (New Haven, Conn.: Yale University Press, 1979).

Clavell, James. *Shogun* (New York: Dell, 1975).

Cohen, Stephen S., and John Zysman. *Manufacturing Matters: The Myth of the Post-Industrial Economy* (New York: Basic Books, 1987).

Comer, James P. "Educating Poor Minority Children," *Scientific American,* 259 (5) (November 1988), 42–48.

"The Competitive Strength of U.S. Industrial Science and Technology: Strategic Issues" (Washington, D.C.: National Science Board, 1992).

Crystal, Graef. *In Search of Excess: The Overcompensation of American Executives* (New York: W. W. Norton, 1991).

———. *The Crystal Report,* 1992–.

Deming, W. Edwards. *Out of the Crisis* (Cambridge, Mass.: MIT Center for Advanced Engineering Study, 1986).

Dertovzos, Michael L., Richard K. Lester, and Robert M. Solow. *Made in America: Regaining the Productive Edge* (Cambridge, Mass.: MIT Press, 1989).

Dietrich, William S. *In the Shadow of the Rising Sun* (University Park: Pennsylvania State University Press, 1991).

Doi, Takeo. *The Anatomy of Dependence* (Tokyo and New York: Kodansha International, 1973).

Drucker, Peter F. *The Frontiers of Management* (New York: Harper & Row, 1986).

———. *The New Realities: In Government and Politics, in Economics and Business, in Society and World View* (New York: HarperCollins, 1989).

———. "The Theory of the Business," *Harvard Business Review,* March–April 1993, pp. 95–104.

Engelmann, Bernt. *Wie wir wurden, was wir sind* (Gütersloh, W. Germany: Bertelsmann, 1980).

Fallows, James. *Looking at the Sun* (New York: Pantheon, 1994).

———. *More Like Us* (Boston: Houghton Mifflin, 1989).

Ferguson, Charles H., and Charles R. Morris. *Computer Wars: The Fall of IBM and the Future of Global Technology* (New York: Times Books, 1994).

Fiske, Edward B. *Smart Schools, Smart Kids* (New York: Simon & Schuster, 1991).

Friedman, David. *The Misunderstood Miracle: Industrial Development and Political Change in Japan* (Ithaca, N.Y.: Cornell University Press, 1988).

Friedman, David B., and Richard J. Samuels. "How to Succeed Without Really Flying: The Japanese Aircraft Industry and Japan's Technology Ideology," paper on the MIT Japan Program (Boston: MIT, April 1, 1992).

Friedman, George, and Meredith Lebard. *The Coming War with Japan* (New York: St. Martin's Press, 1991).

Garten, Jeffrey E. *A Cold Peace: America, Japan, Germany and the Struggle for Supremacy* (New York: Times Books, 1992).

Gerlach, Michael. *Alliance Capitalism: The Social Organization of Japanese Business* (Berkeley: University of California Press, 1992).

Goldberger, Susan, R. Kazis, and M. O'Flanagan. *Learning Through Work: Designing and Implementing Quality Worksite Learning for High School Students* (New York: Manpower Demonstration Research Corporation, 1994).

Grundler, Gerhard E., and Arnim V. Manikowsky. *Das Gericht der Sieger* (Munich: Oldenburg, 1967).

Halberstam, David. *The Next Century* (New York: William Morrow, 1991).

———. *The Reckoning* (New York: Avon, 1986).

Hall, Edward T., and Mildred Reed Hall. *Hidden Differences: Doing Business with the Japanese* (New York: Doubleday, 1987).

Hamabata, Matthews Masayuki. *Crested Kimono: Power and Love in the Japanese Business Family* (Ithaca, N.Y.: Cornell University Press, 1990).

Hamilton, Stephen F. *Apprenticeship for Adulthood* (New York: The Free Press, 1990).

Harbour, Jim. "1992 Update to *The Harbour Report, 1989–1992,*" Oct. 2, 1992.

Hare, Mikiso. *Modern Japan: A Historical Survey* (Boulder, Colo.: Westview Press, 1986).

Heiduk, Günter, and Kozo Yamamura, eds. *Technological Competition and Interdependence* (Seattle: University of Washington Press, 1990).

Hoffman, A., ed. *Facts About Germany* (Frankfurt am Main: Societäts-Verlag, 1992).

Hoover's Handbook of World Business 1993 (Austin, Tex.: Reference Press, 1993).

Hoover's Handbook of World Business 1994 (Austin, Tex.: Reference Press, 1994).

Howell, Thomas R., Brent L. Bartlett, and Warren Davis. *Creating Advantage: Semiconductors and Government Industrial Policy in the 1990s* (Washington, D.C.: Semiconductor Industry Association/Dewey Ballantine, 1992).

Industrial Groupings in Japan, 8th ed. (Tokyo: Dodwell Marketing Consultants, 1988–89).

Inoguchi, Takashi, and Daniel I. Okimoto, eds. *The Political Economy of Japan,* vol. 1, *The Changing International Context* (Stanford, Calif.: Stanford University Press, 1988).

Ishihara, Shintaro. *The Japan That Can Say No: Why Japan Will Be First Among Equals* (New York: Simon & Schuster, 1989).

Jarausch, Konrad H. *The Rush to German Unity* (New York: Oxford University Press, 1994).

Johnson, Chalmers. "*Keiretsu:* An Outsider's View," *Insight,* September–October 1990, pp. 15–17.

———. *MITI and the Japanese Miracle* (Stanford, Calif.: Stanford University Press, 1982).

———, Laura D'Andrea Tyson, and John Zysman, eds. *Politics and Productivity: How Japan's Development Strategy Works* (New York: HarperBusiness, 1989).

Johnson, Haynes. *Divided We Fall: Gambling with History in the Nineties* (New York: W. W. Norton, 1994).

———. *Sleepwalking Through History: America in the Reagan Years* (New York: W. W. Norton, 1991).

Journal of Japanese Studies, vol. 9, no. 2 (Summer 1983).

————, vol. 15, no. 1 (Winter 1989).

Kearns, David T., and David Nadler. *Prophets in the Dark: How Xerox Reinvented Itself and Beat Back the Japanese* (New York: HarperBusiness, 1992).

Kearns, Robert. *Zaibatsu America* (New York: The Free Press, 1992).

Keller, Maryann. *Collision: GM, Toyota, Volkswagen and the Race to Own the 21st Century* (New York: Doubleday, 1993).

————. *Rude Awakening* (New York: Harper Perennial, 1989).

Kennedy, Paul. *Preparing for the Twenty-first Century* (New York: Random House, 1993).

————. *The Rise and Fall of the Great Powers* (New York: Random House, 1987).

Kester, Carl W. *Japanese Takeovers: The Global Contest for Corporate Control* (Boston: Harvard Business School Press, 1991).

Krauss, Ellis S., Thomas P. Rholen, and Patricia G. Steinhoff, eds. *Conflict in Japan* (Honolulu: University of Hawaii Press, 1984).

Krugman, Paul. *The Age of Diminished Expectations* (Cambridge, Mass.: MIT Press, 1990).

————. *Peddling Prosperity* (New York: W. W. Norton, 1994).

Kuttner, Robert. *The End of Laissez-faire* (Philadelphia: University of Pennsylvania Press, 1991).

LeFauve, Richard G., and Arnoldo C. Hax. "Managerial and Technological Innovations at Saturn Corporation," *MIT Management,* Spring 1992, pp. 8–19.

Levitan, Sar A., Garth L. Magnum, and Ray Marshall. *Human Resources and Labor Markets: Employment and Training in the American Economy,* 3d ed. (New York: Harper & Row, 1981).

Lodge, George. *Perestroika for America* (Boston: Harvard Business School Press, 1990).

Lorsch, Jay W., with Elizabeth MacIver. *Pawns or Potentates: The Reality of America's Corporate Boards* (Boston: Harvard Business School Press, 1989).

———— and ————, "Corporate Governance and Investment Time Horizons," unpublished paper, Harvard Business School, October 1991.

Magaziner, Ira C., and Mark Patinkin. *The Silent War* (New York: Vintage Books, 1990).

Marsh, David. *The Germans* (New York: St. Martin's Press, 1989).

Marshall, Ray, and Marc Tucker. *Thinking for a Living: Education and the Wealth of Nations* (New York: Basic Books, 1992).

McMillion, Charles W. "21st Century Manufacturing," paper presented to the annual conference of the National Center for Manufacturing Sciences, Anaheim, Calif., May 10, 1994.

Mishel, Lawrence, and Jared Bernstein. *The State of Working America 1992–93,* Economic Policy Institute Series (Armonk, N.Y.: M. E. Sharpe, 1993).

Morita, Akio, with Edwin Reingold and Mitsuko Shimomura. *Made in Japan* (New York: E. P. Dutton, 1986).

Newhouse, John. *The Sporty Game* (New York: Alfred A. Knopf, 1982).

Newman, Katherine S. *Declining Futures: The Withering of the American Dream* (New York: Basic Books, 1993).

Nothdurft, William E. *School Works: Reinventing Public Schools to Create the Workforce of the Future* (Washington, D.C.: The Brookings Institution, 1989).

Ohmae, Kenichi. *The Borderless World* (New York: HarperBusiness, 1990).

Ohno, Taichi. *Toyota Production System: Beyond Large-Scale Production* (Cambridge, Mass.: Productivity Press, 1978).

————, with Setsuo Mito. *Just in Time: For Today and Tomorrow* (Cambridge, Mass.: Productivity Press, 1986).

Okimoto, Daniel I. *Between MITI and the Market* (Stanford, Calif.: Stanford University Press, 1989).

———— and Thomas P. Rohlen. *Inside the Japanese System* (Stanford, Calif.: Stanford University Press, 1988).

————, Takuo Sugano, and Franklin B. Weinstein, eds. *Competitive Edge: The Semiconductor Industry in the U.S. and Japan* (Stanford, Calif.: Stanford University Press, 1984).

Orr, Robert M., Jr. *The Emergence of Japan's Foreign Aid Power* (New York: Columbia University Press, 1990).

Peters, Tom. *Thriving on Chaos: A Handbook for Management Revolution* (New York: Harper & Row, 1987).

Phillips, Kevin P. *Staying on Top* (New York: Random House, 1984).

Porter, Michael E. "Capital Choices: Changing the Way America Invests in Industry," research report (Washington, D.C.: Council on Competitiveness and Harvard Business School, 1992).

————. *The Competitive Advantage of Nations* (New York: The Free Press, 1990).

Prestowitz, Clyde V., Jr. *Trading Places: How We Allowed Japan to Take the Lead* (New York: Basic Books, 1988).

Rauch, Jonathan. *The Outnation: A Search for the Soul of Japan* (Boston: Harvard Business School Press, 1992).

Rehder, Robert R. "Is Saturn Competitive?" *Business Horizons,* March–April 1994, pp. 7–15.

Reich, Robert B. *Tales of a New America* (New York: Vintage Books, 1987).

————. *The Work of Nations: Capitalism in the 21st Century* (New York: Alfred A. Knopf, 1990).

Reischauer, Edwin O. *Japan: The Story of a Nation* (New York: McGraw-Hill, 1990).

————. *The Japanese Today: Change and Continuity* (Cambridge, Mass.: The Belknap Press, 1988).

———— and Albert M. Craig. *Japan: Tradition & Transformation* (Boston: Houghton Mifflin, 1989).

Rozwenc, Edwin Charles. *The Making of American Society* (New York: Alfred A. Knopf, 1978).

Sakai, Kuniyasu. "The Feudal World of Japanese Manufacturing," *Harvard Business Review,* November–December, 1990, pp. 38–49.

Sakai, Kuniyasu, and Hiroshi Sekiyama. *Bunsha: Improving Your Business Through Company Division* (New York: Intercultural Group, 1985).

Science and Engineering Indicators (Washington, D.C.: National Science Foundation, 1993).

Serling, Robert J. *Legend & Legacy: The Story of Boeing and Its People* (New York: St. Martin's Press, 1992).

Sizer, Theodore R. *Horace's Compromise: The Dilemma of the American High School* (Boston: Houghton Mifflin, 1992).

Sleigh, Stephen, Michael Kapsa, and Chris Hall. "Union Busting Is Bad for Business," Graduate School, City University of New York, Occasional Paper no. 12, October 1992.

Smith, Douglas K., and Robert C. Alexander. *Fumbling the Future: How Xerox Invented, Then Ignored, the First Personal Computer* (New York: William Morrow, 1988).

Smyser, W. R. *The Economy of United Germany* (New York: St. Martin's Press, 1992).

Stevenson, Harold W., and James W. Stigler. *The Learning Gap* (New York: Summit Books, 1992).

Suzuki, Daisetz T. *Zen and Japanese Culture* (Princeton, N.J.: Princeton University Press, 1959).

Suzuki, Shunryu. *Zen Mind, Beginner's Mind* (New York: Weatherkill, 1970).

Taber, George M. "The Deal That Saved the Sarnoff Center," *Business for Central New Jersey,* April 2, 1990, pp. 3–8.

Thurow, Lester. *Head to Head* (New York: William Morrow, 1992).

Tolchin, Martin and Susan J. *Selling Our Security* (New York: Alfred A. Knopf, 1992).

"Toward a National Semiconductor Strategy," second annual report (Washington, D.C.: National Advisory Committee on Semiconductors, 1991).

Toyoda, Eiji. *Toyota: Fifty Years in Motion* (Tokyo: Kodansha International, 1985).

Tyson, Laura D'Andrea. *Who's Bashing Whom? Trade Conflict in High-Technology Industries* (Washington, D.C.: Institute for International Economics, 1992).

U.S. General Accounting Office. "Sematech's Efforts to Strengthen the U.S. Semiconductor Industry" (Washington, D.C.: U.S. Government Printing Office, 1990).

U.S. Office of Technology Assessment. *Competing Economies: America, Europe and the Pacific Rim* (Washington, D.C.: U.S. Government Printing Office, 1991).

U.S. Trade Representative. *Foreign Trade Barriers* (Washington, D.C.: U.S. Government Printing Office, 1994).

Vogel, Ezra. *Japan as Number 1: Lessons for America* (New York: Harper, 1979).

Warshofsky, Fred. *The Chip War* (New York: Scribner's, 1989).

Watson, Alan. *The Germans: Who Are They Now?* (Chicago: Edition Q, 1992).

White, Merry. *The Japanese Educational Challenge* (New York: The Free Press, 1987).

Whiting, Robert. *You Gotta Have Wa* (New York: Vintage Books, 1990).

van Wolferen, Karel. *The Enigma of Japanese Power* (New York: Vintage Books, 1990).

Womack, James P., Daniel T. Jones, and Daniel Ross. *The Machine That Changed the World* (New York: Rawson Associates, 1990).

Yamamoto, Harumi. "The Lifetime Employment System Begins to Unravel," *Japan Quarterly,* October–December 1993, pp. 381–386.

Yamamura, Kozo, ed. *Japanese Investment in the United States: Should We Be Concerned?* (Seattle, Wash.: Society for Japanese Studies, 1989).

———, ed. *Japan's Economic Structure: Should It Change?* (Seattle, Wash.: Society for Japanese Studies, 1990).

——— and Yasukichi Yasuba, eds. *The Political Economy of Japan,* vol. 1, *The Domestic Transformation* (Stanford, Calif.: Stanford University Press, 1987).

Notes

Introduction

1. Stephen R. Covey, *The 7 Habits of Highly Effective People* (New York: Simon & Schuster/Fireside, 1989), p. 40.

2. Gary Hamel and C. K. Prahalad, "Strategy as Stretch and Leverage," *Harvard Business Review,* March–April 1993, p. 77.

3. Niccolò Machiavelli, *The Chief Works and Others* (Durham, N.C.: Duke University Press, 1965), p. 26.

4. Don Petersen, interview with the author, Feb. 2, 1991.

5. Peter F. Drucker, "The Theory of the Business," *Harvard Business Review,* March–April 1993, pp. 95–96.

6. Robert Lawrence, a Harvard economist, estimates that major U.S. multinational firms eliminated 2.2 million U.S.-based jobs from 1977 to 1991; *Fortune,* Dec. 26, 1994, p. 32.

7. *Building a Competitive America,* First Annual Report to the President and Congress (Washington, D.C.: Competitiveness Policy Council, 1992), p. 2 (chart).

8. Paul Krugman, *The Age of Diminished Expectations* (Cambridge, Mass.: MIT Press, 1990), p. 40.

9. Harold W. Stevenson and James W. Stigler, *The Learning Gap* (New York: Summit, 1992), p. 34.

10. Machiavelli, op. cit.

11. David Kearns, interview with the author, Oct. 15, 1993.

12. Jiro Aiko, interview with the author, Feb. 25, 1991.

13. Jack Murphy and William Bradford, interviews with the author, Sept. 8, 1992.

14. E. L. Artzt, speech, Stanford University, Nov. 12, 1987, p. 15.

15. Richard Laube, quoted by Artzt, ibid., p. 15.

16. Artzt, op. cit., p. 7.

17. *The Wall Street Journal,* Sept. 7, 1994, p. 7. In the rankings of the World Competitiveness Report prepared by the International Institute for Management and Development and the World Economic Forum, the authors cautioned that poor secondary school education and work attitudes as well as low savings rates raise the risk of a longer-term U.S. decline if not corrected.

18. "Japan Keeps Pace in U.S. Car Market," *The New York Times,* Jan. 6, 1995, pp. A1, D2.

19. U.S. Special Trade Representative, Foreign Trade Barriers (Washington, D.C.: U.S. Government Printing Office, 1994). For 1994, Foreign Trade Division, U.S. Census Bureau.

20. "Flowing Across the Pacific," Trade Flow Chart, *The New York Times,* Feb. 21, 1994, p. D1.

21. Foreign Trade Division, U.S. Census Bureau, Feb. 24, 1995.

22. For 1979–89, Jeff Faux, "Does America Have the Answer?" paper for International Seminar, Magdalen College, Oxford, Apr. 14–15, 1994; for 1989–92, Lawrence Mishel and Jared Bernstein, *The State of Working America 1992–93,* Economic Policy Institute Series (Armonk, N.Y.: M. E. Sharpe, 1993).

Part One: America Challenged

1. "Poll Shows Charitable Giving, Volunteering Still on Decline," *The Washington Post,* Oct. 19, 1994, p. A24.

2. Jeff Faux, "Does America Have the Answer?" paper for International Seminar, Magdalen College, Oxford, Apr. 14–15, 1994.

3. Paul Krugman, *The Age of Diminished Expectations* (Cambridge, Mass.: MIT Press, 1990), p. 12.

4. Ray Marshall and Marc Tucker, *Thinking for a Living: Education and the Wealth of Nations* (New York: Basic Books, 1992), p. xv.

5. Krugman, op. cit., p. 22.

6. Lester Thurow, *Head to Head* (New York: William Morrow, 1992), p. 29; Ira C. Magaziner and Mark Patinkin, *The Silent War* (New York: Vintage Books, 1990), p. ix.

Chapter 1: New Mind-Set/Old Mind-Set—Challengers Versus Champions

1. Atsushi Asada, interview with the author, Apr. 29, 1993.

2. Robert Whiting, *You Gotta Have Wa* (New York: Vintage Books, 1990), Chap. 1, especially pp. 15–25.

3. In 1991, Nomura Research Institute, Tokyo, estimated that the LCD market in 2000 would be $15 billion; *The Economist,* Apr. 13, 1991. Atsushi Asada, executive vice president of Sharp Electronics Corp., estimated it at $20 billion in an Apr. 29, 1993, interview with the author.

4. *The New York Times,* May 29, 1968, p. 47.

5. George Heilmeier, interview with the author, Mar. 5, 1993.

6. Richard Florida and David Browdy, "The Invention That Got Away," *Technology Review,* August–September 1991, p. 43.

7. A. F. Erbar, "Splitting Up RCA," *Fortune,* Mar. 22, 1982, p. 62.

8. Heilmeier, interview, Dec. 15, 1992.

9. Heilmeier, interview, Mar. 5, 1993.

10. Joe Friel, interview with the author, Mar. 5, 1993.

11. Heilmeier, speech, National Academy of Engineering, Washington, D.C., Sept. 29, 1992.

12. Heilmeier, interview, Mar. 5, 1993.

13. NHK broadcast, spring 1969.

14. Tomio Wada, interview with the author, Apr. 30, 1993.

15. Tadashi Sasaki, interview with the author, Nov. 6, 1991.

16. Sasaki, interview, Nov. 6, 1991.

17. Asada, interview, Apr. 29, 1993.

18. Friel, interview, Mar. 5, 1993.

19. Sasaki, interview, Nov. 6, 1991.

20. Larry Tannas, telephone interview with the author, Nov. 30, 1993.

21. Tannas, interview, Nov. 21, 1991.

22. Asada, interview, Apr. 29, 1993.

23. David Sanger, "Invented in U.S., Spurned in U.S., A Technology Flourishes in Japan," *The New York Times,* Dec. 16, 1990, p. A1.

24. Florida and Browdy, op. cit., p. 47.

25. Ibid., pp. 46–52.

26. Clyde Prestowitz, interview with the author, Mar. 26, 1992.

27. *The New York Times,* Aug. 16, 1993, p. D1; *The New York Times,* Sept. 26, 1991, p. D1. See also International Trade Commission, Publication 2413, "Certain High Information Content Flat Panel Displays and Display Glass Therefor from Japan," Washington, D.C.: U.S. Government Printing Office, August 1991.

28. *The Wall Street Journal,* Oct. 12, 1994, p. B6.

29. *The New York Times,* Apr. 27, 1994, p. A1.

30. Leslie Helm, "Flat Out Competition," *Los Angeles Times,* Jan. 23, 1994, pp. D1, D4.

31. "Japan's Liquid Crystal Gold Rush," *Business Week,* Jan. 17, 1994, p. 76.

32. L. J. Davis, "Did RCA Have to Be Sold?" *The New York Times Magazine,* Sept. 20, 1987, p. 23.

33. George M. Taber, "The Deal That Saved the Sarnoff Center," *Business for Central New Jersey,* Apr. 2, 1990, pp. 3–7.

34. Richard Williams, interview with the author, Mar. 5, 1993.

35. Arno Penzias, interview with the author, June 23, 1991.

36. James A. Carnes, "The Crisis in R&D," *Sarnoff: Fifty Years of Vision,* special supplement (Princeton, N.J.: Sarnoff Laboratory, 1992), p. 8.

37. The National Science Board reported that annual research spending by American industry fell from a peak of $78.8 billion in 1989 to $77.8 billion in 1990 and that nondefense research spending from all sources—government, universities, foundations, and industry—fell from $154.3 billion in 1989 to $151.6 billion in 1990. See *The New York Times,* Feb. 21, 1991, p. A1.

38. "The Competitive Strength of U.S. Industrial Science and Technology: Strategic Issues" (Washington, D.C.: National Science Board, 1992), quoted in *The New York Times,* Aug. 13, 1992, pp. D1, D6.

39. *Science and Engineering Indicators* (Washington, D.C.: National Science Foundation, February 1994), p. 100.

40. *The New York Times,* Nov. 29, 1993, pp. A1, D2.

41. *Building a Competitive America,* First Annual Report to the President and Congress (Washington, D.C.: Competitiveness Policy Council, 1992), pp. 2–3.

42. William J. Broad, "In the Realm of Technology, Japan Looms Ever Larger," *The New York Times,* May 28, 1991, pp. C1, C8.

43. "Big Companies in Japan Trim Research Budgets," *The New York Times,* Nov. 1, 1993, p. D2.

44. "Japanese, in a Painful Recession, Trim Industrial Research Outlays," *The New York Times,* Nov. 29, 1993, pp. A1, D3.

45. Dawon Kahng, interview with the author, June 23, 1991.

46. Gina Kolata, "Japanese Labs in U.S. Luring America's Computer Experts," *The New York Times,* Nov. 11, 1990, pp. A1, A24.

47. Frank Press, interview with the author, June 8, 1991.

48. Heilmeier, interview, March 5, 1993.

Chapter 2: The New Global Game—People, Quality, Flexibility, Trust

1. Matthias Kleinert, interview with the author, Mar. 7, 1991.

2. Roger Smith, "Saturn, Jupiter, Venus and Beyond: Automaking in the Age of Aquarius," *The UMTRI Research Review,* 15(2,3), p. 4.

3. Taichi Ohno, *Toyota Production System: Beyond Large-Scale Production* (Cambridge, Mass.: Productivity Press, 1988), p. 23.

4. Michael E. Porter, *The Competitive Advantage of Nations* (New York: The Free Press, 1990), pp. 377, 376.

5. Richard Smyser, interview with the author, Oct. 30, 1990.

6. Ilja Teutcher, conversation with the author, Jan. 28, 1994.

7. *Test,* January and February 1994 (Berlin: Stiftung Warentest).

8. Kleinert, interview, Mar. 7, 1991.

9. Helmut Werner, interview with the author, Jan. 20, 1993.

10. Horst Rebmann, interview with the author, Apr. 1, 1993.

11. Joe Kokuryo and Malcolm S. Salter, "The U.S. Auto Industry: Scenarios and Choices for the 1990s," Harvard Business School case study (Cambridge, Mass., 1991), Exhibit S-6.

12. Anne B. Fisher, "GM's Unlikely Revolutionist," *Fortune,* Mar. 19, 1984, pp. 106–112.

13. Cary Reich, "The Innovator," *The New York Times Magazine,* Apr. 21, 1985, p. 29.

14. Smith, op. cit.

15. Reich, op. cit., p. 29.

16. *GM in the '80s,* General Motors company film, 1990.

17. Roger Smith, telephone interview with the author, Jan. 18, 1995.

18. Ibid.

19. Reich, op. cit., p. 70.

20. Fisher, op. cit., p. 106.

21. Elmer Johnson, telephone interview with the author, Dec. 18, 1993.

22. Smith, telephone interview, Jan. 18, 1995.

23. *The Wall Street Journal,* Dec. 18, 1987, p. 30.

24. *The New York Times,* March 15, 1989, p. D4.

25. Smith, telephone interview, Jan. 18, 1995.

26. James P. Womack, Daniel T. Jones, and Daniel Roos, *The Machine That Changed the World* (New York: Rawson Associates, 1990), p. 81.

27. John Holusha, "Roger Smith's Troubled Second Act," *The New York Times,* Jan. 12, 1986, pp. F1, F23.

28. Johnson, telephone interview, Dec. 18, 1993.

29. Fisher, op. cit., pp. 106–112.

30. Thomas Wyman, telephone interview with the author, Aug. 27, 1992.

31. Harry J. Pearce, interview with the author, Mar. 20, 1993.

32. Wyman, telephone interview, Aug. 27, 1992.

33. Pearce, interview, Mar. 20, 1993.

34. Ohno, op. cit., p. xiv.

35. Alex Taylor III, "GM's $11,000,000,000 Turnaround," *Fortune,* Oct. 17, 1994, p. 68.

36. Kim Clark, "Working Papers of the MIT Commission on Industrial Productivity," vol. 1, pp. 26–33; also Womack et al., op. cit., pp. 110–111.

37. Donald Petersen, conversation with the author, Feb. 2, 1991; Harold A. Poling, interview with the author, May 16, 1991.

38. Ichizou Suzuki, Nippondenso, interview with the author, Jan. 28, 1993.

39. Kozo Yamamura, interview with the author, Feb. 28, 1992.

40. Kuniyasu Sakai, "The Feudal World of Japanese Manufacturing," *Harvard Business Review,* November–December 1990, p. 40.

41. David Friedman, *The Misunderstood Miracle: Industrial Development and Political Change in Japan* (Ithaca, N.Y.: Cornell University Press, 1988), pp. 10–22.

42. Karel van Wolferen, interview with the author, June 16, 1991.

43. Maryann Keller, *Collision: GM, Toyota, Volkswagen and the Race to Own the 21st Century* (New York: Doubleday, 1993), pp. 161–163.

44. John Paul MacDuffie, interview with the author, Nov. 19, 1992.

45. Mikio Kitano, interview with the author, Jan. 26, 1993.

46. Chris Donnegan, interview with the author, Oct. 14, 1992.

47. Kitano, interview, Jan. 25, 1993.

48. Philip Condit, interview with the author, July 28, 1992.

49. Womack et al., op. cit., pp. 96–98.

50. Ohno, op. cit., p. 23.

51. Tatsushi Nakayama, interview with the author, Apr. 24, 1993.

52. Kazuwaki Gotoh, interview with the author, Apr. 23, 1993.

53. Werner, interview, Mar. 31, 1993.

54. Werner, interview, Jan. 20, 1993.

55. Bruno Sacco, interview with the author, Jan. 20, 1993.

56. Dieter Zetsche, interview with the author, Apr. 1, 1993.

57. Jörg Schuster, interview with the author, Apr. 1, 1993.

58. Rebmann, interview, Apr. 1, 1993.

59. Zetsche, interview, Apr. 1, 1993.

60. Johnson, interview, Dec. 20, 1993.

61. Michael Damer, interview with the author, May 22, 1991.

62. Bill Childs, interview with the author, May 22, 1991.

63. Damer, interview, May 22, 1991.

64. James Womack, interview with the author, Feb. 19, 1991.

65. Kan Higashi, interview with the author, Mar. 1, 1991.

66. Childs, interview, May 22, 1991.

67. Higashi, interview, Mar. 1, 1991.

68. Agreement between New United Motor Manufacturing, Inc., and the United Auto Workers, July 1, 1988, p. 4.

69. Damer, interview, May 22, 1991.

70. NUMMI-UAW Agreement, op. cit., p. 45.

71. Womack et al., op. cit., p. 77.

72. Smith, telephone interview, Jan. 18, 1995.

73. Johnson, interview, Dec. 20, 1993.

74. Jim Harbour, interview with the author, Mar. 24, 1993.

75. Dick Lynch, interview with the author, Mar. 1, 1993.

76. Art Dobbins, interview with the author, Mar. 1, 1993.

77. Terry Mitler, interview with the author, Dec. 17, 1992.

78. Barbara Bell, interview with the author, Dec. 17, 1992.

79. *The New York Times,* July 29, 1994, pp. D1, D2; *The New York Times,* Feb. 1, 1995, pp. D1, D2.

80. Taylor, op. cit., p. 66.

81. *The New York Times,* Oct. 5, 1994, p. D1.

82. Pearce, interview, Mar. 20, 1993.

83. Pearce, quoted in Taylor, op. cit., Oct. 17, 1994, p. 74.

Chapter 3: The Success Reflex

1. Steve Lohr, "On the Road with Chairman Lou," *The New York Times,* June 26, 1994, sec. 3, pp. 1, 6.

2. Robert J. Corrigan, interview with the author, Dec. 4, 1992.

3. Glenn Henry, interview with the author, June 8, 1993.

4. Henry, interviews with the author, Feb. 4 and 6, 1994.

5. *Hoover's Handbook of American Business 1993* (Austin, Tex.: Reference Press, 1993), p. 2.

6. *The New York Times,* April 30, 1985, p. D5.

7. Joel Birnbaum, Bob Evans, and John Moussouris, interviews with the author, March 2–3, 1992.

8. Henry, interview, June 8, 1993.

9. Henry, interview, June 8, 1993.

10. Charles H. Ferguson and Charles R. Morris, *Computer Wars: The Fall of IBM and the Future of Global Technology* (New York: Times Books, 1994), p. xii.

11. See Marie Anchordoguy, *Computers Inc.: Japan's Challenge to IBM* (Cambridge, Mass.: Harvard University Press, 1989), especially Chap. 1.

12. The author heard this story from various sources, including Akio Mikuni, a Japanese financial expert, Oct. 22, 1992, and Glenn Fukushima, former deputy U.S. trade representative, Oct. 23, 1992.

13. Ferguson and Morris, op. cit., pp. 12–13.

14. Andy Grove, interview with the author, Mar. 4, 1992.

15. Paul B. Carroll, "Akers to IBM Employees: Wake UP!" *The Wall Street Journal,* May 29, 1991, pp. B1, B2.

16. John Akers, quoted in Carroll, ibid.

17. Ferguson and Morris, op. cit., pp. 37–38.

18. James C. McGroddy, interview with the author, Mar. 9, 1993.

19. McGroddy, interview with the author, Dec. 4, 1992.

20. Peter Drucker, "The Theory of the Business," *Harvard Business Review,* September–October 1994, pp. 95–104.

21. Henry, interview, June 8, 1993.

22. Charles Ferguson, interview with the author, Mar. 8, 1993.

23. Ferguson, interview, Mar. 8, 1993.

24. Dave Bradley, interview with the author, Apr. 2, 1992.

25. *PC Week,* Jan. 29, 1985, p. 122.

26. Bradley, interview, Apr. 2, 1992.

27. Ferguson and Morris, op. cit., pp. 55–65.

28. Ferguson, interview, Mar. 8, 1993.

29. Corrigan, interview, Dec. 4, 1992.

30. McGroddy, interview, Mar. 9, 1993.

31. Kurt Engelman, interview with the author, Jan. 4, 1993.

32. Anthony Santelli, interview with the author, Jan. 7, 1993.

33. Gregory E. Kinnear, interview with the author, Jan. 7, 1993.

34. Samuel Semel, interview with the author, Jan. 7, 1993.

35. Corrigan, interview, Dec. 14, 1993.

36. Corrigan, interview, Dec. 4, 1992.

37. International Data Corp., quoted in *AFP-Extel News,* Aug. 26, 1993; *The New York Times,* Jan. 24, 1995, pp. D1, D2.

38. David Kirkpatrick, "What's Driving the New PC Shakeout?" *Fortune,* pp. 109–122.

39. "IBM's Head of PC Unit Resigns Post," *The New York Times,* May 3, 1994, p. D1; "IBM's Earnings Jump Surprises Wall Street," *The Washington Post,* pp. D1, D5.

40. "The Custer Connection," *The Economist,* Apr. 9, 1994, pp. 69–70; "Maintaining a Mainframe of Mind," *The Washington Post,* Apr. 6, 1994, pp. D1, D5.

41. Nick Donofrio, interview with the author, Dec. 14, 1993.

42. *The New York Times,* Mar. 25, 1994, p. D1.

43. *The Wall Street Journal,* Apr. 27, 1993, p. A3.

44. "Lou Gerstner's First 30 Days," *Fortune,* May 31, 1993, p. 58.

45. "The Custer Connection," p. 70.

46. Steve Lohr, op. cit.

47. Lou Gerstner, "Dear Colleague" letter, Sept. 13, 1993, p. 1.

48. Henry, interview, Feb. 6, 1994.

49. Ferguson, telephone interview, Aug. 4, 1994.

50. Laurie Hays, "Gerstner Is Struggling As He Tries to Change Ingrained IBM Culture," *The Wall Street Journal,* May 13, 1994.

51. Lohr, op. cit., p. D6.

Part Two: Education

Chapter 4: School—Where the Race Begins

1. Sachiko Ikeda, interview with the author, Apr. 26, 1993.
2. Celeste Moore, interview with the author, Mar. 3, 1993.
3. Ilse Lindenberger, interview with the author, Mar. 30, 1993.
4. Tom Rohlen, interview with the author, Apr. 26, 1993.
5. Harold W. Stevenson and James W. Stigler, *The Learning Gap* (New York: Summit Books, 1992), p. 17.
6. Rohlen, interview, Apr. 26, 1993.
7. Rohlen, interview, Nov. 20, 1992.
8. Ikeda, interview, Apr. 26, 1993.
9. Stevenson and Stigler, op. cit., pp. 33–43.
10. Rohlen, interviews, Nov. 20, 1992, and Apr. 26, 1993.
11. Gien Miwa, interview with the author, Apr. 26, 1993.
12. Miwa, interview, Apr. 26, 1993.
13. Rohlen, interview, Apr. 26, 1993.
14. Stevenson and Stigler, op. cit., pp. 25, 82–84.
15. Tatsushi Nakayama, interview with the author, Mar. 3, 1993.
16. Nakayama, interview, Apr. 25, 1993.
17. Stevenson and Stigler, op. cit., pp. 54, 61, 68–70.
18. Moore, interview, Mar. 3, 1993.
19. Amy Streeter, interview with the author, Mar. 3, 1993.
20. Anne Heald, interview with the author, Oct. 15, 1993.
21. Stevenson and Stigler, op. cit., p. 41.
22. "Hard Science," ranking in science subjects compiled by the International Association for the Evaluation of Educational Achievement, *The New York Times,* Mar. 24, 1991, p. E4, showed American ten-year-olds ranking eighth behind Japan, Korea, Finland, Sweden, Hungary, Canada, and Italy. At age fourteen, Americans ranked thirteenth.
23. Education Secretary Richard W. Riley, in a speech at Georgetown University, Washington, D.C., Feb. 17, 1994, made a similar connection between poor school performance and parental help on homework, citing a 1993 school survey that found that "half the students with below-average grades reported that their parents had spent little or no time with them on school work."
24. Raymond Utter, interview with the author, Mar. 3, 1993.
25. Christie Utter, interview with the author, Mar. 3, 1993.
26. Lindenberger, interview, Mar. 30, 1993.
27. Claudia Schuster, interview with the author, Apr. 5, 1993.
28. Frau Scholz, interview with the author, Jan. 19, 1993.
29. Jörg Schuster, interview with the author, Apr. 5, 1993.
30. Schuster, interview, Apr. 5, 1993.

Chapter 5: High School—The Neglected Majority

1. Bert Grover, interview with the author, May 18, 1993.
2. Lester Thurow, interview with the author, Mar. 8, 1993.
3. Ray Marshall and Marc Tucker, *Thinking for a Living: Education and the Wealth of Nations* (New York: Basic Books, 1992), p. xiii.
4. Ibid., p. 64; Bert Grover, interviews with the author, Oct. 18, 1992, and May 18, 1993.

5. *America's Choice: High Skills or Low Wages!* Report of the Commission on the Skills of the American Workforce (Rochester, N.Y.: National Center on Education and the Economy, 1990), pp. 3, 14.

6. Williams C. Bainbridge and Charles Harrison, "How Are the Schools?," chart in special section, "Retooling the Schools," *The Wall Street Journal,* Mar. 31, 1989, p. R30.

7. Joellen Lightle, interview with the author, Mar. 2, 1993.

8. Grover, interview, May 18, 1993.

9. Lightle, interview, Mar. 2, 1993.

10. Lightle, interview, Mar. 3, 1993.

11. Walter Kennon, interview with Kathleen McCleery, Jan. 26, 1993.

12. Bill Oakes, interview with the author, Mar. 3, 1993.

13. Laurence Steinberg, telephone interview with Steve Johnson, Mar. 3, 1994.

14. Laurence Steinberg and S. M. Dornbusch, cited in Steven Waldman and Karen Springen, "Too Old, Too Fast," *Newsweek,* Nov. 16, 1992, p. 80.

15. Waldman and Springen, ibid., pp. 80–88, especially p. 81.

16. Jerry Keister, interview with the author, Mar. 2, 1993.

17. Lightle, interview, Mar. 3, 1993.

18. Jason Fuller, interview with the author, Mar. 4, 1993.

19. Ted Lewman, interview with the author, Mar. 3, 1993.

20. Grover, interview, May 18, 1993.

21. Alan Watson, *The Germans: Who Are They Now?* (Chicago: Edition Q, 1992), p. 165.

22. A. Hoffmann, ed., *Facts About Germany* (Frankfurt am Main: Societäts-Verlag, 1992) pp. 342–344.

23. Watson, op. cit., p. 169.

24. Ibid., p. 170.

25. German embassy, research data, Mar. 29, 1994.

26. Lester Thurow, *Head to Head* (New York: William Morrow, 1992), pp. 273ff.

27. Werner Rebham, interview with the author, Mar. 11, 1991.

28. Hartmut Welzel, interview with the author, Mar. 4, 1991.

29. Roland Wacker, interview with the author, Mar. 30, 1993.

30. Reinhold Wendel, interview with the author, Mar. 30, 1993.

31. Wacker, interview, Apr. 5, 1993.

32. Gerhard and Erika Wacker, interview with the author, Apr. 1, 1993.

33. R. Wacker, interview, Apr. 5, 1993.

34. Helmut Werner, interview with the author, Mar. 31, 1993.

35. Nicole Rose, interview with the author, Mar. 29, 1993.

36. Helmut Walker, interview with the author, Mar. 29, 1993.

37. Hilmar Kopper, interview with the author, Apr. 8, 1993.

38. Thurow, interview with the author, Mar. 8, 1993.

39. Steven R. Weisman, "How Do Japan's Students Do It? They Cram," *The New York Times,* Apr. 27, 1992, p. A1.

40. Teacher Suzuki, interview with the author, Jan. 29, 1993.

41. Deputy Principal Takei and Dean Kawai, interview with the author, Jan. 29, 1993.

42. Vance Grant, U.S. Department of Education, interview with Anne Lawrence, Mar. 31, 1992.

43. Tom Rohlen, interview with the author, Apr. 27, 1993.

44. Rohlen, interview, Apr. 27, 1993.

45. Minoru Ogiso, interview with the author, Apr. 27, 1993.

46. Hiro Imai, class, April 26, 1993.

47. Imai, interview with the author, Apr. 27, 1993.

48. Yasuteru Iyoda, interview with Steve York, July 1, 1993.

49. Imai, interview with Miho Kometani, Mar. 9, 1994.

50. *America's Choice,* pp. 4, 47, 46.
51. Marshall and Tucker, op. cit., p. 69.
52. *America's Choice,* pp. 24–26.
53. Labor Secretary Robert Reich, speech, Washington, D.C., Mar. 3, 1994.
54. Tom Kean, interview with the author, Oct. 15, 1993.

Chapter 6: Harlem—Teaching Habits of Mind

1. Deborah Meier, interview with the author, June 12, 1992.
2. Paul Schwarz, interview with the author, May 24, 1993.
3. Tom Kean, interview with the author, Oct. 15, 1993.
4. Meier, interview, June 12, 1992.
5. Schwarz, interview, May 24, 1993.
6. Shadia Alvarez, interview with the author, May 24, 1993.
7. Meier, interview, June 12, 1992.
8. Erran Matthews, interview with the author, May 24, 1993.
9. Schwarz, interview, May 24, 1993.
10. Carlos Lavazzeri IV, interview with the author, May 24, 1993.
11. Alvarez, interview, May 24, 1993.
12. Altagracia Faisal, interview with the author, May 26, 1993.
13. Meier, interview, May 25, 1993.
14. Meier, interview, May 25, 1993.
15. Marty Tuminaro and Shirley Hawkinson, interviews with the author, May 25, 1993.
16. Meier, interview, Apr. 13, 1992.
17. Meier, interview, June 12, 1992.
18. Schwarz, interview, May 24, 1993.
19. Meier, interview, May 25, 1993.
20. Meier, interview, June 12, 1992.
21. Joe Walter, interview with the author, May 26, 1993.
22. Semeika Smith, telephone interview with Susan Gray, May 20, 1993.
23. Theodore R. Sizer, *Horace's Compromise: The Dilemma of the American High School* (Boston: Houghton Mifflin, 1992), pp. 225–227.
24. Tuminaro, interview, May 25, 1993.
25. Lavazzeri, graduation committee oral exam, May 26, 1993.
26. Paul Schwarz, David Feldman, Chyann Higgs, Carlos Lavazzeri IV, graduation committee, May 26, 1993.
27. Meier, interview, May 25, 1993.
28. Schwarz, interview, May 20, 1994.
29. Matthews, interview, May 25, 1993.
30. See Sizer, op. cit.; also, "Dewey Disciple," *The Wall Street Journal,* Sept. 11, 1992, p. B4.
31. Carrie Holden, telephone interview with Steve Johnson, Coalition of Essential Schools, Sept. 14, 1994.
32. James P. Comer, "Educating Poor Minority Children," *Scientific American,* 259 (5) (November 1988), pp. 42–48.
33. David Kearns, telephone interview with the author, May 18, 1994.
34. *The New York Times,* Dec. 17, 1993, pp. A1, A36.
35. Education Commission of the States, "Measuring the Progress of Systemic Reform in Education," report to *Fortune* magazine's Sixth Annual Education Summit, November 1993.
36. Ibid.
37. Kean, interview, Oct. 15, 1993.

Chapter 7: Wisconsin—Business and School as Partners

1. John Torinus, interview with the author, May 19, 1993.
2. Brenda Radoll, interview with the author, May 19, 1993.
3. Bert Grover, telephone interview with the author, Sept. 15, 1994.
4. Grover, interview, May 18, 1993.
5. Ibid.
6. Grover, telephone interview, Sept. 15, 1994.
7. Grover, interview, June 20, 1991.
8. Pam Baumann, interview with the author, May 18, 1993.
9. Gary Baumann, interview with the author, May 18, 1993.
10. Eric Baumann, interview with the author, May 18, 1993.
11. Doug Paape, interview with the author, May 18, 1993.
12. Cindy Schey, interview with the author, May 19, 1993.
13. E. Baumann, interview, May 18, 1993.
14. E. Baumann, interview, May 18, 1993.
15. G. Baumann, telephone interview, Sept. 15, 1994.
16. Torinus, interview, May 19, 1993.
17. Radoll, interview, May 19, 1993.
18. Torinus, telephone interview, Sept. 15, 1994.
19. Torinus, telephone interview, Sept. 15, 1994.
20. Torinus, interview, May 18, 1993.
21. Grover, telephone interview, Sept. 15, 1994.
22. Wayne Rowley, interview with the author, Sept. 11, 1992.
23. Lois Ann Porter, interview with the author, Feb. 10, 1992.
24. Susan Goldberger, R. Kazis, and M. O'Flanagan, *Learning Through Work: Designing and Implementing Quality Worksite Learning for High School Students* (New York: Manpower Demonstration Research Corporation, 1994).
25. *The New York Times,* Apr. 23, 1994, p. A9.
26. President William Clinton, interview with the author, Dec. 1, 1993.
27. Ibid.
28. Tom Kean, interview with the author, Oct. 15, 1993.
29. Anne Heald, interview with the author, Oct. 15, 1993.

Part Three: Business

Chapter 8: People

1. Koremasa Anami, interview with the author, Nov. 20, 1992.
2. Wolfgang Wenzel, interview with the author, Jan. 15, 1993.
3. Tom Usher, interview with the author, Aug. 4, 1993.
4. In an interview with the author on Mar. 15, 1994, Professor Haruo Shimada of Keio University, a specialist on Japanese employment practices, provided the estimate that about 40 percent of Japan's workforce is covered by lifetime employment provisions.
5. Takeo Doi, *The Anatomy of Dependence* (Tokyo and New York: Kodansha International, 1973), pp. 14–16, 84–95.
6. Eisuke Sakakibara, interview with the author, Apr. 19, 1993.
7. *Metal Bulletin,* Feb. 21, 1994, p. 16.
8. Anami, interview, Nov. 22, 1992.
9. Etsuya Washio, interview with the author, Oct. 22, 1992.
10. Toshihiro Okuyama, interview with the author, May 10, 1993.
11. Nobuyuki Abe, interview with the author, May 10, 1993.
12. Abe, interview, May 10, 1993.

13. Jun Ishikawa, interview with the author, Feb. 3, 1993.

14. Masaru Hirayama, interview with the author, May 11, 1993.

15. Harumi Yamamoto, "The Lifetime Employment System Begins to Unravel," *Japan Quarterly,* October–December 1993, pp. 381–383.

16. Natsuomi Wakamura, interview with the author, Feb. 3, 1993.

17. Hironori Yano, conversation with the author, Mar. 15, 1994.

18. Yamamoto, op. cit., pp. 383–384; Robert Chiapetta, "Restructuring Japanese Style," *Inside/Outside Japan,* February 1994, p. 3.

19. "Gaze Fixed on the Far Horizon," *Financial Times,* Nov. 8, 1993, pp. 5–6.

20. "Steelmakers Suffer Losses, Cut Dividends," Kyodo News Service, Mar. 8, 1994.

21. *The Economist,* Sept. 3, 1994, p. 102.

22. "Japanese Life Employment System Under Pressure," Reuters, Feb. 22, 1994.

23. Japan Productivity Institute, survey, May 19–June 30, 1993.

24. John Paul MacDuffie, telephone interview, Oct. 14, 1994.

25. Abe, interview, May 10, 1993.

26. Yoshihisa Hayashi, interview with the author, Feb. 1, 1993.

27. Usher, interview, Aug. 4, 1993.

28. Tim Reeves, interview with the author, Dec. 20, 1992.

29. "Steelmaking's Decline," chart, *The Washington Post,* Apr. 12, 1992, p. A26.

30. Andy Keyso, interview with the author, Dec. 19, 1992.

31. Nancy Mapes, interview with the author, Dec. 19, 1992.

32. Joe Vandergrift, interview with the author, Dec. 20, 1992.

33. Reeves, interview, Dec. 20, 1993.

34. Reeves, interview, July 15, 1993.

35. Vandergrift, telephone interview with Steve Johnson, Mar. 23, 1994.

36. Ross Koppel and Alice Hoffmann, "What Do We Do to and for the Unemployed?" paper presented to conference of the American Sociological Association, January 1994, pp. 14–27.

37. Lamar Lewin, "Low Pay and Closed Doors Greet Young in Job Market," *The New York Times,* Mar. 10, 1994, pp. A1, B12.

38. Dirk Johnson, "Family Struggles to Make Do After Fall from Middle Class," *The New York Times,* Mar. 11, 1994, pp. A1, A14.

39. Louis Uchitelle, "Stanching the Loss of Good Jobs," *The New York Times,* Jan. 31, 1993, pp. F1, F6.

40. Lewin, op. cit., p. B12.

41. "Recovery's Weak Spot Is Wages," *The Washington Post,* Mar. 9, 1994, p. A1.

42. General Federal Labor Agency, *This Week in Germany,* Mar. 11, 1994, p. 5; *This Week in Germany,* June 17, 1994, p. 4.

43. W. R. Smyser, *The Economy of United Germany* (New York: St. Martin's Press, 1992), pp. 79–83.

44. Average German factory wages at 1993 exchange rates were $26 per hour, $10 more than in America and Japan. See Silvia Nasar, "The American Economy Back on Top," *The New York Times,* Feb. 27, 1994, sec. 3, pp. 1, 6.

45. Wenzel, comments at meeting, Jan. 15, 1993.

46. Uwe May, interview with Melinda Crane-Engel, Nov. 11, 1994.

47. Wolfgang Kobernick, interview with the author, Jan. 12, 1993.

48. May, interview, Nov. 11, 1994.

49. Peter Harmel, interview with the author, Jan. 13, 1993.

50. Wenzel, interview with the author, Jan. 15, 1993.

Chapter 9: Partnership

1. Don Petersen, interview with the author, Feb. 2, 1991.

2. Bob Rutovic, interview with Kathleen McCleery, Apr. 23, 1993.

3. Reg Anson, interview with the author, May 27, 1993.

4. Petersen, interview, Feb. 2, 1991.

5. Harold A. "Red" Poling, interview with the author, May 16, 1991.

6. Petersen, interview, Feb. 2, 1991.

7. David Halberstam, *The Reckoning* (New York: Avon, 1986), pp. 312–314.

8. John Holusha, "W. Edwards Deming, Expert on Business Management, Dies at 93," *The New York Times,* Dec. 21, 1993, p. C8.

9. W. Edwards Deming, *Out of the Crisis* (Cambridge, Mass.: MIT Center for Advanced Engineering Study, 1986), pp. 26, 97.

10. See ibid., Chap. 2, especially his Fourteen Points for management, pp. 23–24; also Chap. 3, sections on leadership and worker relations, p. 134.

11. Petersen, interview, Feb. 1, 1991.

12. Ernest Savoie, interview with the author, Apr. 9, 1991.

13. Petersen, interview, Feb. 2, 1991.

14. Reg Anson, Arnold Banks, and Lucius Evans, interviews with the author, May 27, 1993; Roland Dennis, interview with Kathleen McCleery, Apr. 23, 1993.

15. Poling, interview, May 16, 1991.

16. Poling, interview, May 28, 1993.

17. Petersen, interview, Feb. 1, 1991.

18. Barry Bluestone and Irving Bluestone, *Negotiating the Future: A Labor Perspective on American Business* (New York: Basic Books, 1992), pp. 176–177.

19. Jim Harbour, "The South Side of Chicago," *Automotive Industries,* November 1992, p. 9.

20. Anson, interview, May 27, 1993.

21. Banks, interview, May 27, 1993.

22. Jim Harbour, "1992 Update to *The Harbour Report, 1989–1992,*" Oct. 2, 1992, pp. 1–4; Harbour, op. cit., p. 9.

23. Chicago *Sun-Times,* Dec. 9, 1992, p. 3A.

24. Evans, interview, May 27, 1993.

25. Anson, interview, May 27, 1993.

26. Savoie, interview, Apr. 9, 1991.

27. Anson, interview, May 27, 1993.

28. Banks, interview, May 27, 1993.

29. Anson, interview, May 27, 1993.

30. Anson, interview, May 27, 1993.

31. Rutovic, interview, Apr. 23, 1993.

32. Deborah Kent, interview with the author, May 27, 1993.

33. Ron Dooley and Joe Robertson, interviews with the author, May 27, 1993.

34. Heidi Tillotson, interview with the author, May 27, 1993.

35. Banks, interview, May 27, 1993.

Chapter 10: Power Sharing

1. Richard Smyser, interview with the author, Nov. 19, 1992.

2. Edzard Reuter, interview with the author, Mar. 30, 1993.

3. Richard G. "Skip" LeFauve, telephone interview with the author, Sept. 14, 1994.

4. Reuter, interview, Mar. 30, 1993.

5. Hilmar Kopper, interview with the author, Apr. 8, 1993.

6. Karl Feuerstein, interview with the author, Jan. 23, 1993.

7. Helmut Werner, interview with the author, Apr. 4, 1993.

8. W. R. Smyser, *The Economy of United Germany* (New York: St. Martin's Press, 1992), pp. 79–83.

9. Alan Watson, *The Germans: Who Are They Now?* (Chicago: Edition Q, 1992), pp. 159–

160. He quotes the autobiography of Christabel Bielenberg calling Berlin "a frozen sea of shattered ruins."

10. Reuter, interview, Mar. 30, 1993.

11. Karl Heinz Kaske, quoted in Watson, op. cit., p. 166.

12. Smyser, op. cit., p. 140.

13. Watson, op. cit., p. 163; David Marsh, *The Germans* (New York: St. Martin's Press, 1989), p. 120.

14. Wolfgang Roth, interview with the author, Mar. 4, 1991.

15. Eberhard von Kuenheim, interview with the author, Mar. 11, 1991.

16. Erich Klemm and Helmut Petri, interviews with the author, Mar. 31, 1993.

17. Reuter, interview, Mar. 30, 1993.

18. Franz Steinkühler, interview with the author, Oct. 30, 1992.

19. Steinkühler, interview, Apr. 1, 1993.

20. Steinkühler, interview, Apr. 8, 1993.

21. *The New York Times,* May 21, 1993, p. D2.

22. Hilmar Kopper, interview with the author, Apr. 8, 1993.

23. Kopper, interview, Sept. 21, 1992.

24. Kopper, interview, Apr. 8, 1993.

25. Daimler-Benz, press release, Apr. 13, 1994, pp. 1–3.

26. Feuerstein, interview, Mar. 26, 1993.

27. Jörg Barczynski, interview with the author, Nov. 11, 1994.

28. Steve Silvia, interview with Stefan Sagner, Apr. 2, 1994; *Der Spiegel,* Nov. 29, 1993, p. 114.

29. Department of Labor, press release, Feb. 9, 1994.

30. Stephen Sleigh, Michael Kapsa, and Chris Hall, "Union Busting Is Bad for Business," Graduate School, City University of New York, Occasional Paper no. 12, October 1992.

31. Al Weygand, interview with the author, Mar. 23, 1993.

32. Robert L. Rose and Alex Kotlowitz, "Back to Bickering," *The Wall Street Journal,* Nov. 23, 1992, pp. A1, A9.

33. Caterpillar entry, *Hoover's Handbook of American Business 1993* (Austin, Tex.: Reference Press, 1993), pp. 1–5.

34. Donald Fites, interview with the author, Mar. 23, 1993.

35. Weygand, interview, Mar. 23, 1993.

36. Terry Thorstenson, letter to the author, Apr. 13, 1993.

37. Fites, interview, Mar. 23, 1993.

38. Rose and Kotlowitz, op. cit., p. A9.

39. Peoria *Journal Star,* Mar. 9, 1993, and Mar. 18, 1993.

40. Thorstenson, telephone conversation, Dec. 17, 1992.

41. For 1992, see Caterpillar entry, *Hoover's Handbook,* p. 4; for 1993, see *Fortune,* Apr. 18, 1994, pp. 220–221.

42. "Strike at 'Cat' Becomes Stand for Way of Life," *The Washington Post,* July 3, 1994, p. A3; "Caterpillar Tries to Fill Strikers' Jobs," *The New York Times,* June 24, 1994, p. D3.

43. *Business Week,* February 6, 1995, p. 38.

44. "For Now, the UAW Can't Keep Cat from Purring," *Business Week,* Oct. 3, 1994; "UAW's Long Strike Fails to Crimp Output at Caterpillar's Plants," *The Wall Street Journal,* Oct. 4, 1994, pp. A1, A9.

45. *Business Week,* February 6, 1995, p. 38.

46. Marsh Campbell, telephone interview with Kathleen McCleery, Feb. 10, 1994.

47. J. Burgess Winter, speech, Chicago, July 26, 1993.

48. See Saul Rubinstein, Michael Bennett, and Thomas Kochan, "The Saturn Partnership: Co-Management and the Reinvention of the Local Union," paper for Work in America Institute, June 1993, pp. 1–6; Robert R. Rehder, "Is Saturn Competitive?" *Business Horizons,* March–April 1994, pp. 7–10.

49. Richard G. LeFauve and Arnoldo C. Hax, "Managerial and Technological Innovations at Saturn Corporation," *MIT Management,* Spring 1992, pp. 8–10.

50. Rubinstein et al., op. cit., pp. 15–16; author's emphasis.

51. LeFauve, telephone interview, Sept. 13, 1994.

52. LeFauve, quoted in Rubinstein et al., op. cit., p. 12.

53. Gregg Martin, telephone interview with the author, Sept. 13, 1994.

54. "Suddenly, Saturn's Orbit Is Getting Wobbly," *Business Week,* Feb. 28, 1994, p. 34.

55. Rubinstein et al., op. cit., pp. 10–14.

56. LeFauve, telephone interview, Sept. 14, 1994.

57. "Saturn Design Teams Turn on a Dime," *The Washington Post,* July 6, 1992, p. A11.

58. LeFauve, quoted in Rubinstein et al., op. cit., p. 19.

59. "Saturn: Labor's Love Lost?" *Business Week,* Feb. 8, 1993, p. 122.

60. *The Wall Street Journal,* Jan. 15, 1993, p. A3.

61. *The Wall Street Journal,* Apr. 5, 1993, p. A4.

62. Martin, telephone interviews, Sept. 14, 1994, and Jan. 17, 1995.

63. *The New York Times,* Aug. 11, 1993, pp. A1, A10.

64. Roger Smith, telephone interview with author, Jan. 18, 1995.

65. James Bennet, "Saturn, GM's Big Hope, Is Taking Its First Lumps," *The New York Times,* Mar. 29, 1994, pp. A1, D2.

66. LeFauve, telephone interview, Sept. 14, 1994.

67. *The Wall Street Journal,* Oct. 5, 1994, p. A5.

Chapter 11: Stakeholders Versus Shareholders

1. Hilmar Kopper, interview with the author, Apr. 8, 1993.

2. Michael Porter, "Capital Choices: Changing the Way America Invests in Industry," research report (Washington, D.C.: Council on Competitiveness and Harvard Business School, 1992), pp. 3, 5.

3. Lester Thurow, interview with the author, Mar. 8, 1993.

4. *Science and Engineering Indicators* (Washington, D.C.: National Science Foundation, February 1994), p. 100.

5. Competitiveness Policy Council, *First Annual Report,* March 1992, pp. 2–3.

6. Porter, op. cit., pp. 3, 6, 25–26.

7. Supplement to *OECD Observer,* no. 188, June–July 1994, pp. 24–25.

8. "Deutsche Bank Buys Control of Daimler," *Facts on File World News Digest,* 1975, pp. 31, 33.

9. W. R. Smyser, *The Economy of United Germany* (New York: St. Martin's Press, 1992), p. 89.

10. Kopper, interview, Apr. 8, 1993.

11. See Porter, op. cit., pp. 33–66, especially pp. 54–55.

12. Edzard Reuter, interview with the author, Mar. 30, 1993.

13. "Mighty German Banks Face Curb," *The New York Times,* Nov. 7, 1989, pp. D1, D6.

14. John Dornberg, "The Spreading Might of Deutsche Bank," *The New York Times Magazine,* Sept. 23, 1990, pp. 26, 30, 60.

15. Deutsche Bank, annual report, 1993, p. 82.

16. Dornberg, op. cit., p. 28, confirmed by Hilmar Kopper to the author.

17. Alan Watson, *The Germans: Who Are They Now?* (Chicago: Edition Q, 1992), p. 173.

18. Jonathan Carr, "Daimler-Benz Buys Majority Stake in AEG," *Financial Times,* Oct. 15, 1985, p. 1.

19. In 1994, Metallgesellschaft, a huge machine-tool firm and a Deutsche Bank client, nearly went under because of huge losses in oil-futures trading; another client, Jürgen Schneider, a big commercial developer, suddenly vanished, skipping out on $750 million in loans from Deutsche

Bank. Critics charged that Deutsche Bank was too cozy with clients, at the price of proper vigilance. *The New York Times,* Apr. 26, 1994, p. D2.

20. "Whose Firm, Whose Money?" *The Economist,* May 5, 1990, p. 9.

21. Jay W. Lorsch, with Elizabeth MacIver, *Pawns or Potentates: The Reality of America's Corporate Boards* (Boston: Harvard Business School Press, 1989), p. 3.

22. David Henry, "High Churnover," *Forbes,* Mar. 10, 1986, p. 146.

23. Michael Gerlach, "*Keiretsu* Organization in the Japanese Economy," in Chalmers Johnson, Laura D'Andrea Tyson, and John Zysman, eds., *Politics and Productivity: How Japan's Development Strategy Works* (New York: HarperBusiness, 1989), p. 158.

24. Jay W. Lorsch and Elizabeth A. MacIver, "Corporate Governance and Investment Time Horizons," unpublished paper, Harvard Business School, October 1991, p. 15, quoted by permission.

25. Lorsch with MacIver, op. cit., 1989, p. 3.

26. Laurence Zuckerman, "Shades of the Go-Go 80s: Takeovers in a Comeback," *The New York Times,* Nov. 3, 1994, p. A1.

27. Margaret M. Blair, "CEO Pay: Why Such a Contentious Issue?" *The Brookings Review,* Winter 1994, p. 26.

28. Haynes Johnson, *Sleepwalking Through History: America in the Reagan Years* (New York: W. W. Norton, 1991), p. 432.

29. Philip R. O'Connell, "A Timely Halt to the Raiders' Shell Game," *The New York Times,* Dec. 22, 1985, sec. 3, p. 2.

30. Johnson, op. cit., pp. 432–437.

31. Thurow, interview, Mar. 8, 1993.

32. Alfred P. Chandler, Jr., *The Visible Hand: The Managerial Revolution in American Business* (Cambridge, Mass.: The Belknap Press, 1977), pp. 497–500.

33. Ibid., pp. 492–493. Generally, I have relied on Chaps. 12 and 13 and the conclusion.

34. Lorsch and MacIver, op. cit., 1991, pp. 15–17.

35. Quoted in "From the Bridge to the Boiler Room," *The Economist,* May 5, 1990, p. 11.

36. Ibid.

37. "Directors, Wake Up!" *Fortune,* June 16, 1992, p. 86.

38. Myles Mace, quoted in Lorsch with MacIver, op. cit., 1989, p. 4.

39. Graef Crystal, interview with the author, Mar. 12, 1993.

40. Lorsch and MacIver, op. cit., 1991, p. 21.

41. Thurow, interview, Mar. 8, 1993.

42. Carl Icahn, quoted in "From the Bridge to the Boiler Room," p. 10.

43. *The Economist,* Feb. 1, 1992, p. 19.

44. *The New York Times,* Jan. 20, 1992, p. D8.

45. "Quote the Maven, Cut Some More," *The Washington Post,* Jan. 29, 1992, p. G1.

46. "Paycheck Peeping," *The New York Times,* Mar. 1, 1992, sec. 7, p. 1.

47. "Executive Pay: The Shareholders Strike Back," *Time,* May 4, 1992, pp. 46–48.

48. "Executive Pay: The Party Ain't Over Yet," *Business Week,* Apr. 26, 1993, pp. 56–64.

49. "That Eye-popping Executive Pay: Is Anybody Worth This Much?" *Business Week,* Apr. 25, 1994, pp. 52–99.

50. Crystal, interview, Mar. 12, 1993.

51. Crystal, telephone interview, Apr. 22, 1994.

52. Crystal, telephone interview, Apr. 22, 1994.

53. *Fortune,* June 17, 1991, p. 76.

54. "Executive Pay," op. cit., p. 47.

55. Bevis Longstreth, "CEO Pay: Don't Let the Government Decide," *The Washington Post,* Mar. 17, 1992, p. A23.

56. Peter Passell, "Those Big Executive Salaries May Mask a Bigger Problem," *The New York Times,* Apr. 20, 1992, pp. A1, D5.

57. "Die Topverdiener der Nation" ("The Nation's Top Earners"), *Forbes* (German ed.), Mar. 3, 1990, pp. 141–169.

58. David Sanger, "In Japan's Bad Times, Chiefs Say Sorry and Cut Their Pay," *The New York Times,* Apr. 11, 1992, pp. A1, A42.

59. "Best Practices in Corporate Restructuring," *Wyatt's 1993 Survey of Corporate Restructuring* (Chicago: The Wyatt Company, 1993), p. 34.

60. Blair, op. cit., p. 26.

61. Ibid., pp. 26–27.

62. Ibid.

63. "World Stock Markets—Ten-Year Total Returns, 1983–1993," Morgan Stanley, research paper, 1994.

64. Thomas Wyman, telephone interview with the author, Aug. 27, 1992.

65. Harry Pearce, interview with the author, Mar. 20, 1993.

66. Elmer Johnson, telephone interview with the author, Dec. 20, 1993.

67. Wyman, telephone interview, Aug. 27, 1992.

68. *The Economist,* Aug. 10, 1991, p. 64.

69. Johnson, telephone interview, Dec. 20, 1993.

70. Wyman, telephone interview, Aug. 27, 1992.

71. *The Washington Post,* Apr. 4, 1990.

72. *The New York Times,* Apr. 12, 1992, p. A1.

73. Wyman, telephone interview, Aug. 27, 1992.

74. Warren Brown and Frank Swoboda, "An Outside Director's Coup Inside GM," *The Washington Post,* Apr. 12, 1992, pp. H1, H4.

75. "Directors, Wake Up!" p. 89.

76. Ibid. pp. 85–90.

77. "Boardrooms: The Ties That Blind?" *Business Week,* May 2, 1994, pp. 112–113.

78. Crystal, interview, Apr. 22, 1994.

79. Dale Hanson, telephone interview with Steve Johnson, May 4, 1994.

80. *Business Week,* Oct. 3, 1994, p. 114.

81. "Their Cup Runneth Over—Again," *Business Week,* Mar. 28, 1994, pp. 26–27.

82. "The King Is Dead," *Fortune,* Jan. 11, 1993, p. 34.

83. Robert C. Pozen, "Institutional Investors: The Reluctant Activists," *Harvard Business Review,* January–February 1994, pp. 140–149.

84. *The New York Times,* Mar. 29, 1994, p. D6; *The Wall Street Journal,* Mar. 29, 1994, p. A4.

85. Jay Lorsch, telephone interview with the author, May 4, 1994.

86. Lorsch and MacIver, op. cit., 1991, p. 22.

87. Margaret M. Blair, *Ownership and Control: Rethinking Corporate Governance for the Twenty-first Century* (Washington, D.C.: The Brookings Institution, 1995); manuscript cited by permission, pp. 286–306.

88. Porter, op. cit., pp. 73–90, especially p. 78.

89. Ibid., pp. 76–97.

90. Ibid., p. 16.

91. "A Firm of Their Own," *The Economist,* June 11, 1994, pp. 59–60.

92. Joseph Raphael Blasi and Douglas Lynn Krause, *The New Owners: The Mass Emergence of Employee Ownership in Public Companies and What It Means to American Business* (New York: HarperBusiness, 1992), pp. 2–3.

93. Tom Usher, interview with the author, Aug. 4, 1993.

94. Lynn Williams, interview with the author, Mar. 14, 1994.

Chapter 12: The Network

1. Chalmers Johnson, *"Keiretsu:* An Outsider's View," *Insight,* September–October, 1990, p. 15.

2. Naohiro Amaya, quoted by Robert Kearns, *Zaibatsu America* (New York: The Free Press, 1992), pp. 170–171.

3. Kenneth Courtis, interview with the author, May 12, 1993.

4. Michael Gerlach, *Alliance Capitalism: The Social Organization of Japanese Business* (Berkeley: University of California Press, 1992), pp. 55, 74–75.

5. Ibid., p. 129.

6. Michael Gerlach, "*Keiretsu* Organization in the Japanese Economy: Analysis and Trade Implications," in Chalmers Johnson, Laura D'Andrea Tyson, and John Zysman, eds., *Politics and Productivity: How Japan's Development Strategy Works* (New York: HarperBusiness, 1989), pp. 155–163.

7. Paul Blustein, "Japan's Corporate Connections Create Challenge for U.S. Business," *The Washington Post,* Oct. 6, 1991, pp. A1, A35.

8. Marie Anchordoguy, interview with the author, May 3, 1993.

9. Amaya, op. cit., pp. 170–171.

10. Johnson, op. cit.

11. Kozo Yamamura, interview with the author, Feb. 28, 1992.

12. Clyde V. Prestowitz, Jr., *Trading Places: How We Allowed Japan to Take the Lead* (New York: Basic Books, 1988), p. 160.

13. Clyde Prestowitz, interview with the author, Mar. 26, 1992.

14. Gerlach, op. cit., 1992, pp. 81–86.

15. Courtis, interview, May 12, 1993.

16. Kearns, op. cit., p. 159.

17. Tsuneo Wakai, interview with the author, May 12, 1993.

18. *Hoover's Handbook of World Business 1993* (Austin, Tex.: Reference Press, 1993), Mitsubishi entry, pp. 1–2.

19. Karel van Wolferen, *The Enigma of Japanese Power* (New York: Vintage Books, 1990), p. 47.

20. Nine of Mitsubishi's twenty-nine core companies did business totaling $267 billion in 1993. Mitsubishi Corporation's trading volume was $155 billion. Mitsubishi Electric, Mitsubishi Heavy Industries, Mitsubishi Motors, and five other large Mitsubishi firms grossed another $112 billion. See *Fortune,* "The World's Largest Industrial Corporations," July 26, 1993, pp. 191–204.

21. David E. Sanger, "Unusual Path to the Top at Mitsubishi," *The New York Times,* Apr. 13, 1992, pp. D1, D3.

22. Minoru Makihara, interview with the author, Apr. 19, 1993.

23. *Industrial Grouping in Japan,* 8th ed. (Tokyo: Dodwell Marketing Consultants, 1988–89), p. 9.

24. Makihara, interviews, Apr. 19, 1993, and Feb. 1, 1993.

25. *Business Week,* Sept. 24, 1990, p. 101.

26. Gerlach, op. cit., pp. 240–245.

27. Makihara, interview, Apr. 19, 1993.

28. Takeshi Hashimoto, interview with the author, Feb. 3, 1993.

29. Makihara, interview, Apr. 19, 1993.

30. Courtis, interview, May 12, 1993.

31. "Mighty Mitsubishi Is on the Move," *Business Week,* Sept. 24, 1990, pp. 98–101.

32. Ibid., pp. 105–106.

33. Jack Brooks, letter to Janet D. Steiger, chairman, Federal Trade Commission, Mar. 20, 1990.

34. *The New York Times,* Feb. 24, 1992, p. D5; Apr. 4, 1992, p. 43.

35. *The New York Times,* Feb. 18, 1995, pp. 37, 49.

36. Wolferen, op. cit., p. 393.

37. Laura D'Andrea Tyson, *Who's Bashing Whom? Trade Conflict in High-Technology Industries* (Washington, D.C.: Institute for International Economics, 1992), p. 83.

38. Robert L. Cutts, "Capitalism in Japan: Cartels and *Keiretsu*," *Harvard Business Review*, July–August 1992, p. 50.

39. For a documented analysis of the depressing effect of *keiretsu* on Japanese imports, see Robert Z. Lawrence, "Efficient or Exclusionist? The Import Behavior of Japanese Corporate Groups" (Washington, D.C.: The Brookings Institution, Papers on Economic Activity, 1:1991).

40. David E. Sanger, "Settlement by Japanese Builders," *The New York Times*, Nov. 24, 1989, p. D1; *International Trade Reporter*, 7(30) (July 25, 1990), p. 1115.

41. Steven R. Weisman, "Foreigners Are Crying Foul over Japan Airport Contract," *The New York Times*, Nov. 23, 1990, p. D1.

42. "Japan-U.S. Trade; Turbulence over Kansai," *The Economist*, June 14, 1986, p. 68; "Section 301 Investigation: USTR Finds Japan Discrimination against U.S. Firms but Rules out Retaliation," *International Construction Newsletter*, 14(9) (December 1989), pp. 1–2.

43. Makihara, interview, Apr. 19, 1993.

44. "Japanese Industrial Policy: The Postwar Record and the Case of Supercomputers," in U.S. Office of Technology Assessment, *Competing Economies: America, Europe and the Pacific Rim* (Washington, D.C.: U.S. Government Printing Office, 1991), pp. 253–267.

45. Takehito Kato, interview with the author, May 13, 1993.

46. Kato, interview, May 13, 1993; Marie Anchordoguy, "Japanese-American Conflict and Super-Computers," *Political Science Quarterly*, 109(1) (Spring 1994) pp. 58–59.

47. Anchordoguy, interview, May 3, 1993.

48. Tyson, op. cit., p. 78.

49. Yoshikazu Hori, interview with the author, May 13, 1993.

50. Hori, interview, May 13, 1993; Anchordoguy, interview, May 3, 1993.

51. Hori and Kato, interviews, May 3, 1993.

52. Anchordoguy, interview, May 3, 1993.

53. Chalmers Johnson, telephone interview with Steve Johnson, May 5, 1994.

54. U.S. Trade Representative, *Foreign Trade Barriers* (Washington, D.C.: U.S. Government Printing Office, 1994), pp. 144–145.

55. Tyson, op. cit., p. 109.

56. *The New York Times*, Sept. 15, 1994, p. D3.

57. *The New York Times*, Jan. 10, 1992, p. A1.

Chapter 13: Counterattack

1. Bob Galvin, interview with the author, June 14, 1993.

2. George Fisher, interview with the author, June 9, 1993.

3. Ira Wolf, interview with the author, Nov. 4, 1991.

4. Galvin, interview, June 14, 1993.

5. *The New York Times*, Feb. 15, 1994, p. D7.

6. Clyde V. Prestowitz, Jr., *Trading Places: How We Allowed Japan to Take the Lead* (New York: Basic Books, 1988), p. 238.

7. Fisher, interview, May 21, 1991.

8. Jim Caile, interview with the author, Dec. 17, 1991.

9. Susumu Cho, interview with the author, Feb. 8, 1993.

10. *The New York Times*, Aug. 20, 1982, p. D5.

11. "The Rival Japan Respects," *Business Week*, Nov. 13, 1989, p. 108.

12. Fisher, interview, May 21, 1991.

13. Galvin, interview, June 14, 1993.

14. Fisher, interview, June 9, 1993.

15. Galvin, interview, June 14, 1993.

16. Fisher, interview, May 21, 1991.

17. Richard Bretow, interview with the author, Dec. 17, 1991.

18. Ed Bales, interview with the author, Dec. 18, 1991.

19. Galvin, interview, June 14, 1993.

20. Fisher, interview, June 9, 1993.

21. Fisher, interview, June 9, 1993.

22. Lee Trevino, Motorola ad, 1993.

23. *The New York Times,* Nov. 7, 1984, p. D5; Gordon Graff, "Cellular Phones: The Big Payoffs Are Still on Hold," *The New York Times,* June 23, 1985, sec. 3, p. 7.

24. Susan Hooker, interview with the author, Dec. 17, 1991.

25. Hooker, interview, Dec. 17, 1991; Albert Brashear, interviews, May 21, 1991, and Dec. 17, 1991.

26. Wolf Pavlok, interview with the author, June 15, 1993.

27. Brashear, Hooker, and Ron Sidlowski, interviews with the author, Dec. 17, 1991.

28. Fisher, interview, June 9, 1993.

29. Miriam Nielsen, interview with the author, June 15, 1993.

30. William Wiggenhorn, interview with the author, June 14, 1993.

31. Wiggenhorn, interview, June 14, 1993.

32. Nielsen, interview, June 15, 1993.

33. Galvin, interview, June 14, 1993.

34. Galvin, interview, June 14, 1993.

35. Galvin, interview, June 14, 1993.

36. Fisher, interview, June 9, 1993.

37. Fisher, interview, June 9, 1993.

38. Ira Wolf, interview, Nov. 4, 1991.

39. Caile, interview, Dec. 17, 1991.

40. Prestowitz, op. cit., p. 212.

41. Ibid., pp. 287–300.

42. Wolf, interview, Nov. 4, 1991.

43. Brashear, interview, May 21, 1991.

44. Wolf, interview, Nov. 4, 1991.

45. *The New York Times,* Feb. 15, 1994, pp. A1, D7.

46. "Accord Will Allow U.S. Cellular Phones in Japan," *The New York Times,* Mar. 13, 1993, p. A8.

47. Cho, interview, May 12, 1993.

48. Fisher, interview, June 9, 1993.

Part Four: Public/Private

1. See Jeffrey E. Garten, *A Cold Peace: America, Japan, Germany, and the Struggle for Supremacy* (New York: Times Books, 1992), pp. 17–19 and 83–102; and Chalmers Johnson, *MITI and the Japanese Miracle* (Stanford, Calif.: Stanford University Press, 1982), pp. 20–25.

Chapter 14: Europe's Grand Coalition

1. Frank Shrontz, interview with the author, Mar. 31, 1992.

2. Laura D'Andrea Tyson, *Who's Bashing Whom? Trade Conflict in High-Technology Industries* (Washington, D.C.: Institute for International Economics, 1992), p. 157.

3. Jürgen Thomas, interview with the author, Apr. 14, 1993.

4. My account draws on interviews with Boeing Vice Presidents Larry Clarkson and Robert George, Boeing and Airbus public relations officials, and two press accounts: Jeff Cole, "Boeing's Dominance of Aircraft Industry Is Beginning to Erode," *The Wall Street Journal,* July 9, 1992, pp. A1, A4; and Agis Salpukas, "Lease Deal by Airbus and United," *The New York Times,* July 9, 1992, p. D1.

5. Larry Clarkson, interview with the author, Mar. 16, 1993.

6. Shrontz, interview, Mar. 31, 1992.

7. Thomas, interview, Apr. 14, 1993.

8. Clarkson, interview, Mar. 16, 1993.

9. Tyson, op. cit., pp. 169–172.

10. Frank Shrontz, "Staying #1: The Global Challenge," speech to Council on Foreign Relations, New York, Jan. 23, 1992.

11. Donna Mikov, interview with the author, July 29, 1992.

12. Richard W. Stevenson, "Will Aerospace Be the Next Casualty?" *The New York Times,* Mar. 15, 1992, sec. 3, pp. 1, 6.

13. Ira C. Magaziner and Mark Patinkin, *The Silent War* (New York: Vintage Books, 1989), p. 257.

14. John Newhouse, *The Sporty Game* (New York: Alfred A. Knopf, 1982), pp. 123–126; ibid., pp. 235–250.

15. Alfred Herrhausen, speech to stockholders, May 10, 1989; Hilmar Kopper, interview with the author, Sept. 21, 1992; Helmut Hartmann, interview with the author, Jan. 11, 1993.

16. Tyson, op. cit., p. 157.

17. Magaziner and Patinkin, op. cit., p. 244.

18. Newhouse, op. cit., p. 28.

19. Magaziner and Patinkin, op. cit., pp. 245–248.

20. Gustav Humbert, interview with the author, Apr. 13, 1993.

21. Steve Greenhouse, "There's No Stopping Airbus Now," *The New York Times,* June 23, 1991, sec. 3, pp. 1, 6.

22. Haluk Taysi and Theodore Benien, joint interview with the author, May 4, 1992.

23. *International Herald Tribune,* Aug. 19, 1994, p. 17.

24. Phil Condit, interview with the author, Mar. 15, 1993.

25. *The Wall Street Journal,* Mar. 4, 1993, pp. A3, A4.

26. Clarkson, interview, Mar. 16, 1993.

27. Clyde Prestowitz, interview with the author, Mar. 26, 1992.

28. Tom Baker, quoted in "The Japanese Connection," *Portland Oregonian,* Mar. 1, 1992, p. C1.

29. David B. Friedman and Richard J. Samuels, "How to Succeed Without Really Flying: The Japanese Aircraft Industry and Japan's Technology Ideology" (Cambridge, Mass.: paper MITJP 92-01, Massachusetts Institute of Technology, the Japan Program, 1992), pp. 1–7.

30. Richard Samuels and Benjamin C. Whipple, "Defense Production and Industrial Development: The Case of Japanese Aircraft," in Chalmers Johnson, Laura D'Andrea Tyson, and John Zysman, eds., *Politics and Productivity: How Japan's Development Strategy Works* (New York: HarperBusiness, 1989), p. 275.

31. Samuels and Whipple, op. cit., pp. 275, 300.

32. Nasakazu Toyoda, interview with the author, May 12, 1993.

33. *Aerospace Facts and Figures 1990–91* (Washington, D.C.: Aerospace Industries Association of America, Inc., 1991), p. 22.

34. Boeing public relations officials, interviews with the author, Feb. 26, 1992, July 28, 1992, and Mar. 15–17, 1993.

35. Samuels and Whipple, op. cit., pp. 289–290.

36. Shoichi Shiraishi, interview with the author, Oct. 21, 1992.

37. Toyoda, interview with the author, May 12, 1993.

38. Sharaishi, interview, Apr. 22, 1993.

39. Toyoda, interview, May 12, 1993.

40. "Boeing Talks to Suppliers About Projects," *The New York Times,* Sept. 9, 1993, p. D5.

41. Interview, Feb. 2, 1993.

42. Dean Thornton, quoted in Tyson, op. cit., p. 192.

43. Condit, interview, Mar. 15, 1993.

44. Condit, interview, July 28, 1992.
45. Condit, interview, Mar. 15, 1993.
46. Condit, interview, Mar. 15, 1993.
47. Gordon McKinzie, interview with the author, Mar. 17, 1993.
48. Condit, interview, Mar. 15, 1993.
49. "Boeing 777 Takes Flight," *The Boeing Company 1994 Midyear Report,* Seattle, July 26, 1994, p. 3.
50. Sir Robert Ayling, interview with the author, Mar. 17, 1993.
51. *The New York Times,* Apr. 2, 1992, pp. A1, C2.
52. Clarkson, interview, Mar. 16, 1993.
53. *The New York Times,* Feb. 17, 1994, p. A1.

Chapter 15: America's Industrial Partnership

1. Thomas R. Howell, Brent L. Bartlett, and Warren Davis, *Creating Advantage: Semiconductors and Government Industrial Policy in the 1990s* (Washington, D.C.: Semiconductor Industry Association/Dewey Ballantine, 1992), p. v.
2. Andy Grove, interview with the author, June 2, 1993.
3. "Total Semiconductor World Market Sales and Shares for 1982–93" (Washington, D.C.: Semiconductor Industry Association, 1994).
4. Bill Spencer, interview with the author, June 7, 1993.
5. Marie Anchordoguy, *Computers Inc: Japan's Challenge to IBM* (Cambridge, Mass.: Harvard University Press, 1989), pp. 43–58.
6. Peter Drucker, *The New Realities: In Government and Politics, in Economics and Business, in Society and World View* (New York: Harper, 1989), pp. 130–131.
7. Howell et al., op. cit., p. 23.
8. Grove, interview, June 2, 1993.
9. Craig Fields, interview with the author, Mar. 11, 1992.
10. U.S. General Accounting Office, "Sematech's Efforts to Strengthen the U.S. Semiconductor Industry" (Washington, D.C.: U.S. Government Printing Office, 1990), p. 4.
11. Ken Olsen, interview with the author, Feb. 19, 1991.
12. James Fallows, "Looking at the Sun," *The Atlantic,* November 1993, p. 87.
13. "Toward a National Semiconductor Strategy," second annual report (Washington, D.C.: National Advisory Committee on Semiconductors, 1991), p. 11.
14. Stuart Auerbach, "U.S. Relied on Foreign-made Parts for Weapons," *The Washington Post,* Mar. 25, 1991, pp. A1, A17.
15. Fallows, op. cit., p. 84.
16. "Japan's Hidden War Role," *U.S. News & World Report,* Mar. 4, 1991, pp. 46–47.
17. Auerbach, op. cit.
18. Taizo Watanabe, quoted in ibid., p. A17.
19. "Uncle Sam's Helping Hand," *The Economist,* Apr. 2, 1994, p. 78.
20. *The New York Times,* Feb. 13, 1987, pp. A1, D5.
21. "Uncle Sam's Helping Hand," p. 78.
22. Fred Warshofsky, *The Chip War* (New York: Scribner's, 1989), pp. 367–369, describes IBM's contribution of its 4-megabit DRAM, and AT&T, its 64,000-bit chip.
23. Wolfgang Ganser, interview with the author, Mar. 12, 1991.
24. "Wonder Chips," *Business Week,* July 4, 1994, pp. 86–92.
25. Papken der Terossian, interview with the author, June 2, 1993.
26. der Terossian, interview, June 2, 1993.
27. Martin and Susan J. Tolchin, *Selling Our Security* (New York: Alfred A. Knopf, 1992), pp. 115–121.
28. Andrew Pollack, "The Challenge of Keeping U.S. Technology at Home," *The New York Times,* Dec. 10, 1989, p. A1; *Electronic News,* 35 (1788) (December 11, 1989), p. 1.

29. William Spencer and Russell G. Weinstock, telephone interviews with the author, July 13, 1994.

30. Spencer, interview, June 7, 1993.

31. Grove, interview, June 2, 1993.

32. der Terossian, interview, June 2, 1993.

33. der Terossian, interview, June 2, 1993.

34. Spencer, interview, June 7, 1993.

35. Weinstock, interview, July 13, 1994; Spencer, interview, Nov. 21, 1994.

36. Spencer, interview, July 13, 1994.

37. Spencer, interview, June 7, 1993.

38. Grove, interview, June 2, 1993.

39. Katie Hafner, "Does Industrial Policy Work? Lessons from Sematech," *The New York Times,* Nov. 7, 1993, p. F5.

40. The government contributed $100 million a year from FY 1988 through FY 1993; and $90 million in FY 1994 and FY 1995.

41. T. J. Rodgers, interview with Kathleen McCleery, June 3, 1993.

42. Grove, interview, June 2, 1993.

43. Howell et al., op. cit., pp. iv–v.

44. Bill Spencer, letter to the author, Sept. 23, 1994.

45. Robert Cohen, study, cited in Robert Kuttner, *The Washington Post,* Dec. 19, 1991, p. A21.

46. Thomas E. Ricks, "Senate Clears $252 Billion Bill That Underscores Industrial Policy," *The Wall Street Journal,* July 5, 1994, p. A14.

47. Memo quoted in Jack Anderson and Michael Binstein, "Reinventing Research," *The Washington Post,* Nov. 7, 1993, p. C7.

48. Budget of the United States Government, Fiscal Year 1996, Chapter VII, February 7, 1995.

49. *Promoting Long-Term Prosperity,* Third Annual Report to the President and Congress (Washington, D.C.: Competitiveness Policy Council, 1994), pp. 19–23.

50. William Safire, "Son of Synfuels," *The New York Times,* Oct. 11, 1993, p. A17; Gary Chapman, "The High-Tech Gravy Train," *The New York Times,* May 31, 1993, p. A21.

51. Matthew Wald, "Government Dream Car," *The New York Times,* Sept. 30, 1993, pp. A1, D7.

52. "Turning Plowshares, or Electric Cars, into Swords," *The New York Times,* Mar. 16, 1994, pp. A1, D5.

53. *The Washington Post,* June 8, 1994, pp. F1, F2.

54. "National Flat Panel Display Initiative," press release, U.S. Department of Defense, Apr. 28, 1994.

Chapter 16: The Unfinished Agenda

1. Ray Marshall, interview with the author, Oct. 15, 1993.

2. Bob Galvin, interview with the author, June 14, 1993.

3. David Kearns, interview with the author, Oct. 15, 1993.

4. Marshall, interview, Oct. 15, 1993.

5. Galvin, interview, June 14, 1993.

6. W. Edwards Deming, *Out of the Crisis* (Cambridge, Mass.: MIT Center for Advanced Engineering Study, 1986), pp. 23, 62–63, 107–108.

7. Ibid., p. 1.

8. Alfred P. Sloan, quoted in David A. Whetten and Kim S. Cameron, "Organizational-Level Productivity Initiatives: The Case of Downsizing," paper, July 1992, p. 1.

9. "Best Practices in Corporate Restructuring," *Wyatt's 1993 Survey of Corporate Restructuring* (Chicago: The Wyatt Company, 1993), p. 5.

10. Andrea Knox, "Most Cuts in Jobs Don't Help Firms, Survey Indicates," *The Philadelphia Inquirer,* Mar. 9, 1992, p. D1.

11. George J. Church, "We're #1 and It Hurts," *Time,* Oct. 24, 1994, p. 56.

12. James R. Emshoff and Teri E. Demlinger, *The New Rules of the Game* (New York: HarperCollins, 1991), p. x.

13. Kim S. Cameron, "Strategies for Successful Organizational Downsizing," paper, University of Michigan, Table 1.

14. David A. Whetten and Kim S. Cameron, "Organizational-Level Productivity Initiatives: The Case for Downsizing," Report to NRC Committee on Human Factors (Urbana: University of Illinois, 1992), p. 5.

15. "1991 AMA Survey on Downsizing and Assistance to Displaced Workers" (New York: American Management Association, 1994), pp. 1–7.

16. *Wyatt's 1993 Survey,* op. cit., pp. 34–35, 46–47.

17. Louis Uchitelle, "U.S. Corporations Expanding Abroad at a Quicker Pace," *The New York Times,* July 25, 1994, pp. A1, D2.

18. Robert Reich, speech, Washington, D.C., Nov. 22, 1994, p. 2.

19. Charles W. McMillion, "21st Century Manufacturing," paper (Anaheim, Calif.: conference of the National Center for Manufacturing Sciences, May 10, 1994), pp. 1–8.

20. Joseph Stiglitz, and study by Nancy Birdsall and Richard Sabot, quoted in "Economics of Equality: A New View," *The New York Times,* Jan. 8, 1993, p. D1.

21. Church, op. cit., pp. 50–51.

22. *The Wall Street Journal,* Sept. 7, 1994, p. A7.

23. "Backing Off the Baldrige," *Business Week,* Aug. 8, 1994, p. 56.

24. John Paul MacDuffie, telephone interview with the author, Oct. 14, 1994.

25. "Detroit, Check Your Rearview Mirror," *Business Week,* June 6, 1994, p. 26.

26. Church, op. cit., p. 55.

27. "Masters of Just Some Trades," McKinsey & Company chart, *The New York Times,* Oct. 22, 1993, p. D1.

28. Ken Courtis, interview with the author, May 19, 1994.

29. Michael Porter, Executive Summary, "Capital Choices: Changing the Way America Invests in Industry," research report (Washington, D.C.: Council on Competitiveness and Harvard Business School, 1992), p. 19.

30. James Renier, "Social Issues," in *Promoting Long-Term Prosperity,* Third Annual Report to the President and Congress (Washington, D.C.: Competitiveness Policy Council, 1994), pp. 34–35.

31. Peter Applebome, "Employers Wary of School Systems," *The New York Times,* Feb. 20, 1995, pp. A1, A11.

32. Ibid.

33. Louis S. Richman, "The New Yorker Elite," *Fortune,* Aug. 22, 1994, pp. 56–66.

34. *Fortune,* June 27, 1994, p. 68.

35. Louis V. Gerstner Jr., "Our Schools Are Failing. Do We Care?" *The New York Times,* May 27, 1994, p. A27.

Index

Aaron, Hank, 7
Abe, Nobuyuki, 201, 205
Abrams tank, 384
Acme, 291
Adenauer, Konrad, 238–39
Advanced Micro Devices, 380, 385, 395
Advanced Research Projects Agency
    (ARPA), 375, 400
"adversarial trade," 380
AEG corporation, 244, 269, 311
Aérospatiale, 356, 357
Aiko, Jiro, xxvi
Airbus 300B, 357
Airbus A310, 358
Airbus A320, 351, 352, 358, 372
Airbus A321, 358
Airbus A330, 358, 370, 373
Airbus A340, 358, 370
Airbus Industrie, 263, 350–60, 366, 369,
    406
    Boeing's rivalry with, 350–53, 355,
        356–57, 360, 373
    emergence of, 356–57
    growth of, 357–60
    integration concept and, 357
    production operations of, 358
    success of, 360
    technical innovations of, 358–59
    work units of, 358

aircraft industry, 350–76
    Airbus's technical innovations and,
        358–59
    Boeing-Airbus rivalry and, 350–53,
        355, 373
    Boeing-Japanese partnership and,
        360–62, 364–69
    Bush administration and, 374, 375
    computer industry and, 359, 367–68
    emergence of Airbus and, 351, 353
    Friendship Clubs and, 364–67
    government assistance and, 353–55,
        399
    importance of, 355
    in Japan, 362–67
    launch customers and, 362
    technology and, 352, 355, 358–59,
        367–68
    U.S. dominance and, 353–54, 355
    see also individual manufacturers
Air France, 356, 358, 373
Akers, John, 73, 75, 77–78, 81, 90–91,
    92, 93, 285
Akihabara district, 336, 340
alliance capitalism, 265–69
Allied Signal, 290
All Nippon Airways, 362, 370, 416
Alvarez, Shadia, 155, 159, 165, 168
amae, 199

Amaya, Naohiro, 293, 296
AMD, 298
American Airlines, 186, 370
American Express, 274, 285, 286
American Management Association, 410
Ampex, 23
Anami, Koremasa, 196, 200
Anchordoguy, Marie, 296, 313, 314
Andrews, Dennis, 74
Anheuser-Busch, 411
Annenberg, Walter, 171
Anson, Reg, 216, 220, 224, 225, 226–27, 230, 231
  Arnold Banks and, 232–33
Apollo spacecraft, 379
Apple, 26, 80, 83, 89, 91, 416
apprentice system:
  Boston program and, 186
  German high school system and, 134, 136–38
  Pennsylvania program and, 186–87
  John Torinus and, 180–84
  Tulsa formula and, 186
  unemployment rate and, 135
  at West Bend High School, 184–85
  Wisconsin system and, 173, 176, 178–84
Araskog, Rand, 279, 286
Aristech Chemical Corporation, 308, 309
Arkansas, 185
Armstrong, Anne L., 281
Artzt, E. L., xxviii
Asada, Atsushi, 6, 21, 24, 26
Asahi Glass, 301, 308
AT&T, 27, 28, 253, 321, 324, 337–38, 380, 385, 391, 393, 409
Atari, 83
Augustine, Norman, 32, 385
Australia, 306, 398
Austria, 206
automation, 39
  "Chicago gun" and, 229
  GM and, 42–45, 46, 68–69
  Motorola and, 330

U.S. Steel and, 205–6
  see also technology
automobile industry, xvii-xviii, 34–71, 77, 361, 413
  ease of manufacturing and, 58
  Japanese competition and, 40, 41, 42, 43, 47–49
  labor-management relations and, 35, 44–45, 55–66, 70
  mass marketing and, 41–45
  MIT studies of, 46, 49, 58, 64
  quality mind-set and, 36–40
  Toyota production system and, 48–60
  transformation of, 34–36
  see also specific manufacturers
Avis, 290
Avon, 286
Axel Springer, 279
Ayling, Robert, 373

"Baby Benz," 61
Baker, Tom, 362
Baker Oil Tools, 186
Bales, Ed, 325
BankAmerica, 409
Banks, Arnold, 223, 224, 226, 230
  Anson and, 232–33
Banquet Foods, 17
Barr, William, 309
Barton, Glenn, 251
"basic oxygen" technology, 206
Baumann, Eric, 177–80, 183, 184
Baumann, Gary, 178, 180
Baumann, Mrs., 178, 180
Bechtel, 311
Bell, Barbara, 69
Bellcore, 31
Bell Laboratories, 27, 28, 30, 324
Bennett, Michael, 255–56, 258–59
Benz, Karl, 34, 38
Bethlehem Steel, 286, 291
"Big Iron," 81
Birnbaum, Joel, 74
Bismarck, Otto von, 268, 348, 356
Blair, Margaret, 279, 289

Blue Springs High School, 128–30, 133, 143, 145
BMW, 36, 38, 40, 240
BOAC, 356
boards of directors, *see* corporate boards of directors
Boeing, xxiv, 35, 58, 263, 302, 306, 348, 349, 406
    Airbus rivalry with, 350–53, 355, 356–57, 360, 373
    customers in design process of, 369–72
    Japanese collaboration with, 360–62, 364–69, 374, 416
    public-private partnership and, 374–76
    Saudi deal pursued for, 375
    777 aircraft design and, 367–68
    teamwork mind-set of, 369
    Toyota as model for, 368–69
    United bid and, 350–53
    U.S. trade deficit and, 355
Boeing B-17 Flying Fortress, 354
Boeing B-29 Superfortress, 254
Boeing KC-135 Stratotanker, 354
Boeing 707, 354
Boeing 737, 351, 352, 364, 372
Boeing 747, 354, 358, 364, 367, 372
Boeing 757, 364
Boeing 777, 361, 362, 364, 365, 367–70, 372, 373
Bosnia, xx
Boston, Mass., 186
"Bottom Up" strategy, 57–60
Bradford, William, xxvii
Brennan, Edward, 285
Bretow, Richard, 325
Bridgestone, 263
British Aerospace, 356, 373
British Airways, 370, 373
Brody, T. Peter, 24–26
Brookings Institution, 279, 289
Brooks, Jack, 309
Brown, George H., 10
Buick, 42
Bureau of Labor Statistics, 210

Burroughs, 79
Burton, Daniel F., Jr., 30
Burton, Jim, 287
Bush, George, 29, 170, 250, 310, 316, 379, 392, 398
Bush administration, 151, 287, 381, 384
    aircraft industry and, 374, 375
    computer industry and, 392
    public-private partnership and, 374, 375
    U.S.-Japanese trade and, 309, 310, 315–16, 337, 340
Business Week, 288, 309
buyouts, 271–72

Caile, Jim, 322, 336
calculator market, 20, 22–23, 24
Caldwell, Philip, 218, 225
California Institute of Technology, 281
CalPERS, 285–86, 287, 288
Canada, 4, 308, 398
Canio, Joseph, 285
Canon, 31, 391, 392, 394
capitalism, 193–94, 197
    "alliance," 268
    American, 270–74
    consensus, 237–39, 242–43
    German, 194–95, 197, 347–48
    Japanese, 194, 197
    managerial, 272–74
    network, 294, 296, 300, 307
    power of CEOs and, 273–74
Caravelle airliner, 356
Career School, 128
Cargill, 263
Carnes, James E., 28
Carter, Jimmy, 310, 379, 407
Carter administration, 149
Cary, Frank, 83, 84
Casio, 24
Caterpillar, 247–48, 263, 306
    Aurora plant of, 250, 251
    Employee Satisfaction Process of, 247–48
    Fites's reforms at, 248–49

Caterpillar *(cont'd)*
  pattern bargaining issue and, 249
  UAW conflict with, 248–53
Cathay Pacific, 370
CBS, 281, 282
cellular phone market, 328–30
Central Park East Secondary School,
  153–69
  absences at, 158–59
  advisory system of, 157–58
  code of behavior and, 155
  as community of relationships, 156–57
  community service at, 164
  "culture" of, 156–57
  curriculum of, 163–64
  graduation from, 164–66
  graduation rate of, 153, 167–68
  "habits of mind" approach of,
    154–55, 163
  mentoring at, 157–58
  mutual respect at, 159–60, 161
  oral exams at, 164–67
  parents and, 156, 159
  required portfolios at, 164–67
  "senior institute" of, 165
  size of, 161–62
  student entry into, 156
  success of, 167–69
  teacher empowerment at, 160–62
  tracking in, 162–63
  work internships at, 164
Chamber of Commerce, U.S., 400
Champion International Corporation, 272
Chandler, Alfred, 273
Chevrolet, 42, 70
Chevrolet Nova, 64, 66
Chevron, 290
Chicago Board of Trade, 293
"Chicago gun," 229
chief executive officers (CEOs), 273–82,
  405–6, 409, 413
  Fortune study on, 278–79
  GM board's guidelines and, 288–89
  GM board's revolt and, 285
  Heilmeier on, 32–33

  Keiretsu system and, 305
  Morgan Stanley study on, 280
  organized labor and, 291–92
  power of, 273–75
  reform and, 286
  shareholder groups and, 286
  state laws and, 289
  stock options and pay packages for,
    276–80, 286, 287
  see also corporate boards of directors;
    General Motors corporate board
Childs, Bill, 64, 66
China, People's Republic of, xxv, 106,
  115, 116, 200, 211, 306
Cho, Susumu, 322, 343
Christian Democratic Union, 239
Chrysler, xviii, xxviii, 30, 41, 45, 46, 52,
  58, 70, 228, 249, 282, 285, 291, 306,
  308, 349, 416
CIS countries (former Soviet Union), 306
"city cars," 246
Clarkson, Larry, 352–53, 354, 361–62,
  366, 374–75
Clausel, Richard, 248
Clayton Anti-Trust Act (1914), 375
"clean room," 387–88
Clinton, Bill, 187, 310, 357
  public-private partnership and, 375–76
Clinton administration, 151, 187–88
  computer industry and, 401–2
  corporate boards and, 287
  education and, 187–88
  government-business relationship
    and, 375–76, 399–400
  LCDs and, 26
  Sematech and, 348–49
  U.S.-Japanese trade disputes and,
    310, 315, 316, 337, 342
coal industry, 211
Coalition of Essential Schools, 169–70,
  171
Coca-Cola, 277, 286
Cocke, John, 75
codetermination *(mitbestimmung)*,
  240–44, 246

Cold War, xix, xx, 4, 193, 348, 374, 399
comanagement, *see* Saturn Corporation
Comer, James P., 170, 171
Commerce Department, U.S., 29, 323, 400
communications notebook, 110, 122
communism, 193, 238
Communist Manifesto, The (Marx), 235
Community Learning Centers, 171
Compaq, 80, 84, 88, 89, 90, 91, 285
Competitiveness Policy Council, 29, 30, 400, 417–18
computer chip industry, 381–99
    "clean room" and, 387–88
    free market and, 398
    Perkin-Elmer rescue and, 391
    photolithography process and, 390–93
    Reagan and, 348, 396
    Sematech and recovery of, 395–97
    "steppers" and, 390–92
    technology of, 389–90
    U.S. recovery of, 395–99
computer industry, 72–94
    aircraft control systems and, 359
    aviation design and, 367–68
    Bush administration and, 392
    Clinton administration and, 401–2
    Cray-Japan dispute and, 312–14
    flat-panel displays and, 401
    IBM brain drain and, 74
    Japanese, 76–77
    keiretsu networks and, 298–99
    mainframe mentality and, 78, 80–82
    multimedia PCs and, 75
    PC market and, 78–80, 84–86
    Persian Gulf War and, 383–85
    personal computer boom and, 396
    RISC operating system and, 73, 75
    U.S.-Japanese trade disputes and, 312–14
    see also computer chip industry;
        Sematech; semiconductor industry
Computerland, 87–88
computers, 116–17

Computer Wars (Ferguson and Morris), 76
Concorde, 356
Condit, Phil, 35, 58, 352, 361, 367–70, 371, 373, 374, 394
Co-NECT, 171
Congress, U.S., 77, 236, 392, 400, 402
    antitrust laws and, 385
    corporate reform and, 287
    Goals 2000 Act passed by, 151, 171, 187, 418
    New Deal legislation of, 273
    unemployment pay and, 207
consensus capitalism, 237–39, 242–43
Consumer Reports, 37
Continental Tire, 269
Control Data, 25, 79, 286
Corning Glass, xxii, 253, 408
Coronet Carpets, 17
corporate boards of directors:
    absentee shareholders and, 289
    CEO domination of, 274–75
    CEO stock options and pay packages and, 276–80
    Clinton administration and, 287
    Congress and, 287
    Crystal's experience with, 275, 276–77, 278
    employee ownership and, 290–91
    German, 239–44, 266–67
    of GM, *see* General Motors corporate board
    government and, 287
    Harvard study on, 263–64, 290, 416, 417
    Icahn on, 276
    institutional investors and, 290
    labor representatives on, 291–92, 416
    New Deal legislation and, 290
    reform of, 263, 266, 273, 275, 283–91, 416, 417
    relationship investing and, 286
    shareholder groups and, 285–289
    stakeholders on, 288–92, 416–17
    see also chief executive officers

Corrigan, Bob, 72, 85–86, 90, 91, 92, 93
Corry, Charles A., 291
Council of Economic Advisers, 310
Council on Competitiveness, 263, 271, 290, 416, 417
Courtis, Kenneth, 293, 414
Covey, Stephen R., xvii
Cray Research, 312–14
Creating Advantage, 377, 398
Crystal, Graef, 275–77, 278, 287
CSA, 356, 357
Cypress Semiconductors, 397

Dai-Ichi Kangyo network, 300
Daimler, Gottlieb, 36, 38
Daimler-Benz, 34, 38, 61, 249, 255, 274
  Deutsche Bank and, 240, 243, 264–66, 269, 357
  Fokker acquisition and, 244–45
  foreign investment in, 264–65
  labor-management relations at, 234–46, 264–66
  power sharing at, 234–44
  reserves of, 244–45
  Reuter's diversification strategy and, 266–67
  stakeholder mind-set at, 264–68
  supervisory board of, 239–44
dango (secret meeting), 310–12
Dassault Aviation, 368
David Sarnoff Laboratories, 9–10, 11, 14, 22
  RCA's demise and, 27–28
DDI, 337, 338, 339, 340
"decision rings," 257
Deere and Company, 249
Defense Advanced Research Projects, (DARPA), 380, 381, 392, 400
Defense Department, U.S., 26, 29, 77, 348, 350, 354, 374, 375, 378, 379, 380, 383–84, 385, 399–400, 401
Defense Science Board, 383, 385
Dell Computer Corporation, 73, 74, 80
Delta Airlines, 370

Deming, W. Edwards, 56, 216, 230, 231, 254, 325, 409
  Ford Motor and, 217, 218–19, 222
  management philosophy of, 218–19
Democratic Party, U.S., 379
Dennis, Roland, 220
derTerossian, Papken, 390–91, 393, 394–95
Desert Storm, Operation, 384
Deutsche Airbus, 350, 353, 357, 359
Deutsche Bank, 140–41, 262, 414
  Daimler-Benz and, 240, 243, 264–66, 269, 357
  history of, 268–69
  industry and, 268–69
  Krupp and, 269
Dewey, John, 169
Dial, 286
Diamond-Star Motor Corporation, 308
Digital Equipment, 79, 285, 380, 382
Discovery, 202
Dobbins, Art, 69
Dodwell's *Industrial Groupings in Japan,* 303–4
dollar, U.S., xxix
  yen and, 310, 414
Donnegan, Chris, 57, 59
Donofrio, Nick, 92
Douglas aircraft, 354
"downsizing," 204, 209
  American Management Association and, 410
  loyalty and, 411
  shortcomings of, 409–12
  steel industry and, 209, 215
  stock market and, 279
  U.S. economy and, 411–12
  Wyatt and Company and, 411
Dresser Industries, xxvii, 35
Drucker, Peter, xx, 81, 221, 380
Duderstadt, James J., 29
Du Pont, 28, 302

Eastern Airlines, 247, 351, 358
Eastman Kodak, 28, 30, 263, 274, 285, 308, 349

Eaton Manufacturing, 253
Economist, 92, 270, 274
Edgar Thompson Works, 206
education, education reform, 97–189,
    406, 407
  Annenberg gift and, 171
  apprenticeships and, *see* apprentice
    system
  assessment of, 417–20
  Boston program and, 186
  Clinton administration and, 187–88
  James P. Comer and, 170, 171
  curriculum and, 127, 163–64, 174–76,
    185
  general diploma and, 127, 128–29,
    174–75, 185
  in Germany, *see* German elementary
    school education; German high
    school system
  high-performance strategy and,
    417–20
  homework and, 117, 118, 122, 144
  in Japan, *see* Japanese elementary
    school education; Japanese high
    school system
  at Motorola University, 333–34
  national standards for, 116, 171
  New American Schools Development
    Corp. and, 170–71
  parents and, 109–11, 116, 117–18,
    122–24, 156, 159, 170, 178
  partnering and, 121–22
  Pennsylvania program and, 186–87
  reform opposition and, 172, 176–77,
    188
  school year in, 118, 143
  size and, 135, 161–62
  Sizer coalition and, 169–70, 171
  tracking and, *see* tracking
  Tulsa formula for, 186
  University of Pennsylvania study on,
    418
  in U.S., *see* Central Park East
    Secondary School; United States
    elementary school education;
    United States high school system;
    Wisconsin education system
  U.S. failure in, 148–50
Educational Quality of the Workforce
    study, 418
Education Commission of the States, 172
Education Department, Wisconsin,
    176–77
Education Ministry, Japanese, 106, 142,
    143, 314
Education Mom (*kyoiku mama*), 110
Eisner, Michael, 277, 278
elections, U.S.:
  of 1992, 250
  of 1994, 412
Electronic Data Systems, 43, 283
Employee Involvement (EI), 227–29
employee-management relations, *see*
    labor-management relations
employee ownership, 195, 291–92
Employee Satisfaction Process, 247–48
Energy Department, U.S., 400–1
energy industry, 379
Engelman, Kurt, 87–88
Estridge, Don, 83
European Community, 374
Evans, Bob, 74
Evans, Lucius, 220, 224
Everhart, Thomas E., 281
Exxon, 25, 28, 30

Fairchild, 298
Fairless Works, 205, 207–9, 213
Fair Trade Office, Japanese, 310
Faisal, Altagracia, 159
Fanuc, 43
Federal Cartel Office, German, 265
Federal Communications Commission,
    328
Federal Trade Commission, 323
Feldman, David, 166–67
Ferguson, Charles, 76, 82, 85, 86, 94
Feuerstein, Karl, 234–37, 240, 243–46
  Kopper's relationship with, 243
Fiat, 58

Fidelity Investments, 288
Fields, Craig I., 381–82
Financial World, 277
First Aircraft Promotion Law (1954),
 Japanese, 365
Fisher, Charles T., III, 281
Fisher, George, 317, 321–22, 323, 324,
 326, 327, 330, 331, 335, 343–44
Fites, Don, 248–52
Flaherty, Gerry, 251
flat-panel displays, 401. *See also*
 liquid-crystal display
Flick, Friedrich Karl, 264, 265
Fokker Aircraft, 244–45
Forbes, 279
Ford, Henry, 41, 97, 223
Ford Escort, 218
Ford Motor Company, xvii-xix, xx, xxi,
 xxvii, 4, 30, 41, 45, 46, 52, 58, 68,
 70, 195, 216–33, 249, 282, 286, 327,
 349, 406, 407, 411, 413, 415
 command style management of, 220–22
 Deming and, 217, 218–19, 222
 Employee Involvement program at,
 227–29
 Japanese competition and, 216–17
 labor management relations and,
 217–31
 Don Peterson and, xvii–xviii, xx,
 xxvii, 52, 216, 217, 218–19, 220,
 221, 222
 plant jackets at, 225–26
 Poling and, 217–18, 220–21, 224–25
 pride at, 227
 public perception of, 217–18
 quality and, 226–27, 231
 retraining at, 221–22, 225, 230–31
 Romeo plant of, 222
 sense of partnership and, 224–26
 Sharonville plant of, 222
 South Chicago plant of, *see* South
 Chicago Ford plant
 "stop button" and, 226
 Toyota as model for, 217
 transformation of, 220–26
 UAW and, 223, 225, 230, 232
 worker-inspired innovations and,
 229–30
Ford Taurus, 218, 224, 225, 227
Ford Thunderbird, 223
Fortune, xxviii, 14, 42, 275, 277, 409
 CEO pay study by, 278–79
Foundation for Product Testing
 (Stiftung Warentest), 37–38
Fox River Valley Technical College,
 178–79, 184
France, 4, 80, 343, 359–60, 384
 Airbus partnership and, 351, 353
 Mercedes plant in, 246
Frankfurt Auto Show (1991), 40
Fraser, Doug, 225, 291
"Friday Club," 302–4, 306
Friedman, David, 55
Friel, Joe, 16, 22
"Friendship Club," 364–67
Frist, Thomas, Jr., 277
Frito Lay, 79
FSX (Fighter Support/Experimental)
 project, 363–64, 366
Fuji, 30
Fuji Heavy Industries, 364, 365
Fuji (Fuyo) network, 300
Fujitsu, 30, 76–77, 79, 279, 299, 312–13,
 314, 329, 391
Fuller, Jason, 128–33, 137, 138, 145,
 147, 150, 174, 177

Galvin, Bob, 317–20, 321, 323–24, 326,
 330, 334, 335, 339, 343, 396–97,
 398, 405, 408, 409, 411
Galvin, Paul, 321
Galvin Manufacturing, Inc., 321
Ganser, Wolfgang, 387
Gates, Bill, 32, 83
GCA, 391–92
General Dynamics, 363
General Dynamics F-16, 363, 384–85
General Electric, 19, 25, 28, 302, 308,
 409, 414
 RCA taken over by, 27

General Instruments, 263
General Motors (GM), xviii, xxiv, 4, 5, 28, 30, 34, 52, 53, 58, 61, 194, 216, 217, 231–32, 249, 263, 274, 292, 302, 319, 323, 348, 349, 406, 409, 413
  automation at, 42–45, 46, 68–69
  consumers and, 46–48
  corporate board of, *see* General Motors corporate board
  Fairfax plant of, 68–69
  Fremont plant of, 63–64
  labor-management relations at, 44–45, 63–64
  mass marketing mind-set of, 41–45, 47–48, 126–27
  resistance to change at, 67–71
  "rework" at, 55–56
  Saturn division of, *see* Saturn Corporation
  Jack Smith's leadership of, 284
  Roger Smith's "reforms" at, 42–44, 46
  technology obsession of, 42–44
  Toyota's joint venture with, 63–66
General Motors corporate board:
  composition of, 281
  corporate manifesto of, 288–89
  guideline of, 288–89
  revolt of, 283–85
  Roger Smith's finesse of, 280–83, 284, 285
Gephardt, Dick, xxiv
German elementary school education, 118–24
  curriculum and, 120
  ethnic diversity in, 119
  grades in, 120–21
  homework in, 118, 122
  Japanese system compared with, 118
  parent-school relationship in, 122–24
  partnering in, 121–22
  school year in, 118
  seating arrangements in, 121
  teachers' social status in, 118, 123
  tracking in, 118, 122, 123, 124
  unity circle in, 119
German high school system, 134–41, 175
  apprentice training in, 134, 136–38
  high-performance strategy in, 136
  job guarantee and, 139
  as model for Wisconsin system, 175–76, 181–82
  quality and, 136
  scale of, 135
  youth unemployment rate and, 135
German metalworkers, *see* IG Metall
Germans, The (Watson), 134
Germany, Federal Republic of (West), 241, 264
  Adenauer and, 238–39
  postwar recovery of, 238–39, 268–69, 348
Germany, reunified, xix, xxiv, xxviii, xxix, 4, 29, 35, 80, 98, 193, 200, 214, 263, 343, 359, 384, 414
  Airbus partnership and, 351, 353
  banks-business relationship in, 268–69
  capitalism in, 194–95, 197, 347–48
  CEO pay in, 279
  as consumer, 37
  dual-education system of, *see* German high school system
  "economic miracle" of, 237–39
  elementary education system of, *see* German elementary school education
  insider trading in, 242
  1992–94 recession and, 210, 211–12, 237, 241–42, 244, 245, 246
  savings rate of, 264
  steel industry of, 210–14
  unemployment in, 210–11
Germany, Weimar, 238
Gerstner, Lou, 72, 78, 92–94, 419
Getty Oil, 304
Gingrich, Newt, xxiv
Giuliani, Rudolph W., 169
Glass-Steagall Act (1933), 273
Goals 2000 Act (1994), 151, 171, 187, 418
Goizueta, Robert, 277
Goldberg Elementary School, 118–19

Goldberger, Marvin, 281
Goodyear, 263
Gotoh, Kazuwaki, 60
Governor's Commission on Youth, 181
Great Britain, 80, 281, 358, 384
    Airbus partnership and, 351, 353
    CEO pay in, 279
Great Depression, 4, 247
Greyhound, 247
Group of 99, 254
Grove, Andy, 32, 77, 377, 381, 393,
    396–98, 399, 402
Grover, Bert, 126, 127, 129, 133–34,
    173–74, 176, 180, 185, 406
GTE, 25

"habits of mind," 154–55, 163
Hamel, Gary, xvii
hans (learning groups), 108
Hanson, Dale, 285, 286, 288, 289
Harbour, Jim, 68, 223
Harmel, Peter, 214
harmony (wa), 101–2
Harris Corporation, 380
Hartmax, 285
Harvard Business Review, xvii
Harvard Business School, 262, 263, 288,
    290, 417
Hawker-Siddeley, 357
Hawkinson, Shirley, 159, 161
Hayakawa, Tokuji, 19, 20
Hayakawa Electric Company, 19
Hayashi, Yoshihisa, 205
Haymarket riot, 247
Heald, Anne, 188–89
Hegel, G.W.F., 234
Heilmeier, George, 9, 13, 14, 15, 20, 22,
    25, 28
    on CEOs, 32–33
    LCD invention and, 10–12
    NHK broadcast and, 18–19
    on research and development, 31–32
    on Robert Sarnoff, 16–17
Heller, Andy, 74
Henry, Glenn, 72–76, 81–82, 83, 86, 93

Henry, Peggy, 72
Hercules company, 286
Hertz Rent A Car, 17
Hewlett-Packard, 74, 263, 380
Higashi, Kan, 65, 66
Higgs, Chyann, 166–67
high-performance strategy, 407–9
    downsizing and, 410
    education and, 417–20
    German high school system and, 136
    long term and, 415
    technology and, 407–8
Hills, Carla, 315, 340
Hilti International, 186
Hirayama, Masaru, 202–3, 207
Hirsch, Leon, 277
Hitachi, 19, 30, 31, 54, 77, 79, 279, 299,
    312–13, 314, 329, 391
Hitler, Adolf, 211, 238
Hoesch, 211
Homestead strike, 247
Honda, 30, 46, 50, 52, 58, 309
Honda Accord, 223
Honeywell, 418
Hong Kong, 21, 79, 280, 398, 412
Hooker, Susan, 329
horizontal keiretsu, 299
Hosakawa, Morihiro, 342
Hospital Corporation of America,
    277
House of Representatives, U.S., 418
    Judiciary Committee of, 309
Howell, Thomas R., 377
Hudler, Donald W., 260
Hughes Aircraft, 43
Humbert, Gustav, 359
Hutschenreuther, 269
Hyundai, 395

Iacocca, Lee, 285
IBM, 4, 5, 25, 26, 27, 30, 72–94, 194,
    261, 263, 274, 285, 286, 302, 319,
    338, 348, 379, 382, 385, 393, 395,
    401, 406, 409, 416
    achievements of, 76

annual "technical recognition"
 program of, 72–73
brain drain at, 74
computer clones and, 79–80
decline of, 76–78, 84–85, 90
Enterprise Division of, 92
Gerstner's tenure at, 92–94
ingrained corporate culture of, 90–94
Japanese competition and, 76–77
mainframe mentality of, 78, 80–82
mainframe-PC conflict within, 82–85
marketing failure of, 86–90
PC division of, 83–86, 91
Perkin-Elmer rescue and, 391–92
resistance to change in, 74–76, 80–82,
 90–94
RISC operating system and, 73, 75, 93
Sematech and, 380, 386
Standard Product Authority of, 83
ThinkPad 700 laptop of, 86–90
3090–600J mainframe of, 368
IBM Japan, 279
Icahn, Carl, 276, 292
If the Japanese Can, Why Can't We?
 (film), 218
IG Metall (German metalworkers'
 union), 61, 212, 213, 235, 240, 241,
 246, 265
Ikeda, Sachiko, 100, 103–6, 108, 110,
 114, 118, 121
Imai, Hiro, 146–48
Imai, Takashi, 204
Industrial Groupings in Japan,
 Dodwell's, 303–4
industrial networks, *see keiretsu*
Infiniti, 257
InFocus, 26
Inland Steel, 291
Inoue, Tokuta, 30
Institute for Educational Leadership,
 418
institutional investors, 270, 417
 corporate boards and, 290
 Japanese, 294–95
 shareholder mind-set and, 270

Intel, 32, 77, 79, 83, 84, 299, 349, 377,
 380, 381, 385, 386, 391, 393, 395
 microprocessors and, 396
International Association of Machinists
 and Aerospace Workers, 362
International High School, 169
International Trade and Industry
 Ministry (MITI), 239, 312, 338
 adversarial trade and, 380
 aerospace industry and, 363–66
International Trade Commission, U.S.,
 26
Investor Responsibility Research
 Center, 286
Iran, 264–65
Iran hostage crisis, 5
Iraq, 306, 384
Ishikawajima-Harima Heavy Industries,
 364, 365
Italy, 4
ITT, 279, 286
Iwasaki, Yataro, 303
Iyoda, Yasuteru, 145, 147–48

Japan, xix, xxiv, xxvii, 4, 35, 80, 83, 98,
 193, 263, 267, 343, 412
 adversarial trade and, 380
 aircraft industry in, 362–67
 auto industry of, 48–49
 capitalism in, 194, 197
 CEO pay in, 279
 communications industry in, 321
 computer industry of, 76–77
 as consumer market, xxvii–xxviii
 economic deregulation in, 337
 education budget of, 109
 elementary school system of, *see*
  Japanese elementary school
  education
 employee-management relations in,
  197–205
 FSX project of, 363–64, 366
 GNP of, 300
 government-business relationship
  and, 362, 364

Japan *(cont'd)*
  group loyalty and teamwork in
    character of, 58–59
  high school system of, *see* Japanese
    high school system
  kaizen culture of, 8, 20, 23–26, 31
  manufacturing sector in, 21–22
  Marunouchi district in, 300–301
  network capitalism in, 296, 300, 307
  1992–94 recession and, 197–98, 210,
    211–12, 296
  Persian Gulf War and, 384
  postwar era in, 199, 301–2, 363
  research and development programs
    in, 29, 30–31
  savings rate of, 264, 414
  unemployment rate of, 204
  U.S. based labs of, 30–31
  U.S. 1986 trade agreement with, 339,
    340, 396
  U.S. trade disputes with, 309, 310–16,
    337–40, 342
Japan Aircraft Development
  Corporation, 365
Japan Airlines, 204, 279, 362, 370, 416
Japan Defense Agency, 365
Japanese elementary school education,
  101–11
  computers and, 116–17
  German system compared with, 118
  national standards for, 116
  parent-school relationship and,
    109–11, 116, 118
  quality in, 101
  socialization and, 105–6, 111
  students' mistakes in, 104
  teamwork in, 101, 108
  tracking in, 105, 115, 124
  whole person approach in, 107–9
Japanese Federation of Steelworkers,
  200
Japanese high school system, 141–48
  business, industry and, 146–48
  career paths in, 142
  competitive pressure in, 142–43

  dropout rate in, 146
  homework in, 144
  jukus and, 142–43
  personal development in, 144
  post-school support system and,
    141–42, 146–48
  school year in, 143
  students' lifestyle in, 145
  teachers in, 146
Japan Productivity Institute, 204
J. D. Power & Associates, 256
J. I. Case, 249
Jobs for the Future, 186
Johnson, Chalmers, 293, 298, 315
Johnson, Elmer, 45, 63, 67–68, 280,
  281–82, 283
Johnson, Rob, 182
Johnson, Ross, 275
Johnson administration, 378
Johnson & Johnson, 409
J. P. Morgan, 281
JRC, 329
Judo teaching, 102–5
jukus (private cram schools), 142–43
"Just in Time" system, 53–54

Kaifu, Toshiki, 315
kaizen culture, 20, 23–26, 31, 33
Kao, 263
Karstadt, 269
Kaske, Karl Heinz, 238
Kato, Takehito, 312–13
Kawanishi, Tsutomu, 299
Kawanishi, Tsuyoshi, 25
Kawasaki Heavy Industries, 364, 365, 366
Kean, Thomas, 150, 152, 172, 188
Kearns, David, xxvi, xxvii, 170, 171,
  399, 405, 409, 413
keiretsu (industrial network), 293–316
  advantages of, 295–96, 298, 305,
    306–7
  CEOs and, 305
  computer industry and, 298–99
  consensus and, 297, 298
  core of, 295, 300

Cray Research episode and, 312–14
in daily life, 296
early feedback and, 394
government agencies and, 313–14
horizontal, 299
institutional investors and, 294–95
loyalty and, 295
Marounichi district and, 300–301
Mazda rescue and, 297–300
Motorola and, 321, 336–37
murahachibu (ostracization) and, 295
network capitalism and, 294
reciprocal shareholding and, 295
relationships and, 295, 296–97
semiconductor industry and, 382–83
stable shareholders and, 294–96
structure of, 296–97
Sumitomo group of, 298, 299–300
of Toyota, 296–97, 299, 311
U.S.-Japanese trade disputes and,
    310–11
vertical, 299, 311
zaibatsu predecessor of, 301–2
see also Mitsubishi Corporation
Keister, Jerry, 131–32
Keller, Maryann, 42, 285
Kennedy administration, 378
Kennon, Walter, 130
Kent, Deborah, 228–29
Ketelsen, James, 285
King, Frank, 74
Kinnear, Gregory E., 89–90
Kirin Brewery, 301, 305
Kitano, Mikio, 57–58
Kleinert, Matthias, 34, 38
Klemm, Erich, 240
Klöckner-Humboldt-Deutz, 212, 269
Knight-Ridder, 290
Kohl, Helmut, 356–57
Kojima Press, 148
Kokusai, 329
Komatsu, Ltd., 248, 263
Kopper, Hilmar, 140–41, 236, 240, 244,
    245, 247, 262, 265–66, 269
    Feuerstein's relationship with, 243

Korea, Republic of (South), 21, 80, 83,
    98, 200, 202, 211, 398, 412
Korean War, 363
Krupp, 211, 212, 264
    Deutsche Bank and, 269
Kuehler, Jack, 78, 391, 396
Kuenheim, Eberhard von, 240
Kuwait, 264, 306
Kuwait Petroleum Company, 304
Kyocera, 337
kyoiku mama (Education Mom), 110
Kyoto University, 314

Labor Department, U.S., 210
labor-management relations:
    amae and, 199
    automobile industry and, 35, 44–45,
        55–66, 70
    Caterpillar-UAW conflict and, 248–53
    Daimler-Benz and, 234–46, 264–66
    Deming's philosophy of, 218–19
    downsizing strategy in, 209, 215,
        409–12
    early retirement in, 203–4, 212
    Employee Involvement program in,
        227–29
    employee ownership in, 291–92
    employee sovereignty in, 199
    employee-stockholder relationship in,
        203–4, 215
    fear of extremism in, 211
    Ford's authoritarian management
        and, 220–22
    Ford Motor Co., and, 217–31
    Ford turnaround and, 220–26, 227–29
    German restructuring of, 212–14
    GM and, 44–45, 63–64
    group exercises in, 198
    job security in, 200, 230–31
    layoffs in, 206–10
    lifetime employment system in,
        197–200, 320
    loyalty in, 199, 201, 205
    at Nippon Steel, 200–204
    paternalism in, 198

labor-management relations *(cont'd)*
Reagan administration and, 247
retraining in, 199, 200, 201–2, 208–9, 213
ritual induction ceremony in, 198
Saturn experiment and, 254–56, 257, 258, 259
social responsibility in, 210, 211, 212–13, 215
social status in, 199
stockholders in, 207, 210
Taylorism in, 219
technology in, 57–58, 205–6
Toyota and, 55–60
unemployment and, 210–11
unions and, 200, 211, 215, 223, 225, 230, 232
in U.S. history, 247
U.S. mind-set and, 206–7
"wedding ceremony" and, 198
worker-inspired innovations in, 229–30
work teams and, 198
see also Motorola; power sharing
Laox (store), 340–41
Laube, Richard, xxvii
"launch customers," 362
Lavazzeri, Carlos, IV, 158, 159, 165, 166–68
LCD, *see* flat panel display; liquid crystal display
leadership, management and, 31–33
Leahy, John, 360
Learning Gap, The (Stevenson and Stigler), 106–7, 117
learning groups *(hans)*, 108
Lefauve, Richard G. "Skip," 234, 255–56, 258, 261, 408
Lego, Paul, 279, 285
Levi Strauss, xxii, 408, 411
Lewman, Ted, 133
Lexus, 51, 60, 257
Liberal Democratic Party, Japanese, 340
lifetime employment system, 197–200, 320

Lightle, Joellen, 129, 130, 132
Lindenberger, Ilse, 100, 119–23
Linden West Elementary School, 111, 115, 116–17, 118
liquid crystal display (LCD), 11–27, 401
Clinton administration and, 26
invention of, 10–12
RCA's abandonment of, 16–18
Sarnoff and, 14–15
Sharp's development of, 20–22
technological innovations and, 24–26
world market and, 26–27
Lockheed, 353, 356, 358, 360
Lockheed C5A Galaxy, 354
Lorsch, Jay W., 271, 288
Lotus, 74
Lowe, Bill, 84
LSI Logic, 380, 385
LTV, 291
Lufthansa, 356, 358, 373
Lutsky, Mark, 159
Lynch, Dick, 69

McDonald, James, 68
McDonald's, 181
McDonnell, Horace G., 392
McDonnell Douglas, 353, 356, 358, 360, 365, 366–67, 370, 375, 406
McDonnell Douglas MD-11, 370, 373
MacDuffie, John Paul, 57
McGroddy, James, 79, 80, 86
Machiavelli, Niccolò, xvii, xxvi
MacIver, Elizabeth A., 271
"McJobs," 210
McKinsey & Company, 414
McKinzie, Gordon, 370–72
McLaughlin, Ann, 281
Magaziner, Ira, 355
Magma Copper, 195, 261, 408, 411, 415
power sharing at, 253
Maine, 185, 187, 417
Makihara, Minoru, 302–6, 308, 312
Malaysia, 127, 328–30
Malcolm Baldrige National Quality Award, 413

management, leadership and, 31–33
managerial capitalism, 272–74
Marathon Oil, 207
Maris, Roger, 7
Marriott, J. Willard, 281
Marriott Corp., 281
Marshall, Ray, 126, 405, 407–9, 411
Martin Marietta, 32, 385
Marunouchi district, 300–301
Marx, Karl, 235
Maryland, 185, 187
Massachusetts, 286, 417
Matsushita, 19, 31, 320, 323, 329, 336, 340
Matthews, Erran, 156–57, 159, 164, 168
Maverick missile, 384
May, Uwe, 213
Mazda Motors, 58
    keiretsu network rescue of, 297–300
Meier, Deborah, 99, 152–53, 156, 161–63, 165, 167, 169, 172, 406
    "habits of mind" approach of, 154–55
    on mutual respect, 159–60
Meiji Mutual Life Insurance, 301
Meiji Restoration, 348
Meistersinger, Die (Wagner), 37
Mercedes Apprenticeship Center, 128, 136–40
Mercedes Automobile Holding, 265
Mercedes-Benz, 34, 50, 193
    American plant of, 245–46
    "city cars" of, 246
    competitive pressure and, 40
    cutbacks by, 244–46
    power sharing and, 234–37, 244
    quality mind-set of, 36–40
    S-car of, 38–40, 61
    "stop stations" of, 62
    supervisor board of, 234–57
    Toyota doctrine's effect on, 60–63
    workers and, 61, 62–63
Merck, 32, 263
Mercury Sable, 218, 224
Messerschmidt company, 245, 356, 357
Messier, 357

Mexico, 127
Micrascan "stepper," 391, 392, 393–95
Micron Technology, 380
microprocessors, 396
Microsoft, 32, 79, 83
Microunity, 74
Mid-America Printing Company, 179–80
MIPS, 74
Misunderstood Miracle, The (Friedman), 55
Mitbestimmung (codetermination), 240–44, 246
Mitchell, John, 329, 330
Mitler, Terry, 69
Mito (Sharp executive), 22
Mitsubishi A6M Zero, 365
Mitsubishi Bank, 301, 305, 309
Mitsubishi Construction, 301
Mitsubishi Corporation, 31, 54, 264, 329, 340, 391
    Chrysler and, 306, 308
    Friday Club of, 302–4, 306
    history of, 301–2
    international reach of, 306
    keiretsu advantage of, 300–301, 306–7
    Marunouchi district and, 300–302, 306
    postwar era and, 301–2
    President's Council (*shacho-kai*) of, 302–4, 306
    Rockefeller Center acquired by, 307–8, 392
    satellite market and, 305–6
    takeover averted by, 304
    U.S. antitrust laws and, 309
    U.S. assets of, 307–9
    U.S. firms and, 306
Mitsubishi Electric, 301, 305, 308
Mitsubishi Estate Company, 301
Mitsubishi Gas Chemical, 301, 309
Mitsubishi Heavy Industries, 301, 308, 363, 364–65
Mitsubishi *keiretsu*, 300–9
Mitsubishi International, 308
Mitsubishi Motors, 308

Mitsubishi Oil, 304
Mitsubishi Petrochemical, 301, 309
Mitsubishi Plastics, 301
Mitsubishi Rayon, 309
Mitsubishi Steel, 308
Mitsubishi Trust, 309
Mitsui network, 300
Miwa, Gien, 107–9
Mogolescu, Marian, 159
Monsanto, 306
Moore, Celeste, 100, 111–15, 117, 118, 121
   on tracking, 115
Moore, Gordon, 396
Morgan, Lee, 248
Morgan Stanley, 280
Morio, Minoru, 30
Morris, Charles, 76
Mosbacher, Robert, 392
Mostek, 298
Motorola, xxii, xxiv, 26, 195, 263, 286, 299, 317–44, 349, 378, 380, 385, 386, 391, 393, 395, 406, 407, 408, 411, 416
   American workforce and, 328–30
   Arlington plant of, 329–30
   automation at, 330
   cellular phone market and, 328–30
   code of candor at, 324
   deregulation and, 337
   Galvin as CEO of, 317–19
   "healthy spirit of discontent" at, 323–25
   keiretsu and, 321, 336–37
   life employment at, 320
   Micro TAC developed by, 339–40, 342
   new plant decision by, 328–30
   pager market conflict and, 320–25
   quality as paradigm for, 319–20, 325–28
   renewal concept and, 319, 321
   retraining and, 335–42
   Six Sigma program of, 326–28
   U.S. government as ally of, 319–20, 321, 322, 336–38, 340, 342–43

Motorola University, 333
Moussouris, John, 74
Muhammad Reza Shah Pahlavi, 264–65
murahachibu, 295
Murphy, Jack, xxvii, 35
Murphy, Thomas, 42
mutual funds, 270

Nabisco Brands, 275
Nakasone, Yasuhiro, 337, 338
Nakayama, Kazuki, 103–4, 106, 110, 111, 113, 117
Nakayama, Mr., 110–11
Nakayama, Mrs., 110
NASA (North American Space Agency), 350, 354, 374, 400
National Academy of Sciences, 31, 382
National Association of Manufacturers, 400, 419
National Cooperative Research Act (1984), 385
National Labor Relations Board, 252
National Science and Technology Council, 400
National Science Board, 29
National Science Foundation, 29
National Security Agency, 383
National Semiconductor, 298, 380
National Steel, 291
NATO (North Atlantic Treaty Organization), xx
Navy, U.S., 310–12
NBC, 13
NBD Bancorp, 281
NCR Corporation, 380
Neenah High School, 178, 180
network capitalism:
   Japanese, 296, 300, 307
   keiretsu networks and, 294
networks, see keiretsu
New American Schools Development Corporation, 170–71
New Deal, 247, 273, 379
New United Motor Manufacturing Inc. (NUMMI), 64–68, 69

New York, 185, 187, 286
New York Stock Exchange, 293
New York Times, 277, 301
New York Times Magazine, 42, 43
New Youth Connections, 158
New Zealand, 398
NHK (Japanese public broadcasting),
    18, 22
Nielsen, Miriam, 331–33
Nigeria, 200
Nikon, 301, 305, 391, 392, 394
NINO, 269
Nippondenso, 53–54, 147–48, 181, 340
Nippon Electric Corporation (NEC),
    19–20, 30, 79, 263, 299, 312–13,
    314, 323, 329, 340, 391
Nippon Ido, 338, 339, 340–41, 342
Nippon Motorola, Ltd., 317, 322, 341,
    343
Nippon Oil Company, 304
Nippon Steel, 54–55, 196, 197–98, 214,
    230, 263
  employee loyalty 196, 200–5, 230, 263
  retraining by, 200–202
  Space World of, 202
  Yawata Works of, 201–2
Nippon Telephone and Telegraph
    (NTT), 204, 321–22, 337–39, 340
Nissan Motors, 30, 58, 204, 299, 313, 338
Nixon, Richard M., 4
Nomi School, 102–3, 105, 107–9, 110,
    111, 114, 116–17
North American F-86 Sabre, 363
North American Rockwell, 17, 22, 25
North Rhine-Westphalia, 212, 214
Northwest Airlines, 290, 351, 360
Noyce, Bob, 385–86
NYNEX, 409

Oakes, Bill, 130
Occidental Petroleum, 286
O'Connell, Philip R., 272
Ogiso, Minoru, 146
Ohno, Taichi, 34, 50, 58
Oki, 329

Oklahoma, 185–86, 417
Okuyama, Toshihiro, 201
Oldsmobile, 42
Olsen, Ken, 285, 382
OPEC, 359
Opel, John, 81, 84
"open-hearth" technology, 206
Oregon, 185, 187
Osaka University, 314
Outward Bound, 171
Ozawa, Ichiro, 340

Paape, Doug, 179
Packard Bell, 80, 91
pagers market, 320–25
Pahlavi, Muhammad Reza, Shah,
    264–65
Paine-Webber, 290
Pampers, xxvii
Panelvision, 25
Parent-Teacher Association, 117
"patient capital," 25, 305, 356, 406
pattern bargaining, 249
Pavlok, Wolf, 329–30
Pearce, Harry, 47, 48, 70–71, 280, 281
Pennsylvania, 185, 186–87, 417
Pennsylvania, University of, 418
Penzias, Arno, 28
Perkin-Elmer, 391–92
Perot, H. Ross, 43, 283–84
Persian Gulf War, 383–85
personal computers (PCs), 75, 78–80,
    84–86, 401
Petersen, Don, xvii-xviii, xx, xxvii, 52,
    216, 217, 218–19, 220, 221, 222
Pfizer, 281
Phelps Dodge, 247
Philco, 320–21
Philipp Holzmann company, 269
photolithographic process, 390–95
Pickens, T. Boone, 296
Pierson, Jean, 351
Pioneer Electronic Corporation, 203
Pirelli, 269
Pittsburgh Plate Glass, 290

Pittston Coal, 247
Polaroid, 7, 286, 290
Poling, Harold "Red," 52, 230, 408
    Ford's labor relations and, 217–18,
    220–21, 224–25
Pontiac, 70
Pontiac Grand Prix, 68
Porsche, 36
Porter, Michael, 36, 262
Post Office, U.S., 399
Posts and Telecommunications Ministry
    (MPT), Japanese, 337, 338, 340,
    342
Pound, John, 288
Power Game, The: How Washington
    Works (Smith), xxiii
power sharing, 234–61
    American experiments in, 253–54
    American mind-set and, 247–48
    bloc voting and, 243
    Caterpillar-UAW conflict and, 248–53
    codetermination and, 240–44, 246
    consensus capitalism and, 237–43
    Daimler-Benz and, 234–44
    German "economic miracle" and,
    237–39
    Magma Copper and, 253
    Mercedes-Benz and, 234–37, 244
    mind-set of, 242–44
    recession of 1992 and, 244, 245, 246
    Saturn Corp. and, see Saturn
    Corporation
    unions and, 241–42
Pozen, Robert, 288
Prahalad, C. K., xvii
Pratt, Edmund T., Jr., 281
Pratt & Whitney, 366
"precompetitive" technology, 393
President's Council (shacho-kai), 302–4,
    306
Press, Frank, 31, 382
Prestowitz, Clyde, 25, 299, 362
Primerica, 274
Prince, The (Machiavelli), xvii
Printron, 180

Procter & Gamble, xxvii-xxviii, 263,
    281, 284, 290, 409
Pro-Tech program, 186
Pryzbylski, Dan, 329
Pullman strike, 247

Quantas, 370
Quasar, 320

Radoll, Brenda, 173, 183, 184
Ravenswood Aluminum, 247
Raytheon, 25
RCA, xxiv, 4, 6, 25, 43, 194, 263, 319,
    320, 321, 399, 401, 406
    demise of, 27
    diversification approach of, 16–18
    "home run" mind-set of, 8–9
    Japanese visit to, 22
    LCD abandoned by, 16–18
    LCD invented by, 9–12
    leadership failure of, 13–14, 15
    Return on Investment approach of,
    12–13
    success syndrome and, 12–13
Reagan, Ronald, xxiii-xxv, 3, 247, 310,
    316, 338
    computer chip industry and, 348, 396
    government-business partnership and,
    348
    Sematech partnership and, 348,
    377–78, 379, 385, 415
Reagan administration, 149, 247
    government-business relationship
    and, 375–76, 378–79, 401–2
    labor-management relations and, 247
    U.S.-Japanese trade and, 309, 310,
    337–38
"Reaganomics," 379
Rebmann, Horst, 39, 62
recession of 1992–94, 197–98, 203
    in Germany, 210, 211–12, 237,
    241–42, 244, 245, 246
    in Japan, 197–98, 210, 211–12, 296
    power sharing and, 244, 245, 246
    steel industry and, 203, 210, 211–12

reciprocal shareholding, 295
Reeves, Tim, 207–9, 213
Reich, Cary, 43
Reich, Robert, 187, 412
Reinventing Education (Gerstner), 419
relationship investing, 285, 286
Renier, James, 418
Republican Party, U.S., 379
Republic Engineered Steel, xxii, 253
retraining:
    costs of, 334–35
    at Ford, 221–22, 225, 230–31
    labor-management relations and, 199,
        200, 201–2, 208–9, 213
    at Motorola, 335–42
    at Nippon Steel, 200–202
    at Saturn, 256
    steel industry and, 200–202, 213
    technology and, 199, 334
Reuter, Edzard, 234, 236, 238, 240–41,
    244–45, 268, 274
    diversification strategy of, 266–67
Reuther, Victor, 66
reverse engineering, 21, 329
Riester, Walter, 242
RISC operating system, 73, 75, 93
risutora (restructuring), 203
RJR Nabisco, 78, 92, 93, 409
Robinson, James, 285, 286
robots, *see* automation
Rockefeller Center, 307–8, 392
Rockwell International, 186, 380, 401
Rodgers, T. J., 397–98, 399
Rohlen, Tom, 102–3, 104, 106, 109, 116,
    143, 144, 146, 148
Rolls-Royce, 366
Roncevic, Janina, 87
Roosevelt, Franklin D., 273
Rose, Nicole, 140
Ruth, Babe, 6–7
Rutovic, Bob, 216, 227
Ryder System, 286

Sacco, Bruno, 61
Sakakibara, Eisuke, 199

Salomon Brothers, 286
Samsung, 395
Samuels, Richard, 363, 364
Sanger, David, 301
Sango, 148
Santelli, Anthony, 89
Sanwa network, 300
Sarnoff, David, 9, 10, 12, 13, 14–15, 20
Sarnoff, Robert, 13–14, 16
Sasaki, Tadashi, 20, 22
Satellite Communications Corporation,
    305
Saturn Corporation, 43, 46, 195, 254–61,
    415, 416
    airbags and, 258
    conflicts at, 257–58
    creation of, 254–55
    credo of, 255
    "decision rings" of, 257
    dependency on GM and, 259–61
    expansion at, 260
    German system and, 254
    GM mind-set and, 257–59
    goal of, 255
    guiding principles of, 255
    labor-management relations and,
        254–56, 257, 258, 259
    marketing of, 259
    retraining at, 256
    Roger Smith and, 254, 256, 259
    Spring Hill plant of, 256
    Strategic Action Council of, 254
    success of, 256–57, 259
    suppliers and, 257
    UAW and, 254–56, 257, 258, 259
    work units of, 257
Saudi Arabia, 306, 375
Savoie, Ernie, 219–20
Scandanavia, 4
S-car, 38–40, 61
Schaefer, George, 248
Schey, Cindy, 179
Schmidt, Helmut, 265
Scholz, Frau, 122
Schuster, Claudia, 121, 122–23

Schuster, Jörg, 62, 122–23
Schwarz, Paul, 152, 155, 157, 160, 162, 163, 166, 168
Sears, Roebuck, 87, 274, 285, 409
Securities and Exchange Commission (SEC), 287
Securities Exchange Act (1934), 273
Seiko, 20
Self-Defense Forces, Japanese, 363
Sematech:
    aim of, 379–80
    chip fab plant of, 386
    Clinton administration and, 348–49
    collaborative mind-set at, 393–95
    criticism of, 397–98
    early feedback process at, 394
    IBM and, 380, 386
    launching of, 377–78, 385
    members of, 380, 385
    as model for other industries, 399–402, 415–16
    models for, 378–81
    organization of, 380
    photolithographic process and, 390–95
    "precompetitive" technology and, 393
    Reagan and, 348, 377–78, 379, 385, 415
    recovery of U.S. computer chip industry and, 395–97
    SVG and, 390, 392–95
    taxpayers' investment in, 397
Semel, Samuel, 90
Semiconductor Agreement (1986), 316
semiconductor industry, 378
    free market and, 398
    Japanese domination of, 382
    keiretsu networks and, 382–83
    "precompetitive" technology and, 393
    "tool" industry of, 382
Semiconductor Industry Association, U.S., 381, 398
Senate, U.S., 236, 338, 379
Serigraph Co., 180–84
7 Habits of Highly Effective People, The (Covey), xvii

shacho-kai (President's Council), 302–4, 306
Shah of Iran, 264–65
Shamada, Haruo, 57
shareholder mind-set, 269–75
    absentee owners and, 269–71
    CEO's power and, 273–75
    institutional investors and, 270
    managerial capitalism and, 272–74
    1980s buyout era and, 271–72
    see also chief executive officers; corporate boards of directors; stakeholder mind-set
Sharp Inc., xxiv, 6, 9, 31, 193, 262–63, 368
    calculator market and, 20, 22–23, 24
    history of, 19–20
    kaizen culture at, 23–26
    LCD developed by, 20–22
    NHK broadcast and, 18–19, 22
    North American Rockwell and, 22–23
    RCA visited by, 22
    world market and, 26–27
Shatswell, Rich, 128
Sherman Anti-Trust Act (1890), 375
Shiraishi, Koichi, 366
Shrontz, Frank, 350, 353, 355, 370, 374
Sidewinder missile, 384
Siemens, 136, 238, 387
Silicon Valley Group (SVG), 390, 392–95
simultaneous engineering, 52
Singapore, 80, 412
Six Sigma program, 326–28
Sizer, Ted, 165, 169–70, 171
Sky Chefs, 274
Sloan, Alfred P., 409
Smale, John G., 281, 284–85, 289, 291
Smith, Adam, 274, 292
Smith, Jack, 70, 260, 284
Smith, Roger, 34, 47, 50, 55, 57, 70, 77, 216, 217, 292
    GM's corporate board and, 280–83, 284, 285
    GM-Toyota joint venture and, 63–64, 67–68
    labor and, 44–45

"reforms" of, 42–45, 46
Saturn Corp. and, 254, 256, 259
Smith, Semeika, 164
Smyser, Richard, 234, 239
SONY, xxvi, 23–24, 30, 55, 336, 337
South Chicago Ford Plant, 220, 327
    Employee Involvement program at,
        227–29
    golf carts at, 225
    plant jackets at, 225–26
    sense of partnership at, 224–26
South Korea, *see* Korea, Republic of
Southwest Airlines, xxii
Soviet Union, xx, 193, 306, 348
Spacecki, Mary, 185
Space World, 202
Spain, 211, 351, 353, 358
Sparrow missile, 384
Spencer, Bill, 378, 386, 388, 389, 393,
        394–96, 397, 398
SRI International, 27
"stable shareholders," 294–96
stakeholder mind-set, 262–92
    cooperative relationships and,
        267–68
    on corporate boards, 288–92,
        416–17
    corporate reform and, 285–89
    at Daimler-Benz, 264–68
    employee ownership and, 290–91
    German banks and, 268–69
    Harvard study and, 263–64
    see also corporate boards of directors;
        shareholder mind-set
Standard & Poor's, 271, 286
Standard Products Authority, 83
Staples, 87
steel industry:
    American, 196, 200, 205–10, 291
    automation in, 205–6
    downsizing in, 209, 215
    economic prosperity in, 214–15
    German, 210–14
    Japanese, 196–98, 200–5, 230, 263
    layoffs in, 207–10

recession of 1992–94 and, 203, 210,
        211–12
    retraining in, 200–202, 213
Steinberg, Laurence, 130–31
Steinkühler, Franz, 241–42, 243
Stempel, Robert, 283–85
"steppers," 390–92
Stevenson, Harold W., 106–7, 115
Stiftung Warentest (Foundation for
        Product Testing), 37–38
Stigler, James W., 106–7, 115
stock options, 276–80, 286, 287
Strategic Action Council, 254
Strauss, Franz Josef, 356
Strauss, Robert, 321
Streeter, Amy, 115
"structural protectionism," 310
Strukturpolitik (restructuring), 212
Sullivan, Leon, 281
Sumitomo group, 298, 299–300
Sundry, Art, 323–24
Sun Microsystems, 75
Superbird satellite, 305
supercomputers, 312–14
supersonic transport (SST), 354, 356
Switzerland, 413
Synthetic Fuels Corporation, 379

Taiwan, xxv, 21, 79–80, 83, 106, 115,
        116, 202, 398, 412
Tamm, Peter, 279
Tandy, 83
Tannas, Larry, 17, 23
Taylor, Frederick Winslow, 219
T. D. Williams, 186
technology, xxiv, 407
    Airbus's innovations in, 358–59
    aircraft industry and, 352, 355,
        358–59, 367–68
    "basic oxygen," 206
    Boeing 777 and, 367–68
    collaboration and, xxi
    computer chip manufacturing and,
        381–83, 389–90
    flat-panel displays and, 401

technology *(cont'd)*
German affinity for, 36–39
GM's obsession with, 42–44
high-performance strategy and, 407–8
Japan and, 57–58
labor-management relations and,
57–58, 205–6
LCD and, 11–27, 401
"open-hearth," 206
Persian Gulf War and, 383–85
"precompetitive," 393
retraining and, 199, 334
steel industry and, 205–6
U.S. underinvestment in, 28–30
workforce and, 47
Technology Review, 12–13
"techno-nationalism," 363
Tenneco, 285
Test, 37–38
Teutcher, Ilja, 37
Texaco, 304
Texas Instruments, 25, 88, 380, 385, 391,
395
Thailand, 384
Thinking For a Living (Marshall and
Tucker), 126
ThinkPad 700, 87
Thoman, G. Richard, 93
Thomas, Jürgen, 350, 353–54
Thomas Watson Research Center, 27
Thompson, Tommy, 175
Thornton, Dean, 351–52, 366
Thurow, Lester, 126, 141, 262, 273, 276
Thyssen, 211, 212
Tillotson, Heidi, 231–32
Time, 412
Time Warner, 286
Timex, 18, 22
Tokyo Marine and Fire Insurance, 301
Tokyophone, 341
Tokyo Stock Exchange, 293–94
Tokyo University, 314
Tomomatsu, Hiroshi, 51
Torinus, John, 173, 185
apprentice system and, 180–84

Toshiba, 19, 24, 25, 88, 89, 197–98, 204,
299, 329, 391, 395
Toyoda, Shoichiro, 51–52
Toyota Camry, 51, 228
Toyota Corolla, 64
Toyota Corona, 51
Toyota Motor Corp., xxiv, 30, 34, 46,
48–60, 68, 70, 97, 104, 181, 193,
197–98, 217, 223, 224, 226, 232,
254, 263, 309, 338, 368
"Bottom Up" strategy of, 57–60
consumers and, 50
ease of manufacturing at, 58
flexible organization of, 50–52, 55–56,
57
GM's joint venture with, 63–66
"Just in Time" system of, 53–54
keiretsu of, 296–97, 299, 311
labor-management relations at, 55–60
Mercedes-Benz influenced by, 60–63
"rework" and, 55–56
simultaneous engineering by, 52
size of, 51–52
suppliers' relationship with, 53–55
Takaoka plant of, 49–50, 56
teamwork and, 58–60
Tsutsumi plant of, 51, 53, 59–60
Toyota Production System, 58–60
Toyota Tekko, 146
Toyota Windom, 51
Toys "R" Us, 315
tracking:
at Central Park East Secondary
School, 162–63
in German elementary system, 118,
122, 123, 124
in Japanese elementary system, 105,
115, 124
Moore on, 115
in U.S. elementary system, 111,
113–16, 124
Wisconsin system and, 176
Trading Places (Prestowitz), 25
Trevino, Lee, 328
Trotman, Alexander J., 413–14

Tucker, Marc, 126
Tulsa, Okla., 186
Tuminaro, Marty, 161, 166
TWA, 290
Tyson, Laura D'Andrea, 310, 350, 357

United Airlines, 279, 290, 360, 370, 372
    Boeing-Airbus competition and,
        350–53
United Auto Workers Union (UAW),
        44–45, 64, 70, 260, 291
    Caterpillar's conflict with, 248–53
    Ford Motor and, 223, 225, 230, 232
    GM-Toyota joint venture and, 66–67
    Saturn Corp. and, 254–56, 257, 258,
        259
United States:
    antitrust laws of, 309, 375, 385, 415
    average wage in, 210
    downsizing and economy of, 411–12
    educational philosophy of, 112
    foreign technology and, 384–85
    free market orientation of, 348
    individualism in character of, 194
    1980s buyout era in, 271–72
    research and development crisis in,
        28–30
    savings rate of, 264, 414
    shareholder mind-set and, 269–70
    trade deficit of, xxiii, xxix, 310, 338,
        355, 413
United States Chamber of Commerce,
    400
United States elementary school
    education, 111–18
    ability groups in, 115
    after-school activities in, 117
    computers in, 116
    homework in, 117
    individualism in, 112
    parent-school relationship in, 111,
        117–18
    teaching methods in, 100, 111–15, 117,
        118, 121
    tracking in, 111, 113–16, 124

United States high school system,
    128–34
    after-school work in, 130–31
    failure of, 133–34, 148–50
    general education and, 127, 128–29
    personal development in, 144
    work-study programs in, 131–33
    see also Central Park East Secondary
        School
United States Navy, 310–12
United States Post Office, 399
United States Semiconductor Industry
    Association, 381, 398
United Steelworkers Union, 207, 291
"unity circle," 119
University Heights High School, 169
Urban Academy, 169
USAir, 286
Usher, Tom, 196, 205–6, 207, 210,
    291
U.S. Steel, 28, 196, 200, 291
    automation and, 205–6
    Fairless Works of, 205, 207–9
    layoffs and, 207–10
    shareholders and, 207, 210
    union represented on board of, 291
U.S. Surgical, 277
USX, 263, 291
Utter, Christie, 116
Utter, Ray (father), 116, 117
Utter, Raymond L. (son), 113, 115, 116,
    117

Vagelos, Roy, 32
Vandergrift, Joe, 208
van Wolferen, Karel, 56, 302, 310
Verbatim, 308
vertical *keiretsu,* 299, 311
VFW Fokker, 357
Vietnam, 307
Vietnam War, 3–4, 5
Vocational Training Center (Vo-Tech),
    130
Volkswagen, 246
VSG Steel Company, 196, 212, 213–14

wa (harmony), 101–2
Wacker, Roland, 137–39
Wada, Akihiro, 52
Wada, Tomio, 19, 22
Wagner, Richard, 37
Wakai, Tsuneo, 301
Wakamura, Natsuomi, 203
"walk-away lease," 351
Wall Street Journal, 128, 276
Wal-Mart, 79, 210, 263, 178, 278
Walt Disney Co., 277, 278
Walter, Joe, 161, 164
Warburg bank, 281
Washington Post, 277
Washio, Etsuya, 200
Watanabe, Taizo, 384
Watergate scandal, 4
Watson, Alan, 134
Watson, Tom, Jr., 76
Watson, Tom, Sr., 76
Weatherstone, Dennis, 281
Webco, 186
Weinberg, Harvey, 285
Weinberger, Caspar, 379, 384, 385
Weisz, Bill, 329, 330
Welch, Jack, 27, 414
Welzel, Hartmut, 136
Wendel, Reinhold, 138
Wenzel, Wolfgang, 196, 212, 214
Werner, Helmut, 38, 60, 140, 234–37,
    240, 244, 245, 246
West Bend High School, 182
  apprentice system at, 184–85
Westinghouse Electric, 19, 24, 25–26,
    274, 279, 285, 306, 311
Weygand, Al, 248, 250–51
Wheeling-Pittsburgh, 291
Whitmore, Kay, 285
Wiggenhorn, Bill, 334
Williams, Lynn, 291–92
Williams, Richard, 28
Wills, Joan, 418
Wilson, Pete, 287

Winter, J. Burgess, 253
Wisconsin, 286, 417
  Industry, Labor and Human
    Relations Department of, 177
Wisconsin education system, 173–89
  apprentice system and, 173, 176,
    177–84
  business, industry and, 176, 180–86,
    188
  general curriculum and, 174–75
  German model for, 175–76, 181–82
  Bert Grover and, 173–74, 176, 180
  parental involvement and, 178
  revised curriculum of, 175–76, 185
  John Torinus and, 180–84, 185
  tracking in, 176
  union opposition to, 176, 188
Wolf, Ira, 317, 335, 339
Wolf, Stephen, 279, 351–52, 372
Womack, James, 64
Woodside, William, 275
Work Council, 235
World Economic Forum, xxviii, 413
World War II, 199, 238, 268, 301–2, 328,
    354, 384, 399
Wyatt and Company, 411
Wyman, Thomas, 47, 48, 281, 282, 283,
    284

Xerox, xxvi, xxvii, 7, 30, 74, 378, 394
Xerox Parc, 27

Yamamura, Kozo, 54, 298
Yawata Works, 201–2
yen, Japanese, 203
  dollar and, 310, 414
YS-11 consortium, 364
Yutakano High School, 128, 143–44,
    145, 148

zaibatsu, 301–2
Zenith, 24
Zetsche, Dieter, 61, 62

About the Author

HEDRICK SMITH's twenty-six-year career with *The New York Times* took him to Vietnam, Cairo, Paris, and Washington, as well as to Moscow, where his reporting from 1971 to 1974 won him a Pulitzer Prize. His books include the bestsellers *The Russians; The Power Game: How Washington Works;* and *The New Russians.* He is editor-in-residence at the Foreign Policy Institute of the Johns Hopkins School of Advanced International Studies. He has created, reported for, and hosted three PBS TV miniseries: *Inside Gorbachev's Russia; The Power Game;* and *Challenge to America,* which, along with extensive traveling and research, inspired this book. He lives in Maryland with his wife, Susan.

About the Type

This book was set in Times Roman, designed by Stanley Morison specifically for the *Times* of London. The typeface was introduced in the newspaper in 1932. Times Roman has had its greatest success in the United States as a book and commercial typeface, rather than one used in newspapers.